1995 CIVIL PROCEDURE SUPPLEMENT

By

John J. Cound
Professor of Law, University of Minnesota

Jack H. Friedenthal
Dean and Professor of Law, The National Law Center, George Washington University

Arthur R. Miller
Bruce Bromley Professor of Law, Harvard University

John E. Sexton
Dean and Professor of Law, New York University

AMERICAN CASEBOOK SERIES®

WEST PUBLISHING CO.
ST. PAUL, MINN., 1995

COPYRIGHT © 1985, 1987, 1989–1991, 1993, 1994 JACK H. FRIEDENTHAL, ARTHUR R. MILLER & JOHN E. SEXTON
COPYRIGHT © 1995 By JACK H. FRIEDENTHAL, ARTHUR R. MILLER & JOHN E. SEXTON
All rights reserved
Printed in the United States of America

ISBN 0-314-06861-9

Table of Contents

	Page
PART I: Federal Rules of Civil Procedure for the United States District Courts *and* Comparative Federal and State Provisions	1
PART II: Selected Provisions of The Constitution of the United States and of Titles 28 and 42, United States Code *plus* Comparative Federal and State Provisions	228
PART III: Selected State Jurisdictional Statutes *and* Selected State Statutes Governing the Powers of Appellate Courts	285
PART IV: Selected Portions of the Federal Rules of Appellate Procedure	292
PART V: Selected Sample Court Orders and Notices for Controlling Discovery, Pretrial Comferences, and Settlement of Class Action	329
PART VI: Illustrative Litigation Problem *with* Sample Documents	353
PART VII: Local Rules for the United States District Courts for the Southern and Eastern Districts of New York	381
PART VIII: Recent Court Decision	423
PART IX: Updates to Cound, Friedenthal, Miller and Sexton, Civil Procedure, Cases and Materials, 6th Edition	437
PART X: Proposed Rule Amendments	452
PART XI: Index to Comparative Provisions	458

*

1995
CIVIL PROCEDURE
SUPPLEMENT

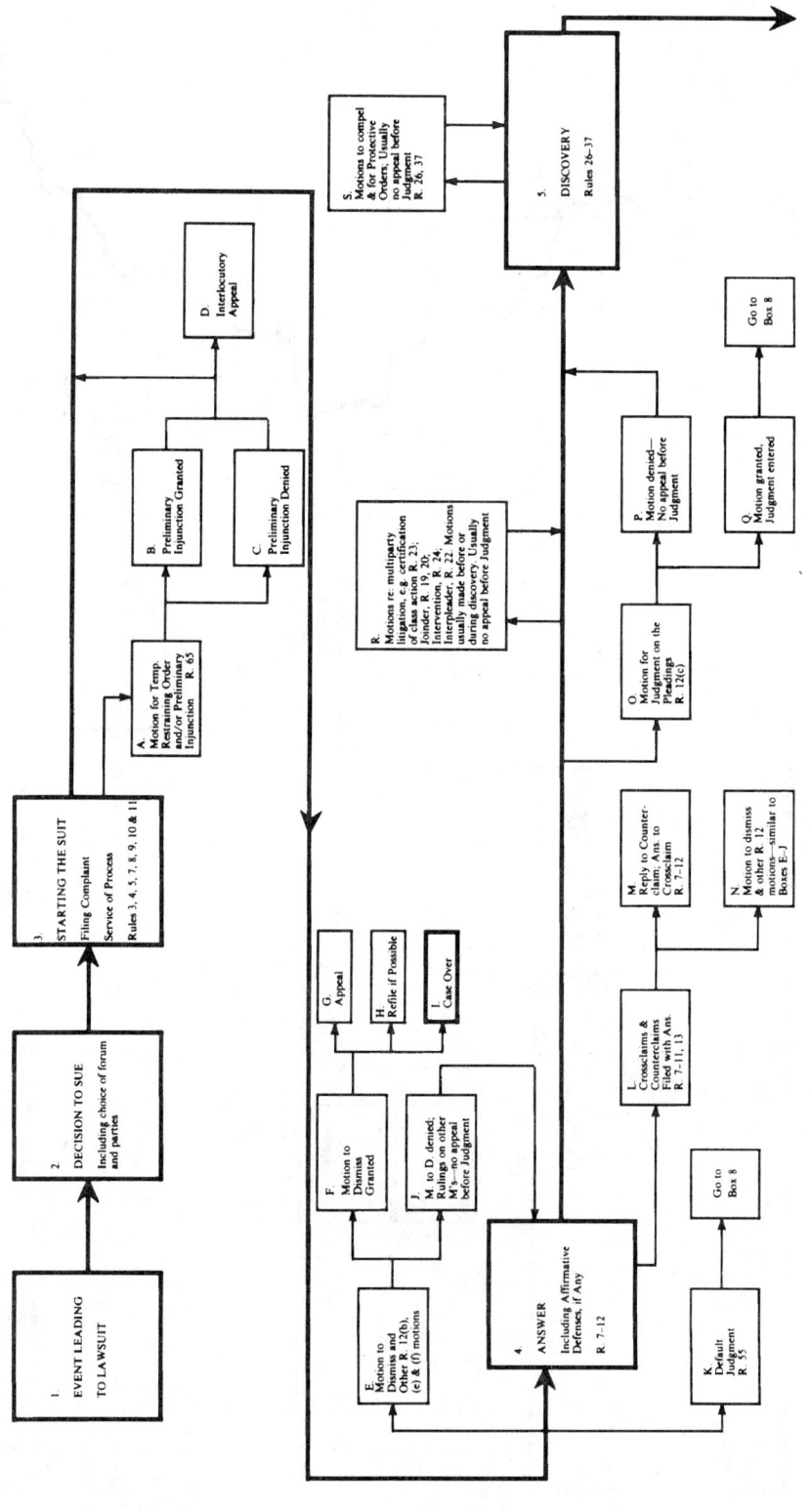

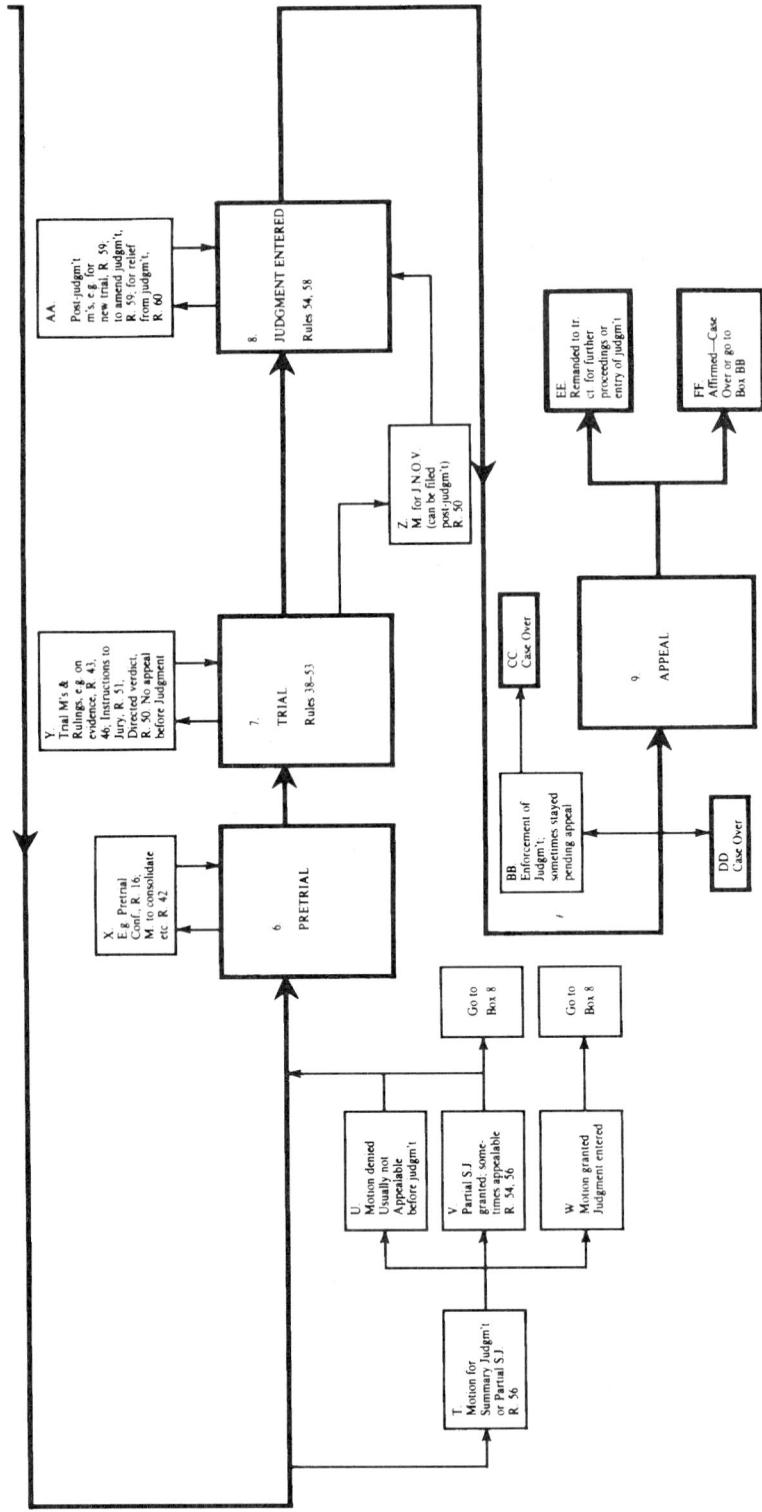

This chart was prepared by Professor Michael J. Goldberg of Widener University School of Law.

Part I

Federal Rules of Civil Procedure for the United States District Courts

and

Comparative Federal and State Provisions

TABLE OF CONTENTS

Federal Rules of Civil Procedure

I. Scope of Rules—One Form of Action

Rule		Page
1.	Scope of Rules	11
2.	One Form of Action	11

II. Commencement of Action; Service of Process, Pleadings, Motions and Orders

3. Commencement of Action 11
4. Summons 12
    (a) Form.
    (b) Issuance.
    (c) Service With Complaint; by Whom Made.
    (d) Waiver of Service; Duty to Save Costs of Service; Request to Waive.
    (e) Service Upon Individuals Within a Judicial District of the United States.
    (f) Service Upon Individuals in a Foreign Country.
    (g) Service Upon Infants and Incompetent Persons.
    (h) Service Upon Corporations and Associations.
    (i) Service Upon the United States, and Its Agencies, Corporations, or Officers.
    (j) Service Upon Foreign, State or Local Governments.
    (k) Territorial Limits of Effective Service.
    (*l*) Proof of Service.
    (m) Time Limit for Service.
    (n) Seizure of Property; Service of Summons Not Feasible.
4.1 Service of Other Process 23
    (a) Generally.
    (b) Enforcement of Orders; Commitment for Civil Contempt.
5. Service and Filing of Pleadings and Other Papers 23
    (a) Service: When Required.
    (b) Same: How Made.
    (c) Same: Numerous Defendants.

RULES OF CIVIL PROCEDURE

Rule		Page
5.	Service and Filing of Pleadings and Other Papers—Continued	
	(d) Filing.	
	(e) Filing With the Court Defined.	
6.	Time	25
	(a) Computation.	
	(b) Enlargement.	
	(c) Rescinded.	
	(d) For Motions—Affidavits.	
	(e) Additional Time After Service by Mail.	

III. Pleadings and Motions

Rule		Page
7.	Pleadings Allowed; Form of Motions	26
	(a) Pleadings.	
	(b) Motions and Other Papers.	
	(c) Demurrers, Pleas, etc., Abolished.	
8.	General Rules of Pleading	27
	(a) Claims for Relief.	
	(b) Defenses; Form of Denials.	
	(c) Affirmative Defenses.	
	(d) Effect of Failure to Deny.	
	(e) Pleading to Be Concise and Direct; Consistency.	
	(f) Construction of Pleadings.	
9.	Pleading Special Matters	32
	(a) Capacity.	
	(b) Fraud, Mistake, Condition of the Mind.	
	(c) Conditions Precedent.	
	(d) Official Document or Act.	
	(e) Judgment.	
	(f) Time and Place.	
	(g) Special Damage.	
	(h) Admiralty and Maritime Claims.	
10.	Form of Pleadings	35
	(a) Caption; Names of Parties.	
	(b) Paragraphs; Separate Statements.	
	(c) Adoption by Reference; Exhibits.	
11.	Signing of Pleadings, Motions, and Other Papers; Representations to Court; Sanctions	36
	(a) Signature.	
	(b) Representations to Court.	
	(c) Sanctions.	
	(d) Inapplicability to Discovery.	
12.	Defenses and Objections—When and How Presented—By Pleading or Motion—Motion for Judgment on the Pleadings	39
	(a) When Presented.	
	(b) How Presented.	
	(c) Motion for Judgment on the Pleadings.	
	(d) Preliminary Hearings.	
	(e) Motion for More Definite Statement.	
	(f) Motion to Strike.	
	(g) Consolidation of Defenses in Motion.	
	(h) Waiver or Preservation of Certain Defenses.	
13.	Counterclaim and Cross-Claim	47
	(a) Compulsory Counterclaims.	
	(b) Permissive Counterclaims.	
	(c) Counterclaim Exceeding Opposing Claim.	

RULES OF CIVIL PROCEDURE

Rule   **Page**

13. Counterclaim and Cross-Claim—Continued
    - (d) Counterclaim Against the United States.
    - (e) Counterclaim Maturing or Acquired After Pleading.
    - (f) Omitted Counterclaim.
    - (g) Cross-Claim Against Co-party.
    - (h) Joinder of Additional Parties.
    - (i) Separate Trials; Separate Judgments.

14. Third Party Practice 49
    - (a) When Defendant May Bring in Third Party.
    - (b) When Plaintiff May Bring in Third Party.
    - (c) Admiralty and Maritime Claims.

15. Amended and Supplemental Pleadings 50
    - (a) Amendments.
    - (b) Amendments to Conform to the Evidence.
    - (c) Relation Back of Amendments.
    - (d) Supplemental Pleadings.

16. Pretrial Conferences; Scheduling; Management 54
    - (a) Pretrial Conferences; Objectives.
    - (b) Scheduling and Planning.
    - (c) Subjects for Consideration at Pretrial Conferences.
    - (d) Final Pretrial Conference.
    - (e) Pretrial Orders.
    - (f) Sanctions.

IV. Parties

17. Parties Plaintiff and Defendant; Capacity 58
    - (a) Real Party in Interest.
    - (b) Capacity to Sue or Be Sued.
    - (c) Infants or Incompetent Persons.

18. Joinder of Claims and Remedies 59
    - (a) Joinder of Claims.
    - (b) Joinder of Remedies; Fraudulent Conveyances.

19. Joinder of Persons Needed for Just Adjudication 61
    - (a) Persons to Be Joined if Feasible.
    - (b) Determination by Court Whenever Joinder Not Feasible.
    - (c) Pleading Reasons for Nonjoinder.
    - (d) Exception of Class Actions.

20. Permissive Joinder of Parties 65
    - (a) Permissive Joinder.
    - (b) Separate Trials.

21. Misjoinder and Non-joinder of Parties 66
22. Interpleader 66
23. Class Actions 68
    - (a) Prerequisites to a Class Action.
    - (b) Class Actions Maintainable.
    - (c) Determination by Order Whether Class Action to Be Maintained; Notice; Judgment; Actions Conducted Partially as Class Actions.
    - (d) Orders in Conduct of Actions.
    - (e) Dismissal or Compromise.

23.1 Derivative Actions by Shareholders 74
23.2 Actions Relating to Unincorporated Associations ... 75

RULES OF CIVIL PROCEDURE

Rule		Page
24.	Intervention	75
	(a) Intervention of Right.	
	(b) Permissive Intervention.	
	(c) Procedure.	
25.	Substitution of Parties	78
	(a) Death.	
	(b) Incompetency.	
	(c) Transfer of Interest.	
	(d) Public Officers; Death or Separation From Office.	

V. Depositions and Discovery

26.	General Provisions Governing Discovery; Duty of Disclosure	79
	(a) Required Disclosures; Methods to Discover Additional Matter.	
	(1) *Initial Disclosures.*	
	(2) *Disclosure of Expert Testimony.*	
	(3) *Pretrial Disclosures.*	
	(4) *Form of Disclosures; Filing.*	
	(5) *Methods to Discover Additional Matter.*	
	(b) Discovery Scope and Limits.	
	(1) *In General.*	
	(2) *Limitations.*	
	(3) *Trial Preparation: Materials.*	
	(4) *Trial Preparation: Experts.*	
	(5) *Claims of Privilege or Protection of Trial Preparation Materials.*	
	(c) Protective Orders.	
	(d) Timing and Sequence of Discovery.	
	(e) Supplementation of Disclosures and Responses.	
	(f) Meeting of Parties; Planning for Discovery.	
	(g) Signing of Disclosures, Discovery Requests, Responses, and Objections.	
27.	Depositions Before Action or Pending Appeal	94
	(a) Before Action.	
	(1) *Petition.*	
	(2) *Notice and Service.*	
	(3) *Order and Examination.*	
	(4) *Use of Deposition.*	
	(b) Pending Appeal.	
	(c) Perpetuation by Action.	
28.	Persons Before Whom Depositions May Be Taken	95
	(a) Within the United States.	
	(b) In Foreign Countries.	
	(c) Disqualification for Interest.	
29.	Stipulations Regarding Discovery Procedure	97
30.	Depositions Upon Oral Examination	97
	(a) When Depositions May Be Taken; When Leave Required.	
	(b) Notice of Examination: General Requirements; Method of Recording; Production of Documents and Things; Deposition of Organization; Deposition by Telephone.	
	(c) Examination and Cross-Examination; Record of Examination; Oath; Objections.	
	(d) Schedule and Duration; Motion to Terminate or Limit Examination.	
	(e) Review by Witness; Changes; Signing.	
	(f) Certification and Filing by Officer; Exhibits; Copies; Notice of Filing.	
	(g) Failure to Attend or to Serve Subpoena; Expenses.	

RULES OF CIVIL PROCEDURE

Rule		Page
31.	Depositions Upon Written Questions	103
	(a) Serving Questions; Notice.	
	(b) Officer to Take Responses and Prepare Record.	
	(c) Notice of Filing.	
32.	Use of Depositions in Court Proceedings	104
	(a) Use of Depositions.	
	(b) Objections to Admissibility.	
	(c) Form of Presentation.	
	(d) Effect of Errors and Irregularities in Depositions.	
	(1) *As to Notice.*	
	(2) *As to Disqualification of Officer.*	
	(3) *As to Taking of Deposition.*	
	(4) *As to Completion and Return of Deposition.*	
33.	Interrogatories to Parties	107
	(a) Availability.	
	(b) Answers and Objections.	
	(c) Scope; Use at Trial.	
	(d) Option to Produce Business Records.	
34.	Production of Documents and Things and Entry Upon Land for Inspection and Other Purposes	110
	(a) Scope.	
	(b) Procedure.	
	(c) Persons Not Parties.	
35.	Physical and Mental Examination of Persons	112
	(a) Order for Examination.	
	(b) Report of Examiner.	
36.	Requests for Admission	114
	(a) Request for Admission.	
	(b) Effect of Admission.	
37.	Failure to Make or Cooperate in Discovery: Sanctions	116
	(a) Motion for Order Compelling Disclosure or Discovery.	
	(1) *Appropriate Court.*	
	(2) *Motion.*	
	(3) *Evasive or Incomplete Disclosure, Answer, or Response.*	
	(4) *Expenses and Sanctions.*	
	(b) Failure to Comply With Order.	
	(1) *Sanctions by Court in District Where Deposition Is Taken.*	
	(2) *Sanctions by Court in Which Action Is Pending.*	
	(c) Failure to Disclose; False or Misleading Disclosure; Refusal to Admit.	
	(d) Failure of Party to Attend at Own Deposition or Serve Answers to Interrogatories or Respond to Request for Inspection.	
	(e) [Abrogated.]	
	(f) [Repealed.]	
	(g) Failure to Participate in the Framing of a Discovery Plan.	

VI. Trials

38.	Jury Trial of Right	122
	(a) Right Preserved.	
	(b) Demand.	
	(c) Same: Specification of Issues.	

RULES OF CIVIL PROCEDURE

Rule		Page
38.	Jury Trial of Right—Continued	
	(d) Waiver.	
	(e) Admiralty and Maritime Claims.	
39.	Trial by Jury or by the Court	123
	(a) By Jury.	
	(b) By the Court.	
	(c) Advisory Jury and Trial by Consent.	
40.	Assignment of Cases for Trial	124
41.	Dismissal of Actions	124
	(a) Voluntary Dismissal: Effect Thereof.	
	(1) *By Plaintiff; by Stipulation.*	
	(2) *By Order of Court.*	
	(b) Involuntary Dismissal: Effect Thereof.	
	(c) Dismissal of Counterclaim, Cross-Claim, or Third-Party Claim.	
	(d) Costs of Previously-Dismissed Action.	
42.	Consolidation; Separate Trials	128
	(a) Consolidation.	
	(b) Separate Trials.	
43.	Taking of Testimony	129
	(a) Form.	
	(b), (c) [Abrogated.]	
	(d) Affirmation in Lieu of Oath.	
	(e) Evidence on Motions.	
	(f) Interpreters.	
44.	Proof of Official Record	129
	(a) Authentication.	
	(1) *Domestic.*	
	(2) *Foreign.*	
	(b) Lack of Record.	
	(c) Other Proof.	
44.1	Determination of Foreign Law	130
45.	Subpoena	131
	(a) Form; Issuance.	
	(b) Service.	
	(c) Protection of Persons Subject to Subpoenas.	
	(d) Duties in Responding to Subpoena.	
	(e) Contempt.	
46.	Exceptions Unnecessary	135
47.	Jurors	135
	(a) Examination of Jurors.	
	(b) Peremptory Challenges.	
	(c) Excuse.	
48.	Number of Jurors—Participation in Verdict	136
49.	Special Verdicts and Interrogatories	137
	(a) Special Verdicts.	
	(b) General Verdict Accompanied by Answer to Interrogatories.	
50.	Judgment as a Matter of Law in Actions Tried by Jury; Alternative Motion for New Trial; Conditional Rulings	138
	(a) Judgment as a Matter of Law.	
	(b) Renewal of Motion for Judgment After Trial; Alternative Motion for New Trial.	
	(c) Same: Conditional Rulings on Grant of Motion.	
	(d) Same: Denial of Motion for Judgment as a Matter of Law.	
51.	Instructions to Jury: Objection	140

RULES OF CIVIL PROCEDURE

Rule		Page
52.	Findings by the Court; Judgment on Partial Findings	142
	(a) Effect.	
	(b) Amendment.	
	(c) Judgment on Partial Findings.	
53.	Masters	143
	(a) Appointment and Compensation.	
	(b) Reference.	
	(c) Powers.	
	(d) Proceedings.	
	(1) *Meetings.*	
	(2) *Witnesses.*	
	(3) *Statement of Accounts.*	
	(e) Report.	
	(1) *Contents and Filing.*	
	(2) *In Non-jury Actions.*	
	(3) *In Jury Actions.*	
	(4) *Stipulation as to Findings.*	
	(5) *Draft Report.*	
	(f) Application to Magistrate Judge.	

VII. Judgment

Rule		Page
54.	Judgments; Costs	146
	(a) Definition; Form.	
	(b) Judgment Upon Multiple Claims or Involving Multiple Parties.	
	(c) Demand for Judgment.	
	(d) Costs; Attorneys' Fees.	
	(1) *Costs Other Than Attorneys' Fees.*	
	(2) *Attorneys' Fees.*	
55.	Default	149
	(a) Entry.	
	(b) Judgment.	
	(1) *By the Clerk.*	
	(2) *By the Court.*	
	(c) Setting Aside Default.	
	(d) Plaintiffs, Counterclaimants, Cross-Claimants.	
	(e) Judgment Against the United States.	
56.	Summary Judgment	151
	(a) For Claimant.	
	(b) For Defending Party.	
	(c) Motion and Proceedings Thereon.	
	(d) Case Not Fully Adjudicated on Motion.	
	(e) Form of Affidavits; Further Testimony; Defense Required.	
	(f) When Affidavits Are Unavailable.	
	(g) Affidavits Made in Bad Faith.	
57.	Declaratory Judgments	156
58.	Entry of Judgment	156
59.	New Trials; Amendment of Judgments	157
	(a) Grounds.	
	(b) Time for Motion.	
	(c) Time for Serving Affidavits.	
	(d) On Initiative of Court.	
	(e) Motion to Alter or Amend a Judgment.	
60.	Relief From Judgment or Order	159
	(a) Clerical Mistakes.	
	(b) Mistakes; Inadvertence; Excusable Neglect; Newly Discovered Evidence; Fraud, etc.	

RULES OF CIVIL PROCEDURE

Rule		Page
61.	Harmless Error	160
62.	Stay of Proceedings to Enforce a Judgment	161

    (a) Automatic Stay; Exceptions—Injunctions, Receiverships, and Patent Accountings.
    (b) Stay on Motion for New Trial or for Judgment.
    (c) Injunction Pending Appeal.
    (d) Stay Upon Appeal.
    (e) Stay in Favor of the United States or Agency Thereof.
    (f) Stay According to State Law.
    (g) Power of Appellate Court Not Limited.
    (h) Stay of Judgment as to Multiple Claims or Multiple Parties.

63.	Inability of a Judge to Proceed	162

VIII. Provisional and Final Remedies

64.	Seizure of Person or Property	162
65.	Injunctions	163

    (a) Preliminary Injunction.
        (1) *Notice.*
        (2) *Consolidation of Hearing With Trial on Merits.*
    (b) Temporary Restraining Order; Notice; Hearing; Duration.
    (c) Security.
    (d) Form and Scope of Injunction or Restraining Order.
    (e) Employer and Employee; Interpleader; Constitutional Cases.

65.1	Security: Proceedings Against Sureties	166
66.	Receivers Appointed by Federal Courts	166
67.	Deposit in Court	167
68.	Offer of Judgment	167
69.	Execution	169

    (a) In General.
    (b) Against Certain Public Officers.

70.	Judgment for Specific Acts; Vesting Title	172
71.	Process in Behalf of and Against Persons Not Parties	172

IX. Special Proceedings

71A.	Condemnation of Property	172

    (a) Applicability of Other Rules.
    (b) Joinder of Properties.
    (c) Complaint.
        (1) *Caption.*
        (2) *Contents.*
        (3) *Filing.*
    (d) Process.
        (1) *Notice; Delivery.*
        (2) *Same; Form.*
        (3) *Service of Notice.*
        (4) *Return; Amendment.*
    (e) Appearance or Answer.
    (f) Amendment of Pleadings.
    (g) Substitution of Parties.
    (h) Trial.
    (i) Dismissal of Action.
        (1) *As of Right.*
        (2) *By Stipulation.*

RULES OF CIVIL PROCEDURE

Rule   **Page**

71A. Condemnation of Property—Continued
    (i) Dismissal of Action—Continued
        (3) *By Order of the Court.*
        (4) *Effect.*
    (j) Deposit and Its Distribution.
    (k) Condemnation Under a State's Power of Eminent Domain.
    (*l*) Costs.

72. Magistrates; Pretrial Matters — 177
    (a) Nondispositive Matters.
    (b) Dispositive Motions and Prisoner Petitions.

73. Magistrate Judges; Trial by Consent and Appeal Options — 178
    (a) Powers; Procedure.
    (b) Consent.
    (c) Normal Appeal Route.
    (d) Optional Appeal Route.

74. Method of Appeal From Magistrate Judge to District Judge Under Title 28, U.S.C. § 636(c)(4) and Rule 73(d) — 178
    (a) When Taken.
    (b) Notice of Appeal; Service.
    (c) Stay Pending Appeal.
    (d) Dismissal.

75. Proceedings on Appeal From Magistrate Judge to District Judge Under Rule 73(d) — 180
    (a) Applicability.
    (b) Record on Appeal.
        (1) *Composition.*
        (2) *Transcript.*
        (3) *Statement in Lieu of Transcript.*
    (c) Time for Filing Briefs.
    (d) Length and Form of Briefs.
    (e) Oral Argument.

76. Judgment of the District Judge on the Appeal Under Rule 73(d) and Costs — 181
    (a) Entry of Judgment.
    (b) Stay of Judgments.
    (c) Costs.

X. District Courts and Clerks

77. District Courts and Clerks — 181
    (a) District Courts Always Open.
    (b) Trials and Hearings; Orders in Chambers.
    (c) Clerk's Office and Orders by Clerk.
    (d) Notice of Orders or Judgments.

78. Motion Day — 182
79. Books and Records Kept by the Clerk and Entries Therein — 182
    (a) Civil Docket.
    (b) Civil Judgments and Orders.
    (c) Indices; Calendars.
    (d) Other Books and Records of the Clerk.

80. Stenographer; Stenographic Report or Transcript as Evidence — 183
    (a), (b) [Abrogated.]
    (c) Stenographic Report or Transcript as Evidence.

RULES OF CIVIL PROCEDURE

Rule   **Page**

XI. General Provisions

81. Applicability in General — 184
    - (a) To What Proceedings Applicable.
    - (b) Scire Facias and Mandamus.
    - (c) Removed Actions.
    - (d) [Abrogated.]
    - (e) Law Applicable.
    - (f) References to Officer of the United States.
82. Jurisdiction and Venue Unaffected — 186
83. Rules by District Courts — 186
84. Forms — 187
85. Title — 187
86. Effective Date — 187
    - (a) [Effective Date of Original Rules].
    - (b) Effective Date of Amendments.
    - (c) Effective Date of Amendments.
    - (d) Effective Date of Amendments.
    - (e) Effective Date of Amendments.

Form   **Page**

1. Summons — 189
1A. Notice of Lawsuit and Request for Waiver of Service of Summons — 190
1B. Waiver of Service of Summons — 191
2. Allegation of Jurisdiction — 192
3. Complaint on a Promissory Note — 193
4. Complaint on an Account — 193
5. Complaint for Goods Sold and Delivered — 194
6. Complaint for Money Lent — 194
7. Complaint for Money Paid by Mistake — 194
8. Complaint for Money Had and Received — 194
9. Complaint for Negligence — 194
10. Complaint for Negligence Where Plaintiff Is Unable to Determine Definitely Whether the Person Responsible Is C.D. or E.F. or Whether Both Are Responsible and Where His Evidence May Justify a Finding of Wilfulness or of Recklessness or of Negligence — 195
11. Complaint for Conversion — 196
12. Complaint for Specific Performance of Contract to Convey Land — 196
13. Complaint on Claim for Debt and to Set Aside Fraudulent Conveyance Under Rule 18(b) — 197
14. Complaint for Negligence Under Federal Employer's Liability Act — 197
15. Complaint for Damages Under Merchant Marine Act — 198
16. Complaint for Infringement of Patent — 199
17. Complaint for Infringement of Copyright and Unfair Competition — 199
18. Complaint for Interpleader and Declaratory Relief — 201
18–A. [Abrogated] — 202
19. Motion to Dismiss, Presenting Defenses of Failure to State a Claim, of Lack of Service of Process, of Improper Venue, and of Lack of Jurisdiction Under Rule 12(b) — 202
20. Answer Presenting Defenses Under Rule 12(b) — 203
21. Answer to Complaint Set Forth in Form 8, With Counterclaim for Interpleader — 204
22. Motion to Bring in Third-Party Defendant [Eliminated] — 204
22–A. Summons and Complaint Against Third-Party Defendant — 205
22–B. Motion to Bring in Third-Party Defendant — 206
23. Motion to Intervene as a Defendant Under Rule 24 — 206
24. Request for Production of Documents, etc., Under Rule 34 — 208
25. Request for Admission Under Rule 36 — 208
26. Allegation of Reason for Omitting Party — 209
27. Notice of Appeal to Court of Appeals Under Rule 73(b) [Abrogated.] — 209

Form		Page
28.	Notice: Condemnation	209
29.	Complaint: Condemnation	210
30.	Suggestion of Death Upon the Record Under Rule 25(a)(1)	212
31.	Judgment on Jury Verdict	212
32.	Judgment on Decision by the Court	213
33.	Notice of Availability of a Magistrate Judge to Exercise Jurisdiction and Appeal Option	213
34.	Consent to Exercise of Jurisdiction by a United States Magistrate Judge, Election of Appeal to District Judge	214
34A.	Order of Reference	215
35.	Report of Parties' Planning Meeting	215

Supplemental Rules for Certain Admiralty and Maritime Claims

Rule		Page
A.	Scope of Rules	217
B.	Attachment and Garnishment: Special Provisions	217
C.	Actions in Rem: Special Provisions	218
D.	Possessory, Petitory, and Partition Actions	220
E.	Actions in Rem and Quasi in Rem: General Provisions	221
F.	Limitation of Liability	225

Comparative Federal and State Provisions

(See Index to Comparative State Provisions, Part XI, infra.)

FEDERAL RULES OF CIVIL PROCEDURE FOR THE UNITED STATES DISTRICT COURTS PLUS COMPARATIVE STATE AND FEDERAL PROVISIONS

I. SCOPE OF RULES—ONE FORM OF ACTION

Rule 1. Scope of Rules

These rules govern the procedure in the United States district courts in all suits of a civil nature whether cognizable as cases at law or in equity or in admiralty, with the exceptions stated in Rule 81. They shall be construed and administered to secure the just, speedy, and inexpensive determination of every action.

Rule 2. One Form of Action

There shall be one form of action to be known as "civil action".

II. COMMENCEMENT OF ACTION; SERVICE OF PROCESS, PLEADINGS, MOTIONS AND ORDERS

Rule 3. Commencement of Action

A civil action is commenced by filing a complaint with the court.

Rule 3   RULES OF CIVIL PROCEDURE

Comparative State Provision

Kansas Statutes Annotated § 60–203(a)

A civil action is commenced at the time of: (1) filing a petition with the clerk of the court, if service of process is obtained or the first publication is made for service by publication within 90 days after the petition is filed, except that the court may extend that time an additional 30 days upon a showing of good cause by the plaintiff; or (2) service of process or first publication, if service of process or first publication is not made within the time specified by provision (1).

Rule 4. Summons

(a) Form. The summons shall be signed by the clerk, bear the seal of the court, identify the court and the parties, be directed to the defendant, and state the name and address of the plaintiff's attorney or, if unrepresented, of the plaintiff. It shall also state the time within which the defendant must appear and defend, and notify the defendant that failure to do so will result in judgment by default against the defendant for the relief demanded in the complaint. The court may allow a summons to be amended.

(b) Issuance. Upon or after filing the complaint, the plaintiff may present a summons to the clerk for signature and seal. If the summons is in proper form, the clerk shall sign, seal, and issue it to the plaintiff for service on the defendant. A summons, or a copy of the summons if addressed to multiple defendants, shall be issued for each defendant to be served.

(c) Service With Complaint; by Whom Made.

(1) A summons shall be served together with a copy of the complaint. The plaintiff is responsible for service of a summons and complaint within the time allowed under subdivision (m) and shall furnish the person effecting service with the necessary copies of the summons and complaint.

(2) Service may be effected by any person who is not a party and who is at least 18 years of age. At the request of the plaintiff, however, the court may direct that service be effected by a United States marshal, deputy United States marshal, or other person or officer specially appointed by the court for that purpose. Such an appointment must be made when plaintiff is to proceed in forma pauperis pursuant to 28 U.S.C. § 1915 or is authorized to proceed as a seaman under 28 U.S.C. § 1916.

(d) Waiver of Service; Duty to Save Costs of Service; Request to Waive.

(1) A defendant who waives service of a summons does not thereby waive any objection to the venue or to the jurisdiction of the court over the person of the defendant.

(2) An individual, corporation, or association that is subject to service under subdivision (e), (f), or (h) and that receives notice of an

action in the manner provided in this paragraph has a duty to avoid unnecessary costs of serving the summons. To avoid costs, the plaintiff may notify such a defendant of the commencement of the action and request that the defendant waive service of a summons. The notice and request

(A) shall be in writing and shall be addressed directly to the defendant, if an individual, or else to an officer or managing or general agent (or other agent authorized by appointment or law to receive service of process) or of a defendant subject to service under subdivision (h);

(B) shall be dispatched through first-class mail or other reliable means;

(C) shall be accompanied by a copy of the complaint and shall identify the court in which it has been filed;

(D) shall inform the defendant, by means of a text prescribed in an official form promulgated pursuant to Rule 84, of the consequences of compliance and of a failure to comply with the request;

(E) shall set forth the date on which the request is sent;

(F) shall allow the defendant a reasonable time to return the waiver, which shall be at least 30 days from the date on which the request is sent, or 60 days from that date if the defendant is addressed outside any judicial district of the United States; and

(G) shall provide the defendant with an extra copy of the notice and request, as well as a prepaid means of compliance in writing.

If a defendant located within the United States fails to comply with a request for waiver made by a plaintiff located within the United States, the court shall impose the costs subsequently incurred in effecting service on the defendant unless good cause for the failure be shown.

(3) A defendant that, before being served with process, timely returns a waiver so requested is not required to serve an answer to the complaint until 60 days after the date on which the request for waiver of service was sent, or 90 days after that date if the defendant was addressed outside any judicial district of the United States.

(4) When the plaintiff files a waiver of service with the court, the action shall proceed, except as provided in paragraph (3), as if a summons and complaint had been served at the time of filing the waiver, and no proof of service shall be required.

(5) The costs to be imposed on a defendant under paragraph (2) for failure to comply with a request to waive service of a summons shall include the costs subsequently incurred in effecting service under subdivision (e), (f), or (h), together with the costs, including a reasonable attorney's fee, of any motion required to collect the costs of service.

Rule 4   RULES OF CIVIL PROCEDURE

(e) Service Upon Individuals Within a Judicial District of the United States. Unless otherwise provided by federal law, service upon an individual from whom a waiver has not been obtained and filed, other than an infant or an incompetent person, may be effected in any judicial district of the United States:

(1) pursuant to the law of the state in which the district court is located, or in which service is effected, for the service of a summons upon the defendant in an action brought in the courts of general jurisdiction of the State; or

(2) by delivering a copy of the summons and of the complaint to the individual personally or by leaving copies thereof at the individual's dwelling house or usual place of abode with some person of suitable age and discretion then residing therein or by delivering a copy of the summons and of the complaint to an agent authorized by appointment or by law to receive service of process.

(f) Service Upon Individuals in a Foreign Country. Unless otherwise provided by federal law, service upon an individual from whom a waiver has not been obtained and filed, other than an infant or an incompetent person, may be effected in a place not within any judicial district of the United States:

(1) by any internationally agreed means reasonably calculated to give notice, such as those means authorized by the Hague Convention on the Service Abroad of Judicial and Extrajudicial Documents; or

(2) if there is no internationally agreed means of service or the applicable international agreement allows other means of service, provided that service is reasonably calculated to give notice:

    (A) in the manner prescribed by the law of the foreign country for service in that country in an action in any of its courts of general jurisdiction; or

    (B) as directed by the foreign authority in response to a letter rogatory or letter of request; or

    (C) unless prohibited by law of the foreign country, by

       (i) delivery to the individual personally of a copy of the summons and the complaint; or

       (ii) any form of mail requiring a signed receipt, to be addressed and dispatched by the clerk of the court to the party to be served; or

(3) by other means not prohibited by international agreement as may be directed by the court.

(g) Service Upon Infants and Incompetent Persons. Service upon an infant or an incompetent person in a judicial district of the United States shall be effected in the manner prescribed by the law of the state in which the service is made for the service of summons or other like process upon any such defendant in an action brought in the courts of general jurisdiction of that state. Service upon an infant or an incompetent person in a place not within any judicial district of the United States shall be effected in the manner prescribed by paragraph (2)(A) or (2)(B) of subdivision (f) or by such means as the court may direct.

(h) Service Upon Corporations and Associations. Unless otherwise provided by federal law, service upon a domestic or foreign corporation or upon a partnership or other unincorporated association that is subject to suit under a common name, and from which a waiver of service has not been obtained and filed, shall be effected:

(1) in judicial district of the United States in the manner prescribed for individuals by subdivision (e)(1), or by delivering a copy of the summons and of the complaint to an officer, a managing or general agent, or to any other agent authorized by appointment or by law to receive service of process and, if the agent is one authorized by statute to receive service and the statute so requires, by also mailing a copy to the defendant, or

(2) in a place not within any judicial district of the United States in any manner prescribed for individuals by subdivision (f) except personal delivery as provided in paragraph (2)(C)(i) thereof.

(i) Service Upon the United States, and Its Agencies, Corporations, or Officers

(1) Service upon the United States shall be effected

(A) by delivering a copy of the summons and of the complaint to the United States attorney for the district in which the action is brought or to an assistant United States attorney or clerical employee designated by the United States attorney in a writing filed with the clerk of the court or by sending a copy of the summons and of the complaint by registered or certified mail addressed to the civil process clerk at the office of the United States attorney and

(B) by also sending a copy of the summons and of the complaint by registered or certified mail to the Attorney General of the United States at Washington, District of Columbia, and

(C) in any action attacking the validity of an order of an officer or agency of the United States not made a party, by also sending a copy of the summons and of the complaint by registered or certified mail to the officer or agency.

(2) Service upon an officer, agency, or corporation of the United States shall be effected by serving the United States in the manner prescribed by paragraph (1) of this subdivision and by also sending a copy of the summons and of the complaint by registered or certified mail to the officer, agency, or corporation.

Rule 4   RULES OF CIVIL PROCEDURE

(3) The court shall allow a reasonable time for service of process under this subdivision for the purpose of curing the failure to serve multiple officers, agencies, or corporations of the United States if the plaintiff has effected service on either the United States attorney or the Attorney General of the United States.

(j) Service Upon Foreign, State, or Local Governments.

(1) Service upon a foreign state or a political subdivision, agency, or instrumentality thereof shall be effected pursuant to 28 U.S.C. § 1608.

(2) Service upon a state, municipal corporation, or other governmental organization subject to suit shall be effected by delivering a copy of the summons and of the complaint to its chief executive officer or by serving the summons and complaint in the manner prescribed by the law of that state for the service of summons or other like process upon any such defendant.

(k) Territorial Limits of Effective Service.

(1) Service of a summons or filing a waiver of service is effective to establish jurisdiction over the person of a defendant

    (A) who could be subjected to the jurisdiction of a court of general jurisdiction in the state in which the district court is located, or

    (B) who is a party joined under Rule 14 or Rule 19 and is served at a place within a judicial district of the United States and not more than 100 miles from the place from which the summons issues, or

    (C) who is subject to the federal interpleader jurisdiction under 28 U.S.C. § 1335, or,

    (D) when authorized by a statute of the United States.

(2) If the exercise of jurisdiction is consistent with the Constitution and laws of the United States, serving a summons or filing a waiver of service is also effective, with respect to claims arising under federal law, to establish personal jurisdiction over the person of any defendant who is not subject to the jurisdiction of the courts of general jurisdiction of any state.

(*l*) Proof of Service. If service is not waived, the person effecting service shall make proof thereof to the court. If service is made by a person other than a United States marshal or deputy United States marshal, the person shall make affidavit thereof. Proof of service in a place not within any judicial district of the United States shall, if effected under paragraph (1) of subdivision (f), be made pursuant to the applicable treaty or convention, and shall, if effected under paragraph (2) or (3) thereof, include a receipt signed by the addressee or other evidence of delivery to the addressee satisfactory to the court. Failure to make proof of service does not affect the validity of the service. The court may allow proof of service to be amended.

(m) Time Limit for Service. If service of the summons and complaint is not made upon a defendant within 120 days after the filing of the complaint, the court, upon motion or on its own initiative after notice to the plaintiff, shall dismiss the action without prejudice as to that defendant or direct that service be effected within a specified time; provided that if the plaintiff shows good cause for the failure, the court shall extend the time for service for an appropriate period. This subdivision does not apply to service in a foreign country pursuant to subdivision (f) or (j)(1).

(n) Seizure of Property; Service of Summons Not Feasible.

(1) If a statute of the United States so provides, the court may assert jurisdiction over property. Notice to claimants of the property shall then be sent in the manner provided by the statute or by service of a summons under this rule.

(2) Upon a showing that personal jurisdiction over a defendant cannot, in the district where the action is brought, be obtained with reasonable efforts by service of summons in any manner authorized by this rule, the court may assert jurisdiction over the defendant's assets found within the district by seizing the assets under the circumstances and in the manner provided by the law of the state in which the district court is located.

Notes on Amendments to Federal Rule 4 and Comparative State Provisions

(a) Amendments in 1993

Rule 4 has been altered in order to facilitate service of the summons and complaint. While some provisions of the old rule have merely been reorganized by the Amendments, other provisions have been added or deleted to improve the service of summons. The provisions of Rule 4 that previously dealt with the service of process other than a summons have been removed to the new Rule 4.1, and, as a result, the caption of Rule 4 has been changed from "Process" to "Summons". Several substantive changes have been made to the rule.

The 1993 Amendment facilitates the issuance and service of a summons in several ways. Subdivision (a) (formerly subdivision (b)) no longer requires that summons follow local rule or statute in special cases, allowing instead a uniform summons form and procedure to be used by all federal courts. Subdivision (b) (formerly subdivision (a)) now makes it clear that it is the plaintiff, and not the clerk, who has the obligation to fill out the summons form. Requirements for service have been broadened to allow service to be made not only pursuant to the laws of the forum state, but, unless the defendant is a minor or incompetent, to be made according to the laws of the state in which service is effected as well.

The Amendment also clarifies the procedure for waiving service. The old Rule 4(c)(2)(C)(ii), stated that a summons and complaint may be served "by mailing a copy of the summons and of the complaint (by first-class mail, postage prepaid) to the person to be served, together with two copies of a notice and acknowledgement. * * *" Further, 4(c)(2)(D) provided for the recovery of costs of service from a defendant who did not return the acknowledgement. While this provision was commonly known as "service by mail", it did not, in fact, effect service on the defendant. Rather, the acknowledgement constituted a waiver of personal service. As amended, Rule 4(d) now clearly sets out the procedure for securing a waiver of service from a defendant and, further, explicitly states that the defendant "has a duty to avoid unnecessary costs of serving the summons." The amended rule sets forth the procedures to be followed when service is waived,

Rule 4   RULES OF CIVIL PROCEDURE

and, at subsection (d)(5), lists what costs are to be recovered from a defendant who fails to waive service.

The reach of the federal courts is broadened by the Amendment. New Rule 4(e) and 4(k) permit service to be effected anywhere in the United States, and further provide that a federal court shall obtain personal jurisdiction over a defendant not subject to the jurisdiction of any single state to the fullest extent permitted under statute and the Constitution.

Rule 4 sets forth several officers who must be served when the United States is a defendant. Under the old rule, the plaintiff had to deal with the danger of failing to serve a required officer, thereby not effecting service on the United States. The revision eliminates this danger by allowing the plaintiff a reasonable time to cure the defect once it is discovered.

Finally, as amended, Rule 4(f) recommends the use of international agreements regarding service of process by permitting service to be effected on individuals in a foreign country by "any internationally agreed means * * * such as those means authorized by the Hague Convention on the Service Abroad of Judicial and Extrajudicial Documents. * * *"

(b) Comparative State Provisions—The Illinois Scheme for Issuing and Serving Process

1. *Issuance of process*

Illinois Compiled Statutes 5/2–201(a)

Every action, unless otherwise expressly provided by statute, shall be commenced by the filing of a complaint. The clerk shall issue summons upon request of the plaintiff. The form and substance of the summons, and of all other process, and the issuance of alias process and the service of copies of pleadings shall be according to rules.

2. *By whom served*

Illinois Compiled Statutes 5/2–202

(a) Process shall be served by a sheriff, or if the sheriff is disqualified, by a coroner of some county of the State. A sheriff of a county with a population of less than 1,000,000 may employ civilian personnel to serve process * * *. The court may, in its discretion upon motion, order service to be made by a private person over 18 years of age and not a party to the action. It is not necessary that service be made by a sheriff or coroner of the county in which service is made. If served or sought to be served by a sheriff or coroner, he or she shall endorse his or her return thereon, and if by a private person the return shall be by affidavit.

(b) Summons may be served upon the defendants wherever they may be found in the State, by any person authorized to serve process. An officer may serve summons in his or her official capacity outside his or her county, but fees for mileage outside the county of the officer cannot be taxed as costs. The person serving the process in a foreign county may make return by mail.

(c) If any sheriff, coroner, or other person to whom any process is delivered, neglects or refuses to make return of the same, the plaintiff may petition the court to enter a rule requiring the sheriff, coroner, or other person, to make return of the process on a day to be fixed by the court, or to show cause on that day why that person should not be attached for contempt of the court. The plaintiff shall then cause a written notice of the rule to be served on the sheriff, coroner, or other person. If good and sufficient cause be not shown to excuse the officer or other person, the court shall adjudge him or her guilty of a contempt, and shall impose punishment as in other cases of contempt.

(d) * * *

3. *Personal service within the state*

Illinois Compiled Statutes 5/2-203(a)

Except as otherwise expressly provided, service of summons upon an individual defendant shall be made (1) by leaving a copy thereof with the defendant personally, (2) by leaving a copy at the defendant's usual place of abode, with some person of the family, of the age of 13 years or upwards, and informing that person of the contents thereof, provided the officer or other person making service shall also send a copy of the summons in a sealed envelope with postage fully prepaid, addressed to the defendant at his or her usual place of abode, or (3) as provided in section 1-2-9.2 of the Illinois Municipal Code with respect to a violation of an ordinance governing parking or standing of vehicles in cities with a population over 500,000. The certificate of the officer or affidavit of the person that he or she has sent the copy in pursuance of this Section is evidence that he or she has done so.

Illinois Compiled Statutes 5/2-204

A private corporation may be served (1) by leaving a copy of the process with its registered agent or any officer or agent of the corporation found anywhere in the State; or (2) in any other manner now or hereafter permitted by law. A private corporation may also be notified by publication and mail in like manner and with like effect as individuals.

Illinois Compiled Statutes 5/2-205

(a) A partnership sued in its firm name may be served by leaving a copy of the process with any partner personally or with any agent of the partnership found anywhere in the State. A partnership sued in its firm name may also be notified by publication and mail in like manner and with like effect as individuals.

(b) When a personal judgment is sought against a known partner for a partnership liability the partner may be served (1) in any manner provided for service on individuals or (2) by leaving a copy of the summons for him or her with any other partner and mailing a copy of the summons in a sealed envelope with postage prepaid, addressed to the partner against whom the judgment is sought at his or her usual place of abode as shown by an affidavit filed in the cause. The certificate of the officer or the affidavit of the other person making service that he or she has mailed the copy in pursuance of this section is evidence that he or she has done so. Service on a nonresident partner against whom a personal judgment is sought may be made by leaving a copy with any other partner, and mailing, as provided herein, only if the cause of action sued on is a partnership liability arising out of the transaction of business within the State.

(c) When a personal judgment is sought against an unknown owner in a suit authorized under Section 6 of "An Act in relation to the use of an assumed name in the conduct or transaction of business in this State", approved July 17, 1941, as amended, service may be made by leaving a copy of the summons with any agent of the business and publishing notice in the manner provided by Section 2-206 of this Act. (Footnote omitted.)

Illinois Compiled Statutes 5/2-205.1

A voluntary unincorporated association sued in its own name may be served by leaving a copy of the process with any officer of the association personally or by leaving a copy of the process at the office of the association with an agent of the association. A voluntary unincorporated association sued in its own name may also be notified by publication and mail in like manner and with like effect as individuals.

Illinois Compiled Statutes 5/2-211

In actions against public, municipal, governmental or quasi-municipal corporations, summons may be served by leaving a copy with the chairperson of the county board or county clerk in the case of a county, with the mayor or city clerk in the case of a city, with the president of the board of trustees or village clerk in the case of a village, with the supervisor or town clerk in the case of a town, and with the president or clerk or other officer corresponding thereto in the case of any other public, municipal, governmental or quasi-municipal corporation or body.

Illinois Compiled Statutes 5/2-212

Any trustee of a corporation or its property or any receiver may be served with summons (1) in any manner provided for service on individuals or corporations, as is appropriate, or (2) by leaving a copy thereof with any agent in the employ of the trustee or receiver anywhere in the State. The trustee or receiver may also be notified by publication and mail in like manner and with like effect as individuals.

4. *Personal service on party not inhabitant of or found within state*

Illinois Compiled Statutes 5/2-208

(a) Personal service of summons may be made upon any party outside the State. If upon a citizen or resident of this State or upon a person who has submitted to the jurisdiction of the courts of this State, it shall have the force and effect of personal service of summons within this State; otherwise it shall have the force and effect of service by publication.

(b) The service of summons shall be made in like manner as service within this State, by any person over 18 years of age not a party to the action. No order of court is required. An affidavit of the server shall be filed stating the time, manner and place of service. The court may consider the affidavit, or any other competent proofs, in determining whether service has been properly made.

(c) No default shall be entered until the expiration of at least 30 days after service. A default judgment entered on such service may be set aside only on a showing which would be timely and sufficient to set aside a default judgment entered on personal service within this State.

5. *Service by publication*

Illinois Compiled Statutes 5/2-206

Whenever, in any action affecting property or status within the jurisdiction of the court, including an action to obtain the specific performance, reformation, or rescission of a contract for the conveyance of land, plaintiff or his or her attorney shall file, at the office of the clerk of the court in which the action is pending, an affidavit showing that the defendant resides or has gone out of this State, or on due inquiry cannot be found, or is concealed within this State, so that process cannot be served upon him or her and stating the place of residence of the defendant, if known, or that upon diligent inquiry his or her place of residence cannot be ascertained, the clerk shall cause publication to be made in some newspaper published in the county in which the action is pending. If there is no newspaper published in that county, then the publication shall be in a newspaper published in an adjoining county in this State, having a circulation in the county in which action is pending. The publication shall contain notice of the pendency of the action, the title of the court, the title of the case, showing the names of the first named plaintiff and the first named defendant, the number of the case, the names of the parties to be served by publication, and the date on or after which default may be entered against such party. The clerk shall also, within 10 days of the first publication of the notice, send a copy thereof by mail, addressed to each defendant whose place of residence is stated in such affidavit. The certificate of the clerk that he or she has sent the copy in pursuance of this Section is evidence that he or she has done so.

Illinois Compiled Statutes 5/2–207

The notice required in the preceding section may be given at any time after the commencement of the action, and shall be published at least once in each week for 3 successive weeks. No default or proceeding shall be taken against any defendant not served with summons, or a copy of the complaint, and not appearing, unless the first publication be at least 30 days prior to the time when the default or other proceeding is sought to be taken.

6. *Service when action based on attachment*

Illinois Compiled Statutes 5/4–101

In any court having competent jurisdiction, a creditor having a money claim, whether liquidated or unliquidated, and whether sounding in contract or tort, may have an attachment against the property of his or her debtor, or that of any one or more of several debtors, either at the time of commencement of the action or thereafter, when the claim exceeds $20, in any one of the following cases:

1. Where the debtor is not a resident of this State.

2. When the debtor conceals himself or herself or stands in defiance of an officer, so that process cannot be served upon him or her.

3. Where the debtor has departed from this State with the intention of having his or her effects removed from this State.

4. Where the debtor is about to depart from this State with the intention of having his or her effects removed from this State.

5. Where the debtor is about to remove his or her property from this State to the injury of such creditor.

6. Where the debtor has within 2 years preceding the filing of the affidavit required, fraudulently conveyed or assigned his or her effects, or a part thereof, so as to hinder or delay his or her creditors.

7. Where the debtor has, within 2 years prior to the filing of such affidavit, fraudulently concealed or disposed of his or her property so as to hinder or delay his or her creditors.

8. Where the debtor is about fraudulently to conceal, assign, or otherwise dispose of his or her property or effects, so as to hinder or delay his or her creditors.

9. Where the debt sued for was fraudulently contracted on the part of the debtor. The statements of the debtor, his or her agent or attorney, which constitute the fraud, shall have been reduced to writing, and his or her signature attached thereto, by himself or herself, agent or attorney.

10. When the debtor is a person convicted of first degree murder or * * * [other serious] felony, or found not guilty by reason of insanity or guilty but mentally ill of first degree murder or * * * [such other felony.]

Illinois Compiled Statutes 5/4–126

The sheriff or any other person authorized to serve summons shall, in like manner as summons are served in ordinary civil cases, summon, wherever they may be found in the State, the persons mentioned in such order of attachment as garnishees and all other persons whom the creditor shall designate as having any property, effects, choses in action or credits in their possession or power, belonging to the defendant, or who are in any way indebted to such defendant, the same as if their names had been inserted in such order for attachment. The persons so summoned shall be considered as garnishees. The return shall state the names of all persons so summoned, and the date of such service on each.

Persons summoned as garnishees shall thereafter hold any property, effects, choses in action or credits in their possession or power belonging to the defendant which are not exempt, subject to the court's order in such proceeding, and shall not pay to the defendant any indebtedness owed to him or her subject to such

Rule 4   RULES OF CIVIL PROCEDURE

order, and such property, effects, choses in action, credits and debts shall be considered to have been attached and the plaintiff's claim to have become a lien thereon pending such action, * * *.

(c) Comparative State Provisions—California Provision for Service of Summons by Mail

California Civil Procedure Code § 415.30

(a) A summons may be served by mail as provided in this section. A copy of the summons and of the complaint shall be mailed (by first-class mail or airmail, postage prepaid) to the person to be served, together with two copies of the notice and acknowledgment provided for in subdivision (b) and a return envelope, postage prepaid, addressed to the sender.

(b) The notice specified in subdivision (a) shall be in substantially the following form:

(Title of court and cause, with action number, to be inserted by the sender prior to mailing)

NOTICE

To: (Here state the name of the person to be served.)

This summons is served pursuant to Section 415.30 of the California Code of Civil Procedure. Failure to complete this form and return it to the sender within 20 days may subject you (or the party on whose behalf you are being served) to liability for the payment of any expenses incurred in serving a summons upon you in any other manner permitted by law. If you are served on behalf of a corporation, unincorporated association (including a partnership), or other entity, this form must be signed in the name of such entity by you or by a person authorized to receive service of process on behalf of such entity. In all other cases, this form must be signed by you personally or by a person authorized by you to acknowledge receipt of summons. Section 415.30 provides that this summons is deemed served on the date of execution of an acknowledgment of receipt of summons.

....
Signature of sender

ACKNOWLEDGMENT OF RECEIPT OF SUMMONS

This acknowledges receipt on (insert date) of a copy of the summons and of the complaint at (insert address).

Date: ....
(Date this acknowledgment is executed)

....
Signature of person acknowledging receipt, with title if acknowledgment is made on behalf of another person

(c) Service of a summons pursuant to this section is deemed complete on the date a written acknowledgment of receipt of summons is executed, if such acknowledgment thereafter is returned to the sender.

(d) If the person to whom a copy of the summons and of the complaint are mailed pursuant to this section fails to complete and return the acknowledgment form set forth in subdivision (b) within 20 days from the date of such mailing, the party to whom the summons was mailed shall be liable for reasonable expenses thereafter incurred in serving or attempting to serve the party by another method permitted by this chapter, and, except for good cause shown, the court in which the action is pending, upon motion, with or without notice, shall award the party such expenses whether or not he is otherwise entitled to recover his costs in the action.

(e) A notice or acknowledgment of receipt in form approved by the Judicial Council is deemed to comply with this section.

Rule 4.1 Service of Other Process

(a) **Generally.** Process other than a summons as provided in Rule 4 or subpoena as provided in Rule 45 shall be served by a United States marshal, a deputy United States marshal, or a person specially appointed for that purpose, who shall make proof of service as provided in Rule 4(1). The process may be served anywhere within the territorial limits of the state in which the district court is located, and, when authorized by a statute of the United States, beyond the territorial limits of that state.

(b) **Enforcement of Orders: Commitment for Civil Contempt.** An order of civil commitment of a person held to be in contempt of a decree or injunction issued to enforce the laws of the United States may be served and enforced in any district. Other orders in civil contempt proceedings shall be served in the state in which the court issuing the order to be enforced is located or elsewhere within the United States if not more than 100 miles from the place at which the order to be enforced was issued.

Note on Adoption of Federal Rule 4.1

Rule 4.1 was adopted in 1993 following the reorganization of Rule 4. Prior to 1993, Rule 4 was entitled "Process" and addressed service of all process. Rule 4 has since been retitled as "Summons" and Rule 4.1 created to govern service of process, other than a summons (governed by Rule 4) and a subpoena (governed by Rule 45).

Rule 4.1(b) provides for nationwide service of orders of civil commitment enforcing decrees of injunctions when issued to compel compliance with federal law. This change replaces the final clause of the second sentence of the former Rule 4. Nationwide service is not mandated by Rule 4.1 in cases where federally-created rights are not at issue.

As noted by the Advisory Committee on Rules, "present law [28 U.S.C. § 3041] permits criminal contempt enforcement against a contemnor wherever that person may be found." Rule 4.1 broadens the scope of the civil contempt service rule to provide greater choice in selecting the most appropriate contempt remedy, be it civil or criminal.

Rule 5. Service and Filing of Pleadings and Other Papers

(a) **Service: When Required.** Except as otherwise provided in these rules, every order required by its terms to be served, every pleading subsequent to the original complaint unless the court otherwise orders because of numerous defendants, every paper relating to discovery required to be served upon a party unless the court otherwise orders, every written motion other than one which may be heard ex parte, and every written notice, appearance, demand, offer of judgment, designation of record on appeal, and similar paper shall be served upon each of the parties. No service need be made on parties in default for failure to

Rule 5   RULES OF CIVIL PROCEDURE

appear except that pleadings asserting new or additional claims for relief against them shall be served upon them in the manner provided for service of summons in Rule 4.

In an action begun by seizure of property, in which no person need be or is named as defendant, any service required to be made prior to the filing of an answer, claim, or appearance shall be made upon the person having custody or possession of the property at the time of its seizure.

(b) Same: How Made. Whenever under these rules service is required or permitted to be made upon a party represented by an attorney the service shall be made upon the attorney unless service upon the party is ordered by the court. Service upon the attorney or upon a party shall be made by delivering a copy to the attorney or party or by mailing it to the attorney or party at the attorney's or party's last known address or, if no address is known, by leaving it with the clerk of the court. Delivery of a copy within this rule means: handing it to the attorney or to the party; or leaving it at the attorney's or party's office with a clerk or other person in charge thereof; or, if there is no one in charge, leaving it in a conspicuous place therein; or, if the office is closed or the person to be served has no office, leaving it at the person's dwelling house or usual place of abode with some person of suitable age and discretion then residing therein. Service by mail is complete upon mailing.

(c) Same: Numerous Defendants. In any action in which there are unusually large numbers of defendants, the court, upon motion or of its own initiative, may order that service of the pleadings of the defendants and replies thereto need not be made as between the defendants and that any cross-claim, counterclaim, or matter constituting an avoidance or affirmative defense contained therein shall be deemed to be denied or avoided by all other parties and that the filing of any such pleading and service thereof upon the plaintiff constitutes due notice of it to the parties. A copy of every such order shall be served upon the parties in such manner and form as the court directs.

(d) Filing. All papers after the complaint required to be served upon a party, together with a certificate of service, shall be filed with the court within a reasonable time after service but the court may on motion of a party or on its own initiative order that depositions upon oral examination and interrogatories, requests for documents, requests for admission, and answers and responses thereto not be filed unless on order of the court or for use in the proceeding.

(e) Filing With the Court Defined. The filing of papers with the court as required by these rules shall be made by filing them with the clerk of the court, except that the judge may permit the papers to be filed with the judge, in which event the judge shall note thereon the filing date and forthwith transmit them to the office of the clerk. A court may, by local rule, permit papers to be filed by facsimile or other electronic means if such means are authorized by and consistent with standards established by the Judicial Conference of the United States. The clerk shall not refuse to accept for filing any paper presented for that purpose solely because it is not presented in proper form as required by these rules or any local rules or practices.

Rule 6. Time

(a) Computation. In computing any period of time prescribed or allowed by these rules, by the local rules of any district court, by order of court, or by any applicable statute, the day of the act, event, or default from which the designated period of time begins to run shall not be included. The last day of the period so computed shall be included, unless it is a Saturday, a Sunday, or a legal holiday or, when the act to be done is the filing of a paper in court, a day on which weather or other conditions have made the office of the clerk of the district court inaccessible, in which event the period runs until the end of the next day which is not one of the aforementioned days. When the period of time prescribed or allowed is less than 11 days, intermediate Saturdays, Sundays, and legal holidays shall be excluded in the computation. As used in this rule and in Rule 77(c), "legal holiday" includes New Year's Day, Birthday of Martin Luther King, Jr., Washington's Birthday, Memorial Day, Independence Day, Labor Day, Columbus Day, Veterans Day, Thanksgiving Day, Christmas Day, and any other day appointed as a holiday by the President or the Congress of the United States, or by the state in which the district court is held.

(b) Enlargement. When by these rules or by a notice given thereunder or by order of court an act is required or allowed to be done at or within a specified time, the court for cause shown may at any time in its discretion (1) with or without motion or notice order the period enlarged if request therefor is made before the expiration of the period originally prescribed or as extended by a previous order, or (2) upon motion made after the expiration of the specified period permit the act to be done where the failure to act was the result of excusable neglect; but it may not extend the time for taking any action under Rules 50(b) and (c)(2), 52(b), 59(b), (d) and (e), 60(b), and 74(a), except to the extent and under the conditions stated in them.

(c) [Rescinded. Feb. 28, 1966, eff. July 1, 1966.]

(d) For Motions—Affidavits. A written motion, other than one which may be heard ex parte, and notice of the hearing thereof shall be served not later than 5 days before the time specified for the hearing, unless a different period is fixed by these rules or by order of the court. Such an order may for cause shown be made on ex parte application. When a motion is supported by affidavit, the affidavit shall be served with the motion; and, except as otherwise provided in Rule 59(c),

Rule 6   RULES OF CIVIL PROCEDURE

opposing affidavits may be served not later than 1 day before the hearing, unless the court permits them to be served at some other time.

(e) Additional Time After Service by Mail. Whenever a party has the right or is required to do some act or take some proceedings within a prescribed period after the service of a notice or other paper upon the party and the notice or paper is served upon the party by mail, 3 days shall be added to the prescribed period.

Note on 1985 Amendments to Federal Rule 6

The amended rule extends the exclusion of intermediate Saturdays, Sundays, and legal holidays to the computation of time periods less than 11 days. Under the prior version of Rule 6, parties bringing motions under rules with 10-day periods could have as few as 5 working days to prepare their motions. This hardship was especially acute in the case of Rules 50(b) and (c)(2), 52(b), 59(b), (d), and (e), and 60(b), which may not be enlarged at the discretion of the court. See Rule 6(b).

III. PLEADINGS AND MOTIONS

Rule 7. Pleadings Allowed; Form of Motions

(a) Pleadings. There shall be a complaint and an answer; a reply to a counterclaim denominated as such; an answer to a cross-claim, if the answer contains a cross-claim; a third-party complaint, if a person who was not an original party is summoned under the provisions of Rule 14; and a third-party answer, if a third-party complaint is served. No other pleading shall be allowed, except that the court may order a reply to an answer or a third-party answer.

(b) Motions and Other Papers.

(1) An application to the court for an order shall be by motion which, unless made during a hearing or trial, shall be made in writing, shall state with particularity the grounds therefor, and shall set forth the relief or order sought. The requirement of writing is fulfilled if the motion is stated in a written notice of the hearing of the motion.

(2) The rules applicable to captions and other matters of form of pleadings apply to all motions and other papers provided for by these rules.

(3) All motions shall be signed in accordance with Rule 11.

(c) Demurrers, Pleas, etc., Abolished. Demurrers, pleas, and exceptions for insufficiency of a pleading shall not be used.

Amendment to Federal Rule 7 and Comparative State Provisions
(a) Addition in 1983 of Rule 7(b)(3)

Rule 7(b)(3) makes clear that an "appropriate sanction" can be obtained against an attorney or party who files a motion in bad faith. One of the reasons sanctions against improper motion practice had been employed infrequently was the lack of clarity of Rule 7. It had stated only generally that the pleading requirements relating to captions, signing, and other matters of form also apply to motions and other papers. The addition of Rule 7(b)(3) explicitly expresses the

PLEADINGS AND MOTIONS — Rule 8

applicability of the signing requirement and the sanctions of Rule 11, which have been amplified. See Amendments to Federal Rule 11, following Rule 11 infra.

(b) *Comparative State Provisions*

Nebraska Revised Statutes § 25–803

The only pleadings allowed are (1) the petition by the plaintiff; (2) the answer or demurrer by the defendant; (3) the demurrer or reply by the plaintiff; and (4) the demurrer to the reply by the defendant.

Nebraska Revised Statutes § 25–820

The plaintiff may demur to one or more of the defenses set up in the answer, stating in his demurrer the grounds thereof; and where the answer contains new matter the plaintiff may reply to such new matter, denying generally or specifically each allegation controverted by him; and he may allege, in ordinary and concise language, and without repetition, any new matter not inconsistent with the petition, constituting a defense to such new matter in the answer.

Rule 8. General Rules of Pleading

(a) Claims for Relief. A pleading which sets forth a claim for relief, whether an original claim, counterclaim, cross-claim, or third-party claim, shall contain (1) a short and plain statement of the grounds upon which the court's jurisdiction depends, unless the court already has jurisdiction and the claim needs no new grounds of jurisdiction to support it, (2) a short and plain statement of the claim showing that the pleader is entitled to relief, and (3) a demand for judgment for the relief the pleader seeks. Relief in the alternative or of several different types may be demanded.

(b) Defenses; Form of Denials. A party shall state in short and plain terms the party's defenses to each claim asserted and shall admit or deny the averments upon which the adverse party relies. If a party is without knowledge or information sufficient to form a belief as to the truth of an averment, the party shall so state and this has the effect of a denial. Denials shall fairly meet the substance of the averments denied. When a pleader intends in good faith to deny only a part or a qualification of an averment, the pleader shall specify so much of it as is true and material and shall deny only the remainder. Unless the pleader intends in good faith to controvert all the averments of the preceding pleading, the pleader may make denials as specific denials of designated averments or paragraphs, or may generally deny all the averments except such designated averments or paragraphs as the pleader expressly admits; but, when the pleader does so intend to controvert all its averments, including averments of the grounds upon which the court's jurisdiction depends, the pleader may do so by general denial subject to the obligations set forth in Rule 11.

(c) Affirmative Defenses. In pleading to a preceding pleading, a party shall set forth affirmatively accord and satisfaction, arbitration and award, assumption of risk, contributory negligence, discharge in bankruptcy, duress, estoppel, failure of consideration, fraud, illegality,

Rule 8   RULES OF CIVIL PROCEDURE

injury by fellow servant, laches, license, payment, release, res judicata, statute of frauds, statute of limitations, waiver, and any other matter constituting an avoidance or affirmative defense. When a party has mistakenly designated a defense as a counterclaim or a counterclaim as a defense, the court on terms, if justice so requires, shall treat the pleading as if there had been a proper designation.

(d) Effect of Failure to Deny. Averments in a pleading to which a responsive pleading is required, other than those as to the amount of damage, are admitted when not denied in the responsive pleading. Averments in a pleading to which no responsive pleading is required or permitted shall be taken as denied or avoided.

(e) Pleading to Be Concise and Direct; Consistency.

(1) Each averment of a pleading shall be simple, concise, and direct. No technical forms of pleading or motions are required.

(2) A party may set forth two or more statements of a claim or defense alternately or hypothetically, either in one count or defense or in separate counts or defenses. When two or more statements are made in the alternative and one of them if made independently would be sufficient, the pleading is not made insufficient by the insufficiency of one or more of the alternative statements. A party may also state as many separate claims or defenses as the party has regardless of consistency and whether based on legal, equitable, or maritime grounds. All statements shall be made subject to the obligations set forth in Rule 11.

(f) Construction of Pleadings. All pleadings shall be so construed as to do substantial justice.

Comparative State Provisions

(a) *Rule 8(a)*

California Civil Procedure Code § 425.10(b)

[A complaint or cross-complaint shall contain:]

A demand for judgment for the relief to which the pleader claims he is entitled. If the recovery of money or damages be demanded, the amount thereof shall be stated, unless the action is brought in the superior court to recover actual or punitive damages for personal injury or wrongful death, in which case the amount thereof shall not be stated.

Georgia Code Annotated § 9–11–8(a)(2)

An original complaint shall contain facts upon which the court's venue depends; and any pleading which sets forth a claim for relief, whether an original claim, counterclaim, a cross-claim, or a third-party claim, shall contain:

(A) A short and plain statement of the claims showing that the pleader is entitled to relief; and

(B) A demand for judgment for the relief to which the pleader deems himself entitled; provided, however, that in actions for medical malpractice, as defined in this Code section, in which a claim for unliquidated damages is made for $10,000.00 or less, the pleadings shall contain a demand for judgment in a sum certain; and, in actions for medical malpractice in which a claim for unliquidated damages is made for a sum exceeding $10,000.00, the demand for judgment shall state that the pleader "demands judgment in excess of $10,000.00," and no further monetary amount shall be stated.

Relief in the alternative or of several different types may be demanded.

Illinois Compiled Statutes 5/2-604

Every complaint and counterclaim shall contain specific prayers for the relief to which the pleader deems himself or herself entitled except that in actions for injury to the person, no ad damnum may be pleaded except to the minimum extent necessary to comply with the circuit rules of assignment where the claim is filed. Relief, whether based on one or more counts, may be requested in the alternative. Prayers for relief which the allegations of the pleadings do not sustain may be objected to on motion or in the answering pleading. In actions for injury to the person, any complaint filed which contains an ad damnum, except to the minimum extent necessary to comply with the circuit rules of assignment where the claim is filed, shall, on motion of a defendant or on the court's own motion, be dismissed without prejudice. Except in case of default, the prayer for relief does not limit the relief obtainable, but where other relief is sought the court shall, by proper orders, and upon terms that may be just, protect the adverse party against prejudice by reason of surprise. In case of default, if relief is sought, whether by amendment, counterclaim, or otherwise, beyond that prayed in the pleading to which the party is in default, notice shall be given the defaulted party as provided by rule.

Nothing in this Section shall be construed as prohibiting the defendant from requesting of the plaintiff by interrogatory the amount of damages which will be sought.

Nebraska Revised Statutes § 25-804

The petition must contain (1) the name of the court and county in which the action is brought, and the names of the parties, plaintiff and defendant; (2) a statement of the facts constituting the cause of action, in ordinary and concise language, and without repetition; and (3) a demand for the relief to which the party supposes himself entitled. If the recovery of money be demanded, the amount of special damages shall be stated but the amount of general damages shall not be stated; and if interest thereon be claimed, the time from which interest is to be computed shall also be stated.

New York Civil Practice Law and Rules 3013

Statements in a pleading shall be sufficiently particular to give the court and parties notice of the transactions, occurrences, or series of transactions or occurrences, intended to be proved and the material elements of each cause of action or defense.

New York Civil Practice Law and Rules 3017(c)

In an action for medical or dental malpractice or in an action against a municipal corporation, as defined in section two of the general municipal law, the complaint, counterclaim, cross-claim, interpleader complaint, and third-party complaint shall contain a prayer for general relief but shall not state the amount of damages to which the pleader deems himself entitled. If the action is brought in the supreme court, the pleading shall also state whether or not the amount of damages sought exceeds the jurisdictional limits of all lower courts which would otherwise have jurisdiction. Provided, however, that a party against whom an action for medical or dental malpractice is brought or the municipal corporation, may at any time request a supplemental demand setting forth the total damages to which the pleader deems himself entitled. A supplemental demand shall be provided by the party bringing the action within fifteen days of the request. In the event the supplemental demand is not served within fifteen days, the court, on motion, may order that it be served. A supplemental demand served pursuant to this subdivision shall be treated in all respects as a demand made pursuant to subdivision (a) of this section.

New York Civil Practice Law and Rules 3041

Any party may require any other party to give a bill of particulars of such party's claim, or a copy of the items of the account alleged in a pleading. * * *

New York Civil Practice Law and Rules 3043

(a) Specified particulars. In actions to recover for personal injuries the following particulars may be required:

(1) The date and approximate time of day of the occurrence;

(2) Its approximate location;

(3) General statement of the acts or omissions constituting the negligence claimed;

(4) Where notice of a condition is a prerequisite, whether actual or constructive notice is claimed;

(5) If actual notice is claimed, a statement of when and to whom it was given;

(6) Statement of the injuries and description of those claimed to be permanent, and in an action designated in * * * [§ 5104(a)] of the insurance law, for personal injuries arising out of negligence in the use or operation of a motor vehicle in this state, in what respect plaintiff has sustained a serious injury, as defined in * * * [§ 5102(d)] of the insurance law, or economic loss greater than basic economic loss, as defined in * * * [§ 5102(a)] of the insurance law;

(7) Length of time confined to bed and to house;

(8) Length of time incapacitated from employment; and

(9) Total amounts claimed as special damages for physicians' services and medical supplies; loss of earnings, with name and address of the employer; hospital expenses; nurses' services.

(b) Supplemental bill of particulars without leave. A party may serve a supplemental bill of particulars with respect to claims of continuing special damages and disabilities without leave of court at any time, but not less than thirty days prior to trial. Provided however that no new cause of action may be alleged or new injury claimed * * *.

(c) Discretion of court. Nothing contained in the foregoing shall be deemed to limit the court in denying in a proper case, any one or more of the foregoing particulars, or in a proper case, in granting other, further or different particulars.

See also North Carolina Rules of Civil Procedure—[Form] (3) Complaint for Negligence as set out following Form 9 of the Appendix of Forms, Federal Rules of Civil Procedure, infra.

(b) *Rule 8(b)*

1. *In general*

Illinois Compiled Statutes 5/2–610

(a) Every answer and subsequent pleading shall contain an explicit admission or denial of each allegation of the pleading to which it relates.

(b) Every allegation, except allegations of damages, not explicitly denied is admitted, unless the party states in his or her pleading that he or she has no knowledge thereof sufficient to form a belief, and attaches an affidavit of the truth of the statement of want of knowledge, or unless the party has had no opportunity to deny.

(c) Denials must not be evasive, but must fairly answer the substance of the allegation denied.

(d) If a party wishes to raise an issue as to the amount of damages only, he or she may do so by stating in his or her pleading that he or she desires to contest only the amount of the damages.

2. *Importance of verification*

California Civil Procedure Code § 431.30(d)

If the complaint is * * * not verified, a general denial is sufficient but only puts in issue the material allegations of the complaint. If the complaint is verified, * * * [then, with exceptions for certain actions] the denial of the allegations shall be made positively or according to the information and belief of the defendant. * * *

California Civil Procedure Code § 446

Every pleading shall be subscribed by the party or his attorney. * * * When the complaint is verified, the answer shall be verified. * * *. [Repealed eff. Jan. 1, 1999]

(c) *Rule 8(c)*

New York Civil Practice Law and Rules 3018(b)

A party shall plead all matters which if not pleaded would be likely to take the adverse party by surprise or would raise issues of fact not appearing on the face of a prior pleading such as arbitration and award, collateral estoppel, culpable conduct claimed in diminution of damages * * *, discharge in bankruptcy, facts showing illegality either by statute or common law, fraud, infancy or other disability of the party defending, payment, release, res judicata, statute of frauds, or statute of limitation. The application of this subdivision shall not be confined to the instances enumerated.

(d) *Rule 8(d)*

Nebraska Revised Statutes § 25–842

Every material allegation of the petition not controverted by the answer, and every material allegation of new matter in the answer not controverted by the reply, shall, for the purposes of the action, be taken as true; but the allegation of new matter in the reply shall be deemed controverted by the adverse party as upon direct denial or avoidance. Allegations of value or amount of damage shall not be considered as true by failure to controvert them.

New York Civil Practice Law and Rules 3018(a)

A party shall deny those statements known or believed by him to be untrue. He shall specify those statements as to the truth of which he lacks knowledge or information sufficient to form a belief and this shall have the effect of a denial. All other statements of a pleading are deemed admitted, except that where no responsive pleading is permitted they are deemed denied or avoided.

(e) *Rule 8(e)(1)*

Colorado Rule of Civil Procedure 8(e)(1)

Each averment of a pleading shall be simple, concise, and direct. When a pleader is without direct knowledge, allegations may be made upon information and belief. No technical forms of pleading or motions are required. Pleadings otherwise meeting the requirements of these rules shall not be considered objectionable for failure to state ultimate facts as distinguished from conclusions of law.

(f) *Rule 8(e)(2)*

Georgia Code Annotated § 9-11-8(e)(2)

A party may set forth two or more statements of a claim or defense alternatively or hypothetically, either in one count or defense or in separate counts or defenses. When two or more statements are made in the alternative and one of them, if made independently, would be sufficient, the pleading is not made insufficient by the insufficiency of one or more of the alternative statements. A party may also state as many separate claims or defenses as he has, regardless of consistency and whether based on legal or on equitable grounds or on both. All statements shall be made subject to the obligations set forth in Code Section 9-11-11.

Rule 9. Pleading Special Matters

(a) Capacity. It is not necessary to aver the capacity of a party to sue or be sued or the authority of a party to sue or be sued in a representative capacity or the legal existence of an organized association of persons that is made a party, except to the extent required to show the jurisdiction of the court. When a party desires to raise an issue as to the legal existence of any party or the capacity of any party to sue or be sued or the authority of a party to sue or be sued in a representative capacity, the party desiring to raise the issue shall do so by specific negative averment, which shall include such supporting particulars as are peculiarly within the pleader's knowledge.

(b) Fraud, Mistake, Condition of the Mind. In all averments of fraud or mistake, the circumstances constituting fraud or mistake shall be stated with particularity. Malice, intent, knowledge, and other condition of mind of a person may be averred generally.

(c) Conditions Precedent. In pleading the performance or occurrence of conditions precedent, it is sufficient to aver generally that all conditions precedent have been performed or have occurred. A denial of performance or occurrence shall be made specifically and with particularity.

(d) Official Document or Act. In pleading an official document or official act it is sufficient to aver that the document was issued or the act done in compliance with law.

(e) Judgment. In pleading a judgment or decision of a domestic or foreign court, judicial or quasijudicial tribunal, or of a board or officer, it is sufficient to aver the judgment or decision without setting forth matter showing jurisdiction to render it.

(f) Time and Place. For the purpose of testing the sufficiency of a pleading, averments of time and place are material and shall be considered like all other averments of material matter.

(g) Special Damage. When items of special damage are claimed, they shall be specifically stated.

(h) Admiralty and Maritime Claims. A pleading or count setting forth a claim for relief within the admiralty and maritime jurisdiction that is also within the jurisdiction of the district court on some other ground may contain a statement identifying the claim as an admiralty or maritime claim for the purposes of Rules 14(c), 38(e), 82, and the Supplemental Rules for Certain Admiralty and Maritime Claims. If the claim is cognizable only in admiralty, it is an admiralty or maritime claim for those purposes whether so identified or not. The amendment of a pleading to add or withdraw an identifying statement is governed by the principles of Rule 15. The reference in Title 28, U.S.C. § 1292(a)(3), to admiralty cases shall be construed to mean admiralty and maritime claims within the meaning of this subdivision (h).

Comparative State Provisions and Notes on Amendment to Federal Rule 9

(a) *Comparative State Provisions*

1. *In General*

New York Civil Practice Law and Rules 3015

(a) Conditions precedent. The performance or occurrence of a condition precedent in a contract need not be pleaded. A denial of performance or occurrence shall be made specifically and with particularity. In case of such denial, the party relying upon the performance or occurrence shall be required to prove on the trial only such performance or occurrence as shall have been so specified.

(b) Corporate status. Where any party is a corporation, the complaint shall so state and, where known, it shall specify the state, country or government by or under whose laws the party was created.

(c) Judgment, decision or determination. A judgment, decision or other determination of a court, judicial or quasi-judicial tribunal, or of a board or officer, may be pleaded without stating matter showing jurisdiction to render it.

(d) Signatures. Unless specifically denied in the pleadings each signature on a negotiable instrument is admitted.

* * *

New York Civil Practice Law and Rules 3016

(a) Libel or slander. In an action for libel or slander, the particular words complained of shall be set forth in the complaint, but their application to the plaintiff may be stated generally.

(b) Fraud or mistake. Where a cause of action or defense is based upon misrepresentation, fraud, mistake, wilful default, breach of trust or undue influence, the circumstances constituting the wrong shall be stated in detail.

(c) Separation or divorce. In an action for separation or divorce, the nature and circumstances of a party's alleged misconduct, if any, and the time and place of each act complained of, if any, shall be specified in the complaint or counterclaim as the case may be.

(d) Judgment. In an action on a judgment, the complaint shall state the extent to which any judgment recovered by the plaintiff against the defendant, or against a person jointly liable with the defendant, on the same cause of action has been satisfied.

(e) Law of foreign country. Where a cause of action or defense is based upon the law of a foreign country or its political subdivision, the substance of the foreign law relied upon shall be stated.

(f) Sale and delivery of goods or performing of labor or services. In an action involving the sale and delivery of goods, or the performing of labor or services, or the furnishing of materials, the plaintiff may set forth and number in his verified complaint the items of his claim and the reasonable value or agreed price of each. Thereupon the defendant by his verified answer shall indicate specifically those items he disputes and whether in respect of delivery or performance, reasonable value or agreed price.

* * *

2. *Rule 9(b)*

Delaware Superior Court Rule (Civil) 9(b)

In all averments of fraud, negligence or mistake, the circumstances constituting fraud, negligence or mistake shall be stated with particularity. Malice, intent, knowledge and other condition of mind of a person may be averred generally.

3. *Rule 9(c)*

New Jersey Civil Practice Rule 4:5–8(b)

In pleading the performance or occurrence of conditions precedent, it is sufficient to allege generally that all such conditions have been performed or have occurred. A denial of performance or occurrence shall be made specifically and with particularity, but when so made the party pleading the performance or occurrence has the burden of establishing it.

See also New York Civil Practice Law and Rules 3015(a) set out in 1 above.

(b) *Amendment in 1966 Adding Rule 9(h)*

Rule 9(h) was added by amendment in 1966. The Advisory Committee's Note to the Rule reads as follows:

Certain distinctive features of the admiralty practice must be preserved for what are now suits in admiralty. This raises the question: After unification, when a single form of action is established, how will the counterpart of the present suit in admiralty be identifiable? In part the question is easily answered. Some claims for relief can only be suits in admiralty, either because the admiralty jurisdiction is exclusive or because no nonmaritime ground of federal jurisdiction exists. Many claims, however, are cognizable by the district courts whether asserted in admiralty or in a civil action, assuming the existence of a nonmaritime ground of jurisdiction. Thus at present the pleader has power to determine procedural consequences by the way in which he exercises the classic privilege given by the saving-to-suitors clause (28 U.S.C. § 1333) or by equivalent statutory provisions. For example, a longshoreman's claim for personal injuries suffered by reason of the unseaworthiness of a vessel may be asserted in a suit in admiralty or, if diversity of citizenship exists, in a civil action. One of the important procedural consequences is that in the civil action either party may demand a jury trial, while in the suit in admiralty there is no right to jury trial except as provided by statute.

It is no part of the purpose of unification to inject a right to jury trial into those admiralty cases in which that right is not provided by statute. Similarly, as will be more specifically noted below, there is no disposition to change the present law as to interlocutory appeals in admiralty, or as to the venue of suits in admiralty; and, of course, there is no disposition to inject into the civil practice as it now is the distinctively maritime remedies (maritime attachment and garnishment, actions in rem, possessory, petitory, and partition actions and limitation of liability). The unified rules must therefore provide some device for preserving the present power of the pleader to determine whether these historically maritime procedures shall be applicable to his claim or not; the pleader must be afforded some means of designating his claim as the counterpart of the present suit in admiralty, where its character as such is not clear.

The problem is different from the similar one concerning the identification of claims that were formerly suits in equity. While that problem is not free from complexities, it is broadly true that the modern counterpart of the suit in equity is distinguishable from the former action at law by the character of the relief sought. This mode of identification is possible in only a limited category of admiralty cases. In large numbers of cases the relief sought in admiralty is simple money damages, indistinguishable from the remedy afforded by the common law. This is true, for example, in the case of the longshoreman's action for personal injuries stated above. After unification has abolished the distinction between civil actions and suits in admiralty, the complaint in such an action would be almost completely ambiguous as to the pleader's intentions regarding the procedure invoked. The allegation of diversity of citizenship might be regarded as a clue indicating an intention to proceed as at present under the saving-to-suitors clause; but this, too, would be ambiguous if there were also reference to the admiralty jurisdiction, and the pleader ought not be required to forego mention of all available jurisdictional grounds.

Other methods of solving the problem were carefully explored, but the Advisory Committee concluded that the preferable solution is to allow the pleader who now has power to determine procedural consequences by filing a suit in admiralty to exercise that power under unification, for the limited instances in which procedural differences will remain, by a simple statement in his pleading to the effect that the claim is an admiralty or maritime claim.

The choice made by the pleader in identifying or in failing to identify his claim as an admiralty or maritime claim is not an irrevocable election. The rule provides that the amendment of a pleading to add or withdraw an identifying statement is subject to the principles of Rule 15.

Rule 10. Form of Pleadings

(a) Caption; Names of Parties. Every pleading shall contain a caption setting forth the name of the court, the title of the action, the file number, and a designation as in Rule 7(a). In the complaint the title of the action shall include the names of all the parties, but in other pleadings it is sufficient to state the name of the first party on each side with an appropriate indication of other parties.

(b) Paragraphs; Separate Statements. All averments of claim or defense shall be made in numbered paragraphs, the contents of each of which shall be limited as far as practicable to a statement of a single set of circumstances; and a paragraph may be referred to by number in all succeeding pleadings. Each claim founded upon a separate transaction or occurrence and each defense other than denials shall be stated in a separate count or defense whenever a separation facilitates the clear presentation of the matters set forth.

(c) Adoption by Reference; Exhibits. Statements in a pleading may be adopted by reference in a different part of the same pleading or in another pleading or in any motion. A copy of any written instrument which is an exhibit to a pleading is a part thereof for all purposes.

Comparative State Provisions
(a) *Rule 10(b)*

Illinois Compiled Statutes 5/2–613(a)

Parties may plead as many causes of action, counterclaims, defenses, and matters in reply as they may have, and each shall be separately designated and numbered.

Rule 10 RULES OF CIVIL PROCEDURE

Illinois Compiled Statutes 5/2–603(b)

Each separate cause of action upon which a separate recovery might be had shall be stated in a separate count or counterclaim, as the case may be and each count, counterclaim, defense or reply, shall be separately pleaded, designated and numbered, and each shall be divided into paragraphs numbered consecutively, each paragraph containing, as nearly as may be, a separate allegation.

(b) *Rule 10(c)*

Michigan Court Rule 2.113(F)

Exhibits; Written Instruments.

(1) If a claim or defense is based on a written instrument, a copy of the instrument or its pertinent parts must be attached to the pleading as an exhibit unless the instrument is

(a) a matter of public record in the county in which the action is commenced and its location in the record is stated in the pleading;

(b) in the possession of the adverse party and the pleading so states;

(c) inaccessible to the pleader and the pleading so states, giving the reason; or

(d) of a nature that attaching the instrument would be unnecessary or impractical and the pleading so states, giving the reason.

(2) An exhibit attached or referred to under subrule (F)(1)(a) or (b) is a part of the pleading for all purposes.

Michigan Court Rule 2.113(G)

Adoption by Reference. Statements in a pleading may be adopted by reference only in another part of the same pleading.

Rule 11. Signing of Pleadings, Motions, and Other Papers; Representations to Court; Sanctions

(a) Signature. Every pleading, written motion, and other paper shall be signed by at least one attorney of record in the attorney's individual name, or, if the party is not represented by an attorney, shall be signed by the party. Each paper shall state the signer's address and telephone number, if any. Except when otherwise specifically provided by rule or statute, pleadings need not be verified or accompanied by affidavit. An unsigned paper shall be stricken unless omission of the signature is corrected promptly after being called to the attention of the attorney or party.

(b) Representations to Court. By presenting to the court (whether by signing, filing, submitting, or later advocating) a pleading, written motion, or other paper, an attorney or unrepresented party is certifying that to the best of the person's knowledge, information, and belief formed after an inquiry reasonable under the circumstances,—

(1) it is not being presented or maintained for any improper purpose, such as to harass or to cause unnecessary delay or needless increase in the cost of litigation;

(2) the claims, defenses, and other legal contentions therein are warranted by existing law or by a nonfrivolous argument for the extension, modification, or reversal of existing law or the establishment of new law;

(3) the allegations and other factual contentions have evidentiary support or, if specifically so identified, are likely to have evidentiary support after a reasonable opportunity for further investigation or discovery; and

(4) the denials of factual contentions are warranted on the evidence or, if specifically so identified, are reasonably based on a lack of information and belief.

(c) Sanctions. If, after notice and a reasonable opportunity to respond, the court determines that subdivision (b) has been violated, the court may, subject to the conditions stated below, impose an appropriate sanction upon the attorneys, law firms, or parties that have violated subdivision (b) or are responsible for the violation.

(1) *How Initiated.*

(A) *By Motion.* A motion for sanctions under this rule shall be made separately from other motions or requests, and shall describe the specific conduct alleged to violate subdivision (b). It shall be served as provided in Rule 5, but shall not be filed with, or presented to, the court unless, within 21 days (or such other period as the court may prescribe), the challenged paper, claim, defense, contention, allegation or denial is not withdrawn or appropriately corrected. If warranted, the court may award to the party prevailing on the motion the reasonable expenses and attorney's fees incurred in presenting or opposing the motion. Absent exceptional circumstances, a law firm shall be held jointly responsible for violations committed by its partners, associates, and employees.

(B) *On Court's Initiative.* On its own initiative, the court may enter an order describing the specific conduct that appears to violate subdivision (b) and directing an attorney, law firm, or party to show cause why it has not violated subdivision (b) with respect thereto.

(2) *Nature of Sanction; Limitations.* A sanction imposed for violation of this rule shall be limited to what is sufficient to deter comparable conduct by others similarly situated. Subject to the limitations in subparagraphs (A) and (B), the sanction may consist of, or include, directives of a nonmonetary nature, an order to pay a penalty into court, or, if imposed on motion and warranted for effective deterrence, an order directing payment to the movant of some or all of the reasonable attorney's fees and other expenses incurred as a direct result of the violation.

(A) Monetary sanctions may not be awarded against a represented party for a violation of subdivision (b)(2).

Rule 11   RULES OF CIVIL PROCEDURE

(B) Monetary sanctions may not be awarded on the court's initiative unless the court issues its order to show cause before a voluntary dismissal or settlement of the claims made by or against the party which is, or whose attorneys are, to be sanctioned.

(3) *Order.* When imposing sanctions, the court shall describe the conduct determined to constitute a violation of this rule and explain the basis for the sanction imposed.

(d) Inapplicability to Discovery. Subdivisions (a) through (c) of this rule do not apply to disclosures and discovery requests, responses, objections, and motions that are subject to the provisions of Rules 26 through 37.

Note on Amendment to Federal Rule 11 and Comparative State Provisions

(a) *Amendment in 1993 to Federal Rule 11*

Several revisions to Rule 11 were adopted in 1993 to address problems that have arisen from application of the 1983 amendments to the Rule. While the purpose of the Rule, to provide sanctions for litigants and attorneys who attempt to thwart the goals of the Federal Rules of Civil Procedure set forth in Rule 1, remains the same, the Rule has been altered to attempt to reduce the large number of motions for sanctions presented under the old Rule.

The amended Rule broadens the duty of an attorney or pro se litigant to warrant that representations to the court, by any means and at any time, are proper, as defined in subdivision (b)(1)–(4). The inclusion of the phrase "later advocating" in subdivision (b) makes clear that the duty to make truthful representations to the court is an ongoing one. Therefore, factual contentions in initial pleadings which fail to be sustained by information obtained through discovery may not, under the new Rule, continue to be advocated. The pleading party making such a contention, however, need only cease advocating the unsustainable contention and is under no duty to formally amend the initial pleading.

Two provisions included in the amended Rule 11 are expected to limit the high volume of requests for sanctions prevailing under the old Rule. First, the new Rule provides, in subdivision (c)(1)(A), that motions for sanctions under the rule should be served according to Rule 5, but not filed with the court unless the attorney served fails to withdraw or appropriately correct the challenged document or contention. This "safe harbor" provision allows an attorney possibly in violation of Rule 11 to voluntarily act to avoid potential sanctions.

A second major change to Rule 11 is that sanctions, whether prompted by motion or issued at the court's own initiative, are no longer mandatory. Subdivision (c) states that "[i]f * * * the court determines that subdivision (b) has been violated, **the court may** * * * impose and appropriate sanction." The former rule required that a court "shall impose" appropriate sanctions if a violation of the rule occurred. Additionally, the new rule makes clear that not only the attorney in violation of the rule, but also that attorney's firm, may be sanctioned, in effect overturning the Supreme Court's decision in Pavelic & Leflore v. Marvel Entertainment Group, 493 U.S. 120, 110 S.Ct. 456, 107 L.Ed.2d 438 (1989).

Finally, the language contained in subdivision (d) of the revised Rule has been added to make clear that the provisions of Rule 11 are inapplicable to discovery. Certification standards for discovery are contained in Rules 26(g) and 37.

(b) *Comparative State Provisions*

Georgia Code Annotated § 9–11–11(b)

Except when otherwise specifically provided by rule or statute, pleadings need not be verified or accompanied by affidavit.

Georgia Code Annotated § 9–10–111

In all cases where the plaintiff files a pleading with an affidavit attached to the effect that the facts stated in the pleading are true to the best of his knowledge and belief, the defendant shall in like manner verify any answer. If the defendant is a corporation, the affidavit may be made by the president, vice-president, superintendent, or any officer or agent who knows, or whose official duty it is to know, about the matters set out in the answer.

Georgia Code Annotated § 19–5–5(a)

The action for divorce shall be brought by written petition and process, the petition being verified by the petitioner.

Pennsylvania Rule of Civil Procedure 1024

(a) Every pleading containing an averment of fact not appearing of record in the action or containing a denial of fact shall state that the averment or denial is true upon the signer's personal knowledge or information and belief and shall be verified. The signer need not aver the source of his information or expectation of ability to prove the averment or denial at the trial. A pleading may be verified upon personal knowledge as to a part and upon information and belief as to the remainder.

(b) If a pleading contains averments which are inconsistent in fact, the verification shall state that the affiant has been unable after reasonable investigation to ascertain which of the inconsistent averments, specifying them, are true but that he has knowledge or information sufficient to form a belief that one of them is true.

(c) The verification shall be made by one or more of the parties filing the pleading unless all the parties (1) lack sufficient knowledge or information, or (2) are outside the jurisdiction of the court and the verification of none of them can be obtained within the time allowed for filing the pleading. In such cases, the verification may be made by any person having sufficient knowledge or information and belief and shall set forth the source of his information as to matters not stated upon his own knowledge and the reason why the verification is not made by a party.

Rule 12. Defenses and Objections—When and How Presented—By Pleading or Motion—Motion for Judgment on the Pleadings

(a) When Presented.

(1) Unless a different time is prescribed in a statute of the United States, a defendant shall serve an answer

 (A) within 20 days after being served with the summons and complaint, or

 (B) if service of the summons has been timely waived on request under Rule 4(d), within 60 days after the date when the request for waiver was sent, or within 90 days after that date if the defendant was addressed outside any judicial district of the United States.

(2) A party served with a pleading stating a cross-claim against that party shall serve an answer thereto within 20 days after being served. The plaintiff shall serve a reply to a counterclaim in the answer within 20 days after service of the answer, or, if a reply is ordered by the court,

Rule 12 RULES OF CIVIL PROCEDURE

within 20 days after service of the order, unless the order otherwise directs.

(3) The United States or an agency thereof shall serve an answer to the complaint or to a cross-claim, or a reply to a counterclaim, within 60 days after the service upon the United States attorney of the pleading in which the claim is asserted.

(4) Unless a different time is fixed by court order, the service of a motion permitted under this rule alters these periods of time as follows,

(A) if the court denies the motion or postpones its disposition until the trial on the merits, the responsive pleading shall be served within 10 days after notice of the court's action; or

(B) if the court grants a motion for a more definite statement, the responsive pleading shall be served within 10 days after the service of the more definite statement.

(b) How Presented. Every defense, in law or fact, to a claim for relief in any pleading, whether a claim, counterclaim, cross-claim, or third-party claim, shall be asserted in the responsive pleading thereto if one is required, except that the following defenses may at the option of the pleader be made by motion: (1) lack of jurisdiction over the subject matter, (2) lack of jurisdiction over the person, (3) improper venue, (4) insufficiency of process, (5) insufficiency of service of process, (6) failure to state a claim upon which relief can be granted, (7) failure to join a party under Rule 19. A motion making any of these defenses shall be made before pleading if a further pleading is permitted. No defense or objection is waived by being joined with one or more other defenses or objections in a responsive pleading or motion. If a pleading sets forth a claim for relief to which the adverse party is not required to serve a responsive pleading, the adverse party may assert at the trial any defense in law or fact to that claim for relief. If, on a motion asserting the defense numbered (6) to dismiss for failure of the pleading to state a claim upon which relief can be granted, matters outside the pleading are presented to and not excluded by the court, the motion shall be treated as one for summary judgment and disposed of as provided in Rule 56, and all parties shall be given reasonable opportunity to present all material made pertinent to such a motion by Rule 56.

(c) Motion for Judgment on the Pleadings. After the pleadings are closed but within such time as not to delay the trial, any party may move for judgment on the pleadings. If, on a motion for judgment on the pleadings, matters outside the pleadings are presented to and not excluded by the court, the motion shall be treated as one for summary judgment and disposed of as provided in Rule 56, and all parties shall be given reasonable opportunity to present all material made pertinent to such a motion by Rule 56.

PLEADINGS AND MOTIONS — Rule 12

(d) Preliminary Hearings. The defenses specifically enumerated (1)–(7) in subdivision (b) of this rule, whether made in a pleading or by motion, and the motion for judgment mentioned in subdivision (c) of this rule shall be heard and determined before trial on application of any party, unless the court orders that the hearing and determination thereof be deferred until the trial.

(e) Motion for More Definite Statement. If a pleading to which a responsive pleading is permitted is so vague or ambiguous that a party cannot reasonably be required to frame a responsive pleading, the party may move for a more definite statement before interposing a responsive pleading. The motion shall point out the defects complained of and the details desired. If the motion is granted and the order of the court is not obeyed within 10 days after notice of the order or within such other time as the court may fix, the court may strike the pleading to which the motion was directed or make such order as it deems just.

(f) Motion to Strike. Upon motion made by a party before responding to a pleading or, if no responsive pleading is permitted by these rules, upon motion made by a party within 20 days after the service of the pleading upon the party or upon the court's own initiative at any time, the court may order stricken from any pleading any insufficient defense or any redundant, immaterial, impertinent, or scandalous matter.

(g) Consolidation of Defenses in Motion. A party who makes a motion under this rule may join with it any other motions herein provided for and then available to the party. If a party makes a motion under this rule but omits therefrom any defense or objection then available to the party which this rule permits to be raised by motion, the party shall not thereafter make a motion based on the defense or objection so omitted, except a motion as provided in subdivision (h)(2) hereof on any of the grounds there stated.

(h) Waiver or Preservation of Certain Defenses.

(1) A defense of lack of jurisdiction over the person, improper venue, insufficiency of process, or insufficiency of service of process is waived (A) if omitted from a motion in the circumstances described in subdivision (g), or (B) if it is neither made by motion under this rule nor included in a responsive pleading or an amendment thereof permitted by Rule 15(a) to be made as a matter of course.

(2) A defense of failure to state a claim upon which relief can be granted, a defense of failure to join a party indispensable under Rule 19, and an objection of failure to state a legal defense to a claim may be made in any pleading permitted or ordered under Rule 7(a), or by motion for judgment on the pleadings, or at the trial on the merits.

(3) Whenever it appears by suggestion of the parties or otherwise that the court lacks jurisdiction of the subject matter, the court shall dismiss the action.

Rule 12 RULES OF CIVIL PROCEDURE

Comparative State Provisions and Notes on Amendments to Federal Rule 12

(a) *Rule 12(a)*

Maryland Rule 2–321

(a) General Rule. A party shall file an answer to an original complaint, counterclaim, cross-claim, or third-party claim within 30 days after being served, except as provided by sections (b) and (c) of this Rule.

(b) Exceptions.

(1) A defendant who is served with an original pleading outside of the State but within the United States shall file an answer within 60 days after being served.

(2) A defendant who is served with an original pleading by publication or posting, pursuant to Rule 2–122, shall file an answer within the time specified in the notice.

(3) A person [whose required agent is] * * * served with an original pleading by service upon the State Department of Assessments and Taxation, the Insurance Commissioner, or some other agency of the State authorized by statute to receive process shall file an answer within 60 days after being served.

(4) The United States or an officer or agency of the United States served with an original pleading pursuant to Rule 2–124(f) shall file an answer within 60 days after being served.

(5) A defendant who is served with an original pleading outside of the United States shall file an answer within 90 days after being served.

(6) If rules for special proceedings, or statutes of this State or of the United States, provide for a different time to answer, the answer shall be filed as provided by those rules or statutes.

(c) Automatic Extension. When a motion is filed pursuant to Rule 2–322, the time for filing an answer is extended without special order to 15 days after entry of the court's order on the motion or, if the court grants a motion for a more definite statement, to 15 days after the service of the more definite statement.

Missouri Rule of Civil Procedure 55.25(a)

A defendant shall file an answer within thirty days after the service of the summons and petition upon him, except where service by mail is had, in which event a defendant shall file an answer within thirty days after the acknowledgment of receipt of summons and petition or return registered or certified mail receipt is filed in the case, or within forty-five days after the first publication of notice if neither personal service nor service by mail is had.

(b) *Rule 12(b)*

1. *In general*

Nebraska Revised Statutes § 25–806

The defendant may demur to the petition only when it appears on its face (1) that the court has no jurisdiction of the person of the defendant or the subject of the action; (2) that the plaintiff has not legal capacity to sue; (3) that there is another action pending between the same parties for the same cause; (4) that there is a defect of parties, plaintiff or defendant; (5) that several causes of action are improperly joined; or (6) that the petition does not state facts sufficient to constitute a cause of action.

PLEADINGS AND MOTIONS — Rule 12

Nebraska Revised Statutes § 25-807

The demurrer shall specify distinctly the grounds of objection to the petition. Unless it do so, it shall be regarded as objecting only that the petition does not state facts sufficient to constitute a cause of action.

Nebraska Revised Statutes § 25-808

When any of the defects enumerated in section 25-806 do not appear upon the face of the petition, the objection may be taken by answer, and if no objection be taken either by demurrer or answer, the defendant shall be deemed to have waived the same, except only the objection to the jurisdiction of the court, and that the petition does not state facts sufficient to constitute a cause of action.

Nebraska Revised Statutes § 25-810

The defendant may demur to one or more of the several causes of action stated in the petition and answer as to the residue.

Indiana Rules of Trial Procedure, Trial Rule 8(E)(3)

All motions and pleadings of any kind addressed to two [2] or more paragraphs of any pleading, or filed by two [2] or more parties, shall be taken and construed as joint, separate, and several motions or pleadings to each of such paragraphs and by and against each of such parties. All motions or pleadings containing two [2] or more subject-matters shall be taken and construed as separate and several as to each subject-matter. All objections to rulings made by two [2] or more parties shall be taken and construed as the joint, separate, and several objections of each of such parties.

A complaint filed by or against two [2] or more plaintiffs shall be taken and construed as joint, separate, and several as to each of said plaintiffs.

2. *Challenging jurisdiction over the subject matter*

California Civil Procedure Code § 396

If an action or proceeding is commenced in a court which lacks jurisdiction of the subject matter thereof, as determined by the complaint of petition, if there is a court of this state which has such jurisdiction, the action or proceeding shall not be dismissed (except as provided in Section 399, and subdivision 1 of Section 581) but shall, on the application of either party, or on the court's own motion, be transferred to a court having jurisdiction of the subject matter which may be agreed upon by the parties, or, if they do not agree, to a court having such jurisdiction which is designated by law as a proper court for the trial or determination thereof, and it shall thereupon be entered and prosecuted in the court to which it is transferred as if it had been commenced therein, all prior proceedings being saved. In any such case, if summons is served prior to the filing of the action or proceeding in the court to which it is transferred, as to any defendant, so served, who has not appeared in the action or proceeding, the time to answer or otherwise plead shall date from service upon such defendant of written notice of filing of such action or proceeding in the court to which it is transferred.

If an action or proceeding is commenced in or transferred to a court which has jurisdiction of the subject matter thereof as determined by the complaint or petition, and it thereafter appears from the verified pleadings, or at the trial, or hearing, that the determination of the action or proceeding, or of a cross-complaint, will necessarily involve the determination of questions not within the jurisdiction of the court, in which the action or proceeding is pending, the court, whenever such lack of jurisdiction appears, must suspend all further proceedings therein and transfer the action or proceeding and certify the pleadings (or if the pleadings be oral, a transcript of the same), and all papers and proceedings therein to a court having jurisdiction thereof which may be agreed upon by the parties, or, it they do not agree, to a court having such jurisdiction which is designated by law as a proper court for the trial or determination thereof.

Rule 12 RULES OF CIVIL PROCEDURE

An action or proceeding which is transferred under the provisions of this section shall be deemed to have been commenced at the time the complaint or petition was filed in the court from which it was originally transferred.

Nothing herein shall be construed to preclude or affect the right to amend the pleadings as provided in this code.

Nothing herein shall be construed to require the superior court to transfer any action or proceeding because the judgment to be rendered, as determined at the trial or hearing, is one which might have been rendered by a municipal or justice court in the same county or city and county.

In any case where the lack of jurisdiction is due solely to an excess in the amount of the demand, the excess may be remitted and the action may continue in the court where it is pending.

Upon the making of an order for such transfer, proceedings shall be had as provided in Section 399 of this code, the costs and fees thereof, and of filing the case in the court to which transferred, to be paid by the party filing the pleading in which the question outside the jurisdiction of the court appears unless the court ordering the transfer shall otherwise direct.

3. *Challenging venue*

Illinois Compiled Statutes 5/2–104(b)

All objections of improper venue are waived by a defendant unless a motion to transfer to a proper venue is made by the defendant on or before the date upon which he or she is required to appear or within any further time that may be granted him or her to answer or move with respect to the complaint, except that if a defendant upon whose residence venue depends is dismissed upon motion of plaintiff, a remaining defendant may promptly move for transfer as though the dismissed defendant had not been a party.

4. *Challenging personal jurisdiction, process, and service of process*

Illinois Compiled Statutes 5/2–301

(a) Prior to filing any other pleading or motion, a special appearance may be made either in person or by attorney for the purpose of objecting to the jurisdiction of the court over the person of the defendant. A special appearance may be made as to an entire proceeding or as to any cause of action involved therein. Every appearance, prior to judgment, not in compliance with the foregoing is a general appearance.

(b) If the reasons for objection are not apparent from the papers on file in the case, the special appearance shall be supported by affidavit setting forth the reasons. In ruling upon the objection, the court shall consider all matters apparent from the papers on file in the case, affidavits submitted by any party, and any evidence adduced upon disputed issues of fact. No determination of any issue of fact in connection with the objection is a determination of the merits of the case or any aspect thereof. A decision adverse to the objector does not preclude the objector from making any motion or defense which he or she might otherwise have made.

(c) If the court sustains the objection, an appropriate order shall be entered. Error in ruling against the defendant on the objection is waived by the defendant's taking part in further proceedings in the case, unless the objection is on the ground that the defendant is not amenable to process issued by a court of this State.

New York Civil Practice Law and Rules 320(c)

When the court's jurisdiction is not based upon personal service on the defendant, an appearance is not equivalent to personal service upon the defendant:

PLEADINGS AND MOTIONS — Rule 12

1. [In quasi-in-rem attachment actions] * * * if jurisdiction is based solely upon a levy on defendant's property within the state pursuant to an order of attachment; or

2. [In in rem actions] * * * if an objection to jurisdiction * * * is asserted by motion or in the answer as provided in rule 3211, unless the defendant proceeds with the defense after asserting the objection to jurisdiction and the objection is not ultimately sustained.

Minnesota Rule of Civil Procedure 4.04(b)(2)

* * *

When quasi in rem jurisdiction has been obtained, a party defending such action thereby submits personally to the jurisdiction of the court. An appearance solely to contest the validity of such quasi in rem jurisdiction is not such a submission.

(c) *Rule 12(d)*

California Civil Procedure Code § 597

When the answer pleads that the action is barred by the statute of limitations, or by a prior judgment, or that another action is pending upon the same cause of action, or sets up any other defense not involving the merits of the plaintiff's cause of action but constituting a bar or ground of abatement to the prosecution thereof, the court may, either upon its own motion or upon the motion of any party, proceed to the trial of the special defense or defenses before the trial of any other issue in the case * * *.

California Civil Procedure Code § 597.5

[In a malpractice action against a doctor, dentist, nurse, or other medical professional] * * * if the answer pleads that the action is barred by the statute of limitations, and if any party so moves or the court upon its own motion requires, the issues raised thereby must be tried separately and before any other issues in the case are tried. * * *

(d) *Rule 12(e)*

1. *Amendments in 1946 to Rule 12(e)*

Prior to 1946 Rule 12(e) read:

Before responding to a pleading or, if no responsive pleading is permitted by these rules, within 20 days after the service of the pleading upon him, a party may move for a more definite statement or for a bill of particulars of any matter which is not averred with sufficient definiteness or particularity to enable him properly to prepare his responsive pleading or to prepare for trial. The motion shall point out the defects complained of and the details desired. If the motion is granted and the order of the court is not obeyed within 10 days after notice of the order or within such other time as the court may fix, the court may strike the pleading to which the motion was directed or make such order as it deems just. A bill of particulars becomes a part of the pleading which it supplements.

The Advisory Committee commented on the alterations as follows:

Subdivision (e). References in this subdivision to a bill of particulars have been deleted, and the motion provided for is confined to one for a more definite statement, to be obtained only in cases where the movant cannot reasonably be required to frame an answer or other responsive pleading to the pleading in question. With respect to preparations for trial, the party is properly relegated to the various methods of examination and discovery provided in the rules for that purpose. * * *

Rule 12(e) as originally drawn has been the subject of more judicial rulings than any other part of the rules, and has been much criticized by commentators, judges and members of the bar. See general discussion and cases cited in 1 Moore's Federal Practice, 1938, Cum.Supplement, § 12.07, under "Page 657"; also, Holtzoff, New Federal Procedure and the Courts, 1940, 35–41. * * * The tendency of some courts freely to grant extended bills of particulars has served to neutralize any helpful benefits derived from Rule 8, and has overlooked the intended use of the rules on depositions and discovery. The words "or to prepare for trial"—eliminated by the proposed amendment—have sometimes been seized upon as grounds for compulsory statement in the opposing pleading of all the details which the movant would have to meet at the trial. On the other hand, many courts have in effect read these words out of the rule. See Walling v. Alabama Pipe Co., W.D.Mo.1942, 3 F.R.D. 159, 6 Fed.Rules Serv. 12e.244, Case 7 * * *. And it has been urged from the bench that the phrase be stricken. Poole v. White, N.D.W.Va.1941, 5 Fed.Rules Serv. 12e.231, Case 4, 2 F.R.D. 40. See also Bowles v. Gabel, W.D.Mo.1946, 9 Fed.Rules Serv. 12e.244, Case 10 ("The courts have never favored that portion of the rules which undertook to justify a motion of this kind for the purpose of aiding counsel in preparing his case for trial.").

2. *Comparative state provisions*

California Civil Procedure Code § 430.10

The party against whom a complaint or cross-complaint has been filed may object, by demurrer or answer as provided in Section 430.30, to the pleading on any one or more of the following grounds:

* * *

(f) The pleading is uncertain. As used in this subdivision, "uncertain" includes ambiguous and unintelligible.

(g) In an action founded upon a contract, it cannot be ascertained from the pleading whether the contract is written, is oral, or is implied by conduct.

* * *

Nebraska Revised Statutes § 25–833

* * * [W]hen the allegations of a pleading are so indefinite and uncertain that the precise nature of the charge or defense is not apparent, the court may require the pleading to be made definite and certain by amendment.

(e) *Rule 12(f)*

1. *Challenging an insufficient defense*

New York Civil Practice Law and Rules 3211

* * *

(b) A party may move for judgment dismissing one or more defenses, on the ground that a defense is not stated or has no merit.

(c) Upon the hearing of a motion made under subdivision (a) or (b), either party may submit any evidence that could properly be considered on a motion for summary judgment. Whether or not issue has been joined, the court, after adequate notice to the parties, may treat the motion as a motion for summary judgment. The court may, when appropriate for the expeditious disposition of the controversy, order immediate trial of the issues raised on the motion.

* * *

2. *Striking irrelevant, impertinent matter*

New York Civil Practice Law and Rules 3024(b)

A party may move to strike any scandalous or prejudicial matter unnecessarily inserted in a pleading.

(f) *Rule 12(h)*

1. *Amendments in 1966 to Rule 12(h)*

Prior to 1966 Rule 12(h) read:

A party waives all defenses and objections which he does not present either by motion as hereinbefore provided or, if he has made no motion, in his answer or reply, except * * * [that defenses under 12(b)(1), 12(b)(6) and 12(b)(7) may be raised at any time before or at trial by pleading or motion.]

The Advisory Committee commented on the 1966 changes as follows:

The question has arisen whether an omitted defense which cannot be made the basis of a second motion may nevertheless be pleaded in the answer. Subdivision (h) called for waiver of "* * * defenses and objections which he [defendant] does not present * * * by motion * * * or, if he has made no motion, in his answer * * *." If the clause "if he has made no motion," was read literally, it seemed that the omitted defense was waived and could not be pleaded in the answer. On the other hand, the clause might be read as adding nothing of substance to the preceding words; in that event it appeared that a defense was not waived by reason of being omitted from the motion and might be set up in the answer. The decisions were divided. * * *

Amended subdivision (h)(1)(A) eliminates the ambiguity and states that certain specified defenses which were available to a party when he made a preanswer motion, but which he omitted from the motion, are waived. The specified defenses are lack of jurisdiction over the person, improper venue, insufficiency of process, and insufficiency of service of process (see Rule 12(b)(2)–(5)). A party who by motion invites the court to pass upon a threshold defense should bring forward all the specified defenses he then has and thus allow the court to do a reasonably complete job. The waiver reinforces the policy of subdivision (g) forbidding successive motions.

By amended subdivision (h)(1)(B), the specified defenses, even if not waived by the operation of (A), are waived by the failure to raise them by a motion under Rule 12 or in the responsive pleading or any amendment thereof to which the party is entitled as a matter of course. The specified defenses are of such a character that they should not be delayed and brought up for the first time by means of an application to the court to amend the responsive pleading.

Since the language of the subdivisions is made clear, the party is put on fair notice of the effect of his actions and omissions and can guard himself against unintended waiver. It is to be noted that while the defenses specified in subdivision (h)(1) are subject to waiver as there provided, the more substantial defenses of failure to state a claim upon which relief can be granted, failure to join a party indispensable under Rule 19, and failure to state a legal defense to a claim (see Rule 12(b)(6), (7), (f)), as well as the defense of lack of jurisdiction over the subject matter (see Rule 12(b)(1)), are expressly preserved against waiver by amended subdivision (h)(2) and (3).

2. *Comparative state provisions*

See Nebraska Revised Statutes § 25–808, as set out in (b)1. above, in connection with Federal Rule 12(b).

Rule 13. Counterclaim and Cross-Claim

(a) Compulsory Counterclaims. A pleading shall state as a counterclaim any claim which at the time of serving the pleading, the pleader has against any opposing party, if it arises out of the transaction or occurrence that is the subject matter of the opposing party's claim and does not require for its adjudication the presence of third parties of whom the court cannot acquire jurisdiction. But the pleader need not state the claim if (1) at the time the action was commenced the claim was the subject of another pending action, or (2) the opposing party brought suit upon the claim by attachment or other process by which the court did not acquire jurisdiction to render a personal judgment on that claim, and the pleader is not stating any counterclaim under this Rule 13.

(b) Permissive Counterclaims. A pleading may state as a counterclaim any claim against an opposing party not arising out of the transaction or occurrence that is the subject matter of the opposing party's claim.

(c) Counterclaim Exceeding Opposing Claim. A counterclaim may or may not diminish or defeat the recovery sought by the opposing party. It may claim relief exceeding in amount or different in kind from that sought in the pleading of the opposing party.

(d) Counterclaim Against the United States. These rules shall not be construed to enlarge beyond the limits now fixed by law the right to assert counterclaims or to claim credits against the United States or an officer or agency thereof.

(e) Counterclaim Maturing or Acquired After Pleading. A claim which either matured or was acquired by the pleader after serving a pleading may, with the permission of the court, be presented as a counterclaim by supplemental pleading.

(f) Omitted Counterclaim. When a pleader fails to set up a counterclaim through oversight, inadvertence, or excusable neglect, or when justice requires, the pleader may by leave of court set up the counterclaim by amendment.

(g) Cross-Claim Against Co-party. A pleading may state as a cross-claim any claim by one party against a co-party arising out of the transaction or occurrence that is the subject matter either of the original action or of a counterclaim therein or relating to any property that is the subject matter of the original action. Such cross-claim may include a claim that the party against whom it is asserted is or may be liable to the cross-claimant for all or part of a claim asserted in the action against the cross-claimant.

(h) Joinder of Additional Parties. Persons other than those made parties to the original action may be made parties to a counterclaim or cross-claim in accordance with the provisions of Rules 19 and 20.

(i) Separate Trials; Separate Judgments. If the court orders separate trials as provided in Rule 42(b), judgment on a counterclaim or cross-claim may be rendered in accordance with the terms of Rule 54(b) when the court has jurisdiction so to do, even if the claims of the opposing party have been dismissed or otherwise disposed of.

PLEADINGS AND MOTIONS — Rule 14

Notes on Amendments to Federal Rule 13 and Comparative State Provisions

(a) *Amendments in 1963 to Federal Rule 13(a)*

Rule 13(a)(2) was added by amendment in 1963. The Advisory Committee's Note on the change reads as follows:

When a defendant, if he desires to defend his interest in property, is obliged to come in and litigate in a court to whose jurisdiction he could not ordinarily be subjected, fairness suggests that he should not be required to assert counterclaims, but should rather be permitted to do so at his election. If, however, he does elect to assert a counterclaim, it seems fair to require him to assert any other which is compulsory within the meaning of Rule 13(a). Clause (2), added by amendment to Rule 13(a), carries out this idea. It will apply to various cases described in Rule 4(e), as amended, where service is effected through attachment or other process by which the court does not acquire jurisdiction to render a personal judgment against the defendant. Clause (2) will also apply to actions commenced in State courts jurisdictionally grounded on attachment or the like, and removed to the Federal courts.

(b) *Comparative State Provisions*

1. *Rules 13(a) and 13(b)*

Michigan Court Rule 2.203(B)

A pleader may join as either independent or alternate claims as many claims, legal or equitable, as the pleader has against an opposing party. If a claim is one previously cognizable only after another claim has been prosecuted to a conclusion, the two claims may be joined in a single action; but the court may grant relief only in accordance with the substantive rights of the parties.

Nebraska Revised Statutes § 25–811

The answer shall contain (1) a general or specific denial of each material allegation of the petition controverted by the defendant; and (2) a statement of any new matter constituting a defense, counterclaim or setoff, in ordinary and concise language and without repetition.

2. *Rule 13(g)*

New York Civil Practice Law and Rules 3019(b)

A cross-claim may be any cause of action in favor of one or more defendants or a person whom a defendant represents against one or more defendants, a person whom a defendant represents or a defendant and other persons alleged to be liable. A cross-claim may include a claim that the party against whom it is asserted is or may be liable to the cross-claimant for all or part of a claim asserted in the action against the cross-claimant.

Rule 14. Third Party Practice

(a) When Defendant May Bring in Third Party. At any time after commencement of the action a defending party, as a third-party plaintiff, may cause a summons and complaint to be served upon a person not a party to the action who is or may be liable to the third-party plaintiff for all or part of the plaintiff's claim against the third-party plaintiff. The third-party plaintiff need not obtain leave to make the service if the third-party plaintiff files the third-party complaint not later than 10 days after serving the original answer. Otherwise the third-party plaintiff must obtain leave on motion upon notice to all parties to the action. The person served with the summons and third-party complaint, hereinafter called the third-party defendant, shall make any defenses to the third-party plaintiff's claim as provided in Rule 12 and any counterclaims against the third-party plaintiff and cross-claims against other third-party defendants as provided in Rule 13. The third-party defendant may assert against the plaintiff any defenses which the third-party plaintiff has to the plaintiff's claim. The third-party defendant may also assert any claim against the plaintiff arising out of the transaction or occurrence that is the subject matter of the plaintiff's claim against the third-party plaintiff. The plaintiff may assert any claim against the third-party defendant arising out of the transaction or occurrence that is the subject matter of the plaintiff's claim against the third-party plaintiff, and the third-party defendant thereupon shall assert any defenses as provided in Rule 12 and any counterclaims and cross-claims as provided in Rule 13. Any party may move to strike the third-party claim, or for its severance or separate trial. A third-party defendant may proceed under this rule against any person not a party to the action who is or may be liable to the third-party defendant for all or part of the claim made in the action against the third-party defendant. The third-party complaint, if within the admiralty and maritime jurisdiction, may be in rem against a vessel, cargo, or other property subject to admiralty or maritime process in rem, in which case references in this rule to the summons include the warrant of arrest, and references to the third-party plaintiff or defendant include, where appropriate, the claimant of the property arrested.

(b) When Plaintiff May Bring in Third Party. When a counterclaim is asserted against a plaintiff, the plaintiff may cause a third party to be brought in under circumstances which under this rule would entitle a defendant to do so.

(c) Admiralty and Maritime Claims. When a plaintiff asserts an admiralty or maritime claim within the meaning of Rule 9(h), the defendant or claimant, as a third-party plaintiff, may bring in a third-party defendant who may be wholly or partly liable, either to the plaintiff or to the third-party plaintiff, by way of remedy over, contribution, or otherwise on account of the same transaction, occurrence, or series of transactions or occurrences. In such a case the third-party plaintiff may also demand judgment against the third-party defendant in favor of the plaintiff, in which event the third-party defendant shall make any defenses to the claim of the plaintiff as well as to that of the third-party plaintiff in the manner provided in Rule 12, and the action shall proceed as if the plaintiff had commenced it against the third-party defendant as well as the third-party plaintiff.

Rule 15. Amended and Supplemental Pleadings

(a) Amendments. A party may amend the party's pleading once as a matter of course at any time before a responsive pleading is served or, if the pleading is one to which no responsive pleading is permitted and the action has not been placed upon the trial calendar, the party may so amend it at any time within 20 days after it is served. Otherwise a party may amend the party's pleading only by leave of court or by written consent of the adverse party; and leave shall be freely given when justice so requires. A party shall plead in response to an amended pleading within the time remaining for response to the original pleading or within 10 days after service of the amended pleading, whichever period may be the longer, unless the court otherwise orders.

(b) Amendments to Conform to the Evidence. When issues not raised by the pleadings are tried by express or implied consent of the parties, they shall be treated in all respects as if they had been raised in the pleadings. Such amendment of the pleadings as may be necessary to cause them to conform to the evidence and to raise these issues may be made upon motion of any party at any time, even after judgment; but failure so to amend does not affect the result of the trial of these issues. If evidence is objected to at the trial on the ground that it is not within the issues made by the pleadings, the court may allow the pleadings to be amended and shall do so freely when the presentation of the merits of the action will be subserved thereby and the objecting party fails to satisfy the court that the admission of such evidence would prejudice the party in maintaining the party's action or defense upon the merits. The court may grant a continuance to enable the objecting party to meet such evidence.

(c) Relation Back of Amendments. An amendment of a pleading relates back to the date of the original pleading when

(1) relation back is permitted by the law that provides the statute of limitations applicable to the action, or

(2) the claim or defense asserted in the amended pleading arose out of the conduct, transaction, or occurrence set forth or attempted to be set forth in the original pleading, or

(3) the amendment changes the party or the naming of the party against whom a claim is asserted if the foregoing provision (2) is satisfied and, within the period provided by Rule 4(m) for service of the summons and complaint, the party to be brought in by amendment (A) has received such notice of the institution of the action that the party will not be prejudiced in maintaining a defense on the merits, and (B) knew or should have known that, but for a mistake concerning the identity of the proper party, the action would have been brought against the party.

The delivery or mailing of process to the United States Attorney, or his designee, or the Attorney General of the United States, or an agency or officer who would have been a proper defendant if named, satisfies the requirement of subparagraphs (A) and (B) of this paragraph (3) with respect to the United States or any agency or officer thereof to be brought into the action as a defendant.

Rule 15   RULES OF CIVIL PROCEDURE

(d) Supplemental Pleadings. Upon motion of a party the court may, upon reasonable notice and upon such terms as are just, permit the party to serve a supplemental pleading setting forth transactions or occurrences or events which have happened since the date of the pleading sought to be supplemented. Permission may be granted even though the original pleading is defective in its statement of a claim for relief or defense. If the court deems it advisable that the adverse party plead to the supplemental pleading, it shall so order, specifying the time therefor.

Comparative State Provisions and Notes on Amendments to Federal Rule 15

(a) *Rule 15(a)*

New York Civil Practice Law and Rules 3025(a) & (b)

(a) A party may amend his pleading once without leave of court within twenty days after its service, or at any time before the period for responding to it expires, or within twenty days after service of a pleading responding to it.

(b) A party may amend his pleading, or supplement it by setting forth additional or subsequent transactions or occurrences, at any time by leave of court or by stipulation of all parties. Leave shall be freely given upon such terms as may be just including the granting of costs and continuances.

(b) *Rule 15(b)*

California Civil Procedure Code § 469

No variance between the allegation in a pleading and the proof is to be deemed material, unless it has actually misled the adverse party to his prejudice in maintaining his action or defense upon the merits. Whenever it appears that a party has been so misled, the Court may order the pleading to be amended upon such terms as may be just.

California Civil Procedure Code § 470

Where the variance is not material, as provided in Section 469 the Court may direct the fact to be found according to the evidence, or may order an immediate amendment, without costs.

California Civil Procedure Code § 471

Where, however, the allegation of the claim or defense to which the proof is directed, is unproved, not in some particular or particulars only, but in its general scope and meaning, it is not to be deemed a case of variance, within the meaning of Sections 469 and 470, but a failure of proof.

(c) *Rule 15(c)*

1. *Relation back of amendments to the claim*

New Jersey Civil Practice Rule 4:9-3

Whenever the claim or defense asserted in the amended pleading arose out of the conduct, transaction or occurrence set forth or attempted to be set forth in the original pleading, the amendment relates back to the date of the original pleading; but the court, in addition to its power to allow amendments may, upon terms, permit the statement of a new or different claim or defense in the pleading. * * *

2. *Relation back of amendments adding parties*

(i) *Amendments in 1991 to Federal Rule 15(c)*

The amendment has two major parts. First, it provides that an amendment relates back to the time the original pleading was filed whenever "relation back is permitted by the law that provides the statute of limitations applicable to the action." Second, it overturns the Supreme Court decision in Schiavone v. Fortune, 477 U.S. 21, 106 S.Ct. 2379, 91 L.Ed.2d 18 (1986), by modifying what is now the second sentence of Rule 15(c) to provide that an amendment *changing the name of a party* relates back to the time of the original pleading under the same circumstances as an amendment *changing a party*.

(ii) *Amendments in 1966 to Federal Rule 15(c)*

Prior to the 1966 amendments, Rule 15(c) contained only what is now its first sentence. The Advisory Committee commented upon the additions as follows:

Rule 15(c) is amplified to state more clearly when an amendment of a pleading changing the party against whom a claim is asserted (including an amendment to correct a misnomer or misdescription of a defendant) shall "relate back" to the date of the original pleading.

The problem has arisen most acutely in certain actions by private parties against officers or agencies of the United States. Thus an individual denied social security benefits by the Secretary of Health, Education, and Welfare may secure review of the decision by bringing a civil action against that officer within sixty days. 42 U.S.C. § 405(g) (Supp. III, 1962). In several recent cases the claimants instituted timely action but mistakenly named as defendant the United States, the Department of HEW, the "Federal Security Administration" (a nonexistent agency), and a Secretary who had retired from the office nineteen days before. Discovering their mistakes, the claimants moved to amend their complaints to name the proper defendant; by this time the statutory sixty-day period had expired. The motions were denied on the ground that the amendment "would amount to the commencement of a new proceeding and would not relate back in time so as to avoid the statutory provision * * * that suit be brought within sixty days. * * *" *Cohn v. Federal Security Adm.*, 199 F.Supp. 884, 885 (W.D.N.Y. 1961) * * *.

Relation back is intimately connected with the policy of the statute of limitations. The policy of the statute limiting the time for suit against the Secretary of HEW would not have been offended by allowing relation back in the situations described above. For the government was put on notice of the claim within the stated period—in the particular instances, by means of the initial delivery of process to a responsible government official (see Rule 4(d)(4) and (5)). In these circumstances, characterization of the amendment as a new proceeding is not responsive to the reality, but is merely question-begging; and to deny relation back is to defeat unjustly the claimant's opportunity to prove his case.

* * * In actions between private parties, the problem of relation back of amendments changing defendants has generally been better handled by the courts, but incorrect criteria have sometimes been applied, leading sporadically to doubtful results. * * * Rule 15(c) has been amplified to provide a general solution. * * *

The relation back of amendments changing plaintiffs is not expressly treated in revised Rule 15(c) since the problem is generally easier. Again the chief consideration of policy is that of the statute of limitations, and the attitude taken in revised Rule 15(c) toward change of defendants extends by analogy to amendments changing plaintiffs. Also relevant is the amendment of Rule 17(a) (real party in interest). To avoid forfeitures of just claims, revised Rule 17(a) would provide that no action shall be dismissed on the ground that it is not prosecuted in the name of the real party in interest until a reasonable time has been allowed for correction of the defect in the manner there stated.

Rule 15   RULES OF CIVIL PROCEDURE

(iii) *Comparative State Provision*

Illinois Compiled Statutes 5/2–616(d)

A cause of action against a person not originally named a defendant is not barred by lapse of time under any statute or contract prescribing or limiting the time within which an action may be brought or right asserted, if all the following terms and conditions are met: (1) the time prescribed or limited had not expired when the original action was commenced; (2) failure to join the person as a defendant was inadvertent; (3) service of summons was in fact had upon the person, his or her agent or partner, as the nature of the defendant made appropriate, even though he or she was served in the wrong capacity or as agent of another, or upon a trustee who has title to but no power of management or control over real property constituting a trust of which the person is a beneficiary; (4) the person, within the time that the action might have been brought or the right asserted against him or her, knew that the original action was pending and that it grew out a transaction or occurrence involving or concerning him or her; and (5) it appears from the original and amended pleadings that the cause of action asserted in the amended pleading grew out of the same transaction or occurrence set up in the original pleading, even though the original pleading was defective in that it failed to allege the performance of some act or the existence of some fact or some other matter which is a necessary condition precedent to the right of recovery when the condition precedent has in fact been performed, and even though the person was not named originally as a defendant. For the purpose of preserving the cause of action under those conditions, an amendment adding the person as a defendant relates back to the date of the filing of the original pleading so amended.

(d) *Rule 15(d)*

See New York Civil Practice Law and Rules 3025(b) as set out in connection with Federal Rule 15(a), supra.

Rule 16. Pretrial Conferences; Scheduling; Management

(a) Pretrial Conferences; Objectives. In any action, the court may in its discretion direct the attorneys for the parties and any unrepresented parties to appear before it for a conference or conferences before trial for such purposes as

(1) expediting the disposition of the action;

(2) establishing early and continuing control so that the case will not be protracted because of lack of management;

(3) discouraging wasteful pretrial activities;

(4) improving the quality of the trial through more thorough preparation, and;

(5) facilitating the settlement of the case.

(b) Scheduling and Planning. Except in categories of actions exempted by district court rule as inappropriate, the district judge, or a magistrate judge when authorized by district court rule, shall, after receiving the report from the parties under Rule 26(f) or after consulting with the attorneys for the parties and any unrepresented parties by a scheduling conference, telephone, mail, or other suitable means, enter a scheduling order that limits the time

(1) to join other parties and to amend the pleadings;

PLEADINGS AND MOTIONS — **Rule 16**

(2) to file motions; and

(3) to complete discovery.

The scheduling order may also include

(4) modifications of the times for disclosures under Rules 26(a) and 26(e)(1) and of the extent of discovery to be permitted;

(5) the date or dates for conferences before trial, a final pretrial conference, and trial; and

(6) any other matters appropriate in the circumstances of the case.

The order shall issue as soon as practicable but in any event within 90 days after the appearance of a defendant and within 120 days after the complaint has been served on a defendant. A schedule shall not be modified except upon a showing of good cause and by leave of the district judge or, when authorized by local rule, by a magistrate judge.

(c) Subjects for Consideration at Pretrial Conferences. At any conference under this rule consideration may be given, and the court may take appropriate action, with respect to

(1) the formulation and simplification of the issues, including the elimination of frivolous claims or defenses;

(2) the necessity or desirability of amendments to the pleadings;

(3) the possibility of obtaining admissions of fact and of documents which will avoid unnecessary proof, stipulations regarding the authenticity of documents, and advance rulings from the court on the admissibility of evidence;

(4) the avoidance of unnecessary proof and of cumulative evidence, and limitations or restrictions on the use of testimony under Rule 702 of the Federal Rules of Evidence;

(5) the appropriateness and timing of summary adjudication under Rule 56;

(6) the control and scheduling of discovery, including orders affecting disclosures and discovery pursuant to Rule 26 and Rules 29 through 37;

(7) the identification of witness[es] and documents, the need and schedule for filing and exchanging pretrial briefs, and the date or dates for further conferences and for trial;

(8) the advisability of referring matters to a magistrate judge or master;

(9) settlement and the use of special procedures to assist in resolving the dispute when authorized by statute or local rule;

(10) the form and substance of the pretrial order;

(11) the disposition of pending motions;

Rule 16   RULES OF CIVIL PROCEDURE

(12) the need for adopting special procedures for managing potentially difficult or protracted actions that may involve complex issues, multiple parties, difficult legal questions, or unusual proof problems;

(13) an order for a separate trial pursuant to Rule 42(b) with respect to a claim, counterclaim, cross-claim, or third-party claim, or with respect to any particular issue in the case;

(14) an order directing a party or parties to present evidence early in the trial with respect to a manageable issue that could, on the evidence, be the basis for a judgment as matter of law under Rule 50(a) or a judgment on partial findings under Rule 52(c);

(15) an order establishing a reasonable limit on time allowed for presenting evidence; and

(16) such other matters as may facilitate the just, speedy, and inexpensive disposition of the action.

At least one of the attorneys for each party participating in any conference before trial shall have authority to enter into stipulations and to make admissions regarding all matters that the participants may reasonably anticipate may be discussed. If appropriate, the court may require that a party or its representative be present or reasonably available by telephone in order to consider possible settlement of the dispute.

(d) Final Pretrial Conference. Any final pretrial conference shall be held as close to the time of trial as reasonable under the circumstances. The participants at any such conference shall formulate a plan for trial, including a program for facilitating the admission of evidence. The conference shall be attended by at least one of the attorneys who will conduct the trial for each of the parties and by any unrepresented parties.

(e) Pretrial Orders. After any conference held pursuant to this rule, an order shall be entered reciting the action taken. This order shall control the subsequent course of the action unless modified by a subsequent order. The order following a final pretrial conference shall be modified only to prevent manifest injustice.

(f) Sanctions. If a party or party's attorney fails to obey a scheduling or pretrial order, or if no appearance is made on behalf of a party at a scheduling or pretrial conference, or if a party or party's attorney is substantially unprepared to participate in the conference, or if a party or party's attorney fails to participate in good faith, the judge, upon motion or the judge's own initiative, may make such orders with regard thereto as are just, and among others any of the orders provided in Rule 37(b)(2)(B), (C), (D). In lieu of or in addition to any other sanction, the judge shall require the party or the attorney representing the party or both to pay the reasonable expenses incurred because of any noncompliance with this rule, including attorney's fees, unless the judge

PLEADINGS AND MOTIONS — Rule 16

finds that the noncompliance was substantially justified or that other circumstances make an award of expenses unjust.

Amendments to Federal Rule 16 and Comparative State Provisions

(a) *Amendment in 1983 and 1993 to Federal Rule 16*

The purpose of the 1983 changes was to alter the focus of pretrial conferences to encompass all aspects of case management and not merely the conduct of the trial. The most dramatic addition was the mandatory scheduling order that must be prepared even in the absence of a formal pretrial conference (unless the case is exempted by local rule).

In 1993, Rule 16(c) was modified to broaden the scope of what may be considered at pretrial conferences. Paragraph (c)(4) now explicitly authorizes the court to consider the limits on the proposed use of expert testimony. While the old Rule referred only to "the avoidance of unnecessary proof and of cumulative evidence," the new Rule specifically allows restrictions on expert testimony where, according to the Notes of the Advisory Committee such testimony "would be unduly expensive given the needs of the case and the other evidence available at trial."

Paragraph (c)(5) was added to allow parties to discuss at pretrial conferences the possibility of summary judgment under Rule 56. Paragraph (c)(6) emphasizes that control of the discovery process is an appropriate goal of the pretrial process. Paragraph (c)(9) was revised to refer to alternative dispute resolution techniques, especially those authorized by local rule or statute which may be mandatory.

(b) *Comparative State Provisions*

New Jersey Civil Practice Rule 4:25–1

(a) Actions to Be Pretried. Pretrial conferences shall be held in all contested actions in the Chancery Division, General Equity, and in all actions brought in lieu of Prerogative Writs. Pretrial conferences in other causes may be held in the discretion of the court either on its own motion or upon a party's written request. The request of a party for a pretrial conference shall include a statement of the facts and reasons supporting the request. * * *

(b) Pretrial Order. The court shall make a pretrial order to be dictated in open court upon the conclusion of the conference and signed forthwith by the judge and attorneys, which shall recite specifically:

(1) A concise descriptive statement of the nature of the action.

(2) The admissions or stipulations of the parties with respect to the cause of action pleaded by plaintiff or defendant-counterclaimant.

(3) The factual and legal contentions of the plaintiff as to the liability of the defendant.

(4) The factual and legal contentions of the defendant as to nonliability and affirmative defenses.

(5) All claims as to damages and the extent of injury, and admissions or stipulations with respect thereto, and this shall limit the claims thereto at the trial. * * *

(6) Any amendments to the pleadings made at the conference * * *.

(7) A specification of the issues to be determined at the trial including all special evidence problems to be determined at trial * * *.

(8) A specification of the legal issues raised by the pleadings which are abandoned or otherwise disposed of. * * *

(9) A list of the exhibits marked in evidence by consent.

(10) Any limitation on the number of expert witnesses.

(11) Any direction with respect to the filing of briefs. * * *

(12) In special circumstances the order of opening and closing to the jury at the trial.

(13) Any other matters which have been agreed upon in order to expedite the disposition of the case.

(14) In the event that a particular member or associate of a firm is to try a case, or if outside trial counsel is to try the case, the name must be specifically set forth. No change in such designated trial counsel shall be made without leave of court if such change will interfere with the trial schedule. * * *

(15) The estimated length of the trial.

(16) When the case shall be placed on the weekly call.

When entered, the pretrial order becomes part of the record, supersedes the pleadings where inconsistent therewith, and controls the subsequent course of action unless modified at or before the trial or pursuant to R. 4:9-2 to prevent manifest injustice. The matter of settlement may be discussed at the sidebar, but it shall not be mentioned in the order.

* * *

IV. PARTIES

Rule 17. Parties Plaintiff and Defendant; Capacity

(a) Real Party in Interest. Every action shall be prosecuted in the name of the real party in interest. An executor, administrator, guardian, bailee, trustee of an express trust, a party with whom or in whose name a contract has been made for the benefit of another, or a party authorized by statute may sue in that person's own name without joining the party for whose benefit the action is brought; and when a statute of the United States so provides, an action for the use or benefit of another shall be brought in the name of the United States. No action shall be dismissed on the ground that it is not prosecuted in the name of the real party in interest until a reasonable time has been allowed after objection for ratification of commencement of the action by, or joinder or substitution of, the real party in interest; and such ratification, joinder, or substitution shall have the same effect as if the action had been commenced in the name of the real party in interest.

(b) Capacity to Sue or Be Sued. The capacity of an individual, other than one acting in a representative capacity, to sue or be sued shall be determined by the law of the individual's domicile. The capacity of a corporation to sue or be sued shall be determined by the law under which it was organized. In all other cases capacity to sue or be sued shall be determined by the law of the state in which the district court is held, except (1) that a partnership or other unincorporated association, which has no such capacity by the law of such state, may sue or be sued in its common name for the purpose of enforcing for or against it a substantive right existing under the Constitution or laws of the United States, and (2) that the capacity of a receiver appointed by a court of the United States to sue or be sued in a court of the United States is governed by Title 28, U.S.C. §§ 754 and 959(a).

(c) **Infants or Incompetent Persons.** Whenever an infant or incompetent person has a representative, such as a general guardian, committee, conservator, or other like fiduciary, the representative may sue or defend on behalf of the infant or incompetent person. An infant or incompetent person who does not have a duly appointed representative may sue by a next friend or by a guardian ad litem. The court shall appoint a guardian ad litem for an infant or incompetent person not otherwise represented in an action or shall make such other order as it deems proper for the protection of the infant or incompetent person.

Notes on Amendments in 1966 to Federal Rule 17(a)

In 1966 Federal Rule 17(a) was amended to add the provision prohibiting dismissal until a reasonable time has been allowed for ratification, joinder, or substitution of the real party in interest.

The Advisory Committee commented on this provision as follows:

This provision keeps pace with the law as it is actually developing. Modern decisions are inclined to be lenient when an honest mistake has been made in choosing the party in whose name the action is to be filed * * *. The provision should not be misunderstood or distorted. It is intended to prevent forfeiture when determination of the proper party to sue is difficult or when an understandable mistake has been made. It does not mean, for example, that, following an airplane crash in which all aboard were killed, an action may be filed in the name of John Doe (a fictitious person), as personal representative of Richard Roe (another fictitious person), in the hope that at a later time the attorney filing the action may substitute the real name of the real personal representative of a real victim, and have the benefit of suspension of the limitation period. * * *

Rule 18. Joinder of Claims and Remedies

(a) **Joinder of Claims.** A party asserting a claim to relief as an original claim, counterclaim, cross-claim, or third-party claim, may join, either as independent or as alternate claims, as many claims, legal, equitable, or maritime, as the party has against an opposing party.

(b) **Joinder of Remedies; Fraudulent Conveyances.** Whenever a claim is one heretofore cognizable only after another claim has been prosecuted to a conclusion, the two claims may be joined in a single action; but the court shall grant relief in that action only in accordance with the relative substantive rights of the parties. In particular, a plaintiff may state a claim for money and a claim to have set aside a conveyance fraudulent as to that plaintiff, without first having obtained a judgment establishing the claim for money.

Notes on Amendments to Federal Rule 18 and Comparative State Provisions

(a) *Amendments in 1966 to Rule 18(a)*

Prior to 1966, Rule 18(a) read as follows:

(a) **Joinder of Claims.** The plaintiff in his complaint or in a reply setting forth a counterclaim and the defendant in an answer setting forth a counterclaim may join either as independent or as alternate claims as many claims either legal or equitable or both as he may have against an opposing party. There may be a like joinder of claims when there are multiple parties if the requirements of Rules 19, 20, and 22 are satisfied. There may be a like joinder of cross-claims or third-party claims if the requirements of Rules 13 and 14 respectively are satisfied.

The Advisory Committee commented on the amendments as follows:

* * *

The liberal policy regarding joinder of claims in the pleadings extends to cases with multiple parties. However, the language used in the second sentence of Rule 18(a)—"if the requirements of Rules 19 [necessary joinder of parties], 20 [permissive joinder of parties], and 22 [interpleader] are satisfied"—has led some courts to infer that the rules regulating joinder of parties are intended to carry back to Rule 18(a) and to impose some special limits on joinder of claims in multiparty cases. In particular, Rule 20(a) has been read as restricting the operation of Rule 18(a) in certain situations in which a number of parties have been permissively joined in an action. In *Federal Housing Admr. v. Christianson*, 26 F.Supp. 419 (D.Conn.1939), the indorsee of two notes sued the three comakers of one note, and sought to join in the action a count on a second note which had been made by two of the three defendants. There was no doubt about the propriety of the joinder of the three parties defendant, for a right to relief was being asserted against all three defendants which arose out of a single "transaction" (the first note) and a question of fact or law "common" to all three defendants would arise in the action. See the text of Rule 20(a). The court, however, refused to allow the joinder of the count on the second note, on the ground that this right to relief, assumed to arise from a distinct transaction, did not involve a question common to all the defendants but only two of them. * * *

If the court's view is followed, it becomes necessary to enter at the pleading stage into speculations about the exact relation between the claim sought to be joined against fewer than all the defendants properly joined in the action, and the claims asserted against all the defendants. * * * Thus if it could be found in the *Christianson* situation that the claim on the second note arose out of the same transaction as the claim on the first or out of a transaction forming part of a "series," and that any question of fact or law with respect to the second note also arose with regard to the first, it would be held that the claim on the second note could be joined in the complaint. * * * Such pleading niceties provide a basis for delaying and wasteful maneuver. It is more compatible with the design of the rules to allow the claim to be joined in the pleading, leaving the question of possible separate trial of that claim to be later decided. * * * It is instructive to note that the court in the *Christianson* case, while holding that the claim on the second note could not be joined as a matter of pleading, held open the possibility that both claims would later be consolidated for trial under Rule 42(a). See 26 F.Supp. 419.

Rule 18(a) is now amended not only to overcome the *Christianson* decision and similar authority, but also to state clearly, as a comprehensive proposition, that a party asserting a claim (an original claim, counterclaim, cross-claim, or third-party claim) may join as many claims as he has against an opposing party.
* * *

It is emphasized that amended Rule 18(a) deals only with pleading. As already indicated, a claim properly joined as a matter of pleading need not be proceeded with together with the other claims if fairness or convenience justifies separate treatment.

* * *

Free joinder of claims and remedies is one of the basic purposes of unification of the admiralty and civil procedure. The amendment accordingly provides for the inclusion in the rule of maritime claims as well as those which are legal and equitable in character.

(b) *Comparative State Provisions*

Michigan Court Rule 2.203

(A) Compulsory Joinder.

(1) In a pleading that states a claim against an opposing party, the pleader must join every claim that the pleader has against that opposing party

at the time of serving the pleading, if it arises out of the transaction or occurrence that is the subject matter of the action and does not require for its adjudication the presence of third parties over whom the court cannot acquire jurisdiction.

(2) Failure to object in a pleading, by motion, or at a pretrial conference to improper joinder of claims or failure to join claims required to be joined constitutes a waiver of the joinder rules, and the judgment shall only merge the claims actually litigated. This rule does not affect collateral estoppel or the prohibition against relitigation of a claim under a different theory.

(B) Permissive Joinder. A pleader may join as either independent or alternate claims as many claims, legal or equitable, as the pleader has against an opposing party. If a claim is one previously cognizable only after another claim has been prosecuted to a conclusion, the two claims may be joined in a single action; but the court may grant relief only in accordance with the substantive rights of the parties.

* * *

Nebraska Revised Statutes § 25–701

The plaintiff may unite several causes of action in the same petition, whether they be such as have heretofore been denominated legal or equitable, or both, when they are included in any of the following classes: (1) The same transaction or transactions connected with the same subject of action; (2) contracts, express or implied; (3) injuries with or without force to person and property or either; (4) injuries to character; (5) claims to recover possession of personal property, with or without damages for the withholding thereof; (6) claims to recover real property with or without damages for the withholding thereof and the rents and profits of the same; and (7) claims against a trustee by virtue of a contract, or by operation of law.

Nebraska Revised Statutes § 25–702

Except for product liability actions, the causes of action so united must affect all the parties to the action, and not require different places of trial.

Rule 19. Joinder of Persons Needed for Just Adjudication

(a) Persons to Be Joined if Feasible. A person who is subject to service of process and whose joinder will not deprive the court of jurisdiction over the subject matter of the action shall be joined as a party in the action if (1) in the person's absence complete relief cannot be accorded among those already parties, or (2) the person claims an interest relating to the subject of the action and is so situated that the disposition of the action in the person's absence may (i) as a practical matter impair or impede the person's ability to protect that interest or (ii) leave any of the persons already parties subject to a substantial risk of incurring double, multiple, or otherwise inconsistent obligations by reason of the claimed interest. If the person has not been so joined, the court shall order that the person be made a party. If the person should join as a plaintiff but refuses to do so, the person may be made a defendant, or, in a proper case, an involuntary plaintiff. If the joined party objects to venue and joinder of that party would render the venue of the action improper, that party shall be dismissed from the action.

(b) Determination by Court Whenever Joinder Not Feasible. If a person as described in subdivision (a)(1)–(2) hereof cannot be made a party, the court shall determine whether in equity and good conscience the action should proceed among the parties before it, or should be dismissed, the absent person being thus regarded as indispensable. The factors to be considered by the court include: first, to what extent a judgment rendered in the person's absence might be prejudicial to the person or those already parties; second, the extent to which, by protective provisions in the judgment, by the shaping of relief, or other measures, the prejudice can be lessened or avoided; third, whether a judgment rendered in the person's absence will be adequate; fourth, whether the plaintiff will have an adequate remedy if the action is dismissed for nonjoinder.

(c) Pleading Reasons for Nonjoinder. A pleading asserting a claim for relief shall state the names, if known to the pleader, of any persons as described in subdivision (a)(1)–(2) hereof who are not joined, and the reasons why they are not joined.

(d) Exception of Class Actions. This rule is subject to the provisions of Rule 23.

Notes on Amendments to Federal Rule 19

Prior to 1966, Rule 19 read as follows:

(a) Necessary Joinder. Subject to the provisions of Rule 23 and of subdivision (b) of this rule, persons having a joint interest shall be made parties and be joined on the same side as plaintiffs or defendants. When a person who should join as a plaintiff refuses to do so, he may be made a defendant or, in proper cases, an involuntary plaintiff.

(b) Effect of Failure to Join. When persons who are not indispensable, but who ought to be parties if complete relief is to be accorded between those already parties, have not been made parties and are subject to the jurisdiction of the court as to both service of process and venue and can be made parties without depriving the court of jurisdiction of the parties before it, the court shall order them summoned to appear in the action. The court in its discretion may proceed in the action without making such persons parties, if its jurisdiction over them as to either service of process or venue can be acquired only by their consent or voluntary appearance or if, though they are subject to its jurisdiction, their joinder would deprive the court of jurisdiction of the parties before it; but the judgment rendered therein does not affect the rights or liabilities of absent persons.

(c) Same: Names of Omitted Persons and Reasons for Non-Joinder to be Pleaded. In any pleading in which relief is asked, the pleader shall set forth the names, if known to him, of persons who ought to be parties if complete relief is to be accorded between those already parties, but who are not joined, and shall state why they are omitted.

The Advisory Committee noted the alterations as follows:

Whenever feasible, the persons materially interested in the subject of an action—see the more detailed description of these persons in the discussion of new subdivision (a) below—should be joined as parties so that they may be heard and a complete disposition made. When this comprehensive joinder cannot be accomplished—a situation which may be encountered in Federal courts because of limitations on service of process, subject matter jurisdiction, and venue—the case should be examined pragmatically and a choice made between the alternatives of proceeding with the action in the absence of particular interested persons, and dismissing the action.

Even if the court is mistaken in its decision to proceed in the absence of an interested person, it does not by that token deprive itself of the power to adjudicate as between the parties already before it through proper service of process. But the court can make a legally binding adjudication only between the parties actually joined in the action. It is true that an adjudication between the parties before the court may on occasion adversely affect the absent person as a practical matter, or leave a party exposed to a later inconsistent recovery by the absent person. These are factors which should be considered in deciding whether the action should proceed, or should rather be dismissed; but they do not themselves negate the court's power to adjudicate as between the parties who have been joined.

Defects in the Original Rule

The foregoing propositions were well understood in the older equity practice, see Hazard, *Indispensable Party: The Historical Origin of a Procedural Phantom,* 61 Colum.L.Rev. 1254 (1961), and Rule 19 could be and often was applied in consonance with them. But experience showed that the rule was defective in its phrasing and did not point clearly to the proper basis of decision.

Textual defects. * * *

(2) The word "indispensable," appearing in original subdivision (b), was apparently intended as an inclusive reference to the interested persons in whose absence it would be advisable, all factors having been considered, to dismiss the action. Yet the sentence implied that there might be interested persons, not "indispensable," in whose absence the action ought also to be dismissed. Further, it seemed at least superficially plausible to equate the word "indispensable" with the expression "having a joint interest," appearing in subdivision (a). * * * But persons holding an interest technically "joint" are not always so related to an action that it would be unwise to proceed without joining all of them, whereas persons holding an interest not technically "joint" may have this relation to an action. See Reed, *Compulsory Joinder of Parties in Civil Actions,* 55 Mich.L.Rev. 327, 356 ff., 483 (1957).

(3) The use of "indispensable" and "joint interest" in the context of original Rule 19 directed attention to the technical or abstract character of the rights or obligations of the persons whose joinder was in question, and correspondingly distracted attention from the pragmatic considerations which should be controlling.

(4) The original rule, in dealing with the feasibility of joining a person as a party to the action, besides referring to whether the person was "subject to the jurisdiction of the court as to both service of process and venue," spoke of whether the person could be made a party "without depriving the court of jurisdiction of the parties before it." The second quoted expression used "jurisdiction" in the sense of the competence of the court over the subject matter of the action, and in this sense the expression was apt. However, by a familiar confusion, the expression seems to have suggested to some that the absence from the lawsuit of a person who was "indispensable" or "who ought to be [a] part[y]" itself deprived the court of the power to adjudicate as between the parties already joined. * * *

Failure to point to correct basis of decision. The original rule did not state affirmatively what factors were relevant in deciding whether the action should proceed or be dismissed when joinder of interested persons was infeasible. In some instances courts did not undertake the relevant inquiry or were misled by the "jurisdiction" fallacy. In other instances there was undue preoccupation with abstract classifications of rights or obligations, as against consideration of the particular consequences of proceeding with the action and the ways by which these consequences might be ameliorated by the shaping of final relief or other precautions.

Although these difficulties cannot be said to have been general, analysis of the cases showed that there was good reason for attempting to strengthen the rule. * * *

The Amended Rule

Subdivision (a) now defines the persons whose joinder in the action is desirable. Clause (1) stresses the desirability of joining those persons in whose absence the court would be obliged to grant partial or "hollow" rather than complete relief to the parties before the court. The interests that are being furthered here are not only those of the parties, but also that of the public in avoiding repeated lawsuits on the same essential subject matter. Clause (2)(i) recognizes the importance of protecting the person whose joinder is in question against the practical prejudice to him which may arise through a disposition of the action in his absence. Clause (2)(ii) recognizes the need for considering whether a party may be left, after the adjudication, in a position where a person not joined can subject him to a double or otherwise inconsistent liability. See Reed, *supra*, 55 Mich.L.Rev. at 330, 338 * * *.

If a person as described in subdivision (a)(1)–(2) is amenable to service of process and his joinder would not deprive the court of jurisdiction in the sense of competence over the action, he should be joined as a party; and if he has not been joined, the court should order him to be brought into the action. If a party joined has a valid objection to the venue and chooses to assert it, he will be dismissed from the action.

Subdivision (b). When a person as described in subdivision (a)(1)–(2) cannot be made a party, the court is to determine whether in equity and good conscience the action should proceed among the parties already before it, or should be dismissed. That this decision is to be made in the light of pragmatic considerations has often been acknowledged by the courts. See *Roos v. Texas Co.*, 23 F.2d 171 (2d Cir. 1927), cert. denied, 277 U.S. 587 (1928); *Niles-Bement-Pond Co. v. Iron Moulders' Union*, 254 U.S. 77, 80 (1920). The subdivision sets out four relevant considerations drawn from the experience revealed in the decided cases. The factors are to a certain extent overlapping, and they are not intended to exclude other considerations which may be applicable in particular situations.

The *first factor* brings in a consideration of what a judgment in the action would mean to the absentee. Would the absentee be adversely affected in a practical sense, and if so, would the prejudice be immediate and serious, or remote and minor? The possible collateral consequences of the judgment upon the parties already joined are also to be appraised. Would any party be exposed to a fresh action by the absentee, and if so, how serious is the threat? * * *

The *second factor* calls attention to the measures by which prejudice may be averted or lessened. The "shaping of relief" is a familiar expedient to this end. See, *e.g.*, the award of money damages in lieu of specific relief where the latter might affect an absentee adversely. *Ward v. Deavers*, 203 F.2d 72 (D.C.Cir.1953) * * *.

The *third factor*—whether an "adequate" judgment can be rendered in the absence of a given person—calls attention to the extent of the relief that can be accorded among the parties joined. It meshes with the other factors, especially the "shaping of relief" mentioned under the second factor. * * *

The *fourth factor,* looking to the practical effects of a dismissal, indicates that the court should consider whether there is any assurance that the plaintiff, if dismissed, could sue effectively in another forum where better joinder would be possible. * * *

The subdivision uses the word "indispensable" only in a conclusory sense, that is, a person is "regarded as indispensable" when he cannot be made a party and, upon consideration of the factors above-mentioned, it is determined that in his absence it would be preferable to dismiss the action, rather than to retain it.

* * *

Subdivision (c) parallels the predecessor subdivision (c) of Rule 19. In some situations it may be desirable to advise a person who has not been joined of the fact that the action is pending, and in particular cases the court in its discretion may itself convey this information by directing a letter or other informal notice to the absentee.

Rule 20. Permissive Joinder of Parties

(a) Permissive Joinder. All persons may join in one action as plaintiffs if they assert any right to relief jointly, severally, or in the alternative in respect of or arising out of the same transaction, occurrence, or series of transactions or occurrences and if any question of law or fact common to all these persons will arise in the action. All persons (and any vessel, cargo or other property subject to admiralty process in rem) may be joined in one action as defendants if there is asserted against them jointly, severally, or in the alternative, any right to relief in respect of or arising out of the same transaction, occurrence, or series of transactions or occurrences and if any question of law or fact common to all defendants will arise in the action. A plaintiff or defendant need not be interested in obtaining or defending against all the relief demanded. Judgment may be given for one or more of the plaintiffs according to their respective rights to relief, and against one or more defendants according to their respective liabilities.

(b) Separate Trials. The court may make such orders as will prevent a party from being embarrassed, delayed, or put to expense by the inclusion of a party against whom the party asserts no claim and who asserts no claim against the party, and may order separate trials or make other orders to prevent delay or prejudice.

Comparative State Provisions

Michigan Court Rule 2.206(A)

(1) All persons may join in one action as plaintiffs

(a) if they assert a right to relief jointly, severally, or in the alternative, in respect of or arising out of the same transaction, occurrence, or series of transactions or occurrences and if a question of law or fact common to all of the plaintiffs will arise in the action; or

(b) if their presence in the action will promote the convenient administration of justice.

(2) All persons may be joined in one action as defendants

(a) if there is asserted against them jointly, severally, or in the alternative, a right to relief in respect of or arising out of the same transaction, occurrence, or series of transactions or occurrences and if a question of law or fact common to all of the defendants will arise in the action; or

(b) if their presence in the action will promote the convenient administration of justice.

(3) A plaintiff or defendant need not be interested in obtaining or defending against all the relief demanded. Judgment may be rendered for one or more of the parties against one or more of the parties as the rights and liabilities of the parties are determined.

New York Civil Practice Law and Rules 1002(a) & (b)

(a) Persons who assert any right to relief jointly, severally, or in the alternative arising out of the same transaction, occurrence, or series of transactions or occurrences, may join in one action as plaintiffs if any common question of law or fact would arise.

Rule 20 RULES OF CIVIL PROCEDURE

(b) Persons against whom there is asserted any right to relief jointly, severally, or in the alternative, arising out of the same transaction, occurrence, or series of transactions or occurrences, may be joined in one action as defendants if any common question of law or fact would arise.

* * *

Rule 21. Misjoinder and Non-joinder of Parties

Misjoinder of parties is not ground for dismissal of an action. Parties may be dropped or added by order of the court on motion of any party or of its own initiative at any stage of the action and on such terms as are just. Any claim against a party may be severed and proceeded with separately.

Rule 22. Interpleader

(1) Persons having claims against the plaintiff may be joined as defendants and required to interplead when their claims are such that the plaintiff is or may be exposed to double or multiple liability. It is not ground for objection to the joinder that the claims of the several claimants or the titles on which their claims depend do not have a common origin or are not identical but are adverse to and independent of one another, or that the plaintiff avers that the plaintiff is not liable in whole or in part to any or all of the claimants. A defendant exposed to similar liability may obtain such interpleader by way of cross-claim or counterclaim. The provisions of this rule supplement and do not in any way limit the joinder of parties permitted in Rule 20.

(2) The remedy herein provided is in addition to and in no way supersedes or limits the remedy provided by Title 28, U.S.C. §§ 1335, 1397, and 2361. Actions under those provisions shall be conducted in accordance with these rules.

Comparative State Provisions
California Civil Procedure Code § 386

(a) A defendant, against whom an action is pending upon a contract, or for specific personal property, may, at any time before answer, upon affidavit that a person not a party to the action makes against him, and without any collusion with him, a demand upon such contract, or for such property, upon notice to such person and the adverse party, apply to the court for an order to substitute such person in his place, and discharge him from liability to either party, on his depositing in court the amount claimed on the contract, or delivering the property or its value to such person as the court may direct; and the court may, in its discretion, make the order; or such defendant may file a verified cross-complaint in interpleader, admitting that he has no interest in such amount or such property claimed, or in a portion of such amount or such property and alleging that all or such portion of the amount or property is demanded by parties to such action or cross-action and apply to the court upon notice to such parties for an order to deliver such property or portion thereof or its value to such person as the court shall direct. And whenever conflicting claims are or may be made upon a person for or relating to personal property, or the performance of an obligation, or any portion thereof, such person may bring an action against the conflicting claimants to compel them to interplead and litigate their several claims. The order of substitution may be made and the action of interpleader may be maintained, and the applicant or interpleading party be discharged from liability to all or any of the conflicting claimants, although their titles or claims have not a common origin, or are not identical but are adverse to and independent of one another.

(b) Any person, firm, corporation, association or other entity against whom double or multiple claims are made, or may be made, by two or more persons which are such that they may give rise to double or multiple liability, may bring an action against the claimants to compel them to interplead and litigate their several claims.

When the person, firm, corporation, association or other entity against whom such claims are made, or may be made, is a defendant in an action brought upon one or more of such claims, it may either file a verified cross-complaint in interpleader, admitting that it has no interest in the money or property claimed, or in only a portion thereof, and alleging that all or such portion is demanded by parties to such action, and apply to the court upon notice to such parties for an order to deliver such money or property or such portion thereof to such person as the court shall direct; or may bring a separate action against the claimants to compel them to interplead and litigate their several claims. The action of interpleader may be maintained although the claims have not a common origin, are not identical but are adverse to and independent of one another, or the claims are unliquidated and no liability on the part of the party bringing the action or filing the cross-complaint has arisen. The applicant or interpleading party may deny liability in whole or in part to any or all of the claimants. The applicant or interpleading party may join as a defendant in such action any other party against whom claims are made by one or more of the claimants or such other party may interplead by cross-complaint; provided, however, that such claims arise out of the same transaction or occurrence.

* * *

New York Civil Practice Law and Rules 216

(a) **Action to recover money.** 1. No action for the recovery of any sum of money due and payable under or on account of a contract, or for any part thereof, shall be commenced by any person who has made claim to the sum, after the expiration of one year from the giving of notice, as hereinafter provided, to the claimant that an action commenced by another person is pending to recover the sum, or any part thereof, exceeding fifty dollars in amount. This limitation shall not be construed to enlarge the time within which the cause of action of the claimant would otherwise be barred.

2. If any person shall make claim for the recovery of any sum of money due and payable under or on account of a contract, and an action has theretofore been, or shall thereafter be, commenced by another person to recover the sum, or any part thereof, exceeding fifty dollars in amount, the defendant in such action may, within twenty days from the date of service upon him of the complaint or from the date of receipt by him of the claim, whichever occurs later, make a motion before the court in which the action is pending for an order permitting the defendant to give notice to the claimant that the action is pending. The court in which the action is pending shall grant the order where it appears that a person not a party to the action has made claim against the defendant for the sum of money, or any part thereof, exceeding fifty dollars in amount; that the action was brought without collusion between the defendant and the plaintiff; and that the claimant cannot, with due diligence, be served with process in such a manner as to obtain jurisdiction over his person. The order shall provide, among such other terms and conditions as justice may require, that notice shall be given to the claimant by sending by registered mail a copy of the summons and complaint in the action and the order and a notice addressed to the claimant at his last known address. In the event that registration of mail directed to any country or part thereof shall be discontinued or suspended, notice to a claimant whose last known address is within such country or part thereof shall be given by ordinary mail, under such terms and conditions as the court may direct. Proof that the notice has been mailed shall be filed within ten days from the date of the order; otherwise the

order becomes inoperative. Upon such filing, notice shall be deemed to have been given on the tenth day after the date of such order.

3. Upon proof by affidavit or otherwise, to the satisfaction of the court, that the conditions of this subdivision have been satisfied and that there is no collusion between the claimant and the defendant, the court shall make an order staying further prosecution of the action for a period not to exceed one year from the date when the notice shall have been given to the claimant. At the time of the granting of such order or at any time thereafter, the court, upon the motion of any party, shall, as a condition of the granting of the order or its continuation, impose upon the defendant such terms as justice may require as to the furnishing of an undertaking in an amount to be fixed by the court. The stay shall be vacated and the undertaking, if any has been given, may be discharged or modified, as justice may require, upon proof to the court by any party to the action that the claimant has intervened or has instituted another action in any court of this state to recover the said sum of money, or any part thereof, exceeding fifty dollars.

4. A motion for any relief as prescribed in this subdivision shall be made on notice to all other parties to the action.

5. Whenever claims are made by two or more persons, each claiming to be, to the exclusion of the other, the duly authorized deputy, officer or agent to demand, receive, collect, sue for or recover the same sum of money due and payable under or on account of a contract, or any part thereof, exceeding fifty dollars in amount, for and on behalf of the same person, each person making such a claim shall be deemed an adverse claimant. Notwithstanding that an action has been commenced in the name of or on behalf of the person for whom he claims to be the duly authorized deputy, officer or agent, any such adverse claimant may be notified of the pendency of an action as provided in this subdivision and may intervene in the action and be designated as claiming to be or as the alleged deputy, officer or agent.

6. Whenever an action has been commenced for the recovery of any sum of money exceeding fifty dollars due and payable under or on account of a contract and the records of the defendant show that a person other than the plaintiff has the right, exclusive of other deputies, officers or agents of the plaintiff, to demand, sue for and recover the same sum of money, or any part thereof, exceeding fifty dollars in amount, either in his own name, on his own behalf, or as the authorized deputy, officer or agent for the plaintiff, and the defendant has received no notice of transfer, revocation, or other change in right or authority acceptable to it, the person so appearing on the records shall be deemed to have made an adverse claim to the sum of money and may be treated as an adverse claimant.

(b) Action to recover property. When an action has been commenced to recover specific personal property, including certificates of stocks, bonds, notes or other securities or obligations, exceeding fifty dollars in value, held by the defendant within the state, or to enforce a vested or contingent interest or lien upon such property, and a person not a party to the action asserts a claim to the whole or any part of the same property or to a right, interest or lien upon it which is adverse to the plaintiff's claim, and the court in which the action is pending has no jurisdiction over the adverse claimant to direct the issuance of process or if the same be issued it would be without effect notwithstanding that the action seeks to have declared, enforced, regulated, defined or limited, rights, interests or liens upon specific personal property within the state, the defendant in the action may within twenty days from the date of service upon him of the complaint or within twenty days of the date of the receipt by him of the adverse claim, whichever shall occur later, make a motion before the court for leave to give notice to the adverse claimant of the pending action in the same manner as provided in subdivision (a). Upon the granting of such an order, the provisions of subdivision (a) shall apply insofar as they are compatible with the subject matter of the action.

Rule 23. Class Actions

(a) Prerequisites to a Class Action. One or more members of a class may sue or be sued as representative parties on behalf of all only if

(1) the class is so numerous that joinder of all members is impracticable, (2) there are questions of law or fact common to the class, (3) the claims or defenses of the representative parties are typical of the claims or defenses of the class, and (4) the representative parties will fairly and adequately protect the interests of the class.

(b) Class Actions Maintainable. An action may be maintained as a class action if the prerequisites of subdivision (a) are satisfied, and in addition:

(1) the prosecution of separate actions by or against individual members of the class would create a risk of

(A) inconsistent or varying adjudications with respect to individual members of the class which would establish incompatible standards of conduct for the party opposing the class, or

(B) adjudications with respect to individual members of the class which would as a practical matter be dispositive of the interests of the other members not parties to the adjudications or substantially impair or impede their ability to protect their interests; or

(2) the party opposing the class has acted or refused to act on grounds generally applicable to the class, thereby making appropriate final injunctive relief or corresponding declaratory relief with respect to the class as a whole; or

(3) the court finds that the questions of law or fact common to the members of the class predominate over any questions affecting only individual members, and that a class action is superior to other available methods for the fair and efficient adjudication of the controversy. The matters pertinent to the findings include: (A) the interest of members of the class in individually controlling the prosecution or defense of separate actions; (B) the extent and nature of any litigation concerning the controversy already commenced by or against members of the class; (C) the desirability or undesirability of concentrating the litigation of the claims in the particular forum; (D) the difficulties likely to be encountered in the management of a class action.

(c) Determination by Order Whether Class Action to Be Maintained; Notice; Judgment; Actions Conducted Partially as Class Actions.

(1) As soon as practicable after the commencement of an action brought as a class action, the court shall determine by order whether it is to be so maintained. An order under this subdivision may be conditional, and may be altered or amended before the decision on the merits.

(2) In any class action maintained under subdivision (b)(3), the court shall direct to the members of the class the best notice practicable under the circumstances, including individual notice to all members who can be identified through reasonable effort. The notice shall advise each

member that (A) the court will exclude the member from the class if the member so requests by a specified date; (B) the judgment, whether favorable or not, will include all members who do not request exclusion; and (C) any member who does not request exclusion may, if the member desires, enter an appearance through counsel.

(3) The judgment in an action maintained as a class action under subdivision (b)(1) or (b)(2), whether or not favorable to the class, shall include and describe those whom the court finds to be members of the class. The judgment in an action maintained as a class action under subdivision (b)(3), whether or not favorable to the class, shall include and specify or describe those to whom the notice provided in subdivision (c)(2) was directed, and who have not requested exclusion, and whom the court finds to be members of the class.

(4) When appropriate (A) an action may be brought or maintained as a class action with respect to particular issues, or (B) a class may be divided into subclasses and each subclass treated as a class, and the provisions of this rule shall then be construed and applied accordingly.

(d) Orders in Conduct of Actions. In the conduct of actions to which this rule applies, the court may make appropriate orders: (1) determining the course of proceedings or prescribing measures to prevent undue repetition or complication in the presentation of evidence or argument; (2) requiring, for the protection of the members of the class or otherwise for the fair conduct of the action, that notice be given in such manner as the court may direct to some or all of the members of any step in the action, or of the proposed extent of the judgment, or of the opportunity of members to signify whether they consider the representation fair and adequate, to intervene and present claims or defenses, or otherwise to come into the action; (3) imposing conditions on the representative parties or on intervenors; (4) requiring that the pleadings be amended to eliminate therefrom allegations as to representation of absent persons, and that the action proceed accordingly; (5) dealing with similar procedural matters. The orders may be combined with an order under Rule 16, and may be altered or amended as may be desirable from time to time.

(e) Dismissal or Compromise. A class action shall not be dismissed or compromised without the approval of the court, and notice of the proposed dismissal or compromise shall be given to all members of the class in such manner as the court directs.

Notes on Amendments to Federal Rule 23 and Comparative State Provision

(a) *Amendments in 1966 to Rule 23*

Prior to 1966 the basic subject matter of current Rule 23 was covered in Rules 23(a) and (c), which read as follows:

(a) Representation. If persons constituting a class are so numerous as to make it impracticable to bring them all before the court, such of them, one or more, as will fairly insure the adequate representation of all may, on behalf of all, sue or be sued, when the character of the right sought to be enforced for or against the class is

(1) joint, or common, or secondary in the sense that the owner of a primary right refuses to enforce that right and a member of the class thereby becomes entitled to enforce it;

(2) several, and the object of the action is the adjudication of claims which do or may affect specific property involved in the action; or

(3) several, and there is a common question of law or fact affecting the several rights and a common relief is sought.

(c) Dismissal or Compromise. A class action shall not be dismissed or compromised without the approval of the court. If the right sought to be enforced is one defined in paragraph (1) of subdivision (a) of this rule notice of the proposed dismissal or compromise shall be given to all members of the class in such manner as the court directs. If the right is one defined in paragraphs (2) or (3) of subdivision (a) notice shall be given only if the court requires it.

The Advisory Committee noted the changes as follows:

Difficulties with the original rule. The categories of class actions in the original rule were defined in terms of the abstract nature of the rights involved: the so-called "true" category was defined as involving "joint, common, or secondary rights"; the "hybrid" category, as involving "several" rights related to "specific property"; the "spurious" category, as involving "several" rights affected by a common question and related to common relief. It was thought that the definitions accurately described the situations amenable to the class-suit device, and also would indicate the proper extent of the judgment in each category, which would in turn help to determine the *res judicata* effect of the judgment if questioned in a later action. Thus the judgments in "true" and "hybrid" class actions would extend to the class (although in somewhat different ways); the judgment in a "spurious" class action would extend only to the parties including intervenors. See Moore, *Federal Rules of Civil Procedure: Some Problems Raised by the Preliminary Draft*, 25 Geo.L.J. 551, 570–76 (1937).

In practice the terms "joint," "common," etc., which were used as the basis of the Rule 23 classification proved obscure and uncertain. * * *

Nor did the rule provide an adequate guide to the proper extent of the judgments in class actions. First, we find instances of the courts classifying actions as "true" or intimating that the judgments would be decisive for the class where these results seemed appropriate but were reached by dint of depriving the word "several" of coherent meaning. * * * Second, we find cases classified by the courts as "spurious" in which, on a realistic view, it would seem fitting for the judgments to extend to the class. * * *

The "spurious" action envisaged by original Rule 23 was in any event an anomaly because, although denominated a "class" action and pleaded as such, it was supposed not to adjudicate the rights or liabilities of any person not a party. It was believed to be an advantage of the "spurious" category that it would invite decisions that a member of the "class" could, like a member of the class in a "true" or "hybrid" action, intervene on an ancillary basis without being required to show an independent basis of Federal jurisdiction, and have the benefit of the date of the commencement of the action for purposes of the statute of limitations. See 3 *Moore's Federal Practice* ¶¶ 23.10[1], 23.12 (2d ed. 1963). These results were attained in some instances but not in others. * * * The results, however, can hardly depend upon the mere appearance of a "spurious" category in the rule; they should turn on more basic considerations. See discussion of subdivision (c)(1) below.

Finally, the original rule did not squarely address itself to the question of the measures that might be taken during the course of the action to assure procedural fairness, particularly giving notice to members of the class, which may in turn be related in some instances to the extension of the judgment to the class. * * *

Rule 23   RULES OF CIVIL PROCEDURE

The amended rule describes in more practical terms the occasions for maintaining class actions; provides that all class actions maintained to the end as such will result in judgments including those whom the court finds to be members of the class, whether or not the judgment is favorable to the class; and refers to the measures which can be taken to assure the fair conduct of these actions.

Subdivision (a) states the prerequisites for maintaining any class action in terms of the numerousness of the class making joinder of the members impracticable, the existence of questions common to the class, and the desired qualifications of the representative parties. * * * These are necessary but not sufficient conditions for a class action. * * * Subdivision (b) describes the additional elements which in varying situations justify the use of a class action.

Subdivision (b)(1). The difficulties which would be likely to arise if resort were had to separate actions by or against the individual members of the class here furnish the reasons for, and the principal key to, the propriety and value of utilizing the class-action device. The considerations stated under clauses (A) and (B) are comparable to certain of the elements which define the persons whose joinder in an action is desirable as stated in Rule 19(a), as amended. * * *

Clause (A): One person may have rights against, or be under duties toward, numerous persons constituting a class, and be so positioned that conflicting or varying adjudications in lawsuits with individual members of the class might establish incompatible standards to govern his conduct. The class action device can be used effectively to obviate the actual or virtual dilemma which would thus confront the party opposing the class. * * * To illustrate: Separate actions by individuals against a municipality to declare a bond issue invalid or condition or limit it, to prevent or limit the making of a particular appropriation or to compel or invalidate an assessment, might create a risk of inconsistent or varying determinations. In the same way, individual litigations of the rights and duties of riparian owners, or of landowners' rights and duties respecting a claimed nuisance, could create a possibility of incompatible adjudications. Actions by or against a class provide a ready and fair means of achieving unitary adjudication. * * *

Clause (B): This clause takes in situations where the judgment in a nonclass action by or against an individual member of the class, while not technically concluding the other members, might do so as a practical matter. The vice of an individual action would lie in the fact that the other members of the class, thus practically concluded, would have had no representation in the lawsuit. In an action by policy holders against a fraternal benefit association attacking a financial reorganization of the society, it would hardly have been practical, if indeed it would have been possible, to confine the effects of a validation of the reorganization to the individual plaintiffs. Consequently a class action was called for with adequate representation of all members of the class. * * * The same reasoning applies to an action which charges a breach of trust by an indenture trustee or other fiduciary similarly affecting the members of a large class of security holders or other beneficiaries, and which requires an accounting or like measures to restore the subject of the trust. * * *

In various situations an adjudication as to one or more members of the class will necessarily or probably have an adverse practical effect on the interests of other members who should therefore be represented in the lawsuit. This is plainly the case when claims are made by numerous persons against a fund insufficient to satisfy all claims. A class action by or against representative members to settle the validity of the claims as a whole, or in groups, followed by separate proof of the amount of each valid claim and proportionate distribution of the fund, meets the problem. * * * Similar problems, however, can arise in the absence of a fund either present or potential. A negative or mandatory injunction secured by one of a numerous class may disable the opposing party from performing claimed duties toward the other members of the class or materially affect his ability to do so. An adjudication as to movie "clearances and runs" nominally affecting only one exhibitor would often have practical effects on all the exhibitors in the same territorial area. * * * Assuming a sufficiently numerous class of exhibitors, a class action would be advisable. (Here representation of subclasses of exhibitors could become necessary; see subdivision (c)(3)(B).)

Subdivision (b)(2). This subdivision is intended to reach situations where a party has taken action or refused to take action with respect to a class, and final relief of an injunctive nature or of a corresponding declaratory nature, settling the legality of the behavior with respect to the class as a whole, is appropriate. Declaratory relief "corresponds" to injunctive relief when as a practical matter it affords injunctive relief or serves as a basis for later injunctive relief. The subdivision does not extend to cases in which the appropriate final relief relates exclusively or predominantly to money damages. Action or inaction is directed to a class within the meaning of this subdivision even if it has taken effect or is threatened only as to one or a few members of the class, provided it is based on grounds which have general application to the class.

Illustrative are various actions in the civil-rights field where a party is charged with discriminating unlawfully against a class, usually one whose members are incapable of specific enumeration. * * *

Subdivision (b)(3). In the situations to which this subdivision relates, class-action treatment is not as clearly called for as in those described above, but it may nevertheless be convenient and desirable depending upon the particular facts. Subdivision (b)(3) encompasses those cases in which a class action would achieve economies of time, effort, and expense, and promote uniformity of decision as to persons similarly situated, without sacrificing procedural fairness or bringing about other undesirable results. * * *

The court is required to find, as a condition of holding that a class action may be maintained under this subdivision, that the questions common to the class predominate over the questions affecting individual members. It is only where this predominance exists that economies can be achieved by means of the class-action device. In this view a fraud perpetrated on numerous persons by the use of similar misrepresentations may be an appealing situation for a class action, and it may remain so despite the need, if liability is found, for separate determination of the damages suffered by individuals within the class. On the other hand, although having some common core, a fraud case may be unsuited for treatment as a class action if there was material variation in the representations made or in the kinds or degrees of reliance by the persons to whom they were addressed. * * *

That common questions predominate is not itself sufficient to justify a class action under subdivision (b)(3), for another method of handling the litigious situation may be available which has greater practical advantages. Thus one or more actions agreed to by the parties as test or model actions may be preferable to a class action; or it may prove feasible and preferable to consolidate actions. * * * To reinforce the point that the court with the aid of the parties ought to assess the relative advantages of alternative procedures for handling the total controversy, subdivision (b)(3) requires, as a further condition of maintaining the class action, that the court shall find that that procedure is "superior" to the others in the particular circumstances.

* * *

Subdivision (c)(2) makes special provision for class actions maintained under subdivision (b)(3). As noted in the discussion of the latter subdivision, the interests of the individuals in pursuing their own litigations may be so strong here as to warrant denial of a class action altogether. Even when a class action is maintained under subdivision (b)(3), this individual interest is respected. Thus the court is required to direct notice to the members of the class of the right of each member to be excluded from the class upon his request. A member who does not request exclusion may, if he wishes, enter an appearance in the action through his counsel; whether or not he does so, the judgment in the action will embrace him.

* * *

Subdivision (c)(3). * * *

Hitherto, in a few actions conducted as "spurious" class actions and thus nominally designed to extend only to parties and others intervening *before* the determination of liability, courts have held or intimated that class members might be permitted to intervene *after* a decision on the merits favorable to their interests, in order to secure the benefits of the decision for themselves, although they would presumably be unaffected by an unfavorable decision. * * * Under proposed subdivision (c)(3), one-way intervention is excluded; the action will have been early determined to be a class or nonclass action, and in the former case the judgment, whether or not favorable, will include the class, as above stated.

Although thus declaring that the judgment in a class action includes the class, as defined, subdivision (c)(3) does not disturb the recognized principle that the court conducting the action cannot predetermine the *res judicata* effect of the judgment; this can be tested only in a subsequent action. * * * The court, however, in framing the judgment in any suit brought as a class action, must decide what its extent or coverage shall be, and if the matter is carefully considered, questions of *res judicata* are less likely to be raised at a later time and if raised will be more satisfactorily answered. * * *

(b) *Comparative State Provision*

California Civil Procedure Code § 382

* * * [W]hen the question is one of a common or general interest, of many persons, or when the parties are numerous, and it is impracticable to bring them all before the court, one or more may sue or defend for the benefit of all.

Rule 23.1 Derivative Actions by Shareholders

In a derivative action brought by one or more shareholders or members to enforce a right of a corporation or of an unincorporated association, the corporation or association having failed to enforce a right which may properly be asserted by it, the complaint shall be verified and shall allege (1) that the plaintiff was a shareholder or member at the time of the transaction of which the plaintiff complains or that the plaintiff's share or membership thereafter devolved on the plaintiff by operation of law, and (2) that the action is not a collusive one to confer jurisdiction on a court of the United States which it would not otherwise have. The complaint shall also allege with particularity the efforts, if any, made by the plaintiff to obtain the action the plaintiff desires from the directors or comparable authority and, if necessary, from the shareholders or members, and the reasons for the plaintiff's failure to obtain the action or for not making the effort. The derivative action may not be maintained if it appears that the plaintiff does not fairly and adequately represent the interests of the shareholders or members similarly situated in enforcing the right of the corporation or association. The action shall not be dismissed or compromised without the approval of the court, and notice of the proposed dismissal or compromise shall be given to shareholders or members in such manner as the court directs.

Notes on the Adoption in 1966 of Federal Rule 23.1

Prior to 1966 the substance of Rule 23.1 was contained in Rules 23 (b) and (c). Rule 23(b) stated:

Secondary Action by Shareholders. In an action brought to enforce a secondary right on the part of one or more shareholders in an association, incorporated or unincorporated, because the association refuses to enforce rights which may properly be asserted by it, the complaint shall be verified by oath and shall aver (1) that the plaintiff was a shareholder at the time of the transaction of which he complains or that his share thereafter devolved on him by operation of law and (2) that the action is not a collusive one to confer on a court of the United States jurisdiction of any action of which it would not otherwise have jurisdiction. The complaint shall also set forth with particularity the efforts of the plaintiff to secure from the managing directors or trustees and, if necessary, from the shareholders such action as he desires, and the reasons for his failure to obtain such action or the reasons for not making such effort.

For former Rule 23(c) see the note following Rule 23.

The Advisory Committee commented as follows on the changes:

A derivative action by a shareholder of a corporation or by a member of an unincorporated association has distinctive aspects which require the special provisions set forth in the new rule. The next-to-the-last sentence recognizes that the question of adequacy of representation may arise when the plaintiff is one of a group of shareholders or members. *Cf.* 3 *Moore's Federal Practice* ¶ 23.08 (2d ed. 1963).

The court has inherent power to provide for the conduct of the proceedings in a derivative action, including the power to determine the course of the proceedings and require that any appropriate notice be given to shareholders or members.

Rule 23.2 Actions Relating to Unincorporated Associations

An action brought by or against the members of an unincorporated association as a class by naming certain members as representative parties may be maintained only if it appears that the representative parties will fairly and adequately protect the interests of the association and its members. In the conduct of the action the court may make appropriate orders corresponding with those described in Rule 23(d), and the procedure for dismissal or compromise of the action shall correspond with that provided in Rule 23(e).

Notes on the Adoption in 1966 of Federal Rule 23.2

The substance of Rule 23.2 was not directly treated prior to its addition in 1966. The Advisory Committee's Notes to the Rule read as follows:

Although an action by or against representatives of the membership of an unincorporated association has often been viewed as a class action, the real or main purpose of this characterization has been to give "entity treatment" to the association when for formal reasons it cannot sue or be sued as a jural person under Rule 17(b). See Louisell & Hazard, *Pleading and Procedure: State and Federal* 718 (1962); 3 *Moore's Federal Practice* ¶ 23.08 (2d ed. 1963) * * *. Rule 23.2 deals separately with these actions, referring where appropriate to Rule 23.

Rule 24. Intervention

(a) Intervention of Right. Upon timely application anyone shall be permitted to intervene in an action: (1) when a statute of the United States confers an unconditional right to intervene; or (2) when the applicant claims an interest relating to the property or transaction which is the subject of the action and the applicant is so situated that the disposition of the action may as a practical matter impair or impede the applicant's ability to protect that interest, unless the applicant's interest is adequately represented by existing parties.

(b) Permissive Intervention. Upon timely application anyone may be permitted to intervene in an action: (1) when a statute of the United States confers a conditional right to intervene; or (2) when an applicant's claim or defense and the main action have a question of law or fact in common. When a party to an action relies for ground of claim or defense upon any statute or executive order administered by a federal or state governmental officer or agency or upon any regulation, order, requirement or agreement issued or made pursuant to the statute or executive order, the officer or agency upon timely application may be permitted to intervene in the action. In exercising its discretion the court shall consider whether the intervention will unduly delay or prejudice the adjudication of the rights of the original parties.

(c) Procedure. A person desiring to intervene shall serve a motion to intervene upon the parties as provided in Rule 5. The motion shall state the grounds therefor and shall be accompanied by a pleading setting forth the claim or defense for which intervention is sought. The same procedure shall be followed when a statute of the United States gives a right to intervene. When the constitutionality of an act of Congress affecting the public interest is drawn in question in any action to which the United States or an officer, agency, or employee thereof is not a party, the court shall notify the Attorney General of the United States as provided in Title 28, U.S.C. § 2403. When the constitutionality of any statute of a State affecting the public interest is drawn in question in any action in which that State or any agency, offices, or employee thereof is not a party, the court shall notify the attorney general of the State as provided in Title 28, U.S.C. § 2403. A party challenging the constitutionality of legislation should call the attention of the court to its consequential duty, but failure to do so is not a waiver of any constitutional right otherwise timely asserted.

Notes on Amendments to Federal Rule 24 and Comparative State Provisions

(a) *Amendments in 1966 to Rule 24(a)*

Prior to 1966, Rules 24(a)(2) and (3) provided a right to intervene as follows:

(2) when the representation of the applicant's interest by existing parties is or may be inadequate and the applicant is or may be bound by a judgment in the action; or (3) when the applicant is so situated as to be adversely affected by a distribution or other disposition of property which is in the custody or subject to the control or disposition of the court or an officer thereof.

The amendment eliminated this language and substituted the present Rule 24(a)(2). The Advisory Committee's Notes on the Amendment read as follows:

In attempting to overcome certain difficulties which have arisen in the application of present Rule 24(a)(2) and (3), this amendment draws upon the revision of the related Rules 19 (joinder of persons needed for just adjudication) and 23 (class actions), and the reasoning underlying that revision.

Rule 24(a)(3) as amended in 1948 provided for intervention of right where the applicant established that he would be adversely affected by the distribution or disposition of property involved in an action to which he had not been made a party. Significantly, some decided cases virtually disregarded the language of this provision. Thus Professor Moore states: "The concept of a fund has been applied so loosely that it is possible for a court to find a fund in almost any in personam action." 4 Moore's Federal Practice, par. 24.09[3], at 55 (2d ed. 1962), and see, e.g., Formulabs, Inc. v. Hartley Pen Co., 275 F.2d 52 (9th Cir. 1960). This development was quite natural, for Rule 24(a)(3) was unduly restricted. If an absentee would be substantially affected in a practical sense by the determination made in an action, he should, as a general rule, be entitled to intervene, and his right to do so should not depend on whether there is a fund to be distributed or otherwise disposed of. Intervention of right is here seen to be a kind of counterpart to Rule 19(a)(2)(i) on joinder of persons needed for a just adjudication: where, upon motion of a party in an action, an absentee should be joined so that he may protect his interest which as a practical matter may be substantially impaired by the disposition of the action, he ought to have a right to intervene in the action on his own motion. See Louisell & Hazard, Pleading and Procedure: State and Federal 749–50 (1962).

The general purpose of original Rule 24(a)(2) was to entitle an absentee, purportedly represented by a party, to intervene in the action if he could establish with fair probability that the representation was inadequate. Thus, where an action is being prosecuted or defended by a trustee, a beneficiary of the trust should have a right to intervene if he can show that the trustee's representation of his interest probably is inadequate; similarly a member of a class should have the right to intervene in a class action if he can show the inadequacy of the representation of his interest by the representative parties before the court.

Original Rule 24(a)(2), however, made it a condition of intervention that "the applicant is or may be bound by a judgment in the action," and this created difficulties with intervention in class actions. If the "bound" language was read literally in the sense of res judicata, it could defeat intervention in some meritorious cases. A member of a class to whom a judgment in a class action extended by its terms (see Rule 23(c)(3), as amended) might be entitled to show in a later action, when the judgment in the class action was claimed to operate as res judicata against him, that the "representative" in the class action had not in fact adequately represented him. If he could make this showing, the class-action judgment might be held not to bind him. See Hansberry v. Lee, 311 U.S. 32 (1940). If a class member sought to intervene in the class action proper, while it was still pending, on grounds of inadequacy of representation, he could be met with the argument: if the representation was in fact inadequate, he would not be "bound" by the judgment when it was subsequently asserted against him as res judicata, hence he was not entitled to intervene; if the representation was in fact adequate, there was no occasion or ground for intervention. * * * This reasoning might be linguistically justified by original Rule 24(a)(2); but it could lead to poor results. * * * A class member who claims that his "representative" does not adequately represent him, and is able to establish that proposition with sufficient probability, should not be put to the risk of having a judgment entered in the action which by its terms extends to him, and be obliged to test the validity of the judgment as applied to his interest by a later collateral attack. Rather he should, as a general rule, be entitled to intervene in the action.

The amendment provides that an applicant is entitled to intervene in an action when his position is comparable to that of a person under Rule 19(a)(2)(i), as amended, unless his interest is already adequately represented in the action by existing parties. The Rule 19(a)(2)(i) criterion imports practical considerations, and the deletion of the "bound" language similarly frees the rule from undue preoccupation with strict considerations of res judicata.

The representation whose adequacy comes into question under the amended rule is not confined to formal representation like that provided by a trustee for his beneficiary or a representative party in a class action for a member of the class. A party to an action may provide practical representation to the absentee seeking intervention although no such formal relationship exists between them, and the adequacy of this practical representation will then have to be weighed. * * *

Rule 24   RULES OF CIVIL PROCEDURE

An intervention of right under the amended rule may be subject to appropriate conditions or restrictions responsive among other things to the requirements of efficient conduct of the proceedings.

(b) Comparative State Provision

Ohio Revised Code Annotated § 2307.27

In an action for the recovery of real or personal property, a person claiming an interest in the property, on his application, may be made a party.

Rule 25. Substitution of Parties

(a) Death.

(1) If a party dies and the claim is not thereby extinguished, the court may order substitution of the proper parties. The motion for substitution may be made by any party or by the successors or representatives of the deceased party and, together with the notice of hearing, shall be served on the parties as provided in Rule 5 and upon persons not parties in the manner provided in Rule 4 for the service of a summons, and may be served in any judicial district. Unless the motion for substitution is made not later than 90 days after the death is suggested upon the record by service of a statement of the fact of the death as provided herein for the service of the motion, the action shall be dismissed as to the deceased party.

(2) In the event of the death of one or more of the plaintiffs or of one or more of the defendants in an action in which the right sought to be enforced survives only to the surviving plaintiffs or only against the surviving defendants, the action does not abate. The death shall be suggested upon the record and the action shall proceed in favor of or against the surviving parties.

(b) Incompetency. If a party becomes incompetent, the court upon motion served as provided in subdivision (a) of this rule may allow the action to be continued by or against the party's representative.

(c) Transfer of Interest. In case of any transfer of interest, the action may be continued by or against the original party, unless the court upon motion directs the person to whom the interest is transferred to be substituted in the action or joined with the original party. Service of the motion shall be made as provided in subdivision (a) of this rule.

(d) Public Officers; Death or Separation From Office.

(1) When a public officer is a party to an action in an official capacity and during its pendency dies, resigns, or otherwise ceases to hold office, the action does not abate and the officer's successor is automatically substituted as a party. Proceedings following the substitution shall be in the name of the substituted party, but any misnomer not affecting the substantial rights of the parties shall be disregarded. An order of substitution may be entered at any time, but the omission to enter such an order shall not affect the substitution.

DEPOSITIONS AND DISCOVERY — **Rule 26**

(2) A public officer who sues or is sued in an official capacity may be described as a party by the officer's official title rather than by name; but the court may require the officer's name to be added.

V. DEPOSITIONS AND DISCOVERY

Rule 26. General Provisions Governing Discovery; Duty of Disclosure

(a) Required Disclosures; Methods to Discover Additional Matter.

(1) *Initial Disclosures.* Except to the extent otherwise stipulated or directed by order or local rule, a party shall, without awaiting a discovery request, provide to other parties;

(A) the name and, if known, the address and telephone number of each individual likely to have discoverable information relevant to disputed facts alleged with particularity in the pleadings, identifying the subjects of the information;

(B) a copy of, or a description by category and location of, all documents, data compilations, and tangible things in the possession, custody, or control of the party that are relevant to the disputed facts alleged with particularity in the pleadings;

(C) a computation of any category of damages claimed by the disclosing party, making available for inspection and copying as under Rule 34 the documents or other evidentiary material, not privileged or protected from disclosure, on which such computation is based, including materials bearing on the nature and extent of injuries suffered; and

(D) for inspection copying as under Rule 34 any insurance agreement under which any person carrying on an insurance business may be liable to satisfy part or all of a judgment which may be entered in the action or to indemnify or reimburse for payments made to satisfy the judgment.

Unless otherwise stipulated or directed by the court, these disclosures shall be made at or within 10 days after the meeting of the parties under subdivision (f). A party shall make its initial disclosures based on the information then reasonably available to it and is not excused from making its disclosure because it has not fully completed its investigation of the case or because it challenges the sufficiency of another party's disclosures or because another party has not made its disclosures.

(2) *Disclosure of Expert Testimony.*

(A) In addition to the disclosures required by paragraph (1), a party shall disclose to other parties the identity of any person who may be used at trial to present evidence under Rules 702, 703, or 705 of the Federal Rules of Evidence.

(B) Except as otherwise stipulated or directed by the court, this disclosure shall, with respect to a witness who is retained or specially employed to provide expert testimony in the case or whose duties as an employee of the party regularly involve giving expert testimony, be accompanied by a written report prepared and signed by the witness. The report shall contain a complete statement of all opinions to be expressed and the basis and reasons therefor; the data or other information considered by the witness in forming the opinions; any exhibits to be used as a summary of or support for the opinions; the qualifications of the witness, including a list of all publications authored by the witness within the preceding ten years; the compensation to be paid for the study and testimony; and a listing of any other cases in which the witness has testified as an expert at trial or by deposition within the preceding four years.

(C) These disclosures shall be made at the times and in the sequence directed by the court. In the absence of other directions from the court or stipulation by the parties, the disclosures shall be made at least 90 days before the trial date or the date the case is to be ready for trial or, if the evidence is intended solely to contradict, or rebut evidence on the same subject matter identified by another party under paragraph (2)(B), within 30 days after the disclosure made by such other party. The parties shall supplement these disclosures when required under subdivision (e)(1).

(3) *Pretrial Disclosures.* In addition to the disclosures required in the preceding paragraphs, a party shall provide to other parties the following information regarding the evidence that it may present at trial other than solely for impeachment purposes:

(A) the name and, if not previously provided, the address and telephone number of each witness, separately identifying those whom the party expects to present and those whom the party may call if the need arises;

(B) the designation of those witnesses whose testimony is expected to be presented by means of a deposition and, if not taken by stenographic means, a transcript of the pertinent portions of the deposition testimony; and

(C) an appropriate identification of each document or other exhibit, including summaries of other evidence, separately identifying those which the party expects to offer and those which the party may offer if the need arises.

Unless otherwise directed by the court, these disclosures shall be made at least 30 days before trial. Within 14 days thereafter, unless a different time is specified by the court, a party may serve and file a list disclosing (i) any objections to the use under Rule 32(a) of a deposition designated by another party under subparagraph (B) and (ii) any objection, together with the grounds therefor, that may be made to the

DEPOSITIONS AND DISCOVERY — Rule 26

admissibility of materials identified under subparagraph (C). Objections not so disclosed, other than objections under Rules 402 and 403 of the Federal Rules of Evidence, shall be deemed waived unless excused by the court for good cause shown.

(4) *Form of Disclosures; Filing.* Unless otherwise directed by order or local rule, all disclosures under paragraphs (1) through (3) shall be made in writing, signed, served, and promptly filed with the court.

(5) *Methods to Discover Additional Matter.* Parties may obtain discovery by one or more of the following methods: depositions upon oral examination or written questions; written interrogatories; production of documents or things or permission to enter upon land or other property under Rule 34 or 45(a)(1)(C), for inspection and other purposes; physical and mental examinations; and requests for admission.

(b) Discovery Scope and Limits. Unless otherwise limited by order of the court in accordance with these rules, the scope of discovery is as follows:

(1) *In General.* Parties may obtain discovery regarding any matter, not privileged, which is relevant to the subject matter involved in the pending action, whether it relates to the claim or defense of the party seeking discovery or to the claim or defense of any other party, including the existence, description, nature, custody, condition and location of any books, documents, or other tangible things and the identity and location of persons having knowledge of any discoverable matter. The information sought need not be admissible at the trial if the information sought appears reasonably calculated to lead to the discovery of admissible evidence.

(2) *Limitations.* By order or by local rule, the court may alter the limits in these rules on the number of depositions and interrogatories and may also limit the length of depositions under Rule 30 and the number of requests under Rule 36. The frequency or extent of use of the discovery methods otherwise permitted under these rules and any local rule shall be limited by the court if it determines that: (i) the discovery sought is unreasonably cumulative or duplicative, or is obtainable from some other source that is more convenient, less burdensome, or less expensive; (ii) the party seeking discovery has had ample opportunity by discovery in the action to obtain the information sought; or (iii) the burden or expense of the proposed discovery outweighs its likely benefit, taking into account the needs of the case, the amount in controversy, the parties' resources, the importance of the issues at stake in the litigation, and the importance of the proposed discovery in resolving the issues. The court may act upon its own initiative after reasonable notice or pursuant to a motion under subdivision (c).

(3) *Trial Preparation: Materials.* Subject to the provisions of subdivision (b)(4) of this rule, a party may obtain discovery of documents and tangible things otherwise discoverable under subdivision (b)(1) of

this rule and prepared in anticipation of litigation or for trial by or for another party or by or for that other party's representative (including the other party's attorney, consultant, surety, indemnitor, insurer, or agent) only upon a showing that the party seeking discovery has substantial need of the materials in the preparation of the party's case and that the party is unable without undue hardship to obtain the substantial equivalent of the materials by other means. In ordering discovery of such materials when the required showing has been made, the court shall protect against disclosure of the mental impressions, conclusions, opinions, or legal theories of an attorney or other representative of a party concerning the litigation.

A party may obtain without the required showing a statement concerning the action or its subject matter previously made by that party. Upon request, a person not a party may obtain without the required showing a statement concerning the action or its subject matter previously made by that person. If the request is refused, the person may move for a court order. The provisions of Rule 37(a)(4) apply to the award of expenses incurred in relation to the motion. For purposes of this paragraph, a statement previously made is (A) a written statement signed or otherwise adopted or approved by the person making it, or (B) a stenographic, mechanical, electrical, or other recording, or a transcription thereof, which is a substantially verbatim recital of an oral statement by the person making it and contemporaneously recorded.

(4) *Trial Preparation: Experts.*

(A) A party may depose any person who has been identified as an expert whose opinions may be presented at trial. If a report from the expert is required under subdivision (a)(2)(B), the deposition shall not be conducted until after the report is provided.

(B) A party may, through interrogatories or by deposition, discover facts known or opinions held by an expert who has been retained or specially employed by another party in anticipation of litigation or preparation for trial and who is not expected to be called as a witness at trial only as provided in Rule 35(b) or upon a showing of exceptional circumstances under which it is impracticable for the party seeking discovery to obtain facts or opinions on the same subject by other means.

(C) Unless manifest injustice would result, (i) the court shall require that the party seeking discovery pay the expert a reasonable fee for time spent in responding to discovery under this subdivision; and (ii) with respect to discovery obtained under subdivision (b)(4)(B) of this rule the court shall require the party seeking discovery to pay the other party a fair portion of the fees and expenses reasonably incurred by the latter party in obtaining facts and opinions from the expert.

DEPOSITIONS AND DISCOVERY   **Rule 26**

(5) *Claims of Privilege or Protection of Trial Preparation Materials.* When a party withholds information otherwise discoverable under these rules by claiming that it is privileged or subject to protection as trial preparation material, the party shall make the claim expressly and shall describe the nature of the documents, communications, or things not produced or disclosed in a manner that, without revealing information itself privileged or protected, will enable other parties to assess the applicability of the privilege or protection.

(c) Protective Orders. Upon motion by a party or by the person from whom discovery is sought, accompanied by a certificate that the movant in good faith has conferred or attempted to confer with other affected parties in an effort to resolve the dispute without court action, and for good cause shown, the court in which the action is pending or alternatively, on matters relating to a deposition, the court in the district where the deposition is to be taken may make any order which justice requires to protect a party or person from annoyance, embarrassment, oppression, or undue burden or expense, including one or more of the following: (1) that the disclosure or discovery not be had; (2) that the disclosure or discovery may be had only on specified terms and conditions, including a designation of the time or place; (3) that the discovery may be had only by a method of discovery other than that selected by the party seeking discovery; (4) that certain matters not be inquired into, or that the scope of the disclosure or discovery be limited to certain matters; (5) that the discovery be conducted with no one present except persons designated by the court; (6) that a deposition after being sealed be opened only by order of the court; (7) that a trade secret or other confidential research, development, or commercial information not be revealed or be revealed only in a designated way; (8) that the parties simultaneously file specified documents or information enclosed in sealed envelopes to be opened as directed by the court.

If the motion for a protective order is denied in whole or in part, the court may, on such terms and conditions as are just, order that any party or other person provide or permit discovery. The provisions of Rule 37(a)(4) apply to the award of expenses incurred in relation to the motion.

(d) Timing and Sequence of Discovery. Except when authorized under these rules or by local rule, order, or agreement of the parties, a party may not seek discovery from any source before the parties have met and conferred as required by subdivision (f). Unless the court upon motion, for the convenience of parties and witnesses and in the interests of justice, orders otherwise, methods of discovery may be used in any sequence, and the fact that a party is conducting discovery, whether by deposition or otherwise, shall not operate to delay another party's discovery.

Rule 26 — RULES OF CIVIL PROCEDURE

(e) Supplementation of Disclosures and Responses. A party who has made a disclosure under subdivision (a) or responded to a request for discovery with a disclosure or response is under a duty to supplement or correct the disclosure or response to include information thereafter acquired if ordered by the court or in the following circumstances:

(1) A party is under a duty to supplement at appropriate intervals its disclosures under subdivision (a) if the party learns that in some material respect the information disclosed is incomplete or incorrect and if the additional or corrective information has not otherwise been made known to the other parties during the discovery process or in writing. With respect to testimony of an expert from whom a report is required under subdivision (a)(2)(B) the duty extends both to information contained in the report and to information provided through a deposition of the expert, and any additions or other changes to this information shall be disclosed by the time the party's disclosures under Rule 26(a)(3) are due.

(2) A party is under a duty seasonably to amend a prior response to an interrogatory, request for production, or request for admission if the party learns that the response is in some material respect incomplete or incorrect and if the additional or corrective information has not otherwise been made known to the other parties during the discovery process or in writing.

(f) Meeting of Parties; Planning for Discovery. Except in actions exempted by local rule or when otherwise ordered, the parties shall, as soon as practicable and in any event at least 14 days before a scheduling conference is held or a scheduling order is due under Rule 16(b), meet to discuss the nature and basis of their claims and defenses and the possibilities for a prompt settlement or resolution of the case, to make or arrange for the disclosures required by subdivision (a)(1), and to develop a proposed discovery plan. The plan shall indicate the parties' views and proposals concerning:

(1) what changes should be made in the timing, form, or requirement for disclosures under subdivision (a) or local rule, including a statement as to when disclosures under subdivision (a)(1) were made or will be made;

(2) the subjects on which discovery may be needed, when discovery should be completed, and whether discovery should be conducted in phases or be limited to or focused upon particular issues;

(3) what changes should be made in the limitations on discovery imposed under these rules or by local rule, and what other limitations should be imposed; and

(4) any other orders that should be entered by the court under subdivision (c) or under Rule 16(b) and (c).

The attorneys of record and all unrepresented parties that have appeared in the case are jointly responsible for arranging and being present or represented at the meeting, for attempting in good faith to agree on the proposed discovery plan, and for submitting to the court within 10 days after the meeting a written report outlining the plan.

(g) Signing of Disclosures, Discovery Requests, Responses, and Objections.

(1) Every disclosure made pursuant to subdivision (a)(1) or subdivision (a)(3) shall be signed by at least one attorney of record in the attorney's individual name, whose address shall be stated. An unrepresented party shall sign the disclosure and state the party's address. The signature of the attorney or party constitutes a certification that to the best of the signer's knowledge, information, and belief formed after a reasonable inquiry, the disclosure is complete and correct as of the time it is made.

(2) Every discovery request, response, or objection made by a party represented by an attorney shall be signed by at least one attorney of record in the attorney's individual name, whose address shall be stated. An unrepresented party shall sign the request, response, or objection and state the party's address. The signature of the attorney or party constitutes a certification that to the best of the signer's knowledge, information, and belief, formed after a reasonable inquiry, the request, response, or objection is: (A) consistent with these rules and warranted by existing law or a good faith argument for the extension, modification, or reversal of existing law; (B) not interposed for any improper purpose, such as to harass or to cause unnecessary delay or needless increase in the cost of litigation; and (C) not unreasonable or unduly burdensome or expensive, given the needs of the case, the discovery already had in the case, the amount in controversy, and the importance of the issues at stake in the litigation.

If a request, response, or objection, is not signed, it shall be stricken unless it is signed promptly after the omission is called to the attention of the party making the request, response, or objection, and a party shall not be obligated to take any action with respect to it until it is signed.

(3) If without substantial justification a certification is made in violation of the rule, the court, upon motion or upon its own initiative, shall impose upon the person who made the certification, the party on whose behalf the disclosure, request, response, or objection is made, or both, an appropriate sanction, which may include an order to pay the amount of the reasonable expenses incurred because of the violation, including a reasonable attorney's fee.

Notes on Amendments to Federal Rule 26 and Comparative State Provisions

(a) *Advisory Committee Comments on Substantive Alterations in Rule 26 Made in 1993*

Major revisions to Rule 26 were adopted in 1993 to facilitate the exchange of pertinent information between parties early in the case. The Advisory Committee on Rules, in the Notes to the amended Rule 26, state that the revisions were based, in part, on the experience of district courts which had previously adopted similar automatic disclosure provisions. It is important to note that some of the significant new changes, such as those in 26(a) and 26(f), state that they can be superseded by local court rules. Although trial courts have been able to control discovery on a case-by-case basis, they have not been formally permitted to sidestep a Federal Rule provision entirely. This new approach raises important questions regarding the value of procedural uniformity among the federal courts.

Subdivision (a) of Rule 26 was amended to include subparagraphs (1)–(4), which impose a duty to disclose basic information necessary for parties to prepare for trial. Subparagraph (1) states that parties must now automatically exchange information such as the names of witnesses, copies of pertinent documents, computations of damages and insurance data.

Subparagraph (2) imposes a duty to disclose information regarding expert testimony, usually within 90 days before the trial date. The revision clarifies the more vague requirement in old Rule 26 that the "substance" of expert testimony be revealed by requiring that experts retained to provide testimony submit detailed and complete written reports. This requirement, along with Rule 37(c)(1), which provides that ordinarily a party will be unable to use expert testimony not so disclosed, is intended to provide parties with basic information about the testimony of the expert. Revised Rule 26(b)(4)(A) now authorizes depositions of experts, but only after the expert's report has been served.

Subparagraph (3) requires that parties automatically exchange information regarding the use of witnesses, trial deposition testimony and exhibits at least 30 days before trial.

Subparagraph (5) is amended to reflect changes to Rule 45 regarding inspection by non-parties of documents and premises without deposition.

Subdivision (b) is substantially revised, in part for organizational clarity and in part to implement provisions which limit the discovery process. Of the substantive revisions, subparagraph (4)(A) is revised to show that experts may be deposed, but as noted in subdivision (a)(2)(B), only after the expert has submitted the required detailed report. Subparagraph (4)(C), regarding compensation of experts, is revised to reflect changes in (4)(A).

Subparagraph (5) has been added to place upon a party an affirmative duty to disclose to other parties if it is withholding materials based on a claim of privilege or work product protection. The party claiming privilege must provide enough information to support its claim to enable other parties to evaluate the applicability of the claim. Sanctions may be imposed under Rule 37(b)(2) for violating this provision.

Subdivision (c) is revised to require parties to confer and attempt to resolve discovery disputes in good faith prior to seeking a protective order from the court.

Subdivision (d) is revised to prohibit the commencement of formal discovery until the parties have met pursuant to revised rule 26(f). Exceptions to this Rule are allowed under Rule 30(a)(2)(C) (deposition of a person about to leave the country) and by local rule, order or stipulation.

Subdivision (e) provides that parties are subject to a continuing duty to supplement disclosures made pursuant to Rule 26(a)(1)–(3). In addition, the revised rule clarifies that the duty to supplement formal discovery requests applies to interrogatories, requests for production, and requests for admissions, but not ordinarily to deposition testimony. Only when opinions expressed by an expert in deposition change is there a duty to supplement deposition responses.

Subdivision (f) is revised to remove provisions relating to a conference with the court regarding discovery. As noted by the Advisory Committee on Rules, "[t]his change does not signal any lessening of the importance of judicial supervision," but rather results from the relocation of such provisions to amended Rule 16 which addresses the court's role in directing the discovery process.

Subdivision (g), newly added, requires all disclosures be signed. In keeping with the revisions to Rule 11, which state that Rule is no longer applicable to discovery matters, the signature requirement is now included directly in Rule 26.

(b) *Advisory Committee Comments on Substantive Alterations in Rule 26 Made in 1970*

The Advisory Committee commented on changes in Rule 26 as follows:

Subdivision (b)(2)—Insurance Policies. [This provision was altered in 1993 and is now covered in Rule 26(a)(1)(D).] Both the cases and commentators are sharply in conflict on the question whether defendant's liability insurance coverage is subject to discovery in the usual situation when the insurance coverage is not itself admissible and does not bear on another issue in the case. * * *

The amendment resolves this issue in favor of disclosure. Most of the decisions denying discovery, some explicitly, reason from the text of Rule 26(b) that it permits discovery only of matters which will be admissible in evidence or appear reasonably calculated to lead to such evidence; they avoid considerations of policy, regarding them as foreclosed. * * *. Some note also that facts about a defendant's financial status are not discoverable as such, prior to judgment with execution unsatisfied, and fear that, if courts hold insurance coverage discoverable, they must extend the principle to other aspects of the defendant's financial status. The cases favoring disclosure rely heavily on the practical significance of insurance in the decisions lawyers make about settlement and trial preparation. In *Clauss v. Danker,* 264 F.Supp. 246 (S.D.N.Y.1967), the court held that the rules forbid disclosure but called for an amendment to permit it.

Disclosure of insurance coverage will enable counsel for both sides to make the same realistic appraisal of the case, so that settlement and litigation strategy are based on knowledge and not speculation. It will conduce to settlement and avoid protracted litigation in some cases, though in others it may have an opposite effect. The amendment is limited to insurance coverage, which should be distinguished from any other facts concerning defendant's financial status (1) because insurance is an asset created specifically to satisfy the claim; (2) because the insurance company ordinarily controls the litigation; (3) because information about coverage is available only from defendant or his insurer; and (4) because disclosure does not involve a significant invasion of privacy. * * *

In no instance does disclosure make the facts concerning insurance coverage admissible in evidence.

Subdivision (b)(3)—Trial Preparation: Materials. Some of the most controversial and vexing problems to emerge from the discovery rules have arisen out of requests for the production of documents or things prepared in anticipation of litigation or for trial. The existing rules make no explicit provision for such materials. Yet, two verbally distinct doctrines have developed, each conferring a qualified immunity on these materials—the "good cause" requirement in Rule 34 (now generally held applicable to discovery of documents via deposition under Rule 45 and interrogatories under Rule 33) and the work-product doctrine of *Hickman v. Taylor,* 329 U.S. 495 (1947). Both demand a showing of justification before production can be had, the one of "good cause" and the other variously described in the *Hickman* case: "necessity or justification," "denial * * * would unduly prejudice the preparation of petitioner's case," or "cause hardship or injustice" 329 U.S. at 509–510. * * *

The major difficulties visible in the existing case law are (1) confusion and disagreement as to whether "good cause" is made out by a showing of relevance and lack of privilege, or requires an additional showing of necessity, (2) confusion and disagreement as to the scope of the *Hickman* work-product doctrine, particularly whether it extends beyond work actually performed by lawyers, and (3) the resulting difficulty of relating the "good cause" required by Rule 34 and the "necessity or justification" of the work-product doctrine, so that their respective roles and the distinctions between them are understood. * * *

The rules are amended by eliminating the general requirement of "good cause" from Rule 34 but retaining a requirement of a special showing for trial preparation materials in this subdivision. The required showing is expressed, not in terms of "good cause" whose generality has tended to encourage confusion and controversy, but in terms of the elements of the special showing to be made: substantial need of the materials in the preparation of the case and inability without undue hardship to obtain the substantial equivalent of the materials by other means.

These changes conform to the holdings of the cases, when viewed in light of their facts. Apart from trial preparation, the fact that the materials sought are documentary does not in and of itself require a special showing beyond relevance and absence of privilege. * * *

Elimination of a "good cause" requirement from Rule 34 and the establishment of a requirement of a special showing in this subdivision will eliminate the confusion caused by having two verbally distinct requirements of justification that the courts have been unable to distinguish clearly. Moreover, the language of the subdivision suggests the factors which the courts should consider in determining whether the requisite showing has been made. The importance of the materials sought to the party seeking them in preparation of his case and the difficulty he will have obtaining them by other means are factors noted in the *Hickman* case. The courts should also consider the likelihood that the party, even if he obtains the information by independent means, will not have the substantial equivalent of the documents the production of which he seeks.

* * *

Materials assembled in the ordinary course of business, or pursuant to public requirements unrelated to litigation, or for other nonlitigation purposes are not under the qualified immunity provided by this subdivision. *Goosman v. A. Duie Pyle, Inc.*, 320 F.2d 45 (4th Cir.1963); *cf. United States v. New York Foreign Trade Zone Operators, Inc.*, 304 F.2d 792 (2d Cir.1962). No change is made in the existing doctrine, noted in the *Hickman* case, that one party may discover relevant facts known or available to the other party, even though such facts are contained in a document which is not itself discoverable.

Treatment of Lawyers; Special Protection of Mental Impressions, Conclusions, Opinions, and Legal Theories Concerning the Litigation.—The courts are divided as to whether the work-product doctrine extends to the preparatory work only of lawyers. The *Hickman* case left this issue open since the statements in that case were taken by a lawyer. * * *

Subdivision (b)(3) reflects the trend of the cases by requiring a special showing, not merely as to materials prepared by an attorney, but also as to materials prepared in anticipation of litigation or preparation for trial by or for a party or any representative acting on his behalf. The subdivision then goes on to protect against disclosure [of] the mental impressions, conclusions, opinions, or legal theories concerning the litigation of an attorney or other representative of a party. The *Hickman* opinion drew special attention to the need for protecting an attorney against discovery of memoranda prepared from recollection of oral interviews. The courts have steadfastly safeguarded against disclosure of lawyers' mental impressions and legal theories, as well as mental impressions and subjective evaluations of investigators and claim-agents. In enforcing this provision of the subdivision, the courts will sometimes find it necessary to order disclosure of a document but with portions deleted. * * *

Party's Right to Own Statement.—An exception to the requirement of this subdivision enables a party to secure production of his own statement without any special showing. The cases are divided. * * *

Courts which treat a party's statement as though it were that of any witness overlook the fact that the party's statement is, without more, admissible in evidence. Ordinarily, a party gives a statement without insisting on a copy because he does not yet have a lawyer and does not understand the legal consequences of his actions. Thus, the statement is given at a time when he functions at a disadvantage. Discrepancies between his trial testimony and earlier statement may result from lapse of memory or ordinary inaccuracy; a written statement produced for the first time at trial may give such discrepancies a prominence which they do not deserve. In appropriate cases the court may order a party to be deposed before his statement is produced. * * *

Witness' Right to Own Statement.—A second exception to the requirement of this subdivision permits a non-party witness to obtain a copy of his own statement without any special showing. Many, though not all, of the considerations supporting a party's right to obtain his statement apply also to the non-party witness. Insurance companies are increasingly recognizing that a witness is entitled to a copy of his statement and are modifying their regular practice accordingly.

Subdivision (b)(4)—Trial Preparation: Experts. * * *

Subsection (b)(4)(A) deals with discovery of information obtained by or through experts who will be called as witnesses at trial. The provision is responsive to problems suggested by a relatively recent line of authorities. Many of these cases present intricate and difficult issues as to which expert testimony is likely to be determinative. Prominent among them are food and drug, patent, and condemnation cases. * * *

In cases of this character, a prohibition against discovery of information held by expert witnesses produces in acute form the very evils that discovery has been created to prevent. Effective cross-examination of an expert witness requires advance preparation. The lawyer even with the help of his own experts frequently cannot anticipate the particular approach his adversary's expert will take or the data on which he will base his judgment on the stand. McGlothlin, *Some Practical Problems in Proof of Economic, Scientific, and Technical Facts*, 23 F.R.D. 467, 478 (1958). A California study of discovery and pretrial in condemnation cases notes that the only substitute for discovery of experts' valuation materials is "lengthy—and often fruitless—cross-examination during trial," and recommends pretrial exchange of such material. Calif.Law Rev.Comm'n, *Discovery in Eminent Domain Proceedings*, 707–710 (Jan.1963). Similarly, effective rebuttal requires advance knowledge of the line of testimony of the other side. If the latter is foreclosed by a rule against discovery, then the narrowing of issues and elimination of surprise which discovery normally produces are frustrated. * * *

Past judicial restrictions on discovery of an adversary's expert, particularly as to his opinions, reflect the fear that one side will benefit unduly from the other's better preparation. The procedure established in subsection (b)(4)(A) holds the risk to a minimum. Discovery is limited to trial witnesses, and may be obtained only at a time when the parties know who their expert witnesses will be. A party must as a practical matter prepare his own case in advance of that time, for he can hardly hope to build his case out of his opponent's experts. * * *

Subdivision (b)(4)(B) deals with an expert who has been retained or specially employed by the party in anticipation of litigation or preparation for trial (thus excluding an expert who is simply a general employee of the party not specially employed on the case), but who is not expected to be called as a witness. Under its provisions, a party may discover facts known or opinions held by such an expert only on a showing of exceptional circumstances under which it is impracticable for the party seeking discovery to obtain facts or opinions on the same subject by other means. * * *

Subdivision (d)—Sequence and Priority. This new provision is concerned with the sequence in which parties may proceed with discovery and with related problems of timing. The principal effects of the new provision are first, to eliminate any fixed priority in the sequence of discovery, and second, to make clear and explicit the court's power to establish priority by an order issued in a particular case.

A priority rule developed by some courts, which confers priority on the party who first serves notice of taking a deposition, is unsatisfactory in several important respects:

First, this priority rule permits a party to establish a priority running to all depositions as to which he has given earlier notice. Since he can on a given day serve notice of taking many depositions he is in a position to delay his adversary's taking of depositions for an inordinate time. * * *

Second, since notice is the key to priority, if both parties wish to take depositions first a race results. See *Caldwell–Clements, Inc. v. McGraw–Hill Pub. Co.,* 11 F.R.D. 156 (S.D.N.Y.1951) (description of tactics used by parties). But the existing rules on notice of deposition create a race with runners starting from different positions. The plaintiff may not give notice without leave of court until 20 days after commencement of the action, whereas the defendant may serve notice at any time after commencement. Thus, a careful and prompt defendant can almost always secure priority. This advantage of defendants is fortuitous, because the purpose of requiring plaintiff to wait 20 days is to afford defendant an opportunity to obtain counsel, not to confer priority.

Third, although courts have ordered a change in the normal sequence of discovery on a number of occasions, *e.g., Kaeppler v. James H. Matthews & Co.,* 200 F.Supp. 229 (E.D.Pa.1961); *Park & Tilford Distillers Corp. v. Distillers Co.,* 19 F.R.D. 169 (S.D.N.Y.1956), and have at all times avowed discretion to vary the usual priority, most commentators are agreed that courts in fact grant relief only for "the most obviously compelling reasons." * * *

It is contended by some that there is no need to alter the existing priority practice. In support, it is urged that there is no evidence that injustices in fact result from present practice and that, in any event, the courts can and do promulgate local rules, as in New York, to deal with local situations and issue orders to avoid possible injustice in particular cases.

Subdivision (d) is based on the contrary view that the rule of priority based on notice is unsatisfactory and unfair in its operation. Subdivision (d) follows an approach adapted from Civil Rule 4 of the District Court for the Southern District of New York. That rule provides that starting 40 days after commencement of the action, unless otherwise ordered by the court, the fact that one party is taking a deposition shall not prevent another party from doing so "concurrently." In practice, the depositions are not usually taken simultaneously; rather, the parties work out arrangements for alternation in the taking of depositions. One party may take a complete deposition and then the other, or, if the depositions are extensive, one party deposes for a set time, and then the other. See, *Caldwell–Clements, Inc. v. McGraw–Hill Pub. Co.,* 11 F.R.D. 156 (S.D.N.Y.1951).

In principle, one party's initiation of discovery should not wait upon the other's completion, unless delay is dictated by special considerations. Clearly the principle is feasible with respect to all methods of discovery other than depositions. And the experience of the Southern District of New York shows that the principle can be applied to depositions as well. The courts have not had an increase in motion business on this matter. * * *

Subdivision (e)—Supplementation of Responses. The rules do not now state whether interrogatories (and questions at deposition as well as requests for inspection and admissions) impose a "continuing burden" on the responding party to supplement his answers if he obtains new information. The issue is acute when new information renders substantially incomplete or inaccurate an answer which was complete and accurate when made. It is essential that the rules provide an answer to this question. The parties can adjust to a rule either way, once they know what it is. See 4 *Moore's Federal Practice* ¶ 33.25[4] (2d ed. 1966).

Arguments can be made both ways. Imposition of a continuing burden reduces the proliferation of additional sets of interrogatories. Some courts have adopted local rules establishing such a burden. * * * On the other hand, there are serious objections to the burden, especially in protracted cases. Although the party signs the answers, it is his lawyer who understands their significance and bears the responsibility to bring answers up to date. In a complex case all sorts of information reaches the party, who little understands its bearing on answers previously given to interrogatories. In practice, therefore, the lawyer under a continuing burden must periodically recheck all interrogatories and canvass all new information. * * *

The duty will normally be enforced, in those limited instances where it is imposed, through sanctions imposed by the trial court, including exclusion of evidence, continuance, or other action, as the court may deem appropriate.

(c) *Note on the Addition of Rule 26(g) in 1983*

Rule 26(g) was added to require every discovery request, or response or objection thereto, to be signed by an attorney of record or by the party if he or she is not represented by an attorney. In harmony with changes in Rules 7 and 11, Rule 26(g) provides for an "appropriate sanction" to be imposed on an attorney, or party, or both, if a certificate is made in violation of the rule.

(d) *Comparative State Provisions*

1. *Rule 26(a)—Required Disclosure*

Arizona Rule of Civil Procedure 26.1

(a) Duty to Disclose, Scope. Within the times set forth in subdivision (b), each party shall disclose in writing to every other party:

(1) The factual basis of the claim or defense. In the event of multiple claims or defenses, the factual basis for each claim or defense.

(2) The legal theory upon which each claim or defense is based including, where necessary for a reasonable understanding of the claim or defense, citations of pertinent legal or case authorities.

(3) The names, addresses, and telephone numbers of any witnesses whom the disclosing party expects to call at trial with a designation of the subject matter about which each witness might be called to testify.

(4) The names and addresses of all persons whom the party believes may have knowledge or information relevant to the events, transactions, or occurrences that gave rise to the action, and the nature of the knowledge or information each such individual is believed to possess.

(5) The names and addresses of all persons who have given statements, whether written or recorded, signed or unsigned, and the custodian of the copies of those statements.

(6) The name and address of each person whom the disclosing party expects to call as an expert witness at trial, the subject matter on which the expert is expected to testify, the substance of the facts and opinions to which the expert is expected to testify, a summary of the grounds for each opinion, the qualifications of the witness and the name and address of the custodian of copies of any reports prepared by the expert.

(7) A computation and the measure of damage alleged by the disclosing party and the documents or testimony on which such computation and measure are based and the names, addresses, and telephone numbers of all damage witnesses.

(8) The existence, location, custodian, and general description of any tangible evidence or relevant documents that the disclosing party plans to use at trial and relevant insurance agreements.

(9) A list of the documents or, in the case of voluminous documentary information, a list of the categories of documents, known by a party to exist whether or not in the party's possession, custody or control and which that party believes may be relevant to the subject matter of the action, and those which appear reasonably calculated to lead to the discovery of admissible evidence, and the date(s) upon which those documents will be made, or have been made, available for inspection and copying. Unless good cause is stated for not doing so, a copy of each document listed shall be served with the disclosure. If production is not made, the name and address of the custodian of the document shall be indicated. A party who produces documents for inspection shall produce them as they are kept in the usual course of business.

Rule 26 RULES OF CIVIL PROCEDURE

2. *Rule 26(b)—Scope of Discovery*

Minnesota Rule of Civil Procedure 26.02(c)

[The Minnesota rule is identical to Federal Rule 26(b)(3) except that the second sentence of the second paragraph reads, "Upon request, a *party or other person* may obtain without the required showing a statement concerning the action or its subject matter previously made by that person *who is not a party*." (Emphasis added.)]

New York Civil Practice Law and Rules 3101

(a) Generally. There shall be full disclosure of all matter material and necessary in the prosecution or defense of an action, regardless of the burden of proof, by:

(1) a party, or the officer, director, member, agent or employee of a party;

(2) a person who possessed a cause of action or defense asserted in the action;

(3) a person about to depart from the state, or without the state, or residing at a greater distance from the place of trial than one hundred miles, or so sick or infirm as to afford reasonable grounds of belief that he will not be able to attend the trial, or a person authorized to practice medicine, dentistry or podiatry who has provided medical, dental or podiatric care or diagnosis to the party demanding disclosure, or who has been retained by him as an expert witness; and

(4) any other person, upon notice stating the circumstances or reasons such disclosure is sought or required.

(b) Privileged matter. Upon objection by a person entitled to assert the privilege, privileged matter shall not be obtainable.

(c) Attorney's work product. The work product of an attorney shall not be obtainable.

(d) Trial preparation. 1. Experts. (i) Upon request, each party shall identify each person whom the party expects to call as an expert witness at trial and shall disclose in reasonable detail the subject matter on which each expert is expected to testify, the substance of the facts and opinions on which each expert is expected to testify, the qualifications of each expert witness and a summary of the grounds for each expert's opinion. However, where a party for good cause shown retains an expert an insufficient period of time before the commencement of trial to give appropriate notice thereof, the party shall not thereupon be precluded from introducing the expert's testimony at the trial solely on grounds of noncompliance with this paragraph. In that instance, upon motion of any party, made before or at trial, or on its own initiative, the court may make whatever order may be just. In an action for medical, dental or podiatric malpractice, a party, in responding to a request, may omit the names of medical, dental or podiatric experts but shall be required to disclose all other information concerning such experts otherwise required by this paragraph.

(ii) In an action for medical, dental or podiatric malpractice, any party may, by written offer made to and served upon all other parties and filed with the court, offer to disclose the name of, and to make available for examination upon oral deposition, any person the party making the offer expects to call as an expert witness at trial. Within twenty days of service of the offer, a party shall accept or reject the offer by serving a written reply upon all parties and filing a copy thereof with the court. Failure to serve a reply within twenty days of service of the offer shall be deemed a rejection of the offer. If all parties accept the offer, each party shall be required to produce his or her expert witness for examination upon oral deposition upon receipt of a notice to take oral deposition in accordance with rule thirty-one hundred seven of this chapter. If any party, having made or accepted the offer, fails to make that party's expert available for oral deposition, that party shall be precluded from offering expert testimony at the trial of the action.

(iii) Further disclosure concerning the expected testimony of any expert may be obtained only by court order upon a showing of special circumstances and subject to restrictions as to scope and provisions concerning fees and expenses as the court may deem appropriate. However, a party, without court order, may take the testimony of a person authorized to practice medicine or dentistry or podiatry who is the party's treating or retained expert, as described in paragraph three of subdivision (a) of this section, in which event any other party shall be entitled to the full disclosure authorized by this article with respect to that expert without court order.

* * *

2. Materials. ... [Identical in substance to the first paragraph of Federal Rule 26(b)(3).]

(e) Party's statement. A party may obtain a copy of his own statement.

(f) Contents of insurance agreement. * * *

(g) Accident reports. Except as otherwise provided by law, in addition to any other matter which may be subject to disclosure, there shall be full disclosure of any written report of an accident prepared in the regular course of business operations or practices of any person, firm, corporation, association or other public or private entity * * *.

2. *Rule 26(d)—Sequence and Timing of Discovery*

New York Civil Practice Law and Rules 3106

(a) Normal priority. After an action is commenced, any party may take the testimony of any person by deposition upon oral or written questions. Leave of the court, granted on motion, shall be obtained if notice of the taking of the deposition of a party is served by the plaintiff before that party's time for serving a responsive pleading has expired.

(b) Witnesses. Where the person to be examined is not a party or a person who at the time of taking the deposition is an officer, director, member or employee of a party, he shall be served with a subpoena. Unless the court orders otherwise, on motion with or without notice, such subpoena shall be served at least twenty days before the examination. Where a motion for a protective order against such an examination is made, the witness shall be notified by the moving party that the examination is stayed.

(c) Prisoners. The deposition of a person confined under legal process may be taken only by leave of the court.

(d) Designation of deponent. A party desiring to take the deposition of a particular officer, director, member or employee of a person shall include in the notice or subpoena served upon such person the identity, description or title of such individual. Such person shall produce the individual so designated unless they shall have, no later than ten days prior to the scheduled deposition, notified the requesting party that another individual would instead be produced and the identity, description or title of such individual is specified. If timely notification has been so given, such other individual shall instead be produced.

3. *Rule 26(e)—Supplementation of Responses*

New Jersey Civil Practice Rule 4:17-7

* * * [I]f a party who has furnished answers to interrogatories thereafter obtains information that renders such answers incomplete or inaccurate, amended answers shall be served not later than 20 days prior to the first date fixed for trial. Thereafter amendments may be allowed only for extraordinary or compelling reasons and to prevent manifest injustice, and upon such terms as the court directs. In no case shall amendments be allowed at trial where it appears that the evidence sought to be introduced was known to the party seeking such leave, more than 10 days prior to trial.

Rule 27. Depositions Before Action or Pending Appeal

(a) Before Action.

(1) *Petition.* A person who desires to perpetuate testimony regarding any matter that may be cognizable in any court of the United States may file a verified petition in the United States district court in the district of the residence of any expected adverse party. The petition shall be entitled in the name of the petitioner and shall show: 1, that the petitioner expects to be a party to an action cognizable in a court of the United States but is presently unable to bring it or cause it to be brought, 2, the subject matter of the expected action and the petitioner's interest therein, 3, the facts which the petitioner desires to establish by the proposed testimony and the reasons for desiring to perpetuate it, 4, the names or a description of the persons the petitioner expects will be adverse parties and their addresses so far as known, and 5, the names and addresses of the persons to be examined and the substance of the testimony which the petitioner expects to elicit from each, and shall ask for an order authorizing the petitioner to take the depositions of the persons to be examined named in the petition, for the purpose of perpetuating their testimony.

(2) *Notice and Service.* The petitioner shall thereafter serve a notice upon each person named in the petition as an expected adverse party, together with a copy of the petition, stating that the petitioner will apply to the court, at a time and place named therein, for the order described in the petition. At least 20 days before the date of hearing the notice shall be served either within or without the district or state in the manner provided in Rule 4(d) for service of summons; but if such service cannot with due diligence be made upon any expected adverse party named in the petition, the court may make such order as is just for service by publication or otherwise, and shall appoint, for persons not served in the manner provided in Rule 4(d), an attorney who shall represent them, and, in case they are not otherwise represented, shall cross-examine the deponent. If any expected adverse party is a minor or incompetent the provisions of Rule 17(c) apply.

(3) *Order and Examination.* If the court is satisfied that the perpetuation of the testimony may prevent a failure or delay of justice, it shall make an order designating or describing the persons whose depositions may be taken and specifying the subject matter of the examination and whether the depositions shall be taken upon oral examination or written interrogatories. The depositions may then be taken in accordance with these rules; and the court may make orders of the character provided for by Rules 34 and 35. For the purpose of applying these rules to depositions for perpetuating testimony, each reference therein to the court in which the action is pending shall be deemed to refer to the court in which the petition for such deposition was filed.

DEPOSITIONS AND DISCOVERY — Rule 28

(4) *Use of Deposition.* If a deposition to perpetuate testimony is taken under these rules or if, although not so taken, it would be admissible in evidence in the courts of the state in which it is taken, it may be used in any action involving the same subject matter subsequently brought in a United States district court, in accordance with the provisions of Rule 32(a).

(b) Pending Appeal. If an appeal has been taken from a judgment of a district court or before the taking of an appeal if the time therefor has not expired, the district court in which the judgment was rendered may allow the taking of the depositions of witnesses to perpetuate their testimony for use in the event of further proceedings in the district court. In such case the party who desires to perpetuate the testimony may make a motion in the district court for leave to take the depositions, upon the same notice and service thereof as if the action was pending in the district court. The motion shall show (1) the names and addresses of persons to be examined and the substance of the testimony which the party expects to elicit from each; (2) the reasons for perpetuating their testimony. If the court finds that the perpetuation of the testimony is proper to avoid a failure or delay of justice, it may make an order allowing the depositions to be taken and may make orders of the character provided for by Rules 34 and 35, and thereupon the depositions may be taken and used in the same manner and under the same conditions as are prescribed in these rules for depositions taken in actions pending in the district court.

(c) Perpetuation by Action. This rule does not limit the power of a court to entertain an action to perpetuate testimony.

Comparative State Provision
Rule 27(a)(1)

New York Civil Practice Law and Rules 3102(c)

Before an action is commenced, disclosure to aid in bringing an action, to preserve information or to aid in arbitration, may be obtained, but only by court order. The court may appoint a referee to take testimony.

Rule 28. Persons Before Whom Depositions May Be Taken

(a) Within the United States. Within the United States or within a territory or insular possession subject to the jurisdiction of the United States, depositions shall be taken before an officer authorized to administer oaths by the laws of the United States or of the place where the examination is held, or before a person appointed by the court in which the action is pending. A person so appointed has power to administer oaths and take testimony. The term officer as used in Rules 30, 31 and 32 includes a person appointed by the court or designated by the parties under Rule 29.

Rule 28 RULES OF CIVIL PROCEDURE

(b) In Foreign Countries. Depositions may be taken in a foreign country (1) pursuant to any applicable treaty or convention, or (2) pursuant to a letter of request (whether or not captioned a letter rogatory), or (3) on notice before a person authorized to administer oaths in the place where the examination is held, either by the law thereof or by the law of the United States, or (4) before a person commissioned by the court, and a person so commissioned shall have the power by virtue of the commission to administer any necessary oath and take testimony. A commission or letter of request shall be issued on application and notice and on terms that are just and appropriate. It is not requisite to the issuance of a commission or a letter of request that the taking of the deposition in any other manner is impracticable or inconvenient; and both a commission and a letter of request may be issued in proper cases. A notice or commission may designate the person before whom the deposition is to be taken either by name or descriptive title. A letter of request may be addressed "To the Appropriate Authority in [here name the country]." When a letter of request or any other device is used pursuant to any applicable treaty or convention, it shall be captioned in the form prescribed by that treaty or convention. Evidence obtained in response to a letter of request need not be excluded merely because it is not a verbatim transcript, because the testimony was not taken under oath, or because of any similar departure from the requirements for depositions taken within the United States under these rules.

(c) Disqualification for Interest. No deposition shall be taken before a person who is a relative or employee or attorney or counsel of any of the parties, or is a relative or employee of such attorney or counsel, or is financially interested in the action.

Notes on Amendments to Federal Rule 28 and Related Federal and State Acts Providing Judicial Assistance to Foreign Tribunals

(a) *Amendments in 1993 and 1963 to Federal Rule 28(b)*

The 1993 changes were primarily linguistic, substituting the term "letter of request" for "letter rogatory" to conform to the Hague Convention.

It was in 1963 that Rule 28(b) was altered to facilitate the taking of depositions abroad. The Advisory Committee discussed the 1963 changes as follows:

The amendment of clause (1) is designed to facilitate depositions in foreign countries by enlarging the class of persons before whom the depositions may be taken on notice. The class is no longer confined, as at present, to a secretary of embassy or legation, consul general, consul, vice consul, or consular agent of the United States. In a country that regards the taking of testimony by a foreign official in aid of litigation pending in a court of another country as an infringement upon its sovereignty, it will be expedient to notice depositions before officers of the country in which the examination is taken. * * *

Clause (2) of amended subdivision (b), like the corresponding provision of subdivision (a) dealing with depositions taken in the United States, makes it clear that the appointment of a person by commission in itself confers power upon him to administer any necessary oath.

It has been held that a letter rogatory will not be issued unless the use of a notice or commission is shown to be impossible or impracticable. * * * The intent of the fourth sentence of the amended subdivision is to overcome this judicial antipathy and to permit a sound choice between depositions under a letter rogatory and on notice or by commission in the light of all the circumstances. In a case in which the foreign country will compel a witness to attend or testify in aid of a letter rogatory but not in aid of a commission, a letter rogatory may be preferred on the ground that it is less expensive to execute, even if there is plainly no need for compulsory process. A letter rogatory may also be preferred when it cannot be demonstrated that a witness will be recalcitrant or when the witness states that he is willing to testify voluntarily, but the contingency exists that he will change his mind at the last moment. In the latter case, it may be advisable to issue both a commission and a letter rogatory, the latter to be executed if the former fails. The choice between a letter rogatory and a commission may be conditioned by other factors, including the nature and extent of the assistance that the foreign country will give to the execution of either.

In executing a letter rogatory the courts of other countries may be expected to follow their customary procedure for taking testimony. See *United States* v. *Paraffin Wax, 2255 Bags,* 23 F.R.D. 289 (E.D.N.Y.1959). In many non-common-law countries the judge questions the witness, sometimes without first administering an oath, the attorneys put any supplemental questions either to the witness or through the judge, and the judge dictates a summary of the testimony, which the witness acknowledges as correct. * * * The last sentence of the amended subdivision provides, contrary to the implications of some authority, that evidence recorded in such a fashion need not be excluded on that account. * * * Whether or to what degree the value or weight of the evidence may be affected by the method of taking or recording the testimony is left for determination according to the circumstances of the particular case * * *; the testimony may indeed be so devoid of substance or probative value as to warrant its exclusion altogether.

Some foreign countries are hostile to allowing a deposition to be taken in their country, especially by notice or commission, or to lending assistance in the taking of a deposition. Thus compliance with the terms of amended subdivision (b) may not in all cases ensure completion of a deposition abroad. Examination of the law and policy of the particular foreign country in advance of attempting a deposition is therefore advisable. See 4 *Moore's Federal Practice* ¶¶ 28.05–28.08 (2d ed. 1950).

(b) *Judicial Assistance to Foreign Tribunals*

See 28 U.S.C. § 1782(a) and the comparative state provision set forth in Part II, infra.

Rule 29. Stipulations Regarding Discovery Procedure

Unless otherwise directed by the court, the parties may by written stipulation (1) provide that depositions may be taken before any person, at any time or place, upon any notice, and in any manner and when so taken may be used like other depositions, and (2) modify other procedures governing or limitations placed upon discovery, except that stipulations extending the time provided in Rules 33, 34, and 36 for responses to discovery may, if they would interfere with any time set for completion of discovery, for hearing of a motion, or for trial, be made only with the approval of the court.

Rule 30. Depositions Upon Oral Examination

(a) When Depositions May Be Taken; When Leave Required.

(1) A party may take the testimony of any person, including a party, by deposition upon oral examination without leave of court except as

Rule 30   RULES OF CIVIL PROCEDURE

provided in paragraph (2). The attendance of witnesses may be compelled by subpoena as provided in Rule 45.

(2) A party must obtain leave of court, which shall be granted to the extent consistent with the principles stated in Rule 26(b)(2), if the person to be examined is confined in prison or if, without the written stipulation of the parties,

    (A) a proposed deposition would result in more than ten depositions being taken under this rule or Rule 31 by the plaintiffs, or by the defendants, or by third-party defendants;

    (B) the person to be examined already has been deposed in the case; or

    (C) a party seeks to take a deposition before the time specified in Rule 26(d) unless the notice contains a certification, with supporting facts, that the person to be examined is expected to leave the United States and be unavailable for examination in this country unless deposed before that time.

(b) Notice of Examination: General Requirements; Method of Recording; Production of Documents and Things; Deposition of Organization; Deposition by Telephone.

(1) A party desiring to take the deposition of any person upon oral examination shall give reasonable notice in writing to every other party to the action. The notice shall state the time and place for taking the deposition and the name and address of each person to be examined, if known, and, if the name is not known, a general description sufficient to identify the person or the particular class or group to which the person belongs. If a subpoena duces tecum is to be served on the person to be examined, the designation of the materials to be produced as set forth in the subpoena shall be attached to or included in the notice.

(2) The party taking the deposition shall state in the notice the method by which the testimony shall be recorded. Unless the court orders otherwise, it may be recorded by sound, sound-and-visual, or stenographic means, and the party taking the deposition shall bear the cost of the recording. Any party may arrange for a transcription to be made from the recording of a deposition taken by nonstenographic means.

(3) With prior notice to the deponent and other parties, any party may designate another method to record the deponent's testimony in addition to that specified by the person taking the deposition. The additional record or transcript shall be made at that party's expense unless the court otherwise orders.

(4) Unless otherwise agreed by the parties, a deposition shall be conducted before an officer appointed or designated under Rule 28 and shall begin with a statement on the record by the officer that includes (A) the officer's name and business address; (B) the date, time, and

place of the deposition; (C) the name of the deponent; (D) the administration of the oath or affirmation to the deponent; and (E) an identification of all persons present. If the deposition is recorded other than stenographically, the officer shall repeat items (A) through (C) at the beginning of each unit of recorded tape or other recording medium. The appearance or demeanor of deponents or attorneys shall not be distorted through camera or sound-recording techniques. At the end of the deposition, the officer shall state on the record that the deposition is complete and shall set forth any stipulations made by counsel concerning the custody of the transcript or recording and the exhibits, or concerning other pertinent matters.

(5) The notice to a party deponent may be accompanied by a request made in compliance with Rule 34 for the production of documents and tangible things at the taking of the deposition. The procedure of Rule 34 shall apply to the request.

(6) A party may in the party's notice and in a subpoena name as the deponent a public or private corporation or a partnership or association or governmental agency and describe with reasonable particularity the matters on which examination is requested. In that event, the organization so named shall designate one or more officers, directors, or managing agents, or other persons who consent to testify on its behalf, and may set forth, for each person designated, the matters on which the person will testify. A subpoena shall advise a non-party organization of its duty to make such a designation. The persons so designated shall testify as to matters known or reasonably available to the organization. This subdivision (b)(6) does not preclude taking a deposition by any other procedure authorized in these rules.

(7) The parties may stipulate in writing or the court may upon motion order that a deposition be taken by telephone or other remote electronic means. For the purposes of the rule and Rules 28(a), 37(a)(1), and 37(b)(1), a deposition taken by such means is taken in the district and at the place where the deponent is to answer questions.

(c) Examination and Cross-Examination; Record of Examination; Oath; Objections. Examination and cross-examination of witnesses may proceed as permitted at the trial under the provisions of the Federal Rules of Evidence except Rules 103 and 615. The officer before whom the deposition is to be taken shall put the witness on oath or affirmation and shall personally, or by someone acting under the officer's direction and in the officer's presence, record the testimony of the witness. The testimony shall be taken stenographically or recorded by any other method authorized by subdivision (b)(2) of this rule. All objections made at the time of the examination to the qualifications of the officer taking the deposition, to the manner of taking it, to the evidence presented, to the conduct of any party, or to any other aspect of the proceedings shall be noted by the officer upon the record of the

Rule 30   RULES OF CIVIL PROCEDURE

deposition; but the examination shall proceed, with the testimony being taken subject to the objections. In lieu of participating in the oral examination, parties may serve written questions in a sealed envelope on the party taking the deposition and the party taking the deposition shall transmit them to the officer, who shall propound them to the witness and record the answers verbatim.

(d) Schedule and Duration; Motion to Terminate or Limit Examination.

(1) Any objection to evidence during a deposition shall be stated concisely and in a non-argumentative and non-suggestive manner. A party may instruct a deponent not to answer only when necessary to preserve a privilege, to enforce a limitation on evidence directed by the court, or to present a motion under paragraph (3).

(2) By order or local rule, the court may limit the time permitted for the conduct of a deposition, but shall allow additional time consistent with Rule 26(b)(2) if needed for a fair examination of the deponent or if the deponent or another party impedes or delays the examination. If the court finds such an impediment, delay, or other conduct that has frustrated the fair examination of the deponent, it may impose upon the person responsible an appropriate sanction, including the reasonable costs and attorney's fees incurred by any parties as a result thereof.

(3) At any time during a deposition, on motion of a party or of the deponent and upon a showing that the examination is being conducted in bad faith or in such a manner as unreasonable to annoy, embarrass, or oppress the deponent or party, the court in which the action is pending or the court in the district where the deposition is being taken may order the officer conducting the examination to cease forthwith from taking the deposition, or may limit the scope and manner of the taking of the deposition as provided in Rule 26(c). If the order made terminates the examination, it shall be presumed thereafter only upon the order of the court in which the action is pending. Upon demand of the objecting party or deponent, the taking of the deposition shall be suspended for the time necessary to make a motion for an order. The provisions of Rule 37(a)(4) apply to the award of expenses incurred in relation to the motion.

(e) Review by Witness; Changes; Signing. If requested by the deponent or a party before completion of the deposition, the deponent shall have 30 days after being notified by the officer that the transcript or recording is available in which to review the transcript or recording and, if there are changes in form or substance, to sign a statement reciting such changes and the reasons given by the deponent for making them. The officer shall indicate in the certificate prescribed by subdivision (f)(1) whether any review was requested and, if so, shall append any changes made by the deponent during the period allowed.

DEPOSITIONS AND DISCOVERY — Rule 30

(f) Certification and Filing by Officer; Exhibits; Copies; Notice of Filing.

(1) The officer shall certify that the witness was duly sworn by the officer and that the deposition is a true record of the testimony given by the witness. This certificate shall be in writing and accompany the record of the deposition. Unless otherwise ordered by the court, the officer shall securely seal the deposition in an envelope or package indorsed with the title of the action and marked "Deposition of [here insert name of witness]" and shall promptly file it with the court in which the action is pending or send it to the attorney who arranged for the transcript or recording, who shall store it under conditions that will protect it against loss, destruction, tampering, or deterioration. Documents and things produced for inspection during the examination of the witness, shall, upon the request of a party, be marked for identification and annexed to the deposition and may be inspected and copied by any party, except that if the person producing the materials desires to retain them the person may (A) offer copies to be marked for identification and annexed to the deposition and to serve thereafter as originals if the person affords to all parties fair opportunity to verify the copies by comparison to the originals, or (B) offer the originals to be marked for identification, after giving to each party an opportunity to inspect and copy them, in which event the materials may then be used in the same manner as if annexed to the deposition. Any party may move for an order that the original be annexed to and returned with the deposition to the court, pending final disposition of the case.

(2) Unless otherwise ordered by the court or agreed by the parties, the officer shall retain stenographic notes of any deposition taken stenographically or a copy of the recording of any deposition taken by another method. Upon payment of reasonable charges therefor, the officer shall furnish a copy of the transcript or other recording of the deposition to any party or to the deponent.

(g) Failure to Attend or to Serve Subpoena; Expenses.

(1) If the party giving the notice of the taking of a deposition fails to attend and proceed therewith and another party attends in person or by attorney pursuant to the notice, the court may order the party giving the notice to pay to such other party the reasonable expenses incurred by that party and that party's attorney in attending, including reasonable attorney's fees.

(2) If the party giving the notice of the taking of a deposition of a witness fails to serve a subpoena upon the witness and the witness because of such failure does not attend, and if another party attends in person or by attorney because that party expects the deposition of that witness to be taken, the court may order the party giving the notice to pay to such other party the reasonable expenses incurred by that party

Rule 30   RULES OF CIVIL PROCEDURE

and that party's attorney in attending, including reasonable attorney's fees.

Notes on Amendments to Federal Rule 30

(a) *Amendments in 1993 to Rule 30*

Rule 30, in an effort to limit costs of discovery, has been modified to limit the number of depositions. Paragraph (a)2(A), containing this new limit, provides that absent leave of court or stipulation among the parties, a party is limited to ten (10) depositions. Paragraph (a)2(B) limits the number of times a witness may be deposed by requiring leave of court if a party wishes to depose a witness more than once.

Subdivision (b) has been revised to allow parties to record deposition testimony by nonstenographic means without first obtaining permission of other counsel. Parties choosing to record only by video- or audiotape should be cognizant that a transcript of such recordings will be required if the testimony is later offered as evidence at trial or on a dispositive motion under Rule 56, pursuant to Rules 26(a)(3)(B) and 32(c).

Subparagraph (b)(3) now allows parties, at their own expense, to record a deposition by any means, in addition to the method designated, and subparagraph (7) is revised to include technological improvements in the taking of depositions. In addition to the use of telephones, authorized by the 1980 Amendment to Rule 30, other remote electronic means such as satellite television are now allowed by stipulation or court order.

Subparagraph (c) is revised to clarify when other witnesses may attend a depositions. The revised Rule provides that other witnesses (potential deponents) are not automatically excluded by request, but that exclusion can be ordered pursuant to Rule 26(c)(5) when appropriate.

Subdivision (d)(2) has been added to clarify the court's authority to limit the length of depositions and to sanction attorneys, parties and non-party witnesses for the use of dilatory and obstructive tactics, and subparagraph (3) clarifies the court's authority to impose sanctions for conduct in violation of the provisions of Rule 30(d)(1).

Subdivision (e) has been modified to require pre-filing review by the deponent only if requested before the deposition is completed. Recognizing the difficulty reporters often have in obtaining signatures for pre-filing review, such signatures are now waived unless review is requested and changes are made.

(b) *Amendments in 1970 to Rule 30*

The 1970 amendments to Rule 30 included a number of important alterations in the deposition practice.

The Advisory Committee commented on these alterations as follows:

Subdivision (b)(5). A provision is added to enable a party, through service of notice, to require another party to produce documents or things at the taking of his deposition. This may now be done as to a nonparty deponent through use of a subpoena duces tecum as authorized by Rule 45, but some courts have held that documents may be secured from a party only under Rule 34. See 2A Barron & Holtzoff, *Federal Practice and Procedure* § 644.1 n. 83.2, § 792 n. 16 (Wright ed. 1961). With the elimination of "good cause" from Rule 34, the reason for this restrictive doctrine has disappeared. * * * If the discovering party insists on examining many and complex documents at the taking of the deposition, thereby causing undue burdens on others, the latter may, under Rules 26(c) or 30(d), apply for a court order that the examining party proceed via Rule 34 alone.

Subdivision (b)(6). A new provision is added, whereby a party may name a corporation, partnership, association, or governmental agency as the deponent and designate the matters on which he requests examination, and the organization shall then name one or more of its officers, directors, or managing agents, or other persons consenting to appear and testify on its behalf with respect to matters known or reasonably available to the organization. *Cf.* Alberta Sup.Ct.R. 255. The organization may designate persons other than officers, directors, and managing agents, but only with their consent. Thus, an employee or agent who has an independent or conflicting interest in the litigation—for example, in a personal injury case—can refuse to testify on behalf of the organization. * * *

The new procedure should be viewed as an added facility for discovery, one which may be advantageous to both sides as well as an improvement in the deposition process. It will reduce the difficulties now encountered in determining, prior to the taking of a deposition, whether a particular employee or agent is a "managing agent." See Note, *Discovery Against Corporations Under the Federal Rules,* 47 Iowa L.Rev. 1006–1016 (1962). It will curb the "bandying" by which officers or managing agents of a corporation are deposed in turn but each disclaims knowledge of facts that are clearly known to persons in the organization and thereby to it. *Cf. Haney v. Woodward & Lothrop, Inc.,* 330 F.2d 940, 944 (4th Cir.1964). The provision should also assist organizations which find that an unnecessarily large number of their officers and agents are being deposed by a party uncertain of who in the organization has knowledge. Some courts have held that under the existing rules a corporation should not be burdened with choosing which person is to appear for it. *E.g., United States v. Gahagan Dredging Corp.,* 24 F.R.D. 328, 329 (S.D.N.Y.1958). This burden is not essentially different from that of answering interrogatories under Rule 33, and is in any case lighter than that of an examining party ignorant of who in the corporation has knowledge. * * *

(c) *Amendments in 1980 to Rule 30*

The Advisory Committee commented as follows on the 1980 addition of Rule 30(b)(7):

> Depositions by telephone are now authorized by Rule 29 upon stipulation of the parties. The amendment authorizes that method by order of the court. The final sentence is added to make it clear that when a deposition is taken by telephone it is taken in the district and at the place where the witness is to answer the questions rather than that where the questions are propounded.

Rule 31. Depositions Upon Written Questions

(a) Serving Questions; Notice.

(1) A party may take the testimony of any person, including a party, by deposition upon written questions without leave of court except as provided in paragraph (2). The attendance of witnesses may be compelled by the use of subpoena provided in Rule 45.

(2) A party must obtain leave of court, which shall be granted to the extent consistent with the principles stated in Rule 26(b)(2), if the person to be examined is confined in prison or if, without the written stipulation of the parties:

(A) a proposed deposition would result in more than ten depositions being taken under this rule or Rule 30 by the plaintiffs, or by the defendants, or by third-party defendants;

(B) the person to be examined has already been deposed in the case; or

(C) a party seeks to take a deposition before the time specified in Rule 26(d).

(3) A party desiring to take a deposition upon written questions shall serve them upon every other party with a notice stating (1) the

Rule 31   RULES OF CIVIL PROCEDURE

name and address of the person who is to answer them, if known, and if the name is not known, a general description sufficient to identify the person or the particular class or group to which the person belongs, and (2) the name or descriptive title and address of the officer before whom the deposition is to be taken. A deposition upon written questions may be taken of a public or private corporation or a partnership or association or governmental agency in accordance with the provisions of Rule 30(b)(6).

(4) Within 14 days after the notice and written questions are served, a party may serve cross questions upon all other parties. Within 7 days after being served with the cross questions, a party may serve redirect questions upon all other parties. Within 7 days after being served with redirect questions, a party may serve recross questions upon all other parties. The court may for cause shown enlarge or shorten the time.

(b) Officer to Take Responses and Prepare Record. A copy of the notice and copies of all questions served shall be delivered by the party taking the deposition to the officer designated in the notice, who shall proceed promptly, in the manner provided by Rule 30(c), (e), and (f), to take the testimony of the witness in response to the questions and to prepare, certify, and file or mail the deposition, attaching thereto the copy of the notice and the questions received by the officer.

(c) Notice of Filing. When the deposition is filed the party taking it shall promptly give notice thereof to all other parties.

Rule 32. Use of Depositions in Court Proceedings

(a) Use of Depositions. At the trial or upon the hearing of a motion or an interlocutory proceeding, any part or all of a deposition, so far as admissible under the rules of evidence applied as though the witness were then present and testifying, may be used against any party who was present or represented at the taking of the deposition or who had reasonable notice thereof, in accordance with any of the following provisions:

(1) Any deposition may be used by any party for the purpose of contradicting or impeaching the testimony of deponent as a witness, or for any other purpose permitted by the Federal Rules of Evidence.

(2) The deposition of a party or of anyone who at the time of taking the deposition was an officer, director, or managing agent, or a person designated under Rule 30(b)(6) or 31(a) to testify on behalf of a public or private corporation, partnership or association or governmental agency which is a party may be used by an adverse party for any purpose.

(3) The deposition of a witness, whether or not a party, may be used by any party for any purpose if the court finds:

(A) that the witness is dead; or

(B) that the witness is at a greater distance than 100 miles from the place of trial or hearing, or is out of the United States, unless it appears that the absence of the witness was procured by the party offering the deposition; or

(C) that the witness is unable to attend or testify because of age, illness, infirmity, or imprisonment; or

(D) that the party offering the deposition has been unable to procure the attendance of the witness by subpoena; or

(E) upon application and notice, that such exceptional circumstance exist as to make it desirable, in the interest of justice and with due regard to the importance of presenting the testimony of witnesses orally in open court, to allow the deposition to be used.

A deposition taken without leave of court pursuant to a notice under Rule 30(a)(2)(C) shall not be used against a party who demonstrates that, when served with the notice, it was unable through the exercise of diligence to obtain counsel to represent it at the taking of the deposition; nor shall a deposition be used against a party who, having received less than 11 days notice of the deposition, has promptly upon receiving such notice filed a motion for a protective order under Rule 26(c)(2) requesting that the deposition not be held or be held at a different time or place and such motion is pending at the time the deposition is held.

(4) If only part of a deposition is offered in evidence by a party, an adverse party may require the offeror to introduce any other part which ought in fairness to be considered with the part introduced, and any party may introduce any other parts.

Substitution of parties pursuant to Rule 25 does not affect the right to use depositions previously taken; and, when an action has been brought in any court of the United States or of any State and another action involving the same subject matter is afterward brought between the same parties or their representatives or successors in interest, all depositions lawfully taken and duly filed in the former action may be used in the latter as if originally taken therefor. A deposition previously taken may also be used as permitted by the Federal Rules of Evidence.

(b) Objections to Admissibility. Subject to the provisions of Rule 28(b) and subdivision (d)(3) of this rule, objection may be made at the trial or hearing to receiving in evidence any deposition or part thereof for any reason which would require the exclusion of the evidence if the witness were then present and testifying.

(c) Form of Presentation. Except as otherwise directed by the court, a party offering deposition testimony pursuant to this rule may offer it in stenographic or nonstenographic form, but, if in nonstenographic form, the party shall also provide the court with a transcript of the portions so offered. On request of any party in a case tried before a jury, deposition testimony offered other than for impeachment purposes shall be presented in nonstenographic form, if available, unless the court for good cause orders otherwise.

(d) Effect of Errors and Irregularities in Depositions.

(1) *As to Notice.* All errors and irregularities in the notice for taking a deposition are waived unless written objection is promptly served upon the party giving the notice.

(2) *As to Disqualification of Officer.* Objection to taking a deposition because of disqualification of the officer before whom it is to be taken is waived unless made before the taking of the deposition begins or as soon thereafter as the disqualification becomes known or could be discovered with reasonable diligence.

(3) *As to Taking of Deposition.*

(A) Objections to the competency of a witness or to the competency, relevancy, or materiality of testimony are not waived by failure to make them before or during the taking of the deposition, unless the ground of the objection is one which might have been obviated or removed if presented at that time.

(B) Errors and irregularities occurring at the oral examination in the manner of taking the deposition, in the form of the questions or answers, in the oath or affirmation, or in the conduct of parties, and errors of any kind which might be obviated, removed, or cured if promptly presented, are waived unless seasonable objection thereto is made at the taking of the deposition.

(C) Objections to the form of written questions submitted under Rule 31 are waived unless served in writing upon the party propounding them within the time allowed for serving the succeeding cross or other questions and within 5 days after service of the last questions authorized.

(4) *As to Completion and Return of Deposition.* Errors and irregularities in the manner in which the testimony is transcribed or the deposition is prepared, signed, certified, sealed, indorsed, transmitted, filed, or otherwise dealt with by the officer under Rules 30 and 31 are waived unless a motion to suppress the deposition or some part thereof is made with reasonable promptness after such defect is, or with due diligence might have been, ascertained.

Comparative State Provisions
Rule 32(a)

Michigan Court Rule 2.302(B)(4)(d)

A party may depose a witness that he or she expects to call as an expert at trial. The deposition may be taken at any time before trial on reasonable notice to the opposite party, and may be offered as evidence at trial as provided in MCR 2.308(A)(1). The court need not adjourn the trial because of the unavailability of expert witnesses or their depositions.

Michigan Court Rule 2.308(A)

Depositions or parts thereof shall be admissible at trial or on the hearing of a motion or in an interlocutory proceeding only as provided in the Michigan Rules of Evidence. [Replaced, effective 12–1–89.]

Rule 33. Interrogatories to Parties

(a) Availability. Without leave of court or written stipulation, any party may serve upon any other party written interrogatories, not exceeding 25 in number including all discrete subparts, to be answered by the party served or, if the party served is a public or private corporation or a partnership or association or governmental agency, by any officer or agent, who shall furnish such information as is available to the party. Leave to serve additional interrogatories shall be granted to the extent consistent with the principles of Rule 26(b)(2). Without leave of court or written stipulation, interrogatories may not be served before the time specified in Rule 26(d).

(b) Answers and Objections.

(1) Each interrogatory shall be answered separately and fully in writing under oath, unless it is objected to, in which event the objecting party shall state the reasons for objection and shall answer to the extent the interrogatory is not objectionable.

(2) The answers are to be signed by the person making them, and the objections signed by the attorney making them.

(3) The party upon whom the interrogatories have been served shall serve a copy of the answers, and objections if any, within 30 days after the service of the interrogatories. A shorter or longer time may be directed by the court or, in the absence of such an order, agreed to in writing by the parties.

(4) All grounds for an objection to an interrogatory shall be stated with specificity. Any ground not stated in a timely objection is waived unless the party's failure to object is excused by the court for good cause shown.

(5) The party submitting the interrogatories may move for an order under Rule 37(a) with respect to any objection to or other failure to answer an interrogatory.

(c) Scope; Use at Trial. Interrogatories may relate to any matters which can be inquired into under Rule 26(b)(1), and the answers may be used to the extent permitted by the rules of evidence.

An interrogatory otherwise proper is not necessarily objectionable merely because an answer to the interrogatory involves an opinion or contention that relates to fact or the application of law to fact, but the court may order that such an interrogatory need not be answered until after designated discovery has been completed or until a pre-trial conference or other later time.

Rule 33 RULES OF CIVIL PROCEDURE

(d) Option to Produce Business Records. Where the answer to an interrogatory may be derived or ascertained from the business records of the party upon whom the interrogatory has been served or from an examination, audit or inspection of such business records, including a compilation, abstract or summary thereof and the burden of deriving or ascertaining the answer is substantially the same for the party serving the interrogatory as for the party served, it is a sufficient answer to such interrogatory to specify the records from which the answer may be derived or ascertained and to afford to the party serving the interrogatory reasonable opportunity to examine, audit or inspect such records and to make copies, compilations, abstracts or summaries. A specification shall be in sufficient detail to permit the interrogating party to locate and to identify, as readily as can the party served, the records from which the answer may be ascertained.

Notes on Amendments to Federal Rule 33 and Comparative Provisions

(a) *Amendments in 1970 to Rule 33*

The Advisory Committee commented on the 1970 amendments to Federal Rule 33 as follows:

Subdivision * * * *[(c)]*. There are numerous and conflicting decisions on the question whether and to what extent interrogatories are limited to matters "of fact," or may elicit opinions, contentions, and legal conclusions. * * *

Rule 33 is amended to provide that an interrogatory is not objectionable merely because it calls for an opinion or contention that relates to fact or the application of law to fact. Efforts to draw sharp lines between facts and opinions have invariably been unsuccessful, and the clear trend of the cases is to permit "factual" opinions. As to requests for opinions or contentions that call for the application of law to fact, they can be most useful in narrowing and sharpening the issues, which is a major purpose of discovery. * * * On the other hand, under the new language interrogatories may not extend to issues of "pure law," i.e., legal issues unrelated to the facts of the case. * * *

Subdivision * * * *[(d)]*. This is a new subdivision, adapted from Calif.Code Civ.Proc. [§ 2030(f)(2)] * * *, relating especially to interrogatories which require a party to engage in burdensome or expensive research into his own business records in order to give an answer. * * * The interrogating party is protected against abusive use of this provision through the requirement that the burden of ascertaining the answer be substantially the same for both sides. A respondent may not impose on an interrogating party a mass of records as to which research is feasible only for one familiar with the records. At the same time, the respondent unable to invoke this subdivision does not on that account lose the protection available to him under new Rule 26(c) against oppressive or unduly burdensome or expensive interrogatories. And even when the respondent successfully invokes the subdivision, the court is not deprived of its usual power, in appropriate cases, to require that the interrogating party reimburse the respondent for the expense of assembling his records and making them intelligible.

(b) *Amendments in 1980 to What Is Now Rule 33(d)*

The last sentence of Rule 33(d) * * * was added in 1980. The Advisory Committee commented as follows:

The Committee is advised that parties upon whom interrogatories are served have occasionally responded by directing the interrogating party to a mass of business records or by offering to make all of their records available, justifying the response by the option provided by this subdivision. Such practices are an abuse of the option. A party who is permitted by the terms of this subdivision to offer records for inspection in lieu of answering an interrogatory should offer them in a manner that permits the same direct and economical access that is available to the party. If the information sought exists in the form of compilations, abstracts or summaries then available to the responding party, those should be made available to the interrogating party. The final sentence is added to make it clear that a responding party has the duty to specify, by category and location, the records from which answers to interrogatories can be derived.

(c) *Amendments in 1993 to Rule 33*

Revisions to Rule 33 have been made to limit interrogatory practice. The Advisory Committee on Rules, in commenting on the changes, stated:

> Because Rule 26(a)(1)(3) requires disclosure of much of the information previously obtained by this form of discovery, there should be less occasion to use [Rule 33]. Experience in over half of the district courts has confirmed that limitations on the number of interrogatories are useful and manageable.

(d) *Local Federal Rules*

United States District Court, Northern District, Illinois, General Rule 9(g)

No party shall serve on any other party more than twenty (20) interrogatories in the aggregate without leave of court. Subparagraphs of any interrogatory shall relate directly to the subject matter of the interrogatory. Any party desiring to serve additional interrogatories shall file a written motion setting forth the proposed additional interrogatories and the reasons establishing good cause for their use. Any such motion shall be subject to the provisions of Rule 13 of the General Rules of this Court. [Added 6–20–75.]

See also Local Rules, United States District Court for the Southern District of New York, Civil Rule 46, Part VII, infra.

(e) *Comparative State Provisions*

1. *Scope of Usage as to Claims and Parties*

New York Civil Practice Law and Rules 3130

1. Except as otherwise provided herein, after commencement of an action, any party may serve upon any other party written interrogatories. Except in a matrimonial action, a party may not serve written interrogatories on another party and also demand a bill of particulars of the same party pursuant to section 3041. In the case of an action to recover damages for personal injury, injury to property or wrongful death predicated solely on * * * negligence, a party shall not be permitted to serve interrogatories on and conduct a deposition of the same party * * * without leave of court.

2. After commencement of a matrimonial action or proceeding, upon motion brought by either party, upon such notice to the other party and to the non-party from whom financial disclosure is sought, and given in such manner as the court shall direct, the court may order a non-party to respond under oath to written interrogatories limited to furnishing financial information concerning a party, and further provided such information is both reasonable and necessary in the prosecution or the defense of such matrimonial action or proceeding.

2. *Limitations on Detail Required in Response*

California Civil Procedure Code § 2030(f)(2)

If the answer to an interrogatory would necessitate the preparation or the making of a compilation, abstract, audit, or summary of or from the documents of the party to whom the interrogatory is directed, and if the burden or expense of preparing or making it would be substantially the same for the party propounding the interrogatory as for the responding party, it is a sufficient answer to that interrogatory to refer to this subdivision and to specify the writings from which the answer may be derived or ascertained. This specification shall be in sufficient detail to permit the propounding party to locate and to identify, as readily as the responding party can, the writings from which the answer may be ascertained. The responding party shall then afford to the propounding party a reasonable opportunity to examine, audit, or inspect these documents and to make copies, compilations, abstracts, or summaries of them.

3. *Restriction on Number of Interrogatories Allowed*
Minnesota Rule of Civil Procedure 33.01(a)

Any party may serve upon any other party written interrogatories. Interrogatories may, without leave of court, be served upon the plaintiff after commencement of the action, and upon any other party with or after service of the summons and complaint upon that party. No party may serve more than a total of 50 interrogatories upon any other party unless permitted to do so by the court upon motion, notice and a showing of a good cause. In computing the total number of interrogatories each subdivision of separate questions shall be counted as an interrogatory.

Rule 34. Production of Documents and Things and Entry Upon Land for Inspection and Other Purposes

(a) Scope. Any party may serve on any other party a request (1) to produce and permit the party making the request, or someone acting on the requestor's behalf, to inspect and copy, any designated documents (including writings, drawings, graphs, charts, photographs, phono-records, and other data compilations from which information can be obtained, translated, if necessary, by the respondent through detection devices into reasonably usable form), or to inspect and copy, test, or sample any tangible things which constitute or contain matters within the scope of Rule 26(b) and which are in the possession, custody or control of the party upon whom the request is served; or (2) to permit entry upon designated land or other property in the possession or control of the party upon whom the request is served for the purpose of inspection and measuring, surveying, photographing, testing, or sampling the property or any designated object or operation thereon, within the scope of Rule 26(b).

(b) Procedure. The request shall set forth, either by individual item or by category, the items to be inspected, and describe each with reasonable particularity. The request shall specify a reasonable time, place, and manner of making the inspection and performing the related acts. Without leave of court or written stipulation, a request may not be served before the time specified in Rule 26(d).

The party upon whom the request is served shall serve a written response within 30 days after the service of the request. A shorter or longer time may be directed by the court or, in the absence of such an order, agreed to in writing by the parties, subject to Rule 29. The response shall state, with respect to each item or category, that inspection and related activities will be permitted as requested, unless the request is objected to, in which event the reasons for the objection shall be stated. If objection is made to part of an item or category, the part shall be specified and inspection permitted of the remaining parts. The

DEPOSITIONS AND DISCOVERY **Rule 34**

party submitting the request may move for an order under Rule 37(a) with respect to any objection to or other failure to respond to the request or any part thereof, or any failure to permit inspection as requested.

A party who produces documents for inspection shall produce them as they are kept in the usual course of business or shall organize and label them to correspond with the categories in the request.

(c) Persons Not Parties. A person not a party to the action may be compelled to produce documents and things or to submit to an inspection as provided in Rule 45.

Notes on Amendments to Federal Rule 34 and Comparative State Provisions

(a) *Amendments in 1970 to Rule 34*

The Advisory Committee commented on the 1970 amendments to Rule 34 as follows:

Rule 34 is revised to accomplish the following major changes in the existing rule: (1) to eliminate the requirement of good cause; (2) to have the rule operate extrajudicially; (3) to include testing and sampling as well as inspecting or photographing tangible things; and (4) to make clear that the rule does not preclude an independent action for analogous discovery against persons not parties.

Subdivision (a). * * * The good cause requirement was originally inserted in Rule 34 as a general protective provision in the absence of experience with the specific problems that would arise thereunder. As the note to Rule 26(b)(3) on trial preparation materials makes clear, good cause has been applied differently to varying classes of documents, though not without confusion. It has often been said in court opinions that good cause requires a consideration of need for the materials and of alternative means of obtaining them, i. e., something more than relevance and lack of privilege. But the overwhelming proportion of the cases in which the formula of good cause has been applied to require a special showing are those involving trial preparation. In practice, the courts have not treated documents as having a special immunity to discovery simply because of their being documents. Protection may be afforded to claims of privacy or secrecy or of undue burden or expense under what is now Rule 26(c) (previously Rule 30(b)). To be sure, an appraisal of "undue" burden inevitably entails consideration of the needs of the party seeking discovery. With special provisions added to govern trial preparation materials and experts, there is no longer any occasion to retain the requirement of good cause.

The revision of Rule 34 to have it operate extrajudicially, rather than by court order, is to a large extent a reflection of existing law office practice. The Columbia Survey shows that of the litigants seeking inspection of documents or things, only about 25 percent filed motions for court orders. This minor fraction nevertheless accounted for a significant number of motions. About half of these motions were uncontested and in almost all instances the party seeking production ultimately prevailed. Although an extrajudicial procedure will not drastically alter existing practice under Rule 34—it will conform to it in most cases—it has the potential of saving court time in a substantial though proportionately small number of cases tried annually. * * *

Subdivision (c). Rule 34 as revised continues to apply only to parties. Comments from the bar make clear that in the preparation of cases for trial it is occasionally necessary to enter land or inspect large tangible things in the possession of a person not a party, and that some courts have dismissed independent actions in the nature of bills in equity for such discovery on the ground that Rule 34 is preemptive. While an ideal solution to this problem is to provide for discovery against persons not parties in Rule 34, both the jurisdictional and procedural problems are very complex. For the present, this subdivision makes

Rule 34 RULES OF CIVIL PROCEDURE

clear that Rule 34 does not preclude independent actions for discovery against persons not parties.

(b) *Amendment in 1980 to Rule 34(b)*

The last paragraph of Rule 34(b) was added in 1980 to proscribe the practice of some litigants of deliberately mixing critical documents with many others in order to obscure significance.

(c) *Comparative State Provisions*

New York Civil Practice Law and Rules 3120

(a) As against party:

1. After commencement of an action, any party may serve on any other party notice:

(i) to produce and permit the party seeking discovery, or someone acting on his behalf, to inspect, copy, test or photograph any specifically designated documents or any things which are in the possession, custody or control of the party served; or

(ii) to permit entry upon designated land or other property in the possession, custody or control of the party served for the purpose of inspecting, measuring, surveying, sampling, testing, photographing or recording by motion pictures or otherwise the property or any specifically designated object or operation thereon.

2. The notice shall specify the time, which shall be not less than twenty days after service of the notice, and the place and manner of making the inspection, copy, test or photograph, or of the entry upon the land or other property * * *.

(b) As against non-party. A person not a party may be directed by order to do whatever a party may be directed to do under subdivision (a). The motion for such order shall be on notice to all adverse parties; the non-party shall be served with the notice of motion in the same manner as a summons. The order shall contain, in addition to such specifications as the notice is required to contain under paragraph two of subdivision (a), provision for the defraying of the expenses of the non-party.

Rule 35. Physical and Mental Examination of Persons

(a) Order for Examination. When the mental or physical condition (including the blood group) of a party, or of a person in the custody or under the legal control of a party, is in controversy, the court in which the action is pending may order the party to submit to a physical or mental examination by a suitably licensed or certified examiner or to produce for examination the person in the party's custody or legal control. The order may be made only on motion for good cause shown and upon notice to the person to be examined and to all parties and shall specify the time, place, manner, conditions, and scope of the examination and the person or persons by whom it is to be made.

(b) Report of Examiner.

(1) If requested by the party against whom an order is made under Rule 35(a) or the person examined, the party causing the examination to be made shall deliver to the requestor a copy of a detailed written report of the examiner setting out the physician's findings, including results of all tests made, diagnoses and conclusions, together with like reports of all earlier examinations of the same condition. After delivery the party

causing the examination shall be entitled upon request to receive from the party against whom the order is made a like report of any examination, previously or thereafter made, of the same condition, unless, in the case of a report of examination of a person not a party, the party shows that such party is unable to obtain it. The court on motion may make an order against a party requiring delivery of a report on such terms as are just, and if a physician fails or refuses to make a report the court may exclude the physician's testimony if offered at the trial.

(2) By requesting and obtaining a report of the examination so ordered or by taking the deposition of the examiner, the party examined waives any privilege the party may have in that action or any other involving the same controversy, regarding the testimony of every other person who has examined or may thereafter examine the party in respect of the same mental or physical condition.

(3) This subdivision applies to examinations made by agreement of the parties, unless the agreement expressly provides otherwise. This subdivision does not preclude discovery of a report of an examiner or the taking of a deposition of the examiner in accordance with the provisions of any other rule.

Notes on Amendments to Federal Rule 35 and Comparative State Provisions

(a) *Amendments in 1970 to Rule 35*

The Advisory Committee commented on the 1970 amendment to Rule 35 as follows:

Subdivision (a). Rule 35(a) has hitherto provided only for an order requiring a party to submit to an examination. It is desirable to extend the rule to provide for an order against the party for examination of a person in his custody or under his legal control. As appears from the provisions of amended Rule 37(b)(2) and the comment under that rule, an order to "produce" the third person imposes only an obligation to use good faith efforts to produce the person.

The amendment will settle beyond doubt that a parent or guardian suing to recover for injuries to a minor may be ordered to produce the minor for examination. Further, the amendment expressly includes blood examination within the kinds of examinations that can be ordered under the rule.

(b) *Amendment in 1991 to Rule 35*

The 1991 amendment eliminated the requirement that an examination be carried out by a physician, or, in the case of a mental examination, by a physician or psychologist. Instead, an order for an examination is proper if carried out "by a suitably licensed or certified examiner."

(c) *Comparative State Provisions*

1. *Rule 35(a)*

Minnesota Rule of Civil Procedure 35.01

In an action in which the physical or mental condition or the blood relationship of a party, or of an agent of a party, or of a person under control of a party, is in controversy, the court in which the action is pending may order the party to submit to, or produce such agent or person for, a mental, physical, or blood examination by a suitably licensed or certified examiner. The order may be made only on motion for good cause shown and upon notice to the party or person to be examined and to all other parties and shall specify the time, place, manner, conditions, and scope of the examination and the person or persons by whom it is made.

2. *Rule 35(b)*

New York Civil Practice Law and Rules 3121(b)

A copy of a detailed written report of the examining physician setting out his findings and conclusions shall be delivered by the party seeking the examination to any party requesting to exchange therefor a copy of each report in his control of an examination made with respect to the mental or physical condition in controversy.

Rule 36. Requests for Admission

(a) Request for Admission. A party may serve upon any other party a written request for the admission, for purposes of the pending action only, of the truth of any matters within the scope of Rule 26(b)(1) set forth in the request that relate to statements or opinions of fact or of the application of law to fact, including the genuineness of any documents described in the request. Copies of documents shall be served with the request unless they have been or are otherwise furnished or made available for inspection and copying. Without leave of court or written stipulation, requests for admission may not be served before the time specified in Rule 26(d).

Each matter of which an admission is requested shall be separately set forth. The matter is admitted unless, within 30 days after service of the request, or within such shorter or longer time as the court may allow or the parties may agree to in writing, subject to Rule 29, the party to whom the request is directed serves upon the party requesting the admission a written answer or objection addressed to the matter, signed by the party or by the party's attorney. If objection is made, the reasons therefor shall be stated. The answer shall specifically deny the matter or set forth in detail the reasons why the answering party cannot truthfully admit or deny the matter. A denial shall fairly meet the substance of the requested admission, and when good faith requires that a party qualify an answer or deny only a part of the matter of which an admission is requested, the party shall specify so much of it as is true and qualify or deny the remainder. An answering party may not give lack of information or knowledge as a reason for failure to admit or deny unless the party states that the party has made reasonable inquiry and that the information known or readily obtainable by the party is insufficient to enable the party to admit or deny. A party who considers that a matter of which an admission has been requested presents a genuine issue for trial may not, on that ground alone, object to the request; the party may, subject to the provisions of Rule 37(c), deny the matter or set forth reasons why the party cannot admit or deny it.

The party who has requested the admissions may move to determine the sufficiency of the answers or objections. Unless the court determines that an objection is justified, it shall order that an answer be served. If the court determines that an answer does not comply with the requirements of this rule, it may order either that the matter is admitted or that an amended answer be served. The court may, in lieu of these orders, determine that final disposition of the request be made at a pre-trial conference or at a designated time prior to trial. The provisions of Rule 37(a)(4) apply to the award of expenses incurred in relation to the motion.

(b) Effect of Admission. Any matter admitted under this rule is conclusively established unless the court on motion permits withdrawal or amendment of the admission. Subject to the provisions of Rule 16 governing amendment of a pre-trial order, the court may permit withdrawal or amendment when the presentation of the merits of the action will be subserved thereby and the party who obtained the admission fails to satisfy the court that withdrawal or amendment will prejudice that party in maintaining the action or defense on the merits. Any admission made by a party under this rule is for the purpose of the pending action only and is not an admission for any other purpose nor may it be used against the party in any other proceeding.

Notes on Amendments to Federal Rule 36

The 1970 amendments made several important changes in Rule 36. The Advisory Committee commented on these changes as follows:

Subdivision (a). As revised, the subdivision provides that a request may be made to admit any matters within the scope of Rule 26(b) that relate to statements or opinions of fact or of the application of law to fact. It thereby eliminates the requirement that the matters be "of fact." This change resolves conflicts in the court decisions as to whether a request to admit matters of "opinion" and matters involving "mixed law and fact" is proper under the rule. * * *

Not only is it difficult as a practical matter to separate "fact" from "opinion," see 4 *Moore's Federal Practice* ¶ 36.04 (2d ed. 1966); *cf.* 2A Barron & Holtzoff, *Federal Practice and Procedure* 317 (Wright ed. 1961), but an admission on a matter of opinion may facilitate proof or narrow the issues or both. An admission of a matter involving the application of law to fact may, in a given case, even more clearly narrow the issues. For example, an admission that an employee acted in the scope of his employment may remove a major issue from the trial. * * *

Courts have also divided on whether an answering party may properly object to request for admission as to matters which that party regards as "in dispute." * * * The proper response in such cases is an answer. The very purpose of the request is to ascertain whether the answering party is prepared to admit or regards the matter as presenting a genuine issue for trial. In his answer, the party may deny, or he may give as his reason for inability to admit or deny the existence of a genuine issue. The party runs no risk of sanctions if the matter is genuinely in issue, since Rule 37(c) provides a sanction of costs only when there are no good reasons for a failure to admit.

* * *

Another sharp split of authority exists on the question whether a party may base his answer on lack of information or knowledge without seeking out additional information. One line of cases has held that a party may answer on the basis of such knowledge as he has at the time he answers. * * *

The rule as revised adopts the majority view, as in keeping with a basic principle of the discovery rules that a reasonable burden may be imposed on the parties when its discharge will facilitate preparation for trial and ease the trial process. It has been argued against this view that one side should not have the burden of "proving" the other side's case. The revised rule requires only that the answering party make reasonable inquiry and secure such knowledge and information as are readily obtainable by him. In most instances, the investigation will be necessary either to his own case or to preparation for rebuttal. Even when it is not, the information may be close enough at hand to be "readily obtainable." Rule 36 requires only that the party state that he has taken these steps. The sanction for failure of a party to inform himself before he answers lies in the award of costs after trial, as provided in Rule 37(c). * * *

A problem peculiar to Rule 36 arises if the responding party serves answers that are not in conformity with the requirements of the rule—for example, a denial is not "specific," or the explanation of inability to admit or deny is not "in detail." Rule 36 now makes no provision for court scrutiny of such answers before trial, and it seems to contemplate that defective answers bring about admissions just as effectively as if no answer had been served. Some cases have so held. * * *

Giving a defective answer the automatic effect of an admission may cause unfair surprise. A responding party who purported to deny or to be unable to admit or deny will for the first time at trial confront the contention that he has made a binding admission. Since it is not always easy to know whether a denial is "specific" or an explanation is "in detail," neither party can know how the court will rule at trial and whether proof must be prepared. Some courts, therefore, have entertained motions to rule on defective answers. They have at times ordered that amended answers be served, when the defects were technical, and at other times have declared that the matter was admitted. * * * The rule as revised conforms to the latter practice.

Subdivision (b). The rule does not now indicate the extent to which a party is bound by his admission. Some courts view admissions as the equivalent of sworn testimony. * * * At least in some jurisdictions a party may rebut his own testimony, e. g., *Alamo v. Del Rosario*, 98 F.2d 328 (D.C.Cir.1938), and by analogy an admission made pursuant to Rule 36 may likewise be thought rebuttable. * * * In *McSparran v. Hanigan*, 225 F.Supp. 628, 636–637 (E.D.Pa.1963), the court held that an admission is conclusively binding, though noting the confusion created by prior decisions.

The new provisions give an admission a conclusively binding effect, for purposes only of the pending action, unless the admission is withdrawn or amended. In form and substance a Rule 36 admission is comparable to an admission in pleadings or a stipulation drafted by counsel for use at trial, rather than to an evidentiary admission of a party. * * *

Rule 37. Failure to Make or Cooperate in Discovery: Sanctions

(a) Motion for Order Compelling Disclosure or Discovery. A party, upon reasonable notice to other parties and all persons affected thereby, may apply for an order compelling disclosure or discovery as follows:

(1) *Appropriate Court.* An application for an order to a party shall be made to the court in which the action is pending. An application for an order to a person who is not a party shall be made to the court in the district where the discovery is being, or is to be, taken.

(2) *Motion.*

(A) If a party fails to make a disclosure required by Rule 26(a), any other party may move to compel disclosure and for appropriate sanctions. The motion must include a certification that the movant has in good faith conferred or attempted to confer with the party not making the disclosure in an effort to secure the disclosure without court action.

(B) If a deponent fails to answer a question propounded or submitted under Rules 30 or 31, or a corporation or other entity fails to make a designation under Rule 30(b)(6) or 31(a), or a party fails to answer an interrogatory submitted under Rule 33, or if a party, in response to a request for inspection submitted under Rule 34, fails to respond that inspection will be permitted as requested or fails to permit inspection as requested, the discovering party may move for an order compelling an answer, or a designation, or an order compelling inspection in accordance with the request. The motion must include a certification that the movant has in good faith conferred or attempted to confer with the person or party failing to make the discovery in an effort to secure the information or material without court action. When taking a deposition on oral examination, the proponent of the question may complete or adjourn the examination before applying for an order.

(3) *Evasive or Incomplete Disclosure, Answer, or Response.* For purposes of this subdivision an evasive or incomplete disclosure, answer, or response is to be treated as a failure to disclose, answer, or respond.

(4) *Expenses and Sanctions.*

(A) If the motion is granted or if the disclosure or requested discovery is provided after the motion was filed, the court shall, after affording an opportunity to be heard, require the party or deponent whose conduct necessitated the motion or the party or attorney advising such conduct or both of them to pay to the moving party the reasonable expenses incurred in making the motion, including attorney's fees, unless the court finds that the motion was filed without the movant's first making a good faith effort to obtain the disclosure or discovery without court action, or that the opposing party's nondisclosure, response, or objection was substantially justified, or that other circumstances make an award of expenses unjust.

(B) If the motion is denied, the court may enter any protective order authorized under Rule 26(c) and shall, after affording an opportunity to be heard, require the moving party or the attorney filing the motion or both of them to pay to the party or deponent who opposed the motion the reasonable expenses incurred in opposing the motion, including attorney's fees, unless the court finds that the making of the motion was substantially justified or that other circumstances make an award of expenses unjust.

(C) If the motion is granted in part and denied in part, the court may enter any protective order authorized under Rule 26(c) and may, after affording an opportunity to be heard, apportion the reasonable expenses incurred in relation to the motion among the parties and persons in a just manner.

(b) Failure to Comply With Order.

(1) *Sanctions by Court in District Where Deposition Is Taken.* If a deponent fails to be sworn or to answer a question after being directed to do so by the court in the district in which the deposition is being taken, the failure may be considered a contempt of that court.

(2) *Sanctions by Court in Which Action Is Pending.* If a party or an officer, director, or managing agent of a party or a person designated under Rule 30(b)(6) or 31(a) to testify on behalf of a party fails to obey an order to provide or permit discovery, including an order made under subdivision (a) of this rule or Rule 35, or if a party fails to obey an order entered under Rule 26(f), the court in which the action is pending may make such orders in regard to the failure as are just, and among others the following:

(A) An order that the matters regarding which the order was made or any other designated facts shall be taken to be established for the purposes of the action in accordance with the claim of the party obtaining the order;

(B) An order refusing to allow the disobedient party to support or oppose designated claims or defenses, or prohibiting that party from introducing designated matters in evidence;

(C) An order striking out pleadings or parts thereof, or staying further proceedings until the order is obeyed, or dismissing the action or proceeding or any part thereof, or rendering a judgment by default against the disobedient party;

(D) In lieu of any of the foregoing orders or in addition thereto, an order treating as a contempt of court the failure to obey any orders except an order to submit to a physical or mental examination;

(E) Where a party has failed to comply with an order under Rule 35(a) requiring that party to produce another for examination, such orders as are listed in paragraphs (A), (B), and (C) of this subdivision, unless the party failing to comply shows that that party is unable to produce such person for examination.

In lieu of any of the foregoing orders or in addition thereto, the court shall require the party failing to obey the order or the attorney advising that party or both to pay the reasonable expenses, including attorney's fees, caused by the failure, unless the court finds that the failure was substantially justified or that other circumstances make an award of expenses unjust.

(c) Failure to Disclose; False or Misleading Disclosure; Refusal to Admit.

(1) A party that without substantial justification fails to disclose information as required by Rule 26(a) or 26(e)(1) shall not, unless such

failure is harmless, be permitted to use as evidence at trial, at a hearing, or on a motion, any witness or information not so disclosed. In addition or in lieu of this sanction, the court, on motion after affording opportunity to be heard, may impose other appropriate sanctions. In addition to requiring payment of reasonable expenses, including attorney's fees, caused by the failure, these sanctions may include any actions authorized under subparagraphs (A), (B), and (C) of subdivision (b)(2) of this rule and may include informing the jury of the failure to make the disclosure.

(2) If a party fails to admit the genuineness of any document or the truth of any matter requested under Rule 36, and if the party requesting the admissions thereafter proves the genuineness of the document or the truth of the matter, the requesting party may apply to the court for an order requiring the other party to pay the party the reasonable expenses incurred in making that proof, including reasonable attorney's fees. The court shall make the order unless it finds that (A) the request was held objectionable pursuant to Rule 36(a), or (B) the admission sought was of no substantial importance, or (C) the party failing to admit had reasonable ground to believe that the party might prevail on the matter, or (D) there was other good reason for the failure to admit.

(d) Failure of Party to Attend at Own Deposition or Serve Answers to Interrogatories or Respond to Request for Inspection. If a party or an officer, director, or managing agent of a party or a person designated under Rule 30(b)(6) or 31(a) to testify on behalf of a party fails (1) to appear before the officer who is to take the deposition, after being served with a proper notice, or (2) to serve answers or objections to interrogatories submitted under Rule 33, after proper service of the interrogatories, or (3) to serve a written response to a request for inspection submitted under Rule 34, after proper service of the request, the court in which the action is pending on motion may make such orders in regard to the failure as are just, and among others it may take any action authorized under paragraphs (A), (B), and (C) of subdivision (b)(2) of this rule. Any motion specifying a failure under clauses (2) or (3) of this subdivision shall include a certification that the movant in good faith has conferred or attempted to confer with the party failing to answer or respond in an effort to obtain such answer or response without court action. In lieu of any order or in addition thereto, the court shall require the party failing to act or the attorney advising that party or both to pay the reasonable expenses, including attorney's fees, caused by the failure, unless the court finds that the failure was substantially justified or that other circumstances make an award of expenses unjust.

The failure to act described in this subdivision may not be excused on the ground that the discovery sought is objectionable unless the party failing to act has applied for a protective order as provided by Rule 26(c).

Rule 37   RULES OF CIVIL PROCEDURE

(e) [Abrogated]

(f) [Repealed. Pub.L. 96–481, Title II, § 205(a), Oct. 21, 1980, 94 Stat. 2330.]

(g) Failure to Participate in the Framing of a Discovery Plan. If a party or a party's attorney fails to participate in good faith in the development and submission of a proposed discovery plan as required by Rule 26(f), the court may, after opportunity for hearing, require such party or attorney to pay to any other party the reasonable expenses, including attorney's fees, caused by the failure.

Notes on Amendments to Federal Rule 37 and Comparative Federal and State Provisions

(a) *Amendments in 1993 to Federal Rule 37*

Rule 37 has been revised to reflect the revisions made to Rule 26(a) mandating the automatic exchange of information without formal discovery. Subdivision (a)(2)(A) has been added to provide a method for compelling disclosure where a party fails to fully comply with Rule 26(a). Under (c)(1) of the revised rule, if the information is important evidence for the non-disclosing party, the party seeking to compel disclosure may, as an alternative measure, ask the court to exclude the evidence at trial.

Language has been added to paragraph (d) and to subparagraph (a)(2)(B) which requires litigants to use informal means of resolving discovery disputes before filing a motion to compel compliance. Paragraph (a)(3), as revised, clarifies that evasive or incomplete disclosures and answers to requests for production of documents and interrogatories will be treated as failures to respond and may serve as the basis for sanctions under Rule 37(a).

Subdivision (c) provides that as a sanction for failing to automatically disclose information required by Rule 26(a) or 26(e)(1), a party will be prohibited from using such information at trial. Unlike the old version of the rule, this provision is self-executing and does not require the opposing party to make a motion. The inclusion of the requirement that the failure to disclose must be "without substantial justification" and the exception from sanctions where the failure to disclose is harmless serve to mitigate the harshness of this rule.

(b) *Comparative Provisions*

Rule 37(a)

1. *Local Federal Rules*

United States District Court, Northern District, California, Civil Rule 230-4

(a) Conference Required. The court will entertain no motion pursuant to Rules 26 through 37, Federal Rules of Civil Procedure, unless counsel shall have previously conferred concerning all disputed issues. If counsel for the moving party seeks to arrange such a conference and counsel for the party against whom the motion will be made willfully refuses or fails to confer, the judge (in the absence of a prior order dispensing for good cause with such a conference) may order the payment of reasonable expenses, including attorney's fees, pursuant to Rule 37(a)(4), Federal Rules of Civil Procedure and Local Rule 100-3.

(b) Certificate of Compliance. At the time of filing any motion with respect to Rules 26 through 37, Federal Rules of Civil Procedure, counsel for the moving party shall serve and file a certificate of compliance with this Rule.

* * *

United States District Court, Northern District, Illinois, General Rule 12k

To curtail undue delay and expense in the administration of justice, this court shall hereafter refuse to hear any and all motions for discovery and production of documents under Rules 26 through 37 of the Federal Rules of Civil Procedure, unless the motion includes a statement (1) that after personal consultation and sincere attempts to resolve differences they are unable to reach an accord, or (2) counsel's attempts to engage in such personal consultation were unsuccessful due to no fault of counsel's. Where the consultation occurred, this statement shall recite, in addition, the date, time and place of such conference, and the names of all parties participating therein. Where counsel was unsuccessful in engaging in such consultation, the statement shall recite the efforts made by counsel to engage in consultation.

2. *Comparative State Provision*

California Civil Procedure Code § 2023

(a) Misuses of the discovery process include, but are not limited to, the following:

(1) Persisting, over objection and without substantial justification, in an attempt to obtain information or materials that are outside the scope of permissible discovery.

(2) Using a discovery method in a manner that does not comply with its specified procedures.

(3) Employing a discovery method in a manner or to an extent that causes unwarranted annoyance, embarrassment, or oppression, or undue burden and expense.

(4) Failing to respond or submit to an authorized method of discovery.

(5) Making, without substantial justification, an unmeritorious objection or evasive response to discovery.

(6) Making an evasive response to discovery.

(7) Disobeying a court order to provide discovery.

(8) Making or opposing, unsuccessfully and without substantial justification, a motion to compel or to limit discovery.

(9) Failing to confer in person, by telephone, or by letter with an opposing party or attorney in a reasonable and good faith attempt to resolve informally any dispute concerning discovery, if the section governing a particular discovery motion requires the filing of a declaration stating facts showing that such an attempt has been made. Notwithstanding the outcome of the particular discovery motion, the court shall impose a monetary sanction ordering that any party or attorney who fails to confer as required pay the reasonable expenses, including attorney's fees, incurred by anyone as a result of that conduct.

(b) To the extent authorized by the section governing any particular discovery method or any other provision of this article, the court, after notice to any affected party, person, or attorney, and after opportunity for hearing, may impose the following sanctions against anyone engaging in conduct that is a misuse of the discovery process.

(1) The court may impose a monetary sanction ordering that one engaging in the misuse of the discovery process, or any attorney advising that conduct, or both pay the reasonable expenses, including attorney's fees, incurred by anyone as a result of that conduct. The court may also impose this sanction on one unsuccessfully asserting that another has engaged in the misuse of the discovery process, or on any attorney who advised that assertion, or on both. If a monetary sanction is authorized by any provision of this article, the court shall impose that sanction unless it finds that the one subject to the sanction acted with substantial justification or that other circumstances make the sanction unjust.

(2) The court may impose an issue sanction ordering that designed facts shall be taken as established in the action in accordance with the claim of the party adversely affected by the misuse of the discovery process. The court may also impose an issue sanction by an order prohibiting any party engaging in the misuse of the discovery process from supporting or opposing designated claims or defenses.

(3) The court may impose an evidence sanction by an order prohibiting any party engaging in the misuse of the discovery process from introducing designated matters in evidence.

(4) The court may impose a terminating sanction by one of the following orders:

(A) An order striking out the pleadings or parts of the pleadings of any party engaging in the misuse of the discovery process.

(B) An order staying further proceedings by that party until an order for discovery is obeyed.

(C) An order dismissing the action, or any part of the action, of that party.

(D) An order rendering a judgment by default against that party.

(5) The court may impose a contempt sanction by an order treating the misuse of the discovery process as a contempt of court.

(c) A request for a sanction shall, in the notice of motion, identify every person, party, and attorney against whom the sanction is sought, and specify the type of sanction sought. The notice of motion shall be supported by a memorandum of points and authorities, and accompanied by a declaration setting forth facts supporting the amount of any monetary sanction sought.

VI. TRIALS

Rule 38. Jury Trial of Right

(a) Right Preserved. The right of trial by jury as declared by the Seventh Amendment to the Constitution or as given by a statute of the United States shall be preserved to the parties inviolate.

(b) Demand. Any party may demand a trial by jury of any issue triable of right by a jury by (1) serving upon the other parties a demand therefor in writing at any time after the commencement of the action and not later than 10 days after the service of the last pleading directed to such issue, and (2) filing the demand as required by Rule 5(d). Such demand may be indorsed upon a pleading of the party.

(c) Same: Specification of Issues. In the demand a party may specify the issues which the party wishes so tried; otherwise the party shall be deemed to have demanded trial by jury for all the issues so triable. If the party has demanded trial by jury for only some of the issues, any other party within 10 days after service of the demand or such lesser time as the court may order, may serve a demand for trial by jury of any other or all of the issues of fact in the action.

(d) Waiver. The failure of a party to serve and file a demand as required by this rule constitutes a waiver by the party of trial by jury. A demand for trial by jury made as herein provided may not be withdrawn without the consent of the parties.

(e) Admiralty and Maritime Claims. These rules shall not be construed to create a right to trial by jury of the issues in an admiralty or maritime claim within the meaning of Rule 9(h).

Federal and State Provisions Governing the Right to Jury Trial

(a) Constitutional Provisions

United States Constitution, 7th Amendment

In Suits at common law, where the value in controversy shall exceed twenty dollars, the right of trial by jury shall be preserved, and no fact tried by a jury shall be otherwise re-examined in any Court of the United States than according to the rules of the common law.

Pennsylvania Constitution Art. 1, § 6

Trial by jury shall be as heretofore, and the right thereof remain inviolate. The General Assembly may provide, however, by law, that a verdict may be rendered by not less than five-sixths of the jury in any civil case.

Virginia Constitution Art. 1, § 11

* * *

That in controversies respecting property, and in suits between man and man, trial by jury is preferable to any other, and ought to be held sacred. The General Assembly may limit the number of jurors for civil cases in courts of record to not less than five.

(b) State Statute on Demand and Waiver

New York Civil Practice Law and Rules 4103

When it appears in the course of a trial by the court that the relief required, although not originally demanded by a party, entitles the adverse party to a trial by jury of certain issues of fact, the court shall give the adverse party an opportunity to demand a jury trial of such issues. Failure to make such demand within the time limited by the court shall be deemed a waiver of the right to trial by jury. Upon such demand, the court shall order a jury trial of any issues of fact which are required to be tried by jury.

Rule 39. Trial by Jury or by the Court

(a) By Jury. When trial by jury has been demanded as provided in Rule 38, the action shall be designated upon the docket as a jury action. The trial of all issues so demanded shall be by jury, unless (1) the parties or their attorneys of record, by written stipulation filed with the court or by an oral stipulation made in open court and entered in the record, consent to trial by the court sitting without a jury or (2) the court upon motion or of its own initiative finds that a right of trial by jury of some or all of those issues does not exist under the Constitution or statutes of the United States.

(b) By the Court. Issues not demanded for trial by jury as provided in Rule 38 shall be tried by the court; but, notwithstanding the failure of a party to demand a jury in an action in which such a demand

Rule 39   RULES OF CIVIL PROCEDURE

might have been made of right, the court in its discretion upon motion may order a trial by a jury of any or all issues.

(c) Advisory Jury and Trial by Consent. In all actions not triable of right by a jury the court upon motion or of its own initiative may try any issue with an advisory jury or, except in actions against the United States when a statute of the United States provides for trial without a jury, the court, with the consent of both parties, may order a trial with a jury whose verdict has the same effect as if trial by jury had been a matter of right.

Rule 40. Assignment of Cases for Trial

The district courts shall provide by rule for the placing of actions upon the trial calendar (1) without request of the parties or (2) upon request of a party and notice to the other parties or (3) in such other manner as the courts deem expedient. Precedence shall be given to actions entitled thereto by any statute of the United States.

Rule 41. Dismissal of Actions

(a) Voluntary Dismissal: Effect Thereof.

(1) *By Plaintiff; by Stipulation.* Subject to the provisions of Rule 23(e), of Rule 66, and of any statute of the United States, an action may be dismissed by the plaintiff without order of court (i) by filing a notice of dismissal at any time before service by the adverse party of an answer or of a motion for summary judgment, whichever first occurs, or (ii) by filing a stipulation of dismissal signed by all parties who have appeared in the action. Unless otherwise stated in the notice of dismissal or stipulation, the dismissal is without prejudice, except that a notice of dismissal operates as an adjudication upon the merits when filed by a plaintiff who has once dismissed in any court of the United States or of any state an action based on or including the same claim.

(2) *By Order of Court.* Except as provided in paragraph (1) of this subdivision of this rule, an action shall not be dismissed at the plaintiff's instance save upon order of the court and upon such terms and conditions as the court deems proper. If a counterclaim has been pleaded by a defendant prior to the service upon the defendant of the plaintiff's motion to dismiss, the action shall not be dismissed against the defendant's objection unless the counterclaim can remain pending for independent adjudication by the court. Unless otherwise specified in the order, a dismissal under this paragraph is without prejudice.

(b) Involuntary Dismissal: Effect Thereof. For failure of the plaintiff to prosecute or to comply with these rules or any order of court, a defendant may move for dismissal of an action or of any claim against the defendant. Unless the court in its order for dismissal otherwise specifies, a dismissal under this subdivision and any dismissal not provided for in this rule, other than a dismissal for lack of jurisdiction, for improper venue, or for failure to join a party under Rule 19, operates as an adjudication upon the merits.

(c) Dismissal of Counterclaim, Cross-Claim, or Third-Party Claim. The provisions of this rule apply to the dismissal of any counterclaim, cross-claim, or third-party claim. A voluntary dismissal by the claimant alone pursuant to paragraph (1) of subdivision (a) of this rule shall be made before a responsive pleading is served or, if there is none, before the introduction of evidence at the trial or hearing.

(d) Costs of Previously-Dismissed Action. If a plaintiff who has once dismissed an action in any court commences an action based upon or including the same claim against the same defendant, the court may make such order for the payment of costs of the action previously dismissed as it may deem proper and may stay the proceedings in the action until the plaintiff has complied with the order.

Comparative Provisions and Notes on Amendments to Federal Rule 41

(a) *Rule 41(a)*

Illinois Compiled Statutes 5/2–1009(a)

The plaintiff may, at any time before trial or hearing begins, upon notice to each party who has appeared or each such party's attorney, and upon payment of costs, dismiss his or her action or any part thereof as to any defendant, without prejudice, by order filed in the cause. Thereafter the plaintiff may dismiss, only on terms fixed by the court (1) upon filing a stipulation to that effect signed by the defendant, or (2) on motion specifying the ground for dismissal, which shall be supported by affidavit or other proof. After a counterclaim has been pleaded by a defendant no dismissal may be had as to the defendant except by the defendant's consent.

(b) *Rule 41(b)*

1. *Amendments in 1963 to Federal Rule 41(b)*

Prior to 1963 the second sentence of Rule 41(b) providing for a dismissal upon completion of plaintiff's presentation of evidence was not restricted to non-jury cases. The purpose of the amendment was set forth by the Advisory Committee as follows:

Under the present text of the second sentence of this subdivision, the motion for dismissal at the close of the plaintiff's evidence may be made in a case tried to a jury as well as in a case tried without a jury. But, when made in a jury-tried case, this motion overlaps the motion for a directed verdict under Rule 50(a), which is also available in the same situation. It has been held that the standard to be applied in deciding the Rule 41(b) motion at the close of the plaintiff's evidence in a jury-tried case is the same as that used upon a motion for a directed verdict made at the same stage; and, just as the court need not make findings pursuant to Rule 52(a) when it directs a verdict, so in a jury-tried case it may omit these findings in granting the Rule 41(b) motion. See generally *O'Brien v. Westinghouse Electric Corp.*, 293 F.2d 1, 5–10 (3d Cir.1961).

As indicated by the discussion in the *O'Brien* case, the overlap has caused confusion. Accordingly, the second and third sentences of Rule 41(b) are amended to provide that the motion for dismissal at the close of the plaintiff's evidence shall apply only to nonjury cases (including cases tried with an advisory jury). Hereafter the correct motion in jury-tried cases will be the motion for a directed verdict. This involves no change of substance. * * *

The first sentence of Rule 41(b), providing for dismissal for failure to prosecute or to comply with the Rules or any order of court, and the general provisions of the last sentence remain applicable in jury as well as non-jury cases.

* * *

2. *Local Federal Rules*

United States District Court, Eastern District, California, Civil Rule 271

(a) *Dismissal Calendar.* Each Judge will maintain an individual dismissal or status conference calendar. Unless the Judge otherwise orders, semiannually each year the Clerk shall order the call of all civil cases which have been pending for more than six months and in which the plaintiff has failed to take action for six months. In the discretion of the Judge, civil cases may be added to or deleted from the call of cases on the dismissal calendar.

(b) *Responses to Dismissal Notice.* Pursuant to the notice requirements of LR 230, the Clerk shall notify all parties to show cause by affidavit filed in duplicate why such action should or should not be dismissed for lack of prosecution. All such affidavits opposing dismissal shall be filed no later than (sic) filing date required by LR 230 for opposition briefs; all affidavits supporting dismissal shall be filed no later than the date required by LR 230 for reply briefs. Failure to file a timely response to the dismissal notice may subject counsel or parties to monetary sanctions and/or may result in denial of the right to oppose or urge dismissal and to present oral arguments at the hearing, or may be deemed to be an admission that the failure to prosecute has resulted in prejudice to the opposing side. [Amended 8-3-89]

(c) *Hearing.* Filing of a certificate of readiness or a stipulation to continue or drop the action from the Court's calendar or any other action taken by the parties (except a voluntary dismissal in strict conformity with FR Civ P 41(a)) will not remove an action from the dismissal calendar absent express approval of the Court. Prior to the hearing, the Court may, sua sponte, drop the action from the dismissal calendar or may continue the hearing to a later date, with or without specific directions for action by the parties.

(d) *Disposition.* At the hearing, the Court may:

(1) dismiss the action for lack of prosecution or for other good reason,

(2) continue the matter to a later date for further proceedings, with or without specific directions to the parties,

(3) set the action for status conference or pretrial conference, or

(4) drop the action from the dismissal calendar if the facts so warrant, with or without such additional orders as may be appropriate.

(e) *Motions to Dismiss for Lack of Prosecution.* This Rule does not impair the right of a party to move for dismissal under the provisions of FR Civ P 41(b).

United States District Court, Eastern District, Michigan, Former Rule 5(b)

[This rule was deleted effective Sept. 12, 1994.]

Sanctions Affecting the Outcome of the Litigation (civil only). Abandonment, failure to prosecute, or failure to defend diligently may be found should counsel for any party fail to appear before the Court at pre-trial conference or should counsel fail to complete the necessary preparation for pre-trial or trial. Judgment may be entered against the defaulting party either with respect to a specific issue or on the entire case. Alternatively, the failures of counsel listed in this section may result in the imposition of sanctions authorized by Local Rule 5(c). After the case is at issue as to the party suffering the dismissal or default pursuant to this Rule, the Court shall direct that notice shall be given to the affected litigant of the sanction and the basis for its imposition.

3. *Comparative State Provisions*

California Civil Procedure Code § 583.210

(a) The summons and complaint shall be served upon a defendant within three years after the action is commenced against the defendant. For the purpose of this subdivision an action is commenced at the time the complaint is filed.

(b) Return of summons or other proof of service shall be made within 60 days after the time the summons and complaint must be served upon a defendant.

California Civil Procedure Code § 583.310

An action shall be brought to trial within five years after the action is commenced against the defendant.

California Civil Procedure Code § 583.320

(a) If a new trial is granted in the action the action shall again be brought to trial within the following times:

(1) If a trial is commenced but no judgment is entered because of a mistrial or because a jury is unable to reach a decision, within three years after the order of the court declaring the mistrial or the disagreement of the jury is entered.

(2) If after judgment a new trial is granted and no appeal is taken, within three years after the order granting the new trial is entered.

(3) If on appeal an order granting a new trial is affirmed or a judgment is reversed and the action remanded for a new trial, within three years after the remittitur is filed by the clerk of the trial court.

(b) Nothing in this section requires that an action again be brought to trial before expiration of the time prescribed in Section 583.310.

California Civil Procedure Code § 583.330

The parties may extend the time within which an action must be brought to trial pursuant to this article by the following means:

(a) By written stipulation. The stipulation need not be filed but, if it is not filed, the stipulation shall be brought to the attention of the court if relevant to a motion for dismissal.

(b) By oral agreement made in open court, if entered in the minutes of the court or a transcript is made.

California Civil Procedure Code § 583.360

(a) An action shall be dismissed by the court on its own motion or on motion of the defendant, after notice to the parties, if the action is not brought to trial within the time prescribed in this article.

(b) The requirements of this article are mandatory and are not subject to extension, excuse, or exception except as expressly provided by statute.

California Civil Procedure Code § 583.410(a)

The court may in its discretion dismiss an action for delay in prosecution pursuant to this article on its own motion or on motion of the defendant if to do so appears to the court appropriate under the circumstances of the case.

California Civil Procedure Code § 583.420

(a) The court may not dismiss an action pursuant to this article for delay in prosecution except after one of the following conditions has occurred:

(1) Service is not made within two years after the action is commenced against the defendant.

(2) The action is not brought to trial within the following times:

(A) Three years after the action is commenced against the defendant unless otherwise prescribed by rule under subparagraph (B).

(B) Two years after the action is commenced against the defendant if the Judicial Council by rule adopted pursuant to Section 583.410 so prescribes for the court because of the condition of the court calendar or for other reasons affecting the conduct of litigation or the administration of justice.

(3) A new trial is granted and the action is not again brought to trial within the following times:

(A) If a trial is commenced but no judgment is entered because of a mistrial or because a jury is unable to reach a decision, within two years after the order of the court declaring the mistrial or the disagreement of the jury is entered.

(B) If after judgment a new trial is granted and no appeal is taken, within two years after the order granting the new trial is entered.

(C) If on appeal an order granting a new trial is affirmed or a judgment is reversed and the action remanded for a new trial, within two years after the remittitur is filed by the clerk of the trial court.

(b) The times provided in subdivision (a) shall be computed in the manner provided for computation of the comparable times under Articles 2 (commencing with Section 583.210) and 3 (commencing with Section 583.310).

Indiana Rules of Trial Procedure, Trial Rule 41(E)

Whenever there has been a failure to comply with these rules or when no action has been taken in a civil case for a period of sixty [60] days, the court, on motion of a party or on its own motion shall order a hearing for the purpose of dismissing such case. The court shall enter an order of dismissal at plaintiff's costs if the plaintiff shall not show sufficient cause at or before such hearing. Dismissal may be withheld or reinstatement of dismissal may be made subject to the condition that the plaintiff comply with these rules and diligently prosecute the action and upon such terms that the court in its discretion determines to be necessary to assure such diligent prosecution.

Rule 42. Consolidation; Separate Trials

(a) Consolidation. When actions involving a common question of law or fact are pending before the court, it may order a joint hearing or trial of any or all the matters in issue in the actions; it may order all the actions consolidated; and it may make such orders concerning proceedings therein as may tend to avoid unnecessary costs or delay.

(b) Separate Trials. The court, in furtherance of convenience or to avoid prejudice, or when separate trials will be conducive to expedition and economy, may order a separate trial of any claim, cross-claim, counterclaim, or third-party claim, or of any separate issue or of any number of claims, cross-claims, counterclaims, third-party claims, or issues, always preserving inviolate the right of trial by jury as declared by the Seventh Amendment to the Constitution or as given by a statute of the United States.

Comparative State Provisions
(a) *Rule 42(a)*

New York Civil Practice Law and Rules 602

(a) Generally. When actions involving a common question of law or fact are pending before a court, the court, upon motion, may order a joint trial of any or all the matters in issue, may order the actions consolidated, and may make such other orders concerning proceedings therein as may tend to avoid unnecessary costs or delay.

(b) Cases pending in different courts. Where an action is pending in the supreme court it may, upon motion, remove to itself an action pending in another court and consolidate it or have it tried together with that in the supreme court. Where an action is pending in the county court, it may, upon motion, remove to itself an action pending in a city, municipal, district or justice court in the county and consolidate it or have it tried together with that in the county court.

(b) *Rule 42(b)*

New York Civil Practice Law and Rules 1002(c)

It shall not be necessary that each plaintiff be interested in obtaining, or each defendant be interested in defending against, all the relief demanded or as to every claim included in an action; but the court may make such orders as will prevent a party from being embarrassed, delayed, or put to expense by the inclusion of a party against whom he asserts no claim and, who asserts no claim against him, and may order separate trials or make other orders to prevent prejudice.

Rule 43. Taking of Testimony

(a) Form. In all trials the testimony of witnesses shall be taken orally in open court, unless otherwise provided by an Act of Congress or by these rules, the Federal Rules of Evidence, or other rules adopted by the Supreme Court.

(b), (c) [Abrogated]

(d) Affirmation in Lieu of Oath. Whenever under these rules an oath is required to be taken, a solemn affirmation may be accepted in lieu thereof.

(e) Evidence on Motions. When a motion is based on facts not appearing of record the court may hear the matter on affidavits presented by the respective parties, but the court may direct that the matter be heard wholly or partly on oral testimony or deposition.

(f) Interpreters. The court may appoint an interpreter of its own selection and may fix the interpreter's reasonable compensation. The compensation shall be paid out of funds provided by law or by one or more of the parties as the court may direct, and may be taxed ultimately as costs, in the discretion of the court.

Rule 44. Proof of Official Record

(a) Authentication.

(1) *Domestic.* An official record kept within the United States, or any state, district, or commonwealth, or within a territory subject to the administrative or judicial jurisdiction of the United States, or an entry therein, when admissible for any purpose, may be evidenced by an official publication thereof or by a copy attested by the officer having the legal custody of the record, or by the officer's deputy, and accompanied by a certificate that such officer has the custody. The certificate may be

made by a judge of a court of record of the district or political subdivision in which the record is kept, authenticated by the seal of the court, or may be made by any public officer having a seal of office and having official duties in the district or political subdivision in which the record is kept, authenticated by the seal of the officer's office.

(2) *Foreign.* A foreign official record, or an entry therein, when admissible for any purpose, may be evidenced by an official publication thereof; or a copy thereof, attested by a person authorized to make the attestation, and accompanied by a final certification as to the genuineness of the signature and official position (i) of the attesting person, or (ii) of any foreign official whose certificate of genuineness of signature and official position relates to the attestation or is in a chain of certificates of genuineness of signature and official position relating to the attestation. A final certification may be made by a secretary of embassy or legation, consul general, consul, vice consul, or consular agent of the United States, or a diplomatic or consular official of the foreign country assigned or accredited to the United States. If reasonable opportunity has been given to all parties to investigate the authenticity and accuracy of the documents, the court may, for good cause shown, (i) admit an attested copy without final certification or (ii) permit the foreign official record to be evidenced by an attested summary with or without a final certification. The final certification is unnecessary if the record and the attestation are certified as provided in a treaty or convention to which the United States and the foreign country in which the official record is located are parties.

(b) Lack of Record. A written statement that after diligent search no record or entry of a specified tenor is found to exist in the records designated by the statement, authenticated as provided in subdivision (a) (1) of this rule in the case of a domestic record, or complying with the requirements of subdivision (a) (2) of this rule for a summary in the case of a foreign record, is admissible as evidence that the records contain no such record or entry.

(c) Other Proof. This rule does not prevent the proof of official records or of entry or lack of entry therein by any other method authorized by law.

Rule 44.1 Determination of Foreign Law

A party who intends to raise an issue concerning the law of a foreign country shall give notice by pleadings or other reasonable written notice. The court, in determining foreign law, may consider any relevant material or source, including testimony, whether or not submitted by a party or admissible under the Federal Rules of Evidence. The court's determination shall be treated as a ruling on a question of law.

Notes by Advisory Committee on Adoption of Federal Rule 44.1

Rule 44.1 was added by amendment to furnish Federal courts with a uniform and effective procedure for raising and determining an issue concerning the law of a foreign country.

To avoid unfair surprise, the *first sentence* of the new rule requires that a party who intends to raise an issue of foreign law shall give notice thereof. The uncertainty under Rule 8(a) about whether foreign law must be pleaded * * * is eliminated by the provision that the notice shall be "written" and "reasonable." It may, but need not be, incorporated in the pleadings. In some situations the pertinence of foreign law is apparent from the outset; accordingly the necessary investigation of that law will have been accomplished by the party at the pleading stage, and the notice can be given conveniently in the pleadings. In other situations the pertinence of foreign law may remain doubtful until the case is further developed. A requirement that notice of foreign law be given only through the medium of the pleadings would tend in the latter instances to force the party to engage in a peculiarly burdensome type of investigation which might turn out to be unnecessary; and correspondingly the adversary would be forced into a possibly wasteful investigation. * * *

The *second sentence* of the new rule describes the materials to which the court may resort in determining an issue of foreign law. Heretofore the district courts, applying Rule 43(a), have looked in certain cases to State law to find the rules of evidence by which the content of foreign-country law is to be established. The State laws vary; some embody procedures which are inefficient, time consuming, and expensive. * * * In all events the ordinary rules of evidence are often inapposite to the problem of determining foreign law and have in the past prevented examination of material which could have provided a proper basis for the determination. * * *

The new rule refrains from imposing an obligation on the court to take "judicial notice" of foreign law because this would put an extreme burden on the court in many cases; and it avoids use of the concept of "judicial notice" in any form because of the uncertain meaning of that concept as applied to foreign law. See, *e.g.*, Stern, *Foreign Law in the Courts: Judicial Notice and Proof*, 45 Calif.L.Rev. 23, 43 (1957). Rather the rule provides flexible procedures for presenting and utilizing material on issues of foreign law by which a sound result can be achieved with fairness to the parties.

Under the *third sentence*, the court's determination of an issue of foreign law is to be treated as a ruling on a question of "law," not "fact," so that appellate review will not be narrowly confined by the "clearly erroneous" standard of Rule 52(a). * * *

Rule 45. Subpoena

(a) Form; Issuance.

(1) Every subpoena shall

(A) state the name of the court from which it is issued; and

(B) state the title of the action, the name of the court in which it is pending, and its civil action number; and

(C) command each person to whom it is directed to attend and give testimony or to produce and permit inspection and copying of designated books, documents or tangible things in the possession, custody or control of that person, or to permit the inspection of premises, at a time and place therein specified; and

(D) set forth the text of subdivisions (c) and (d) of this rule.

Rule 45   RULES OF CIVIL PROCEDURE

A command to produce evidence or to permit inspection may be joined with a command to appear at trial or hearing or at deposition, or may be issued separately.

(2) A subpoena commanding attendance at a trial or hearing shall issue from the court for the district in which the hearing or trial is to be held. A subpoena for attendance at a deposition shall issue from the court for the district designated by the notice of deposition as the district in which the deposition is to be taken. If separate from a subpoena commanding the attendance of a person, a subpoena for production or inspection shall issue from the court for the district in which the production or inspection is to be made.

(3) The clerk shall issue a subpoena, signed but otherwise in blank, to a party requesting it, who shall complete it before service. An attorney as officer of the court may also issue and sign a subpoena on behalf of

(A) a court in which the attorney is authorized to practice; or

(B) a court for a district in which a deposition or production is compelled by the subpoena, if the deposition or production pertains to an action pending in a court in which the attorney is authorized to practice.

(b) Service.

(1) A subpoena may be served by any person who is not a party and is not less than 18 years of age. Service of a subpoena upon a person named therein shall be made by delivering a copy thereof to such person and, if the person's attendance is commanded, by tendering to that person the fees for one day's attendance and the mileage allowed by law. When the subpoena is issued on behalf of the United States or an officer or agency thereof, fees and mileage need not be tendered. Prior notice of any commanded production of documents and things or inspection of premises before trial shall be served on each party in the manner prescribed by Rule 5(b).

(2) Subject to the provisions of clause (ii) of subparagraph (c)(3)(A) of this rule, a subpoena may be served at any place within the district of the court by which it is issued, or at any place without the district that is within 100 miles of the place of the deposition, hearing, trial, production, or inspection specified in the subpoena or at any place within the state where a state statute or rule of court permits service of a subpoena issued by a state court of general jurisdiction sitting in the place of the deposition, hearing, trial, production, or inspection specified in the subpoena. When a statute of the United States provides therefor, the court upon proper application and cause shown may authorize the service of a subpoena at any other place. A subpoena directed to a witness in a foreign country who is a national or resident of the United States shall issue under the circumstances and in the manner and be served as provided in Title 28, U.S.C. § 1783.

(3) Proof of service when necessary shall be made by filing with the clerk of the court by which the subpoena is issued a statement of the date and the manner of service and of the names of the persons served, certified by the person who made the service.

(c) Protection of Persons Subject to Subpoenas.

(1) A party or an attorney responsible for the issuance and service of a subpoena shall take reasonable steps to avoid imposing undue burden or expense on a person subject to that subpoena. The court on behalf of which the subpoena was issued shall enforce this duty and impose upon the party or attorney in breach of this duty an appropriate sanction, which may include, but is not limited to, lost earnings and a reasonable attorney's fee.

(2)(A) A person commanded to produce and permit inspection and copying of designated books, papers, documents or tangible things, or inspection of premises need not appear in person at the place of production or inspection unless commanded to appear for deposition, hearing or trial.

(B) Subject to paragraph (d)(2) of this rule, a person commanded to produce and permit inspection and copying may, within 14 days after service of the subpoena or before the time specified for compliance if such time is less than 14 days after service, serve upon the party or attorney designated in the subpoena written objection to inspection or copying of any or all of the designated materials or of the premises. If objection is made, the party serving the subpoena shall not be entitled to inspect and copy the materials or inspect the premises except pursuant to an order of the court by which the subpoena was issued. If objection has been made, the party serving the subpoena may, upon notice to the person commanded to produce, move at any time for an order to compel the production. Such an order to compel production shall protect any person who is not a party or an officer of a party from significant expense resulting from the inspection and copying commanded.

(3)(A) On timely motion, the court by which a subpoena was issued shall quash or modify the subpoena if it

(i) fails to allow reasonable time for compliance;

(ii) requires a person who is not a party or an officer of a party to travel to a place more than 100 miles from the place where that person resides, is employed or regularly transacts business in person, except that, subject to provisions of clause (c)(3)(B)(iii) of this rule, such a person may in order to attend trial be commanded to travel from any such place within the state in which the trial is held, or

(iii) requires disclosure of privileged or other protected matter and no exception or waiver applies, or

(iv) subjects a person to undue burden.

Rule 45 RULES OF CIVIL PROCEDURE

(B) If a subpoena

(i) requires disclosure of a trade secret or other confidential research, development, or commercial information, or

(ii) requires disclosure of an unretained expert's opinion or information not describing specific events or occurrences in dispute and resulting from the expert's study made not at the request of any party, or

(iii) requires a person who is not a party or an officer of a party to incur substantial expense to travel more than 100 miles to attend trial, the court may, to protect a person subject to or affected by the subpoena, quash or modify the subpoena or, if the party in whose behalf the subpoena is issued shows a substantial need for the testimony or material that cannot be otherwise met without undue hardship and assures that the person to whom the subpoena is addressed will be reasonably compensated, the court may order appearance or production only upon specified conditions.

(d) Duties in Responding to Subpoena.

(1) A person responding to a subpoena to produce documents shall produce them as they are kept in the usual course of business or shall organize and label them to correspond with the categories in the demand.

(2) When information subject to a subpoena is withheld on a claim that it is privileged or subject to protection as trial preparation materials, the claim shall be made expressly and shall be supported by a description of the nature of the documents, communications, or things not produced that is sufficient to enable the demanding party to contest the claim.

(e) Contempt. Failure by any person without adequate excuse to obey a subpoena served upon that person may be deemed a contempt of the court from which the subpoena is issued. An adequate cause for failure to obey exists when a subpoena purports to require a non-party to attend or produce at a place not within the limits provided by clause (ii) of subparagraph (c)(3)(A).

Notes on Amendments to Federal Rule 45 and Comparative State Provisions

(a) *Amendments in 1991 to Rule 45*

In 1991 Rule 45 was modified in a number of significant respects. Rule 45(c)(2)(A) was added to provide that a subpoena may be issued for the production of documents and other items without requiring the person in possession to be summoned to a deposition as Rule 45 previously required. Indeed current Rule 45(c) was entirely new and was added to provide protection for any person who has been served with a subpoena. The purpose of the provision is to ensure that such a person be given reasonable time to comply and not be faced with other undue burdens.

(b) *Comparative State Provisions*

Nebraska Revised Statutes § 25-1223

The clerks of the several courts and judges of the county courts shall, on application of any person having a cause or any matter pending in court, issue a subpoena for witnesses, under the seal of the court, inserting all the names required by the applicant in one subpoena, which may be served by any person not interested in the action, or by the sheriff, coroner or constable * * *.

Nebraska Revised Statutes § 25-1224

The subpoena shall be directed to the person therein named, requiring him to attend at a particular time and place, to testify as a witness; and it may contain a clause directing the witness to bring with him any book, writing or other thing under his control, which he is bound by law to produce as evidence.

Nebraska Revised Statutes § 25-1227(1)

Witnesses in civil cases cannot be compelled to attend a trial in the district court out of the state where they are served, nor at a distance of more than one hundred miles from the place of their residence, or from the place where they are served with a subpoena, unless within the same county. Witnesses in civil cases shall not be obliged to attend a deposition outside the county of their residence, or outside the county where the subpoena is served.

Nebraska Revised Statutes § 25-1228(1)

* * * [A] witness may demand his traveling fees, and fee for one day's attendance, when the subpoena is served upon him, and if the same be not paid the witness shall not be obliged to obey the subpoena. * * *

See also New York Civil Practice Law and Rules 3120(b) as set out following Federal Rule 34, supra.

Rule 46. Exceptions Unnecessary

Formal exceptions to rulings or orders of the court are unnecessary; but for all purposes for which an exception has heretofore been necessary it is sufficient that a party, at the time the ruling or order of the court is made or sought, makes known to the court the action which the party desires the court to take or the party's objection to the action of the court and the grounds therefor; and, if a party has no opportunity to object to a ruling or order at the time it is made, the absence of an objection does not thereafter prejudice the party.

Rule 47. Jurors

(a) Examination of Jurors. The court may permit the parties or their attorneys to conduct the examination of prospective jurors or may itself conduct the examination. In the latter event, the court shall permit the parties or their attorneys to supplement the examination by such further inquiry as it deems proper or shall itself submit to the prospective jurors such additional questions of the parties or their attorneys as it deems proper.

(b) Peremptory Challenges. The court shall allow the number of peremptory challenges provided by 28 U.S.C. § 1870.

Rule 47   RULES OF CIVIL PROCEDURE

(c) Excuse. The court may for good cause excuse a juror from service during trial or deliberation.

Comparative State Provisions

California Rule of Court 228

    This rule applies to all civil jury trials. To select a fair and impartial jury, the trial judge shall examine the prospective jurors [* * *. Upon] completion of the initial examination the trial judge shall permit counsel for each party who so requests to submit additional questions which the judges shall put to the jurors. Upon request of counsel, the trial judge shall permit counsel to supplement the judge's examination by oral and direct questioning of any of the prospective jurors. The scope of the additional questions or supplemental examination shall be within reasonable limits prescribed by the trial judge in the judge's sound discretion.

    The court may, upon stipulation by counsel for all parties appearing in the action, permit counsel to examine the prospective jurors outside a judge's presence.

South Carolina Code § 14-7-1020

    The court shall, on motion of either party in the suit, examine on oath any person who is called as a juror to know whether he is related to either party, has any interest in the cause, has expressed or formed any opinion, or is sensible of any bias or prejudice therein, and the party objecting to the juror may introduce any other competent evidence in support of the objection. If it appears to the court that the juror is not indifferent in the cause, he must be placed aside as to the trial of that cause and another must be called.

Rule 48. Number of Jurors—Participation in Verdict

    The court shall seat a jury of not fewer than six and not more than twelve members and all jurors shall participate in the verdict unless excused from service by the court pursuant to Rule 47(c). Unless the parties otherwise stipulate, (1) the verdict shall be unanimous and (2) no verdict shall be taken from a jury reduced in size to fewer than six members.

Comparative State Provisions

Minnesota Constitution Art. 1, § 4

    The right of trial by jury shall remain inviolate, and shall extend to all cases at law without regard to the amount in controversy. A jury trial may be waived by the parties in all cases in the manner prescribed by law. The legislature may provide that the agreement of five-sixths of a jury in a civil action or proceeding, after not less than six hours' deliberation, is a sufficient verdict. The legislature may provide for the number of jurors * * * provided that the jury have at least six members.

Virginia Code § 8.01-359

    A. Five persons from a panel of eleven shall constitute a jury in a civil case when the amount involved exclusive of interest and costs does not exceed [specified] jurisdictional limits. ... Seven persons from a panel of thirteen shall constitute a jury in all other civil cases except that when a special jury is allowed, twelve persons from a panel of twenty shall constitute the jury.

    * * *

    D. In any civil case in which the consent of the plaintiff and defendant shall be entered of record, it shall be lawful for the plaintiff to select one person who is eligible as a juror and for the defendant to select another, and for the two so selected to select a third of like qualifications, and the three so selected shall constitute a jury in the case. They shall take the oath required of jurors, and hear and determine the issue, and any two concurring shall render a verdict in like manner and with like effect as a jury of seven.

Rule 49. Special Verdicts and Interrogatories

(a) **Special Verdicts.** The court may require a jury to return only a special verdict in the form of a special written finding upon each issue of fact. In that event the court may submit to the jury written questions susceptible of categorical or other brief answer or may submit written forms of the several special findings which might properly be made under the pleadings and evidence; or it may use such other method of submitting the issues and requiring the written findings thereon as it deems most appropriate. The court shall give to the jury such explanation and instruction concerning the matter thus submitted as may be necessary to enable the jury to make its findings upon each issue. If in so doing the court omits any issue of fact raised by the pleadings or by the evidence, each party waives the right to a trial by jury of the issue so omitted unless before the jury retires the party demands its submission to the jury. As to an issue omitted without such demand the court may make a finding; or, if it fails to do so, it shall be deemed to have made a finding in accord with the judgment on the special verdict.

(b) **General Verdict Accompanied by Answer to Interrogatories.** The court may submit to the jury, together with appropriate forms for a general verdict, written interrogatories upon one or more issues of fact the decision of which is necessary to a verdict. The court shall give such explanation or instruction as may be necessary to enable the jury both to make answers to the interrogatories and to render a general verdict, and the court shall direct the jury both to make written answers and to render a general verdict. When the general verdict and the answers are harmonious, the appropriate judgment upon the verdict and answers shall be entered pursuant to Rule 58. When the answers are consistent with each other but one or more is inconsistent with the general verdict, judgment may be entered pursuant to Rule 58 in accordance with the answers, notwithstanding the general verdict, or the court may return the jury for further consideration of its answers and verdict or may order a new trial. When the answers are inconsistent with each other and one or more is likewise inconsistent with the general verdict, judgment shall not be entered, but the court shall return the jury for further consideration of its answers and verdict or shall order a new trial.

Comparative State Provisions

Wisconsin Statutes Annotated § 805.12(1)

Unless it orders otherwise, the court shall direct the jury to return a special verdict. The verdict shall be prepared by the court in the form of written questions relating only to material issues of ultimate fact and admitting a direct answer. The jury shall answer in writing. In cases founded upon negligence, the court need not submit separately any particular respect in which the party was allegedly negligent. The court may also direct the jury to find upon particular questions of fact.

Wisconsin Statutes Annotated § 805.12(2)

When some material issue of ultimate fact not brought to the attention of the trial court but essential to sustain the judgment is omitted from the verdict, the issue shall be deemed determined by the court in conformity with its judgment and the failure to request a finding by the jury on the issue shall be deemed a waiver of jury trial on that issue.

Rule 50. Judgment as a Matter of Law in Actions Tried by Jury; Alternative Motion for New Trial; Conditional Rulings*

(a) Judgment as a Matter of Law.

(1) If during a trial by jury a party has been fully heard on an issue and there is no legally sufficient evidentiary basis for a reasonable jury to find for that party on that issue, the court may determine the issue against that party and may grant a motion for judgment as matter of law against that party with respect to a claim or defense that cannot under the controlling law be maintained without a favorable finding on that issue.

(2) Motions for judgment as a matter of law may be made at any time before submission of the case to the jury. Such a motion shall specify the judgment sought and the law and the facts on which the moving party is entitled to the judgment.

(b) Renewal of Motion for Judgment After Trial; Alternative Motion for New Trial.

Whenever a motion for a judgment as a matter of law made at the close of all evidence is denied or for any reason is not granted, the court is deemed to have submitted the action to the jury subject to a later determination of the legal questions raised by the motion. Such a motion may be renewed by service and filing not later than 10 days after entry of judgment. A motion for a new trial under Rule 59 may be joined with a renewal of the motion for judgment as a matter of law, or a new trial may be requested in the alternative. If a verdict was returned, the court may, in disposing of the renewed motion, allow the judgment to stand or may reopen the judgment and either order a new trial or direct the entry of judgment as a matter of law. If no verdict was returned, the court may, in disposing of the renewed motion, direct the entry of judgment as a matter of law or may order a new trial.

(c) Same: Conditional Rulings on Grant of Motion.

(1) If the renewed judgment as a matter of law is granted, the court shall also rule on the motion for a new trial, if any, by determining whether it should be granted if the judgment is thereafter vacated or

* Proposed amendments to Rule 50 are found in Part X of this Supplement.

reversed, and shall specify the grounds for granting or denying the motion for the new trial. If the motion for a new trial is thus conditionally granted, the order thereon does not affect the finality of the judgment. In case the motion for a new trial has been conditionally granted and the judgment is reversed on appeal, the new trial shall proceed unless the appellate court has otherwise ordered. In case the motion for a new trial has been conditionally denied, the appellee on appeal may assert error in that denial; and if the judgment is reversed on appeal, subsequent proceedings shall be in accordance with the order of the appellate court.

(2) The party against whom judgment as a matter of law has been rendered may serve a motion for a new trial pursuant to Rule 59 not later than 10 days after entry of the judgment.

(d) Same: Denial of Motion for Judgment as a Matter of Law. If the motion for judgment as a matter of law is denied, the party who prevailed on that motion may, as appellee, assert grounds entitling the party to a new trial in the event the appellate court concludes that the trial court erred in denying the motion for judgment. If the appellate court reverses the judgment, nothing in this rule precludes it from determining that the appellee is entitled to a new trial, or from directing the trial court to determine whether a new trial shall be granted.

Comparative State Provisions and Notes on Amendments to Federal Rule 50

(a) *Rules 50(a) and (b)—Comparative State Provisions*

New York Civil Practice Law and Rules 4404(a)

After a trial of a cause of action or issue triable of right by a jury, upon the motion of any party or on its own initiative, the court may set aside a verdict or any judgment entered thereon and direct that judgment be entered in favor of a party entitled to judgment as a matter of law or it may order a new trial of a cause of action or separable issue where the verdict is contrary to the weight of the evidence, in the interest of justice or where the jury cannot agree after being kept together for as long as is deemed reasonable by the court.

Indiana Rules of Trial Procedure, Trial Rule 50

(A) Where all or some of the issues in a case tried before a jury or an advisory jury are not supported by sufficient evidence or a verdict thereon is clearly erroneous as contrary to the evidence because the evidence is insufficient to support it, the court shall withdraw such issues from the jury and enter judgment thereon or shall enter judgment thereon notwithstanding a verdict. * * *

(B) Every case tried by a jury is made subject to the right of the court, before or after the jury is discharged, to enter final judgment on the evidence, without directing a verdict thereon.

(b) *Notes on Amendments in 1963 Adding Rules 50(c) and (d)*

The Advisory Committee commented on Rules 50(c) and (d), which were added in 1963, as follows:

Subdivision (c) deals with the situation where a party joins a motion for a new trial with his motion for judgment n.o.v., or prays for a new trial in the alternative, and the motion for judgment n.o.v. is granted. The procedure to be followed in making rulings on the motion for the new trial, and the consequences of the rulings thereon, were partly set out in *Montgomery Ward & Co. v. Duncan,* 311 U.S. 243, 253, 61 S.Ct. 189, 85 L.Ed. 147 (1940), and have been further elaborated in later cases. * * * However, courts as well as counsel have often misunderstood the procedure, and it will be helpful to summarize the proper practice in the text of the rule. The amendments do not alter the effects of a jury verdict or the scope of appellate review.

In the situation mentioned, *subdivision (c)(1)* requires that the court make a "conditional" ruling on the new-trial motion, *i.e.,* a ruling which goes on the assumption that the motion for judgment n. o. v. was erroneously granted and will be reversed or vacated; and the court is required to state its grounds for the conditional ruling. Subdivision (c)(1) then spells out the consequences of a reversal of the judgment in the light of the conditional ruling on the new-trial motion.

If the motion for new trial has been conditionally granted, and the judgment is reversed, "the new trial shall proceed unless the appellate court has otherwise ordered." The party against whom the judgment n.o.v. was entered below may, as appellant, besides seeking to overthrow that judgment, also attack the conditional grant of the new trial. And the appellate court, if it reverses the judgment n. o. v., may in an appropriate case also reverse the conditional grant of the new trial and direct that judgment be entered on the verdict. * * *

If the motion for a new trial has been conditionally denied, and the judgment is reversed, "subsequent proceedings shall be in accordance with the order of the appellate court." The party in whose favor judgment n. o. v. was entered below may, as appellee, besides seeking to uphold that judgment, also urge on the appellate court that the trial court committed error in conditionally denying the new trial. The appellee may assert this error in his brief, without taking a cross-appeal. * * * If the appellate court concludes that the judgment cannot stand, but accepts the appellee's contention that there was error in the conditional denial of the new trial, it may order a new trial in lieu of directing the entry of judgment upon the verdict.

Subdivision (c)(2), which also deals with the situation where the trial court has granted the motion for judgment n. o. v., states that the verdict-winner may apply to the trial court for a new trial pursuant to Rule 59 after the judgment n. o. v. has been entered against him. In arguing to the trial court in opposition to the motion for judgment n. o. v., the verdict-winner may, and often will, contend that he is entitled, at the least, to a new trial, and the court has a range of discretion to grant a new trial or (where plaintiff won the verdict) to order a dismissal of the action without prejudice instead of granting judgment n. o. v. * * *

Subdivision (d) deals with the situation where judgment has been entered on the jury verdict, the motion for judgment n. o. v. and any motion for a new trial having been denied by the trial court. The verdict-winner, as appellee, besides seeking to uphold the judgment, may urge upon the appellate court that in case the trial court is found to have erred in entering judgment on the verdict, there are grounds for granting him a new trial instead of directing the entry of judgment for his opponent. In appropriate cases the appellate court is not precluded from itself directing that a new trial be had. * * *

Rule 51. Instructions to Jury: Objection

At the close of the evidence or at such earlier time during the trial as the court reasonably directs, any party may file written requests that the court instruct the jury on the law as set forth in the requests. The court shall inform counsel of its proposed action upon the requests prior to their arguments to the jury. The court, at its election, may instruct the jury before or after argument, or both. No party may assign as error the giving or the failure to give an instruction unless that party objects thereto before the jury retires to consider its verdict, stating distinctly the matter objected to and the grounds of the objection. Opportunity shall be given to make the objection out of the hearing of the jury.

Notes on Amendment to Federal Rule 51 and Comparative State Provisions

(a) *1987 Amendment to Federal Rule 51*

In 1987, on recommendation of the Advisory Committee, Rule 51 was amended to give the court discretion to instruct the jury either before or after the argument. See generally Raymond, *Merits and Demerits of the Missouri System of Instructing Juries*, 5 St. Louis U.L.J. 317 (1959).

(b) *Comparative State Provisions*

Georgia Code Annotated § 5-5-24

(a) Except as otherwise provided in this Code section, in all civil cases, no party may complain of the giving or the failure to give an instruction to the jury unless he objects thereto before the jury returns its verdict, stating distinctly the matter to which he objects and the grounds of his objection. Opportunity shall be given to make the objection out of the hearing of the jury. Objection need not be made with the particularity formerly required of assignments of error and need only be as reasonably definite as the circumstances will permit. * * *

(b) In all cases, at the close of the evidence or at such earlier time during the trial as the court reasonably directs, any party may present to the court written requests that it instruct the jury on the law as set forth therein. Copies of requests shall be given to opposing counsel for their consideration prior to the charge of the court. The court shall inform counsel of its proposed action upon the requests prior to their arguments to the jury but shall instruct the jury after the arguments are completed. The trial judge shall file with the clerk all requests submitted to him, whether given in charge or not.

(c) Notwithstanding any other provision of this Code section, the appellate courts shall consider and review erroneous charges where there has been a substantial error in the charge which was harmful as a matter of law, regardless of whether objection was made hereunder or not.

Minnesota Rule of Civil Procedure 51

At the close of the evidence or at such earlier time during the trial as the court reasonably directs, any party may file written requests that the court instruct the jury on the law as set forth in the requests. The court shall inform the counsel of its proposed action upon the requests prior to their arguments to the jury, and such action shall be made a part of the record. The court shall instruct the jury before or after closing arguments of counsel except, in the discretion of the court, preliminary instructions need not be repeated. The instructions may be in writing and, in the discretion of the court, one complete copy may be taken to the jury room when the jury retires to deliberate. No party may assign as error unintentional misstatements and verbal errors or omissions in the charge, unless that party objects thereto before the jury retires to consider its verdict, stating specifically the matter to which he objects and the ground of his objections. An error in the instructions with respect to fundamental law or controlling principle may be assigned in a motion for a new trial though it was not otherwise called to the attention of the court.

Mississippi Code Annotated § 11-7-155

The judge in any civil cause shall not sum up or comment on the testimony, or charge the jury as to the weight of evidence.

Illinois Supreme Court Rule 239

(a) Use of IPI Instructions; Requirements of Other Instructions.
Whenever Illinois Pattern Jury Instructions (IPI) contains an instruction applica-

ble in a civil case, giving due consideration to the facts and the prevailing law, and the court determines that the jury should be instructed on the subject, the IPI instruction shall be used, unless the court determines that it does not accurately state the law. Whenever IPI does not contain an instruction on a subject on which the court determines that the jury should be instructed, the instruction given on that subject should be simple, brief, impartial, and free from argument.

(b) **Court's Instructions.** At any time before or during the trial, the court may direct counsel to prepare designated instructions. Counsel shall comply with the direction and copies of instructions so prepared shall be marked "Court's Instruction." Counsel may object at the conference on instructions to any instruction prepared at the court's direction, regardless of who prepared it, and the court shall rule on these objections as well as objections to other instructions. The grounds of the objections shall be particularly specified.

(c) **Procedure.** Each instruction shall be accompanied by a copy and a copy shall be delivered to opposing counsel. In addition to numbering the copies and indicating who tendered them, as required by section 2-1107 of the Code of Civil Procedure, the copy shall contain a notation substantially as follows:

"IPI No. _____" or "IPI No. _____ Modified" or "Not in IPI" as the case may be. All objections made at the conference and the rulings thereon shall be shown in the report of proceedings.

Rule 52. Findings by the Court; Judgment on Partial Findings*

(a) **Effect.** In all actions tried upon the facts without a jury or with an advisory jury, the court shall find the facts specially and state separately its conclusions of law thereon, and judgment shall be entered pursuant to Rule 58; and in granting or refusing interlocutory injunctions the court shall similarly set forth the findings of fact and conclusions of law which constitute the grounds of its action. Requests for findings are not necessary for purposes of review. Findings of fact, whether based on oral or documentary evidence, shall not be set aside unless clearly erroneous, and due regard shall be given to the opportunity of the trial court to judge of the credibility of the witnesses. The findings of a master, to the extent that the court adopts them, shall be considered as the findings of the court. It will be sufficient if the findings of fact and conclusions of law are stated orally and recorded in open court following the close of the evidence or appear in an opinion or memorandum of decision filed by the court. Findings of fact and conclusions of law are unnecessary on decisions of motions under Rules 12 or 56 or any other motion except as provided in subdivision (c) of this rule.

(b) **Amendment.** Upon motion of a party made not later than 10 days after entry of judgment the court may amend its findings or make additional findings and may amend the judgment accordingly. The motion may be made with a motion for a new trial pursuant to Rule 59. When findings of fact are made in actions tried by the court without a jury, the question of the sufficiency of the evidence to support the findings may thereafter be raised whether or not the party raising the question has made in the district court an objection to such findings or has made a motion to amend them or a motion for judgment.

---

* Proposed amendments to Rule 52 are found in Part X of this Supplement.

(c) Judgment on Partial Findings. If during a trial without a jury a party has been fully heard on an issue and the court finds against the party on that issue, the court may enter judgment as a matter of law against that party with respect to a claim or defense that cannot under the controlling law be maintained or defeated without a favorable finding on that issue, or the court may decline to render any judgment until the close of all the evidence. Such a judgment shall be supported by findings of fact and conclusions of law as required by subdivision (a) of this rule.

Notes on Amendments to Rule 52 and Comparative State Provisions

(a) *Amendment in 1985*

The purpose of the 1985 amendment was to make certain that the "clearly erroneous" standard applies when the trial court's decision is based solely on documentary evidence as well as when it is based on oral testimony. Previously, appellate courts were divided on the matter, some holding that the scope of review is broader when witness credibility is not involved. The change was designed to support the integrity of the trial court's findings of fact, thus to promote judicial economy by discouraging retrial at the appellate level.

(b) *Amendment in 1983*

Rule 52(a) was amended to provide explicitly that the district judge may make the findings of fact and conclusions of law required in nonjury cases orally. The objective is to lighten the burden on the trial court in preparing findings in nonjury cases. It should also reduce the number of published district court opinions that embrace written findings.

(c) *Comparative State Provision*

Oklahoma Statutes Annotated Tit. 12, § 611

Upon the trial of questions of fact by the court, it shall not be necessary for the court to state its findings, except generally, for the plaintiff or defendant, unless one of the parties request it, with the view of excepting to the decision of the court upon the questions of law involved in the trial; in which case the court shall state, in writing, the findings of fact found, separately from the conclusions of law.

Rule 53. Masters

(a) Appointment and Compensation. The court in which any action is pending may appoint a special master therein. As used in these rules the word "master" includes a referee, an auditor, an examiner, and an assessor. The compensation to be allowed to a master shall be fixed by the court, and shall be charged upon such of the parties or paid out of any fund or subject matter of the action, which is in the custody and control of the court as the court may direct; provided that this provision for compensation shall not apply when a United States magistrate judge is designated to serve as a master. The master shall not retain the master's report as security for the master's compensation; but when the party ordered to pay the compensation allowed by the court does not pay it after notice and within the time prescribed by the court, the master is entitled to a writ of execution against the delinquent party.

(b) Reference. A reference to a master shall be the exception and not the rule. In actions to be tried by a jury, a reference shall be made only when the issues are complicated; in actions to be tried without a jury, save in matters of account and of difficult computation of damages, a reference shall be made only upon a showing that some exceptional condition requires it. Upon the consent of the parties, a magistrate judge may be designated to serve as a special master without regard to the provisions of this subdivision.

(c) Powers. The order of reference to the master may specify or limit the master's powers and may direct the master to report only upon particular issues or to do or perform particular acts or to receive and report evidence only and may fix the time and place for beginning and closing the hearings and for the filing of the master's report. Subject to the specifications and limitations stated in the order, the master has and shall exercise the power to regulate all proceedings in every hearing before the master and to do all acts and take all measures necessary or proper for the efficient performance of the master's duties under the order. The master may require the production before the master of evidence upon all matters embraced in the reference, including the production of all books, papers, vouchers, documents, and writings applicable thereto. The master may rule upon the admissibility of evidence unless otherwise directed by the order of reference and has the authority to put witnesses on oath and may examine them and may call the parties to the action and examine them upon oath. When a party so requests, the master shall make a record of the evidence offered and excluded in the same manner and subject to the same limitations as provided in the Federal Rules of Evidence for a court sitting without a jury.

(d) Proceedings.

(1) *Meetings.* When a reference is made, the clerk shall forthwith furnish the master with a copy of the order of reference. Upon receipt thereof unless the order of reference otherwise provides, the master shall forthwith set a time and place for the first meeting of the parties or their attorneys to be held within 20 days after the date of the order of reference and shall notify the parties or their attorneys. It is the duty of the master to proceed with all reasonable diligence. Either party, on notice to the parties and master, may apply to the court for an order requiring the master to speed the proceedings and to make the report. If a party fails to appear at the time and place appointed, the master may proceed ex parte or, in the master's discretion, adjourn the proceedings to a future day, giving notice to the absent party of the adjournment.

(2) *Witnesses.* The parties may procure the attendance of witnesses before the master by the issuance and service of subpoenas as provided in Rule 45. If without adequate excuse a witness fails to appear or give

evidence, the witness may be punished as for a contempt and be subjected to the consequences, penalties, and remedies provided in Rules 37 and 45.

(3) *Statement of Accounts.* When matters of accounting are in issue before the master, the master may prescribe the form in which the accounts shall be submitted and in any proper case may require or receive in evidence a statement by a certified public accountant who is called as a witness. Upon objection of a party to any of the items thus submitted or upon a showing that the form of statement is insufficient, the master may require a different form of statement to be furnished, or the accounts or specific items thereof to be proved by oral examination of the accounting parties or upon written interrogatories or in such other manner as the master directs.

(e) Report.

(1) *Contents and Filing.* The master shall prepare a report upon the matters submitted to the master by the order of reference and, if required to make findings of fact and conclusions of law, the master shall set them forth in the report. The master shall file the report with the clerk of the court and serve on all parties notice of the filing. In an action to be tried without a jury, unless otherwise directed by the order of reference, the master shall file with the report a transcript of the proceedings and of the evidence and the original exhibits. Unless otherwise directed by the order of reference, the master shall serve a copy of the report on each party.

(2) *In Non-jury Actions.* In an action to be tried without a jury the court shall accept the master's findings of fact unless clearly erroneous. Within 10 days after being served with notice of the filing of the report any party may serve written objections thereto upon the other parties. Application to the court for action upon the report and upon objections thereto shall be by motion and upon notice as prescribed in Rule 6(d). The court after hearing may adopt the report or may modify it or may reject it in whole or in part or may receive further evidence or may recommit it with instructions.

(3) *In Jury Actions.* In an action to be tried by a jury the master shall not be directed to report the evidence. The master's findings upon the issues submitted to the master are admissible as evidence of the matters found and may be read to the jury, subject to the ruling of the court upon any objections in point of law which may be made to the report.

(4) *Stipulation as to Findings.* The effect of a master's report is the same whether or not the parties have consented to the reference; but, when the parties stipulate that a master's findings of fact shall be final, only questions of law arising upon the report shall thereafter be considered.

Rule 53. RULES OF CIVIL PROCEDURE

(5) *Draft Report.* Before filing the master's report a master may submit a draft thereof to counsel for all parties for the purpose of receiving their suggestions.

(f) Application to Magistrate Judge. A magistrate judge is subject to this rule only when the order referring a matter to the magistrate judge expressly provides that the reference is made under this Rule.

Amendments to Rule 53 and Comparative State Provisions

(a) *Amendments in 1983 to Rule 53*

Because the federal courts now have full time magistrates, serving at government expense, the changes eliminated as unnecessary a clause of the first sentence in Rule 53(a) providing for "standing masters."

In addition Rule 53(b) was altered to provide that upon consent of the parties a magistrate may be appointed to serve as a special master even though "exceptional circumstances" do not exist. The latter requirement would still apply to appointment of others for whose services the parties would be required to pay.

The new subdivision (f) responded to the confusion resulting from the dual authority for references of pretrial matters to magistrates. Under the rule, the appointment of a master, without consent of the parties, to supervise discovery would require some exceptional condition (Rule 53(b)) and would subject the proceedings to the report procedures of Rule 53(e). This subdivision, therefore, establishes a presumption that the limitations of Rule 53 are not applicable unless the reference is specifically made subject to Rule 53.

(b) *Comparative State Provisions*

(1) *Rules 53(a) and (b)*

New York Civil Practice Law and Rules 4317

(a) Upon consent of the parties. The parties may stipulate that any issue shall be determined by a referee. Upon the filing of the stipulation with the clerk, the clerk shall forthwith enter an order referring the issue for trial to the referee named therein. * * *

(b) Without consent of the parties. On motion of any party or on its own initiative, the court may order a reference to determine a cause of action or an issue where the trial will require the examination of a long account, including actions to foreclose mechanic's liens; or to determine an issue of damages separately triable and not requiring a trial by jury; or where otherwise authorized by law.

(2) *Rules 53(c)(2) and (3)*

New Jersey Civil Practice Rule 4:41-5(b) & (c)

(b) In an action to be tried without a jury the court shall accept the master's findings of fact unless contrary to the weight of the evidence. * * *

(c) In an action to be tried by a jury the findings of the master upon the issues submitted to him are admissible as evidence of the matters found, and may together with the evidence taken before the master be read to the jury, subject to the ruling of the court upon objections to the report or the evidence.

VII. JUDGMENT

Rule 54. Judgments; Costs

(a) Definition; Form. "Judgment" as used in these rules includes a decree and any order from which an appeal lies. A judgment shall not contain a recital of pleadings, the report of a master, or the record of prior proceedings.

(b) Judgment Upon Multiple Claims or Involving Multiple Parties. When more than one claim for relief is presented in an action, whether as a claim, counterclaim, cross-claim, or third-party claim, or when multiple parties are involved, the court may direct the entry of a final judgment as to one or more but fewer than all of the claims or parties only upon an express determination that there is no just reason for delay and upon an express direction for the entry of judgment. In the absence of such determination and direction, any order or other form of decision, however designated, which adjudicates fewer than all the claims or the rights and liabilities of fewer than all the parties shall not terminate the action as to any of the claims or parties, and the order or other form of decision is subject to revision at any time before the entry of judgment adjudicating all the claims and the rights and liabilities of all the parties.

(c) Demand for Judgment. A judgment by default shall not be different in kind from or exceed in amount that prayed for in the demand for judgment. Except as to a party against whom a judgment is entered by default, every final judgment shall grant the relief to which the party in whose favor it is rendered is entitled, even if the party has not demanded such relief in the party's pleadings.

(d) Costs; Attorneys' Fees.

(1) *Costs Other Than Attorneys' Fees.* Except when express provision therefor is made either in a statute of the United States or in these rules, costs other than attorneys' fees shall be allowed as of course to the prevailing party unless the court otherwise directs; but costs against the United States, its officers, and agencies shall be imposed only to the extent permitted by law. Such costs may be taxed by the clerk on one day's notice. On motion served within 5 days thereafter, the action of the clerk may be reviewed by the court.

(2) *Attorneys' Fees.*

(A) Claims for attorneys' fees and related nontaxable expenses shall be made by motion unless the substantive law governing the action provides for the recovery of such fees as an element of damages to be proved at trial.

(B) Unless otherwise provided by statute or order of the court, the motion must be filed and served no later than 14 days after the entry of judgment; must specify the judgment and the statute, rule, or other grounds entitling the moving party to the award; and must state the amount or provide a fair estimate of the amount sought. If directed by the court, the motion shall also disclose the terms of any agreement with respect to fees to be paid for the services for which the claim is made.

Rule 54   RULES OF CIVIL PROCEDURE

(C) On request of a party or class member, the court shall afford an opportunity for adversary submissions with respect to the motion in accordance with Rule 43(e) or Rule 78. The court may determine issues of liability for fees before receiving submissions bearing on issues of evaluation of services for which liability is imposed by the court. The court shall find the facts and state its conclusions of law as provided in Rule 52(a), and a judgment shall be set forth in a separate document as provided in Rule 58.

(D) By local rule the court may establish special procedures by which issues relating to such fees may be resolved without extensive evidentiary hearings. In addition, the court may refer issues relating to the value of services to a special master under Rule 53 without regard to the provisions of subdivision (b) thereof and may refer a motion for attorneys' fees to a magistrate judge under Rule 72(b) as if it were a dispositive pretrial matter.

(E) The provisions of subparagraphs (A) through (D) do not apply to claims for fees and expenses as sanctions for violations of these rules or under 28 U.S.C. § 1927.

Notes on Amendments to Federal Rule 54 and Comparative State Provisions

(a) *Amendments in 1948 to Rule 54(b)*

Rule 54(b) originally read as follows:

When more than one claim for relief is presented in an action, the court at any stage, upon a determination of the issues material to a particular claim and all counterclaims arising out of the transaction or occurrence which is the subject matter of the claim, may enter a judgment disposing of such claim. The judgment shall terminate the action with respect to the claim so disposed of and the action shall proceed as to the remaining claims. In case a separate judgment is so entered, the court by order may stay its enforcement until the entering of a subsequent judgment or judgments and may prescribe such conditions as are necessary to secure the benefit thereof to the party in whose favor the judgment is entered.

In 1946 the Advisory Committee commented as follows on proposed amendments to the Rule which were promulgated in 1948:

The historic rule in the federal courts has always prohibited piecemeal disposal of litigation * * *. Rule 54(b) was originally adopted in view of the wide scope and possible content of the newly created "civil action" in order to avoid the possible injustice of a delay in judgment of a distinctly separate claim to await adjudication of the entire case. It was not designed to overturn the settled federal rule stated above * * *.

Unfortunately, this was not always understood, and some confusion ensued. Hence situations arose where district courts made a piecemeal disposition of an action and entered what the parties thought amounted to a judgment, although a trial remained to be had on other claims similar or identical with those disposed of. In the interim the parties did not know their ultimate rights, and accordingly took an appeal, thus putting the finality of the partial judgment in question. While most appellate courts have reached a result generally in accord with the intent of the rule, yet there have been divergent precedents and division of views which have served to render the issues more clouded to the parties appellant. It hardly seems a case where multiplicity of precedents will tend to remove the problem from debate. * * *

In view of the difficulty thus disclosed, the Advisory Committee * * * attempted to redefine the original rule with particular stress upon the interlocutory nature of partial judgments which did not adjudicate all claims arising out of a single transaction or occurrence. * * * The Committee, however, became convinced on careful study of its own proposals that the seeds of ambiguity still remained, and that it had not completely solved the problem of piecemeal appeals. After extended consideration, it concluded that a retention of the older federal rule was desirable, and that this rule needed only the exercise of a discretionary power to afford a remedy in the infrequent harsh case to provide a simple, definite, workable rule. * * *

In 1961 the Advisory Committee again commented as follows:

A serious difficulty has * * * arisen because the rule speaks of claims but nowhere mentions parties. A line of cases had developed in the circuits consistently holding the rule to be inapplicable to the dismissal, even with the requisite trial court determination, of one or more but fewer than all defendants jointly charged in an action, *i.e.,* charged with various forms of concerted or related wrongdoing or related liability. * * * For purposes of Rule 54(b) it was arguable that there were as many "claims" as there were parties defendant and that the rule in its present text applied where fewer than all of the parties were dismissed, * * * but the Courts of Appeals are now committed to an opposite view.

* * *

(b) *Comparative State Provisions*

1. *Rule 54(b)*

Texas Rule of Civil Procedure 301

* * * Only one final judgment shall be rendered in any cause except where it is otherwise specially provided by law. Judgment may, in a proper case, be given for or against one or more of several plaintiffs, and for or against one or more of several defendants or intervenors.

2. *Rule 54(c)*

Georgia Code Annotated § 9–11–54(c)(1)

A judgment by default shall not be different in kind from or exceed in amount that prayed for in the demand for judgment. Except as to a party against whom a judgment is entered by default, every final judgment shall grant the relief to which the party in whose favor it is rendered is entitled, even if the party has not demanded such relief in his pleadings; but the court shall not give the successful party relief, though he may be entitled to it, where the propriety of the relief was not litigated and the opposing party had no opportunity to assert defenses to such relief.

Rule 55. Default

(a) Entry. When a party against whom a judgment for affirmative relief is sought has failed to plead or otherwise defend as provided by these rules and that fact is made to appear by affidavit or otherwise, the clerk shall enter the party's default.

(b) Judgment. Judgment by default may be entered as follows:

(1) *By the Clerk.* When the plaintiff's claim against a defendant is for a sum certain or for a sum which can by computation be made certain, the clerk upon request of the plaintiff and upon affidavit of the amount due shall enter judgment for that amount and costs against the

defendant, if the defendant has been defaulted for failure to appear and is not an infant or incompetent person.

(2) *By the Court.* In all other cases the party entitled to a judgment by default shall apply to the court therefor; but no judgment by default shall be entered against an infant or incompetent person unless represented in the action by a general guardian, committee, conservator, or other such representative who has appeared therein. If the party against whom judgment by default is sought has appeared in the action, the party (or, if appearing by representative, the party's representative) shall be served with written notice of the application for judgment at least 3 days prior to the hearing on such application. If, in order to enable the court to enter judgment or to carry it into effect, it is necessary to take an account or to determine the amount of damages or to establish the truth of any averment by evidence or to make an investigation of any other matter, the court may conduct such hearings or order such references as it deems necessary and proper and shall accord a right of trial by jury to the parties when and as required by any statute of the United States.

(c) Setting Aside Default. For good cause shown the court may set aside an entry of default and, if a judgment by default has been entered, may likewise set it aside in accordance with Rule 60(b).

(d) Plaintiffs, Counterclaimants, Cross-Claimants. The provisions of this rule apply whether the party entitled to the judgment by default is a plaintiff, a third-party plaintiff, or a party who has pleaded a cross-claim or counterclaim. In all cases a judgment by default is subject to the limitations of Rule 54(c).

(e) Judgment Against the United States. No judgment by default shall be entered against the United States or an officer or agency thereof unless the claimant establishes a claim or right to relief by evidence satisfactory to the court.

Comparative State Provision

Florida Rule of Civil Procedure 1.500

(a) By the Clerk. When a party against whom affirmative relief is sought has failed to file or serve any paper in the action, the party seeking relief may have the clerk enter a default against the party failing to serve or file such paper.

(b) By the Court. When a party against whom affirmative relief is sought has failed to plead or otherwise defend as provided by these rules or any applicable statute or any order of court, the court may enter a default against such party; provided that if such party has filed or served any paper in the action, he shall be served with notice of the application for default.

(c) Right to Plead. A party may plead or otherwise defend at any time before default is entered. If a party in default files any paper after the default is entered, the clerk shall notify the party of the entry of the default. * * *

(d) Setting Aside Default. The court may set aside a default and if a final judgment consequent thereon has been entered, the court may set it aside in accordance with Rule 1.540(b).

(e) Final Judgment. Final judgments after default may be entered by the court at any time but no judgment may be entered against an infant or incompetent person unless represented in the action by a general guardian, committee, conservator or other representative who has appeared * * *. If it is necessary to take an account or to determine the amount of damages or to establish the truth of any averment by evidence or to make an investigation of any other matter to enable the court to enter judgment or to effectuate it, the court may receive affidavits, make references or conduct hearings as it deems necessary and shall accord a right of trial by jury to the parties when required by the Constitution or any statute.

Rule 56. Summary Judgment

(a) For Claimant. A party seeking to recover upon a claim, counterclaim, or cross-claim or to obtain a declaratory judgment may, at any time after the expiration of 20 days from the commencement of the action or after service of a motion for summary judgment by the adverse party, move with or without supporting affidavits for a summary judgment in the party's favor upon all or any part thereof.

(b) For Defending Party. A party against whom a claim, counterclaim, or cross-claim is asserted or a declaratory judgment is sought may, at any time, move with or without supporting affidavits for a summary judgment in the party's favor as to all or any part thereof.

(c) Motion and Proceedings Thereon. The motion shall be served at least 10 days before the time fixed for the hearing. The adverse party prior to the day of hearing may serve opposing affidavits. The judgment sought shall be rendered forthwith if the pleadings, depositions, answers to interrogatories, and admissions on file, together with the affidavits, if any, show that there is no genuine issue as to any material fact and that the moving party is entitled to a judgment as a matter of law. A summary judgment, interlocutory in character, may be rendered on the issue of liability alone although there is a genuine issue as to the amount of damages.

(d) Case Not Fully Adjudicated on Motion. If on motion under this rule judgment is not rendered upon the whole case or for all the relief asked and a trial is necessary, the court at the hearing of the motion, by examining the pleadings and the evidence before it and by interrogating counsel, shall if practicable ascertain what material facts exist without substantial controversy and what material facts are actually and in good faith controverted. It shall thereupon make an order specifying the facts that appear without substantial controversy, including the extent to which the amount of damages or other relief is not in controversy, and directing such further proceedings in the action as are just. Upon the trial of the action the facts so specified shall be deemed established, and the trial shall be conducted accordingly.

(e) Form of Affidavits; Further Testimony; Defense Required. Supporting and opposing affidavits shall be made on personal knowledge, shall set forth such facts as would be admissible in evidence, and shall show affirmatively that the affiant is competent to testify to

Rule 56   RULES OF CIVIL PROCEDURE

the matters stated therein. Sworn or certified copies of all papers or parts thereof referred to in an affidavit shall be attached thereto or served therewith. The court may permit affidavits to be supplemented or opposed by depositions, answers to interrogatories, or further affidavits. When a motion for summary judgment is made and supported as provided in this rule, an adverse party may not rest upon the mere allegations or denials of the adverse party's pleading, but the adverse party's response, by affidavits or as otherwise provided in this rule, must set forth specific facts showing that there is a genuine issue for trial. If the adverse party does not so respond, summary judgment, if appropriate, shall be entered against the adverse party.

(f) When Affidavits Are Unavailable. Should it appear from the affidavits of a party opposing the motion that the party cannot for reasons stated present by affidavit facts essential to justify the party's opposition, the court may refuse the application for judgment or may order a continuance to permit affidavits to be obtained or depositions to be taken or discovery to be had or may make such other order as is just.

(g) Affidavits Made in Bad Faith. Should it appear to the satisfaction of the court at any time that any of the affidavits presented pursuant to this rule are presented in bad faith or solely for the purpose of delay, the court shall forthwith order the party employing them to pay to the other party the amount of the reasonable expenses which the filing of the affidavits caused the other party to incur, including reasonable attorney's fees, and any offending party or attorney may be adjudged guilty of contempt.

Comparative State Provisions and Notes on Amendments and Proposed Amendments to Federal Rule 56

(a) *Comparative State Provisions*

California Civil Procedure Code § 437c

(a) Any party may move for summary judgment in any action or proceeding if it is contended that the action has no merit or that there is no defense thereto. The motion may be made at any time after 60 days have elapsed since the general appearance in the action or proceeding of each party against whom the motion is directed or at such earlier time after the general appearance as the court * * * may direct. Notice of the motion and supporting papers shall be served on all other parties to the action at least 28 days before the time appointed for hearing. However, if the notice is served by mail, the required 28-day period of notice shall be increased by five days if the place of address is within the State of California, 10 days if the place of address is outside the State of California but within the United States, and 20 days if the place of address is outside the United States. The motion shall be heard no later than 30 days before the date of trial, unless the court for good cause orders otherwise. The filing of such motion shall not extend the time within which a party must otherwise file a responsive pleading.

(b) The motion shall be supported by affidavits, declarations, admissions, answers to interrogatories, depositions and matters of which judicial notice shall or may be taken. The supporting papers shall include a separate statement setting forth plainly and concisely all material facts which the moving party contends are undisputed. Each of the material facts stated shall be followed by a reference to the supporting evidence. The failure to comply with this requirement of a separate statement may in the court's discretion constitute a sufficient ground for denial of the motion.

Any opposition to the motion shall be served and filed not less than 14 days preceding the noticed or continued date of hearing, unless the court for good cause orders otherwise. The opposition, where appropriate, shall consist of affidavits, declarations, admissions, answers to interrogatories, depositions and matters of which judicial notice shall or may be taken. The opposition papers shall include a separate statement which responds to each of the material facts contended by the moving party to be undisputed, indicating whether the opposing party agrees or disagrees that those facts are undisputed. The statement also shall set forth plainly and concisely any other material facts which the opposing party contends are disputed. Each material fact contended by the opposing party to be disputed shall be followed by a reference to the supporting evidence. Failure to comply with this requirement of a separate statement may constitute a sufficient ground, in the court's discretion, for granting the motion.

Any reply to the opposition shall be served and filed by the moving party not less than five days preceding the noticed or continued date of hearing, unless the court for good cause orders otherwise.

Evidentiary objections not made at the hearing shall be deemed waived.

Section 1005 and subdivision (a) of Section 1013, extending the time within which a right may be exercised or an act may be done, do not apply to this section.

Any incorporation by reference of matter in the court's file shall set forth with specificity the exact matter to which reference is being made and shall not incorporate the entire file.

(c) The motion for summary judgment shall be granted if all the papers submitted show that there is no triable issue as to any material fact and that the moving party is entitled to a judgment as a matter of law. In determining whether the papers show that there is no triable issue as to any material fact the court shall consider all of the evidence set forth in the papers, except that to which objections have been made and sustained by the court, and all inferences reasonably deducible from the evidence, except summary judgment shall not be granted by the court based on inferences reasonably deducible from the evidence, if contradicted by other inferences or evidence, which raise a triable issue as to any material fact.

(d) Supporting and opposing affidavits or declarations shall be made by any person on personal knowledge, shall set forth admissible evidence, and shall show affirmatively that the affiant is competent to testify to the matters stated therein. Any objections based on the failure to comply with the requirements of this subdivision shall be made at the hearing or shall be deemed waived.

(e) If a party is otherwise entitled to a summary judgment pursuant to this section, summary judgment shall not be denied on grounds of credibility or for want of cross-examination of witnesses furnishing affidavits or declarations in support of the summary judgment, except that summary judgment may be denied in the discretion of the court, where the only proof of a material fact offered in support of the summary judgment is an affidavit or declaration made by an individual who was the sole witness to that fact; or where a material fact is an individual's state of mind, or lack thereof, and that fact is sought to be established solely by the individual's affirmation thereof.

(f) If it is contended that one or more causes of action within an action has no merit or that there is no defense thereto, or that there is no merit to an affirmative defense as to any cause of action, or both, or that there is no merit to a claim for damages, as specified in Section 3294 of the Civil Code, or that one or more defendants either owed or did not owe a duty to the plaintiff or plaintiffs, any party may move for summary adjudication as to that cause or causes of action, that affirmative defense, that claim for damages, or that issue of duty. A cause of action has no merit if one or more of the elements of the cause of action, even if not separately pleaded, cannot be established. A motion may be made by itself or as an alternative to a motion for summary judgment and shall proceed in all procedural respects as a motion for summary judgment. However, a party may not move for summary judgment based on issues asserted in a prior motion for summary adjudication and denied by the court, unless that party establishes to the satisfaction of the court, newly discovered facts or circumstances supporting the issues reasserted in the summary judgment motion.

(g) Upon the denial of a motion for summary judgment, on the ground that there is a triable issue as to one or more material facts, the court shall, by written or oral order, specify one or more material facts raised by the motion as to which the court has determined there exists a triable controversy. This determination shall specifically refer to the evidence proffered in support of and in opposition to the motion which indicates that a triable controversy exists. Upon the grant of a motion for summary judgment, on the ground that there is no triable issue of material fact, the court shall, by written or oral order, specify the reasons for its determination. The order shall specifically refer to the evidence proffered in support of, and if applicable in opposition to, the motion which indicates that no triable issue exists. The court shall also state its reasons for any other determination. The court shall record its determination by court reporter or written order.

(h) If it appears from the affidavits submitted in opposition to a motion for summary judgment or summary adjudication or both that facts essential to justify opposition may exist but cannot, for reasons stated, then be presented, the court shall deny the motion, or order a continuance to permit affidavits to be obtained or discovery to be had or may make any other order as may be just.

(i) If the court determines at any time that any of the affidavits are presented in bad faith or solely for purposes of delay, the court shall order the party presenting the affidavits to pay the other party the amount of the reasonable expenses which the filing of the affidavits caused the other party to incur. Sanctions shall not be imposed pursuant to this subdivision except on notice contained in a party's papers, or on the court's own noticed motion, and after an opportunity to be heard.

(j) Except where a separate judgment may properly be awarded in the action, no final judgment shall be entered on a motion for summary judgment prior to the termination of such action, but the final judgment shall, in addition to any matters determined in the action, award judgment as established by the summary proceeding herein provided for.

(k) In actions which arise out of an injury to the person or to property, when a motion for summary judgment was granted on the basis that the defendant was without fault, no other defendant during trial, over plaintiff's objection, may attempt to attribute fault to or comment on the absence or involvement of the defendant who was granted the motion.

(*l*) A summary judgment entered under this section is an appealable judgment as in other cases. Upon entry of any order pursuant to this section except the entry of summary judgment, a party may, within 20 days after service upon him or her of a written notice of entry of the order, petition an appropriate reviewing court for a peremptory writ. If the notice is served by mail, the initial period within which to file the petition shall be increased by five days if the place of address is within the State of California, 10 days if the place of address is outside the State of California but within the United States, and 20 days if the place of address is outside the United States. The superior court may, for good cause, and prior to the expiration of the initial period, extend the time for one additional period not to exceed 10 days.

* * *

(p) Nothing in this section shall be construed to extend the period for trial provided by Section 1170.5.

California Civil Procedure Code § 436

The court may, upon a motion made pursuant to Section 435, or at any time in its discretion, and upon terms it deems proper:

(a) Strike out any irrelevant, false, or improper matter inserted in any pleading.

(b) Strike out all or any part of any pleading not drawn or filed in conformity with the laws of this State, a court rule, or an order of the court.

(b) *Notes on Amendments in 1963 to Rule 56(e)*

The 1963 amendment added the last two sentences to present Rule 56(e). The Advisory Committee's Notes on the alteration read as follows:

The last two sentences are added to overcome a line of cases, chiefly in the Third Circuit, which has impaired the utility of the summary judgment device. A typical case is as follows: A party supports his motion for summary judgment by affidavits or other evidentiary matter sufficient to show that there is no genuine issue as to a material fact. The adverse party, in opposing the motion, does not produce any evidentiary matter, or produces some but not enough to establish that there is a genuine issue for trial. Instead, the adverse party rests on averments of his pleadings which on their face present an issue. In this situation Third Circuit cases have taken the view that summary judgment must be denied, at least if the averments are "well-pleaded," and not supposititious, conclusory, or ultimate.
* * *

The very mission of the summary judgment procedure is to pierce the pleadings and to assess the proof in order to see whether there is a genuine need for trial. The Third Circuit doctrine, which permits the pleadings themselves to stand in the way of granting an otherwise justified summary judgment, is incompatible with the basic purpose of the rule. * * *

It is hoped that the amendment will contribute to the more effective utilization of the salutary device of summary judgment.

The amendment is not intended to derogate from the solemnity of the pleadings. Rather it recognizes that, despite the best efforts of counsel to make his pleadings accurate, they may be overwhelmingly contradicted by the proof available to his adversary.

Nor is the amendment designed to affect the ordinary standards applicable to the summary judgment motion. So, for example: Where an issue as to a material fact cannot be resolved without observation of the demeanor of witnesses in order to evaluate their credibility, summary judgment is not appropriate. Where the evidentiary matter in support of the motion does not establish the absence of a genuine issue, summary judgment must be denied even if no opposing evidentiary matter is presented. And summary judgment may be inappropriate where the party opposing it shows under subdivision (f) that he cannot at the time present facts essential to justify his opposition.

(c) *Proposed Amendments in 1991 to Rule 56*

The proposal involved an extensive rewriting of Rule 56, but generally did not change its basic substance. One significant alteration would have allowed the trial court to "summarily establish as a matter of law any facts that are not genuinely controverted or it may establish law to control further proceedings in an action." At present a court, pursuant to Rule 56(d), may establish the existence of facts, but only if a motion for summary judgment has been made and the court is unable to render judgment on the entire case. There is no current provision with respect to the establishment of law.

A second significant provision would specifically have permitted a party seeking relief, in addition to producing material to support the existence of facts to be established, to make "reference to any absence of probative evidence enabling an opposing party to satisfy a burden of producing evidence or proof." The ability of a party to rely upon the absence of probative evidence by which an opposing party could meet his or her burden of proof was the subject of controversy in the Supreme Court case of Celotex Corp. v. Catrett, 477 U.S. 317, 106 S.Ct. 2548, 91 L.Ed.2d 265 (1986), in which none of the opinions commanded a majority of the Court.

Rule 57. Declaratory Judgments

The procedure for obtaining a declaratory judgment pursuant to Title 28 U.S.C. § 2201, shall be in accordance with these rules, and the right to trial by jury may be demanded under the circumstances and in the manner provided in Rules 38 and 39. The existence of another adequate remedy does not preclude a judgment for declaratory relief in cases where it is appropriate. The court may order a speedy hearing of an action for a declaratory judgment and may advance it on the calendar.

Rule 58. Entry of Judgment

Subject to the provisions of Rule 54(b): (1) upon a general verdict of a jury, or upon a decision by the court that a party shall recover only a sum certain or costs or that all relief shall be denied, the clerk, unless the court otherwise orders, shall forthwith prepare, sign, and enter the judgment without awaiting any direction by the court; (2) upon a decision by the court granting other relief, or upon a special verdict or a general verdict accompanied by answers to interrogatories, the court shall promptly approve the form of the judgment, and the clerk shall thereupon enter it. Every judgment shall be set forth on a separate document. A judgment is effective only when so set forth and when entered as provided in Rule 79(a). Entry of the judgment shall not be delayed, nor the time for appeal extended, in order to tax costs or award fees, except that, when a timely motion for attorneys' fees is made under Rule 54(d)(2), the court, before a notice of appeal has been filed and become effective, may order that the motion have the same effect under 4(a)(4) of the Federal Rules of Appellate Procedure as a timely motion under Rule 59. Attorneys shall not submit forms of judgment except upon direction of the court, and these directions shall not be given as a matter of course.

Notes on 1963 Amendments to Federal Rule 58

Rule 58 as originally promulgated read as follows:

Unless the court otherwise directs and subject to the provisions of Rule 54(b), judgment upon the verdict of a jury shall be entered forthwith by the clerk; but the court shall direct the appropriate judgment to be entered upon a special verdict or upon a general verdict accompanied by answers to interrogatories returned by a jury pursuant to Rule 49. When the court directs that a party recover only money or costs or that all relief be denied, the clerk shall enter judgment forthwith upon receipt by him of the directions; but when the court directs entry of judgment for other relief, the judge shall promptly settle or approve the form of the judgment and direct that it be entered by the clerk. The notation of a judgment in the civil docket as provided by Rule 79(a) constitutes the entry of the judgment; and the judgment is not effective before such entry. The entry of the judgment shall not be delayed for the taxing of costs.

The Advisory Committee commented on the 1963 amendments as follows:

Under the present rule a distinction has sometimes been made between judgments on general jury verdicts, on the one hand, and, on the other, judgments upon decisions of the court that a party shall recover only money or costs or that all relief shall be denied. In the first situation, it is clear that the clerk should enter the judgment without awaiting a direction by the court unless the court otherwise orders. In the second situation it was intended that the clerk should similarly enter the judgment forthwith upon the court's decision; but because of the separate listing in the rule, and the use of the phrase "upon receipt * * * of the direction," the rule has sometimes been interpreted as requiring the clerk to await a separate direction of the court. All these judgments are usually uncomplicated, and should be handled in the same way. The amended rule accordingly deals with them as a single group in clause (1) (substituting the expression "only a sum certain" for the present expression "only money"), and requires the clerk to prepare, sign, and enter them forthwith, without awaiting court direction, unless the court makes a contrary order. * * * The more complicated judgments described in clause (2) must be approved by the court before they are entered.

* * *

Hitherto some difficulty has arisen, chiefly where the court has written an opinion or memorandum containing some apparently directive or dispositive words * * *. Clerks on occasion have viewed these opinions or memoranda as being in themselves a sufficient basis for entering judgment in the civil docket as provided by Rule 79(a). However, where the opinion or memoranda has not contained all the elements of a judgment, or where the judge has later signed a formal judgment, it has become a matter of doubt whether the purported entry of judgment was effective, starting the time running for postverdict motions and for the purpose of appeal. * * *

The amended rule eliminates these uncertainties by requiring that there be a judgment set out on a separate document—distinct from any opinion or memorandum—which provides the basis for the entry of judgment. That judgments shall be on separate documents is also indicated in Rule 79(b) * * *.

Rule 59. New Trials; Amendment of Judgments *

(a) Grounds. A new trial may be granted to all or any of the parties and on all or part of the issues (1) in an action in which there has been a trial by jury, for any of the reasons for which new trials have heretofore been granted in actions at law in the courts of the United States; and (2) in an action tried without a jury, for any of the reasons for which rehearings have heretofore been granted in suits in equity in the courts of the United States. On a motion for a new trial in an action tried without a jury, the court may open the judgment if one has been entered, take additional testimony, amend findings of fact and conclusions of law or make new findings and conclusions, and direct the entry of a new judgment.

(b) Time for Motion. A motion for a new trial shall be served not later than 10 days after the entry of the judgment.

(c) Time for Serving Affidavits. When a motion for new trial is based upon affidavits they shall be served with the motion. The opposing party has 10 days after such service within which to serve opposing affidavits, which period may be extended for an additional period not exceeding 20 days either by the court for good cause shown or by the parties by written stipulation. The court may permit reply affidavits.

(d) On Initiative of Court. Not later than 10 days after entry of judgment the court of its own initiative may order a new trial for any reason for which it might have granted a new trial on motion of a party.

---

* Proposed amendments to Rule 59 are found in Part X of this Supplement.

Rule 59   RULES OF CIVIL PROCEDURE

After giving the parties notice and an opportunity to be heard on the matter, the court may grant a motion for a new trial, timely served, for a reason not stated in the motion. In either case, the court shall specify in the order the grounds therefor.

(e) Motion to Alter or Amend a Judgment. A motion to alter or amend the judgment shall be served not later than 10 days after entry of the judgment.

Comparative State Provisions

(a) *Rule 59(a)*

Minnesota Rule of Civil Procedure 59.01

A new trial may be granted to all or any of the parties and on all or part of the issues for any of the following causes:

(1) Irregularity in the proceedings of the court, referee, jury, or prevailing party, or any order or abuse of discretion, whereby the moving party was deprived of a fair trial;

(2) Misconduct of the jury or prevailing party;

(3) Accident or surprise which could not have been prevented by ordinary prudence;

(4) Material evidence, newly discovered, which with reasonable diligence could not have been found and produced at the trial;

(5) Excessive or insufficient damages, appearing to have been given under the influence of passion or prejudice;

(6) Errors of law occurring at the trial, and objected to at the time or, if no objection need have been made under Rules 46 and 51, plainly assigned in the notice of motion;

(7) The verdict, decision, or report is not justified by the evidence, or is contrary to law; but, unless it be so expressly stated in the order granting a new trial, it shall not be presumed, on appeal, to have been made on the ground that the verdict, decision, or report was not justified by the evidence.

On a motion for a new trial in an action tried without a jury, the court may open the judgment if one has been entered, take additional testimony, amend findings of fact and conclusions of law or make new findings and conclusions, and direct entry of a new judgment.

Missouri Statutes Annotated § 510.330

A new trial may be granted for any of the reasons for which new trials have heretofore been granted. A new trial may be granted to all or any of the parties and on all or part of the issues after trial by jury, court or referee. On a motion for a new trial in an action tried without a jury, the court may open the judgment if one has been entered, take additional testimony, amend findings of fact or make new findings, and direct the entry of a new judgment. Only one new trial shall be allowed on the ground that the verdict is against the weight of the evidence. Every order allowing a new trial shall specify of record the ground or grounds on which said new trial is granted.

(b) *Rule 59(b)*

Minnesota Rule of Civil Procedure 59.03

A notice of motion for a new trial shall be served within 15 days after a general verdict or service of notice by a party of the filing of the decision or order; and the motion shall be heard within 30 days after such general verdict or notice of filing, unless the time for hearing be extended by the court within the 30 days period for good cause shown.

Rule 60. Relief From Judgment or Order

(a) Clerical Mistakes. Clerical mistakes in judgments, orders or other parts of the record and errors therein arising from oversight or omission may be corrected by the court at any time of its own initiative or on the motion of any party and after such notice, if any, as the court orders. During the pendency of an appeal, such mistakes may be so corrected before the appeal is docketed in the appellate court, and thereafter while the appeal is pending may be so corrected with leave of the appellate court.

(b) Mistakes; Inadvertence; Excusable Neglect; Newly Discovered Evidence; Fraud, etc. On motion and upon such terms as are just, the court may relieve a party or a party's legal representative from a final judgment, order, or proceeding for the following reasons: (1) mistake, inadvertence, surprise, or excusable neglect; (2) newly discovered evidence which by due diligence could not have been discovered in time to move for a new trial under Rule 59(b); (3) fraud (whether heretofore denominated intrinsic or extrinsic), misrepresentation, or other misconduct of an adverse party; (4) the judgment is void; (5) the judgment has been satisfied, released, or discharged, or a prior judgment upon which it is based has been reversed or otherwise vacated, or it is no longer equitable that the judgment should have prospective application; or (6) any other reason justifying relief from the operation of the judgment. The motion shall be made within a reasonable time, and for reasons (1), (2), and (3) not more than one year after the judgment, order, or proceeding was entered or taken. A motion under this subdivision (b) does not affect the finality of a judgment or suspend its operation. This rule does not limit the power of a court to entertain an independent action to relieve a party from a judgment, order, or proceeding, or to grant relief to a defendant not actually personally notified as provided in Title 28, U.S.C., § 1655, or to set aside a judgment for fraud upon the court. Writs of coram nobis, coram vobis, audita querela, and bills of review and bills in the nature of a bill of review, are abolished, and the procedure for obtaining any relief from a judgment shall be by motion as prescribed in these rules or by an independent action.

Comparative State Provisions

(a) In General

Georgia Code Annotated § 9-11-60

(a) * * *

(b) Methods of direct attack. A judgment may be attacked by motion for a new trial or motion to set aside. Judgments may be attacked by motion only in the court of rendition.

Rule 60   RULES OF CIVIL PROCEDURE

(c) Motion for new trial. A motion for new trial must be predicated upon some intrinsic defect which does not appear upon the face of the record or pleadings.

(d) Motion to set aside. A motion may be brought to set aside a judgment based upon:

    (1) Lack of jurisdiction over the person or the subject matter;

    (2) Fraud, accident, or mistake or the acts of the adverse party unmixed with the negligence or fault of the movant; or

    (3) A nonamendable defect which appears upon the face of the record or pleadings. Under this paragraph, it is not sufficient that the complaint or other pleading fails to state a claim upon which relief can be granted, but the pleadings must affirmatively show no claim in fact existed.

(e) Complaint in equity. The use of a complaint in equity to set aside a judgment is prohibited.

(f) Procedure; time of relief. * * * Motions for new trial must be brought within the time prescribed by law. In all other instances, all motions to set aside judgments shall be brought within three years from entry of the judgment complained of.

(g) Clerical mistakes. Clerical mistakes in judgments, orders, or other parts of the record and errors therein arising from oversight or omission may be corrected by the court at any time of its own initiative or on the motion of any party and after such notice, if any, as the court orders.

(h) Law of the case rule. The law of the case rule is abolished; but generally judgments and orders shall not be set aside or modified without just cause and, in setting aside or otherwise modifying judgments and orders, the court shall consider whether rights have vested thereunder and whether or not innocent parties would be injured thereby; provided, however, that any ruling by the Supreme Court or the Court of Appeals in a case shall be binding in all subsequent proceedings in that case in the lower court and in the Supreme Court or the Court of Appeals as the case may be.

(b) Perjury as a Ground for Relief

Missouri Rule of Civil Procedure 78.01

[On January 1, 1975, Rule 78.01 was revised to eliminate all references to specific grounds for a new trial. The legislative note makes clear that the revision was not intended to alter or eliminate any ground upon which new trials previously were permitted. Prior to the change Rule 78.01 read in part as follows:] * * * The court may award a new trial of any issue upon good cause shown and in any case where there has been * * * a fraud or deceit practiced by one party on the other or the court is satisfied that perjury or mistake has been committed by a witness, and is also satisfied that an improper verdict or finding was occasioned by any such matters * * *, it shall, on motion of the proper party, grant a new trial * * *.

Rule 61. Harmless Error

No error in either the admission or the exclusion of evidence and no error or defect in any ruling or order or in anything done or omitted by the court or by any of the parties is ground for granting a new trial or for setting aside a verdict or for vacating, modifying or otherwise disturbing a judgment or order, unless refusal to take such action appears to the court inconsistent with substantial justice. The court at every stage of the proceeding must disregard any error or defect in the proceeding which does not affect the substantial rights of the parties.

Rule 62. Stay of Proceedings to Enforce a Judgment

(a) Automatic Stay; Exceptions—Injunctions, Receiverships, and Patent Accountings. Except as stated herein, no execution shall issue upon a judgment nor shall proceedings be taken for its enforcement until the expiration of 10 days after its entry. Unless otherwise ordered by the court, an interlocutory or final judgment in an action for an injunction or in a receivership action, or a judgment or order directing an accounting in an action for infringement of letters patent, shall not be stayed during the period after its entry and until an appeal is taken or during the pendency of an appeal. The provisions of subdivision (c) of this rule govern the suspending, modifying, restoring, or granting of an injunction during the pendency of an appeal.

(b) Stay on Motion for New Trial or for Judgment. In its discretion and on such conditions for the security of the adverse party as are proper, the court may stay the execution of or any proceedings to enforce a judgment pending the disposition of a motion for a new trial or to alter or amend a judgment made pursuant to Rule 59, or of a motion for relief from a judgment or order made pursuant to Rule 60, or of a motion for judgment in accordance with a motion for a directed verdict made pursuant to Rule 50, or of a motion for amendment to the findings or for additional findings made pursuant to Rule 52(b).

(c) Injunction Pending Appeal. When an appeal is taken from an interlocutory or final judgment granting, dissolving, or denying an injunction, the court in its discretion may suspend, modify, restore, or grant an injunction during the pendency of the appeal upon such terms as to bond or otherwise as it considers proper for the security of the rights of the adverse party. If the judgment appealed from is rendered by a district court of three judges specially constituted pursuant to a statute of the United States, no such order shall be made except (1) by such court sitting in open court or (2) by the assent of all the judges of such court evidenced by their signatures to the order.

(d) Stay Upon Appeal. When an appeal is taken the appellant by giving a supersedeas bond may obtain a stay subject to the exceptions contained in subdivision (a) of this rule. The bond may be given at or after the time of filing the notice of appeal or of procuring the order allowing the appeal, as the case may be. The stay is effective when the supersedeas bond is approved by the court.

(e) Stay in Favor of the United States or Agency Thereof. When an appeal is taken by the United States or an officer or agency thereof or by direction of any department of the Government of the United States and the operation or enforcement of the judgment is stayed, no bond, obligation, or other security shall be required from the appellant.

(f) Stay According to State Law. In any state in which a judgment is a lien upon the property of the judgment debtor and in

Rule 62. RULES OF CIVIL PROCEDURE

which the judgment debtor is entitled to a stay of execution, a judgment debtor is entitled, in the district court held therein, to such stay as would be accorded the judgment debtor had the action been maintained in the courts of that state.

(g) Power of Appellate Court Not Limited. The provisions in this rule do not limit any power of an appellate court or of a judge or justice thereof to stay proceedings during the pendency of an appeal or to suspend, modify, restore, or grant an injunction during the pendency of an appeal or to make any order appropriate to preserve the status quo or the effectiveness of the judgment subsequently to be entered.

(h) Stay of Judgment as to Multiple Claims or Multiple Parties. When a court has ordered a final judgment under the conditions stated in Rule 54(b), the court may stay enforcement of that judgment until the entering of a subsequent judgment or judgments and may prescribe such conditions as are necessary to secure the benefit thereof to the party in whose favor the judgment is entered.

Rule 63. Inability of a Judge to Proceed

If a trial or hearing has been commenced and the judge is unable to proceed, any other judge may proceed with it upon certifying familiarity with the record and determining that the proceedings in the case may be completed without prejudice to the parties. In a hearing or trial without a jury, the successor judge shall at the request of a party recall any witness whose testimony is material and disputed and who is available to testify again without undue burden. The successor judge may also recall any other witness.

VIII. PROVISIONAL AND FINAL REMEDIES

Rule 64. Seizure of Person or Property

At the commencement of and during the course of an action, all remedies providing for seizure of person or property for the purpose of securing satisfaction of the judgment ultimately to be entered in the action are available under the circumstances and in the manner provided by the law of the state in which the district court is held, existing at the time the remedy is sought, subject to the following qualifications: (1) any existing statute of the United States governs to the extent to which it is applicable; (2) the action in which any of the foregoing remedies is used shall be commenced and prosecuted or, if removed from a state court, shall be prosecuted after removal, pursuant to these rules. The remedies thus available include arrest, attachment, garnishment, replevin, sequestration, and other corresponding or equivalent remedies, however designated and regardless of whether by state procedure the remedy is ancillary to an action or must be obtained by an independent action.

Comparative State Provisions

New York Civil Practice Law and Rules 6201

An order of attachment may be granted in any action, except a matrimonial action, where the plaintiff has demanded and would be entitled, in whole or in part, or in the alternative, to a money judgment against one or more defendants, when:

1. the defendant is a nondomiciliary residing within the state, or is a foreign corporation not qualified to do business in the state; or

2. the defendant resides or is domiciled in the state and cannot be personally served despite diligent efforts to do so; or

3. the defendant, with intent to defraud his creditors or frustrate the enforcement of a judgment that might be rendered in plaintiff's favor, has assigned, disposed of, encumbered or secreted property, or removed it from the state or is about to do any of these acts; or

4. the action is brought by the victim * * * of a crime * * * to recover damages sustained as a result of such crime * * *.

5. the cause of action is based on a judgment, decree or order of a court of the United States or of any other court which is entitled to full faith and credit in this state, or on a [recognized foreign] judgment * * *.

Rule 65. Injunctions

(a) Preliminary Injunction.

(1) *Notice.* No preliminary injunction shall be issued without notice to the adverse party.

(2) *Consolidation of Hearing With Trial on Merits.* Before or after the commencement of the hearing of an application for a preliminary injunction, the court may order the trial of the action on the merits to be advanced and consolidated with the hearing of the application. Even when this consolidation is not ordered, any evidence received upon an application for a preliminary injunction which would be admissible upon the trial on the merits becomes part of the record on the trial and need not be repeated upon the trial. This subdivision (a)(2) shall be so construed and applied as to save to the parties any rights they may have to trial by jury.

(b) Temporary Restraining Order; Notice; Hearing; Duration.

A temporary restraining order may be granted without written or oral notice to the adverse party or that party's attorney only if (1) it clearly appears from specific facts shown by affidavit or by the verified complaint that immediate and irreparable injury, loss, or damage will result to the applicant before the adverse party or that party's attorney can be heard in opposition, and (2) the applicant's attorney certifies to the court in writing the efforts, if any, which have been made to give the notice and the reasons supporting the claim that notice should not be required. Every temporary restraining order granted without notice shall be indorsed with the date and hour of issuance; shall be filed forthwith in the clerk's office and entered of record; shall define the injury and state why it is irreparable and why the order was granted without notice; and shall expire by its terms within such time after entry, not to exceed 10 days, as the court fixes, unless within the time so fixed the order, for good cause shown, is extended for a like period or unless the party against whom the order is directed consents that it may be extended for a longer period. The reasons for the extension shall be entered of record. In case a temporary restraining order is granted without notice, the motion for a preliminary injunction shall be set down for hearing at the earliest possible time and takes precedence of all matters except older matters of the same character; and when the motion comes on for hearing the party who obtained the temporary restraining order shall proceed with the application for a preliminary injunction and, if the party does not do so, the court shall dissolve the temporary restraining order. On 2 days' notice to the party who obtained the temporary restraining order without notice or on such shorter notice to that party as the court may prescribe, the adverse party may appear and move its dissolution or modification and in that event the court shall proceed to hear and determine such motion as expeditiously as the ends of justice require.

(c) Security. No restraining order or preliminary injunction shall issue except upon the giving of security by the applicant, in such sum as the court deems proper, for the payment of such costs and damages as may be incurred or suffered by any party who is found to have been wrongfully enjoined or restrained. No such security shall be required of the United States or of an officer or agency thereof.

The provisions of Rule 65.1 apply to a surety upon a bond or undertaking under this rule.

(d) Form and Scope of Injunction or Restraining Order. Every order granting an injunction and every restraining order shall set forth the reasons for its issuance; shall be specific in terms; shall describe in reasonable detail, and not by reference to the complaint or other document, the act or acts sought to be restrained; and is binding only upon the parties to the action, their officers, agents, servants, employees, and attorneys, and upon those persons in active concert or participation with them who receive actual notice of the order by personal service or otherwise.

(e) Employer and Employee; Interpleader; Constitutional Cases. These rules do not modify any statute of the United States relating to temporary restraining orders and preliminary injunctions in actions affecting employer and employee; or the provisions of Title 28, U.S.C. § 2361, relating to preliminary injunctions in actions of interpleader or in the nature of interpleader; or Title 28, U.S.C. § 2284, relating to actions required by Act of Congress to be heard and determined by a district court of three judges.

Notes on Amendments to Federal Rule 65 and Comparative State Provision

(a) *Notes on Amendments in 1966 to Federal Rules 65(a) and (b)*

The 1966 amendments added Rule 65(a)(2) and clause (2) in Rule 65(b). The Advisory Committee's Notes on these amendments read as follows:

Subdivision (a)(2). This new subdivision provides express authority for consolidating the hearing of an application for a preliminary injunction with the trial on the merits. The authority can be exercised with particular profit when it appears that a substantial part of the evidence offered on the application will be relevant to the merits and will be presented in such form as to qualify for admission on the trial proper. Repetition of evidence is thereby avoided. The fact that the proceedings have been consolidated should cause no delay in the disposition of the application for the preliminary injunction, for the evidence will be directed in the first instance to that relief, and the preliminary injunction, if justified by the proof, may be issued in the course of the consolidated proceedings. Furthermore, to consolidate the proceedings will tend to expedite the final disposition of the action. It is believed that consolidation can be usefully availed of in many cases.

The subdivision further provides that even when consolidation is not ordered, evidence received in connection with an application for a preliminary injunction which would be admissible on the trial on the merits forms part of the trial record. This evidence need not be repeated on the trial. On the other hand, repetition is not altogether prohibited. That would be impractical and unwise. For example, a witness testifying comprehensively on the trial who has previously testified upon the application for a preliminary injunction might sometimes be hamstrung in telling his story if he could not go over some part of his prior testimony to connect it with his present testimony. So also, some repetition of testimony may be called for where the trial is conducted by a judge who did not hear the application for the preliminary injunction. In general, however, repetition can be avoided with an increase of efficiency in the conduct of the case and without any distortion of the presentation of evidence by the parties.

Since an application for a preliminary injunction may be made in an action in which, with respect to all or part of the merits, there is a right to trial by jury, it is appropriate to add the caution appearing in the last sentence of the subdivision. In such a case the jury will have to hear all the evidence bearing on its verdict, even if some part of the evidence has already been heard by the judge alone on the application for the preliminary injunction.

The subdivision is believed to reflect the substance of the best current practice and introduces no novel conception.

Subdivision (b). In view of the possibly drastic consequences of a temporary restraining order, the opposition should be heard, if feasible, before the order is granted. Many judges have properly insisted that, when time does not permit of formal notice of the application to the adverse party, some expedient, such as telephonic notice to the attorney for the adverse party, be resorted to if this can reasonably be done. On occasion, however, temporary restraining orders have been issued without any notice when it was feasible for some fair, although informal, notice to be given. * * *

Heretofore the first sentence of subdivision (b), in referring to a notice "served" on the "adverse party" on which a "hearing" could be held, perhaps invited the interpretation that the order might be granted without notice if the circumstances did not permit of a formal hearing on the basis of a formal notice. The subdivision is amended to make it plain that informal notice, which may be communicated to the attorney rather than the adverse party, is to be preferred to no notice at all.

Before notice can be dispensed with, the applicant's counsel must give his certificate as to any efforts made to give notice and the reasons why notice should not be required. This certificate is in addition to the requirement of an affidavit or verified complaint setting forth the facts as to the irreparable injury which would result before the opposition could be heard.

* * *

(b) *Comparative State Provision*

New York Civil Practice Law and Rules 6301

A preliminary injunction may be granted in any action where it appears that the defendant threatens or is about to do, or is doing or procuring or suffering to be done, an act in violation of the plaintiff's rights respecting the subject of the action, and tending to render the judgment ineffectual, or in any action where the plaintiff has demanded and would be entitled to a judgment restraining the defendant from the commission or continuance of an act, which, if committed or continued during the pendency of the action, would produce injury to the plaintiff. A temporary restraining order may be granted pending a hearing for a preliminary injunction where it appears that immediate and irreparable injury, loss or damage will result unless the defendant is restrained before the hearing can be had.

Rule 65.1 Security: Proceedings Against Sureties

Whenever these rules, including the Supplemental Rules for Certain Admiralty and Maritime Claims, require or permit the giving of security by a party, and security is given in the form of a bond or stipulation or other undertaking with one or more sureties, each surety submits to the jurisdiction of the court and irrevocably appoints the clerk of the court as the surety's agent upon whom any papers affecting the surety's liability on the bond or undertaking may be served. The surety's liability may be enforced on motion without the necessity of an independent action. The motion and such notice of the motion as the court prescribes may be served on the clerk of the court, who shall forthwith mail copies to the sureties if their addresses are known.

Rule 66. Receivers Appointed by Federal Courts

An action wherein a receiver has been appointed shall not be dismissed except by order of the court. The practice in the administration of estates by receivers or by other similar officers appointed by the court shall be in accordance with the practice heretofore followed in the courts of the United States or as provided in rules promulgated by the district courts. In all other respects the action in which the appointment of a receiver is sought or which is brought by or against a receiver is governed by these rules.

Comparative State Provision

New York Civil Practice Law and Rules 6401

(a) Upon motion of a person having an apparent interest in property which is the subject of an action in the supreme or a county court, a temporary receiver of the property may be appointed, before or after service of summons and at any time prior to judgment, or during the pendency of an appeal, where there is danger that the property will be removed from the state, or lost, materially injured or destroyed. * * *

(b) The court appointing a receiver may authorize him to take and hold real and personal property, and sue for, collect and sell debts or claims, upon such conditions and for such purposes as the court shall direct. A receiver shall have no power to employ counsel unless expressly so authorized by order of the court. Upon motion of the receiver or a party, powers granted to a temporary receiver may be extended or limited or the receivership may be extended to another action involving the property.

* * *

Rule 67. Deposit in Court

In an action in which any part of the relief sought is a judgment for a sum of money or the disposition of a sum of money or the disposition of any other thing capable of delivery, a party, upon notice to every other party, and by leave of court, may deposit with the court all or any part of such sum or thing, whether or not that party claims all or any part of the sum or thing. The party making the deposit shall serve the order permitting deposit on the clerk of the court. Money paid into court under this rule shall be deposited and withdrawn in accordance with the provisions of Title 28, U.S.C. §§ 2041, and 2042; the Act of June 26, 1934, c. 756, § 23, as amended (48 Stat. 1236, 58 Stat. 845), U.S.C., Title 31, § 725v; or any like statute. The fund shall be deposited in an interest-bearing account or invested in an interest-bearing instrument approved by the court.

Amendments in 1983 to Federal Rule 67

The first alteration to Rule 67 made clear that a litigant could deposit money or other property with the court even though that litigant continues to claim an interest in such property. The second alteration provided that money so deposited shall be invested in an interest bearing account or instrument approved by the court.

Rule 68. Offer of Judgment

At any time more than 10 days before the trial begins, a party defending against a claim may serve upon the adverse party an offer to allow judgment to be taken against the defending party for the money or property or to the effect specified in the offer, with costs then accrued. If within 10 days after the service of the offer the adverse party serves written notice that the offer is accepted, either party may then file the offer and notice of acceptance together with proof of service thereof and thereupon the clerk shall enter judgment. An offer not accepted shall be deemed withdrawn and evidence thereof is not admissible except in a proceeding to determine costs. If the judgment finally obtained by the offeree is not more favorable than the offer, the offeree must pay the costs incurred after the making of the offer. The fact that an offer is made but not accepted does not preclude a subsequent offer. When the liability of one party to another has been determined by verdict or order or judgment, but the amount or extent of the liability remains to be determined by further proceedings, the party adjudged liable may make an offer of judgment, which shall have the same effect as an offer made before trial if it is served within a reasonable time not less than 10 days prior to the commencement of hearings to determine the amount or extent of liability.

Rule 68   RULES OF CIVIL PROCEDURE

Proposed Amendments to Federal Rule 68 and Comparative State Provisions

(a) Proposed Amendments

The Advisory Committee on the Federal Rules once circulated a draft proposal that would have altered the rule dramatically. In the main, the suggested rule provided for sanctions against any party who unreasonably refuses an offer to settle whether or not that party ultimately prevails in the action. The trial judge would be permitted to impose any "appropriate sanction" in light of all of the circumstances of the case.

(b) Comparative State Provisions

New York Civil Practice Law and Rules 3219

At any time not later than ten days before trial, any party against whom a cause of action based upon contract, expressed or implied, is asserted, and against whom a separate judgment may be taken, may, without court order, deposit with the clerk of the court for safekeeping, an amount deemed by him to be sufficient to satisfy the claim asserted against him, and serve upon the claimant a written tender of payment to satisfy such claim. * * * Within ten days after such deposit the claimant may withdraw the amount deposited upon filing a duly acknowledged statement that the withdrawal is in satisfaction of the claim. The clerk shall thereupon enter judgment dismissing the pleading setting forth the claim, without costs.

* * * If the tender is not accepted and the claimant fails to obtain a more favorable judgment, he shall not recover interest or costs from the time of the offer, but shall pay costs for defending against the claim from that time. A tender shall not be made known to the jury.

* * *

New York Civil Practice Law and Rules 3220

At any time not later than ten days before trial, any party against whom a cause of action based upon contract, express or implied, is asserted may serve upon the claimant a written offer to allow judgment to be taken against him for a sum therein specified, with costs then accrued, if the party against whom the claim is asserted fails in his defense. If within ten days thereafter the claimant serves a written notice that he accepts the offer, and damages are awarded to him on the trial, they shall be assessed in the sum specified in the offer. If the offer is not so accepted and the claimant fails to obtain a more favorable judgment, he shall pay the expenses necessarily incurred by the party against whom the claim is asserted, for trying the issue of damages from the time of the offer. The expenses shall be ascertained by the judge or referee before whom the case is tried. An offer under this rule shall not be made known to the jury.

New York Civil Practice Law and Rules 3221

Except in a matrimonial action, at any time not later than ten days before trial, any party against whom a claim is asserted, and against whom a separate judgment may be taken, may serve upon the claimant a written offer to allow judgment to be taken against him for a sum or property or to the effect therein specified, with costs then accrued. If within ten days thereafter the claimant serves a written notice that he accepts the offer, either party may file the summons, complaint and offer, with proof of acceptance, and thereupon the clerk shall enter judgment accordingly. If the offer is not accepted and the claimant fails to obtain a more favorable judgment, he shall not recover costs from the time of the offer, but shall pay costs from that time. An offer of judgment shall not be made known to the jury.

Rule 69. Execution

(a) In General. Process to enforce a judgment for the payment of money shall be a writ of execution, unless the court directs otherwise. The procedure on execution, in proceedings supplementary to and in aid of a judgment, and in proceedings on and in aid of execution shall be in accordance with the practice and procedure of the state in which the district court is held, existing at the time the remedy is sought, except that any statute of the United States governs to the extent that it is applicable. In aid of the judgment or execution, the judgment creditor or a successor in interest when that interest appears of record, may obtain discovery from any person, including the judgment debtor, in the manner provided in these rules or in the manner provided by the practice of the state in which the district court is held.

(b) Against Certain Public Officers. When a judgment has been entered against a collector or other officer of revenue under the circumstances stated in Title 28, U.S.C. § 2006, or against an officer of Congress in an action mentioned in the Act of March 3, 1875, ch. 130, § 8 (18 Stat. 401), U.S.C. Title 2, § 118, and when the court has given the certificate of probable cause for the officer's act as provided in those statutes, execution shall not issue against the officer or the officer's property but the final judgment shall be satisfied as provided in such statutes.

State Provisions Exempting Property from Execution
New York Civil Practice Law and Rules 5205

(a) **Exemption for personal property.** The following personal property when owned by any person is exempt from application to the satisfaction of a money judgment except where the judgment is for the purchase price of the exempt property or was recovered by a domestic, laboring person or mechanic for work performed by that person in such capacity:

1. all stoves kept for use in the judgment debtor's dwelling house and necessary fuel therefor for sixty days; one sewing machine with its appurtenances;

2. the family bible, family pictures, and school books used by the judgment debtor or in the family; and other books, not exceeding fifty dollars in value, kept and used as part of the family or judgment debtor's library;

3. a seat or pew occupied by the judgment debtor or the family in a place of public worship;

4. domestic animals with the necessary food for those animals for sixty days, provided that the total value of such animals and food does not exceed four hundred fifty dollars; all necessary food actually provided for the use of the judgment debtor or his family for sixty days;

5. all wearing apparel, household furniture, one mechanical, gas or electric refrigerator, one radio receiver, one television set, crockery, tableware and cooking utensils necessary for the judgment debtor and the family;

6. a wedding ring; a watch not exceeding thirty-five dollars in value; and

7. necessary working tools and implements, including those of a mechanic, farm machinery, team, professional instruments, furniture and library, not exceeding six hundred dollars in value, together with the necessary

food for the team for sixty days, provided, however, that the articles specified in this paragraph are necessary to the carrying on of the judgment debtor's profession or calling.

(b) Exemption of cause of action and damages for taking or injuring exempt personal property. A cause of action, to recover damages for taking or injuring personal property exempt from application to the satisfaction of a money judgment, is exempt from application to the satisfaction of a money judgment. A money judgment and its proceeds arising out of such a cause of action is exempt, for one year after the collection thereof, from application to the satisfaction of a money judgment.

(c) Trust exemption. * * * [A]ll property while held in trust for a judgment debtor, where the trust has been created by, or the fund so held in trust has proceeded from, a person other than the judgment debtor, is exempt from application to the satisfaction of a money judgment. * * *

(d) Income exemptions. The following personal property is exempt from application to the satisfaction of a money judgment, except such part as a court determines to be unnecessary for the reasonable requirements of the judgment debtor and his dependents:

1. ninety per cent of the income or other payments from a trust the principal of which is exempt under subdivision (c) [and one hundred per cent of income from keogh and other retirement plans];

2. ninety per cent of the earnings of the judgment debtor for his personal services rendered within sixty days before, and at any time after, an income execution is delivered to the sheriff or a motion is made to secure the application of the judgment debtor's earnings to the satisfaction of the judgment; and

3. payments pursuant to an award in a matrimonial action, for the support of a wife, where the wife is the judgment debtor, or for the support of a child, where the child is the judgment debtor; where the award was made by a court of the state, determination of the extent to which it is unnecessary shall be made by that court.

(e) Exemptions to members of armed forces. The pay and bounty of a non-commissioned officer, musician or private in the armed forces of the United States or the state of New York; a land warrant, pension or other reward granted by the United States, or by a state, for services in the armed forces; a sword, horse, medal, emblem or device of any kind presented as a testimonial for services rendered in the armed forces of the United States or a state; and the uniform, arms and equipments which were used by a person in the service, are exempt from application to the satisfaction of a money judgment; provided, however, that the provisions of this subdivision shall not apply to the satisfaction of any order or money judgment for the support of a person's child, spouse, or former spouse.

(f) Exemption for unpaid milk proceeds. Ninety per cent of any money or debt due or to become due to the judgment debtor for the sale of milk produced on a farm operated by him and delivered for his account to a milk dealer licensed pursuant to article twenty-one of the agriculture and markets law is exempt from application to the satisfaction of a money judgment.

(g) Security deposit exemption. Money deposited as security for the rental of real property to be used as the residence of the judgment debtor or the judgment debtor's family; and money deposited as security with a gas, electric, water, steam, telegraph or telephone corporation, or a municipality rendering equivalent utility services, for services to judgment debtor's residence or the residence of judgment debtor's family, are exempt from application to the satisfaction of a money judgment.

(h) The following personal property is exempt from application to the satisfaction of money judgment, except such part as a court determines to be unnecessary for the reasonable requirements of the judgment debtor and his dependents:

1. any and all medical and dental accessions to the human body and all personal property or equipment that is necessary or proper to maintain or assist in sustaining or maintaining one or more major life activities or is utilized to provide mobility for a person with a permanent disability; and

2. any guide dog, service dog or hearing dog, as those terms are defined in section one hundred eight of the agriculture and markets law, or any animal trained to aid or assist a person with a permanent disability and actually being so used by such person, together with any and all food or feed for any such dog or other animal.

(i) * * *

New York Civil Practice Law and Rules 5206

(a) **Exemption of homestead.** Property of one of the following types, not exceeding ten thousand dollars in value above liens and encumbrances, owned and occupied as a principal residence, is exempt from application to the satisfaction of a money judgment, unless the judgment was recovered wholly for the purchase price thereof:

1. a lot of land with a dwelling thereon,
2. shares of stock in a cooperative apartment corporation,
3. units of a condominium apartment, or
4. a mobile home.

But no exempt homestead shall be exempt from taxation or from sale for nonpayment of taxes or assessments.

(b) **Homestead exemption after owner's death.** The homestead exemption continues after the death of the person in whose favor the property was exempted for the benefit of the surviving spouse and surviving children until the majority of the youngest surviving child and until the death of the surviving spouse.

(c) **Suspension of occupation as affecting homestead.** The homestead exemption ceases if the property ceases to be occupied as a residence by a person for whose benefit it may so continue, except where the suspension of occupation is for a period not exceeding one year, and occurs in consequence of injury to, or destruction of, the dwelling house upon the premises.

(d) **Exemption of homestead exceeding ten thousand dollars in value.** The exemption of a homestead is not void because the value of the property exceeds ten thousand dollars but the lien of a judgment attaches to the surplus.

(e) **Sale of homestead exceeding ten thousand dollars in value.** A judgment creditor may commence a special proceeding in the county in which the homestead is located against the judgment debtor for the sale, by a sheriff or receiver, of a homestead exceeding ten thousand dollars in value. The court may direct that the notice of petition be served upon any other person. The court, if it directs such a sale, shall so marshal the proceeds of the sale that the right and interest of each person in the proceeds shall correspond as nearly as may be to his right and interest in the property sold. Money, not exceeding ten thousand dollars, paid to a judgment debtor, as representing his interest in the proceeds, is exempt for one year after the payment, unless, before the expiration of the year, he acquires an exempt homestead, in which case, the exemption ceases with respect to so much of the money as was not expended for the purchase of that property; and the exemption of the property so acquired extends to every debt against which the property sold was exempt. Where the exemption of property sold as prescribed in this subdivision has been continued after the judgment debtor's death, or where he dies after the sale and before payment to him of his portion of the proceeds of the sale, the court may direct that portion of the proceeds which represents his interest be invested for the benefit of the person or persons entitled to the benefit of the exemption, or be otherwise disposed of as justice requires.

(f) **Exemption of burying ground.** Land, set apart as a family or private burying ground, is exempt from application to the satisfaction of a money judgment, upon the following conditions only:

    1. a portion of it must have been actually used for that purpose;

    2. it must not exceed in extent one-fourth of an acre; and

    3. it must not contain any building or structure, except one or more vaults or other places of deposit for the dead, or mortuary monuments.

Rule 70. Judgment for Specific Acts; Vesting Title

If a judgment directs a party to execute a conveyance of land or to deliver deeds or other documents or to perform any other specific act and the party fails to comply within the time specified, the court may direct the act to be done at the cost of the disobedient party by some other person appointed by the court and the act when so done has like effect as if done by the party. On application of the party entitled to performance, the clerk shall issue a writ of attachment or sequestration against the property of the disobedient party to compel obedience to the judgment. The court may also in proper cases adjudge the party in contempt. If real or personal property is within the district, the court in lieu of directing a conveyance thereof may enter a judgment divesting the title of any party and vesting it in others and such judgment has the effect of a conveyance executed in due form of law. When any order or judgment is for the delivery of possession, the party in whose favor it is entered is entitled to a writ of execution or assistance upon application to the clerk.

Rule 71. Process in Behalf of and Against Persons Not Parties

When an order is made in favor of a person who is not a party to the action, that person may enforce obedience to the order by the same process as if a party; and, when obedience to an order may be lawfully enforced against a person who is not a party, that person is liable to the same process for enforcing obedience to the order as if a party.

IX. SPECIAL PROCEEDINGS

Rule 71A. Condemnation of Property

(a) **Applicability of Other Rules.** The Rules of Civil Procedure for the United States District Courts govern the procedure for the condemnation of real and personal property under the power of eminent domain, except as otherwise provided in this rule.

(b) **Joinder of Properties.** The plaintiff may join in the same action one or more separate pieces of property, whether in the same or different ownership and whether or not sought for the same use.

(c) **Complaint.**

(1) *Caption.* The complaint shall contain a caption as provided in Rule 10(a), except that the plaintiff shall name as defendants the

property, designated generally by kind, quantity, and location, and at least one of the owners of some part of or interest in the property.

(2) *Contents.* The complaint shall contain a short and plain statement of the authority for the taking, the use for which the property is to be taken, a description of the property sufficient for its identification, the interests to be acquired, and as to each separate piece of property a designation of the defendants who have been joined as owners thereof or of some interest therein. Upon the commencement of the action, the plaintiff need join as defendants only the persons having or claiming an interest in the property whose names are then known, but prior to any hearing involving the compensation to be paid for a piece of property, the plaintiff shall add as defendants all persons having or claiming an interest in that property whose names can be ascertained by a reasonably diligent search of the records, considering the character and value of the property involved and the interests to be acquired, and also those whose names have otherwise been learned. All others may be made defendants under the designation "Unknown Owners." Process shall be served as provided in subdivision (d) of this rule upon all defendants, whether named as defendants at the time of the commencement of the action or subsequently added, and a defendant may answer as provided in subdivision (e) of this rule. The court meanwhile may order such distribution of a deposit as the facts warrant.

(3) *Filing.* In addition to filing the complaint with the court, the plaintiff shall furnish to the clerk at least one copy thereof for the use of the defendants and additional copies at the request of the clerk or of a defendant.

(d) Process.

(1) *Notice; Delivery.* Upon the filing of the complaint the plaintiff shall forthwith deliver to the clerk joint or several notices directed to the defendants named or designated in the complaint. Additional notices directed to defendants subsequently added shall be so delivered. The delivery of the notice and its service have the same effect as the delivery and service of the summons under Rule 4.

(2) *Same; Form.* Each notice shall state the court, the title of the action, the name of the defendant to whom it is directed, that the action is to condemn property, a description of the defendant's property sufficient for its identification, the interest to be taken, the authority for the taking, the uses for which the property is to be taken, that the defendant may serve upon the plaintiff's attorney an answer within 20 days after service of the notice, and that the failure so to serve an answer constitutes a consent to the taking and to the authority of the court to proceed to hear the action and to fix the compensation. The notice shall conclude with the name of the plaintiff's attorney and an address within the district in which action is brought where the attorney may be served.

Rule 71A   RULES OF CIVIL PROCEDURE

The notice need contain a description of no other property than that to be taken from the defendants to whom it is directed.

(3) *Service of Notice.*

A. Personal Service. Personal service of the notice (but without copies of the complaint) shall be made in accordance with Rule 4 upon a defendant whose residence is known and who resides within the United States or a territory subject to the administration or judicial jurisdiction of the United States.

B. Service by Publication. Upon the filing of a certificate of the plaintiff's attorney stating that the attorney believes a defendant cannot be personally served, because after diligent inquiry within the state in which the complaint is filed the defendant's place of residence cannot be ascertained by the plaintiff or, if ascertained, that it is beyond the territorial limits of personal service as provided in this rule, service of the notice shall be made on this defendant by publication in a newspaper published in the county where the property is located, or if there is no such newspaper, then in a newspaper having a general circulation where the property is located, once a week for not less than three successive weeks. Prior to the last publication, a copy of the notice shall also be mailed to a defendant who cannot be personally served as provided in this rule but whose place of residence is then known. Unknown owners may be served by publication in like manner by a notice addressed to "Unknown Owners."

Service by publication is complete upon the date of the last publication. Proof of publication and mailing shall be made by certificate of the plaintiff's attorney, to which shall be attached a printed copy of the published notice with the name and dates of the newspaper marked thereon.

(4) *Return; Amendment.* Proof of service of the notice shall be made and amendment of the notice or proof of its service allowed in the manner provided for the return and amendment of the summons under Rule 4.

(e) Appearance or Answer. If a defendant has no objection or defense to the taking of the defendant's property, the defendant may serve a notice of appearance designating the property in which the defendant claims to be interested. Thereafter, the defendant shall receive notice of all proceedings affecting it. If a defendant has any objection or defense to the taking of the property, the defendant shall serve an answer within 20 days after the service of notice upon the defendant. The answer shall identify the property in which the defendant claims to have an interest, state the nature and extent of the interest claimed, and state all the defendant's objections and defenses to the taking of the property. A defendant waives all defenses and objections not so presented, but at the trial of the issue of just compensation, whether or not the defendant has previously appeared or answered, the defendant may present evidence as to the amount of the compensation to be paid for the property, and the defendant may share in the distribution of the award. No other pleading or motion asserting any additional defense or objection shall be allowed.

(f) Amendment of Pleadings. Without leave of court, the plaintiff may amend the complaint at any time before the trial of the issue of compensation and as many times as desired, but no amendment shall be made which will result in a dismissal forbidden by subdivision (i) of this rule. The plaintiff need not serve a copy of an amendment, but shall serve notice of the filing, as provided in Rule 5(b), upon any party affected thereby who has appeared and, in the manner provided in subdivision (d) of this rule, upon any party affected thereby who has not appeared. The plaintiff shall furnish to the clerk of the court for the use of the defendants at least one copy of each amendment, and shall furnish additional copies on the request of the clerk or of a defendant. Within the time allowed by subdivision (e) of this rule a defendant may serve an answer to the amended pleading, in the form and manner and with the same effect as there provided.

(g) Substitution of Parties. If a defendant dies or becomes incompetent or transfers an interest after the defendant's joinder, the court may order substitution of the proper party upon motion and notice of hearing. If the motion and notice of hearing are to be served upon a person not already a party, service shall be made as provided in subdivision (d)(3) of this rule.

(h) Trial. If the action involves the exercise of the power of eminent domain under the law of the United States, any tribunal specially constituted by an Act of Congress governing the case for the trial of the issue of just compensation shall be the tribunal for the determination of that issue; but if there is no such specially constituted tribunal any party may have a trial by jury of the issue of just compensation by filing a demand therefor within the time allowed for answer or within such further time as the court may fix, unless the court in its discretion orders that, because of the character, location, or quantity of the property to be condemned, or for other reasons in the interest of justice, the issue of compensation shall be determined by a commission of three persons appointed by it.

In the event that a commission is appointed the court may direct that not more than two additional persons serve as alternate commissioners to hear the case and replace commissioners who, prior to the time when a decision is filed, are found by the court to be unable or disqualified to perform their duties. An alternate who does not replace a regular commissioner shall be discharged after the commission renders its final decision. Before appointing the members of the commission and alternates the court shall advise the parties of the identity and qualifications of each prospective commissioner and alternate and may permit the parties to examine each such designee. The parties shall not be permitted or required by the court to suggest nominees. Each party shall have the right to object for valid cause to the appointment of any person as a commissioner or alternate. If a commission is appointed it shall have the powers of a master provided in subdivision (c) of Rule 53 and proceedings before it shall be governed by the provisions of paragraphs (1) and (2) of subdivision (d) of Rule 53. Its action and report shall be determined by a majority and its findings and report shall have the effect, and be dealt with by the court in accordance with the practice, prescribed in paragraph (2) of subdivision (e) of Rule 53. Trial of all issues shall otherwise be by the court.

(i) Dismissal of Action.

(1) *As of Right.* If no hearing has begun to determine the compensation to be paid for a piece of property and the plaintiff has not acquired the title or a lesser interest in or taken possession, the plaintiff may dismiss the action as to that property, without an order of the court, by filing a notice of dismissal setting forth a brief description of the property as to which the action is dismissed.

(2) *By Stipulation.* Before the entry of any judgment vesting the plaintiff with title or a lesser interest in or possession of property, the action may be dismissed in whole or in part, without an order of the court, as to any property by filing a stipulation of dismissal by the plaintiff and the defendant affected thereby; and, if the parties so stipulate, the court may vacate any judgment that has been entered.

(3) *By Order of the Court.* At any time before compensation for a piece of property has been determined and paid and after motion and hearing, the court may dismiss the action as to that property, except that it shall not dismiss the action as to any part of the property of which the plaintiff has taken possession or in which the plaintiff has taken title or a lesser interest, but shall award just compensation for the possession, title or lesser interest so taken. The court at any time may drop a defendant unnecessarily or improperly joined.

(4) *Effect.* Except as otherwise provided in the notice, or stipulation of dismissal, or order of the court, any dismissal is without prejudice.

(j) Deposit and Its Distribution. The plaintiff shall deposit with the court any money required by law as a condition to the exercise of the power of eminent domain; and, although not so required, may make a deposit when permitted by statute. In such cases the court and attorneys shall expedite the proceedings for the distribution of the money so deposited and for the ascertainment and payment of just compensation. If the compensation finally awarded to any defendant exceeds the amount which has been paid to that defendant on distribution of the deposit, the court shall enter judgment against the plaintiff and in favor of that defendant for the deficiency. If the compensation finally awarded to any defendant is less than the amount which has been paid to that defendant, the court shall enter judgment against that defendant and in favor of the plaintiff for the overpayment.

(k) Condemnation Under a State's Power of Eminent Domain. The practice as herein prescribed governs in actions involving the exercise of the power of eminent domain under the law of a state, provided that if the state law makes provision for trial of any issue by jury, or for trial of the issue of compensation by jury or commission or both, that provision shall be followed.

(*l*) Costs. Costs are not subject to Rule 54(d).

Rule 72. Magistrates; Pretrial Matters

(a) Nondispositive Matters. A magistrate judge to whom a pretrial matter not dispositive of a claim or defense of a party is referred to hear and determine shall promptly conduct such proceedings as are required and when appropriate enter into the record a written order setting forth the disposition of the matter. Within 10 days after being served with a copy of the magistrate judge's order, a party may serve and file objections to the order; a party may not thereafter assign as error a defect in the magistrate judge's order to which objection was not timely made. The district judge to whom the case is assigned shall consider such objections and shall modify or set aside any portion of the magistrate judge's order found to be clearly erroneous or contrary to law.

(b) Dispositive Motions and Prisoner Petitions. A magistrate judge assigned without consent of the parties to hear a pretrial matter dispositive of a claim or defense of a party or a prisoner petition challenging the conditions of confinement shall promptly conduct such proceedings as are required. A record shall be made of all evidentiary proceedings before the magistrate judge, and a record may be made of such other proceedings as the magistrate judge deems necessary. The magistrate judge shall enter into the record a recommendation for disposition of the matter, including proposed findings of fact when appropriate. The clerk shall forthwith mail copies to all parties.

A party objecting to the recommended disposition of the matter shall promptly arrange for the transcription of the record, or portions of it as all parties may agree upon or the magistrate judge deems sufficient, unless the district judge otherwise directs. Within 10 days after being served with a copy of the recommended disposition, a party may serve and file specific, written objections to the proposed findings and recommendations. A party may respond to another party's objections within 10 days after being served with a copy thereof. The district judge to whom the case is assigned shall make a de novo determination upon the record, or after additional evidence, of any portion of the magistrate judge's disposition to which specific written objection has been made in accordance with this rule. The district judge may accept, reject, or modify the recommended decision, receive further evidence, or recommit the matter to the magistrate judge with instructions.

Rule 73. Magistrate Judges; Trial by Consent and Appeal Options

(a) Powers; Procedure. When specially designated to exercise such jurisdiction by local rule or order of the district court and when all parties consent thereto, a magistrate judge may exercise the authority provided by Title 28, U.S.C. § 636(c) and may conduct any or all proceedings, including a jury or nonjury trial, in a civil case. A record of the proceedings shall be made in accordance with the requirements of Title 28, U.S.C. § 636(c)(7).

(b) Consent. When a magistrate judge has been designated to exercise civil trial jurisdiction, the clerk shall give written notice to the parties of their opportunity to consent to the exercise by a magistrate of civil jurisdiction over the case, as authorized by Title 28, U.S.C. § 636(c). If, within the period specified by local rule, the parties agree to a magistrate judge's exercise of such authority, they shall execute and file a joint form of consent or separate forms of consent setting forth such election.

A district judge, magistrate judge, or other court official may again advise the parties of the availability of the magistrate judge, but, in so doing, shall also advise the parties that they are free to withhold consent without adverse substantive consequences. A district judge or magistrate judge shall not be informed of a party's response to the clerk's notification, unless all parties have consented to the referral of the matter to a magistrate judge.

The district judge, for good cause shown on the judge's motion, or under extraordinary circumstances shown by a party, may vacate a reference of a civil matter to a magistrate judge under this subdivision.

(c) Normal Appeal Route. In accordance with Title 28, U.S.C. § 636(c)(3), unless the parties otherwise agree to the optional appeal route provided for in subdivision (d) of this rule, appeal from a judgment entered upon direction of a magistrate judge in proceedings under this rule will lie to the court of appeals as it would from a judgment of the district court.

(d) Optional Appeal Route. In accordance with Title 28, U.S.C. § 636(c)(4), at the time of reference to a magistrate judge, the parties may consent to appeal on the record to a judge of the district court and thereafter, by petition only, to the court of appeals.

Rule 74. Method of Appeal From Magistrate Judge to District Judge Under Title 28, U.S.C. § 636(c)(4) and Rule 73(d)

(a) When Taken. When the parties have elected under Rule 73(d) to proceed by appeal to a district judge from an appealable decision made by a magistrate judge under the consent provisions of Title 28, U.S.C. § 636(c)(4), an appeal may be taken from the decision of a magistrate judge by filing with the clerk of the district court a notice of appeal within 30 days of the date of entry of the judgment appealed from; but if the United States or an officer or agency thereof is a party, the notice of appeal may be filed by any party within 60 days of such entry. If a timely notice of appeal is filed by a party, any other party may file a notice of appeal within 14 days thereafter, or within the time otherwise prescribed by this subdivision, whichever period last expires.

The running of the time for filing a notice of appeal is terminated as to all parties by the timely filing of any of the following motions with the magistrate judge by any party, and the full time for appeal from the judgment entered by the magistrate judge commences to run anew from entry of any of the following orders: (1) granting or denying a motion for judgment under Rule 50(b); (2) granting or denying a motion under Rule 52(b) to amend or make additional findings of fact, whether or not an alteration of the judgment would be required if the motion is granted; (3) granting or denying a motion under Rule 59 to alter or amend the judgment; (4) denying a motion for a new trial under Rule 59.

An interlocutory decision or order by a magistrate judge which, if made by a district judge, could be appealed under any provision of law, may be appealed to a district judge, by filing a notice of appeal within 15 days after entry of the decision or order, provided the parties have elected to appeal to a district judge under Rule 73(d). An appeal of such interlocutory decision or order shall not stay the proceedings before the magistrate judge unless the magistrate judge or district judge shall so order.

Upon a showing of excusable neglect, the magistrate judge may extend the time for filing a notice of appeal upon motion filed not later than 20 days after the expiration of the time otherwise prescribed by this rule.

(b) Notice of Appeal; Service. The notice of appeal shall specify the party or parties taking the appeal, designate the judgment, order or part thereof appealed from, and state that the appeal is to a judge of the district court. The clerk shall mail copies of the notice to all other parties and note the date of mailing in the civil docket.

(c) Stay Pending Appeal. Upon a showing that the magistrate judge has refused or otherwise failed to stay the judgment pending appeal to the district judge under Rule 73(d), the appellant may make application for a stay to the district judge with reasonable notice to all parties. The stay may be conditioned upon the filing in the district court of a bond or other appropriate security.

(d) Dismissal. For failure to comply with these rules or any local rule or order, the district judge may take such action as is deemed appropriate, including dismissal of the appeal. The district judge also

Rule 74   RULES OF CIVIL PROCEDURE

may dismiss the appeal upon the filing of a stipulation signed by all parties, or upon motion and notice by the appellant.

Rule 75. Proceedings on Appeal From Magistrate Judge to District Judge Under Rule 73(d)

(a) Applicability. In proceedings under Title 28, U.S.C. § 636(c), when the parties have previously elected under Rule 73(d) to appeal to a district judge rather than to the court of appeals, this rule shall govern the proceedings on appeal.

(b) Record on Appeal.

(1) *Composition.* The original papers and exhibits filed with the clerk of the district court, the transcript of the proceedings, if any, and the docket entries shall constitute the record on appeal. In lieu of this record the parties, within 10 days after the filing of the notice of appeal, may file a joint statement of the case showing how the issues presented by the appeal arose and were decided by the magistrate judge, and setting forth only so many of the facts averred and proved or sought to be proved as are essential to a decision of the issues presented.

(2) *Transcript.* Within 10 days after filing the notice of appeal the appellant shall make arrangements for the production of a transcript of such parts of the proceedings as the appellant deems necessary. Unless the entire transcript is to be included, the appellant, within the time provided above, shall serve on the appellee and file with the court a description of the parts of the transcript which the appellant intends to present on the appeal. If the appellee deems a transcript of other parts of the proceedings to be necessary, within 10 days after the service of the statement of the appellant, the appellee shall serve on the appellant and file with the court a designation of additional parts to be included. The appellant shall promptly make arrangements for the inclusion of all such parts unless the magistrate judge, upon motion, exempts the appellant from providing certain parts, in which case the appellee may provide for their transcription.

(3) *Statement in Lieu of Transcript.* If no record of the proceedings is available for transcription, the parties shall, within 10 days after the filing of the notice of appeal, file a statement of the evidence from the best available means to be submitted in lieu of the transcript. If the parties cannot agree they shall submit a statement of their differences to the magistrate judge for settlement.

(c) Time for Filing Briefs. Unless a local rule or court order otherwise provides, the following time limits for filing briefs shall apply.

(1) The appellant shall serve and file the appellant's brief within 20 days after the filing of the transcript, statement of the case, or statement of the evidence.

(2) The appellee shall serve and file the appellee's brief within 20 days after service of the brief of the appellant.

(3) The appellant may serve and file a reply brief within 10 days after service of the brief of the appellee.

(4) If the appellee has filed a cross-appeal, the appellee may file a reply brief limited to the issues on the cross-appeal within 10 days after service of the reply brief of the appellant.

(d) Length and Form of Briefs. Briefs may be typewritten. The length and form of briefs shall be governed by local rule.

(e) Oral Argument. The opportunity for the parties to be heard on oral argument shall be governed by local rule.

Rule 76. Judgment of the District Judge on the Appeal Under Rule 73(d) and Costs

(a) Entry of Judgment. When the parties have elected under Rule 73(d) to appeal from a judgment of the magistrate judge to a district judge, the clerk shall prepare, sign, and enter judgment in accordance with the order or decision of the district judge following an appeal from a judgment of the magistrate judge, unless the district judge directs otherwise. The clerk shall mail to all parties a copy of the order or decision of the district judge.

(b) Stay of Judgments. The decision of the district judge shall be stayed for 10 days during which time a party may petition the district judge for rehearing, and a timely petition shall stay the decision of the district judge pending disposition of a petition for rehearing. Upon the motion of a party, the decision of the district judge may be stayed in order to allow a party to petition the court of appeals for leave to appeal.

(c) Costs. Except as otherwise provided by law or ordered by the district judge, costs shall be taxed against the losing party; if a judgment of the magistrate judge is affirmed in part or reversed in part, or is vacated, costs shall be allowed only as ordered by the district judge. The cost of the transcript, if necessary for the determination of the appeal, and the premiums paid for bonds to preserve rights pending appeal shall be taxed as costs by the clerk.

X. DISTRICT COURTS AND CLERKS

Rule 77. District Courts and Clerks

(a) District Courts Always Open. The district courts shall be deemed always open for the purpose of filing any pleading or other proper paper, of issuing and returning mesne and final process, and of making and directing all interlocutory motions, orders, and rules.

(b) Trials and Hearings; Orders in Chambers. All trials upon the merits shall be conducted in open court and so far as convenient in a regular court room. All other acts or proceedings may be done or conducted by a judge in chambers, without the attendance of the clerk or other court officials and at any place either within or without the district; but no hearing, other than one ex parte, shall be conducted outside the district without the consent of all parties affected thereby.

(c) Clerk's Office and Orders by Clerk. The clerk's office with the clerk or a deputy in attendance shall be open during business hours on all days except Saturdays, Sundays, and legal holidays, but a district court may provide by local rule or order that its clerk's office shall be open for specified hours on Saturdays or particular legal holidays other than New Year's Day, Washington's Birthday, Memorial Day, Independence Day, Labor Day, Columbus Day, Veterans Day, Thanksgiving Day, and Christmas Day. All motions and applications in the clerk's office for issuing mesne process, for issuing final process to enforce and execute judgments, for entering defaults or judgments by default, and for other proceedings which do not require allowance or order of the court are grantable of course by the clerk; but the clerk's action may be suspended or altered or rescinded by the court upon cause shown.

(d) Notice of Orders or Judgments. Immediately upon the entry of an order or judgment the clerk shall serve a notice of the entry by mail in the manner provided for in Rule 5 upon each party who is not in default for failure to appear, and shall make a note in the docket of the mailing. Any party may in addition serve a notice of such entry in the manner provided in Rule 5 for the service of papers. Lack of notice of the entry by the clerk does not affect the time to appeal or relieve or authorize the court to relieve a party for failure to appeal within the time allowed, except as permitted in Rule 4(a) of the Federal Rules of Appellate Procedure.

Rule 78. Motion Day

Unless local conditions make it impracticable, each district court shall establish regular times and places, at intervals sufficiently frequent for the prompt dispatch of business, at which motions requiring notice and hearing may be heard and disposed of; but the judge at any time or place and on such notice, if any, as the judge considers reasonable may make orders for the advancement, conduct, and hearing of actions.

To expedite its business, the court may make provision by rule or order for the submission and determination of motions without oral hearing upon brief written statements of reasons in support and opposition.

Rule 79. Books and Records Kept by the Clerk and Entries Therein

(a) Civil Docket. The clerk shall keep a book known as "civil docket" of such form and style as may be prescribed by the Director of the Administrative Office of the United States Courts with the approval of the Judicial Conference of the United States, and shall enter therein each civil action to which these rules are made applicable. Actions shall be assigned consecutive file numbers. The file number of each action shall be noted on the folio of the docket whereon the first entry of the action is made. All papers filed with the clerk, all process issued and returns made thereon, all appearances, orders, verdicts, and judgments shall be entered chronologically in the civil docket on the folio assigned to the action and shall be marked with its file number. These entries shall be brief but shall show the nature of each paper filed or writ issued and the substance of each order or judgment of the court and of the returns showing execution of process. The entry of an order or judgment shall show the date the entry is made. When in an action trial by jury has been properly demanded or ordered the clerk shall enter the word "jury" on the folio assigned to that action.

(b) Civil Judgments and Orders. The clerk shall keep, in such form and manner as the Director of the Administrative Office of the United States Courts with the approval of the Judicial Conference of the United States may prescribe, a correct copy of every final judgment or appealable order, or order affecting title to or lien upon real or personal property, and any other order which the court may direct to be kept.

(c) Indices; Calendars. Suitable indices of the civil docket and of every civil judgment and order referred to in subdivision (b) of this rule shall be kept by the clerk under the direction of the court. There shall be prepared under the direction of the court calendars of all actions ready for trial, which shall distinguish "jury actions" from "court actions."

(d) Other Books and Records of the Clerk. The clerk shall also keep such other books and records as may be required from time to time by the Director of the Administrative Office of the United States Courts with the approval of the Judicial Conference of the United States.

Rule 80. Stenographer; Stenographic Report or Transcript as Evidence

(a), (b) [Abrogated]

(c) Stenographic Report or Transcript as Evidence. Whenever the testimony of a witness at a trial or hearing which was stenographically reported is admissible in evidence at a later trial, it may be proved by the transcript thereof duly certified by the person who reported the testimony.

Rule 81. RULES OF CIVIL PROCEDURE

XI. GENERAL PROVISIONS

Rule 81. Applicability in General

(a) To What Proceedings Applicable.

(1) These rules do not apply to prize proceedings in admiralty governed by Title 10, U.S.C. §§ 7651–7681. They do not apply to proceedings in bankruptcy or proceedings in copyright under Title 17, U.S.C., except in so far as they may be made applicable thereto by rules promulgated by Supreme Court of the United States. They do not apply to mental health proceedings in the United States District Court for the District of Columbia.

(2) These rules are applicable to proceedings for admission to citizenship, habeas corpus, and quo warranto, to the extent that the practice in such proceedings is not set forth in statutes of the United States and has heretofore conformed to the practice in civil actions. The writ of habeas corpus, or order to show cause, shall be directed to the person having custody of the person detained. It shall be returned within 3 days unless for good cause shown additional time is allowed which in cases brought under 28 U.S.C. § 2254 shall not exceed 40 days, and in all other cases shall not exceed 20 days.

(3) In proceedings under Title 9, U.S.C., relating to arbitration, or under the Act of May 20, 1926, ch. 347, § 9 (44 Stat. 585), U.S.C., Title 45, § 159, relating to boards of arbitration of railway labor disputes, these rules apply only to the extent that matters of procedure are not provided for in those statutes. These rules apply to proceedings to compel the giving of testimony or production of documents in accordance with a subpoena issued by an officer or agency of the United States under any statute of the United States except as otherwise provided by statute or by rules of the district court or by order of the court in the proceedings.

(4) These rules do not alter the method prescribed by the Act of February 18, 1922, c. 57, § 2 (42 Stat. 388), U.S.C., Title 7, § 292; or by the Act of June 10, 1930, c. 436, § 7 (46 Stat. 534), as amended, U.S.C., Title 7, § 499g(c), for instituting proceedings in the United States district courts to review orders of the Secretary of Agriculture; or prescribed by the Act of June 25, 1934, c. 742, § 2 (48 Stat. 1214), U.S.C., Title 15, § 522, for instituting proceedings to review orders of the Secretary of the Interior; or prescribed by the Act of February 22, 1935, c. 18, § 5 (49 Stat. 31), U.S.C., Title 15, § 715d(c), as extended, for instituting proceedings to review orders of petroleum control boards; but the conduct of such proceedings in the district courts shall be made to conform to these rules as far as applicable.

(5) These rules do not alter the practice in the United States district courts prescribed in the Act of July 5, 1935, c. 372, §§ 9 and 10 (49 Stat.

453), as amended, U.S.C., Title 29, §§ 159 and 160, for beginning and conducting proceedings to enforce orders of the National Labor Relations Board; and in respects not covered by those statutes, the practice in the district courts shall conform to these rules so far as applicable.

(6) These rules apply to proceedings for enforcement or review of compensation orders under the Longshoremen's and Harbor Workers' Compensation Act, Act of March 4, 1927, c. 509, §§ 18, 21 (44 Stat. 1434, 1436), as amended, U.S.C., Title 33, §§ 918, 921, except to the extent that matters of procedure are provided for in that Act. The provisions for service by publication and for answer in proceedings to cancel certificates of citizenship under the Act of June 27, 1952, c. 477, Title III, c. 2, § 340 (66 Stat. 260), U.S.C., Title 8, § 1451, remain in effect.

(7) [Abrogated]

(b) Scire Facias and Mandamus. The writs of scire facias and mandamus are abolished. Relief heretofore available by mandamus or scire facias may be obtained by appropriate action or by appropriate motion under the practice prescribed in these rules.

(c) Removed Actions. These rules apply to civil actions removed to the United States district courts from the state courts and govern procedure after removal. Repleading is not necessary unless the court so orders. In a removed action in which the defendant has not answered, the defendant shall answer or present the other defenses or objections available under these rules within 20 days after the receipt through service or otherwise of a copy of the initial pleading setting forth the claim for relief upon which the action or proceeding is based, or within 20 days after the service of summons upon such initial pleading, then filed, or within 5 days after the filing of the petition for removal, whichever period is longest. If at the time of removal all necessary pleadings have been served, a party entitled to trial by jury under Rule 38 shall be accorded it, if the party's demand therefor is served within 10 days after the petition for removal is filed if the party is the petitioner, or if not the petitioner within 10 days after service on the party of the notice of filing the petition. A party who, prior to removal, has made an express demand for trial by jury in accordance with state law, need not make a demand after removal. If state law applicable in the court from which the case is removed does not require the parties to make express demands in order to claim trial by jury, they need not make demands after removal unless the court directs that they do so within a specified time if they desire to claim trial by jury. The court may make this direction on its own motion and shall do so as a matter of course at the request of any party. The failure of a party to make demand as directed constitutes a waiver by that party of trial by jury.

(d) [Abrogated]

(e) Law Applicable. Whenever in these rules the law of the state in which the district court is held is made applicable, the law applied in the District of Columbia governs proceedings in the United States District Court for the District of Columbia. When the word "state" is used, it includes, if appropriate, the District of Columbia. When the term "statute of the United States" is used, it includes, so far as concerns proceedings in the United States District Court for the District of Columbia, any Act of Congress locally applicable to and in force in the District of Columbia. When the law of a state is referred to, the word "law" includes the statutes of that state and the state judicial decisions construing them.

(f) References to Officer of the United States. Under any rule in which reference is made to an officer or agency of the United States, the term "officer" includes a district director of internal revenue, a former district director or collector of internal revenue, or the personal representative of a deceased district director or collector of internal revenue.

Rule 82. Jurisdiction and Venue Unaffected

These rules shall not be construed to extend or limit the jurisdiction of the United States district courts or the venue of actions therein. An admiralty or maritime claim within the meaning of Rule 9(h) shall not be treated as a civil action for the purposes of Title 28, U.S.C. §§ 1391–93.

Rule 83. Rules by District Courts *

Each district court by action of a majority of the judges thereof may from time to time, after giving appropriate public notice and an opportunity to comment, make and amend rules governing its practice not inconsistent with these rules. A local rule so adopted shall take effect upon the date specified by the district court and shall remain in effect unless amended by the district court or abrogated by the judicial council of the circuit in which the district is located. Copies of rules and amendments so made by the district court shall upon their promulgation be furnished to the judicial council and the Administrative Office of the United States Courts and be made available to the public. In all cases not provided for by rule, the district judges and magistrates may regulate their practice in any manner not inconsistent with these rules or those of the district in which they act.

1985 Amendment to Rule 83

The 1985 alteration enhances the local rulemaking process by requiring appropriate public notice of proposed rules and an opportunity to comment on them. It attempts to assure that the expert advice of practitioners and scholars is made available to the district court before local rules are promulgated.

* Proposed amendments to Rule 83 are found in Part X of this Supplement.

Rule 84. Forms

The forms contained in the Appendix of Forms are sufficient under the rules and are intended to indicate the simplicity and brevity of statement which the rules contemplate.

Notes on the 1946 Amendment to Federal Rule 84

In 1946 Rule 84 was amended to state that the forms were sufficient under the rules. The Advisory Committee commented as follows:

The amendment serves to emphasize that the forms contained in the Appendix of Forms are sufficient to withstand attack under the rules under which they are drawn, and that the practitioner using them may rely on them to that extent. The circuit courts of appeals generally have upheld the use of the forms as promoting desirable simplicity and brevity of statement. Sierocinski v. E. I. DuPont DeNemours & Co. (CCA3d, 1939) 103 F.2d 843; Swift & Co. v. Young (CCA4th, 1939) 107 F.2d 170; Sparks v. England (CCA8th, 1940) 113 F.2d 579; Ramsouer v. Midland Valley R. Co. (CCA8th, 1943) 135 F.2d 101. And the forms as a whole have met with widespread approval in the courts. See cases cited in 1 Moore's Federal Practice (1938), Cum.Supplement § 8.07, under "Page 554"; see also Commentary, The Official Forms, 1941, 4 Fed. Rules Serv. 954. In Cook, "Facts" and "Statements of Fact", 1937, 4 U.Chi.L.Rev. 233, 245–246, it is said with reference to what is now Rule 84: "... pleaders in the federal courts are not to be left to guess as to the meaning of [the] language" in Rule 8(a) regarding the form of the complaint. "All of which is as it should be. In no other way can useless litigation be avoided." Ibid. The amended rule will operate to discourage isolated results such as those found in Washburn v. Moorman Mfg. Co. (S.D.Cal. 1938) 25 F.Supp. 546; Employers Mutual Liability Ins. Co. of Wisconsin v. Blue Line Transfer Co. (W.D.Mo.1941) 5 Fed.Rules Serv. 12e.235, Case 2.

Rule 85. Title

These rules may be known and cited as the Federal Rules of Civil Procedure.

Rule 86. Effective Date

(a) [Effective Date of Original Rules]. These rules will take effect on the day which is 3 months subsequent to the adjournment of the second regular session of the 75th Congress, but if that day is prior to September 1, 1938, then these rules will take effect on September 1, 1938. They govern all proceedings in actions brought after they take effect and also all further proceedings in actions then pending, except to the extent that in the opinion of the court their application in a particular action pending when the rules take effect would not be feasible or would work injustice, in which event the former procedure applies.

(b) Effective Date of Amendments. The amendments adopted by the Supreme Court on December 27, 1946, and transmitted to the Attorney General on January 2, 1947, shall take effect on the day which is three months subsequent to the adjournment of the first regular session of the 80th Congress, but, if that day is prior to September 1, 1947, then these amendments shall take effect on September 1, 1947. They govern all proceedings in actions brought after they take effect and also all further proceedings in actions then pending, except to the extent that in the opinion of the court their application in a particular action pending when the amendments take effect would not be feasible or would work injustice, in which event the former procedure applies.

(c) Effective Date of Amendments. The amendments adopted by the Supreme Court on December 29, 1948, and transmitted to the Attorney General on December 31, 1948, shall take effect on the day following the adjournment of the first regular session of the 81st Congress.

(d) Effective Date of Amendments. The amendments adopted by the Supreme Court on April 17, 1961, and transmitted to the Congress on April 18, 1961, shall take effect on July 19, 1961. They govern all proceedings in actions brought after they take effect and also all further proceedings in actions then pending, except to the extent that in the opinion of the court their application in a particular action pending when the amendments take effect would not be feasible or would work injustice, in which event the former procedure applies.

(e) Effective Date of Amendments. The amendments adopted by the Supreme Court on January 21, 1963, and transmitted to the Congress on January 21, 1963, shall take effect on July 1, 1963. They govern all proceedings in actions brought after they take effect and also all further proceedings in actions then pending, except to the extent that in the opinion of the court their application in a particular action pending when the amendments take effect would not be feasible or would work injustice, in which event the former procedure applies.

APPENDIX OF FORMS

(See Rule 84)

Introductory Statement

1. The following forms are intended for illustration only. They are limited in number. No attempt is made to furnish a manual of forms. Each form assumes the action to be brought in the Southern District of New York. If the district in which an action is brought has divisions, the division should be indicated in the caption.

2. Except where otherwise indicated each pleading, motion, and other paper should have a caption similar to that of the summons, with the designation of the particular paper substituted for the word "Summons". In the caption of the summons and in the caption of the complaint all parties must be named but in other pleadings and papers, it is sufficient to state the name of the first party on either side, with an appropriate indication of other parties. See Rules 4(b), 7(b)(2), and 10(a).

3. In Form 3 and the forms following, the words, "Allegation of jurisdiction," are used to indicate the appropriate allegation in Form 2.

4. Each pleading, motion, and other paper is to be signed in his individual name by at least one attorney of record (Rule 11). The attorney's name is to be followed by his address as indicated in Form 3. In forms following Form 3 the signature and address are not indicated.

5. If a party is not represented by an attorney, the signature and address of the party are required in place of those of the attorney.

Form 1.

SUMMONS

UNITED STATES DISTRICT COURT FOR THE
SOUTHERN DISTRICT OF NEW YORK

Civil Action, File Number _____

A. B., Plaintiff
    v.   *Summons*

C. D., Defendant

To the above-named Defendant:

You are hereby summoned and required to serve upon _____, plaintiff's attorney, whose address is _____, an answer to

Form 1   RULES OF CIVIL PROCEDURE

the complaint which is herewith served upon you, within 20[1] days after service of this summons upon you, exclusive of the day of service. If you fail to do so, judgment by default will be taken against you for the relief demanded in the complaint.

_____,
Clerk of Court.

[Seal of the U. S. District Court]

Dated _____

(This summons is issued pursuant to Rule 4
of the Federal Rules of Civil Procedure)

Form 1–A.

NOTICE OF LAWSUIT AND REQUEST FOR WAIVER OF SERVICE OF SUMMONS

TO: _____(A)_____ [as _____(B)_____ of _____(C)_____]

A lawsuit has been commenced against you (or the entity on whose behalf you are addressed). A copy of the complaint is attached to this notice. It has been filed in the United States District Court for the _____(D)_____ and has been assigned docket number _____(E)_____.

This is not a formal summons or notification from the court, but rather my request that you sign and return the enclosed waiver of service in order to save the cost of serving you with a judicial summons and an additional copy of the complaint. The cost of service will be avoided if I receive a signed copy of the waiver within _____(F)_____ days after the date designated below as the date on which this Notice and Request is sent. I enclose a stamped and addressed envelope (or other means of cost-free return) for your use. An extra copy of the waiver is also attached for your records.

If you comply with this request and return the signed waiver, it will be filed with the court and no summons will be served on you. The action will then proceed as if you had been served on the date the waiver is filed, except that you will not be obligated to answer the complaint before 60 days from the date designated below as the date on which this notice is sent (or before 90 days from that date if your address is not in any judicial district of the United States).

If you do not return the signed waiver within the time indicated, I will take appropriate steps to effect formal service in a manner authorized by the Federal Rules of Civil Procedure and will then, to the extent

---

[1] If the United States or an officer or agency thereof is a defendant, the time to be inserted as to it is 60 days.

APPENDIX OF FORMS — Form 1-B

authorized by those Rules, ask the court to require you (or the party on whose behalf you are addressed) to pay the full costs of such service. In that connection, please read the statement concerning the duty of parties to waive the service of the summons, which is set forth on the reverse side (or at the foot) of the waiver form.

I affirm that this request is being sent to you on behalf of the plaintiff, this ___ day of _____, ___.

_____
Signature of Plaintiff's Attorney
or Unrepresented Plaintiff

Notes:

A—Name of individual defendant (or name of officer or agent of corporate defendant)

B—Title, or other relationship of individual to corporate defendant

C—Name of corporate defendant, if any

D—District

E—Docket number of action

F—Addressee must be given at least 30 days (60 days if located in foreign country) in which to return waiver

Form 1-B.

WAIVER OF SERVICE OF SUMMONS

TO: (name of plaintiff's attorney or unrepresented plaintiff)

I acknowledge receipt of your request that I waive service of a summons in the action of   (caption of action) , which is case number   (docket number)   in the United States District Court for the   (district) . I have also received a copy of the complaint in the action, two copies of this instrument, and a means by which I can return the signed waiver to you without cost to me.

I agree to save the cost of service of a summons and an additional copy of the complaint in this lawsuit by not requiring that I (or the entity on whose behalf I am acting) be served with judicial process in the manner provided by Rule 4.

I (or the entity on whose behalf I am acting) will retain all defenses or objections to the lawsuit or to the jurisdiction or venue of the court except for objections based on a defect in the summons or in the service of the summons.

I understand that a judgment may be entered against me (or the party on whose behalf I am acting) if an answer or motion under Rule 12 is not served upon you within 60 days after   (date request was sent) , or within 90 days after that date if the request was sent outside the United States.

Form 1-B   RULES OF CIVIL PROCEDURE

Date   Signature
       Printed/typed name: _____
         [as _____]
         [of _____]

To be printed on reverse side of the waiver form or set forth at the foot of the form:

Duty to Avoid Unnecessary Costs of Service of Summons

Rule 4 of the Federal Rules of Civil Procedure requires certain parties to cooperate in saving unnecessary costs of service of the summons and complaint. A defendant located in the United States who, after being notified of an action and asked by a plaintiff located in the United States to waive service of a summons, fails to do so will be required to bear the cost of such service unless good cause be shown for its failure to sign and return the waiver.

It is not good cause for a failure to waive service that a party believes that the complaint is unfounded, or that the action has been brought in an improper place or in a court that lacks jurisdiction over the subject matter of the action or over its person or property. A party who waives service of the summons retains all defenses and objections (except any relating to the summons or to the service of the summons), and may later object to the jurisdiction of the court or to the place where the action has been brought.

A defendant who waives service must within the time specified on the waiver form serve on the plaintiff's attorney (or unrepresented plaintiff) a response to the complaint and must also file a signed copy of the response with the court. If the answer or motion is not served within this time, a default judgment may be taken against that defendant. By waiving service, a defendant is allowed more time to answer than if the summons had been actually served when the request for waiver of service was received.

Form 2.

ALLEGATION OF JURISDICTION

(a) Jurisdiction founded on diversity of citizenship and amount.

Plaintiff is a [citizen of the State of Connecticut] [corporation incorporated under the laws of the State of Connecticut having its principal place of business in the State of Connecticut] and defendant is a corporation incorporated under the laws of the State of New York having its principal place of business in a State other than the State of Connecticut. The matter in controversy exceeds, exclusive of interest and costs, the sum of fifty thousand dollars.

(b) Jurisdiction founded on the existence of a Federal question.

The action arises under [the Constitution of the United States, Article ___, Section ___]; [the ___ Amendment to the Constitution of the United States, Section ___]; [the Act of ___, ___ Stat. ___; U.S.C., Title ___, § ___]; [the Treaty of the United States (here describe the treaty)], as hereinafter more fully appears.

(c) Jurisdiction founded on the existence of a question arising under particular statutes.

The action arises under the Act of ___, ___ Stat. ___; U.S.C., Title ___, § ___, as hereinafter more fully appears.

(d) Jurisdiction founded on the admiralty or maritime character of the claim.

This is a case of admiralty and maritime jurisdiction, as hereinafter more fully appears. [If the pleader wishes to invoke the distinctively maritime procedures referred to in Rule 9(h), add the following or its substantial equivalent: This is an admiralty or maritime claim within the meaning of Rule 9(h).]

Form 3.

COMPLAINT ON A PROMISSORY NOTE

1. Allegation of jurisdiction.

2. Defendant on or about June 1, 1935, executed and delivered to plaintiff a promissory note [in the following words and figures: (here set out the note verbatim)]; [a copy of which is hereto annexed as Exhibit A]; [whereby defendant promised to pay to plaintiff or order on June 1, 1936 the sum of _____ dollars with interest thereon at the rate of six percent * * * per annum].

3. Defendant owes to plaintiff the amount of said note and interest.

Wherefore plaintiff demands judgment against defendant for the sum of _____ dollars, interest, and costs.

Signed: _____
Attorney for Plaintiff

Address: _____

Form 4.

COMPLAINT ON AN ACCOUNT

1. Allegation of jurisdiction.

2. Defendant owes plaintiff _____ dollars according to the account hereto annexed as Exhibit A.

Wherefore (etc. as in Form 3).

Form 5.

COMPLAINT FOR GOODS SOLD AND DELIVERED

1. Allegation of jurisdiction.

2. Defendant owes plaintiff _____ dollars for goods sold and delivered by plaintiff to defendant between June 1, 1936 and December 1, 1936.

Wherefore (etc. as in Form 3).

Form 6.

COMPLAINT FOR MONEY LENT

1. Allegation of jurisdiction.

2. Defendant owes plaintiff _____ dollars for money lent by plaintiff to defendant on June 1, 1936.

Wherefore (etc. as in Form 3).

Form 7.

COMPLAINT FOR MONEY PAID BY MISTAKE

1. Allegation of jurisdiction.

2. Defendant owes plaintiff _____ dollars for money paid by plaintiff to defendant by mistake on June 1, 1936, under the following circumstances: [here state the circumstances with particularity—see Rule 9(b)].

Wherefore (etc. as in Form 3).

Form 8.

COMPLAINT FOR MONEY HAD AND RECEIVED

1. Allegation of jurisdiction.

2. Defendant owes plaintiff _____ dollars for money had and received from one G. H. on June 1, 1936, to be paid by defendant to plaintiff.

Wherefore (etc. as in Form 3).

Form 9.

COMPLAINT FOR NEGLIGENCE

1. Allegation of jurisdiction.

APPENDIX OF FORMS   Form 10

2. On June 1, 1936, in a public highway called Boylston Street in Boston, Massachusetts, defendant negligently drove a motor vehicle against plaintiff who was then crossing said highway.

3. As a result plaintiff was thrown down and had his leg broken and was otherwise injured, was prevented from transacting his business, suffered great pain of body and mind, and incurred expenses for medical attention and hospitalization in the sum of one thousand dollars.

Wherefore plaintiff demands judgment against defendant in the sum of _____ dollars and costs.

Comparative State Provision
North Carolina Rules of Civil Procedure—[Form] (3) Complaint for Negligence

1. On _____, 19__, at [name of place where accident occurred], defendant negligently drove a motor vehicle against plaintiff who was then crossing said street.

2. Defendant was negligent in that:

(a) Defendant drove at an excessive speed.

(b) Defendant drove through a red light.

(c) Defendant failed to yield the right-of-way to plaintiff in a marked crosswalk.

3. As a result plaintiff was thrown down and had his leg broken and was otherwise injured, was prevented from transacting his business, suffered great pain of body and mind, and incurred expenses for medical attention and hospitalization [in the sum of one thousand dollars] (or) [in an amount not yet determined].

Wherefore, plaintiff demands judgment against defendant in the sum of _____ dollars and costs.

See also New York Civil Practice Law and Rules 3041, 3043, as set out in connection with Federal Rule 8(a), supra.

Form 10.

COMPLAINT FOR NEGLIGENCE WHERE PLAINTIFF IS UNABLE TO DETERMINE DEFINITELY WHETHER THE PERSON RESPONSIBLE IS C. D. OR E. F. OR WHETHER BOTH ARE RESPONSIBLE AND WHERE HIS EVIDENCE MAY JUSTIFY A FINDING OF WILFULNESS OR OF RECKLESSNESS OR OF NEGLIGENCE

A. B., Plaintiff
v.   } *Complaint*
C. D. and E. F., Defendants

1. Allegation of jurisdiction.

2. On June 1, 1936, in a public highway called Boylston Street in Boston, Massachusetts, defendant C. D. or defendant E. F., or both

Form 10   RULES OF CIVIL PROCEDURE

defendants C. D. and E. F. wilfully or recklessly or negligently drove or caused to be driven a motor vehicle against plaintiff who was then crossing said highway.

3. As a result plaintiff was thrown down and had his leg broken and was otherwise injured, was prevented from transacting his business, suffered great pain of body and mind, and incurred expenses for medical attention and hospitalization in the sum of one thousand dollars.

Wherefore plaintiff demands judgment against C. D. or against E. F. or against both in the sum of _____ dollars and costs.

Form 11.

COMPLAINT FOR CONVERSION

1. Allegation of jurisdiction.

2. On or about December 1, 1936, defendant converted to his own use ten bonds of the _____ Company (here insert brief identification as by number and issue) of the value of _____ dollars, the property of plaintiff.

Wherefore plaintiff demands judgment against defendant in the sum of _____ dollars, interest, and costs.

Form 12.

COMPLAINT FOR SPECIFIC PERFORMANCE OF CONTRACT TO CONVEY LAND

1. Allegation of jurisdiction.

2. On or about December 1, 1936, plaintiff and defendant entered into an agreement in writing a copy of which is hereto annexed as Exhibit A.

3. In accord with the provisions of said agreement plaintiff tendered to defendant the purchase price and requested a conveyance of the land, but defendant refused to accept the tender and refused to make the conveyance.

4. Plaintiff now offers to pay the purchase price.

Wherefore plaintiff demands (1) that defendant be required specifically to perform said agreement, (2) damages in the sum of one thousand dollars, and (3) that if specific performance is not granted plaintiff have judgment against defendant in the sum of _____ dollars.

APPENDIX OF FORMS Form 14

Form 13.

COMPLAINT ON CLAIM FOR DEBT AND TO SET ASIDE FRAUDULENT CONVEYANCE UNDER RULE 18(b)

A.B., Plaintiff
     v. } *Complaint*
C.D. and E.F., Defendants

1. Allegation of jurisdiction.

2. Defendant C.D. on or about ___ executed and delivered to plaintiff a promissory note [in the following words and figures: (here set out the note verbatim)]; [a copy of which is hereto annexed as Exhibit A]; [whereby defendant C.D. promised to pay to plaintiff or order on ___ the sum of five thousand dollars with interest thereon at the rate of ___ percent. per annum].

3. Defendant C.D. owes to plaintiff the amount of said note and interest.

4. Defendant C.D. on or about ___ conveyed all his property, real and personal [or specify and describe] to defendant E.F. for the purpose of defrauding plaintiff and hindering and delaying the collection of the indebtedness evidenced by the note above referred to.

Wherefore plaintiff demands:

(1) That plaintiff have judgment against defendant C.D. for ___ dollars and interest; (2) that the aforesaid conveyance to defendant E.F. be declared void and the judgment herein be declared a lien on said property; (3) that plaintiff have judgment against the defendants for costs.

Form 14.

COMPLAINT FOR NEGLIGENCE UNDER FEDERAL EMPLOYER'S LIABILITY ACT

1. Allegation of jurisdiction.

2. During all the times herein mentioned defendant owned and operated in interstate commerce a railroad which passed through a tunnel located at ___ and known as Tunnel No. ___.

3. On or about June 1, 1936, defendant was repairing and enlarging the tunnel in order to protect interstate trains and passengers and freight from injury and in order to make the tunnel more conveniently usable for interstate commerce.

4. In the course of thus repairing and enlarging the tunnel on said day defendant employed plaintiff as one of its workmen, and negligently put plaintiff to work in a portion of the tunnel which defendant had left unprotected and unsupported.

Form 14   RULES OF CIVIL PROCEDURE

5. By reason of defendant's negligence in thus putting plaintiff to work in that portion of the tunnel, plaintiff was, while so working pursuant to defendant's orders, struck and crushed by a rock, which fell from the unsupported portion of the tunnel, and was (here describe plaintiff's injuries).

6. Prior to these injuries, plaintiff was a strong, able-bodied man, capable of earning and actually earning ___ dollars per day. By these injuries he has been made incapable of any gainful activity, has suffered great physical and mental pain, and has incurred expense in the amount of ___ dollars for medicine, medical attendance, and hospitalization.

Wherefore plaintiff demands judgment against defendant in the sum of ___ dollars and costs.

Form 15.

COMPLAINT FOR DAMAGES UNDER MERCHANT MARINE ACT

1. Allegation of jurisdiction. [If the pleader wishes to invoke the distinctively maritime procedures referred to in Rule 9(h), add the following or its substantial equivalent: This is an admiralty or maritime claim within the meaning of Rule 9(h).]

2. During all the times herein mentioned defendant was the owner of the steamship _____ and used it in the transportation of freight for hire by water in interstate and foreign commerce.

3. During the first part of (month and year) at _____ plaintiff entered the employ of defendant as an able seaman on said steamship under seamen's articles of customary form for a voyage from _____ ports to the Orient and return at a wage of _____ dollars per month and found, which is equal to a wage of _____ dollars per month as a shore worker.

4. On June 1, 1936, said steamship was about _____ days out of the port of _____ and was being navigated by the master and crew on the return voyage to _____ ports. (Here describe weather conditions and the condition of the ship and state as in an ordinary complaint for personal injuries the negligent conduct of defendant.)

5. By reason of defendant's negligence in thus (brief statement of defendant's negligent conduct) and the unseaworthiness of said steamship, plaintiff was (here describe plaintiff's injuries).

6. Prior to these injuries, plaintiff was a strong, able-bodied man, capable of earning and actually earning _____ dollars per day. By these injuries he has been made incapable of any gainful activity; has suffered great physical and mental pain, and has incurred expense in the amount of _____ dollars for medicine, medical attendance, and hospitalization.

Wherefore plaintiff demands judgment against defendant in the sum of _____ dollars and costs.

Form 16.

COMPLAINT FOR INFRINGEMENT OF PATENT

1. Allegation of jurisdiction.

2. On May 16, 1934, United States Letters Patent No. __ were duly and legally issued to plaintiff for an invention in an electric motor; and since that date plaintiff has been and still is the owner of those Letters Patent.

3. Defendant has for a long time past been and still is infringing those Letters Patent by making, selling, and using electric motors embodying the patented invention, and will continue to do so unless enjoined by this court.

4. Plaintiff has placed the required statutory notice on all electric motors manufactured and sold by him under said Letters Patent, and has given written notice to defendant of his said infringement.

Wherefore plaintiff demands a preliminary and final injunction against continued infringement, an accounting for damages, and an assessment of interest and costs against defendant.

Form 17.

COMPLAINT FOR INFRINGEMENT OF COPYRIGHT AND UNFAIR COMPETITION

1. Allegation of jurisdiction.

2. Prior to March, 1936, plaintiff, who then was and ever since has been a citizen of the United States, created and wrote an original book, entitled _____.

3. This book contains a large amount of material wholly original with plaintiff and is copyrightable subject matter under the laws of the United States.

4. Between March 2, 1936, and March 10, 1936, plaintiff complied in all respects with the Act of (give citation) and all other laws governing copyright, and secured the exclusive rights and privileges in and to the copyright of said book, and received from the Register of Copyrights a certificate of registration, dated and identified as follows: "March 10, 1936, Class _____, No. _____."

5. Since March 10, 1936, said book has been published by plaintiff and all copies of it made by plaintiff or under his authority or license have been printed, bound, and published in strict conformity with the provisions of the Act of _____ and all other laws governing copyright.

Form 17   RULES OF CIVIL PROCEDURE

6. Since March 10, 1936, plaintiff has been and still is the sole proprietor of all rights, title, and interest in and to the copyright in said book.

7. After March 10, 1936, defendant infringed said copyright by publishing and placing upon the market a book entitled _____, which was copied largely from plaintiff's copyrighted book, entitled _____.

8. A copy of plaintiff's copyrighted book is hereto attached as "Exhibit 1"; and a copy of defendant's infringing book is hereto attached as "Exhibit 2."

9. Plaintiff has notified defendant that defendant has infringed the copyright of plaintiff, and defendant has continued to infringe the copyright.

10. After March 10, 1936, and continuously since about _____, defendant has been publishing, selling and otherwise marketing the book entitled _____, and has thereby been engaging in unfair trade practices and unfair competition against plaintiff's irreparable damage.

Wherefore plaintiff demands:

(1) That defendant, his agents, and servants be enjoined during the pendency of this action and permanently from infringing said copyright of said plaintiff in any manner, and from publishing, selling, marketing or otherwise disposing of any copies of the book entitled _____.

(2) That defendant be required to pay to plaintiff such damages as plaintiff has sustained in consequence of defendant's infringement of said copyright and said unfair trade practices and unfair competition and to account for

(a) all gains, profits and advantages derived by defendant by said trade practices and unfair competition and

(b) all gains, profits, and advantages derived by defendant by his infringement of plaintiff's copyright or such damages as to the court shall appear proper within the provisions of the copyright statutes, but not less than two hundred and fifty dollars.

(3) That defendant be required to deliver up to be impounded during the pendency of this action all copies of said book entitled _____ in his possession or under his control and to deliver up for destruction all infringing copies and all plates, molds, and other matter for making such infringing copies.

(4) That defendant pay to plaintiff the costs of this action and reasonable attorney's fees to be allowed to the plaintiff by the court.

(5) That plaintiff have such other and further relief as is just.

Form 18.

COMPLAINT FOR INTERPLEADER
AND DECLARATORY RELIEF

1. Allegation of jurisdiction.

2. On or about June 1, 1935, plaintiff issued to G.H. a policy of life insurance whereby plaintiff promised to pay to K.L. as beneficiary the sum of _____ dollars upon the death of G.H. The policy required the payment by G.H. of a stipulated premium on June 1, 1936, and annually thereafter as a condition precedent to its continuance in force.

3. No part of the premium due June 1, 1936, was ever paid and the policy ceased to have any force or effect on July 1, 1936.

4. Thereafter, on September 1, 1936, G.H. and K.L. died as the result of a collision between a locomotive and the automobile in which G.H. and K.L. were riding.

5. Defendant C.D. is the duly appointed and acting executor of the will of G.H.; defendant E.F. is the duly appointed and acting executor of the will of K.L.; defendant X.Y. claims to have been duly designated as beneficiary of said policy in place of K.L.

6. Each of defendants, C.D., E.F., and X.Y. is claiming that the above-mentioned policy was in full force and effect at the time of the death of G.H.; each of them is claiming to be the only person entitled to receive payment of the amount of the policy and has made demand for payment thereof.

7. By reason of these conflicting claims of the defendants, plaintiff is in great doubt as to which defendant is entitled to be paid the amount of the policy, if it was in force at the death of G.H.

Wherefore plaintiff demands that the court adjudge:

(1) That none of the defendants is entitled to recover from plaintiff the amount of said policy or any part thereof.

(2) That each of the defendants be restrained from instituting any action against plaintiff for the recovery of the amount of said policy or any part thereof.

(3) That, if the court shall determine that said policy was in force at the death of G.H., the defendants be required to interplead and settle between themselves their rights to the money due under said policy, and that plaintiff be discharged from all liability in the premises except to the person whom the court shall adjudge entitled to the amount of said policy.

(4) That plaintiff recover its costs.

Form 18–A RULES OF CIVIL PROCEDURE

Form 18–A. [Abrogated]

Form 19.

MOTION TO DISMISS, PRESENTING DEFENSES OF FAILURE TO STATE A CLAIM, OF LACK OF SERVICE OF PROCESS, OF IMPROPER VENUE, AND OF LACK OF JURISDICTION UNDER RULE 12(b)

The defendant moves the court as follows:

1. To dismiss the action because the complaint fails to state a claim against defendant upon which relief can be granted.

2. To dismiss the action or in lieu thereof to quash the return of service of summons on the grounds (a) that the defendant is a corporation organized under the laws of Delaware and was not and is not subject to service of process within the Southern District of New York, and (b) that the defendant has not been properly served with process in this action, all of which more clearly appears in the affidavits of M.N. and X.Y. hereto annexed as Exhibit A and Exhibit B respectively.

3. To dismiss the action on the ground that it is in the wrong district because (a) the jurisdiction of this court is invoked solely on the ground that the action arises under the Constitution and laws of the United States and (b) the defendant is a corporation incorporated under the laws of the State of Delaware and is not licensed to do or doing business in the Southern District of New York, all of which more clearly appears in the affidavits of K.L. and V.W. hereto annexed as Exhibits C and D respectively.

4. To dismiss the action on the ground that the court lacks jurisdiction because the amount actually in controversy is less than ten thousand dollars exclusive of interest and costs.

Signed: _____,
Attorney for Defendant.

Address: _____

Notice of Motion

To: _____
Attorney for Plaintiff.

Please take notice, that the undersigned will bring the above motion on for hearing before this Court at Room ___, United States Court House, Foley Square, City of New York, on the ___ day of _____, 193__, at 10 o'clock in the forenoon of that day or as soon thereafter as counsel can be heard.

Signed: _____,
Attorney for Defendant.

Address: _____

Form 20.

ANSWER PRESENTING DEFENSES UNDER RULE 12(b)

First Defense

The complaint fails to state a claim against defendant upon which relief can be granted.

Second Defense

If defendant is indebted to plaintiffs for the goods mentioned in the complaint, he is indebted to them jointly with G.H. G.H. is alive; is a citizen of the State of New York and a resident of this district, is subject to the jurisdiction of this court, as to both service of process and venue; can be made a party without depriving this court of jurisdiction of the present parties, and has not been made a party.

Third Defense

Defendant admits the allegation contained in paragraphs 1 and 4 of the complaint; alleges that he is without knowledge or information sufficient to form a belief as to the truth of the allegations contained in paragraph 2 of the complaint; and denies each and every other allegation contained in the complaint.

Fourth Defense

The right of action set forth in the complaint did not accrue within six years next before the commencement of this action.

Counterclaim

(Here set forth any claim as a counterclaim in the manner in which a claim is pleaded in a complaint. No statement of the grounds on which the court's jurisdiction depends need be made unless the counterclaim requires independent grounds of jurisdiction.)

Cross-Claim Against Defendant M.N.

(Here set forth the claim constituting a cross-claim against defendant M.N. in the manner in which a claim is pleaded in a complaint. The statement of grounds upon which the court's jurisdiction depends need not be made unless the cross-claim requires independent grounds of jurisdiction.)

Form 21.

ANSWER TO COMPLAINT SET FORTH IN FORM 8, WITH COUNTERCLAIM FOR INTERPLEADER

Defense

Defendant admits the allegations stated in paragraph 1 of the complaint; and denies the allegations stated in paragraph 2 to the extent set forth in the counterclaim herein.

Counterclaim for Interpleader

1. Defendant received the sum of _____ dollars as a deposit from E.F.

2. Plaintiff has demanded the payment of such deposit to him by virtue of an assignment of it which he claims to have received from E.F.

3. E.F. has notified the defendant that he claims such deposit, that the purported assignment is not valid, and that he holds the defendant responsible for the deposit.

Wherefore defendant demands:

(1) That the court order E.F. to be made a party defendant to respond to the complaint and to this counterclaim.[1]

(2) That the court order the plaintiff and E.F. to interplead their respective claims.

(3) That the court adjudge whether the plaintiff or E.F. is entitled to the sum of money.

(4) That the court discharge defendant from all liability in the premises except to the person it shall adjudge entitled to the sum of money.

(5) That the court award to the defendant its costs and attorney's fees.

Form 22.

MOTION TO BRING IN THIRD–PARTY DEFENDANT

[The contents of Form 22 are eliminated; they are adequately covered by Forms 22–A and 22–B.]

---

[1] Rule 13(h) provides for the court ordering parties to a counterclaim, but who are not parties to the original action, to be brought in as defendants.

Form 22-A.

SUMMONS AND COMPLAINT AGAINST THIRD-PARTY DEFENDANT

UNITED STATES DISTRICT COURT FOR THE
SOUTHERN DISTRICT OF NEW YORK

Civil Action, File Number _____

A.B., Plaintiff
v.
C.D., Defendant and Third-Party Plaintiff
v.
E.F., Third-Party Defendant
} Summons

To the above-named Third-Party Defendant:

You are hereby summoned and required to serve upon _____, plaintiff's attorney whose address is _____, and upon _____, who is attorney for C.D., defendant and third-party plaintiff, and whose address is _____, and answer to the third-party complaint which is herewith served upon you within 20 days after the service of this summons upon you exclusive of the day of service. If you fail to do so, judgment by default will be taken against you for the relief demanded in the third-party complaint. There is also served upon you herewith a copy of the complaint of the plaintiff which you may but are not required to answer.

_____,
Clerk of Court.

[Seal of District Court]

Dated _____

UNITED STATES DISTRICT COURT FOR THE
SOUTHERN DISTRICT OF NEW YORK

Civil Action, File Number _____

A.B., Plaintiff
v.
C.D., Defendant and Third-Party Plaintiff
v.
E.F., Third-Party Defendant
} Third-Party Complaint

1. Plaintiff A.B. has filed against defendant C.D. a complaint, a copy of which is hereto attached as "Exhibit A."

Form 22–A RULES OF CIVIL PROCEDURE

2. (Here state the grounds upon which C.D. is entitled to recover from E.F., all or part of what A.B. may recover from C.D. The statement should be framed as in an original complaint.)

Wherefore C.D. demands judgment against third-party defendant E.F. for all sums [1] that may be adjudged against defendant C.D. in favor of plaintiff A.B.

Signed: _____
Attorney for C.D.,
Third-Party Plaintiff

Address: _____

Form 22–B.

MOTION TO BRING IN THIRD-PARTY DEFENDANT

Defendant moves for leave, as third-party plaintiff, to cause to be served upon E.F. a summons and third-party complaint, copies of which are hereto attached as Exhibit X.

Signed: _____
Attorney for Defendant C.D.

Address: _____

Notice of Motion

(Contents the same as in Form 19. The notice should be addressed to all parties to the action.)

Exhibit X

(Contents the same as in Form 22–A.)

Form 23.

MOTION TO INTERVENE AS A DEFENDANT UNDER RULE 24

(Based upon the complaint, Form 16)

United States District Court for the Southern District of New York

Civil Action, File Number _____

A.B., plaintiff
v.
C.D., defendant
E.F., applicant for intervention
} *Motion to intervene as a defendant*

---

[1] Make appropriate change where C.D. is entitled to only partial recovery-over against E.F.

Form 24

E.F. moves for leave to intervene as a defendant in this action, in order to assert the defenses set forth in his proposed answer, of which a copy is hereto attached, on the ground that he is the manufacturer and vendor to the defendant, as well as to others, of the articles alleged in the complaint to be an infringement of plaintiff's patent, and as such has a defense to plaintiff's claim presenting both questions of law and of fact which are common to the main action.*

Signed: _____,
          Attorney for E.F., Applicant for Intervention.
Address: _____

Notice of Motion

(Contents the same as in Form 19)

United States District Court for the Southern District of New York

Civil Action, File Number _____

A.B., plaintiff)
     v.   ) *Intervener's Answer*
C.D., defendant)
E.F., intervener)

First Defense

Intervener admits the allegations stated in paragraphs 1 and 4 of the complaint; denies the allegations in paragraph 3, and denies the allegations in paragraph 2 in so far as they assert the legality of the issuance of the Letters Patent to plaintiff.

Second Defense

Plaintiff is not the first inventor of the articles covered by the Letters Patent specified in his complaint, since articles substantially identical in character were previously patented in Letters Patent granted to intervener on January 5, 1920.

Signed: _____,
          Attorney for E.F., Intervener
Address: _____

---

* For other grounds of intervention, either of right or in the discretion of the court, see Rule 24(a) and (b).

Form 24.

REQUEST FOR PRODUCTION OF DOCUMENTS, ETC., UNDER RULE 34

Plaintiff A.B. requests defendant C.D. to respond within _____ days to the following requests:

(1) That defendant produce and permit plaintiff to inspect and to copy each of the following documents:

(Here list the documents either individually or by category and describe each of them.)

(Here state the time, place, and manner of making the inspection and performance of any related acts.)

(2) That defendant produce and permit plaintiff to inspect and to copy, test, or sample each of the following objects:

(Here list the objects either individually or by category and describe each of them.)

(Here state the time, place, and manner of making the inspection and performance of any related acts.)

(3) That defendant permit plaintiff to enter (here describe property to be entered) and to inspect and to photograph, test or sample (here describe the portion of the real property and the objects to be inspected).

(Here state the time, place, and manner of making the inspection and performance of any related acts.)

Signed: _____
Attorney for Plaintiff.

Address: _____

Form 25.

REQUEST FOR ADMISSION UNDER RULE 36

Plaintiff A.B. requests defendant C.D. within _____ days after service of this request to make the following admissions for the purpose of this action only and subject to all pertinent objections to admissibility which may be interposed at the trial:

1. That each of the following documents, exhibited with this request, is genuine.

(Here list the documents and describe each document.)

2. That each of the following statements is true.

(Here list the statements.)

Signed: _____,
Attorney for Plaintiff.

Address: _____

APPENDIX OF FORMS **Form 28**

Form 26.

ALLEGATION OF REASON FOR OMITTING PARTY

When it is necessary, under Rule 19(c), for the pleader to set forth in his pleading the names of persons who ought to be made parties, but who are not so made, there should be an allegation such as the one set out below:

John Doe named in this complaint is not made a party to this action [because he is not subject to the jurisdiction of this court]; [because he cannot be made a party to this action without depriving this court of jurisdiction].

Form 27.

NOTICE OF APPEAL TO COURT OF APPEALS UNDER RULE 73(b)

Abrogated Dec. 4, 1967, eff. July 1, 1968

Form 28.

NOTICE: CONDEMNATION

United States District Court for the Southern District of New York

Civil Action, File Number _____

UNITED STATES OF AMERICA, PLAINTIFF
                v.
1,000 ACRES OF LAND IN [here insert a general location as "City of ...." or "County of ...."], JOHN DOE ET AL., AND UNKNOWN OWNERS, DEFENDANTS
      } Notice.

To (here insert the names of the defendants to whom the notice is directed):

You are hereby notified that a complaint in condemnation has heretofore been filed in the office of the clerk of the United States District Court for the Southern District of New York, in the United States Court House in New York City, New York, for the taking (here state the interest to be acquired, as "an estate in fee simple") for use (here state briefly the use, "as a site for a postoffice building") of the following described property in which you have or claim an interest.

    (Here insert brief description of the property in which the defendants, to whom the notice is directed, have or claim an interest.)

Form 28   RULES OF CIVIL PROCEDURE

The authority for the taking is (here state briefly, as "the Act of _____, _____ Stat. _____, U.S.C.A., Title _____ § _____".)[1]

You are further notified that if you desire to present any objection or defense to the taking of your property you are required to serve your answer on the plaintiff's attorney at the address herein designated within twenty days after _____
_____.[2]

Your answer shall identify the property in which you claim to have an interest, state the nature and extent of the interest you claim, and state all of your objections and defenses to the taking of your property. All defenses and objections not so presented are waived. And in case of your failure so to answer the complaint, judgment of condemnation of that part of the above-described property in which you have or claim an interest will be rendered.

But without answering, you may serve on the plaintiff's attorney a notice of appearance designating the property in which you claim to be interested. Thereafter you will receive notice of all proceedings affecting it. At the trial of the issue of just compensation, whether or not you have previously appeared or answered, you may present evidence as to the amount of the compensation to be paid for your property, and you may share in the distribution of the award.

United States Attorney.
Address _____

(Here state an address within the district where the United States Attorney may be served as "United States Court House, New York, N.Y.")

Dated _____

Form 29.

COMPLAINT: CONDEMNATION

United States District Court for the Southern District of New York

Civil Action, File Number _____

UNITED STATES OF AMERICA, PLAINTIFF)
      v.   )

---

[1] And where appropriate add a citation to any applicable Executive Order.

[2] Here insert the words "personal service of this notice upon you," if personal service is to be made pursuant to subdivision (d)(3)(i) of this rule [Rule 71A]; or, insert the date of the last publication of notice, if service by publication is to be made pursuant to subdivision (d)(3)(ii) of this rule.

APPENDIX OF FORMS — Form 29

1,000 Acres of Land in [here insert a general location as "City of .... " or "County of ...."],
John Doe, et al., and Unknown Owners
DEFENDANTS

Complaint.

1. This is an action of a civil nature brought by the United States of America for the taking of property under the power of eminent domain and for the ascertainment and award of just compensation to the owners and parties in interest.[1]

2. The authority for the taking is (here state briefly, as "the Act of ———, ——— Stat. ———, U.S.C.A., Title ———, § ———").[2]

3. The use for which the property is to be taken is (here state briefly the use, "as a site for a post-office building").

4. The interest to be acquired in the property is (here state the interest as "an estate in fee simple").

5. The property so to be taken is (here set forth a description of the property sufficient for its identification) or (described in Exhibit A hereto attached and made a part hereof).

6. The persons known to the plaintiff to have or claim an interest in the property[3] are:

(Here set forth the names of such persons and the interests claimed.)[4]

7. In addition to the persons named, there are or may be others who have or may claim some interest in the property to be taken, whose names are unknown to the plaintiff and on diligent inquiry have not been ascertained. They are made parties to the action under the designation "Unknown Owners."

---

[1] If the plaintiff is not the United States, but is, for example, a corporation invoking the power of eminent domain delegated to it by the state, then this paragraph 1 of the complaint should be appropriately modified and should be preceded by a paragraph appropriately alleging federal jurisdiction for the action, such as diversity. See Form 2.

[2] And where appropriate add a citation to any applicable Executive Order.

[3] At the commencement of the action the plaintiff need name as defendants only the persons having or claiming an interest in the property whose names are then known, but prior to any hearing involving the compensation to be paid for a particular piece of property the plaintiff must add as defendants all persons having or claiming an interest in that property whose names can be ascertained by an appropriate search of the records and also those whose names have otherwise been learned. See Rule 71A(c)(2).

[4] The plaintiff should designate, as to each separate piece of property, the defendants who have been joined as owners thereof or of some interest therein. See Rule 71A(c)(2).

Form 29 RULES OF CIVIL PROCEDURE

Wherefore the plaintiff demands judgment that the property be condemned and that just compensation for the taking be ascertained and awarded and for such other relief as may be lawful and proper.

United States Attorney.

Address _____

(Here state an address within the district where the United States Attorney may be served, as "United States Court House, New York, N.Y.").

Form 30.

SUGGESTION OF DEATH UPON THE RECORD UNDER RULE 25(a)(1)

A.B. [describe as a party, or as executor, administrator, or other representative or successor of C.D., the deceased party] suggests upon the record, pursuant to Rule 25(a)(1), the death of C.D. [describe as party] during the pendency of this action.

Form 31.

JUDGMENT ON JURY VERDICT

United States District Court for the Southern District of New York

Civil Action, File Number _____

A.B., Plaintiff
v.
C.D., Defendant
} Judgment

This action came on for trial before the Court and a jury, Honorable John Marshall, District Judge, presiding, and the issues having been duly tried and the jury having duly rendered its verdict,

It is Ordered and Adjudged

[that the plaintiff A.B. recover of the defendant C.D. the sum of _____, with interest thereon at the rate of _____ per cent as provided by law, and his costs of action.]

[that the plaintiff take nothing, and that the action be dismissed on the merits, and that the defendant C.D. recover of the plaintiff A.B. his costs of action.]

Dated at New York, New York, this _____ day of _____, 19__.

Clerk of Court

APPENDIX OF FORMS   Form 33

Form 32.

JUDGMENT ON DECISION BY THE COURT

UNITED STATES DISTRICT COURT FOR THE
SOUTHERN DISTRICT OF NEW YORK

Civil Action, File Number _____

A.B., Plaintiff
    v.   } Judgment
C.D., Defendant

This action came on for [trial] [hearing] before the Court, Honorable John Marshall, District Judge, presiding, and the issues having been duly [tried] [heard] and a decision having been duly rendered,

It is Ordered and Adjudged

[that the plaintiff A.B. recover of the defendant C.D. the sum of _____, with interest thereon at the rate of _____ per cent as provided by law, and his costs of action.]

[that the plaintiff take nothing, that the action be dismissed on the merits, and that the defendant C.D. recover of the plaintiff A.B. his costs of action.]

Dated at New York, New York, this _____ day of _____, 19__.

Clerk of Court

Form 33.

NOTICE OF AVAILABILITY OF A MAGISTRATE JUDGE TO EXERCISE JURISDICTION AND APPEAL OPTION

In accordance with the provisions of Title 28, U.S.C. § 636(c), you are hereby notified that a United States magistrate judge of this district court is available to exercise the court's jurisdiction and to conduct any or all proceedings in this case including a jury or nonjury trial, and entry of a final judgment. Exercise of this jurisdiction by a magistrate judge is, however, permitted only if all parties voluntarily consent.

You may, without adverse substantive consequences, withhold your consent, but this will prevent the court's jurisdiction from being exercised by a magistrate judge. If any party withholds consent, the identity of the parties consenting or withholding consent will not be communicated to any magistrate judge or to the district judge to whom the case has been assigned.

An appeal from a judgment entered by a magistrate judge may be taken directly to the United States court of appeals for this judicial

Form 33   RULES OF CIVIL PROCEDURE

circuit in the same manner as an appeal from any other judgment of a district court. Alternatively, upon consent of all parties, an appeal from a judgment entered by a magistrate judge may be taken directly to a district judge. Cases in which an appeal is taken to a district judge may be reviewed by the United States court of appeals for this judicial circuit only by way of petition for leave to appeal.

Copies of the Form for the "Consent to Jurisdiction by a United States Magistrate Judge" and "Election of Appeal to a District Judge" are available from the clerk of the court.

Form 34.

CONSENT TO EXERCISE OF JURISDICTION BY A UNITED STATES MAGISTRATE JUDGE, ELECTION OF APPEAL TO DISTRICT JUDGE

UNITED STATES DISTRICT COURT
_____ DISTRICT OF _____

Plaintiff,)
)
vs.) Docket No. _____
)
Defendant.)

CONSENT TO JURISDICTION BY A UNITED STATES MAGISTRATE JUDGE

In accordance with the provisions of Title 28, U.S.C. § 636(c), the undersigned party or parties to the above-captioned civil matter hereby voluntarily consent to have a United States magistrate judge conduct any and all further proceedings in the case, including trial, and order the entry of a final judgment.

Date   Signature

ELECTION OF APPEAL TO DISTRICT JUDGE

[Do not execute this portion of the Consent Form if you desire that the appeal lie directly to the court of appeals.]

In accordance with the provisions of Title 28, U.S.C. § 636(c)(4), the undersigned party or parties elect to take any appeal in this case to a district judge of this court.

Date   Signature

APPENDIX OF FORMS **Form 35**

Note: Return this form to the Clerk of the Court if you consent to jurisdiction by a magistrate judge. Do not send a copy of this form to any district judge or magistrate judge.

Form 34A.

ORDER OF REFERENCE

UNITED STATES DISTRICT COURT
_____ DISTRICT OF _____

Plaintiff,)	
vs.)	Docket No. _____
Defendant.)	

ORDER OF REFERENCE

IT IS HEREBY ORDERED that the above-captioned matter be referred to United States Magistrate Judge _____ for all further proceedings and entry of judgment in accordance with Title 28, U.S.C. § 636(c) and the consent of the parties.

_____
U.S. District Judge

Form 35.

REPORT OF PARTIES' PLANNING MEETING

[Caption and Names of Parties]

1. Pursuant to Fed.R.Civ.P. 26(f), a meeting was held on ___(date)___ at ___(place)___ and was attended by:

   ___(name)___ for plaintiff(s)
   ___(name)___ for defendant(s) ___(party name)___
   ___(name)___ for defendant(s) ___(party name)___

2. Pre-Discovery Disclosures. The parties [have exchanged] [will exchange by ___(date)___] the information required by [Fed.R.Civ.P. 26(a)(1)] [local rule ___].

3. Discovery Plan. The parties jointly propose to the court the following discovery plan: [Use separate paragraphs or subparagraphs as necessary if parties disagree.]

   Discovery will be needed on the following subjects: ___(brief description of subjects on which discovery will be needed)___

Form 35   RULES OF CIVIL PROCEDURE

All discovery commenced in time to be completed by ___(date)___. [Discovery on ___(issue for early discovery)___ to be completed by ___(date)___.]

Maximum of __ interrogatories by each party to any other party. [Responses due __ days after service.]

Maximum of __ requests for admission by each party to any other party. [Responses due __ days after service.]

Maximum of __ depositions by plaintiff(s) and __ by defendant(s).

Each deposition [other than of _____] limited to maximum of __ hours unless extended by agreement of parties.

Reports from retained experts under Rule 26(a)(2) due:

from plaintiff(s) by ___(date)___

from defendant(s) by ___(date)___

Supplementations under Rule 26(e) due ___(time(s) or interval(s))___.

4. Other Items. [Use separate paragraphs or subparagraphs as necessary if parties disagree.]

The parties [request] [do not request] a conference with the court before entry of the scheduling order.

The parties request a pretrial conference in ___(month and year)___.

Plaintiff(s) should be allowed until ___(date)___ to join additional parties and until ___(date)___ to amend the pleadings.

Defendant(s) should be allowed until ___(date)___ to join additional parties and until ___(date)___ to amend the pleadings.

All potentially dispositive motions should be filed by ___(date)___.

Settlement [is likely] [is unlikely] [cannot be evaluated prior to ___(date)___] [may be enhanced by use of the following alternative dispute resolution procedure: [_____]].

SUPPLEMENTAL RULES

For Certain Admiralty and Maritime Claims

The former Rules of Practice in Admiralty and Maritime Cases, promulgated by the Supreme Court on December 6, 1920, effective March 7, 1921, as revised, amended and supplemented, were rescinded, effective July 1, 1966.

Rule A. Scope of Rules

These Supplemental Rules apply to the procedure in admiralty and maritime claims within the meaning of Rule 9(h) with respect to the following remedies:

(1) Maritime attachment and garnishment;

(2) Actions in rem;

(3) Possessory, petitory, and partition actions;

(4) Actions for exoneration from or limitation of liability.

These rules also apply to the procedure in statutory condemnation proceedings analogous to maritime actions in rem, whether within the admiralty and maritime jurisdiction or not. Except as otherwise provided, references in these Supplemental Rules to actions in rem include such analogous statutory condemnation proceedings.

The general Rules of Civil Procedure for the United States District Courts are also applicable to the foregoing proceedings except to the extent that they are inconsistent with these Supplemental Rules.

Rule B. Attachment and Garnishment: Special Provisions

(1) When Available: Complaint, Affidavit, Judicial Authorization, and Process. With respect to any admiralty or maritime claim in personam a verified complaint may contain a prayer for process to attach the defendant's goods and chattels, or credits and effects in the hands of garnishees to be named in the process to the amount sued for, if the defendant shall not be found within the district. Such a complaint shall be accompanied by an affidavit signed by the plaintiff or the plaintiff's attorney that, to the affiant's knowledge, or to the best of the affiant's information and belief, the defendant cannot be found within the district. The verified complaint and affidavit shall be reviewed by the court and, if the conditions set forth in this rule appear to exist, an order so stating and authorizing process of attachment and garnishment shall issue. Supplemental process enforcing the court's order may be issued by the clerk upon application without further order of the court. If the plaintiff or the plaintiff's attorney certifies that exigent circumstances make review by the court impracticable, the clerk shall issue a

Rule B   SUPPLEMENTAL RULES

summons and process of attachment and garnishment and the plaintiff shall have the burden on a post-attachment hearing under Rule E(4)(f) to show that exigent circumstances existed. In addition, or in the alternative, the plaintiff may, pursuant to Rule 4(e), invoke the remedies provided by state law for attachment and garnishment or similar seizure of the defendant's property. Except for Rule E(8) these Supplemental Rules do not apply to state remedies so invoked.

(2) Notice to Defendant. No judgment by default shall be entered except upon proof, which may be by affidavit, (a) that the plaintiff or the garnishee has given notice of the action to the defendant by mailing to the defendant a copy of the complaint, summons, and process of attachment or garnishment, using any form of mail requiring a return receipt, or (b) that the complaint, summons, and process of attachment or garnishment have been served on the defendant in a manner authorized by Rule 4(d) or (i), or (c) that the plaintiff or the garnishee has made diligent efforts to give notice of the action to the defendant and has been unable to do so.

(3) Answer.

(a) By Garnishee. The garnishee shall serve an answer, together with answers to any interrogatories served with the complaint, within 20 days after service of process upon the garnishee. Interrogatories to the garnishee may be served with the complaint without leave of court. If the garnishee refuses or neglects to answer on oath as to the debts, credits, or effects of the defendant in the garnishee's hands, or any interrogatories concerning such debts, credits, and effects that may be propounded by the plaintiff, the court may award compulsory process against the garnishee. If the garnishee admits any debts, credits, or effects, they shall be held in the garnishee's hands or paid into the registry of the court, and shall be held in either case subject to the further order of the court.

(b) By Defendant. The defendant shall serve an answer within 30 days after process has been executed, whether by attachment of property or service on the garnishee.

1985 Amendment to Rule B(1)

The 1985 alterations were designed to ensure that the rule is consistent with the principles of procedural due process enunciated by the Supreme Court in *Sniadach v. Family Finance Corp.*, 395 U.S. 337 (1969), and later developed in *Fuentes v. Shevin*, 407 U.S. 67 (1972), *Mitchell v. W.T. Grant Co.*, 416 U.S. 600 (1974), and *North Georgia Finishing, Inc. v. Di-Chem, Inc.*, 419 U.S. 601 (1975).

Rule C. Actions in Rem: Special Provisions

(1) When Available. An action in rem may be brought:

(a) To enforce any maritime lien;

(b) Whenever a statute of the United States provides for a maritime action in rem or a proceeding analogous thereto.

Except as otherwise provided by law a party who may proceed in rem may also, or in the alternative, proceed in personam against any person who may be liable.

Statutory provisions exempting vessels or other property owned or possessed by or operated by or for the United States from arrest or seizure are not affected by this rule. When a statute so provides, an action against the United States or an instrumentality thereof may proceed on in rem principles.

(2) Complaint. In actions in rem the complaint shall be verified on oath or solemn affirmation. It shall describe with reasonable particularity the property that is the subject of the action and state that it is within the district or will be during the pendency of the action. In actions for the enforcement of forfeitures for violation of any statute of the United States the complaint shall state the place of seizure and whether it was on land or on navigable waters, and shall contain such allegations as may be required by the statute pursuant to which the action is brought.

(3) Judicial Authorization and Process. Except in actions by the United States for forfeitures for federal statutory violations, the verified complaint and any supporting papers shall be reviewed by the court and, if the conditions for an action in rem appear to exist, an order so stating and authorizing a warrant for the arrest of the vessel or other property that is the subject of the action shall issue and be delivered to the clerk who shall prepare the warrant. If the property is a vessel or a vessel and tangible property on board the vessel, the warrant shall be delivered to the marshal for service. If other property, tangible or intangible is the subject of the action, the warrant shall be delivered by the clerk to a person or organization authorized to enforce it, who may be a marshal, a person or organization contracted with by the United States, a person specially appointed for that purpose, or, if the action is brought by the United States, any officer or employee of the United States. If the property that is the subject of the action consists in whole or in part of freight, or the proceeds of property sold, or other intangible property, the clerk shall issue a summons directing any person having control of the funds to show cause why they should not be paid into court to abide the judgment. Supplemental process enforcing the court's order may be issued by the clerk upon application without further order of the court. If the plaintiff or the plaintiff's attorney certifies that exigent circumstances make review by the court impracticable, the clerk shall issue a summons and warrant for the arrest and the plaintiff shall have the burden on a post-arrest hearing under Rule E(4)(f) to show that exigent circumstances existed. In actions by the United States for forfeitures for federal statutory violations the clerk, upon filing of the complaint, shall forthwith issue a summons and warrant for the arrest of the vessel or other property without requiring a certification of exigent circumstances.

Rule C — SUPPLEMENTAL RULES

(4) Notice. No notice other than the execution of the process is required when the property that is the subject of the action has been released in accordance with Rule E(5). If the property is not released within 10 days after execution of process, the plaintiff shall promptly or within such time as may be allowed by the court cause public notice of the action and arrest to be given in a newspaper of general circulation in the district, designated by order of the court. Such notice shall specify the time within which the answer is required to be filed as provided by subdivision (6) of this rule. This rule does not affect the requirements of notice in actions to foreclose a preferred ship mortgage pursuant to the Act of June 5, 1920, ch. 250, § 30, as amended.

(5) Ancillary Process. In any action in rem in which process has been served as provided by this rule, if any part of the property that is the subject of the action has not been brought within the control of the court because it has been removed or sold, or because it is intangible property in the hands of a person who has not been served with process, the court may, on motion, order any person having possession or control of such property or its proceeds to show cause why it should not be delivered into the custody of the marshal or other person or organization having a warrant for the arrest of the property, or paid into court to abide the judgment; and, after hearing, the court may enter such judgment as law and justice may require.

(6) Claim and Answer; Interrogatories. The claimant of property that is the subject of an action in rem shall file a claim within 10 days after process has been executed, or within such additional time as may be allowed by the court, and shall serve an answer within 20 days after the filing of the claim. The claim shall be verified on oath or solemn affirmation, and shall state the interest in the property by virtue of which the claimant demands its restitution and the right to defend the action. If the claim is made on behalf of the person entitled to possession by an agent, bailee, or attorney, it shall state that the agent, bailee, or attorney is duly authorized to make the claim. At the time of answering the claimant shall also serve answers to any interrogatories served with the complaint. In actions in rem interrogatories may be so served without leave of court.

1985 Amendment to Rule C(3)

The 1985 amendments provide for judicial scrutiny before the issuance of any warrant of arrest. Their purpose is to eliminate any doubt as to the rule's constitutionality under the *Sniadach* line of cases. See 1985 Amendment to Rule B(1), following Rule B, supra.

Rule D. Possessory, Petitory, and Partition Actions

In all actions for possession, partition, and to try title maintainable according to the course of the admiralty practice with respect to a vessel, in all actions so maintainable with respect to the possession of cargo or other maritime property, and in all actions by one or more part owners against the others to obtain security for the return of the vessel from any voyage undertaken without their consent, or by one or more part owners against the others to obtain possession of the vessel for any voyage on giving security for its safe return, the process shall be by a warrant of arrest of the vessel, cargo, or other property, and by notice in the manner provided by Rule B(2) to the adverse party or parties.

Rule E. Actions in Rem and Quasi in Rem: General Provisions

(1) Applicability. Except as otherwise provided, this rule applies to actions in personam with process of maritime attachment and garnishment, actions in rem, and petitory, possessory, and partition actions, supplementing Rules B, C, and D.

(2) Complaint; Security.

(a) Complaint. In actions to which this rule is applicable the complaint shall state the circumstances from which the claim arises with such particularity that the defendant or claimant will be able, without moving for a more definite statement, to commence an investigation of the facts and to frame a responsive pleading.

(b) Security for Costs. Subject to the provisions of Rule 54(d) and of relevant statutes, the court may, on the filing of the complaint or on the appearance of any defendant, claimant, or any other party, or at any later time, require the plaintiff, defendant, claimant, or other party to give security, or additional security, in such sum as the court shall direct to pay all costs and expenses that shall be awarded against the party by any interlocutory order or by the final judgment, or on appeal by any appellate court.

(3) Process.

(a) Territorial Limits of Effective Service. Process in rem and of maritime attachment and garnishment shall be served only within the district.

(b) Issuance and Delivery. Issuance and delivery of process in rem, or of maritime attachment and garnishment, shall be held in abeyance if the plaintiff so requests.

(4) Execution of Process; Marshal's Return; Custody of Property; Procedures for Release.

(a) In General. Upon issuance and delivery of the process, or, in the case of summons with process of attachment and garnishment, when it appears that the defendant cannot be found within the district, the marshal shall forthwith execute the process in accordance with this subdivision (4), making due and prompt return.

(b) Tangible Property. If tangible property is to be attached or arrested, the marshal or other person or organization having the warrant shall take it into the marshal's possession for safe custody. If the

character or situation of the property is such that the taking of actual possession is impracticable, the marshal shall execute the process by affixing a copy thereof to the property in a conspicuous place and by leaving a copy of the complaint and process with the person having possession or the person's agent. In furtherance of the marshal's custody of any vessel the marshal is authorized to make a written request to the collector of customs not to grant clearance to such vessel until notified by the marshal or a deputy marshal or by the clerk that the vessel has been released in accordance with these rules.

(c) Intangible Property. If intangible property is to be attached or arrested the marshal or other person or organization having the warrant shall execute the process by leaving with the garnishee or other obligor a copy of the complaint and process requiring the garnishee or other obligor to answer as provided in Rules B(3)(a) and C(6); or the marshal may accept for payment into the registry of the court the amount owed to the extent of the amount claimed by the plaintiff with interest and costs, in which event the garnishee or other obligor shall not be required to answer unless alias process shall be served.

(d) Directions with Respect to Property in Custody. The marshal or other person or organization having the warrant may at any time apply to the court for directions with respect to property that has been attached or arrested, and shall give notice of such application to any or all of the parties as the court may direct.

(e) Expenses of Seizing and Keeping Property; Deposit. These rules do not alter the provisions of Title 28, U.S.C., § 1921, as amended, relative to the expenses of seizing and keeping property attached or arrested and to the requirement of deposits to cover such expenses.

(f) Procedure for Release from Arrest or Attachment. Whenever property is arrested or attached, any person claiming an interest in it shall be entitled to a prompt hearing at which the plaintiff shall be required to show why the arrest or attachment should not be vacated or other relief granted consistent with these rules. This subdivision shall have no application to suits for seamen's wages when process is issued upon a certification of sufficient cause filed pursuant to Title 46, U.S.C. §§ 603 and 604 or to actions by the United States for forfeitures for violation of any statute of the United States.

(5) Release of Property.

(a) Special Bond. Except in cases of seizures for forfeiture under any law of the United States, whenever process of maritime attachment and garnishment or process in rem is issued the execution of such process shall be stayed, or the property released, on the giving of security, to be approved by the court or clerk, or by stipulation of the parties, conditioned to answer the judgment of the court or of any appellate court. The parties may stipulate the amount and nature of such security. In the event of the inability or refusal of the parties so to

stipulate the court shall fix the principal sum of the bond or stipulation at an amount sufficient to cover the amount of the plaintiff's claim fairly stated with accrued interest and costs; but the principal sum shall in no event exceed (i) twice the amount of the plaintiff's claim or (ii) the value of the property on due appraisement, whichever is smaller. The bond or stipulation shall be conditioned for the payment of the principal sum and interest thereon at 6 per cent per annum.

(b) General Bond. The owner of any vessel may file a general bond or stipulation, with sufficient surety, to be approved by the court, conditioned to answer the judgment of such court in all or any actions that may be brought thereafter in such court in which the vessel is attached or arrested. Thereupon the execution of all such process against such vessel shall be stayed so long as the amount secured by such bond or stipulation is at least double the aggregate amount claimed by plaintiffs in all actions begun and pending in which such vessel has been attached or arrested. Judgments and remedies may be had on such bond or stipulation as if a special bond or stipulation had been filed in each of such actions. The district court may make necessary orders to carry this rule into effect, particularly as to the giving of proper notice of any action against or attachment of a vessel for which a general bond has been filed. Such bond or stipulation shall be indorsed by the clerk with a minute of the actions wherein process is so stayed. Further security may be required by the court at any time.

If a special bond or stipulation is given in a particular case, the liability on the general bond or stipulation shall cease as to that case.

(c) Release by Consent or Stipulation; Order of Court or Clerk; Costs. Any vessel, cargo, or other property in the custody of the marshal or other person or organization having the warrant may be released forthwith upon the marshal's acceptance and approval of a stipulation, bond, or other security, signed by the party on whose behalf the property is detained or the party's attorney and expressly authorizing such release, if all costs and charges of the court and its officers shall have first been paid. Otherwise no property in the custody of the marshal or other officer of the court shall be released without an order of the court; but such order may be entered as of course by the clerk, upon the giving of approved security as provided by law and these rules, or upon the dismissal or discontinuance of the action; but the marshal shall not deliver any property so released until the costs and charges of the officers of the court shall first have been paid.

(d) Possessory, Petitory, and Partition Actions. The foregoing provisions of this subdivision (5) do not apply to petitory, possessory, and partition actions. In such cases the property arrested shall be released only by order of the court, on such terms and conditions and on the giving of such security as the court may require.

(6) Reduction or Impairment of Security. Whenever security is taken the court may, on motion and hearing, for good cause shown, reduce the amount of security given; and if the surety shall be or become insufficient, new or additional sureties may be required on motion and hearing.

(7) Security on Counterclaim. Whenever there is asserted a counterclaim arising out of the same transaction or occurrence with respect to which the action was originally filed, and the defendant or claimant in the original action has given security to respond in damages, any plaintiff for whose benefit such security has been given shall give security in the usual amount and form to respond in damages to the claims set forth in such counterclaim, unless the court, for cause shown, shall otherwise direct; and proceedings on the original claim shall be stayed until such security is given, unless the court otherwise directs. When the United States or a corporate instrumentality thereof as defendant is relieved by law of the requirement of giving security to respond in damages it shall nevertheless be treated for the purposes of this subdivision E(7) as if it had given such security if a private person so situated would have been required to give it.

(8) Restricted Appearance. An appearance to defend against an admiralty and maritime claim with respect to which there has issued process in rem, or process of attachment and garnishment whether pursuant to these Supplemental Rules or to Rule 4(e), may be expressly restricted to the defense of such claim, and in that event shall not constitute an appearance for the purposes of any other claim with respect to which such process is not available or has not been served.

(9) Disposition of Property; Sales.

(a) Actions for Forfeitures. In any action in rem to enforce a forfeiture for violation of a statute of the United States the property shall be disposed of as provided by statute.

(b) Interlocutory Sales. If property that has been attached or arrested is perishable, or liable to deterioration, decay, or injury by being detained in custody pending the action, or if the expense of keeping the property is excessive or disproportionate, or if there is unreasonable delay in securing the release of property, the court, on application of any party or of the marshal, or other person or organization having the warrant may order the property or any portion thereof to be sold; and the proceeds, or so much thereof as shall be adequate to satisfy any judgment, may be ordered brought into court to abide the event of the action; or the court may, on motion of the defendant or claimant, order delivery of the property to the defendant or claimant, upon the giving of security in accordance with these rules.

(c) Sales; Proceeds. All sales of property shall be made by the marshal or a deputy marshal, or by other person or organization having the warrant, or by any other person assigned by the court where the

marshal or other person or organization having the warrant is a party in interest; and the proceeds of sale shall be forthwith paid into the registry of the court to be disposed of according to law.

1985 Amendments to Rule E

New Rule E(4)(f), effective August 1, 1985, makes available the type of prompt post-seizure hearing in proceedings under Supplemental Rules B and C that the Supreme Court has called for in a number of cases arising in other contexts. Rule E(4)(f) is based on a proposal by the Maritime Law Association of the United States and on local admiralty rules in the Eastern and Southern Districts of New York.

Rule E(4)(f) will be triggered by the defendant or any other person with an interest in the property seized. Upon an oral or written application similar to that used in seeking a temporary restraining order, see Rule 65(b), the court will be required to hold a hearing as promptly as possible to determine whether to allow the arrest or attachment to stand. The plaintiff has the burden of showing why the seizure should not be vacated.

Rule F. Limitation of Liability

(1) Time for Filing Complaint; Security. Not later than six months after receipt of a claim in writing, any vessel owner may file a complaint in the appropriate district court, as provided in subdivision (9) of this rule, for limitation of liability pursuant to statute. The owner (a) shall deposit with the court, for the benefit of claimants, a sum equal to the amount or value of the owner's interest in the vessel and pending freight, or approved security therefor, and in addition such sums, or approved security therefor, as the court may from time to time fix as necessary to carry out the provisions of the statutes as amended; or (b) at the owner's option shall transfer to a trustee to be appointed by the court, for the benefit of claimants, the owner's interest in the vessel and pending freight, together with such sums, or approved security therefor, as the court may from time to time fix as necessary to carry out the provisions of the statutes as amended. The plaintiff shall also give security for costs and, if the plaintiff elects to give security, for interest at the rate of 6 percent per annum from the date of the security.

(2) Complaint. The complaint shall set forth the facts on the basis of which the right to limit liability is asserted, and all facts necessary to enable the court to determine the amount to which the owner's liability shall be limited. The complaint may demand exoneration from as well as limitation of liability. It shall state the voyage, if any, on which the demands sought to be limited arose, with the date and place of its termination; the amount of all demands including all unsatisfied liens or claims of lien, in contract or in tort or otherwise, arising on that voyage, so far as known to the plaintiff, and what actions and proceedings, if any, are pending thereon; whether the vessel was damaged, lost, or abandoned, and, if so, when and where; the value of the vessel at the close of the voyage or, in case of wreck, the value of her wreckage, strippings, or proceeds, if any, and where and in whose possession they are; and the amount of any pending freight recovered or recoverable. If the plaintiff elects to transfer the plaintiff's interest in the vessel to a trustee, the complaint must further show any prior paramount liens thereon, and what voyages or trips, if any, she has made since the voyage or trip on which the claims sought to be limited arose, and any existing liens arising upon any such subsequent voyage or trip, with the amounts and causes thereof, and the names and addresses of the lienors, so far as known; and whether the vessel sustained any injury upon or by reason of such subsequent voyage or trip.

(3) Claims Against Owner; Injunction. Upon compliance by the owner with the requirements of subdivision (1) of this rule all claims and proceedings against the owner or the owner's property with respect to the matter in question shall cease. On application of the plaintiff the court shall enjoin the further prosecution of any action or proceeding against the plaintiff or the plaintiff's property with respect to any claim subject to limitation in the action.

(4) Notice to Claimants. Upon the owner's compliance with subdivision (1) of this rule the court shall issue a notice to all persons asserting claims with respect to which the complaint seeks limitation, admonishing them to file their respective claims with the clerk of the court and to serve on the attorneys for the plaintiff a copy thereof on or before a date to be named in the notice. The date so fixed shall not be less than 30 days after issuance of the notice. For cause shown, the court may enlarge the time within which claims may be filed. The notice shall be published in such newspaper or newspapers as the court may direct once a week for four successive weeks prior to the date fixed for the filing of claims. The plaintiff not later than the day of second publication shall also mail a copy of the notice to every person known to have made any claim against the vessel or the plaintiff arising out of the voyage or trip on which the claims sought to be limited arose. In cases involving death a copy of such notice shall be mailed to the decedent at the decedent's last known address, and also to any person who shall be known to have made any claim on account of such death.

(5) Claims and Answer. Claims shall be filed and served on or before the date specified in the notice provided for in subdivision (4) of this rule. Each claim shall specify the facts upon which the claimant relies in support of the claim, the items thereof, and the dates on which the same accrued. If a claimant desires to contest either the right to exoneration from or the right to limitation of liability the claimant shall file and serve an answer to the complaint unless the claim has included an answer.

(6) Information to Be Given Claimants. Within 30 days after the date specified in the notice for filing claims, or within such time as the court thereafter may allow, the plaintiff shall mail to the attorney for each claimant (or if the claimant has no attorney to the claimant) a list setting forth (a) the name of each claimant, (b) the name and address of the claimant's attorney (if the claimant is known to have one), (c) the nature of the claim, i.e., whether property loss, property damage, death, personal injury, etc., and (d) the amount thereof.

(7) Insufficiency of Fund or Security. Any claimant may by motion demand that the funds deposited in court or the security given by the plaintiff be increased on the ground that they are less than the value of the plaintiff's interest in the vessel and pending freight. Thereupon the court shall cause due appraisement to be made of the value of the plaintiff's interest in the vessel and pending freight; and if the court finds that the deposit or security is either insufficient or excessive it shall order its increase or reduction. In like manner any claimant may demand that the deposit or security be increased on the ground that it is insufficient to carry out the provisions of the statutes relating to claims in respect of loss of life or bodily injury; and, after notice and hearing, the court may similarly order that the deposit or security be increased or reduced.

(8) Objections to Claims: Distribution of Fund. Any interested party may question or controvert any claim without filing an objection thereto. Upon determination of liability the fund deposited or secured, or the proceeds of the vessel and pending freight, shall be divided pro rata, subject to all relevant provisions of law, among the several claimants in proportion to the amounts of their respective claims, duly proved, saving, however, to all parties any priority to which they may be legally entitled.

(9) Venue; Transfer. The complaint shall be filed in any district in which the vessel has been attached or arrested to answer for any claim with respect to which the plaintiff seeks to limit liability; or, if the vessel has not been attached or arrested, then in any district in which the owner has been sued with respect to any such claim. When the vessel has not been attached or arrested to answer the matters aforesaid, and suit has not been commenced against the owner, the proceedings may be had in the district in which the vessel may be, but if the vessel is not within any district and no suit has been commenced in any district, then the complaint may be filed in any district. For the convenience of parties and witnesses, in the interest of justice, the court may transfer the action to any district; if venue is wrongly laid the court shall dismiss or, if it be in the interest of justice, transfer the action to any district in which it could have been brought. If the vessel shall have been sold, the proceeds shall represent the vessel for the purposes of these rules.

Part II

Selected Provisions of The Constitution of the United States and of Titles 28 and 42, United States Code
plus
Comparative Federal and State Provisions

TABLE OF CONTENTS

Selected Provisions of the Constitution of the United States

	Page
Article I	230
Article III	231
Article IV	232
Article VI	232
Amendment I	232
Amendment IV	232
Amendment V	232
Amendment VII	233
Amendment IX	233
Amendment X	233
Amendment XI	233
Amendment XIV	233

Selected Provisions of Title 28, United States Code—Judiciary and Judicial Procedure

Section		Page
471.	Requirement for a district court civil justice expense and delay reduction plan	233
472.	Development and implementation of a civil justice expense and delay reduction plan	234
473.	Content of civil justice expense and delay reduction plans	235
474.	Review of district court action	237
475.	Periodic district court assessment	238
476.	Enhancement of judicial information dissemination	238
477.	Model civil justice expense and delay reduction plan	238
478.	Advisory groups	239
479.	Information on litigation management and cost and delay reduction	239

CONSTITUTION OF THE UNITED STATES

(b) *Other Selected Provisions*

Section	Page
1251. Original jurisdiction	240
1253. Direct appeals from decisions of three-judge courts	240
1254. Courts of appeals; certiorari; appeal; certified questions	241
1257. State courts; appeal; certiorari	245
1291. Final decisions of district courts	245
1292. Interlocutory decisions	245
1331. Federal question	249
1332. Diversity of citizenship; amount in controversy; costs	249
1333. Admiralty, maritime and prize cases	250
1334. Bankruptcy cases and proceedings	250
1335. Interpleader	251
1337. Commerce and antitrust regulations	251
1338. Patents, plant variety protection, copyrights, mask works, trademarks and unfair competition	252
1343. Civil rights and elective franchise	253
1345. United States as plaintiff	253
1346. United States as defendant	253
1359. Parties collusively joined or made	254
1361. Action to compel an officer of the United States to perform his duty	254
1367. Supplemental jurisdiction	254
1391. Venue generally	255
1392. Defendants or property in different districts in same State	257
1397. Interpleader	257
1400. Patents and copyrights	257
1401. Stockholder's derivative action	257
1402. United States as defendant	257
1404. Change of venue	258
1406. Cure or waiver of defects	259
1407. Multidistrict litigation	260
1441. Actions removable generally	262
1442. Federal officers sued or prosecuted	262
1443. Civil rights cases	263
1445. Nonremovable actions	263
1446. Procedure for removal	263
1447. Procedure after removal generally	264
1631. Transfer to cure want of jurisdiction	265
1651. Writs	265
1652. State laws as rules of decision	265
1653. Amendment of pleadings to show jurisdiction	266
1655. Lien enforcement; absent defendants	266
1693. Place of arrest in civil action	266
1694. Patent infringement action	267
1695. Stockholder's derivative action	267
1738. State and Territorial statutes and judicial proceedings; full faith and credit	267
1781. Transmittal of letter rogatory or request	267
1782. Assistance to foreign and international tribunals and to litigants before such tribunals	268
1783. Subpoena of person in foreign country	268
1861. Declaration of policy	269
1862. Exemptions	269
1863. Plan for random jury selection	269
1864. Drawing of names from the master jury wheel; completion of juror qualification form	272

SELECTED PROVISIONS

Section	Page
1865. Qualifications for jury service	273
1866. Selection and summoning of jury panels	274
1867. Challenging compliance with selection procedures	276
1868. Maintenance and inspection of records	277
1869. Definitions	277
1870. Challenges	280
1919. Dismissal for lack of jurisdiction	280
1920. Taxation of costs	280
1927. Counsel's liability for excessive costs	280
1963. Registration of judgments of the district courts and the Court of International Trade	280
2071. Rule-making power generally	281
2072. Rules of procedure and evidence; power to prescribe	282
2111. Harmless error	282
2201. Creation of remedy	282
2202. Further relief	283
2283. Stay of State court proceedings	283
2284. Three-judge court; when required; composition; procedure	283
2361. Process and procedure	283
2403. Intervention by United States or a State; constitutional question	284

Selected Provision of Title 42, United States Code—The Public Health and Welfare

Section	Page
1983. Civil action for deprivation of rights	284

Comparative Federal and State Provisions

(See Index to Comparative Provisions, Part XI, infra.)

Selected Provisions of the Constitution of the United States
ARTICLE I.

Section 8. The Congress shall have Power To lay and collect Taxes, Duties, Imposts and Excises, to pay the Debts and provide for the common Defence and general Welfare of the United States; but all Duties, Imposts and Excises shall be uniform throughout the United States;

To borrow Money on the credit of the United States;

To regulate Commerce with foreign Nations, and among the several States, and with the Indian Tribes;

To establish an uniform Rule of Naturalization, and uniform Laws on the subject of Bankruptcies throughout the United States;

* * *

To promote the Progress of Science and useful Arts, by securing for limited Times to Authors and Inventors the exclusive Right to their respective Writings and Discoveries;

To constitute Tribunals inferior to the supreme Court;

* * *

To declare War, grant Letters of Marque and Reprisal, and make Rules concerning Captures on Land and Water;

To raise and support Armies, but no Appropriation of Money to that Use shall be for a longer Term than two Years;

To provide and maintain a Navy;

* * *

To exercise exclusive Legislation in all Cases whatsoever, over such District (not exceeding ten Miles square) as may, by Cession of particular States, and the Acceptance of Congress, become the Seat of the Government of the United States, and to exercise like Authority over all Places purchased by the Consent of the Legislature of the State in which the Same shall be, for the Erection of Forts, Magazines, Arsenals, dock-Yards, and other needful Buildings;—And

To make all Laws which shall be necessary and proper for carrying into Execution the foregoing Powers, and all other Powers vested by this Constitution in the Government of the United States, or in any Department or Officer thereof.

ARTICLE III.

Section 1. The judicial Power of the United States, shall be vested in one supreme Court, and in such inferior Courts as the Congress may from time to time ordain and establish. The Judges, both of the supreme and inferior Courts, shall hold their Offices during good Behaviour, and shall, at stated Times, receive for their Services, a Compensation, which shall not be diminished during their Continuance in Office.

Section 2. The judicial Power shall extend to all Cases, in Law and Equity, arising under this Constitution, the Laws of the United States, and Treaties made, or which shall be made, under their Authority;—to all Cases affecting Ambassadors, other public Ministers and Consuls;—to all Cases of admiralty and maritime Jurisdiction;—to Controversies to which the United States shall be a Party;—to Controversies between two or more States;—between a State and Citizens of another State;—between Citizens of different States;—between Citizens of the same State claiming Lands under Grants of different States, and between a State, or the Citizens thereof, and foreign States, Citizens or Subjects.

In all Cases affecting Ambassadors, other public Ministers and Consuls, and those in which a State shall be Party, the supreme Court shall have original Jurisdiction. In all the other Cases before mentioned, the supreme Court shall have appellate Jurisdiction, both as to Law and Fact, with such Exceptions, and under such Regulations as the Congress shall make.

SELECTED PROVISIONS

The Trial of all Crimes, except in Cases of Impeachment, shall be by Jury; and such Trial shall be held in the State where the said Crimes shall have been committed; but when not committed within any State, the Trial shall be at such Place or Places as the Congress may by Law have directed.

* * *

ARTICLE IV.

Section 1. Full Faith and Credit shall be given in each State to the public Acts, Records, and judicial Proceedings of every other State. And the Congress may by general Laws prescribe the Manner in which such Acts, Records and Proceedings shall be proved, and the Effect thereof.

Section 2. The Citizens of each State shall be entitled to all Privileges and Immunities of Citizens in the several States.

* * *

ARTICLE VI.

* * *

This Constitution, and the Laws of the United States which shall be made in Pursuance thereof; and all Treaties made, or which shall be made, under the Authority of the United States, shall be the supreme Law of the Land; and the Judges in every State shall be bound thereby, any Thing in the Constitution or Laws of any State to the Contrary notwithstanding.

* * *

AMENDMENT I.

Congress shall make no law respecting an establishment of religion, or prohibiting the free exercise thereof; or abridging the freedom of speech, or of the press; or the right of the people peaceably to assemble, and to petition the Government for a redress of grievances.

AMENDMENT IV.

The right of the people to be secure in their persons, houses, papers, and effects, against unreasonable searches and seizures, shall not be violated, and no Warrants shall issue, but upon probable cause, supported by Oath or affirmation, and particularly describing the place to be searched, and the persons or things to be seized.

AMENDMENT V.

No person shall be held to answer for a capital, or otherwise infamous crime, unless on a presentment or indictment of a Grand Jury, except in cases arising in the land or naval forces, or in the Militia, when in actual service in time of War or public danger; nor shall any person be subject for the same offence to be twice put in jeopardy of life or limb;

nor shall be compelled in any criminal case to be a witness against himself, nor be deprived of life, liberty, or property, without due process of law; nor shall private property be taken for public use, without just compensation.

AMENDMENT VII.

In Suits at common law, where the value in controversy shall exceed twenty dollars, the right of trial by jury shall be preserved, and no fact tried by a jury, shall be otherwise re-examined in any Court of the United States, than according to the rules of the common law.

Comparative State Provisions

See the state provisions as set out following Federal Rule of Civil Procedure 38, supra.

AMENDMENT IX.

The enumeration in the Constitution, of certain rights, shall not be construed to deny or disparage others retained by the people.

AMENDMENT X.

The powers not delegated to the United States by the Constitution, nor prohibited by it to the States, are reserved to the States respectively, or to the people.

AMENDMENT XI.

The Judicial power of the United States shall not be construed to extend to any suit in law or equity, commenced or prosecuted against one of the United States by Citizens of another State, or by Citizens or Subjects of any Foreign State.

AMENDMENT XIV.

Section 1. All persons born or naturalized in the United States, and subject to the jurisdiction thereof, are citizens of the United States and of the State wherein they reside. No State shall make or enforce any law which shall abridge the privileges or immunities of citizens of the United States; nor shall any State deprive any person of life, liberty, or property, without due process of law; nor deny to any person within its jurisdiction the equal protection of the laws.

* * *

Section 5. The Congress shall have power to enforce, by appropriate legislation, the provisions of this article.

Selected Provisions of Title 28, United States Code—Judiciary and Judicial Procedure

§ 471. Requirement for a district court civil justice expense and delay reduction plan

There shall be implemented by each United States district court, in accordance with this chapter, a civil justice expense and delay reduction plan. The plan may be a plan developed by such district court or a model plan developed by the Judicial Conference of the United States. The purposes of each plan are to facilitate deliberate adjudication of civil cases on the merits, monitor discovery, improve litigation management, and ensure just, speedy, and inexpensive resolutions of civil disputes.

§ 472. Development and implementation of a civil justice expense and delay reduction plan

(a) The civil justice expense and delay reduction plan implemented by a district court shall be developed or selected, as the case may be, after consideration of the recommendations of an advisory group appointed in accordance with section 478 of this title.

(b) The advisory group of a United States district court shall submit to the court a report, which shall be made available to the public and which shall include—

(1) an assessment of the matters referred to in subsection (c)(1);

(2) the basis for its recommendation that the district court develop a plan or select a model plan;

(3) recommended measures, rules and programs; and

(4) an explanation of the manner in which the recommended plan complies with section 473 of this title.

(c)(1) In developing its recommendations, the advisory group of a district court shall promptly complete a thorough assessment of the state of the court's civil and criminal dockets. In performing the assessment for a district court, the advisory group shall—

(A) determine the condition of the civil and criminal dockets;

(B) identify trends in case filings and in the demands being placed on the court's resources;

(C) identify the principal causes of cost and delay in civil litigation, giving consideration to such potential causes as court procedures and the ways in which litigants and their attorneys approach and conduct litigation; and

(D) examine the extent to which costs and delays could be reduced by a better assessment of the impact of new legislation on the courts.

(2) In developing its recommendations, the advisory group of a district court shall take into account the particular needs and circumstances of the district court, litigants in such court, and the litigants' attorneys.

(3) The advisory group of a district court shall ensure that its recommended actions include significant contributions to be made by the

court, the litigants, and the litigants' attorneys toward reducing cost and delay and thereby facilitating access to the courts.

(d) The chief judge of the district court shall transmit a copy of the plan implemented in accordance with subsection (a) and the report prepared in accordance with subsection (b) of this section to—

(1) the Director of the Administrative Office of the United States Courts;

(2) the judicial council of the circuit in which the district court is located; and

(3) the chief judge of each of the other United States district courts located in such circuit.

§ 473. Content of civil justice expense and delay reduction plans

(a) In formulating the provisions of its civil justice expense and delay reduction plan, each United States district court, in consultation with an advisory group appointed under section 478 of this title, shall consider and may include the following principles and guidelines of litigation management and cost and delay reduction:

(1) systematic, differential treatment of civil cases that tailors the level of individualized and case specific management to such criteria as case complexity, the amount of time reasonably needed to prepare the case for trial, and the judicial and other resources required and available for the preparation and disposition of the case;

(2) early and ongoing control of the pretrial process through involvement of a judicial officer in—

(A) assessing and planning the progress of a case;

(B) setting early, firm trial dates, such that the trial is scheduled to occur within eighteen months after the filing of the complaint, unless a judicial officer certifies that—

(i) the demands of the case and its complexity make such a trial date incompatible with serving the ends of justice; or

(ii) the trial court cannot reasonably be held within such time because of the complexity of the case or the number or complexity of pending criminal cases;

(C) controlling the extent of discovery and the time for completion of discovery, and ensuring compliance with appropriate requested discovery in a timely fashion; and

(D) setting, at the earliest practicable time, deadlines for filing motions and a time framework for their disposition;

(3) for all cases that the court or an individual judicial officer determines are complex and any other appropriate cases, careful and deliberate monitoring through a discovery-case management conference or a series of such conferences at which the presiding judicial officer—

(A) explores the parties' receptivity to, and the propriety of, settlement or proceeding with the litigation;

(B) identifies or formulates the principal issues in contention and, in appropriate cases, provides for the staged resolution or bifurcation of issues for trial consistent with Rule 42(b) of the Federal Rules of Civil Procedure;

(C) prepares a discovery schedule and plan consistent with any presumptive time limits that a district court may set for the completion of discovery and with any procedures a district court may develop to—

(i) identify and limit the volume of discovery available to avoid unnecessary or unduly burdensome or expensive discovery; and

(ii) phase discovery into two or more stages; and

(D) sets, at the earliest practicable time, deadlines for filing motions and a time framework for their disposition;

(4) encouragement of cost-effective discovery through voluntary exchange of information among litigants and their attorneys and through the use of cooperative discovery devices;

(5) conservation of judicial resources by prohibiting the consideration of discovery motions unless accompanied by a certification that the moving party has made a reasonable and good faith effort to reach agreement with opposing counsel on the matters set forth in the motion; and

(6) authorization to refer appropriate cases to alternative dispute resolution programs that—

(A) have been designated for use in a district court; or

(B) the court may make available, including mediation, minitrial, and summary jury trial.

(b) In formulating the provisions of its civil justice expense and delay reduction plan, each United States district court, in consultation with an advisory group appointed under section 478 of this title, shall consider and may include the following litigation management and cost and delay reduction techniques:

(1) a requirement that counsel for each party to a case jointly present a discovery-case management plan for the case at the initial pretrial conference, or explain the reasons for their failure to do so;

(2) a requirement that each party be represented at each pretrial conference by an attorney who has the authority to bind that party regarding all matters previously identified by the court for discussion at the conference and all reasonably related matters;

(3) a requirement that all requests for extensions of deadlines for completion of discovery or for postponement of the trial be signed by the attorney and the party making the request;

(4) a neutral evaluation program for the presentation of the legal and factual basis of a case to a neutral court representative selected by the court at a nonbinding conference conducted early in the litigation;

(5) a requirement that, upon notice by the court, representatives of the parties with authority to bind them in settlement discussions be present or available by telephone during any settlement conference; and

(6) such other features as the district court considers appropriate after considering the recommendations of the advisory group referred to in section 472(a) of this title.

(c) Nothing in a civil justice expense and delay reduction plan relating to the settlement authority provisions of this section shall alter or conflict with the authority of the Attorney General to conduct litigation on behalf of the United States, or any delegation of the Attorney General.

§ 474. Review of district court action

(a)(1) The chief judge of each district court in a circuit and the chief judge of the circuit shall, as a committee—

(A) review each plan and report submitted pursuant to section 472(d) of this title; and

(B) make such suggestions for additional actions or modified actions of that district court as the committee considers appropriate for reducing cost and delay in civil litigation in the district court.

(2) The chief judge of a circuit may designate another judge of the court of appeals of that circuit, and the chief judge of a district court may designate another judge of such court, to perform that chief judge's responsibilities under paragraph (1) of this subsection.

(b) The Judicial Conference of the United States—

(1) shall review each plan and report submitted by a district court pursuant to section 472(d) of this title; and

(2) may request the district court to take additional action if the Judicial Conference determines that such court has not adequately responded to the conditions relevant to the civil and crimi-

nal dockets of the court or to the recommendations of the district court's advisory group.

§ 475. Periodic district court assessment

After developing or selecting a civil justice expense and delay reduction plan, each United States district court shall assess annually the condition of the court's civil and criminal dockets with a view to determining appropriate additional actions that may be taken by the court to reduce cost and delay in civil litigation and to improve the litigation management practices of the court. In performing such assessment, the court shall consult with an advisory group appointed in accordance with section 478 of this title.

§ 476. Enhancement of judicial information dissemination

(a) The Director of the Administrative Office of the United States Courts shall prepare a semiannual report, available to the public, that discloses for each judicial officer—

(1) the number of motions that have been pending for more than six months and the name of each case in which such motion has been pending;

(2) the number of bench trials that have been submitted for more than six months and the name of each case in which such trials are under submission; and

(3) the number and names of cases that have not been terminated within three years after filing.

(b) To ensure uniformity of reporting, the standards for categorization or characterization of judicial actions to be prescribed in accordance with section 481 of this title shall apply to the semiannual report prepared under subsection (a).

§ 477. Model civil justice expense and delay reduction plan

(a)(1) Based on the plans developed and implemented by the United States district courts designated as Early Implementation District Courts pursuant to section 103(c) of the Civil Justice Reform Act of 1990, the Judicial Conference of the United States may develop one or more model civil justice expense and delay reduction plans. Any such model plan shall be accompanied by a report explaining the manner in which the plan complies with section 473 of this title.

(2) The Director of the Federal Judicial Center and the Director of the Administrative Office of the United States Courts may make recommendations to the Judicial Conference regarding the development of any model civil justice expense and delay reduction plan.

(b) The Director of the Administrative Office of the United States Courts shall transmit to the United States district courts and to the

Committees on the Judiciary of the Senate and the House of Representatives copies of any model plan and accompanying report.

§ 478. Advisory groups

(a) Within ninety days after the date of the enactment of this chapter, the advisory group required in each United States district court in accordance with section 472 of this title shall be appointed by the chief judge of each district court, after consultation with the other judges of such court.

(b) The advisory group of a district court shall be balanced and include attorneys and other persons who are representative of major categories of litigants in such court, as determined by the chief judge of such court.

(c) Subject to subsection (d), in no event shall any member of the advisory group serve longer than four years.

(d) Notwithstanding subsection (c), the United States Attorney for a judicial district, or his or her designee, shall be a permanent member of the advisory group for that district court.

(e) The chief judge of a United States district court may designate a reporter for each advisory group, who may be compensated in accordance with guidelines established by the Judicial Conference of the United States.

(f) The members of an advisory group of a United States district court and any person designated as a reporter for such group shall be considered as independent contractors of such court when in the performance of official duties of the advisory group and may not, solely by reason of service on or for the advisory group, be prohibited from practicing law before such court.

§ 479. Information on litigation management and cost and delay reduction

(a) Within four years after the date of the enactment of this chapter, the Judicial Conference of the United States shall prepare a comprehensive report on all plans received pursuant to section 472(d) of this title. The Director of the Federal Judicial Center and the Director of the Administrative Office of the United States Courts may make recommendations regarding such report to the Judicial Conference during the preparation of the report. The Judicial Conference shall transmit copies of the report to the United States district courts and to the Committees on the Judiciary of the Senate and the House of Representatives.

(b) The Judicial Conference of the United States shall, on a continuing basis—

28 § 479 SELECTED PROVISIONS

(1) study ways to improve litigation management and dispute resolution services in the district courts; and

(2) make recommendations to the district courts on ways to improve such services.

(c)(1) The Judicial Conference of the United States shall prepare, periodically revise, and transmit to the United States district courts a Manual for Litigation Management and Cost and Delay Reduction. The Director of the Federal Judicial Center and the Director of the Administrative Office of the United States Courts may make recommendations regarding the preparation of and any subsequent revisions to the Manual.

(2) The Manual shall be developed after careful evaluation of the plans implemented under section 472 of this title, the demonstration program conducted under section 104 of the Civil Justice Reform Act of 1990, and the pilot program conducted under section 105 of the Civil Justice Reform Act of 1990.

(3) The Manual shall contain a description and analysis of the litigation management, cost and delay reduction principles and techniques, and alternative dispute resolution programs considered most effective by the Judicial Conference, the Director of the Federal Judicial Center, and the Director of the Administrative Office of the United States Courts.

§ 1251. Original jurisdiction

(a) The Supreme Court shall have original and exclusive jurisdiction of all controversies between two or more States.

(b) The Supreme Court shall have original but not exclusive jurisdiction of:

(1) All actions or proceedings to which ambassadors, other public ministers, consuls, or vice consuls of foreign states are parties;

(2) All controversies between the United States and a State;

(3) All actions or proceedings by a State against the citizens of another State or against aliens.

§ 1253. Direct appeals from decisions of three-judge courts

Except as otherwise provided by law, any party may appeal to the Supreme Court from an order granting or denying, after notice and hearing, an interlocutory or permanent injunction in any civil action, suit or proceeding required by any Act of Congress to be heard and determined by a district court of three judges.

§ 1254. Courts of appeals; certiorari; appeal; certified questions

Cases in the courts of appeals may be reviewed by the Supreme Court by the following methods:

(1) By writ of certiorari granted upon the petition of any party to any civil or criminal case, before or after rendition of judgment or decree;

(2) By certification at any time by a court of appeals of any question of law in any civil or criminal case as to which instructions are desired, and upon such certification the Supreme Court may give binding instructions or require the entire record to be sent up for decision of the entire matter in controversy.

Related Provisions Regarding Appeals to the Highest Court in a Jurisdiction

(a) *Discretionary Review*

1. *Comparative state provisions*

California Constitution Art. 6, § 11

The Supreme Court has appellate jurisdiction when judgment of death has been pronounced. With that exception courts of appeal have appellate jurisdiction when superior courts have original jurisdiction and in other causes prescribed by statute.

* * *

California Constitution Art. 6, § 12

(a) The Supreme Court may, before decision, transfer to itself a cause in a court of appeal. It may, before decision, transfer a cause from itself to a court of appeal or from one court of appeal or division to another. The court to which a cause is transferred has jurisdiction.

(b) The Supreme Court may review the decision of a court of appeal in any cause.

(c) The Judicial Council shall provide, by rules of court, for the time and procedure for transfer and for review, including, among other things, provisions for the time and procedure for transfer with instructions, for review of all or part of a decision, and for remand as improvidently granted.

(d) This section shall not apply to an appeal involving a judgment of death.

California Rule of Court 28

(a) [Time within which court may order review]

(1) [*On own motion*] If no petition for review is filed, within 30 days after a decision of a Court of Appeal becomes final as to that court the Supreme Court, on its own motion, may order review of the Court of Appeal decision. Within the original 30-day period or any extension of it the Supreme Court may, for good cause, extend the time for one or more additional periods amounting to not more than an additional 60 days in the aggregate. The total time, including extensions shall not exceed 90 days after the decision becomes final as to the Court of Appeal.

(2) [*On petition*] Within 60 days after the filing, as provided in subdivision (b), of the last timely petition for review, the Supreme Court may order review of a Court of Appeal decision. Within the original 60-day period or any extension of it the Supreme Court may, for good cause, extend the time for one or more additional periods amounting to not more than an additional 30 days in the

aggregate. The total time, including extensions, shall not exceed 90 days after the filing of the last timely petition for review.

(b) [Time for filing petition] A party seeking review must serve and file a petition within 10 days after the decision of the Court of Appeal becomes final as to that court, but a petition may not be filed after denial of a transfer to a Court of Appeal in a case within the original jurisdiction of a municipal or justice court. Proof shall be filed of the delivery or mailing of one copy of the petition to the clerk of the Court of Appeal which rendered the decision. The clerk of that court shall transmit to the Clerk of the Supreme Court the original record, briefs, and all original papers and exhibits on file in the cause * * *. If the petition is denied, the Clerk of the Supreme Court shall return them to the clerk of the proper Court of Appeal. If the petition is granted, they shall be retained and properly numbered by the clerk of the Supreme Court.

* * *

New York Civil Practice Law and Rules 5602

(a) Permission of appellate division or court of appeals. An appeal may be taken to the court of appeals by permission of the appellate division granted before application to the court of appeals, or by permission of the court of appeals upon refusal by the appellate division or upon direct application. * * * Permission by the court of appeals for leave to appeal shall be pursuant to rules * * * which shall provide that leave to appeal be granted upon the approval of two judges of the court of appeals. Such appeal may be taken:

1. in an action originating in the supreme court, a county court, a surrogate's court, the family court, the court of claims or an administrative agency or an arbitration,

　(i) from an order of the appellate division which finally determines the action and which is not appealable as of right, or

　(ii) from a final judgment of such court or final determination of such agency or final arbitration award where the appellate division has made an order on a prior appeal in the action which necessarily affects the final judgment, determination or award and the final judgment or determination or award is not appealable as of right pursuant to subdivision (d) of section 5601 of this article; and

2. in a proceeding instituted by or against one or more public officers or a board, commission or other body of public officers or a court or tribunal, from an order of the appellate division which does not finally determine such proceeding, except that the appellate division shall not grant permission to appeal from an order granting or affirming the granting of a new trial or hearing.

(b) Permission of appellate division. An appeal may be taken to the court of appeals by permission of the appellate division:

1. from an order of the appellate division which does not finally determine an action, except an order described in paragraph two of subdivision (a) or subparagraph (iii) of paragraph two of subdivision (b) of this section or in subdivision (c) of section 5601;

2. in an action originating in a court other than the supreme court, a county court, a surrogate's court, the family court, the court of claims or an administrative agency,

　(i) from an order of the appellate division which finally determines the action, and which is not appealable as of right pursuant to paragraph one of subdivision (b) of section 5601, or

　(ii) from a final judgment of such court or a final determination of such agency where the appellate division has made an order on a prior appeal in the action which necessarily affects the final judgment or determination and the final judgment or determination is not appealable as of right pursuant to subdivision (d) of section 5601, or

(iii) from an order of the appellate division granting or affirming the granting of a new trial or hearing where the appellant stipulates that, upon affirmance, judgment absolute shall be entered against him.

2. *Basis for exercise of discretion*

United States Supreme Court Rule 10.1 (Former Rule 17.1)

A review on writ of certiorari is not a matter of right, but of judicial discretion. A petition for a writ of certiorari will be granted only when there are special and important reasons therefor. The following, while neither controlling nor fully measuring the Court's discretion, indicate the character of reasons that will be considered:

(a) When a United States court of appeals has rendered a decision in conflict with the decision of another United States court of appeals on the same matter; or has decided a federal question in a way in conflict with a state court of last resort; or has so far departed from the accepted and usual course of judicial proceedings, or sanctioned such a departure by a lower court, as to call for an exercise of this Court's power of supervision.

(b) When a state court of last resort has decided a federal question in a way that conflicts with the decision of another state court of last resort or of a United States court of appeals.

(c) When a state court or a United States court of appeals has decided an important question of federal law which has not been, but should be, settled by this Court, or has decided a federal question in a way that conflicts with applicable decisions of this Court.

California Rule of Court 29

(a) **[Grounds]** Review by the Supreme Court of a decision of a Court of Appeal will be ordered (1) where it appears necessary to secure uniformity of decision or the settlement of important questions of law; (2) where the Court of Appeal was without jurisdiction of the cause; or (3) where, because of disqualification or other reason, the decision of the Court of Appeal lacks the concurrence of the required majority of qualified judges.

(b) **[Limitations]** As a matter of policy, on petition for review the Supreme Court normally will not consider: (1) any issue that could have been but was not timely raised in the briefs filed in the Court of Appeal; (2) any issue or any material fact that was omitted from or misstated in the opinion of the Court of Appeal, unless the omission or misstatement was called to the attention of the Court of Appeal in a petition for rehearing. All other issues and facts may be presented in the petition for review without the necessity of filing a petition for rehearing.

(b) *Mandatory Review*

Georgia Constitution Art. VI, § 1, ¶ 8

Any court shall transfer to the appropriate court in the state any civil case in which it determines that jurisdiction or venue lies elsewhere.

Georgia Constitution Art. VI, § 5, ¶ 5

In the event of an equal division of the Judges when sitting as a body, the case shall be immediately transmitted to the Supreme Court.

Georgia Constitution Art. VI, § 6, ¶ 2

The Supreme Court shall be a court of review and shall exercise exclusive appellate jurisdiction in the following cases:

(1) All cases involving the construction of a treaty or of the Constitution of the State of Georgia or of the United States and all cases in which the constitutionality of a law, ordinance, or constitutional provision has been drawn in question; and

(2) All cases of election contest.

Georgia Constitution Art. VI, § 6, ¶ 3

Unless otherwise provided by law, the Supreme Court shall have appellate jurisdiction of the following classes of cases:

(1) Cases involving title to land;

(2) All equity cases;

(3) All cases involving wills;

(4) All habeas corpus cases;

(5) All cases involving extraordinary remedies;

(6) All divorce and alimony cases;

(7) All cases certified to it by the Court of Appeals; and

(8) All cases in which a sentence of death was imposed or could be imposed.

Review of all cases shall be as provided by law.

Georgia Constitution, Art. VI, § 6, ¶ 5

The Supreme Court may review by certiorari cases in the Court of Appeals which are of gravity or great public importance.

New York Civil Practice Law and Rules 5601

(a) Dissent. An appeal may be taken to the court of appeals as of right in an action originating in the supreme court, a county court, a surrogate's court, the family court, the court of claims or an administrative agency, from an order of the appellate division which finally determines the action, where there is a dissent by at least two justices on a question of law in favor of the party taking such appeal.

(b) Constitutional grounds. An appeal may be taken to the court of appeals as of right:

1. from an order of the appellate division which finally determines an action where there is directly involved the construction of the constitution of the state or of the United States; and

2. from a judgment of a court of record of original instance which finally determines an action where the only question involved on the appeal is the validity of a statutory provision of the state or of the United States under the constitution of the state or of the United States.

(c) From order granting new trial or hearing, upon stipulation for judgment absolute. An appeal may be taken to the court of appeals as of right in an action originating in the supreme court, a county court, a surrogate's court, the family court, the court of claims or an administrative agency, from an order of the appellate division granting or affirming the granting of a new trial or hearing where the appellant stipulates that, upon affirmance, judgment absolute shall be entered against him.

(d) Based upon non-final determination of appellate division. An appeal may be taken to the court of appeals as of right from a final judgment entered in a court of original instance or from a final determination of an administrative agency or from a final arbitration award, or from an order of the appellate division which finally determines an appeal from such a judgment or determination, where the appellate division has made an order on a prior appeal in the action which necessarily affects the judgment, determination or award and which satisfies the requirements of subdivision (a) or of paragraph one of subdivision (b) except that of finality.

§ 1257. State courts; appeal; certiorari

(a) Final judgments or decrees rendered by the highest court of a State in which a decision could be had, may be reviewed by the Supreme Court by writ of certiorari, where the validity of a treaty or statute of the United States is drawn in question or where the validity of a statute of any State is drawn in question on the ground of its being repugnant to the Constitution, treaties, or laws of the United States, or where any title, right, privilege or immunity is specially set up or claimed under the Constitution or the treaties or statutes of, or any commission held or authority exercised under, the United States.

(b) For purposes of this section, the term "highest court of a State" includes the District of Columbia Court of Appeals.

Related Provision

See United States Supreme Court Rule 10.1 as set out following 28 U.S.C. § 1254, supra.

§ 1291. Final decisions of district courts

The courts of appeals (other than the United States Court of Appeals for the Federal Circuit) shall have jurisdiction of appeals from all final decisions of the district courts of the United States, the United States District Court for the District of the Canal Zone, the District Court of Guam, and the District Court of the Virgin Islands, except where a direct review may be had in the Supreme Court * * *.

Comparative State Provision

See New York Civil Practice Law and Rules 5701 as set out following 28 U.S.C. § 1292, infra.

§ 1292. Interlocutory decisions

(a) Except as provided in subsections (c) and (d) of this section, the courts of appeals shall have jurisdiction of appeals from:

(1) Interlocutory orders of the district courts of the United States, the United States District Court for the District of the Canal Zone, the District Court of Guam, and the District Court of the Virgin Islands, or of the judges thereof, granting, continuing, modifying, refusing or dissolving injunctions, or refusing to dissolve or modify injunctions, except where a direct review may be had in the Supreme Court;

(2) Interlocutory orders appointing receivers, or refusing orders to wind up receiverships or to take steps to accomplish the purposes thereof, such as directing sales or other disposals of property;

(3) Interlocutory decrees of such district courts or the judges thereof determining the rights and liabilities of the parties to admiralty cases in which appeals from final decrees are allowed.

(b) When a district judge, in making in a civil action an order not otherwise appealable under this section, shall be of the opinion that such order involves a controlling question of law as to which there is substantial ground for difference of opinion and that an immediate appeal from the order may materially advance the ultimate termination of the litigation, he shall so state in writing in such order. The Court of Appeals which would have jurisdiction of an appeal of such action may thereupon, in its discretion, permit an appeal to be taken from such order, if application is made to it within ten days after the entry of the order: *Provided, however,* That application for an appeal hereunder shall not stay proceedings in the district court unless the district judge or the Court of Appeals or a judge thereof shall so order.

(c) The United States Court of Appeals for the Federal Circuit shall have exclusive jurisdiction—

(1) of an appeal from an interlocutory order or decree described in subsection (a) or (b) of this section in any case over which the court would have jurisdiction of an appeal under section 1295 of this title; and

(2) of an appeal from a judgment in a civil action for patent infringement which would otherwise be appealable to the United States Court of Appeals for the Federal Circuit and is final except for an accounting.

(d)(1) When the chief judge of the Court of International Trade issues an order under the provisions of section 256(b) of this title, or when any judge of the Court of International Trade, in issuing any other interlocutory order, includes in the order a statement that a controlling question of law is involved with respect to which there is a substantial ground for difference of opinion and that an immediate appeal from that order may materially advance the ultimate termination of the litigation, the United States Court of Appeals for the Federal Circuit may, in its discretion, permit an appeal to be taken from such order, if application is made to that Court within ten days after the entry of such order.

(2) When the chief judge of the United States Court of Federal Claims issues an order under section 798(b) of this title, or when any judge of the United States Court of Federal Claims, in issuing an interlocutory order, includes in the order a statement that a controlling question of law is involved with respect to which there is a substantial ground for difference of opinion and that an immediate appeal from that

order may materially advance the ultimate termination of the litigation, the United States Court of Appeals for the Federal Circuit may, in its discretion, permit an appeal to be taken from such order, if application is made to that Court within ten days after the entry of such order.

(3) Neither the application for nor the granting of an appeal under this subsection shall stay proceedings in the Court of International Trade or in the Court of Federal Claims, as the case may be, unless a stay is ordered by a judge of the Court of International Trade or of the Court of Federal Claims or by the United States Court of Appeals for the Federal Circuit or a judge of that court.

(4)(A) The United States Court of Appeals for the Federal Circuit shall have exclusive jurisdiction of an appeal from an interlocutory order of a district court of the United States, the District Court of Guam, the District Court of the Virgin Islands, or the District Court for the Northern Mariana Islands, granting or denying, in whole or in part, a motion to transfer an action to the United States Court of Federal Claims under section 1631 of this title.

(B) When a motion to transfer an action to the Court of Federal Claims is filed in a district court, no further proceedings shall be taken in the district court until 60 days after the court has ruled upon the motion. If an appeal is taken from the district court's grant or denial of the motion, proceedings shall be further stayed until the appeal has been decided by the Court of Appeals for the Federal Circuit. The stay of proceedings in the district court shall not bar the granting of preliminary or injunctive relief, where appropriate and where expedition is reasonably necessary. However, during the period in which proceedings are stayed as provided in this subparagraph, no transfer to the Court of Federal Claims pursuant to the motion shall be carried out.

(e) The Supreme Court may prescribe rules, in accordance with section 2072 of this title, to provide for an appeal of an interlocutory decision to the courts of appeals that is not otherwise provided for under subsection (a), (b), (c), or (d).

Comparative Federal and State Provisions

(a) *Related Federal Rule*

See Federal Rule of Appellate Procedure 5, Part IV, infra.

(b) *Comparative State Provisions*

Minnesota Rules of Civil Appellate Procedure 103.03

An appeal may be taken to the Court of Appeals:

(a) from a judgment entered in the trial court;

(b) from an order which grants, refuses, dissolves or refuses to dissolve, an injunction;

(c) from an order vacating or sustaining an attachment;

(d) from an order denying a new trial, or from an order granting a new trial if the trial court expressly states therein, or in a memorandum attached thereto, that the order is based exclusively upon errors of law occurring at the trial, and upon no other ground; and the trial court shall specify such errors in its order or memorandum, but upon appeal, such order granting a new trial may be sustained for errors of law prejudicial to respondent other than those specified by the trial court;

(e) from an order which, in effect, determines the action and prevents a judgment from which an appeal might be taken;

(f) from a final order or judgment made or rendered in proceedings supplementary to execution;

(g) * * *

(h) if the trial court certifies that the question presented is important and doubtful, from an order which denies a motion to dismiss for failure to state a claim upon which relief can be granted or from an order which denies a motion for summary judgment.

New York Civil Practice Law and Rules 5701

(a) Appeals as of right. An appeal may be taken to the appellate division as of right in an action, originating in the supreme court or a county court:

1. from any final or interlocutory judgment except one entered subsequent to an order of the appellate division which disposes of all the issues in the action; or

2. from an order not specified in subdivision (b), where the motion it decided was made upon notice and it:

(i) grants, refuses, continues or modifies a provisional remedy; or

(ii) settles, grants or refuses an application to resettle a transcript or statement on appeal; or

(iii) grants or refuses a new trial; except where specific questions of fact arising upon the issues in an action triable by the court have been tried by a jury, pursuant to an order for that purpose, and the order grants or refuses a new trial upon the merits; or

(iv) involves some part of the merits; or

(v) affects a substantial right; or

(vi) in effect determines the action and prevents a judgment from which an appeal might be taken; or

(vii) determines a statutory provision of the state to be unconstitutional, and the determination appears from the reasons given for the decision or is necessarily implied in the decision; or

3. from an order, where the motion it decided was made upon notice, refusing to vacate or modify a prior order, if the prior order would have been appealable as of right under paragraph two had it decided a motion made upon notice.

(b) Orders not appealable as of right. An order is not appealable to the appellate division as of right where it:

1. is made in a proceeding against a body or officer pursuant to article 78; or

2. requires or refuses to require a more definite statement in a pleading; or

3. orders or refuses to order that scandalous or prejudicial matter be stricken from a pleading.

(c) Appeals by permission. An appeal may be taken to the appellate division from any order which is not appealable as of right in an action originating in the supreme court or a county court by permission of the judge who made the order granted before application to a justice of the appellate division; or by permission of a justice of the appellate division in the department to which the appeal could be taken, upon refusal by the judge who made the order or upon direct application.

§ 1331. Federal question

The district courts shall have original jurisdiction of all civil actions arising under the Constitution, laws, or treaties of the United States.

§ 1332. Diversity of citizenship; amount in controversy; costs

(a) The district courts shall have original jurisdiction of all civil actions where the matter in controversy exceeds the sum or value of $50,000, exclusive of interest and costs, and is between—

(1) citizens of different States;

(2) citizens of a State and citizens or subjects of a foreign state;

(3) citizens of different States and in which citizens or subjects of a foreign state are additional parties; and

(4) a foreign state, * * * as plaintiff and citizens of a State or of different States.

For the purposes of this section, section 1335, and section 1441, an alien admitted to the United States for permanent residence shall be deemed a citizen of the State in which such alien is domiciled.

(b) Except when express provision therefor is otherwise made in a statute of the United States, where the plaintiff who files the case originally in the Federal courts is finally adjudged to be entitled to recover less than the sum or value of $50,000, computed without regard to any setoff or counterclaim to which the defendant may be adjudged to be entitled, and exclusive of interest and costs, the district court may deny costs to the plaintiff and, in addition, may impose costs on the plaintiff.

(c) For the purposes of this section and section 1441 of this title—

(1) a corporation shall be deemed a citizen of any State by which it has been incorporated and of the State where it has its principal place of business, except that in any direct action against the insurer of a policy or contract of liability insurance, whether incorporated or unincorporated, to which action the insured is not joined as a party-defendant, such insurer shall be deemed a citizen of the State of which the insured is a citizen, as well as of any State by which the insurer has been incorporated and of the State where it has its principal place of business; and

(2) the legal representative of the estate of a decedent shall be deemed to be a citizen only of the same State as the decedent, and the legal representative of an infant or incompetent shall be deemed to be a citizen only of the same State as the infant or incompetent.

(d) The word "States", as used in this section, includes the Territories, the District of Columbia, and the Commonwealth of Puerto Rico.

§ 1333. Admiralty, maritime and prize cases

The district courts shall have original jurisdiction, exclusive of the courts of the States, of:

(1) Any civil case of admiralty or maritime jurisdiction, saving to suitors in all cases all other remedies to which they are otherwise entitled.

(2) Any prize brought into the United States and all proceedings for the condemnation of property taken as prize.

§ 1334. Bankruptcy cases and proceedings

(a) Except as provided in subsection (b) of this section, the district courts shall have original and exclusive jurisdiction of all cases under title 11.

(b) Notwithstanding any Act of Congress that confers exclusive jurisdiction on a court or courts other than the district courts, the district courts shall have original but not exclusive jurisdiction of all civil proceedings arising under title 11, or arising in or related to cases under title 11.

(c)(1) Nothing in this section prevents a district court in the interest of justice, or in the interest of comity with State courts or respect for State law, from abstaining from hearing a particular proceeding arising under title 11 or arising in or related to a case under title 11.

(2) Upon timely motion of a party in a proceeding based upon a State law claim or State law cause of action, related to a case under title 11 but not arising under title 11 or arising in a case under title 11, with respect to which an action could not have been commenced in a court of the United States absent jurisdiction under this section, the district court shall abstain from hearing such proceeding if an action is commenced, and can be timely adjudicated, in a State forum of appropriate jurisdiction. Any decision to abstain or not to abstain made under this subsection is not reviewable by appeal or otherwise by the court of appeals under section 158(d), 1291, or 1292 of this title or by the Supreme Court of the United States under section 1254 of this title. This subsection shall not be construed to limit the applicability of the stay provided for by section 362 of title 11, United States Code, as such section applies to an action affecting the property of the estate in bankruptcy.

(d) The district court in which a case under title 11 is commenced or is pending shall have exclusive jurisdiction of all of the property, wherever located, of the debtor as of the commencement of such case, and of property of the estate.

§ 1335. Interpleader

(a) The district courts shall have original jurisdiction of any civil action of interpleader or in the nature of interpleader filed by any person, firm, or corporation, association, or society having in his or its custody or possession money or property of the value of $500 or more, or having issued a note, bond, certificate, policy of insurance, or other instrument of value or amount of $500 or more, or providing for the delivery or payment or the loan of money or property of such amount or value, or being under any obligation written or unwritten to the amount of $500 or more, if

(1) Two or more adverse claimants, of diverse citizenship as defined in section 1332 of this title, are claiming or may claim to be entitled to such money or property, or to any one or more of the benefits arising by virtue of any note, bond, certificate, policy or other instrument, or arising by virtue of any such obligation; and if (2) the plaintiff has deposited such money or property or has paid the amount of or the loan or other value of such instrument or the amount due under such obligation into the registry of the court, there to abide the judgment of the court, or has given bond payable to the clerk of the court in such amount and with such surety as the court or judge may deem proper, conditioned upon the compliance by the plaintiff with the future order or judgment of the court with respect to the subject matter of the controversy.

(b) Such an action may be entertained although the titles or claims of the conflicting claimants do not have a common origin, or are not identical, but are adverse to and independent of one another.

§ 1337. Commerce and antitrust regulations

(a) The district courts shall have original jurisdiction of any civil action or proceeding arising under any Act of Congress regulating commerce or protecting trade and commerce against restraints and monopolies * * *.

Related Federal Provisions

United States Code Tit. 15, § 15(a)

Except as provided in subsection (b) [regarding suits by foreign states], any person who shall be injured in his business or property by reason of anything forbidden in the antitrust laws may sue therefor in any district court of the United States in the district in which the defendant resides or is found or has an agent, without respect to the amount in controversy, and shall recover threefold the damages by him sustained, and the cost of suit, including a reasonable attorney's fee. * * *

Proposed Consumer Class Action Act [House of Representatives Bill 839, January 3, 1973]

Sec. 2. Section 5 of the Federal Trade Commission Act (15 U.S.C. 45) is amended by adding at the end thereof the following:

"(m) Consumers who have been damaged by unfair or deceptive acts or practices in commerce are hereby authorized to bring consumer class actions for redress of such damages. Such actions shall be brought as consumer class actions in accordance with section 4 of the Consumer Class Action Act." * * *

Sec. 4. (a)(1) An Act in defraud of consumers which affects commerce is unlawful and the district courts of the United States shall have original jurisdiction without regard to the amount in controversy to entertain civil class actions for redress of such unlawful acts.

(2) For the purposes of this section an "act in defraud of consumers" is—

(A) an unfair or deceptive act or practice which is unlawful within the meaning of section 5(a)(1) of the Federal Trade Commission Act, or

(B) an act that gives rise to a civil action by a consumer or consumers under State, statutory or decisional law for the benefit of consumers. * * *

(c) In the case of any class action brought upon the basis of a violation of consumers' rights under any State law the court shall, in deciding such action, apply the following criteria:

(1) State law relating to the consumers' rights under State statutory or decisional law is adopted as Federal law.

(2) Federal law applicable to each class shall be fashioned upon the law of the State and the State statutory and decisional construction shall be applied as if jurisdiction of the Federal court were based on diversity of citizenship.

(3) In cases of conflict between State statutory and decisional construction and Federal law the latter shall prevail, and Federal law governing the case shall be fashioned from State law not in conflict, as near as may be, and from Federal law.

(4) If, prior to the date of enactment of this Act, a cause was not subject to removal under section 1441 of title 28, United States Code, the adoption of State law as Federal law by this Act shall not authorize the removal of such a cause on the jurisdictional basis of a Federal question.

(d) Whenever a class of consumers prevails in a class action under this Act, including the amendments made by this Act, the court shall award to the attorneys representing such class a reasonable fee based on the value of their services to the class. An award of attorney's fees is to be made in addition to the damages or relief recovered by the class except that attorney's fees may be awarded from money damages or financial penalties which the defendant owes to members of the class who cannot be located with due diligence. Such attorneys' fees awarded by the court shall not exceed 10 percent of the total judgment unless failure to award a greater amount would be manifestly unjust and not commensurate with the efforts of counsel.

§ 1338. Patents, plant variety protection, copyrights, mask works, trademarks and unfair competition

(a) The district courts shall have original jurisdiction of any civil action arising under any Act of Congress relating to patents, plant variety protection, copyrights and trade-marks. Such jurisdiction shall be exclusive of the courts of the states in patent, plant variety protection and copyright cases.

(b) The district courts shall have original jurisdiction of any civil action asserting a claim of unfair competition when joined with a substantial and related claim under the copyright, patent, plant variety protection or trade-mark laws.

(c) Subsections (a) and (b) apply to exclusive rights in mask works under chapter 9 of title 17 to the same extent as such subsections apply to copyrights.

§ 1343. Civil rights and elective franchise

(a) The district courts shall have original jurisdiction of any civil action authorized by law to be commenced by any person:

(1) To recover damages for injury to his person or property, or because of the deprivation of any right or privilege of a citizen of the United States, by any act done in furtherance of any conspiracy mentioned in section 1985 of Title 42;

(2) To recover damages from any person who fails to prevent or to aid in preventing any wrongs mentioned in section 1985 of Title 42 which he had knowledge were about to occur and power to prevent;

(3) To redress the deprivation, under color of any State law, statute, ordinance, regulation, custom or usage, of any right, privilege or immunity secured by the Constitution of the United States or by any Act of Congress providing for equal rights of citizens or of all persons within the jurisdiction of the United States;

(4) To recover damages or to secure equitable or other relief under any Act of Congress providing for the protection of civil rights, including the right to vote.

* * *

§ 1345. United States as plaintiff

Except as otherwise provided by Act of Congress, the district courts shall have original jurisdiction of all civil actions, suits or proceedings commenced by the United States, or by any agency or officer thereof expressly authorized to sue by Act of Congress.

§ 1346. United States as defendant

(a) The district courts shall have original jurisdiction, concurrent with the United States Court of Federal Claims, of:

(1) Any civil action against the United States for the recovery of any internal-revenue tax alleged to have been erroneously or illegally assessed or collected, or any penalty claimed to have been collected without authority or any sum alleged to have been excessive or in any manner wrongfully collected under the internal-revenue laws;

(2) Any other civil action or claim against the United States, not exceeding $10,000 in amount, founded either upon the Constitution, or any Act of Congress, or any regulation of an executive department, or

upon any express or implied contract with the United States, or for liquidated or unliquidated damages in cases not sounding in tort * * *. For the purpose of this paragraph, an express or implied contract with the Army and Air Force Exchange Service, Navy Exchanges, Marine Corps Exchanges, Coast Guard Exchanges, or Exchange Councils of the National Aeronautics and Space Administration shall be considered an express or implied contract with the United States.

(b) Subject to the provisions of chapter 171 of this title, the district courts, together with the United States District Court for the District of the Canal Zone and the District Court of the Virgin Islands, shall have exclusive jurisdiction of civil actions on claims against the United States for money damages, accruing on and after January 1, 1945, for injury or loss of property, or personal injury or death caused by the negligent or wrongful act of omission of any employee of the Government while acting within the scope of his office or employment, under circumstances where the United States, if a private person, would be liable to the claimant in accordance with the law of the place where the act or omission occurred.

(c) The jurisdiction conferred by this section includes jurisdiction of any set-off, counterclaim, or other claim or demand whatever on the part of the United States against any plaintiff commencing an action under this section.

(d) The district courts shall not have jurisdiction under this section of any civil action or claim for a pension.

(e) The district courts shall have original jurisdiction of any civil action against the United States provided in section 6226, 6228(a), 7426, or 7428 * * * or section 7429 of the Internal Revenue Code of 1954.

(f) The district courts shall have exclusive original jurisdiction of civil actions under section 2409a to quiet title to an estate or interest in real property in which an interest is claimed by the United States.

§ 1359. Parties collusively joined or made

A district court shall not have jurisdiction of a civil action in which any party, by assignment or otherwise, has been improperly or collusively made or joined to invoke the jurisdiction of such court.

§ 1361. Action to compel an officer of the United States to perform his duty

The district courts shall have original jurisdiction of any action in the nature of mandamus to compel an officer or employee of the United States or any agency thereof to perform a duty owed to the plaintiff.

§ 1367. Supplemental jurisdiction

(a) Except as provided in subsections (b) and (c) or as expressly provided otherwise by Federal statute, in any civil action of which the district courts have original jurisdiction, the district courts shall have supplemental jurisdiction over all other claims that are so related to claims in the action within such original jurisdiction that they form part of the same case or controversy under Article III of the United States Constitution. Such supplemental jurisdiction shall include claims that involve the joinder or intervention of additional parties.

(b) In any civil action of which the district courts have original jurisdiction founded solely on section 1332 of this title, the district courts shall not have supplemental jurisdiction under subsection (a) over claims by plaintiffs against persons made parties under Rule 14, 19, 20, or 24 of the Federal Rules of Civil Procedure; or over claims by persons proposed to be joined as plaintiffs under Rule 19 of such rules, or seeking to intervene as plaintiffs under Rule 24 of such rules, when exercising supplemental jurisdiction over such claims would be inconsistent with the jurisdictional requirements of section 1332.

(c) The district courts may decline to exercise supplemental jurisdiction over a claim under subsection (a) if—

> (1) the claim raises a novel or complex issue of State law,
>
> (2) the claim substantially predominates over the claim or claims over which the district court has original jurisdiction,
>
> (3) the district court has dismissed all claims over which it has original jurisdiction, or
>
> (4) in exceptional circumstances there are other compelling reasons for declining jurisdiction.

(d) The period of limitations for any claim asserted under subsection (a), and for any other claim in the same action that is voluntarily dismissed at the same time as or after the dismissal of the claim under subsection (a), shall be tolled while the claim is pending and for a period of 30 days after it is dismissed unless State law provides for a longer tolling period.

(e) As used in this section, the term "State" includes the District of Columbia, the Commonwealth of Puerto Rico, and any territory or possession of the United States.

§ 1391. Venue generally

(a) A civil action wherein jurisdiction is founded only on diversity of citizenship may, except as otherwise provided by law, be brought only in (1) a judicial district where any defendant resides, if all defendants reside in the same State, (2) a judicial district in which a substantial part of the events or omissions giving rise to the claim occurred, or a substantial part of property that is the subject of the action is situated, or (3) a judicial district in which the defendants are subject to personal jurisdiction at the time the action is commenced, if there is no district in which the action may otherwise be brought.

(b) A civil action wherein jurisdiction is not founded solely on diversity of citizenship may, except as otherwise provided by law, be brought only [in] * * * (1) a judicial district where any defendant resides, if all defendants reside in the same State, (2) a judicial district in which a substantial part of the events or omissions giving rise to the claim occurred, or a substantial part of property that is the subject of the action is situated, or (3) a judicial district in which any defendant may be found, if there is no district in which the action may otherwise be brought.

(c) For purposes of venue under this chapter, a defendant that is a corporation shall be deemed to reside in any judicial district in which it is subject to personal jurisdiction at the time the action is commenced. In a State which has more than one judicial district and in which a defendant that is a corporation is subject to personal jurisdiction at the time an action is commenced, such corporation shall be deemed to reside in any district in that State within which its contacts would be sufficient to subject it to personal jurisdiction if that district were a separate State, and, if there is no such district, the corporation shall be deemed to reside in the district within which it has the most significant contacts.

(d) An alien may be sued in any district.

(e) A civil action in which a defendant is an officer or employee of the United States or any agency thereof acting in his official capacity or under color of legal authority, or an agency of the United States, or the United States, may, except as otherwise provided by law, be brought in any judicial district in which: (1) a defendant in the action resides, (2) a substantial part of the events or omissions giving rise to the claim occurred, or a substantial part of property that is the subject of the action is situated, or (3) the plaintiff resides if no real property is involved in the action. Additional persons may be joined as parties to any such action in accordance with Federal Rules of Civil Procedure and with such other venue requirements as would be applicable if the United States or one of its officers, employees, or agencies were not a party.

The summons and complaint in such an action shall be served as provided by the Federal Rules of Civil Procedure except that the delivery of the summons and complaint to the officer or agency as required by the rules may be made by certified mail beyond the territorial limits of the district in which the action is brought.

(f) A civil action against a foreign state as defined in section 1603(a) of this title may be brought—

(1) in any judicial district in which a substantial part of the events or omissions giving rise to the claim occurred, or a substantial part of property that is the subject of the action is situated;

(2) in any judicial district in which the vessel or cargo of a foreign state is situated, if the claim is asserted under section 1605(b) of this title;

(3) in any judicial district in which the agency or instrumentality is licensed to do business or is doing business, if the action is brought against an agency or instrumentality of a foreign state as defined in section 1603(b) of this title; or

(4) in the United States District Court for the District of Columbia if the action is brought against a foreign state or political subdivision thereof.

§ 1392. Defendants or property in different districts in same State

(a) Any civil action, not of a local nature, against defendants residing in different districts in the same State, may be brought in any of such districts.

(b) Any civil action, of a local nature, involving property located in different districts in the same State, may be brought in any of such districts.

§ 1397. Interpleader

Any civil action of interpleader or in the nature of interpleader under section 1335 of this title may be brought in the judicial district in which one or more of the claimants reside.

§ 1400. Patents and copyrights

(a) Civil actions, suits, or proceedings arising under any Act of Congress relating to copyrights or exclusive rights in mask works may be instituted in the district in which the defendant or his agent resides or may be found.

(b) Any civil action for patent infringement may be brought in the judicial district where the defendant resides, or where the defendant has committed acts of infringement and has a regular and established place of business.

§ 1401. Stockholder's derivative action

Any civil action by a stockholder on behalf of his corporation may be prosecuted in any judicial district where the corporation might have sued the same defendants.

§ 1402. United States as defendant

(a) Any civil action in a district court against the United States under subsection (a) of section 1346 of this title may be prosecuted only:

(1) Except as provided in paragraph (2), in the judicial district where the plaintiff resides;

(2) In the case of a civil action by a corporation under paragraph (1) of subsection (a) of section 1346, in the judicial district in which is located the principal place of business or principal office or agency of the corporation; or if it has no principal place of business or principal office or agency in any judicial district (A) in the judicial district in which is located the office to which was made the return of the tax in respect of which the claim is made, or (B) if no return was made, in the judicial district in which lies the District of Columbia. Notwithstanding the foregoing provisions of this paragraph a district court, for the convenience of the parties and witnesses, in the interest of justice, may transfer any such action to any other district or division.

(b) Any civil action on a tort claim against the United States under subsection (b) of section 1346 of this title may be prosecuted only in the judicial district where the plaintiff resides or wherein the act or omission complained of occurred.

(c) Any civil action against the United States under subsection (e) of section 1346 of this title may be prosecuted only in the judicial district where the property is situated at the time of levy, or if no levy is made, in the judicial district in which the event occurred which gave rise to the cause of action.

(d) Any civil action under section 2409a to quiet title to an estate or interest in real property in which an interest is claimed by the United States shall be brought in the district court of the district where the property is located or, if located in different districts, in any of such districts.

§ 1404. Change of venue

(a) For the convenience of parties and witnesses, in the interest of justice, a district court may transfer any civil action to any other district or division where it might have been brought.

* * *

Comparative State Provision

Wisconsin Statutes Annotated § 801.63

(1) Stay on initiative of parties. If a court of this state, on motion of any party, finds that trial of an action pending before it should as a matter of substantial justice be tried in a forum outside this state, the court may in conformity with sub. (3) enter an order to stay further proceedings on the action in this state. A moving party under this subsection must stipulate consent to suit in the alternative forum and waive right to rely on statutes of limitation which may have run in the alternative forum after commencement of the action in this state. A stay order may be granted although the action could not have been commenced in the alternative forum without consent of the moving party.

(2) Time for filing and hearing motion. The motion to stay the proceedings shall be filed prior to or with the answer unless the motion is to stay proceedings on a cause raised by counterclaim, in which instance the motion shall be filed prior to or with the reply. The issues raised by this motion shall be tried to the court in advance of any issue going to the merits of the action and shall be joined with objections, if any, raised by answer or motion pursuant to S. 802.06(2). The court shall find separately on each issue so tried and these findings shall be set forth in a single order.

(3) Scope of trial court discretion on motion to stay proceedings. The decision on any timely motion to stay proceedings pursuant to sub. (1) is within the discretion of the court in which the action is pending. In the exercise of that discretion the court may appropriately consider such factors as:

(a) Amenability to personal jurisdiction in this state and in any alternative forum of the parties to the action;

(b) Convenience to the parties and witnesses of trial in this state and in any alternative forum;

(c) Differences in conflict of law rules applicable in this state and in any alternative forum; or

(d) Any other factors having substantial bearing upon the selection of a convenient, reasonable and fair place of trial.

(4) Subsequent modification of order to stay proceedings. Jurisdiction of the court continues over the parties to a proceeding in which a stay has been ordered under this section until a period of 5 years has elapsed since the last order affecting the stay was entered in the court. At any time during which jurisdiction of the court continues over the parties to the proceedings, the court may, on motion and notice to the parties, subsequently modify the stay order and take any further action in the proceeding as the interests of justice require. When jurisdiction of the court over the parties and the proceeding terminates by reason of the lapse of 5 years following the last court order in the action, the clerk of the court in which the stay was granted shall without notice enter an order dismissing the action.

* * *

§ 1406. Cure or waiver of defects

(a) The district court of a district in which is filed a case laying venue in the wrong division or district shall dismiss, or if it be in the interest of justice, transfer such case to any district or division in which it could have been brought.

(b) Nothing in this chapter shall impair the jurisdiction of a district court of any matter involving a party who does not interpose timely and sufficient objection to the venue.

* * *

Comparative State Provisions

Illinois Compiled Statutes 5/2–104(a), (b)

(a) No order or judgment is void because rendered in the wrong venue, except in case of judgment by confession as provided in subsection (c) of Section 2–1301 of this Act. No action shall abate or be dismissed because commenced in the wrong venue if there is a proper venue to which the cause may be transferred. (Footnote omitted.)

(b) All objections of improper venue are waived by a defendant unless a motion to transfer to a proper venue is made by the defendant on or before the date upon which he or she is required to appear or within any further time that may be granted him or her to answer or move with respect to the complaint, except that if a defendant upon whose residence venue depends is dismissed upon motion of plaintiff, a remaining defendant may promptly move for transfer as though the dismissed defendant had not been a party.

See also California Civil Procedure Code § 396 as set out in connection with Federal Rule 12(b), supra.

§ 1407. Multidistrict litigation

(a) When civil actions involving one or more common questions of fact are pending in different districts, such actions may be transferred to any district for coordinated or consolidated pretrial proceedings. Such transfers shall be made by the judicial panel on multidistrict litigation authorized by this section upon its determination that transfers for such proceedings will be for the convenience of parties and witnesses and will promote the just and efficient conduct of such actions. Each action so transferred shall be remanded by the panel at or before the conclusion of such pretrial proceedings to the district from which it was transferred unless it shall have been previously terminated: *Provided, however,* That the panel may separate any claim, cross-claim, counter-claim, or third-party claim and remand any of such claims before the remainder of the action is remanded.

(b) Such coordinated or consolidated pretrial proceedings shall be conducted by a judge or judges to whom such actions are assigned by the judicial panel on multidistrict litigation. For this purpose, upon request of the panel, a circuit judge or a district judge may be designated and assigned temporarily for service in the transferee district by the Chief Justice of the United States or the chief judge of the circuit, as may be required, in accordance with the provisions of chapter 13 of this title. With the consent of the transferee district court, such actions may be assigned by the panel to a judge or judges of such district. The judge or judges to whom such actions are assigned, the members of the judicial panel on multidistrict litigation, and other circuit and district judges designated when needed by the panel may exercise the powers of a district judge in any district for the purpose of conducting pretrial depositions in such coordinated or consolidated pretrial proceedings.

(c) Proceedings for the transfer of an action under this section may be initiated by—

(i) the judicial panel on multidistrict litigation upon its own initiative, or

(ii) motion filed with the panel by a party in any action in which transfer for coordinated or consolidated pretrial proceedings under this section may be appropriate. A copy of such motion shall be filed in the district court in which the moving party's action is pending.

The panel shall give notice to the parties in all actions in which transfers for coordinated or consolidated pretrial proceedings are contemplated, and such notice shall specify the time and place of any hearing to determine whether such transfer shall be made. Orders of the panel to set a hearing and other orders of the panel issued prior to the order either directing or denying transfer shall be filed in the office of the clerk of the district court in which a transfer hearing is to be or has been held. The panel's order of transfer shall be based upon a record of such hearing at which material evidence may be offered by any party to an action pending in any district that would be affected by the proceedings under this section, and shall be supported by findings of fact and conclusions of law based upon such record. Orders of transfer and such other orders as the panel may make thereafter shall be filed in the office of the clerk of the district court of the transferee district and shall be effective when thus filed. The clerk of the transferee district court shall forthwith transmit a certified copy of the panel's order to transfer to the clerk of the district court from which the action is being transferred. An order denying transfer shall be filed in each district wherein there is a case pending in which the motion for transfer has been made.

(d) The judicial panel on multidistrict litigation shall consist of seven circuit and district judges designated from time to time by the Chief Justice of the United States, no two of whom shall be from the same circuit. The concurrence of four members shall be necessary to any action by the panel.

(e) No proceedings for review of any order of the panel may be permitted except by extraordinary writ pursuant to the provisions of title 28, section 1651, United States Code. Petitions for an extraordinary writ to review an order of the panel to set a transfer hearing and other orders of the panel issued prior to the order either directing or denying transfer shall be filed only in the court of appeals having jurisdiction over the district in which a hearing is to be or has been held. Petitions for an extraordinary writ to review an order to transfer or orders subsequent to transfer shall be filed only in the court of appeals having jurisdiction over the transferee district. There shall be no appeal or review of an order of the panel denying a motion to transfer for consolidated or coordinated proceedings.

(f) The panel may prescribe rules for the conduct of its business not inconsistent with Acts of Congress and the Federal Rules of Civil Procedure.

(g) Nothing in this section shall apply to any action in which the United States is a complainant arising under the antitrust laws. "Antitrust laws" as used herein include those acts referred to in the Act of October 15, 1914, as amended (38 Stat. 730; 15 U.S.C. 12), and also include the Act of June 19, 1936 (49 Stat. 1526; 15 U.S.C. 13, 13a, and 13b) and the Act of September 26, 1914, as added March 21, 1938 (52 Stat. 116, 117; 15 U.S.C. 56); but shall not include section 4A of the Act of October 15, 1914, as added July 7, 1955 (69 Stat. 282; 15 U.S.C. 15a).

(h) Notwithstanding the provisions of section 1404 or subsection (f) of this section, the judicial panel on multidistrict litigation may consolidate and transfer with or without the consent of the parties, for both pretrial purposes and for trial, any action brought under section 4C of the Clayton Act.

§ 1441. Actions removable generally

(a) Except as otherwise expressly provided by Act of Congress, any civil action brought in a State court of which the district courts of the United States have original jurisdiction, may be removed by the defendant or the defendants, to the district court of the United States for the district and division embracing the place where such action is pending. For purposes of removal under this chapter, the citizenship of defendants sued under fictitious names shall be disregarded.

(b) Any civil action of which the district courts have original jurisdiction founded on a claim or right arising under the Constitution, treaties or laws of the United States shall be removable without regard to the citizenship or residence of the parties. Any other such action shall be removable only if none of the parties in interest properly joined and served as defendants is a citizen of the State in which such action is brought.

(c) Whenever a separate and independent claim or cause of action within the jurisdiction conferred by section 1331 of this title is joined with one or more otherwise non-removable claims or causes of action, the entire case may be removed and the district court may determine all issues therein, or, in its discretion, may remand all matters in which State law predominates.

(d) Any civil action brought in a State court against a foreign state as defined in section 1603(a) of this title may be removed by the foreign state to the district court of the United States for the district and division embracing the place where such action is pending. Upon removal the action shall be tried by the court without jury. Where removal is based upon this subsection, the time limitations of section 1446(b) of this chapter may be enlarged at any time for cause shown.

(e) The court to which such civil action is removed is not precluded from hearing and determining any claim in such civil action because the State court did not have jurisdiction over that claim.

§ 1442. Federal officers sued or prosecuted

(a) A civil action or criminal prosecution commenced in a State court against any of the following persons may be removed by them to the district court of the United States for the district and division embracing the place wherein it is pending:

(1) Any officer of the United States or any agency thereof, or person acting under him, for any act under color of such office or on account of any right, title or authority claimed under any Act of

Congress for the apprehension or punishment of criminals or the collection of the revenue.

(2) A property holder whose title is derived from any such officer, where such action or prosecution affects the validity of any law of the United States.

(3) Any officer of the courts of the United States, for any Act under color of office or in the performance of his duties.

(4) Any officer of either House of Congress, for any act in the discharge of his official duty under an order of such House.

(b) A personal action commenced in any State court by an alien against any citizen of a State who is, or at the time the alleged action accrued was, a civil officer of the United States and is a nonresident of such State, wherein jurisdiction is obtained by the State court by personal service of process, may be removed by the defendant to the district court of the United States for the district and division in which the defendant was served with process.

§ 1443. Civil rights cases

Any of the following civil actions or criminal prosecutions, commenced in a State court may be removed by the defendant to the district court of the United States for the district and division embracing the place wherein it is pending:

(1) Against any person who is denied or cannot enforce in the courts of such State a right under any law providing for the equal civil rights of citizens of the United States, or of all persons within the jurisdiction thereof;

(2) For any act under color of authority derived from any law providing for equal rights, or for refusing to do any act on the ground that it would be inconsistent with such law.

§ 1445. Nonremovable actions

(a) A civil action in any State court against a railroad or its receivers or trustees, arising under sections 51–60 of Title 45 [Federal Employers' Liability Act], may not be removed to any district court of the United States.

* * *

(c) A civil action in any State court arising under the workmen's compensation laws of such State may not be removed to any district court of the United States.

§ 1446. Procedure for removal

(a) A defendant or defendants desiring to remove any civil action or criminal prosecution from a State court shall file in the district court of the United States for the district and division within which such action is pending a notice of removal signed pursuant to Rule 11 of the Federal Rules of Civil Procedure and containing a short and plain statement of the grounds for removal, together with a copy of all process, pleadings, and orders served upon such defendant or defendants in such action.

(b) The notice of removal of a civil action or proceeding shall be filed within thirty days after the receipt by the defendant, through service or otherwise, of a copy of the initial pleading setting forth the claim for relief upon which such action or proceeding is based, or within thirty days after the service of summons upon the defendant if such initial pleading has then been filed in court and is not required to be served on the defendant, whichever period is shorter.

If the case stated by the initial pleading is not removable, a notice of removal may be filed within thirty days after receipt by the defendant, through service or otherwise, of a copy of an amended pleading, motion, order or other paper from which it may first be ascertained that the case is one which is or has become removable, except that a case may not be removed on the basis of jurisdiction conferred by section 1332 of this title more than 1 year after commencement of the action.

(c) * * * [This section refers solely to criminal matters.]

(d) Promptly after the filing of such notice of removal of a civil action the defendant or defendants shall give written notice thereof to all adverse parties and shall file a copy of the notice with the clerk of such State court, which shall effect removal and the State court shall proceed no further unless and until the case is remanded.

(e) If the defendant or defendants are in actual custody on process issued by the State court, the district court shall issue its writ of habeas corpus, and the marshal shall thereupon take such defendant or defendants into his custody and deliver a copy of the writ to the clerk of such State court.

§ 1447. Procedure after removal generally

(a) In any case removed from a State court, the district court may issue all necessary orders and process to bring before it all proper parties whether served by process issued by the State court or otherwise.

(b) It may require the removing party to file with its clerk copies of all records and proceedings in such State court or may cause the same to be brought before it by writ of certiorari issued to such State court.

(c) A motion to remand the case on the basis of any defect in removal procedure must be made within 30 days after the filing of the notice of removal under section 1446(a). If at any time before final judgment it appears that the district court lacks subject matter jurisdiction, the case shall be remanded. An order remanding the case may require payment of just costs and any actual expenses, including attorney fees, incurred as a result of the removal. A certified copy of the order of remand shall be mailed by the clerk to the clerk of the State court. The State court may thereupon proceed with such case.

(d) An order remanding a case to the State court from which it was removed is not reviewable on appeal or otherwise, except that an order remanding a case to the State court from which it was removed pursuant to section 1443 of this title shall be reviewable by appeal or otherwise.

(e) If after removal the plaintiff seeks to join additional defendants whose joinder would destroy subject matter jurisdiction, the court may deny joinder, or permit joinder and remand the action to the State court.

§ 1631. Transfer to cure want of jurisdiction

Whenever a civil action is filed in a court as defined in section 610 of this title or an appeal, including a petition for review of administrative action, is noticed for or filed with such a court and that court finds that there is a want of jurisdiction, the court shall, if it is in the interest of justice, transfer such action or appeal to any other such court in which the action or appeal could have been brought at the time it was filed or noticed, and the action or appeal shall proceed as if it had been filed in or noticed for the court to which it is transferred on the date upon which it was actually filed in or noticed for the court from which it is transferred.

§ 1651. Writs

(a) The Supreme Court and all courts established by Act of Congress may issue all writs necessary or appropriate in aid of their respective jurisdictions and agreeable to the usages and principles of law.

(b) An alternative writ or rule nisi may be issued by a justice or judge of a court which has jurisdiction.

§ 1652. State laws as rules of decision

The laws of the several states, except where the Constitution or treaties of the United States or Acts of Congress otherwise require or provide, shall be regarded as rules of decision in civil actions in the courts of the United States, in cases where they apply.

Illinois Supreme Court Rule 20

(a) **Certification.** When it shall appear to the Supreme Court of the United States, or to the United States Court of Appeals for the Seventh Circuit, that there are involved in any proceeding before it questions as to the law of this State, which may be determinative of the said cause, and there are no controlling precedents in the decisions of this court, such court may certify such questions of the laws of this State to this court for instructions concerning such questions of State law, which certificate this court, by written opinion, may answer.

(b) **Contents of Certification Order.** A certification order shall contain:

(1) the questions of law to be answered; and

28 § 1652   SELECTED PROVISIONS

(2) a statement of all facts relevant to the questions certified and showing fully the nature of the controversy in which the questions arose.

(c) Record Before Certifying Court. This court may require the original or copies of all or of any portion of the record before the certifying court to be filed with it, if, in the opinion of this court, the record or a portion thereof may be necessary in answering the questions.

(d) Briefs and Argument. Proceedings in this court shall be those provided in these rules governing briefs and oral arguments, except that the time for filing briefs specified in Rule 343 begins to run from the day this court agrees to answer the certified question of law, and the parties retain the same designation as they have in the certifying court.

(e) Costs of Certification. Fees and costs shall be the same as in the civil appeals docketed before this court and shall be equally divided between the parties unless otherwise ordered by the certifying court.

§ 1653. Amendment of pleadings to show jurisdiction

Defective allegations of jurisdiction may be amended, upon terms, in the trial or appellate courts.

§ 1655. Lien enforcement; absent defendants

In an action in a district court to enforce any lien upon or claim to, or to remove any incumbrance or lien or cloud upon the title to, real or personal property within the district, where any defendant cannot be served within the State, or does not voluntarily appear, the court may order the absent defendant to appear or plead by a day certain.

Such order shall be served on the absent defendant personally if practicable, wherever found, and also upon the person or persons in possession or charge of such property, if any. Where personal service is not practicable, the order shall be published as the court may direct, not less than once a week for six consecutive weeks.

If an absent defendant does not appear or plead within the time allowed, the court may proceed as if the absent defendant had been served with process within the State, but any adjudication shall, as regards the absent defendant without appearance, affect only the property which is the subject of the action. When a part of the property is within another district, but within the same state, such action may be brought in either district.

Any defendant not so personally notified may, at any time within one year after final judgment, enter his appearance, and thereupon the court shall set aside the judgment and permit such defendant to plead on payment of such costs as the court deems just.

§ 1693. Place of arrest in civil action

Except as otherwise provided by Act of Congress, no person shall be arrested in one district for trial in another in any civil action in a district court.

§ 1694. Patent infringement action

In a patent infringement action commenced in a district where the defendant is not a resident but has a regular and established place of business, service of process, summons or subpoena upon such defendant may be made upon his agent or agents conducting such business.

§ 1695. Stockholder's derivative action

Process in a stockholder's action in behalf of his corporation may be served upon such corporation in any district where it is organized or licensed to do business or is doing business.

§ 1738. State and Territorial statutes and judicial proceedings; full faith and credit

The Acts of the legislature of any State, Territory, or Possession of the United States, or copies thereof, shall be authenticated by affixing the seal of such State, Territory or Possession thereto.

The records and judicial proceedings of any court of any such State, Territory or Possession, or copies thereof, shall be proved or admitted in other courts within the United States and its Territories and Possessions by the attestation of the clerk and seal of the court annexed, if a seal exists, together with a certificate of a judge of the court that the said attestation is in proper form.

Such Acts, records and judicial proceedings or copies thereof, so authenticated, shall have the same full faith and credit in every court within the United States and its Territories and Possessions as they have by law or usage in the courts of such State, Territory or Possession from which they are taken.

§ 1781. Transmittal of letter rogatory or request

(a) The Department of State has power, directly, or through suitable channels—

(1) to receive a letter rogatory issued, or request made, by a foreign or international tribunal, to transmit it to the tribunal, officer, or agency in the United States to whom it is addressed, and to receive and return it after execution; and

(2) to receive a letter rogatory issued, or request made, by a tribunal in the United States, to transmit it to the foreign or international tribunal, officer, or agency to whom it is addressed, and to receive and return it after execution.

(b) This section does not preclude—

(1) the transmittal of a letter rogatory or request directly from a foreign or international tribunal to the tribunal, officer, or agency

in the United States to whom it is addressed and its return in the same manner; or

(2) the transmittal of a letter rogatory or request directly from a tribunal in the United States to the foreign or international tribunal, officer, or agency to whom it is addressed and its return in the same manner.

§ 1782. Assistance to foreign and international tribunals and to litigants before such tribunals

(a) The district court of the district in which a person resides or is found may order him to give his testimony or statement or to produce a document or other thing for use in a proceeding in a foreign or international tribunal. The order may be made pursuant to a letter rogatory issued, or request made, by a foreign or international tribunal or upon the application of any interested person and may direct that the testimony or statement be given, or the document or other thing be produced, before a person appointed by the court. By virtue of his appointment, the person appointed has power to administer any necessary oath and take the testimony or statement. The order may prescribe the practice and procedure, which may be in whole or part the practice and procedure of the foreign country or the international tribunal, for taking the testimony or statement or producing the document or other thing. To the extent that the order does not prescribe otherwise, the testimony or statement shall be taken, and the document or other thing produced, in accordance with the Federal Rules of Civil Procedure.

* * *

Comparative State Provision

Massachusetts General Laws Annotated c. 233, § 45

A person may be summoned and compelled, in like manner and under the same penalties as are provided for a witness before a court, to give his deposition in a cause pending in a court of any other state or government. Such deposition may be taken before a justice of the peace or a notary public in the commonwealth, or before a commissioner appointed under the authority of the state or government in which the action is pending. If the deposition is taken before such commissioner, the witness may be summoned and compelled to appear before him by process from a justice of the peace or a notary public in the commonwealth.

§ 1783. Subpoena of person in foreign country

(a) A court of the United States may order the issuance of a subpoena requiring the appearance as a witness before it, or before a person or body designated by it, of a national or resident of the United States who is in a foreign country, or requiring the production of a specified document or other thing by him, if the court finds that particular testimony or the production of the document or other thing by him is necessary in the interest of justice, and, in other than a criminal action or proceeding, if the court finds, in addition, that it is not possible to obtain his testimony in admissible form without his personal appearance or to obtain the production of the document or other thing in any other manner.

* * *

§ 1861. Declaration of policy

It is the policy of the United States that all litigants in Federal courts entitled to trial by jury shall have the right to grand and petit juries selected at random from a fair cross section of the community in the district or division wherein the court convenes. It is further the policy of the United States that all citizens shall have the opportunity to be considered for service on grand and petit juries in the district courts of the United States, and shall have an obligation to serve as jurors when summoned for that purpose.

§ 1862. Exemptions

No citizen shall be excluded from service as a grand or petit juror in the district courts of the United States or in the Court of International Trade on account of race, color, religion, sex, national origin, or economic status.

§ 1863. Plan for random jury selection

(a) Each United States district court shall devise and place into operation a written plan for random selection of grand and petit jurors that shall be designed to achieve the objectives of sections 1861 and 1862 of this title, and that shall otherwise comply with the provisions of this title. The plan shall be placed into operation after approval by a reviewing panel consisting of the members of the judicial council of the circuit and either the chief judge of the district whose plan is being reviewed or such other active district judge of that district as the chief judge of the district may designate. The panel shall examine the plan to ascertain that it complies with the provisions of this title. If the reviewing panel finds that the plan does not comply, the panel shall state the particulars in which the plan fails to comply and direct the district court to present within a reasonable time an alternative plan remedying the defect or defects. Separate plans may be adopted for each division or combination of divisions within a judicial district. The district court may modify a plan at any time and it shall modify the plan when so directed by the reviewing panel. The district court shall promptly notify the panel, the Administrative Office of the United States Courts, and the Attorney General of the United States, of the initial adoption and future modifications of the plan by filing copies therewith. Modifications of the plan made at the instance of the district court shall become effective after approval by the panel. Each district court shall submit a report on the jury selection process within its jurisdiction to the Administrative

Office of the United States Courts in such form and at such times as the Judicial Conference of the United States may specify. The Judicial Conference of the United States may, from time to time, adopt rules and regulations governing the provisions and the operation of the plans formulated under this title.

(b) Among other things, such plan shall—

(1) either establish a jury commission, or authorize the clerk of the court, to manage the jury selection process. If the plan establishes a jury commission, the district court shall appoint one citizen to serve with the clerk of the court as the jury commission: *Provided, however*, That the plan for the District of Columbia may establish a jury commission consisting of three citizens. The citizen jury commissioner shall not belong to the same political party as the clerk serving with him. The clerk or the jury commission, as the case may be, shall act under the supervision and control of the chief judge of the district court or such other judge of the district court as the plan may provide. Each jury commissioner shall, during his tenure in office, reside in the judicial district or division for which he is appointed. Each citizen jury commissioner shall receive compensation to be fixed by the district court plan at a rate not to exceed $50 per day for each day necessarily employed in the performance of his duties, plus reimbursement for travel, subsistence, and other necessary expenses * * *.

(2) specify whether the names of prospective jurors shall be selected from the voter registration lists or the lists of actual voters of the political subdivisions within the district or division. The plan shall prescribe some other source or sources of names in addition to voter lists where necessary to foster the policy and protect the rights secured by sections 1861 and 1862 of this title. * * *

(3) specify detailed procedures to be followed by the jury commission or clerk in selecting names from the sources specified in paragraph (2) of this subsection. These procedures shall be designed to ensure the random selection of a fair cross section of the persons residing in the community in the district or division wherein the court convenes. They shall ensure that names of persons residing in each of the counties, parishes, or similar political subdivisions within the judicial district or division are placed in a master jury wheel; and shall insure that each county, parish, or similar political subdivision within the district or division is substantially proportionally represented in the master jury wheel for that judicial district, division, or combination of divisions. For the purposes of determining proportional representation in the master jury wheel, either the number of actual voters at the last general election in each county, parish, or similar political subdivision, or the number

of registered voters if registration of voters is uniformly required throughout the district or division, may be used.

(4) provide for a master jury wheel (or a device similar in purpose and function) into which the names of those randomly selected shall be placed. The plan shall fix a minimum number of names to be placed initially in the master jury wheel, which shall be at least one-half of 1 per centum of the total number of persons on the lists used as a source of names for the district or division; but if this number of names is believed to be cumbersome and unnecessary, the plan may fix a smaller number of names to be placed in the master wheel, but in no event less than one thousand. The chief judge of the district court, or such other district court judge as the plan may provide, may order additional names to be placed in the master jury wheel from time to time as necessary. The plan shall provide for periodic emptying and refilling of the master jury wheel at specified times, the interval for which shall not exceed four years.

(5)(A) except as provided in subparagraph (B), specify those groups of persons or occupational classes whose members shall, on individual request therefor, be excused from jury service. Such groups or classes shall be excused only if the district court finds, and the plan states, that jury service by such class or group would entail undue hardship or extreme inconvenience to the members thereof, and excuse of members thereof would not be inconsistent with sections 1861 and 1862 of this title.

(B) specify that volunteer safety personnel, upon individual request, shall be excused from jury service. For purposes of this subparagraph, the term "volunteer safety personnel" means individuals serving a public agency (as defined in section 1203(6) of title I of the Omnibus Crime Control and Safe Streets Act of 1968) in an official capacity, without compensation, as firefighters or members of a rescue squad or ambulance crew.

(6) specify that the following persons are barred from jury service on the ground that they are exempt: (A) members in active service in the Armed Forces of the United States; (B) members of the fire or police departments of any State, the District of Columbia, any territory or possession of the United States, or any subdivision of a State, the District of Columbia, or such territory or possession; (C) public officers in the executive, legislative, or judicial branches of the Government of the United States, or of any State, the District of Columbia, any territory or possession of the United States, or any subdivision of a State, the District of Columbia, or such territory or possession, who are actively engaged in the performance of official duties.

(7) fix the time when the names drawn from the qualified jury wheel shall be disclosed to parties and to the public. If the plan

permits these names to be made public, it may nevertheless permit the chief judge of the district court, or such other district court judge as the plan may provide, to keep these names confidential in any case where the interests of justice so require.

(8) specify the procedures to be followed by the clerk or jury commission in assigning persons whose names have been drawn from the qualified jury wheel to grand and petit jury panels.

(c) The initial plan shall be devised by each district court and transmitted to the reviewing panel specified in subsection (a) of this section within one hundred and twenty days of the date of enactment of the Jury Selection and Service Act of 1968. The panel shall approve or direct the modification of each plan so submitted within sixty days thereafter. Each plan or modification made at the direction of the panel shall become effective after approval at such time thereafter as the panel directs, in no event to exceed ninety days from the date of approval. Modifications made at the instance of the district court under subsection (a) of this section shall be effective at such time thereafter as the panel directs, in no event to exceed ninety days from the date of modification.

(d) State, local and Federal officials having custody, possession, or control of voter registration lists, lists of actual voters, or other appropriate records shall make such lists and records available to the jury commission or clerks for inspection, reproduction, and copying at all reasonable times as the commission or clerk may deem necessary and proper for the performance of duties under this title. The district courts shall have jurisdiction upon application by the Attorney General of the United States to compel compliance with this subsection by appropriate process.

§ 1864. Drawing of names from the master jury wheel; completion of juror qualification form

(a) From time to time as directed by the district court, the clerk or a district judge shall publicly draw at random from the master jury wheel the names of as many persons as may be required for jury service. The clerk or jury commission may upon order of the court prepare an alphabetical list of the names drawn from the master jury wheel. Any list so prepared shall not be disclosed to any person except pursuant to the district court plan or pursuant to section 1867 or 1868 of this title. The clerk or jury commission shall mail to every person whose name is drawn from the master wheel a juror qualification form accompanied by instructions to fill out and return the form, duly signed and sworn, to the clerk or jury commission by mail within ten days. If the person is unable to fill out the form, another shall do it for him, and shall indicate that he has done so and the reason therefor. In any case in which it appears that there is an omission, ambiguity, or error in a form, the clerk or jury commission shall return the form with instructions to the person to make such additions or corrections as may be necessary and to return the form to the clerk or jury commission within ten days. Any person who fails to return a completed juror qualification form as instructed may be summoned by the clerk or jury commission forthwith to appear before the clerk or jury commission to fill out a juror qualification form. A person summoned to appear because of failure to return a juror qualification form as instructed who personally appears and executes a juror qualification form before the clerk or jury commission may, at the discretion of the district court, except where his prior failure to execute and mail such form was willful, be entitled to receive for such appearance the same fees and travel allowances paid to jurors under section 1871 of this title. At the time of his appearance for jury service, any person may be required to fill out another juror qualification form in the presence of the jury commission or the clerk or the court, at which time, in such cases as it appears warranted, the person may be questioned, but only with regard to his responses to questions contained on the form. Any information thus acquired by the clerk or jury commission may be noted on the juror qualification form and transmitted to the chief judge or such district court judge as the plan may provide.

(b) Any person summoned pursuant to subsection (a) of this section who fails to appear as directed shall be ordered by the district court forthwith to appear and show cause for his failure to comply with the summons. Any person who fails to appear pursuant to such order or who fails to show good cause for noncompliance with the summons may be fined not more than $100 or imprisoned not more than three days, or both. Any person who willfully misrepresents a material fact on a juror qualification form for the purpose of avoiding or securing service as a juror may be fined not more than $100 or imprisoned not more than three days, or both.

§ 1865. Qualifications for jury service

(a) The chief judge of the district court, or such other district court judge as the plan may provide, on his initiative or upon recommendation of the clerk or jury commission, shall determine solely on the basis of information provided on the juror qualification form and other competent evidence whether a person is unqualified for, or exempt, or to be excused from jury service. The clerk shall enter such determination in the space provided on the juror qualification form and in any alphabetical list of names drawn from the master jury wheel. If a person did not appear in response to a summons, such fact shall be noted on said list.

(b) In making such determination the chief judge of the district court, or such other district court judge as the plan may provide, shall deem any person qualified to serve on grand and petit juries in the district court unless he—

(1) is not a citizen of the United States eighteen years old who has resided for a period of one year within the judicial district;

(2) is unable to read, write, and understand the English language with a degree of proficiency sufficient to fill out satisfactorily the juror qualification form;

(3) is unable to speak the English language;

(4) is incapable, by reason of mental or physical infirmity, to render satisfactory jury service; or

(5) has a charge pending against him for the commission of, or has been convicted in a State or Federal court of record of, a crime punishable by imprisonment for more than one year and his civil rights have not been restored.

§ 1866. Selection and summoning of jury panels

(a) The jury commission, or in the absence thereof the clerk, shall maintain a qualified jury wheel and shall place in such wheel names of all persons drawn from the master jury wheel who are determined to be qualified as jurors and not exempt or excused pursuant to the district court plan. From time to time, the jury commission or the clerk shall publicly draw at random from the qualified jury wheel such number of names of persons as may be required for assignment to grand and petit jury panels. The jury commission or the clerk shall prepare a separate list of names of persons assigned to each grand and petit jury panel.

(b) When the court orders a grand or petit jury to be drawn the clerk or jury commission or their duly designated deputies shall issue summonses for the required number of jurors.

Each person drawn for jury service may be served personally, or by registered, certified, or first-class mail addressed to such person at his usual residence or business address.

If such service is made personally, the summons shall be delivered by the clerk or the jury commission or their duly designated deputies to the marshal who shall make such service.

If such service is made by mail, the summons may be served by the marshal or by the clerk, the jury commission or their duly designated deputies, who shall make affidavit of service and shall attach thereto any receipt from the addressee for a registered or certified summons.

(c) Except as provided in section 1865 of this title or in any jury selection plan provision adopted pursuant to paragraph (5) or (6) of section 1863(b) of this title, no person or class of persons shall be disqualified, excluded, excused, or exempt from service as jurors: *Provided*, That any person summoned for jury service may be (1) excused by the court, or by the clerk under supervision of the court if the court's jury selection plan so authorizes, upon a showing of undue hardship or extreme inconvenience, for such period as the court deems necessary, at the conclusion of which such person either shall be summoned again for jury service under subsections (b) and (c) of this section, or if the court's jury selection plan so provides, the name of such person shall be reinserted into the qualified jury wheel for selection pursuant to subsection (a) of this section, or (2) excluded by the court on the ground that such person may be unable to render impartial jury service or that his service as a juror would be likely to disrupt the proceedings, or (3) excluded upon peremptory challenge as provided by law, or (4) excluded pursuant to the procedure specified by law upon a challenge by any party for good cause shown, or (5) excluded upon determination by the court that his service as a juror would be likely to threaten the secrecy of the proceedings, or otherwise adversely affect the integrity of jury deliberations. No person shall be excluded under clause (5) of this subsection unless the judge, in open court, determines that such is warranted and that exclusion of the person will not be inconsistent with sections 1861 and 1862 of this title. The number of persons excluded under clause (5) of this subsection shall not exceed one per centum of the number of persons who return executed jury qualification forms during the period, specified in the plan, between two consecutive fillings of the master jury wheel. The names of persons excluded under clause (5) of this subsection, together with detailed explanations for the exclusions, shall be forwarded immediately to the judicial council of the circuit, which shall have the power to make any appropriate order, prospective or retroactive, to redress any misapplication of clause (5) of this subsection, but otherwise exclusions effectuated under such clause shall not be subject to challenge under the provisions of this title. Any person excluded from a particular jury under clause (2), (3), or (4) of this subsection shall be eligible to sit on another jury if the basis for his initial exclusion would not be relevant to his ability to serve on such other jury.

(d) Whenever a person is disqualified, excused, exempt, or excluded from jury service, the jury commission or clerk shall note in the space provided on his juror qualification form or on the juror's card drawn from the qualified jury wheel the specific reason therefor.

(e) In any two-year period, no person shall be required to (1) serve or attend court for prospective service as a petit juror for a total of more than thirty days, except when necessary to complete service in a particular case, or (2) serve on more than one grand jury, or (3) serve as both a grand and petit juror.

(f) When there is an unanticipated shortage of available petit jurors drawn from the qualified jury wheel, the court may require the marshal to summon a sufficient number of petit jurors selected at random from the voter registration lists, lists of actual voters, or other lists specified in the plan, in a manner ordered by the court consistent with sections 1861 and 1862 of this title.

(g) Any person summoned for jury service who fails to appear as directed shall be ordered by the district court to appear forthwith and show cause for his failure to comply with the summons. Any person who fails to show good cause for noncompliance with a summons may be fined not more than $100 or imprisoned not more than three days, or both.

§ 1867. Challenging compliance with selection procedures

(a) In criminal cases, before the voir dire examination begins, or within seven days after the defendant discovered or could have discovered, by the exercise of diligence, the grounds therefor, whichever is earlier, the defendant may move to dismiss the indictment or stay the proceedings against him on the ground of substantial failure to comply with the provisions of this title in selecting the grand or petit jury.

(b) In criminal cases, before the voir dire examination begins, or within seven days after the Attorney General of the United States discovered or could have discovered, by the exercise of diligence, the grounds therefor, whichever is earlier, the Attorney General may move to dismiss the indictment or stay the proceedings on the ground of substantial failure to comply with the provisions of this title in selecting the grand or petit jury.

(c) In civil cases, before the voir dire examination begins, or within seven days after the party discovered or could have discovered, by the exercise of diligence, the grounds therefor, whichever is earlier, any party may move to stay the proceedings on the ground of substantial failure to comply with the provisions of this title in selecting the petit jury.

(d) Upon motion filed under subsection (a), (b), or (c) of this section, containing a sworn statement of facts which, if true, would constitute a substantial failure to comply with the provisions of this title, the moving party shall be entitled to present in support of such motion the testimony of the jury commission or clerk, if available, any relevant records and papers not public or otherwise available used by the jury commissioner or clerk, and any other relevant evidence. If the court determines that there has been a substantial failure to comply with the provisions of this title in selecting a grand jury, the court shall stay the proceedings pending the selection of a grand jury in conformity with this title or dismiss the indictment, whichever is appropriate. If the court determines that there has been a substantial failure to comply with the provisions of this title in selecting the petit jury, the court shall stay the proceedings pending the selection of a petit jury in conformity with this title.

(e) The procedures prescribed by this section shall be the exclusive means by which a person accused of a Federal crime, the Attorney General of the United States or a party in a civil case may challenge any jury on the ground that such jury was not selected in conformity with the provisions of this title. Nothing in this section shall preclude any person or the United States from pursuing any other remedy, civil or criminal, which may be available for the vindication or enforcement of any law prohibiting discrimination on account of race, color, religion, sex, national origin or economic status in the selection of persons for service on grand or petit juries.

(f) The contents of records or papers used by the jury commission or clerk in connection with the jury selection process shall not be disclosed, except pursuant to the district court plan or as may be necessary in the preparation or presentation of a motion under subsection (a), (b), or (c) of this section, until after the master jury wheel has been emptied and refilled pursuant to section 1863(b)(4) of this title and all persons selected to serve as jurors before the master wheel was emptied have completed such service. The parties in a case shall be allowed to inspect, reproduce, and copy such records or papers at all reasonable times during the preparation and pendency of such a motion. Any person who discloses the contents of any record or paper in violation of this subsection may be fined not more than $1,000 or imprisoned not more than one year, or both.

§ 1868. Maintenance and inspection of records

After the master jury wheel is emptied and refilled pursuant to section 1863(b)(4) of this title, and after all persons selected to serve as jurors before the master wheel was emptied have completed such service, all records and papers compiled and maintained by the jury commission or clerk before the master wheel was emptied shall be preserved in the custody of the clerk for four years or for such longer period as may be ordered by a court, and shall be available for public inspection for the purpose of determining the validity of the selection of any jury.

§ 1869. Definitions

For purposes of this chapter—

(a) "clerk" and "clerk of the court" shall mean the clerk of the district court of the United States, any authorized deputy clerk, and any other person authorized by the court to assist the clerk in the performance of functions under this chapter;

(b) "chief judge" shall mean the chief judge of any district court of the United States;

(c) "voter registration lists" shall mean the official records maintained by State or local election officials of persons registered to vote in either the most recent State or the most recent Federal general election, or, in the case of a State or political subdivision thereof that does not require registration as a prerequisite to voting, other official lists of persons qualified to vote in such election. The term shall also include the list of eligible voters maintained by any Federal examiner pursuant to the Voting Rights Act of 1965 where the names on such list have not been included on the official registration lists or other official lists maintained by the appropriate State or local officials. With respect to the districts of Guam and the Virgin Islands, "voter registration lists" shall mean the official records maintained by territorial election officials of persons registered to vote in the most recent territorial general election;

(d) "lists of actual voters" shall mean the official lists of persons actually voting in either the most recent State or the most recent Federal general election;

(e) "division" shall mean: (1) one or more statutory divisions of a judicial district; or (2) in statutory divisions that contain more than one place of holding court, or in judicial districts where there are no statutory divisions, such counties, parishes, or similar political subdivisions surrounding the places where court is held as the district court plan shall determine: *Provided*, That each county, parish, or similar political subdivision shall be included in some such division;

(f) "district court of the United States", "district court", and "court" shall mean any district court established by chapter 5 of this title, and any court which is created by Act of Congress in a territory and is invested with any jurisdiction of a district court established by chapter 5 of this title;

(g) "jury wheel" shall include any device or system similar in purpose or function, such as a properly programmed electronic data processing system or device;

(h) "juror qualification form" shall mean a form prescribed by the Administrative Office of the United States Courts and approved by the Judicial Conference of the United States, which shall elicit the name, address, age, race, occupation, education, length of residence within the judicial district, distance from residence to place of holding court, prior jury service, and citizenship of a potential juror, and whether he should be excused or exempted from jury service, has any physical or mental infirmity impairing his capacity to serve as juror, is able to read, write, speak and understand the English language, has pending against him any charge for the commission of a State or Federal criminal offense punishable by imprisonment for more than one year, or has been convicted in any State or Federal Court of record of a crime punishable by imprisonment for more than one year and has not had his civil rights restored. The form shall request, but not require, any other information not inconsistent with the provisions of this title and required by the district court plan in the interests of the sound administration of justice. The form also shall elicit the sworn statement that his responses are true to the best of his knowledge. Notarization shall not be required. The form shall contain words clearly informing the person that the furnishing of any information with respect to his religion, national origin, or economic status is not a prerequisite to his qualification for jury service, that such information need not be furnished if the person finds it objectionable to do so, and that information concerning race is required solely to enforce nondiscrimination in jury selection and has no bearing on an individual's qualification for jury service.

(i) "public officer" shall mean a person who is either elected to public office or who is directly appointed by a person elected to public office;

(j) "undue hardship or extreme inconvenience", as a basis for excuse from immediate jury service under section 1866(c)(1) of this chapter, shall mean great distance, either in miles or travel-time, from the place of holding court, grave illness in the family or any other emergency which outweighs in immediacy and urgency the obligation to serve as a juror when summoned, or any other factor which the court determines to constitute an undue hardship or to create an extreme inconvenience to the juror; and in addition, in situations where it is anticipated that a trial or grand jury proceeding may require more than thirty days of service, the court may consider, as a further basis for temporary excuse, severe economic hardship to an employer which would result from the absence of a key employee during the period of such service;

(k) "publicly draw", as referred to in sections 1864 and 1866 of this chapter, shall mean a drawing which is conducted within the district after a reasonable public notice and which is open to the public at large under the supervision of the clerk or jury commission, except that when a drawing is made by means of electronic data processing, "publicly draw" shall mean a drawing which is conducted at a data processing center located in or out of the district, after reasonable public notice given in the district for which juror names are being drawn, and which is open to the public at large under such supervision of the clerk or jury commission as the Judicial Conference of the United States shall by regulation require; and

(*l*) "jury summons" shall mean a summons issued by a clerk of court, jury commission, or their duly designated deputies, containing either a preprinted or stamped seal of court, and containing the name of the issuing clerk imprinted in preprinted, type, or facsimile manner on the summons or the envelopes transmitting the summons.

§ 1870. Challenges

In civil cases, each party shall be entitled to three peremptory challenges. Several defendants or several plaintiffs may be considered as a single party for the purposes of making challenges, or the court may allow additional peremptory challenges and permit them to be exercised separately or jointly.

All challenges for cause or favor, whether to the array or panel or to individual jurors, shall be determined by the court.

§ 1919. Dismissal for lack of jurisdiction

Whenever any action or suit is dismissed in any district court or the Court of International Trade for want of jurisdiction, such court may order the payment of just costs.

§ 1920. Taxation of costs

A judge or clerk of any court of the United States may tax as costs the following:

(1) Fees of the clerk and marshal;

(2) Fees of the court reporter for all or any part of the stenographic transcript necessarily obtained for use in the case;

(3) Fees and disbursements for printing and witnesses;

(4) Fees for exemplification and copies of papers necessarily obtained for use in the case;

(5) Docket fees under section 1923 of this title;

(6) Compensation of court appointed experts, compensation of interpreters, and salaries, fees, expenses, and costs of special interpretation services under section 1828 of this title.

A bill of costs shall be filed in the case and, upon allowance, included in the judgment or decree.

§ 1927. Counsel's liability for excessive costs

Any attorney or other person admitted to conduct cases in any court of the United States or any Territory thereof who so multiplies the proceedings in any case unreasonably and vexatiously may be required by the court to satisfy personally the excess costs, expenses, and attorneys' fees reasonably incurred because of such conduct.

§ 1963. Registration of judgments of the district courts and the Court of International Trade

A judgment in an action for the recovery of money or property entered in any district court or in the Court of International Trade may be registered by filing a certified copy of such judgment in any other district or, with respect to the Court of International Trade, in any judicial district, when the judgment has become final by appeal or expiration of the time for appeal or when ordered by the court that entered the judgment for good cause shown. Such a judgment entered in favor of the United States may be so registered any time after judgment is entered. A judgment so registered shall have the same effect as a judgment of the district court of the district where registered and may be enforced in like manner.

A certified copy of the satisfaction of any judgment in whole or in part may be registered in like manner in any district in which the judgment is a lien.

Comparative State Provisions
Uniform Enforcement of Foreign Judgments Act (1964 Revision) § 2

A copy of any foreign judgment authenticated in accordance with the act of Congress or the statutes of this state may be filed in the office of the Clerk of any [District Court of any city or county] of this state. The Clerk shall treat the foreign judgment in the same manner as a judgment of the [District Court of any city or county] of this state. A judgment so filed has the same effect and is subject to the same procedures, defenses and proceedings for reopening, vacating, or staying as a judgment of a [District Court of any city or county] of this state and may be enforced or satisfied in like manner.

Uniform Enforcement of Foreign Judgments Act (1964 Revision) § 6

The right of a judgment creditor to bring an action to enforce his judgment instead of proceeding under this Act remains unimpaired.

§ 2071. Rule-making power generally

(a) The Supreme Court and all courts established by Act of Congress may from time to time prescribe rules for the conduct of their business. Such rules shall be consistent with Acts of Congress and rules of practice and procedure prescribed under section 2072 of this title.

(b) Any rule prescribed by a court, other than the Supreme Court, under subsection (a) shall be prescribed only after giving appropriate public notice and an opportunity for comment. Such rule shall take effect upon the date specified by the prescribing court and shall have such effect on pending proceedings as the prescribing court may order.

(c)(1) A rule of a district court prescribed under subsection (a) shall remain in effect unless modified or abrogated by the judicial council of the relevant circuit.

(2) Any other rule prescribed by a court other than the Supreme Court under subsection (a) shall remain in effect unless modified or abrogated by the Judicial Conference.

(d) Copies of rules prescribed under subsection (a) by a district court shall be furnished to the judicial council, and copies of all rules prescribed by a court other than the Supreme Court under subsection (a) shall be furnished to the director of the Administrative Office of the United States Courts and made available to the public.

(e) If the prescribing court determines that there is an immediate need for a rule, such court may proceed under this section without public notice and opportunity for comment, but such court shall promptly thereafter afford such notice and opportunity for comment.

(f) No rule may be prescribed by a district court other than under this section.

§ 2072. Rules of procedure and evidence; power to prescribe

(a) The Supreme Court shall have the power to prescribe general rules of practice and procedure and rules of evidence for cases in the United States district courts (including proceedings before magistrates thereof) and courts of appeals.

(b) Such rules shall not abridge, enlarge or modify any substantive right. All laws in conflict with such rules shall be of no further force or effect after such rules have taken effect.

(c) Such rules may define when a ruling of a district court is final for the purposes of appeal under section 1291 of this title.

§ 2111. Harmless error

On the hearing of any appeal or writ of certiorari in any case, the court shall give judgment after an examination of the record without regard to errors or defects which do not affect the substantial rights of the parties.

§ 2201. Creation of remedy

(a) In a case of actual controversy within its jurisdiction, except with respect to Federal taxes other than actions brought under section 7428 of the Internal Revenue Code of 1986 * * *, any court of the United States, upon the filing of an appropriate pleading, may declare the rights and other legal relations of any interested party seeking such declaration, whether or not further relief is or could be sought. Any such declaration shall have the force and effect of a final judgment or decree and shall be reviewable as such.

* * *

Comparative State Provisions
Connecticut Rules for the Superior Court § 390

The court will not render declaratory judgments upon the complaint of any person:

(a) unless he has an interest, legal or equitable, by reason of danger of loss or of uncertainty as to his rights or other jural relations; or

(b) unless there is an actual bona fide and substantial question or issue in dispute or substantial uncertainty of legal relations which requires settlement between the parties; or

(c) where the court shall be of the opinion that the parties should be left to seek redress by some other form of procedure; or

(d) unless all persons having an interest in the subject matter of the complaint are parties to the action or have reasonable notice thereof.

Uniform Declaratory Judgments Act § 6

The court may refuse to render or enter a declaratory judgment or decree where such judgment or decree, if rendered or entered, would not terminate the uncertainty or controversy giving rise to the proceeding.

§ 2202. Further relief

Further necessary or proper relief based on a declaratory judgment or decree may be granted, after reasonable notice and hearing, against any adverse party whose rights have been determined by such judgment.

§ 2283. Stay of State court proceedings

A court of the United States may not grant an injunction to stay proceedings in a State court except as expressly authorized by Act of Congress, or where necessary in aid of its jurisdiction, or to protect or effectuate its judgments.

§ 2284. Three-judge court; when required; composition; procedure

(a) A district court of three judges shall be convened when otherwise required by Act of Congress, or when an action is filed challenging the constitutionality of the apportionment of congressional districts or the apportionment of any statewide legislative body.

(b) In any action required to be heard and determined by a district court of three judges under subsection (a) of this section, the composition and procedure of the court shall be as follows:

(1) Upon the filing of a request for three judges, the judge to whom the request is presented shall, unless he determines that three judges are not required, immediately notify the chief judge of the circuit, who shall designate two other judges, at least one of whom shall be a circuit judge. The judges so designated, and the judge to whom the request was presented, shall serve as members of the court to hear and determine the action or proceeding.

* * *

§ 2361. Process and procedure

In any civil action of interpleader or in the nature of interpleader under section 1335 of this title, a district court may issue its process for all claimants and enter its order restraining them from instituting or prosecuting any proceeding in any State or United States court affecting the property, instrument or obligation involved in the interpleader action until further order of the court. Such process and order shall be returnable at such time as the court or judge thereof directs, and shall be addressed to and served by the United States marshals for the respective districts where the claimants reside or may be found.

Such district court shall hear and determine the case, and may discharge the plaintiff from further liability, make the injunction permanent, and make all appropriate orders to enforce its judgment.

§ 2403. Intervention by United States or a State; constitutional question

(a) In any action, suit or proceeding in a court of the United States to which the United States or any agency, officer or employee thereof is not a party, wherein the constitutionality of any Act of Congress affecting the public interest is drawn in question, the court shall certify such fact to the Attorney General, and shall permit the United States to intervene for presentation of evidence, if evidence is otherwise admissible in the case, and for argument on the question of constitutionality. The United States shall, subject to the applicable provisions of law, have all the rights of a party and be subject to all liabilities of a party as to court costs to the extent necessary for a proper presentation of the facts and law relating to the question of constitutionality.

(b) In any action, suit, or proceeding in a court of the United States to which a State or any agency, officer, or employee thereof is not a party, wherein the constitutionality of any statute of that State affecting the public interest is drawn in question, the court shall certify such fact to the attorney general of the State, and shall permit the State to intervene for presentation of evidence, if evidence is otherwise admissible in the case, and for argument on the question of constitutionality. The State shall, subject to the applicable provisions of law, have all the rights of a party and be subject to all liabilities of a party as to court costs to the extent necessary for a proper presentation of the facts and law relating to the question of constitutionality.

Selected Provision of Title 42, United States Code—The Public Health and Welfare

§ 1983. Civil action for deprivation of rights

Every person who, under color of any statute, ordinance, regulation, custom, or usage, of any State or Territory or the District of Columbia, subjects, or causes to be subjected, any citizen of the United States or other person within the jurisdiction thereof to the deprivation of any rights, privileges, or immunities secured by the Constitution and laws, shall be liable to the party injured in an action at law, suit in equity, or other proper proceeding for redress. For the purposes of this section, any Act of Congress applicable exclusively to the District of Columbia shall be considered to be a statute of the District of Columbia.

Part III

Selected State Jurisdictional Statutes
and
Selected State Statutes Governing the Powers of Appellate Courts

TABLE OF CONTENTS

Selected State Jurisdictional Statutes

Statute		Page
New York Civil Practice Law and Rules 302(a)		285
North Carolina General Statutes	§ 1–75.2	286
	§ 1–75.4	286
	§ 1–75.7	289
	§ 1–75.8	289
Rhode Island General Laws Annotated	§ 9–5–33(a)	289
Uniform Interstate and International Procedure Act	§ 1.02	290
	§ 1.03	290
	§ 1.05	290
Uniform Parentage Act	§ 8(b)	290

Selected State Statutes Governing the Powers of the Appellate Courts

Statute	Page
Alabama Code § 12–2–13	291
California Civil Procedure Code § 909	291

Selected State Jurisdictional Statutes

New York Civil Practice Law and Rules 302(a)

As to a cause of action arising from any of the acts enumerated in this section, a court may exercise personal jurisdiction over any non-domiciliary, or his executor or administrator, who in person or through an agent:

1. transacts any business within the state or contracts anywhere to supply goods or services in the state; or

2. commits a tortious act within the state, except as to a cause of action for defamation of character arising from the act; or

3. commits a tortious act without the state causing injury to person or property within the state, except as to a cause of action for defamation of character arising from the act, if he

(i) regularly does or solicits business, or engages in any other persistent course of conduct, or derives substantial revenue from goods used or consumed or services rendered, in the state, or

(ii) expects or should reasonably expect the act to have consequences in the state and derives substantial revenue from interstate or international commerce; or

4. owns, uses or possesses any real property situated within the state.

North Carolina General Statutes § 1-75.2

Definitions.—In this article the following words have the designated meanings:

(1) "Person" means any natural person, partnership, corporation, body politic, and any unincorporated association, organization, or society which may sue or be sued under a common name.

* * *

North Carolina General Statutes § 1-75.4

Personal jurisdiction, grounds for generally.—A court of this State having jurisdiction of the subject matter has jurisdiction over a person served in an action pursuant to Rule 4(j) or Rule 4(j1) of the Rules of Civil Procedure under any of the following circumstances:

(1) Local Presence or Status.—In any action, whether the claim arises within or without this State, in which a claim is asserted against a party who when service of process is made upon such party:

a. Is a natural person present within this State; or

b. Is a natural person domiciled within this State; or

c. Is a domestic corporation; or

d. Is engaged in substantial activity within this State, whether such activity is wholly interstate, intrastate, or otherwise.

(2) Special Jurisdiction Statutes.—In any action which may be brought under statutes of this State that specifically confer grounds for personal jurisdiction.

(3) Local Act or Omission.—In any action claiming injury to person or property or for wrongful death within or without this State arising out of an act or omission within this State by the defendant.

(4) Local Injury; Foreign Act.—In any action for wrongful death occurring within this State or in any action claiming injury to person or property within this State arising out of an act or omission outside this State by the defendant, provided in addition that at or about the time of the injury either:

SELECTED STATE JURISDICTIONAL STATUTES

    a. Solicitation or services activities were carried on within this State by or on behalf of the defendant; or

    b. Products, materials or things processed, serviced or manufactured by the defendant were used or consumed within this State in the ordinary course of trade.

(5) *Local Services, Goods or Contracts.*—In any action which:

    a. Arises out of a promise, made anywhere to the plaintiff or to some third party for the plaintiff's benefit, by the defendant to perform services within this State or to pay for services to be performed in this State by the plaintiff; or

    b. Arises out of services actually performed for the plaintiff by the defendant within this State, or services actually performed for the defendant by the plaintiff within this State if such performance within this State was authorized or ratified by the defendant; or

    c. Arises out of a promise, made anywhere to the plaintiff or to some third party for the plaintiff's benefit, by the defendant to deliver or receive within this State, or to ship from this State goods, documents of title, or other things of value; or

    d. Relates to goods, documents of title, or other things of value shipped from this State by the plaintiff to the defendant on his order or direction; or

    e. Relates to goods, documents of title, or other things of value actually received by the plaintiff in this State from the defendant through a carrier without regard to where delivery to the carrier occurred.

(6) *Local Property.*—In any action which arises out of:

    a. A promise, made anywhere to the plaintiff or to some third party for the plaintiff's benefit, by the defendant to create in either party an interest in, or protect, acquire, dispose of, use, rent, own, control or possess by either party real property situated in this State; or

    b. A claim to recover for any benefit derived by the defendant through the use, ownership, control or possession by the defendant of tangible property situated within this State either at the time of the first use, ownership, control or possession or at the time the action is commenced; or

    c. A claim that the defendant return, restore, or account to the plaintiff for any asset or thing of value which was within this State at the time the defendant acquired possession or control over it.

(7) *Deficiency Judgment on Local Foreclosure or Resale.*—In any action to recover a deficiency judgment upon an obligation

secured by a mortgage, deed of trust, conditional sale, or other security instrument executed by the defendant or his predecessor to whose obligation the defendant has succeeded and the deficiency is claimed either:

   a. In an action in this State to foreclose such security instrument upon real property, tangible personal property, or an intangible represented by an indispensable instrument, situated in this State; or

   b. Following sale of real or tangible personal property or an intangible represented by an indispensable instrument in this State under a power of sale contained in any security instrument.

(8) Director or Officer of a Domestic Corporation.—In any action against a defendant who is or was an officer or director of a domestic corporation where the action arises out of the defendant's conduct as such officer or director or out of the activities of such corporation while the defendant held office as a director or officer.

(9) Taxes or Assessments.—In any action for the collection of taxes or assessments levied, assessed or otherwise imposed by a taxing authority of this State after the date of ratification of this act.

(10) Insurance or Insurers.—In any action which arises out of a contract of insurance as defined in G.S. 58–3 made anywhere between the plaintiff or some third party and the defendant and in addition either:

   a. The plaintiff was a resident of this State when the event occurred out of which the claim arose; or

   b. The event out of which the claim arose occurred within this State, regardless of where the plaintiff resided.

(11) Personal Representative.—In any action against a personal representative to enforce a claim against the deceased person represented, whether or not the action was commenced during the lifetime of the deceased, where one or more of the grounds stated in subdivisions (2) to (10) of this section would have furnished a basis for jurisdiction over the deceased had he been living.

(12) Marital Relationship.—In any action under Chapter 50 that arises out of the marital relationship within this State, notwithstanding subsequent departure from the State, if the other party to the marital relationship continues to reside in this State.

SELECTED STATE JURISDICTIONAL STATUTES

North Carolina General Statutes § 1-75.7

Personal jurisdiction—Grounds for without service of summons.—A court of this State having jurisdiction of the subject matter may, without serving a summons upon him, exercise jurisdiction in an action over a person:

(1) Who makes a general appearance in an action; * * * or

(2) With respect to any counterclaim asserted against that person in an action which he has commenced in this State.

North Carolina General Statutes § 1-75.8

Jurisdiction in rem or quasi in rem—Grounds for generally.—A court of this State having jurisdiction of the subject matter may exercise jurisdiction in rem or quasi in rem on the grounds stated in this section. A judgment in rem or quasi in rem may affect the interests of a defendant in a status, property or thing acted upon only if process has been served upon the defendant pursuant to Rule 4(k) of the Rules of Civil Procedure. Jurisdiction in rem or quasi in rem may be invoked in any of the following cases:

(1) When the subject of the action is real or personal property in this State and the defendant has or claims any lien or interest therein, or the relief demanded consists wholly or partially in excluding the defendant from any interest or lien therein. This subdivision shall apply whether any such defendant is known or unknown.

(2) When the action is to foreclose, redeem from or satisfy a deed of trust, mortgage, claim or lien upon real or personal property in this State.

(3) When the action is for a divorce or for annulment of marriage of a resident of this State.

(4) When the defendant has property within this State which has been attached or has a debtor within the State who has been garnished. Jurisdiction under this subdivision may be independent of or supplementary to jurisdiction acquired under subdivisions (1), (2) and (3) of this section.

[In Balcon, Inc. v. Sadler, 36 N.C.App. 322, 244 S.E.2d 164 (1978), the court held that subdivision (4) fails to meet standards set forth in Shaffer v. Heitner, 433 U.S. 186, 97 S.Ct. 2569, 53 L.Ed.2d 683 (1977), and is therefor unconstitutional.]

(5) In any other action in which in rem or quasi in rem jurisdiction may be constitutionally exercised.

Rhode Island General Laws Annotated § 9-5-33(a)

Every foreign corporation, every individual not a resident of this state or his executor or administrator, and every partnership or association, composed of any person or persons, not such residents, that shall have the necessary minimum contacts with the state of Rhode Island, shall be subject to the jurisdiction of the state of Rhode Island, and the courts of this state shall hold such foreign corporations and such nonresident individuals or their executors or administrators, and such partnerships or associations amenable to suit in Rhode Island in every case not contrary to the provisions of the constitution or laws of the United States.

Uniform Interstate and International Procedure Act § 1.02

A court may exercise personal jurisdiction over a person domiciled in, organized under the laws of, or maintaining his or its principal place of business in, this state as to any [cause of action] [claim for relief].

Uniform Interstate and International Procedure Act § 1.03

(a) A court may exercise personal jurisdiction over a person, who acts directly or by an agent, as to a [cause of action] [claim for relief] arising from the person's

(1) transacting any business in this state;

(2) contracting to supply services or things in this state;

(3) causing tortious injury by an act or omission in this state;

(4) causing tortious injury in this state by an act or omission outside this state if he regularly does or solicits business, or engages in any other persistent course of conduct, or derives substantial revenue from goods used or consumed or services rendered, in this state; [or]

(5) having an interest in, using, or possessing real property in this state[; or

(6) contracting to insure any person, property, or risk located within this state at the time of contracting].

(b) When jurisdiction over a person is based solely upon this section, only a [cause of action] [claim for relief] arising from acts enumerated in this section may be asserted against him.

Uniform Interstate and International Procedure Act § 1.05

When the court finds that in the interest of substantial justice the action should be heard in another forum, the court may stay or dismiss the action in whole or in part on any conditions that may be just.

Uniform Parentage Act § 8(b)

A person who has sexual intercourse in this State thereby submits to the jurisdiction of the courts of this State as to an action brought under this Act [to establish parentage] with respect to a child who may have been conceived by that act of intercourse. * * *

SELECTED STATE JURISDICTIONAL STATUTES

Selected State Statutes Governing the Powers of the Appellate Courts

Alabama Code § 12-2-13

The supreme court, in deciding each case when there is a conflict between its existing opinion and any former ruling in the case, must be governed by what, in its opinion, at that time is law, without any regard to such former ruling on the law by it; but the right of third persons, acquired on the faith of the former ruling, shall not be defeated or interfered with by or on account of any subsequent ruling.

Comparative Provision

See Georgia Code Annotated § 9-11-60(h) as set out following Federal Rule of Civil Procedure 60, supra.

California Civil Procedure Code § 909

In all cases where trial by jury is not a matter of right or where trial by jury has been waived, the reviewing court may make factual determinations contrary to or in addition to those made by the trial court. The factual determinations may be based on the evidence adduced before the trial court either with or without the taking of evidence by the reviewing court. The reviewing court may for the purpose of making the factual determinations or for any other purpose in the interests of justice, take additional evidence of or concerning facts occurring at any time prior to the decision of the appeal, and may give or direct the entry of any judgment or order and may make any further or other order as the case may require. This section shall be liberally construed to the end among others that, where feasible, causes may be finally disposed of by a single appeal and without further proceedings in the trial court except where in the interests of justice a new trial is required on some or all of the issues.

Part IV

Selected Portions of the Federal Rules of Appellate Procedure

---

TABLE OF RULES

Title I. Applicability of Rules

Rule		Page
1.	Scope of Rules and Title	293
2.	Suspension of Rules	294

Title II. Appeals From Judgments and Orders of District Courts

3.	Appeal as of Right—How Taken	294
3.1	Appeal From a Judgment Entered by a Magistrate Judge in a Civil Case	296
4.	Appeal as of Right—When Taken	296
5.	Appeal by Permission Under 28 U.S.C. § 1292(b)	298
5.1	Appeal by Permission Under 28 U.S.C. § 636(c)(5)	299
6.	Appeals by Allowance in Bankruptcy Proceedings	[Omitted]
7.	Bond for Costs on Appeal in Civil Cases	300
8.	Stay or Injunction Pending Appeal	300
9.	Release in Criminal Cases	[Omitted]
10.	The Record on Appeal	301
11.	Transmission of the Record	303
12.	Docketing the Appeal; Filing a Representation Statement; Filing the Record	304

Title III. Review of Decisions of the United States Tax Court

13.	Review of Decisions of the Tax Court	[Omitted]
14.	Applicability of Other Rules to Review of Decisions of the Tax Court	[Omitted]

Title IV. Review and Enforcement of Orders of Administrative Agencies, Boards, Commissions and Officers

15.	Review or Enforcement of Agency Orders—How Obtained; Intervention	305
15.1	Briefs and Oral Argument in National Labor Relations Board Proceedings	[Omitted]
16.	The Record on Review or Enforcement	[Omitted]
17.	Filing of the Record	[Omitted]
18.	Stay Pending Review	306
19.	Settlement of Judgments Enforcing Orders	307
20.	Applicability of Other Rules to Review or Enforcement of Agency Orders	[Omitted]

APPLICABILITY OF RULES Rule 1

Title V. Extraordinary Writs

Rule		Page
21.	Writs of Mandamus and Prohibition Directed to a Judge or Judges and Other Extraordinary Writs	307

Title VI. Habeas Corpus; Proceedings in Forma Pauperis

22.	Habeas Corpus Proceedings	[Omitted]
23.	Custody of Prisoners in Habeas Corpus Proceedings	[Omitted]
24.	Proceedings in Forma Pauperis	308

Title VII. General Provisions

25.	Filing and Service	309
26.	Computation and Extension of Time	310
26.1	Corporate Disclosure Statement	311
27.	Motions	311
28.	Briefs	312
29.	Brief of an Amicus Curiae	315
30.	Appendix to the Briefs	315
31.	Filing and Service of a Brief	317
32.	Form of Briefs, the Appendix and Other Papers	318
33.	Appeal Conferences	319
34.	Oral Argument	319
35.	Determination of Causes by the Court in Banc	320
36.	Entry of Judgment	321
37.	Interest on Judgments	321
38.	Damages and Costs for Frivolous Appeals	322
39.	Costs	322
40.	Petition for Rehearing	323
41.	Issuance of Mandate; Stay of Mandate	323
42.	Voluntary Dismissal	324
43.	Substitution of Parties	324
44.	Cases Involving Constitutional Questions Where United States Is Not a Party	325
45.	Duties of Clerks	325
46.	Attorneys	326
47.	Rules by Courts of Appeals	327
48.	Masters	328

Forms

Form 1.	Notice of Appeal to a Court of Appeals from a Judgment or Order of a District Court	[Omitted]
Form 2.	Notice of Appeal to a Court of Appeals from a Decision of the Tax Court	[Omitted]
Form 3.	Petition for Review of Order of an Agency, Board, Commission or Officer	[Omitted]
Form 4.	Affidavit to Accompany Motion for Leave to Appeal in Forma Pauperis	[Omitted]

TITLE I. APPLICABILITY OF RULES

Rule 1. Scope of Rules and Title

(a) Scope of Rules. These rules govern procedure in appeals to United States courts of appeals from the United States district courts

293

and the United States Tax Court; in appeals from bankruptcy appellate panels; in proceedings in the courts of appeals for review or enforcement of orders of administrative agencies, boards, commissions and officers of the United States; and in applications for writs or other relief which a court of appeals or a judge thereof is competent to give. When these rules provide for the making of a motion or application in the district court, the procedure for making such motion or application shall be in accordance with the practice of the district court.

(b) Rules Not to Affect Jurisdiction. These rules shall not be construed to extend or limit the jurisdiction of the courts of appeals as established by law.

(c) Title. These rules may be known and cited as the Federal Rules of Appellate Procedure.

(As amended Apr. 30, 1979, eff. Aug. 1, 1979; Apr. 25, 1989, eff. Dec. 1, 1989; Apr. 29, 1994, eff. Dec. 1, 1994.)

Rule 2. Suspension of Rules

In the interest of expediting decision, or for other good cause shown, a court of appeals may, except as otherwise provided in Rule 26(b), suspend the requirements or provisions of any of these rules in a particular case on application of a party or on its own motion and may order proceedings in accordance with its direction.

TITLE II. APPEALS FROM JUDGMENTS AND ORDERS OF DISTRICT COURTS

Rule 3. Appeal as of Right—How Taken

(a) Filing the Notice of Appeal. An appeal permitted by law as of right from a district court to a court of appeals must be taken by filing a notice of appeal with the clerk of the district court within the time allowed by Rule 4. At the time of filing, the appellant must furnish the clerk with sufficient copies of the notice of appeal to enable the clerk to comply promptly with the requirements of subdivision (d) of this Rule 3. Failure of an appellant to take any step other than the timely filing of a notice of appeal does not affect the validity of the appeal, but is ground only for such action as the court of appeals deems appropriate, which may include dismissal of the appeal. Appeals by permission under 28 U.S.C. § 1292(b) and appeals in bankruptcy must be taken in the manner prescribed by Rule 5 and Rule 6 respectively.

(b) Joint or Consolidated Appeals. If two or more persons are entitled to appeal from a judgment or order of a district court and their interests are such as to make joinder practicable, they may file a joint notice of appeal, or may join in appeal after filing separate timely notices of appeal, and they may thereafter proceed on appeal as a single appellant. Appeals may be consolidated by order of the court of appeals upon its own motion or upon motion of a party, or by stipulation of the parties to the several appeals.

(c) Content of the Notice of Appeal. A notice of appeal must specify the party or parties taking the appeal by naming each appellant in either the caption or the body of the notice of appeal. An attorney representing more than one party may fulfill this requirement by describing those parties with such terms as "all plaintiffs," "the defendants," "the plaintiffs A, B, et al.," or "all defendants except X." A notice of appeal filed pro se is filed on behalf of the party signing the notice and the signer's spouse and minor children, if they are parties, unless the notice of appeal clearly indicates a contrary intent. In a class action, whether or not the class has been certified, it is sufficient for the notice to name one person qualified to bring the appeal as representative of the class. A notice of appeal also must designate the judgment, order, or part thereof appealed from, and must name the court to which the appeal is taken. An appeal will not be dismissed for informality of form or title of the notice of appeal, or for failure to name a party whose intent to appeal is otherwise clear from the notice. Form 1 in the Appendix of Forms is a suggested form for a notice of appeal.

(d) Serving the Notice of Appeal. The clerk of the district court shall serve notice of the filing of a notice of appeal by mailing a copy to each party's counsel of record (apart from the appellant's), or, if a party is not represented by counsel, to the party's last known address. The clerk of the district court shall forthwith send a copy of the notice and of the docket entries to the clerk of the court of appeals named in the notice. The clerk of the district court shall likewise send a copy of any later docket entry in the case to the clerk of the court of appeals. When a defendant appeals in a criminal case, the clerk of the district court shall also serve a copy of the notice of appeal upon the defendant, either by personal service or by mail addressed to the defendant. The clerk shall note on each copy served the date when the notice of appeal was filed and, if the notice of appeal was filed in the manner provided in Rule 4(c) by an inmate confined in an institution, the date when the clerk received the notice of appeal. The clerk's failure to serve notice does not affect the validity of the appeal. Service is sufficient notwithstanding the death of a party or the party's counsel. The clerk shall note in the docket the names of the parties to whom the clerk mails copies, with the date of mailing.

(e) Payment of Fees. Upon the filing of any separate or joint notice of appeal from the district court, the appellant shall pay to the clerk of the district court such fees as are established by statute, and also the docket fee prescribed by the Judicial Conference of the United States, the latter to be received by the clerk of the district court on behalf of the court of appeals.

Rule 3   RULES OF APPELLATE PROCEDURE

(As amended Apr. 30, 1979, eff. Aug. 1, 1979; Mar. 10, 1986, eff. July 1, 1986; Apr. 25, 1989, eff. Dec. 1, 1989; Apr. 22, 1993, eff. Dec. 1, 1993; Apr. 29, 1994, eff. Dec. 1, 1994.)

Rule 3.1 Appeal From a Judgment Entered by a Magistrate Judge in a Civil Case

When the parties consent to a trial before a magistrate judge under 28 U.S.C. § 636(c)(1), any appeal from the judgment must be heard by the court of appeals in accordance with 28 U.S.C. § 636(c)(3), unless the parties consent to an appeal on the record to a district judge and thereafter, by petition only, to the court of appeals, in accordance with 28 U.S.C. § 636(c)(4). An appeal under 28 U.S.C. § 636(c)(3) must be taken in identical fashion as an appeal from any other judgment of the district court.

Rule 4. Appeal as of Right—When Taken *

(a) Appeal in a Civil Case.

(1) Except as provided in paragraph (a)(4) of this Rule, in a civil case in which an appeal is permitted by law as of right from a district court to a court of appeals the notice of appeal required by Rule 3 must be filed with the clerk of the district court within 30 days after the date of entry of the judgment or order appealed from; but if the United States or an officer or agency thereof is a party, the notice of appeal may be filed by any party within 60 days after such entry. If a notice of appeal is mistakenly filed in the court of appeals, the clerk of the court of appeals shall note thereon the date when the clerk received the notice and send it to the clerk of the district court and the notice will be treated as filed in the district court on the date so noted.

(2) A notice of appeal filed after the court announces a decision or order but before the entry of the judgment or order is treated as filed on the date of and after the entry.

(3) If one party timely files a notice of appeal, any other party may file a notice of appeal within 14 days after the date when the first notice was filed, or within the time otherwise prescribed by this Rule 4(a), whichever period last expires.

(4) If any party makes a timely motion of a type specified immediately below, the time for appeal for all parties runs from the entry of the order disposing of the last such motion outstanding. This provision applies to a timely motion under the Federal Rules of Civil Procedure:

    (A) for judgment under Rule 50(b);

    (B) to amend or make additional findings of fact under Rule 52(b), whether or not granting the motion would alter the judgment;

---

* Proposed amendments to Rule 4 are found in Part X of this Supplement.

(C) to alter or amend the judgment under Rule 59;

(D) for attorney's fees under Rule 54 if a district court under Rule 58 extends the time for appeal;

(E) for a new trial under Rule 59; or

(F) for relief under Rule 60 if the motion is served within 10 days after the entry of judgment.

A notice of appeal filed after announcement or entry of the judgment but before disposition of any of the above motions is ineffective to appeal from the judgment or order, or part thereof, specified in the notice of appeal, until the date of the entry of the order disposing of the last such motion outstanding. Appellate review of an order disposing of any of the above motions requires the party, in compliance with Appellate Rule 3(c), to amend a previously filed notice of appeal. A party intending to challenge an alteration or amendment of the judgment shall file an amended notice of appeal within the time prescribed by this Rule 4 measured from the entry of the order disposing of the last such motion outstanding. No additional fees will be required for filing an amended notice.

(5) The district court, upon a showing of excusable neglect or good cause, may extend the time for filing a notice of appeal upon motion filed not later than 30 days after the expiration of the time prescribed by this Rule 4(a). Any such motion which is filed before expiration of the prescribed time may be *ex parte* unless the court otherwise requires. Notice of any such motion which is filed after expiration of the prescribed time shall be given to the other parties in accordance with local rules. No such extension shall exceed 30 days past such prescribed time or 10 days from the date of entry of the order granting the motion, whichever occurs later.

(6) The district court, if it finds (a) that a party entitled to notice of the entry of a judgment or order did not receive such notice from the clerk or any party within 21 days of its entry and (b) that no party would be prejudiced, may, upon motion filed within 180 days of entry of the judgment or order or within 7 days of receipt of such notice, whichever is earlier, reopen the time for appeal for a period of 14 days from the date of entry of the order reopening the time for appeal.

(7) A judgment or order is entered within the meaning of this Rule 4(a) when it is entered in compliance with Rules 58 and 79(a) of the Federal Rules of Civil Procedure.

(b) Appeal in a Criminal Case. In a criminal case, a defendant shall file the notice of appeal in the district court within 10 days after the entry either of the judgment or order appealed from, or of a notice of appeal by the Government. A notice of appeal filed after the announcement of a decision, sentence, or order—but before entry of the judgment or order—is treated as filed on the date of and after the entry. If a defendant makes a timely motion specified immediately below, in accordance with the Federal Rules of Criminal Procedure, an appeal from a judgment of conviction must be taken within 10 days after the entry of the order disposing of the last such motion outstanding, or within 10 days after the entry of the judgment of conviction, whichever is later. This provision applies to a timely motion:

(1) for judgment of acquittal;

(2) for arrest of judgment;

(3) for a new trial on any ground other than newly discovered evidence; or

(4) for a new trial based on the ground of newly discovered evidence if the motion is made before or within 10 days after entry of the judgment.

A notice of appeal filed after the court announces a decision, sentence, or order but before it disposes of any of the above motions, is ineffective until the date of the entry of the order disposing of the last such motion outstanding, or until the date of the entry of the judgment of conviction, whichever is later. Notwithstanding the provisions of Rule 3(c), a valid notice of appeal is effective without amendment to appeal from an order disposing of any of the above motions. When an appeal by the government is authorized by statute, the notice of appeal must be filed in the district court within 30 days after (i) the entry of the judgment or order appealed from or (ii) the filing of a notice of appeal by any defendant.

A judgment or order is entered within the meaning of this subdivision when it is entered on the criminal docket. Upon a showing of excusable neglect, the district court may—before or after the time has expired, with or without motion and notice—extend the time for filing a notice of appeal for a period not to exceed 30 days from the expiration of the time otherwise prescribed by this subdivision.

The filing of a notice of appeal under this Rule 4(b) does not divest a district court of jurisdiction to correct a sentence under Fed.R.Crim.P. 35(c), nor does the filing of a motion under Fed.R.Crim.P. 35(c) affect the validity of a notice of appeal filed before entry of the order disposing of the motion.

Rule 5. Appeal by Permission Under 28 U.S.C. § 1292(b)

(a) Petition for Permission to Appeal. An appeal from an interlocutory order containing the statement prescribed by 28 U.S.C. § 1292(b) may be sought by filing a petition for permission to appeal with the clerk of the court of appeals within 10 days after the entry of such order in the district court with proof of service on all other parties to the action in the district court. An order may be amended to include the prescribed statement at any time, and permission to appeal may be sought within 10 days after entry of the order as amended.

(b) Content of Petition; Answer. The petition shall contain a statement of the facts necessary to an understanding of the controlling question of law determined by the order of the district court; a statement of the question itself; and a statement of the reasons why a substantial basis exists for a difference of opinion on the question and why an immediate appeal may materially advance the termination of the litigation. The petition shall include or have annexed thereto a copy of the order from which appeal is sought and of any findings of fact, conclusions of law and opinion relating thereto. Within 7 days after service of the petition an adverse party may file an answer in opposition. The application and answer shall be submitted without oral argument unless otherwise ordered.

(c) Form of Papers; Number of Copies. All papers may be typewritten. An original and three copies must be filed unless the court requires the filing of a different number by local rule or by order in a particular case.

(d) Grant of Permission; Cost Bond; Filing of Record. Within 10 days after the entry of an order granting permission to appeal the appellant shall (1) pay to the clerk of the district court the fees established by statute and the docket fee prescribed by the Judicial Conference of the United States and (2) file a bond for costs if required pursuant to Rule 7. The clerk of the district court shall notify the clerk of the court of appeals of the payment of the fees. Upon receipt of such notice the clerk of the court of appeals shall enter the appeal upon the docket. The record shall be transmitted and filed in accordance with Rules 11 and 12(b). A notice of appeal need not be filed.

(As amended Apr. 30, 1979, eff. Aug. 1, 1979; Apr. 29, 1994, eff. Dec. 1, 1994.)

Rule 5.1 Appeal by Permission Under 28 U.S.C. § 636(c)(5)

(a) Petition for Leave to Appeal; Answer or Cross Petition. An appeal from a district court judgment, entered after an appeal under 28 U.S.C. § 636(c)(4) to a district judge from a judgment entered upon direction of a magistrate judge in a civil case, may be sought by filing a petition for leave to appeal. An appeal on petition for leave to appeal is not a matter of right, but its allowance is a matter of sound judicial discretion. The petition shall be filed with the clerk of the court of appeals within the time provided by Rule 4(a) for filing a notice of appeal, with proof of service on all parties to the action in the district court. A notice of appeal need not be filed. Within 14 days after service of the petition, a party may file an answer in opposition or a cross petition.

Rule 5.1   RULES OF APPELLATE PROCEDURE

(b) Content of Petition; Answer. The petition for leave to appeal shall contain a statement of the facts necessary to an understanding of the questions to be presented by the appeal; a statement of those questions and of the relief sought; a statement of the reasons why in the opinion of the petitioner the appeal should be allowed; and a copy of the order, decree or judgment complained of and any opinion or memorandum relating thereto. The petition and answer shall be submitted to a panel of judges of the court of appeals without oral argument unless otherwise ordered.

(c) Form of Papers; Number of Copies. All papers may be typewritten. An original and three copies must be filed unless the court requires the filing of a different number by local rule or by order in a particular case.

(d) Allowance of the Appeal; Fees; Cost Bond; Filing of Record. Within 10 days after the entry of an order granting the appeal, the appellant shall (1) pay to the clerk of the district court the fees established by statute and the docket fee prescribed by the Judicial Conference of the United States and (2) file a bond for costs if required pursuant to Rule 7. The clerk of the district court shall notify the clerk of the court of appeals of the payment of the fees. Upon receipt of such notice, the clerk of the court of appeals shall enter the appeal upon the docket. The record shall be transmitted and filed in accordance with Rules 11 and 12(b).

(Added Mar. 10, 1986, eff. July 1, 1986, and amended Apr. 22, 1993, eff. Dec. 1, 1993; Apr. 29, 1994, eff. Dec. 1, 1994.)

Rule 7.   Bond for Costs on Appeal in Civil Cases

The district court may require an appellant to file a bond or provide other security in such form and amount as it finds necessary to ensure payment of costs on appeal in a civil case. The provisions of Rule 8(b) apply to a surety upon a bond given pursuant to this rule.

Rule 8.   Stay or Injunction Pending Appeal *

(a) Stay Must Ordinarily Be Sought in the First Instance in District Court; Motion for Stay in Court of Appeals. Application for a stay of the judgment or order of a district court pending appeal, or for approval of a supersedeas bond, or for an order suspending, modifying, restoring or granting an injunction during the pendency of an appeal must ordinarily be made in the first instance in the district court. A motion for such relief may be made to the court of appeals or to a judge thereof, but the motion shall show that application to the district court for the relief sought is not practicable, or that the district court has denied an application, or has failed to afford the relief which the applicant requested, with the reasons given by the district court for its

---

* Proposed amendments to Rule 8 are found in Part X of this Supplement.

action. The motion shall also show the reasons for the relief requested and the facts relied upon, and if the facts are subject to dispute the motion shall be supported by affidavits or other sworn statements or copies thereof. With the motion shall be filed such parts of the record as are relevant. Reasonable notice of the motion shall be given to all parties. The motion shall be filed with the clerk and normally will be considered by a panel or division of the court, but in exceptional cases where such procedure would be impracticable due to the requirements of time, the application may be made to and considered by a single judge of the court.

(b) Stay May Be Conditioned Upon Giving of Bond; Proceedings Against Sureties. Relief available in the court of appeals under this rule may be conditioned upon the filing of a bond or other appropriate security in the district court. If security is given in the form of a bond or stipulation or other undertaking with one or more sureties, each surety submits himself to the jurisdiction of the district court and irrevocably appoints the clerk of the district court as the surety's agent upon whom any papers affecting the surety's liability on the bond or undertaking may be served. A surety's liability may be enforced on motion in the district court without the necessity of an independent action. The motion and such notice of the motion as the district court prescribes may be served on the clerk of the district court, who shall forthwith mail copies to the sureties if their addresses are known.

(c) Stays in Criminal Cases. Stays in criminal cases shall be had in accordance with the provisions of Rule 38(a) of the Federal Rules of Criminal Procedure.

Rule 10. The Record on Appeal *

(a) Composition of the Record on Appeal. The original papers and exhibits filed in the district court, the transcript of proceedings, if any, and a certified copy of the docket entries prepared by the clerk of the district court shall constitute the record on appeal in all cases.

(b) The Transcript of Proceedings; Duty of Appellant to Order; Notice to Appellee if Partial Transcript is Ordered.

(1) Within 10 days after filing the notice of appeal the appellant shall order from the reporter a transcript of such parts of the proceedings not already on file as the appellant deems necessary, subject to local rules of the courts of appeals. The order shall be in writing and within the same period a copy shall be filed with the clerk of the district court. If funding is to come from the United States under the Criminal Justice Act, the order shall so state. If no such parts of the proceedings are to be ordered, within the same period the appellant shall file a certificate to that effect.

---

* Proposed amendments to Rule 10 are found in Part X of this Supplement.

(2) If the appellant intends to urge on appeal that a finding or conclusion is unsupported by the evidence or is contrary to the evidence, the appellant shall include in the record a transcript of all evidence relevant to such finding or conclusion.

(3) Unless the entire transcript is to be included, the appellant shall, within the 10 days time provided in (b)(1) of this Rule 10, file a statement of the issues the appellant intends to present on the appeal and shall serve on the appellee a copy of the order or certificate and of the statement. An appellee who believes that a transcript of other parts of the proceedings is necessary shall, within 10 days after the service of the order or certificate and the statement of the appellant, file and serve on the appellant a designation of additional parts to be included. Unless within 10 days after service of the designation the appellant has ordered such parts, and has so notified the appellee, the appellee may within the following 10 days either order the parts or move in the district court for an order requiring the appellant to do so.

(4) At the time of ordering, a party must make satisfactory arrangements with the reporter for payment of the cost of the transcript.

(c) Statement of the Evidence or Proceedings When no Report Was Made or When the Transcript Is Unavailable. If no report of the evidence or proceedings at a hearing or trial was made, or if a transcript is unavailable, the appellant may prepare a statement of the evidence or proceedings from the best available means, including the appellant's recollection. The statement shall be served on the appellee, who may serve objections or proposed amendments thereto within 10 days after service. Thereupon the statement and any objections or proposed amendments shall be submitted to the district court for settlement and approval and as settled and approved shall be included by the clerk of the district court in the record on appeal.

(d) Agreed Statement as the Record on Appeal. In lieu of the record on appeal as defined in subdivision (a) of this rule, the parties may prepare and sign a statement of the case showing how the issues presented by the appeal arose and were decided in the district court and setting forth only so many of the facts averred and proved or sought to be proved as are essential to a decision of the issues presented. If the statement conforms to the truth, it, together with such additions as the court may consider necessary fully to present the issues raised by the appeal, shall be approved by the district court and shall then be certified to the court of appeals as the record on appeal and transmitted thereto by the clerk of the district court within the time provided by Rule 11. Copies of the agreed statement may be filed as the appendix required by Rule 30.

(e) Correction or Modification of the Record. If any difference arises as to whether the record truly discloses what occurred in the district court, the difference shall be submitted to and settled by that court and the record made to conform to the truth. If anything material to either party is omitted from the record by error or accident or is misstated therein, the parties by stipulation, or the district court either before or after the record is transmitted to the court of appeals, or the court of appeals, on proper suggestion or of its own initiative, may direct that the omission or misstatement be corrected, and if necessary that a supplemental record be certified and transmitted. All other questions as to the form and content of the record shall be presented to the court of appeals.

Rule 11. Transmission of the Record

(a) Duty of Appellant. After filing the notice of appeal the appellant, or in the event that more than one appeal is taken, each appellant, shall comply with the provisions of Rule 10(b) and shall take any other action necessary to enable the clerk to assemble and transmit the record. A single record shall be transmitted.

(b) Duty of Reporter to Prepare and File Transcript; Notice to Court of Appeals; Duty of Clerk to Transmit the Record. Upon receipt of an order for a transcript, the reporter shall acknowledge at the foot of the order the fact that the reporter has received it and the date on which the reporter expects to have the transcript completed and shall transmit the order, so endorsed, to the clerk of the court of appeals. If the transcript cannot be completed within 30 days of receipt of the order the reporter shall request an extension of time from the clerk of the court of appeals and the action of the clerk of the court of appeals shall be entered on the docket and the parties notified. In the event of the failure of the reporter to file the transcript within the time allowed, the clerk of the court of appeals shall notify the district judge and take such other steps as may be directed by the court of appeals. Upon completion of the transcript the reporter shall file it with the clerk of the district court and shall notify the clerk of the court of appeals that the reporter has done so.

When the record is complete for purposes of the appeal, the clerk of the district court shall transmit it forthwith to the clerk of the court of appeals. The clerk of the district court shall number the documents comprising the record and shall transmit with the record a list of documents correspondingly numbered and identified with reasonable definiteness. Documents of unusual bulk or weight, physical exhibits other than documents, and such other parts of the record as the court of appeals may designate by local rule, shall not be transmitted by the clerk unless the clerk is directed to do so by a party or by the clerk of the court of appeals. A party must make advance arrangements with the clerks for the transportation and receipt of exhibits of unusual bulk or weight.

(c) Temporary Retention of Record in District Court for Use in Preparing Appellate Papers. Notwithstanding the provisions of (a) and (b) of this Rule 11, the parties may stipulate, or the district court on motion of any party may order, that the clerk of the district court shall temporarily retain the record for use by the parties in preparing appellate papers. In that event the clerk of the district court shall certify to the clerk of the court of appeals that the record, including the transcript or parts thereof designated for inclusion and all necessary exhibits, is complete for purposes of the appeal. Upon receipt of the brief of the appellee, or at such earlier time as the parties may agree or the court may order, the appellant shall request the clerk of the district court to transmit the record.

(d) [Extension of Time for Transmission of the Record; Reduction of Time.] [Abrogated.]

(e) Retention of the Record in the District Court by Order of Court. The court of appeals may provide by rule or order that a certified copy of the docket entries shall be transmitted in lieu of the entire record, subject to the right of any party to request at any time during the pendency of the appeal that designated parts of the record be transmitted.

If the record or any part thereof is required in the district court for use there pending the appeal, the district court may make an order to that effect, and the clerk of the district court shall retain the record or parts thereof subject to the request of the court of appeals, and shall transmit a copy of the order and of the docket entries together with such parts of the original record as the district court shall allow and copies of such parts as the parties may designate.

(f) Stipulation of Parties that Parts of the Record Be Retained in the District Court. The parties may agree by written stipulation filed in the district court that designated parts of the record shall be retained in the district court unless thereafter the court of appeals shall order or any party shall request their transmittal. The parts thus designated shall nevertheless be a part of the record on appeal for all purposes.

(g) Record for Preliminary Hearing in the Court of Appeals. If prior to the time the record is transmitted a party desires to make in the court of appeals a motion for dismissal, for release, for a stay pending appeal, for additional security on the bond on appeal or on a supersedeas bond, or for any intermediate order, the clerk of the district court at the request of any party shall transmit to the court of appeals such parts of the original record as any party shall designate.

Rule 12. Docketing the Appeal; Filing a Representation Statement; Filing the Record

(a) Docketing the Appeal. Upon receipt of the copy of the notice of appeal and of the docket entries, transmitted by the clerk of the district court pursuant to Rule 3(d), the clerk of the court of appeals shall thereupon enter the appeal upon the docket. An appeal shall be docketed under the title given to the action in the district court, with the appellant identified as such, but if such title does not contain the name of the appellant, the appellant's name, identified as appellant, shall be added to the title.

(b) Filing a Representation Statement. Within 10 days after filing a notice of appeal, unless another time is designated by the court of appeals, the attorney who filed the notice of appeal shall file with the clerk of the court of appeals a statement naming each party represented on appeal by that attorney.

(c) Filing the Record, Partial Record, or Certificate. Upon receipt of the record transmitted pursuant to Rule 11(b), or the partial record transmitted pursuant to Rule 11(e), (f), or (g), or the clerk's certificate under Rule 11(c), the clerk of the court of appeals shall file it and shall immediately give notice to all parties of the date on which it was filed.

TITLE IV. REVIEW AND ENFORCEMENT OF ORDERS OF ADMINISTRATIVE AGENCIES, BOARDS, COMMISSIONS AND OFFICERS

Rule 15. Review or Enforcement of Agency Orders—How Obtained; Intervention

(a) Petition for Review of Order; Joint Petition. Review of an order of an administrative agency, board, commission or officer (hereinafter, the term "agency" shall include agency, board, commission or officer) must be obtained by filing with the clerk of a court of appeals that is authorized to review such order, within the time prescribed by law, a petition to enjoin, set aside, suspend, modify or otherwise review, or a notice of appeal, whichever form is indicated by the applicable statute (hereinafter, the term "petition for review" shall include a petition to enjoin, set aside, suspend, modify or otherwise review, or a notice of appeal). The petition must name each party seeking review either in the caption or in the body of the petition. Use of such terms as "et al.," or "petitioners" or "respondents" is not effective to name the parties. The petition also must designate the respondent and the order or part thereof to be reviewed. Form 3 in the Appendix of Forms is a suggested form of a petition for review. In each case the agency must be named respondent. The United States shall also be a respondent if required by statute, even though not designated in the petition. If two or more persons are entitled to petition the same court for review of the same order and their interests are such as to make joinder practicable, they may file a joint petition for review and may thereafter proceed as a single petitioner.

(b) Application for Enforcement of Order; Answer; Default; Cross-Application for Enforcement. An application for enforcement of an order of an agency shall be filed with the clerk of a court of appeals which is authorized to enforce the order. The application shall contain a concise statement of the proceedings in which the order was entered, the facts upon which venue is based, and the relief prayed. Within 20 days after the application is filed, the respondent shall serve on the petitioner and file with the clerk an answer to the application. If the respondent fails to file an answer within such time, judgment will be awarded for the relief prayed. If a petition is filed for review of an order which the court has jurisdiction to enforce, the respondent may file a cross-application for enforcement.

(c) Service of Petition or Application. A copy of a petition for review or of an application or cross-application for enforcement of an order shall be served by the clerk of the court of appeals on each respondent in the manner prescribed by Rule 3(d), unless a different manner of service is prescribed by an applicable statute. At the time of filing, the petitioner shall furnish the clerk with a copy of the petition or application for each respondent. At or before the time of filing a petition for review, the petitioner shall serve a copy thereof on all parties who shall have been admitted to participate in the proceedings before the agency other than respondents to be served by the clerk, and shall file with the clerk a list of those so served.

(d) Intervention. Unless an applicable statute provides a different method of intervention, a person who desires to intervene in a proceeding under this rule shall serve upon all parties to the proceeding and file with the clerk of the court of appeals a motion for leave to intervene. The motion shall contain a concise statement of the interest of the moving party and the grounds upon which intervention is sought. A motion for leave to intervene or other notice of intervention authorized by an applicable statute shall be filed within 30 days of the date on which the petition for review is filed.

(e) Payment of Fees. When filing any separate or joint petition for review in a court of appeals, the petitioner must pay the clerk of the court of appeals the fees established by statute, and also the docket fee prescribed by the Judicial Conference of the United States.

Rule 18. Stay Pending Review

Application for a stay of a decision or order of an agency pending direct review in the court of appeals shall ordinarily be made in the first instance to the agency. A motion for such relief may be made to the court of appeals or to a judge thereof, but the motion shall show that application to the agency for the relief sought is not practicable, or that application has been made to the agency and denied, with the reasons given by it for denial, or that the action of the agency did not afford the relief which the applicant had requested. The motion shall also show the reasons for the relief requested and the facts relied upon, and if the facts are subject to dispute the motion shall be supported by affidavits or other sworn statements or copies thereof. With the motion shall be filed such parts of the record as are relevant to the relief sought. Reasonable notice of the motion shall be given to all parties to the proceeding in the court of appeals. The court may condition relief under this rule upon the filing of a bond or other appropriate security. The motion shall be filed with the clerk and normally will be considered by a panel or division of the court, but in exceptional cases where such procedure would be impracticable due to the requirements of time, the application may be made to and considered by a single judge of the court.

Rule 19. Settlement of Judgments Enforcing Orders

When an opinion of the court is filed directing the entry of a judgment enforcing in part the order of an agency, the agency shall within 14 days thereafter serve upon the respondent and file with the clerk a proposed judgment in conformity with the opinion. If the respondent objects to the proposed judgment as not in conformity with the opinion, the respondent shall within 7 days thereafter serve upon the agency and file with the clerk a proposed judgment which the respondent deems to be in conformity with the opinion. The court will thereupon settle the judgment and direct its entry without further hearing or argument.

TITLE V. EXTRAORDINARY WRITS

Rule 21. Writs of Mandamus and Prohibition Directed to a Judge or Judges and Other Extraordinary Writs

(a) Mandamus or Prohibition to a Judge or Judges; Petition for Writ; Service and Filing. Application for a writ of mandamus or of prohibition directed to a judge or judges shall be made by filing a petition therefor with the clerk of the court of appeals with proof of service on the respondent judge or judges and on all parties to the action in the trial court. The petition shall contain a statement of the facts necessary to an understanding of the issues presented by the application; a statement of the issues presented and of the relief sought; a statement of the reasons why the writ should issue; and copies of any order or opinion or parts of the record which may be essential to an understanding of the matters set forth in the petition. Upon receipt of the prescribed docket fee, the clerk shall docket the petition and submit it to the court.

(b) Denial; Order Directing Answer. If the court is of the opinion that the writ should not be granted, it shall deny the petition. Otherwise, it shall order that an answer to the petition be filed by the respondents within the time fixed by the order. The order shall be served by the clerk on the judge or judges named respondents and on all other parties to the action in the trial court. All parties below other than the petitioner shall also be deemed respondents for all purposes. Two or more respondents may answer jointly. If the judge or judges named respondents do not desire to appear in the proceeding, they may so advise the clerk and all parties by letter, but the petition shall not thereby be taken as admitted. The clerk shall advise the parties of the dates on which briefs are to be filed, if briefs are required, and of the date of oral argument. The proceeding shall be given preference over ordinary civil cases.

(c) Other Extraordinary Writs. Application for extraordinary writs other than those provided for in subdivisions (a) and (b) of this rule shall be made by petition filed with the clerk of the court of appeals with proof of service on the parties named as respondents. Proceedings on such application shall conform, so far as is practicable, to the procedure prescribed in subdivisions (a) and (b) of this rule.

(d) Form of Papers; Number of Copies. All papers may be typewritten. An original and three copies must be filed unless the court requires the filing of a different number by local rule or by order in a particular case.

(As amended Apr. 29, 1994, eff. Dec. 1, 1994.)

TITLE VI. HABEAS CORPUS; PROCEEDINGS IN FORMA PAUPERIS

Rule 24. Proceedings in Forma Pauperis

(a) Leave to Proceed on Appeal in Forma Pauperis From District Court to Court of Appeals. A party to an action in a district court who desires to proceed on appeal in forma pauperis shall file in the district court a motion for leave so to proceed, together with an affidavit, showing, in the detail prescribed by Form 4 of the Appendix of Forms, the party's inability to pay fees and costs or to give security therefor, the party's belief that that party is entitled to redress, and a statement of the issues which that party intends to present on appeal. If the motion is granted, the party may proceed without further application to the court of appeals and without prepayment of fees or costs in either court or the giving of security therefor. If the motion is denied, the district court shall state in writing the reasons for the denial.

Notwithstanding the provisions of the preceding paragraph, a party who has been permitted to proceed in an action in the district court in forma pauperis, or who has been permitted to proceed there as one who is financially unable to obtain adequate defense in a criminal case, may proceed on appeal in forma pauperis without further authorization unless, before or after the notice of appeal is filed, the district court shall certify that the appeal is not taken in good faith or shall find that the party is otherwise not entitled so to proceed, in which event the district court shall state in writing the reasons for such certification or finding.

If a motion for leave to proceed on appeal in forma pauperis is denied by the district court, or if the district court shall certify that the appeal is not taken in good faith or shall find that the party is otherwise not entitled to proceed in forma pauperis, the clerk shall forthwith serve notice of such action. A motion for leave so to proceed may be filed in the court of appeals within 30 days after service of notice of the action of the district court. The motion shall be accompanied by a copy of the affidavit filed in the district court, or by the affidavit prescribed by the first paragraph of this subdivision if no affidavit has been filed in the district court, and by a copy of the statement of reasons given by the district court for its action.

(b) Leave to Proceed on Appeal or Review in Forma Pauperis in Administrative Agency Proceedings. A party to a proceeding before an administrative agency, board, commission or officer (including, for the purpose of this rule, the United States Tax Court) who desires to proceed on appeal or review in a court of appeals in forma pauperis, when such appeal or review may be had directly in a court of appeals, shall file in the court of appeals a motion for leave so to proceed, together with the affidavit prescribed by the first paragraph of (a) of this Rule 24.

(c) Form of Briefs, Appendices and Other Papers. Parties allowed to proceed in forma pauperis may file briefs, appendices and other papers in typewritten form, and may request that the appeal be heard on the original record without the necessity of reproducing parts thereof in any form.

TITLE VII. GENERAL PROVISIONS

Rule 25. Filing and Service

(a) Filing. A paper required or permitted to be filed in a court of appeals must be filed with the clerk. Filing may be accomplished by mail addressed to the clerk, but filing is not timely unless the clerk receives the papers within the time fixed for filing, except that briefs and appendices are treated as filed on the day of mailing if the most expeditious form of delivery by mail, except special delivery, is used. Papers filed by an inmate confined in an institution are timely filed if deposited in the institution's internal mail system on or before the last day for filing. Timely filing of papers by an inmate confined in an institution may be shown by a notarized statement or declaration (in compliance with 28 U.S.C. § 1746) setting forth the date of deposit and stating that first-class postage has been prepaid. If a motion requests relief that may be granted by a single judge, the judge may permit the motion to be filed with the judge, in which event the judge shall note thereon the filing date and thereafter give it to the clerk. A court of appeals may, by local rule, permit papers to be filed by facsimile or other electronic means, provided such means are authorized by and consistent with standards established by the Judicial Conference of the United States. The clerk must not refuse to accept for filing any paper presented for that purpose solely because it is not presented in proper form as required by these rules or by any local rules or practices.

(b) Service of All Papers Required. Copies of all papers filed by any party and not required by these rules to be served by the clerk shall, at or before the time of filing, be served by a party or person acting for that party on all other parties to the appeal or review. Service on a party represented by counsel shall be made on counsel.

(c) Manner of Service. Service may be personal or by mail. Personal service includes delivery of the copy to a clerk or other responsible person at the office of counsel. Service by mail is complete on mailing.

(d) Proof of Service. Papers presented for filing must contain an acknowledgment of service by the person served or proof of service in the form of a statement of the date and manner of service, of the names of the persons served, and of the addresses to which the papers were mailed or at which they were delivered, certified by the person who made service. Proof of service may appear on or be affixed to the papers filed.

(e) Number of Copies. Whenever these rules require the filing or furnishing of a number of copies, a court may require a different number by local rule or by order in a particular case.

(As amended Mar. 10, 1986, eff. July 1, 1986; Apr. 30, 1991, eff. Dec. 1, 1991; Apr. 22, 1993, eff. Dec. 1, 1993; Apr. 29, 1994, eff. Dec. 1, 1994.)

Rule 26. Computation and Extension of Time

(a) Computation of Time. In computing any period of time prescribed by these rules, by an order of court, or by any applicable statute, the day of the act, event, or default from which the designated period of time begins to run shall not be included. The last day of the period shall be included, unless it is a Saturday, a Sunday, or a legal holiday, or, when the act to be done is the filing of a paper in court, a day on which weather or other conditions have made the office of the clerk inaccessible, in which event the period extends until the end of the next day which is not one of the aforementioned days. When the period of time prescribed or allowed is less than 7 days, intermediate Saturdays, Sundays, and legal holidays shall be excluded in the computation. As used in this rule "legal holiday" includes New Year's Day, Birthday of Martin Luther King, Jr., Washington's Birthday, Memorial Day, Independence Day, Labor Day, Columbus Day, Veterans Day, Thanksgiving Day, Christmas Day, and any other day appointed as a holiday by the President or the Congress of the United States. It shall also include a day appointed as a holiday by the state wherein the district court which rendered the judgment or order which is or may be appealed from is situated, or by the state wherein the principal office of the clerk of the court of appeals in which the appeal is pending is located.

(b) Enlargement of Time. The court for good cause shown may upon motion enlarge the time prescribed by these rules or by its order for doing any act, or may permit an act to be done after the expiration of such time; but the court may not enlarge the time for filing a notice of appeal, a petition for allowance, or a petition for permission to appeal. Nor may the court enlarge the time prescribed by law for filing a petition to enjoin, set aside, suspend, modify, enforce or otherwise review, or a notice of appeal from, an order of an administrative agency, board, commission or officer of the United States, except as specifically authorized by law.

(c) Additional Time After Service by Mail. Whenever a party is required or permitted to do an act within a prescribed period after service of a paper upon that party and the paper is served by mail, 3 days shall be added to the prescribed period.

(As amended Mar. 1, 1971, eff. July 1, 1971.)

Rule 26.1 Corporate Disclosure Statement

Any non-governmental corporate party to a civil or bankruptcy case or agency review proceeding and any non-governmental corporate defendant in a criminal case must file a statement identifying all parent companies, subsidiaries (except wholly-owned subsidiaries), and affiliates that have issued shares to the public. The statement must be filed with a party's principal brief or upon filing a motion, response, petition, or answer in the court of appeals, whichever first occurs, unless a local rule requires earlier filing. Whenever the statement is filed before a party's principal brief, an original and three copies of the statement must be filed unless the court requires the filing of a different number by local rule or by order in a particular case. The statement must be included in front of the table of contents in a party's principal brief even if the statement was previously filed.

(Added Apr. 25, 1989, eff. Dec. 1, 1989, and amended Apr. 30, 1991, eff. Dec. 1, 1991; Apr. 29, 1994, eff. Dec. 1, 1994.)

Rule 27. Motions

(a) Content of motions; response. Unless another form is elsewhere prescribed by these rules, an application for an order or other relief shall be made by filing a motion for such order or relief with proof of service on all other parties. The motion shall contain or be accompanied by any matter required by a specific provision of these rules governing such a motion, shall state with particularity the grounds on which it is based, and shall set forth the order or relief sought. If a motion is supported by briefs, affidavits or other papers, they shall be served and filed with the motion. Any party may file a response in opposition to a motion other than one for a procedural order [for which see subdivision (b)] within 7 days after service of the motion, but motions authorized by Rules 8, 9, 18 and 41 may be acted upon after reasonable notice, and the court may shorten or extend the time for responding to any motion.

(b) Determination of Motions for Procedural Orders. Notwithstanding the provisions of (a) of this Rule 27 as to motions generally, motions for procedural orders, including any motion under Rule 26(b), may be acted upon at any time, without awaiting a response thereto, and pursuant to rule or order of the court, motions for specified types of procedural orders may be disposed of by the clerk. Any party adversely affected by such action may by application to the court request consideration, vacation or modification of such action.

(c) Power of a Single Judge to Entertain Motions. In addition to the authority expressly conferred by these rules or by law, a single judge of a court of appeals may entertain and may grant or deny any request for relief which under these rules may properly be sought by motion, except that a single judge may not dismiss or otherwise determine an appeal or other proceeding, and except that a court of appeals may provide by order or rule that any motion or class of motions must be acted upon by the court. The action of a single judge may be reviewed by the court.

(d) Form of Papers; Number of Copies. All papers relating to a motion may be typewritten. An original and three copies must be filed unless the court requires the filing of a different number by local rule or by order in a particular case.

(As amended Apr. 30, 1979, eff. Aug. 1, 1979; Apr. 25, 1989, eff. Dec. 1, 1989; Apr. 29, 1994, eff. Dec. 1, 1994.)

Rule 28. Briefs

(a) Appellant's Brief. The brief of the appellant must contain, under appropriate headings and in the order here indicated:

(1) A table of contents, with page references, and a table of cases (alphabetically arranged), statutes and other authorities cited, with references to the pages of the brief where they are cited.

(2) A statement of subject matter and appellate jurisdiction. The statement shall include: (i) a statement of the basis for subject matter jurisdiction in the district court or agency, with citation to applicable statutory provisions and with reference to the relevant facts to establish such jurisdiction; (ii) a statement of the basis for jurisdiction in the court of appeals, with citation to applicable statutory provisions and with reference to the relevant facts to establish such jurisdiction; the state-

ment shall include relevant filing dates establishing the timeliness of the appeal or petition for review and (a) shall state that the appeal is from a final order or a final judgment that disposes of all claims with respect to all parties or, if not, (b) shall include information establishing that the court of appeals has jurisdiction on some other basis.

(3) A statement of the issues presented for review.

(4) A statement of the case. The statement shall first indicate briefly the nature of the case, the course of proceedings, and its disposition in the court below. There shall follow a statement of the facts relevant to the issues presented for review, with appropriate references to the record (see subdivision (e)).

(5) A summary of argument. The summary should contain a succinct, clear, and accurate statement of the arguments made in the body of the brief. It should not be a mere repetition of the argument headings.

(6) An argument. The argument must contain the contentions of the appellant on the issues presented, and the reasons therefor, with citations to the authorities, statutes, and parts of the record relied on. The argument must also include for each issue a concise statement of the applicable standard of review; this statement may appear in the discussion of each issue or under a separate heading placed before the discussion of the issues.

(7) A short conclusion stating the precise relief sought.

(b) Appellee's Brief. The brief of the appellee must conform to the requirements of paragraphs (a)(1)–(6), except that none of the following need appear unless the appellee is dissatisfied with the statement of the appellant:

(1) the jurisdictional statement;

(2) the statement of the issues;

(3) the statement of the case;

(4) the statement of the standard of review.

(c) Reply Brief. The appellant may file a brief in reply to the brief of the appellee, and if the appellee has cross-appealed, the appellee may file a brief in reply to the response of the appellant to the issues presented by the cross appeal. No further briefs may be filed except with leave of court. All reply briefs shall contain a table of contents, with page references, and a table of cases (alphabetically arranged), statutes and other authorities cited, with references to the pages of the reply brief where they are cited.

(d) References in Briefs to Parties. Counsel will be expected in their briefs and oral arguments to keep to a minimum references to parties by such designations as "appellant" and "appellee". It promotes clarity to use the designations used in the lower court or in the agency proceedings, or the actual names of parties, or descriptive terms such as "the employee," "the injured person," "the taxpayer," "the ship," "the stevedore," etc.

(e) References in Briefs to the Record. References in the briefs to parts of the record reproduced in the appendix filed with the brief of the appellant (see Rule 30(a)) shall be to the pages of the appendix at which those parts appear. If the appendix is prepared after the briefs are filed, references in the briefs to the record shall be made by one of the methods allowed by Rule 30(c). If the record is reproduced in accordance with the provisions of Rule 30(f), or if references are made in the briefs to parts of the record not reproduced, the references shall be to the pages of the parts of the record involved; e.g., Answer p. 7, Motion for Judgment p. 2, Transcript p. 231. Intelligible abbreviations may be used. If reference is made to evidence the admissibility of which is in controversy, reference shall be made to the pages of the appendix or of the transcript at which the evidence was identified, offered, and received or rejected.

(f) Reproduction of Statutes, Rules, Regulations, etc. If determination of the issues presented requires the study of statutes, rules, regulations, etc. or relevant parts thereof, they shall be reproduced in the brief or in an addendum at the end, or they may be supplied to the court in pamphlet form.

(g) Length of briefs. Except by permission of the court, or as specified by local rule of the court of appeals, principal briefs must not exceed 50 pages, and reply briefs must not exceed 25 pages, exclusive of pages containing the corporate disclosure statement, table of contents, tables of citations, proof of service, and any addendum containing statutes, rules, regulations, etc.

(h) Briefs in cases involving cross appeals. If a cross appeal is filed, the party who first files a notice of appeal, or in the event that the notices are filed on the same day, the plaintiff in the proceeding below shall be deemed the appellant for the purposes of this rule and Rules 30 and 31, unless the parties otherwise agree or the court otherwise orders. The brief of the appellee shall conform to the requirements of subdivision (a)(1)–(6) of this rule with respect to the appellee's cross appeal as well as respond to the brief of the appellant except that a statement of the case need not be made unless the appellee is dissatisfied with the statement of the appellant.

(i) Briefs in Cases Involving Multiple Appellants or Appellees. In cases involving more than one appellant or appellee, including cases consolidated for purposes of the appeal, any number of either may join in a single brief, and any appellant or appellee may adopt by reference any part of the brief of another. Parties may similarly join in reply briefs.

(j) Citation of Supplemental Authorities. When pertinent and significant authorities come to the attention of a party after the party's brief has been filed, or after oral argument but before decision, a party may promptly advise the clerk of the court, by letter, with a copy to all counsel, setting forth the citations. There shall be a reference either to the page of the brief or to a point argued orally to which the citations pertain, but the letter shall without argument state the reasons for the supplemental citations. Any response shall be made promptly and shall be similarly limited.

(As amended Apr. 30, 1979, eff. Aug. 1, 1979; Mar. 10, 1986, eff. July 1, 1986; Apr. 25, 1989, eff. Dec. 1, 1989; Apr. 30, 1991, eff. Dec. 1, 1991; Apr. 22, 1993, eff. Dec. 1, 1993; Apr. 29, 1994, eff. Dec. 1, 1994.)

Rule 29. Brief of an Amicus Curiae

A brief of an amicus curiae may be filed only if accompanied by written consent of all parties, or by leave of court granted on motion or at the request of the court, except that consent or leave shall not be required when the brief is presented by the United States or an officer or agency thereof, or by a State, Territory or Commonwealth. The brief may be conditionally filed with the motion for leave. A motion for leave shall identify the interest of the applicant and shall state the reasons why a brief of an amicus curiae is desirable. Save as all parties otherwise consent, any amicus curiae shall file its brief within the time allowed the party whose position as to affirmance or reversal the amicus brief will support unless the court for cause shown shall grant leave for later filing, in which event it shall specify within what period an opposing party may answer. A motion of an amicus curiae to participate in the oral argument will be granted only for extraordinary reasons.

Rule 30. Appendix to the Briefs

(a) Duty of Appellant to Prepare and File; Content of Appendix; Time for Filing; Number of Copies. The appellant must prepare and file an appendix to the briefs which must contain: (1) the relevant docket entries in the proceeding below; (2) any relevant portions of the pleadings, charge, findings, or opinion; (3) the judgment, order, or decision in question; and (4) any other parts of the record to which the parties wish to direct the particular attention of the court. Except where they have independent relevance, memoranda of law in the district court should not be included in the appendix. The fact that parts of the record are not included in the appendix shall not prevent the parties or the court from relying on such parts.

Unless filing is to be deferred pursuant to the provisions of subdivision (c) of this rule, the appellant must serve and file the appendix with the brief. Ten copies of the appendix must be filed with the clerk, and one copy must be served on counsel for each party separately represented, unless the court requires the filing or service of a different number by local rule or by order in a particular case.

(b) Determination of contents of appendix; cost of producing. The parties are encouraged to agree as to the contents of the appendix. In the absence of agreement, the appellant shall, not later than 10 days after the date on which the record is filed, serve on the appellee a designation of the parts of the record which the appellant intends to include in the appendix and a statement of the issues which the appellant intends to present for review. If the appellee deems it necessary to direct the particular attention of the court to parts of the record not designated by the appellant, the appellee shall, within 10 days after receipt of the designation, serve upon the appellant a designation of those parts. The appellant shall include in the appendix the parts thus designated with respect to the appeal and any cross appeal. In designating parts of the record for inclusion in the appendix, the parties shall have regard for the fact that the entire record is always available to the court for reference and examination and shall not engage in unnecessary designation. The provisions of this paragraph shall apply to cross appellants and cross appellees.

Unless the parties otherwise agree, the cost of producing the appendix shall initially be paid by the appellant, but if the appellant considers that parts of the record designated by the appellee for inclusion are unnecessary for the determination of the issues presented the appellant may so advise the appellee and the appellee shall advance the cost of including such parts. The cost of producing the appendix shall be taxed as costs in the case, but if either party shall cause matters to be included in the appendix unnecessarily the court may impose the cost of producing such parts on the party. Each circuit shall provide by local rule for the imposition of sanctions against attorneys who unreasonably and vexatiously increase the costs of litigation through the inclusion of unnecessary material in the appendix.

(c) Alternative Method of Designating Contents of the Appendix; How References to the Record May Be Made in the Briefs When Alternative Method Is Used. If the court shall so provide by rule for classes of cases or by order in specific cases, preparation of the appendix may be deferred until after the briefs have been filed, and the appendix may be filed 21 days after service of the brief of the appellee. If the preparation and filing of the appendix is thus deferred, the provisions of subdivision (b) of this Rule 30 shall apply, except that the designations referred to therein shall be made by each party at the time each brief is served, and a statement of the issues presented shall be unnecessary.

If the deferred appendix authorized by this subdivision is employed, references in the briefs to the record may be to the pages of the parts of the record involved, in which event the original paging of each part of the record shall be indicated in the appendix by placing in brackets the number of each page at the place in the appendix where that page begins. Or if a party desires to refer in a brief directly to pages of the appendix, that party may serve and file typewritten or page proof copies of the brief within the time required by Rule 31(a), with appropriate references to the pages of the parts of the record involved. In that event, within 14 days after the appendix is filed the party shall serve and file copies of the brief in the form prescribed by Rule 32(a) containing references to the pages of the appendix in place of or in addition to the initial references to the pages of the parts of the record involved. No other changes may be made in the brief as initially served and filed, except that typographical errors may be corrected.

(d) Arrangement of the Appendix. At the beginning of the appendix there shall be inserted a list of the parts of the record which it contains, in the order in which the parts are set out therein, with references to the pages of the appendix at which each part begins. The relevant docket entries shall be set out following the list of contents. Thereafter, other parts of the record shall be set out in chronological order. When matter contained in the reporter's transcript of proceedings is set out in the appendix, the page of the transcript at which such matter may be found shall be indicated in brackets immediately before the matter which is set out. Omissions in the text of papers or of the transcript must be indicated by asterisks. Immaterial formal matters (captions, subscriptions, acknowledgments, etc.) shall be omitted. A question and its answer may be contained in a single paragraph.

(e) Reproduction of Exhibits. Exhibits designated for inclusion in the appendix may be contained in a separate volume, or volumes, suitably indexed. Four copies thereof shall be filed with the appendix and one copy shall be served on counsel for each party separately represented. The transcript of a proceeding before an administrative agency, board, commission or officer used in an action in the district court shall be regarded as an exhibit for the purpose of this subdivision.

(f) Hearing of Appeals on the Original Record Without the Necessity of an Appendix. A court of appeals may by rule applicable to all cases, or to classes of cases, or by order in specific cases, dispense with the requirement of an appendix and permit appeals to be heard on the original record, with such copies of the record, or relevant parts thereof, as the court may require.

(As amended Mar. 30, 1970, eff. July 1, 1970; Mar. 10, 1986, eff. July 1, 1986; Apr. 30, 1991, eff. Dec. 1, 1991; Apr. 30, 1994, eff. Dec. 1, 1994.)

Rule 31. Filing and Service of a Brief

(a) Time for Serving and Filing Briefs. The appellant shall serve and file a brief within 40 days after the date on which the record is filed. The appellee shall serve and file a brief within 30 days after service of the brief of the appellant. The appellant may serve and file a reply brief within 14 days after service of the brief of the appellee, but, except for good cause shown, a reply brief must be filed at least 3 days before argument. If a court of appeals is prepared to consider cases on the merits promptly after briefs are filed, and its practice is to do so, it may shorten the periods prescribed above for serving and filing briefs, either by rule for all cases or for classes of cases, or by order for specific cases.

(b) Number of Copies to Be Filed and Served. Twenty-five copies of each brief must be filed with the clerk, and two copies must be served on counsel for each party separately represented unless the court requires the filing or service of a different number by local rule or by order in a particular case. If a party is allowed to file typewritten ribbon and carbon copies of the brief, the original and three legible copies must be filed with the clerk, and one copy must be served on counsel for each party separately represented.

(c) Consequence of Failure to File Briefs. If an appellant fails to file a brief within the time provided by this rule, or within the time as extended, an appellee may move for dismissal of the appeal. If an appellee fails to file a brief, the appellee will not be heard at oral argument except by permission of the court.

(As amended Mar. 30, 1970, eff. July 1, 1970; Mar. 10, 1986, eff. July 1, 1986; Apr. 29, 1994, eff. Dec. 1, 1994.)

Rule 32. Form of Briefs, the Appendix and Other Papers

(a) Form of Briefs and the Appendix. Briefs and appendices may be produced by standard typographic printing or by any duplicating or copying process which produces a clear black image on white paper. Carbon copies of briefs and appendices may not be submitted without permission of the court, except in behalf of parties allowed to proceed in forma pauperis. All printed matter must appear in at least 11 point type on opaque, unglazed paper. Briefs and appendices produced by the standard typographic process shall be bound in volumes having pages $6\frac{1}{8}$ by $9\frac{1}{4}$ inches and type matter $4\frac{1}{6}$ by $7\frac{1}{6}$ inches. Those produced by any other process shall be bound in volumes having pages not exceeding $8\frac{1}{2}$ by 11 inches and type matter not exceeding $6\frac{1}{2}$ by $9\frac{1}{2}$ inches, with double spacing between each line of text. In patent cases the pages of briefs and appendices may be of such size as is necessary to utilize copies of patent documents. Copies of the reporter's transcript and other papers reproduced in a manner authorized by this rule may be inserted in the appendix; such pages may be informally renumbered if necessary.

If briefs are produced by commercial printing or duplicating firms, or, if produced otherwise and the covers to be described are available, the cover of the brief of the appellant should be blue; that of the appellee, red; that of an intervenor or amicus curiae, green; that of any reply brief, gray. The cover of the appendix, if separately printed, should be white. The front covers of the briefs and of appendices, if separately printed, shall contain: (1) the name of the court and the number of the case; (2) the title of the case (see Rule 12(a)); (3) the nature of the proceeding in the court (e.g., Appeal; Petition for Review) and the name of the court, agency or board below; (4) the title of the document (e.g., Brief for Appellant, Appendix); and (5) the names and addresses of counsel representing the party on whose behalf the document is filed.

(b) Form of Other Papers. Petitions for rehearing shall be produced in a manner prescribed by subdivision (a). Motions and other papers may be produced in like manner, or they may be typewritten upon opaque, unglazed paper 8½ by 11 inches in size. Lines of typewritten text shall be double spaced. Consecutive sheets shall be attached at the left margin. Carbon copies may be used for filing and service if they are legible.

A motion or other paper addressed to the court shall contain a caption setting forth the name of the court, the title of the case, the file number, and a brief descriptive title indicating the purpose of the paper.

Rule 33. Appeal Conferences

The court may direct the attorneys, and in appropriate cases the parties, to participate in one or more conferences to address any matter that may aid in the disposition of the proceedings, including the simplification of the issues and the possibility of settlement. A conference may be conducted in person or by telephone and be presided over by a judge or other person designated by the court for that purpose. Before a settlement conference, attorneys must consult with their clients and obtain as much authority as feasible to settle the case. As a result of a conference, the court may enter an order controlling the course of the proceedings or implementing any settlement agreement.

(As amended Apr. 29, 1994, eff. Dec. 1, 1994.)

Rule 34. Oral Argument

(a) In General; Local Rule. Oral argument shall be allowed in all cases unless pursuant to local rule a panel of three judges, after examination of the briefs and record, shall be unanimously of the opinion that oral argument is not needed. Any such local rule shall provide any party with an opportunity to file a statement setting forth the reasons why oral argument should be heard. A general statement of the criteria employed in the administration of such local rule shall be published in or with the rule and such criteria shall conform substantially to the following minimum standard:

Oral argument will be allowed unless

(1) the appeal is frivolous; or

(2) the dispositive issue or set of issues has been recently authoritatively decided; or

(3) the facts and legal arguments are adequately presented in the briefs and record and the decisional process would not be significantly aided by oral argument.

(b) Notice of Argument; Postponement. The clerk shall advise all parties whether oral argument is to be heard, and if so, of the time and place therefor, and the time to be allowed each side. A request for postponement of the argument or for allowance of additional time must be made by motion filed reasonably in advance of the date fixed for hearing.

(c) Order and Content of Argument. The appellant is entitled to open and conclude the argument. Counsel may not read at length from briefs, records or authorities.

(d) Cross and Separate Appeals. A cross or separate appeal shall be argued with the initial appeal at a single argument, unless the court otherwise directs. If a case involves a cross-appeal, the party who first files a notice of appeal, or in the event that the notices are filed on the same day the plaintiff in the proceeding below, shall be deemed the appellant for the purpose of this rule unless the parties otherwise agree or the court otherwise directs. If separate appellants support the same argument, care shall be taken to avoid duplication of argument.

(e) Non-Appearance of Parties. If the appellee fails to appear to present argument, the court will hear argument on behalf of the appellant, if present. If the appellant fails to appear, the court may hear argument on behalf of the appellee, if present. If neither party appears, the case will be decided on the briefs unless the court shall otherwise order.

(f) Submission on Briefs. By agreement of the parties, a case may be submitted for decision on the briefs, but the court may direct that the case be argued.

(g) Use of Physical Exhibits at Argument; Removal. If physical exhibits other than documents are to be used at the argument, counsel shall arrange to have them placed in the court room before the court convenes on the date of the argument. After the argument counsel shall cause the exhibits to be removed from the court room unless the court otherwise directs. If exhibits are not reclaimed by counsel within a reasonable time after notice is given by the clerk, they shall be destroyed or otherwise disposed of as the clerk shall think best.

Rule 35. Determination of Causes by the Court in Banc

(a) When Hearing or Rehearing in Banc Will Be Ordered. A majority of the circuit judges who are in regular active service may order that an appeal or other proceeding be heard or reheard by the court of appeals in banc. Such a hearing or rehearing is not favored and ordinarily will not be ordered except (1) when consideration by the full court is necessary to secure or maintain uniformity of its decisions, or (2) when the proceeding involves a question of exceptional importance.

(b) Suggestion of a Party for Hearing or Rehearing in Banc. A party may suggest the appropriateness of a hearing or rehearing in banc. No response shall be filed unless the court shall so order. The clerk shall transmit any such suggestion to the members of the panel and the judges of the court who are in regular active service but a vote need not be taken to determine whether the cause shall be heard or reheard in banc unless a judge in regular active service or a judge who was a member of the panel that rendered a decision sought to be reheard requests a vote on such a suggestion made by a party.

(c) Time for Suggestion of a Party for Hearing or Rehearing in Banc; Suggestion Does Not Stay Mandate. If a party desires to suggest that an appeal be heard initially in banc, the suggestion must be made by the date on which the appellee's brief is filed. A suggestion for a rehearing in banc must be made within the time prescribed by Rule 40 for filing a petition for rehearing, whether the suggestion is made in such petition or otherwise. The pendency of such a suggestion whether or not included in a petition for rehearing shall not affect the finality of the judgment of the court of appeals or stay the issuance of the mandate.

(d) Number of Copies. The number of copies that must be filed may be prescribed by local rule and may be altered by order in a particular case.

(As amended Apr. 30, 1979, eff. Aug. 1, 1979; Apr. 29, 1994, eff. Dec. 1, 1994.)

Rule 36. Entry of Judgment

The notation of a judgment in the docket constitutes entry of the judgment. The clerk shall prepare, sign and enter the judgment following receipt of the opinion of the court unless the opinion directs settlement of the form of the judgment, in which event the clerk shall prepare, sign and enter the judgment following final settlement by the court. If a judgment is rendered without an opinion, the clerk shall prepare, sign and enter the judgment following instruction from the court. The clerk shall, on the date judgment is entered, mail to all parties a copy of the opinion, if any, or of the judgment if no opinion was written, and notice of the date of entry of the judgment.

Rule 37. Interest on Judgments

Unless otherwise provided by law, if a judgment for money in a civil case is affirmed, whatever interest is allowed by law shall be payable from the date the judgment was entered in the district court. If a judgment is modified or reversed with a direction that a judgment for money be entered in the district court, the mandate shall contain instructions with respect to allowance of interest.

Rule 38. Damages and Costs for Frivolous Appeals

If a court of appeals determines that an appeal is frivolous, it may, after a separately filed motion or notice from the court and reasonable opportunity to respond, award just damages and single or double costs to the appellee.

(As amended Apr. 29, 1994, eff. Dec. 1, 1994.)

Rule 39. Costs

(a) To Whom Allowed. Except as otherwise provided by law, if an appeal is dismissed, costs shall be taxed against the appellant unless otherwise agreed by the parties or ordered by the court; if a judgment is affirmed, costs shall be taxed against the appellant unless otherwise ordered; if a judgment is reversed, costs shall be taxed against the appellee unless otherwise ordered; if a judgment is affirmed or reversed in part, or is vacated, costs shall be allowed only as ordered by the court.

(b) Costs For and Against the United States. In cases involving the United States or an agency or officer thereof, if an award of costs against the United States is authorized by law, costs shall be awarded in accordance with the provisions of subdivision (a); otherwise, costs shall not be awarded for or against the United States.

(c) Costs of Briefs, Appendices, and Copies of Records. By local rule the court of appeals shall fix the maximum rate at which the cost of printing or otherwise producing necessary copies of briefs, appendices, and copies of records authorized by Rule 30(f) shall be taxable. Such rate shall not be higher than that generally charged for such work in the area where the clerk's office is located and shall encourage the use of economical methods of printing and copying.

(d) Bill of Costs; Objections; Costs to Be Inserted in Mandate or Added Later. A party who desires such costs to be taxed shall state them in an itemized and verified bill of costs which the party shall file with the clerk, with proof of service, within 14 days after the entry of judgment. Objections to the bill of costs must be filed within 10 days of service on the party against whom costs are to be taxed unless the time is extended by the court. The clerk shall prepare and certify an itemized statement of costs taxed in the court of appeals for insertion in the mandate, but the issuance of the mandate shall not be delayed for taxation of costs and if the mandate has been issued before final determination of costs, the statement, or any amendment thereof, shall be added to the mandate upon request by the clerk of the court of appeals to the clerk of the district court.

(e) Costs on Appeal Taxable in the District Courts. Costs incurred in the preparation and transmission of the record, the cost of the reporter's transcript, if necessary for the determination of the appeal, the premiums paid for cost of supersedeas bonds or other bonds to preserve rights pending appeal, and the fee for filing the notice of appeal shall be taxed in the district court as costs of the appeal in favor of the party entitled to costs under this rule.

Rule 40. Petition for Rehearing

(a) Time for Filing; Content; Answer; Action by Court if Granted. A petition for rehearing may be filed within 14 days after entry of judgment unless the time is shortened or enlarged by order or by local rule. However, in all civil cases in which the United States or an agency or officer thereof is a party, the time within which any party may seek rehearing shall be 45 days after entry of judgment unless the time is shortened or enlarged by order. The petition must state with particularity the points of law or fact which in the opinion of the petitioner the court has overlooked or misapprehended and must contain such argument in support of the petition as the petitioner desires to present. Oral argument in support of the petition will not be permitted. No answer to a petition for rehearing will be received unless requested by the court, but a petition for rehearing will ordinarily not be granted in the absence of such a request. If a petition for rehearing is granted, the court may make a final disposition of the cause without reargument or may restore it to the calendar for reargument or resubmission or may make such other orders as are deemed appropriate under the circumstances of the particular case.

(b) Form of Petition; Length. The petition shall be in a form prescribed by Rule 32(a), and copies shall be served and filed as prescribed by Rule 31(b) for the service and filing of briefs. Except by permission of the court, or as specified by local rule of the court of appeals, a petition for rehearing shall not exceed 15 pages.

(As amended Apr. 30, 1979, eff. Aug. 1, 1979; Apr. 29, 1994, eff. Dec. 1, 1994.)

Rule 41. Issuance of Mandate; Stay of Mandate

(a) Date of Issuance. The mandate of the court must issue 7 days after the expiration of the time for filing a petition for rehearing unless such a petition is filed or the time is shortened or enlarged by order. A certified copy of the judgment and a copy of the opinion of the court, if any, and any direction as to costs shall constitute the mandate, unless the court directs that a formal mandate issue. The timely filing of a petition for rehearing will stay the mandate until disposition of the petition unless otherwise ordered by the court. If the petition is denied, the mandate must issue 7 days after entry of the order denying the petition unless the time is shortened or enlarged by order.

(b) Stay of Mandate Pending Petition for Certiorari. A party who files a motion requesting a stay of mandate pending petition to the Supreme Court for a writ of certiorari must file, at the same time, proof of service on all other parties. The motion must show that a petition for certiorari would present a substantial question and that there is good cause for a stay. The stay cannot exceed 30 days unless the period is extended for cause shown or unless during the period of the stay, a notice from the clerk of the Supreme Court is filed showing that the party who has obtained the stay has filed a petition for the writ, in which case the stay will continue until final disposition by the Supreme Court. The court of appeals must issue the mandate immediately when a copy of a Supreme Court order denying the petition for writ of certiorari is filed. The court may require a bond or other security as a condition to the grant or continuance of a stay of the mandate.

(As amended Apr. 29, 1994, eff. Dec. 1, 1994.)

Rule 42. Voluntary Dismissal

(a) Dismissal in the District Court. If an appeal has not been docketed, the appeal may be dismissed by the district court upon the filing in that court of a stipulation for dismissal signed by all the parties, or upon motion and notice by the appellant.

(b) Dismissal in the Court of Appeals. If the parties to an appeal or other proceeding shall sign and file with the clerk of the court of appeals an agreement that the proceeding be dismissed, specifying the terms as to payment of costs, and shall pay whatever fees are due, the clerk shall enter the case dismissed, but no mandate or other process shall issue without an order of the court. An appeal may be dismissed on motion of the appellant upon such terms as may be agreed upon by the parties or fixed by the court.

Rule 43. Substitution of Parties

(a) Death of a Party. If a party dies after a notice of appeal is filed or while a proceeding is otherwise pending in the court of appeals, the personal representative of the deceased party may be substituted as a party on motion filed by the representative or by any party with the clerk of the court of appeals. The motion of a party shall be served upon the representative in accordance with the provisions of Rule 25. If the deceased party has no representative, any party may suggest the death on the record and proceedings shall then be had as the court of appeals may direct. If a party against whom an appeal may be taken dies after entry of a judgment or order in the district court but before a notice of appeal is filed, an appellant may proceed as if death had not occurred. After the notice of appeal is filed substitution shall be effected in the court of appeals in accordance with this subdivision. If a party entitled to appeal shall die before filing a notice of appeal, the notice of appeal may be filed by that party's personal representative, or, if there is no personal representative, by that party's attorney of record within the time prescribed by these rules. After the notice of appeal is filed substitution shall be effected in the court of appeals in accordance with this subdivision.

(b) Substitution for Other Causes. If substitution of a party in the court of appeals is necessary for any reason other than death, substitution shall be effected in accordance with the procedure prescribed in subdivision (a).

(c) Public Officers; Death or Separation From Office.

(1) When a public officer is a party to an appeal or other proceeding in the court of appeals in an official capacity and during its pendency dies, resigns or otherwise ceases to hold office, the action does not abate and the public officer's successor is automatically substituted as a party. Proceedings following the substitution shall be in the name of the substituted party, but any misnomer not affecting the substantial rights of the parties shall be disregarded. An order of substitution may be entered at any time, but the omission to enter such an order shall not affect the substitution.

(2) When a public officer is a party to an appeal or other proceeding in his official capacity the public officer may be described as a party by the public officer's official title rather than by name; but the court may require the public officer's name to be added.

Rule 44. Cases Involving Constitutional Questions Where United States Is Not a Party

It shall be the duty of a party who draws in question the constitutionality of any Act of Congress in any proceeding in a court of appeals to which the United States, or any agency thereof, or any officer or employee thereof, as such officer or employee, is not a party, upon the filing of the record, or as soon thereafter as the question is raised in the court of appeals, to give immediate notice in writing to the court of the existence of said question. The clerk shall thereupon certify such fact to the Attorney General.

Rule 45. Duties of Clerks

(a) General Provisions. The clerk of a court of appeals shall take the oath and give the bond required by law. Neither the clerk nor any deputy clerk shall practice as an attorney or counselor in any court while continuing in office. The court of appeals shall be deemed always open for the purpose of filing any proper paper, of issuing and returning process and of making motions and orders. The office of the clerk with the clerk or a deputy in attendance shall be open during business hours on all days except Saturdays, Sundays, and legal holidays, but a court may provide by local rule or order that the office of its clerk shall be open for specified hours on Saturdays or on particular legal holidays other than New Year's Day, Birthday of Martin Luther King, Jr., Washington's Birthday, Memorial Day, Independence Day, Labor Day, Columbus Day, Veterans Day, Thanksgiving Day and Christmas Day.

(b) The Docket; Calendar; Other Records Required. The clerk shall maintain a docket, in such form and style as may be prescribed by the Director of the Administrative Office of the United States Courts. The clerk shall enter a record of all papers filed with the clerk and all process, orders and judgments. An index of cases contained in the docket shall be maintained as prescribed by the Director of the Administrative Office of the United States Courts.

The clerk shall prepare, under the direction of the court, a calendar of cases awaiting argument. In placing cases on the calendar for argument, the clerk shall give preference to appeals in criminal cases and to appeals and other proceedings entitled to preference by law.

The clerk shall keep such other books and records as may be required from time to time by the Director of the Administrative Office of the United States Courts with the approval of the Judicial Conference of the United States, or as may be required by the court.

(c) Notice of Orders or Judgments. Immediately upon the entry of an order or judgment the clerk shall serve a notice of entry by mail upon each party to the proceeding together with a copy of any opinion respecting the order or judgment, and shall make a note in the docket of the mailing. Service on a party represented by counsel shall be made on counsel.

(d) Custody of Records and Papers. The clerk shall have custody of the records and papers of the court. The clerk shall not permit any original record or paper to be taken from the clerk's custody except as authorized by the orders or instructions of the court. Original papers transmitted as the record on appeal or review shall upon disposition of the case be returned to the court or agency from which they were received. The clerk shall preserve copies of briefs and appendices and other printed papers filed.

Rule 46. Attorneys

(a) Admission to the Bar of a Court of Appeals; Eligibility; Procedure for Admission. An attorney who has been admitted to practice before the Supreme Court of the United States, or the highest court of a state, or another United States court of appeals, or a United States district court (including the district courts for the Canal Zone, Guam and the Virgin Islands), and who is of good moral and professional character, is eligible for admission to the bar of a court of appeals.

An applicant shall file with the clerk of the court of appeals, on a form approved by the court and furnished by the clerk, an application for admission containing the applicant's personal statement showing his eligibility for membership. At the foot of the application the applicant shall take and subscribe to the following oath or affirmation:

I, ..., do solemnly swear (or affirm) that I will demean myself as an attorney and counselor of this court, uprightly and according to law; and that I will support the Constitution of the United States.

Thereafter, upon written or oral motion of a member of the bar of the court, the court will act upon the application. An applicant may be admitted by oral motion in open court, but it is not necessary that the applicant appear before the court for the purpose of being admitted, unless the court shall otherwise order. An applicant shall upon admission pay to the clerk the fee prescribed by rule or order of the court.

(b) Suspension or Disbarment. When it is shown to the court that any member of its bar has been suspended or disbarred from practice in any other court of record, or has been guilty of conduct unbecoming a member of the bar of the court, the member will be subject to suspension or disbarment by the court. The member shall be afforded an opportunity to show good cause, within such time as the court shall prescribe, why the member should not be suspended or disbarred. Upon the member's response to the rule to show cause, and after hearing, if requested, or upon expiration of the time prescribed for a response if no response is made, the court shall enter an appropriate order.

(c) Disciplinary Power of the Court Over Attorneys. A court a appeals may, after reasonable notice and an opportunity to show cause to the contrary, and after hearing, if requested, take any appropriate disciplinary action against any attorney who practices before it for conduct unbecoming a member of the bar or for failure to comply with these rules or any rule of the court.

Rule 47. Rules by Courts of Appeals *

Each court of appeals by action of a majority of the circuit judges in regular active service may from time to time make and amend rules governing its practice not inconsistent with these rules. In all cases not provided for by rule, the courts of appeals may regulate their practice in any manner not inconsistent with these rules. Copies of all rules made by a court of appeals shall upon their promulgation be furnished to the Administrative Office of the United States Courts.

* Proposed amendments to Rule 47 are found in Part X of this Supplement.

Rule 48. Masters

A court of appeals may appoint a special master to hold hearings, if necessary, and to make recommendations as to factual findings and disposition in matters ancillary to proceedings in the court. Unless the order referring a matter to a master specifies or limits the master's powers, a master shall have power to regulate all proceedings in every hearing before the master and to do all acts and take all measures necessary or proper for the efficient performance of the master's duties under the order including, but not limited to, requiring the production of evidence upon all matters embraced in the reference and putting witnesses and parties on oath and examining them. If the master is not a judge or court employee, the court shall determine the master's compensation and whether the cost will be charged to any of the parties.

(As amended Apr. 29, 1994, eff. Dec. 1, 1994.)

Part V

Selected Sample Court Orders and Notices for Controlling Discovery, Pretrial Conferences, and Settlement of Class Action

TABLE OF CONTENTS

	Page
Stipulation and Order Governing Discovery and the Protection and Exchange of Confidential Information	329
Pretrial Order Establishing Schedules for Completion of All Subsequent Steps in a Case	331
Final Pretrial Order	337
Notice of Settlement of Class Action With Proof of Claim Form	341

Stipulation and Order Governing Discovery and the Protection and Exchange of Confidential Information [1]

It is hereby stipulated and agreed by and between the undersigned parties to this action that the following restrictions and procedures shall apply to all documents, testimony, interrogatories, and other information produced, given or exchanged by any party or non-party in the course of pretrial discovery in this action (hereinafter collectively referred to as "Pre-trial Information").

1. All Pre-trial Information shall be treated and deemed as confidential and protected within the meaning of Chancery Court Rule 26(c). In addition to the foregoing, any party or non-party may designate any Pre-trial Information that reflects sensitive internal business or competitive information not relating to proposed transactions or negotiations between or among the parties as "Confidential—Attorneys Only."

2. Unless otherwise ordered by the Court in this proceeding, all Pre-trial Information will be held by the receiving party solely for use in connection with the above-captioned action.

3. Pre-trial Information shall not be disclosed to any person, except:

---

[1] Sussman & Sussman, "Confidentiality Agreements Help Protect Clients," Legal Times of New York, September 1984, p. 6, 36 (reproducing protective order entered in Pennzoil Co. v. Getty Oil Co., No. 7425 (Del. Ch. Jan. 24, 1984)).

SAMPLE COURT ORDERS & NOTICES

(a) outside counsel and to house counsel for the parties;

(b) employees of such counsel assigned to and necessary to assist such counsel in the preparation of this litigation;

(c) officers, directors, or employees of the parties, to the extent deemed necessary by counsel for the prosecution or defense of this litigation;

(d) consultants or experts, to the extent deemed necessary by counsel for the prosecution or defense of the litigation; and

(e) the Court.

4. Pre-trial Information designated "Confidential–Attorneys Only" shall not be disclosed to any person other than those persons included in paragraphs 3(a), 3(b) and 3(c) above.

5. Any person given access to Pre-trial Information pursuant to the terms hereof shall be advised that the documents, material or information are being disclosed pursuant to and subject to the terms of this Stipulation and Order and may not be disclosed other than pursuant to the terms hereof.

6. Pre-trial Information used in connection with any pleading, motion, hearing or trial or otherwise submitted to the Court shall be filed under seal.

7. Inadvertent production of any document or other information during discovery in this action shall be without prejudice to any claim that such material is privileged or protected from discovery as work product within the meaning of Chancery Court Rule 26, and no party shall be held to have waived any rights under Rule 26 by such inadvertent production. Any document or information so produced and subject to a claim of privilege or work product subsequently made shall immediately be returned to the producing party, or expunged, and, in either event, such document or information shall not be introduced into evidence in this or any other proceeding by any person without the consent of the producing party or by order of the Court, nor will such document or information be subject to production in any proceeding by virtue of the fact that it was inadvertently produced in this proceeding.

8. Nothing herein shall preclude any of the parties from, upon twenty-four (24) hours notice to the other parties, making application to the Court for an order modifying any of the terms hereof or contesting or seeking designation of any information as "Confidential—Attorneys Only."

9. The parties agree forthwith to submit this Stipulation and Order to the Court to be "So Ordered" and further agree that, prior to approval by the Court, this Stipulation and Order shall be effective as if approved and, specifically, that any violation of its terms shall be subject to the same sanctions and penalties, including those under Chancery

SAMPLE COURT ORDERS & NOTICES

Court Rule 37 as if this Stipulation and Order had been entered by the Court.

10. At the conclusion of the litigation, all Pre-trial Information and all copies thereof, and all documents designated "Confidential–Attorneys Only" and all copies thereof, shall be promptly returned to the producing parties or, at their written request, destroyed. The return or destruction of such documents shall be certified by the receiving persons.

11. This Stipulation and Order shall inure to the benefit of and be enforceable by non-parties with respect to information produced, given, or exchanged by them in the course of pre-trial discovery.

Pretrial Order Establishing Schedules for Completion of All Subsequent Steps in a Case

Part I. Second Wave and Completion of Discovery [2]

Part II. Designation of Deposition Evidence and Documents for Objections Thereto

Part III. Final Pretrial Briefs, Written Offers of Proof, Written Narrative Summaries of Expert Testimony, and Statements of Uncontroverted Facts

Part IV. Listing of Trial Witnesses

Part V. Filing of Proposed Voir Dire Questions

Part VI. Scheduling Final Pretrial Conference

Part VII. Setting Trial Date

A pretrial conference was held in the above-captioned cause on the _____ day of _____, 19__, wherein or as a result of which the following proceedings were had:

Part I. Second Wave and Completion of Discovery

A. The following interrogatories on behalf of plaintiffs were approved and ordered answered on or before the _____ day of _____, 19__ [list interrogatories].

B. The following requests for production of documents on behalf of plaintiffs were granted and the documents were ordered produced at [insert location] on or before the _____ day of _____, 19__ [list motions approved].

C. Depositions on behalf of plaintiffs of the following persons, at the places and times designated, were approved:

---

[2] Pretrial Order, except for Part VII, taken from "Manual for Complex Litigation," Fifth Edition, For Use With Federal Practice and Procedure by Charles Alan Wright and Arthur R. Miller (West Publishing Co.).

SAMPLE COURT ORDERS & NOTICES

Witness	Company	Location	Date
_____	_____	_____	____
_____	_____	_____	____
_____	_____	_____	____

D. The following interrogatories on behalf of defendants were approved and ordered answered on or before the _____ day of _____, 19__ [list interrogatories].

E. The following requests for production of documents on behalf of defendants were granted and the documents were ordered produced at [insert location] on or before the _____ day of _____, 19__ [list motions approved].

F. Depositions on behalf of defendants of the following persons, at the places and times designated, were approved:

Witness	Company	Location	Date
_____	_____	_____	____
_____	_____	_____	____
_____	_____	_____	____

G. Except as may hereafter be ordered by the Court for good cause shown and in the interest of the just determination of this cause, no discovery in addition to the discovery heretofore ordered shall be taken in this cause.

Part II. Designation of Deposition Testimony, Documents, and Objections Thereto

H. On or before the _____ day of _____, 19__, plaintiffs shall designate those portions of deposition testimony that plaintiffs desire to offer in evidence at the trial.

I. On or before the _____ day of _____, 19__, defendants (1) shall designate the parts of the depositions designated by plaintiffs that defendants seek to require plaintiffs to introduce under Federal Rule of Civil Procedure 32(a)(4), and (2) shall designate such portions of depositions as defendants desire to offer in evidence at the trial.

J. On or before the _____ day of _____, 19__, plaintiffs (1) shall designate the part of the depositions designated by defendants that plaintiffs seek to require defendants to introduce under Federal Rule of Civil Procedure 32(a)(4), and (2) shall counter-designate such portions of the depositions designated by defendants as plaintiffs desire to offer in evidence at the trial.

K. On or before the _____ day of _____, 19__, plaintiffs shall designate those documents they desire to introduce at trial and shall provide each defendant with a copy of each such document.

L. On or before the _____ day of _____, 19__, defendants shall designate those documents they desire to introduce at trial and shall provide each plaintiff with a copy of each such document.

SAMPLE COURT ORDERS & NOTICES

M. On or before the _____ day of _____, 19__, plaintiffs and defendants shall file all objections to designated deposition testimony and exhibits.

Part III. Final Pretrial Briefs, Written Offers of Proof, Written Narrative Summaries of Expert Testimony, and Statements of Uncontroverted Facts

N.[3] Plaintiffs and defendants shall each file two detailed, written pretrial briefs constructed as hereinafter provided. The first such brief shall be filed by the plaintiffs on or before the _____ day of _____, 19__, and shall relate to the claims for relief by plaintiffs against defendants. The second such brief shall be filed by the defendants on or before the _____ day of _____, 19__, and shall relate to the defenses, including affirmative defenses, of the defendants to plaintiffs' claims for relief, and, in a separate section, to the defendants' claims for relief on their counterclaims herein. The third such brief shall be filed by the plaintiffs on or before the _____ day of _____, 19__, and shall relate to plaintiffs' reply to the affirmative matter in the defenses of defendants to plaintiffs' claims for relief, and to plaintiffs' defenses, including affirmative defenses, to defendants' counterclaims for relief. The fourth such brief shall be filed by the defendants on or before the _____ day of _____, 19__, and shall relate to the reply of the defendants to any affirmative matter in the defenses of plaintiffs to the counterclaims of defendants.

Each of the four briefs required to be filed as hereinafter provided shall consist of (1) a detailed narrative statement of the facts proposed to be proved by the party filing the brief, and (2) concise statements of legal contentions of the party filing the brief in support of any affirmative matter contained in the brief and in response to legal contentions made by the adverse party in the next preceding brief. In sections of the pretrial brief there shall be a narrative statement or statement of facts and statements of legal contentions. Neither shall be commingled with the other, and they shall be in the following form:

(1) In support of each claim for relief, whether contained in the complaint or the counterclaim, the party or parties asserting the claim for relief shall set forth in simple declarative sentences, separately numbered, the narration of all facts relied upon in support of the claim or claims for relief herein. Each narrative statement of facts shall be in a separate section and shall be complete in itself and shall contain no recitation of what any witness testified to, or what the adverse party or parties stated or admitted in these or other proceedings, and no reference to the pleadings or other documents or schedules as such; provid-

---

[3] This paragraph of Part III is based upon a pretrial order entered by Chief Judge William H. Becker on June 21, 1967, in Johnson v. Tri-State Motor Transit Co., Civil Action No. 15974-3 (W.D.Mo.), in which both a complaint and a counterclaim were filed.

SAMPLE COURT ORDERS & NOTICES

ed, however, that at the option of a party or parties, any narrative statement of facts may contain references in parentheses to the names of witnesses, depositions, pleadings, exhibits, or other documents, but no party or parties shall be required to admit or deny the accuracy of such references. No narrative statement of facts shall, so far as possible, contain any color words, labels, or legal conclusions; and in no event shall any color word, label, or legal conclusion be commingled with any statement of fact in any sentence or paragraph. Each narrative statement of facts shall be constructed, to the best of the ability of plaintiffs' counsel, so that the opposite party will be able to admit or deny each separate sentence of the statement of facts. Each separate sentence of the statement of facts shall be separately and consecutively numbered.

(2) In each separate section of the pretrial brief containing the statement of legal contentions and authorities in support thereof, all legal contentions and authorities in support of the claim or claims for relief that are the subject for the foregoing narrative statement of facts, necessary to demonstrate the liability of the adverse party or parties to the party or parties filing the brief, shall be separately, clearly, and concisely stated in separately numbered paragraphs. Each such paragraph shall be followed by a citation of authorities in support thereof without quotations therefrom.

(3) The party or parties filing a pretrial brief in defense of a claim or claims for relief shall set forth in a separate section, in separate simple declarative sentences, factual statements admitting or denying each separate sentence contained in the narrative statement of facts of the adverse party in support of its claim for relief, except in instances where a portion of a sentence can be admitted and a portion denied. In those instances the brief shall state clearly the portion of the sentence admitted and the portion denied. Each separate sentence of a brief in response to a narrative statement of facts in support of a claim for relief shall bear the same number as the corresponding sentence in the narrative statement of facts in support of the claim for relief. In a separate portion of the narrative fact statement in response to a narrative fact brief in support of a claim for relief, the responding party shall set forth in a separate narrative statement all affirmative matters of a factual nature relied upon by it in defense (in whole or in part) against the claim or claims for relief. This separate narrative statement of affirmative matters shall be contained in a narrative statement of facts constructed in the same manner as hereinabove provided for a narrative statement of facts in support of a claim for relief.

SAMPLE COURT ORDERS & NOTICES

(4) In response to a brief in support of a claim for relief, the party or parties responding shall, in a separate section of the pretrial brief, set forth a statement of legal contentions and authorities in defense (in whole or in part) against the claim for relief to which the response is made. In this separate section the party or parties shall set forth its legal contentions and authorities in support thereof, directly responding to the legal contentions of the adverse party in support of the claim for relief, and shall separately set forth such additional contentions of the party or parties as may be necessary to demonstrate the nonliability (in whole or in part) of the party or parties filing the brief or briefs. The statement of legal contentions in a brief responding to a brief in support of a claim for relief shall be constructed in the same manner as provided in subparagraph (2) hereinabove for the statement of legal contentions of a party or parties in support of a claim for relief.

(5) Within _____ days after the service of defendant's pretrial brief containing statements of affirmative matter, the plaintiff shall file a reply pretrial brief containing factual statements admitting or denying each separate sentence of the separate narrative statement of affirmative matters of the defendant. This portion of the plaintiff's reply brief shall be constructed in the same manner provided in subparagraph (3) above for defendant's factual statements responding to plaintiff's narrative statement of facts, and shall be in a separate portion of the reply brief.

(6) Within _____ days after the service of defendant's statement of additional legal contentions and authorities in support thereof, plaintiff shall file, in a separate part of its reply brief, its separate statement of additional legal contentions and authorities in support thereof, which shall directly respond to the additional legal contentions of defendant. The statement of legal contentions and authorities in support thereof shall be constructed in the same manner provided in subparagraph (4) above for defendant's pretrial brief, and shall be in a separate portion of the reply brief.

(7) Any factual contention, any legal contention, any claim for relief or defense (in whole or in part), or any affirmative matter not set forth in detail as provided hereinabove shall be deemed abandoned, uncontroverted, or withdrawn in future proceedings, notwithstanding the contents of any pleadings or other papers on file herein, except for factual contentions, legal contentions, claims for relief or defenses thereto, and affirmative matters of which a party may not be aware and could not be aware in the exercise of reasonable diligence at the time of filing the briefs hereinabove provided for. Any matters of which a party was not

aware at the time of filing and of which he could not have been aware in the exercise of diligence at the time of the filing of a brief may be supplemented by a supplemental brief by leave of Court for good cause shown on timely motion therefor.

O. On or before the _____ day of _____, 19__, each plaintiff and each defendant herein shall serve and file written offers of proof on the following issues: (list)

P. On or before the _____ day of _____, 19__, each plaintiff and each defendant herein shall serve and file written narrative summaries setting forth in detail the testimony of each expert whom the party so filing will employ at trial, including a complete listing of all documents, data, and authorities studied by each such expert.

Q. On or before the _____ day of _____, 19__, the parties shall confer and attempt to agree on a joint statement of those factual issues that are without substantial controversy, and agree upon forms of statements of factual issues that are controverted. If the parties are unable to agree upon the uncontroverted factual issues or upon the forms of statements of the controverted factual issues, each party shall separately prepare on or before the _____ day of _____, 19__, a proposed statement thereof.

Part IV. Listing of Trial Witnesses

R. On or before the _____ day of _____, 19__, each plaintiff shall identify each witness it intends to call at trial in its case in chief and state whether such witness will appear in person or by deposition.

S. On or before the _____ day of _____, 19__, each defendant shall identify each witness it intends to call at trial in its case in chief and state whether such witness will appear in person or by deposition.

Part V. Filing of Proposed Voir Dire Questions

T. On or before the _____ day of _____, 19__, all parties shall file in writing (1) proposed topics for questions for voir dire examination of the jury, and (2) separate written requests for instructions to the jury and for special interrogatories. On each request for an instruction to the jury, there shall be noted the source of authorities from which it is derived or on which it is based.

Part VI. Scheduling Final Pretrial Conference

U. A final pretrial conference is set for the _____ day of _____, 19__, beginning at the hour of _____ o'clock, __.m.

V. At the pretrial conference set in paragraph U, final trial plans will be developed and, among other things, the following matters will be considered:

(1) The then undetermined issues of fact and law will be delineated and, to the extent feasible, simplified;

SAMPLE COURT ORDERS & NOTICES

(2) The reception in evidence of documentary matters not precluded by stipulation of fact, subject to such objections, if any, as may be reserved for the trial;

(3) The identity and scope of testimony of witnesses to be called at time of trial and their possible limitation will be considered;

(4) An agreement upon a trial schedule;

(5) The handling of documentary evidence;

(6) Authentication of documents;

(7) Witness lists;

(8) Spokesmen;

(9) Examination of witnesses;

(10) Use of written narrative statements of expert witnesses;

(11) Use of depositions, including the possible use of narrative summaries or verbatim extracts;

(12) Final pretrial briefs filed pursuant to this pretrial order;

(13) Limitation of opening statements;

(14) Current index of the record;

(15) Daily transcripts;

(16) Instructions;

(17) Separation of issues;

(18) Use of and mechanics for special jury verdict, or general verdict with interrogatories;

(19) Possibility of settlement.

Part VII. Setting Trial Date

W. Trial of the above-captioned case shall begin on the _____ day of _____, 19__, at _____ o'clock, __.m.

Dated this _____ day of _____, 19__.

_____
JUDGE

Final Pretrial Order [4]

A final pretrial conference was held in this cause on the _____ day of _____, 19__, wherein the following proceedings were had:

---

[4] Taken from "Manual for Complex Litigation," Fifth Edition, For Use With Federal Practice and Procedure by Charles Alan Wright and Arthur R. Miller (West Publishing Co.). This order is based on a final pretrial order developed by Judge George H. Boldt for use in Public Utility District No. 2 v. General Elec. Co., Civil Action No. 5380 (W.D.Wash.).

SAMPLE COURT ORDERS & NOTICES

A. The following counsel were present representing the plaintiffs: (list).

B. The following counsel were present representing the defendants: (list).

C. The following issues of fact and law were framed, and the following witnesses who may be called at trial and exhibits that may be offered at trial were identified (list):

 (1) Jurisdiction and venue
 (2) Admitted facts
 (3) Plaintiffs' contentions on disputed facts
 (4) Defendants' contentions on disputed facts
 (5) Plaintiffs' contentions on the principal issues of law
 (6) Defendants' contentions on the principal issues of law
 (7) Plaintiffs' exhibits

Exhibit No.	Identification (Description)

 (8) Defendants' exhibits

Exhibit No.	Identification (Description)

 (9) Plaintiffs' witness list

Name	Live or Deposition Testimony

 (10) Defendants' witness list

Name	Live or Deposition Testimony

D. Trial in this cause shall commence on the _____ day of _____, 19__. Court sessions will be held from _____ o'clock a.m. to _____ o'clock p.m. on _____.

 (1) Plaintiffs shall, to the extent possible, present separately the evidence regarding each issue following the order set forth below: (list).

 (2) When plaintiffs' case is completed, defendants shall, to the extent possible, present separately the evidence regarding each issue following the order set forth below: (list).

 (3) Each defendant shall present its evidence in the order in which defendants are named in the caption of this case.

SAMPLE COURT ORDERS & NOTICES

(4) When defendants' case is completed, plaintiffs shall present their rebuttal evidence.

(5) None of the provisions herein shall require witnesses to make multiple appearances to maintain the order of presentation set forth above.

(6) The Court will not receive evidence relating to the period prior to _____ or subsequent to _____.

(7) _____, of counsel for plaintiffs, and _____, of counsel for defendants, are designated to represent all counsel of the parties as liaison counsel to receive notifications and act as spokesmen for co-counsel.

(8) Each motion by any defendant (or any plaintiff) on each objection shall be considered as made by each defendant (or plaintiff) in the same manner and to the same extent as though made separately by each such party, unless otherwise stated.

(9) Unless otherwise authorized by the Court, only one counsel for each party shall examine any witness. Counsel for the respective defendants shall attempt to designate one of their number to handle the cross-examination of any witness. Cross-examination of witnesses shall follow the direct examination, unless otherwise authorized by the Court.

(10) Plaintiffs' opening statements shall be limited to _____. Defendants' opening statements shall be limited to _____. Plaintiffs' and defendants' counsel respectively shall agree on the division of time. If necessary, the Court will make the division.

(11) Daily transcript shall be delivered after adjournment of the Court each day. Corrections shall be suggested at the opening of Court on the second following morning.

(12) (Jury Case) A jury of twelve jurors and _____ alternates shall be selected. Each plaintiff is permitted _____ peremptory challenges. Each defendant is permitted _____ peremptory challenges. The voir dire examination initially shall be conducted on the basis of the following questions:

(Questions (a)–(o) to be asked of the entire panel as a group.)

    (a) This trial in all probability will be a lengthy one. While it is not possible to make a precise estimate, it may last as long as _____ months or more. Is there any reason why you cannot serve as a juror for that duration? What is it?

    (b) Are you or any of your immediate family (spouse, children, parents, or brothers and sisters) or have you or any of your immediate family ever been employed by or represented any of the following: (list plaintiffs)?

SAMPLE COURT ORDERS & NOTICES

(c) Are you or are any of your immediate family (spouse, children, parents, or brothers and sisters) or have you or any of your immediate family ever been employed by or represented any of the following: (list defendants)?

(d) Are you or any of your immediate family stockholders or holders of any other securities or obligations, or have you or any of your immediate family ever been stockholders or holders of any other securities or obligations, of any of the above companies?

(e) Do you or any of your immediate family have any business connections or dealings, or have you or any of your immediate family ever had any business connections or dealings, with any of the above companies? (If so, elicit details.)

(f) Have you or any of your immediate family or any organization you have been associated with ever had any dispute or unpleasantness with any of the above-named companies? If so, was it resolved to your satisfaction?

(g) Do you know any lawyers who are or ever have been associated with any of the following firms: (list)?

(h) Do you have any relatives or friends who are lawyers? (If so, elicit details.)

(i) Have you ever worked for a lawyer or law firm? (If so, elicit details.)

(j) Have you ever served on a federal jury in the past year?

(k) Have you or any of your immediate family ever been involved in a lawsuit as a plaintiff or a defendant? (If so, elicit details.)

(l) Has any one among you ever heard or read anything concerning any proceeding in this cause?

(m) Have you ever discussed this case with anyone?

(n) Would the fact that the defendant (or defendants) in a prior federal criminal proceeding entered a plea of guilty make it difficult or impossible for you to find for the defendants if the evidence shows that plaintiffs were not injured?

(o) Have you formed or expressed an opinion who should prevail in this controversy?

(Questions (p)–(u) to be asked of each juror individually.)

(p) What is your name?

(q) What is your home address?

(r) Are you married? If so: (a) How many children do you have? How old are they? What are the occupations of each

SAMPLE COURT ORDERS & NOTICES

of your adult children, and by whom are they employed? What is the occupation of your spouse? Who is his (her) employer?

(s) Who is your employer?

(t) Briefly describe the work you do.

(u) How long have you been with your present employer? (a) (If less than 10 years:) Would you describe what jobs you have had since 19__?

It is hereby so ORDERED.

Dated this _____ day of _____, 19__.

_____
JUDGE

Notice of Settlement of Class Action With Proof of Claim Form [5]

NOTICE OF CLASS ACTION DETERMINATION AND SETTLEMENT HEARING TO PURCHASERS OF THE FOLLOWING SECURITIES OF THE SINGER COMPANY BETWEEN JANUARY 20, 1973 AND DECEMBER 29, 1975 (INCLUSIVE): (i) SINGER'S COMMON STOCK, PAR VALUE $10 PER SHARE, (ii) SINGER'S $3.50 CUMULATIVE PREFERRED STOCK, STATED VALUE $13 PER SHARE AND (iii) SINGER'S 8% SINKING FUND DEBENTURES DUE JANUARY 15, 1999

AND

PROOF OF CLAIM
UNITED STATES DISTRICT COURT FOR THE DISTRICT
OF NEW JERSEY

THIS NOTICE IS GIVEN pursuant to Rule 23 of the Federal Rules of Civil Procedure and pursuant to an Order of the United States District Court for the District of New Jersey (hereinafter sometimes called the "Court") entered November 14, 1978, to all persons who, during the period from January 20, 1973 through December 29, 1975 purchased (i) shares of Common Stock, par value $10 per share of The Singer Company (hereinafter called the "Company"), or (ii) shares of the Company's $3.50 Cumulative Preferred Stock, stated value $13 per share, or (iii) any of the Company's 8% Sinking Fund Debentures due January 15, 1999 (hereinafter sometimes called the "Class Securities"). Such persons who are not employees of the Company purchasing their

---

[5] Taken from "Manual for Complex Litigation," Fifth Edition, For Use With Federal Practice and Procedure, by Charles Alan Wright and Arthur R. Miller (West Publishing Co.). This notice and proof of claim form were used by the Honorable Stanley S. Brotman in Bullock v. Kircher, Civil Action No. 76–1173 (D.N.J.), and published in the *Wall Street Journal* (Jan. 8, 1979).

shares pursuant to a stock option plan, stock purchase plan or executive incentive plan sponsored or adopted by the Company, and who are not individual defendants in the action or a spouse, child, parent, brother or sister of such defendants, are herein collectively called the "Class."

NATURE OF THE ACTION

The above action entitled Thomas Bullock v. Donald P. Kircher, et al., asserts a claim on behalf of the Class against the Company and certain of its officers and directors. The consolidated complaint, which is brought under the provisions of the Securities Exchange Act of 1934 and Rule 10b–5 adopted by the Securities and Exchange Commission thereunder, alleges, *inter alia*, that the defendants conspired to and did cause certain of the Company's financial statements and other publicly disseminated information to contain material untrue statements and omissions concerning the assets and net worth of the Company and the Company's business generally. Damages are sought on behalf of the members of the Class.

FURTHER PROCEEDINGS

The defendants have filed answers denying, and continue to deny, any liability or any wrongdoing whatever in connection with claims in the action and have asserted various defenses. The Court has not yet passed on the merits of the claims or of any defenses thereto. The giving of this notice is not meant to imply that there has been any violation of the law, or that a recovery after a trial could be had if the action is not settled. Following the joinder of issues in the action, the attorneys for plaintiff engaged in extensive pre-trial discovery, including the review and analysis of tens of thousands of documents produced by defendants and third parties and the taking of in excess of twenty depositions. On the basis of their detailed investigation of the facts and the law relating to the issues involved in this action, they have concluded that the proposed settlement described below is fair to the members of the Class.

THE CLASS

The Court has ruled that the action may, pursuant to Rule 23 of the Federal Rules of Civil Procedure, proceed and be maintained as a class action on behalf of all persons who purchased any of the Class Securities described in the first paragraph of this Notice during the period January 20, 1973 through December 29, 1975.

If you purchased shares of the Company's Common Stock or $3.50 Cumulative Preferred Stock or any of the Company's 8% Sinking Fund Debentures due January 15, 1999 during the period January 20, 1973 through December 29, 1975 and are not related to or affiliated with any of the defendants, and are not an employee of the Company who purchased securities through a plan sponsored or adopted by the Company, you are a member of the Class. Any Class member may, however,

SAMPLE COURT ORDERS & NOTICES

request the Court to exclude him from the Class, provided that such request is made in writing, postmarked on or before March 15, 1979, addressed to:

> Singer Settlement Administration Committee
> c/o Heffler & Company
> P.O. Box 30
> Philadelphia, Pennsylvania 19105

setting forth the name and number of this case (Bullock v. Kircher, Civ. 76–1173); your name and present address; the number of shares, and/or amount of debentures, included in the Class Securities which were purchased by you between January 20, 1973 and December 29, 1975, inclusive; the date(s) of purchase; your address on the date of purchase if the Class Securities were registered in your own name; if the Class Securities were not so registered, the name and address on the date of purchase of the person who was the registered holder of such Class Securities on such date; and your request to be excluded from the Class (all joint owners must sign this request and provide such information). A Class member who has excluded himself from the Class in the manner above specified will not share in the benefits of any favorable judgment or settlement and will not be affected by the proposed settlement described below or bound by any adverse judgment which may be rendered. Any judgment, whether or not favorable to the members of the Class, will include all Class members who have not requested exclusion, whether or not they join or intervene in the action. Any Class member who does not request exclusion may, if he desires, enter an appearance in the action through counsel of his own choice. If he does so, he may be responsible for the fees, costs and disbursements resulting therefrom or relating thereto. Any Class member who does not request exclusion and who does not enter an appearance through his own counsel will be represented by Mssrs. Barrack, Rodos & McMahon, 2000 Market Street, Philadelphia, Pennsylvania 19103, counsel for plaintiff Thomas Bullock in this action.

THE PROPOSED SETTLEMENT

An agreement of settlement has been reached in the action between counsel for the plaintiff and counsel for the defendants, which is embodied in a Stipulation and Agreement of Compromise and Settlement dated November 10, 1978 (the "Settlement Agreement") on file with the Court. As noted above, the attorneys for plaintiff, on the basis of an extensive investigation of the facts and the law relating to the matters complained of, have concluded that the proposed settlement is fair to, and in the best interests of, the Class. While defendants deny all charges of wrongdoing and do not concede liability, they desire to settle the action on the basis proposed in order to put to rest all further controversy, and to avoid substantial expenses and the inconvenience and distraction of burdensome and protracted litigation. The following

SAMPLE COURT ORDERS & NOTICES

description of the proposed settlement is a summary only, and reference is made to the text of the Settlement Agreement for a full statement of the provisions thereof:

1. The Company has established a Settlement Fund of $4,400,000 which has been invested in interest bearing obligations. Such interest will, if the settlement is approved by the Court, inure to the benefit of the Class.

2. The Company has established an Administration Fund of $175,000.

3. The Administration Fund will be used to pay the costs of administering the settlement provided for in the Settlement Agreement, including costs of compiling lists of holders of Class Securities, costs of identifying through informal requests or judicial proceedings beneficial owners of Class Securities, expenses of publishing and mailing notices of the settlement and hearings thereon, and the fees and disbursements of accountants and disbursing agents retained to administer claims of, and payments to, holders of Class Securities.

4. The Settlement Fund and all interest earned thereon will be distributed under the Court's direction and supervision, as follows: (i) in payment of all expenses in excess of $175,000 incurred in the administration of the settlement; (ii) to the extent approved by Order of the Court in payment of the fees, allowances and disbursements of counsel for plaintiff; (iii) the balance (the "Net Settlement Fund") to the members of the Class who file valid Proofs of Claim in accordance with the procedure set forth below in proportion to the Recognized Loss incurred by each such member.

5. *The Recognized Loss* of a member of the Class shall be measured as follows: the actual cost of all shares of the Company's Common Stock, par value $10 per share, and the actual cost of all shares of the Company's $3.50 Cumulative Preferred Stock, stated value $13 per share, and the actual cost of all of the Company's 8% Sinking Fund Debentures due January 15, 1999 purchased by him during the period from January 20, 1973 through December 29, 1975 less the total of: (i) the actual sales price received for such shares or debentures sold on or prior to October 16, 1978, and (ii) as to any such shares or debentures still held after October 16, 1978, (a) the number of such shares of Common Stock multiplied by $18.375 (the closing price for such Common Stock of the Company on October 16, 1978), (b) the number of such shares of Cumulative Preferred Stock multiplied by $35.50 (the closing price for such Cumulative Preferred Stock of the Company on October 16, 1978), and (c) the number of $1,000 multiples of such Sinking Fund Debentures multiplied by $852.50 (the closing price for each $1,000 of such Sinking Fund Debentures on October 16, 1978). The terms "actual cost" and "actual sales price" shall be deemed to include brokerage commissions, stock transfer taxes and other miscellaneous charges (ex-

SAMPLE COURT ORDERS & NOTICES

cepting accrued interest) usually incurred in connection with a purchase or sale. The date of purchase or sale shall be the "contract" or "trade" date, as distinguished from the "settlement" date. Any member of the Class who acquired shares of such Common Stock or shares of such Cumulative Preferred Stock or any such Sinking Fund Debentures by gift or bequest or operation of law shall assume the actual cost of his transferor for the purpose of this paragraph.

6. Any Class member who excludes himself from the Class by following the procedure described above shall not be entitled to any distribution from the Net Settlement Fund.

7. If the proposed settlement is approved by the Court, there will be a dismissal on the merits of all claims, demands and causes of action, without limitation and whether or not heretofore asserted, which plaintiff and each member of the Class (except those who exclude themselves from the Class as provided above) have or may have, or which have been or might have been asserted on their behalf, against the defendants, or any of them, or which have been or might have been asserted against the officers, directors, employees, agents, attorneys, and representatives of the Company and/or the individual defendants, or any of them, in connection with or arising out of any of the matters, transactions and occurrences recited, described or referred to in the pleadings and proceedings herein, and with prejudice to all members of the Class except those Class members who exclude themselves from the Class as provided above.

8. By filing a Proof of Claim, a member of the Class will thereby submit himself to the jurisdiction of the Court, and each Proof of Claim shall be subject to investigation and discovery if deemed necessary by the Settlement Administration Committee pursuant to the Federal Rules of Civil Procedure.

9. Plaintiff or defendants may withdraw from the Settlement Agreement under certain circumstances described in the Settlement Agreement, in which event the Settlement Fund and all interest thereon and the Administration Fund and all interest therein, less any amounts incurred for administering the settlement, shall be returned to the Company.

NOTICE TO BROKERS AND OTHER NOMINEES

The Court has directed each brokerage house, bank and other institutional nominee which purchased Class Securities to forward a copy of the Notice and Proof of Claim to all persons who were the beneficial owners of any Class Securities purchased in your record name during the period January 20, 1973 through January 15, 1976. Adequate quantities of the Notice and Proof of Claim will be mailed to you by the Settlement Administration Committee upon your request.

SAMPLE COURT ORDERS & NOTICES

ATTORNEYS' FEES AND COSTS

Messrs. Barrack, Rodos & McMahon, attorneys for plaintiff Thomas Bullock, and other associated plaintiff's counsel, will apply to the Court, at the hearing described below, for an award of counsel fees not to exceed 25% of the total of the Settlement Fund and the Administration Fund and all interest earned on those funds, plus litigation expenses and disbursements actually incurred. Such award as may be granted by the Court will be paid from the Settlement Fund.

THE HEARING

Pursuant to an order of the Court filed November 14, 1978, a hearing will be held before The Honorable Stanley S. Brotman, or Magistrate Stephen M. Oriofsky to whom this matter may be referred, United States Court House, Fourth and Market Streets, Camden, New Jersey 08101 at 10 a.m. on April 9, 1979 for the purpose of determining whether the proposed settlement is fair, reasonable and adequate and whether it should be approved by the Court and the action dismissed on the merits and with prejudice as provided above and for the purpose of considering plaintiff's counsel's application for fees, allowances and disbursements. The hearing may be adjourned from time to time by the Court at the hearing or at any adjourned session thereof without further notice.

Any member of the Class who has not requested exclusion therefrom may appear at the hearing and show cause, if any he has, why the proposed settlement should not be approved and the action should not be dismissed on the merits and with prejudice and/or present any opposition to the application of plaintiff's counsel for fees, allowances and disbursements, provided that no such person shall be heard, except by special permission of the Court, unless his objection or opposition is made in writing and is filed together with copies of all other papers and briefs to be submitted by him to the Court at the hearing with the Court on or before March 15, 1979, and showing due proof of service on Barrack, Rodos & McMahon, 2000 Market Street, Philadelphia, Pennsylvania 19103; Riker, Danzig, Scherer, Debevoise & Hyland, 744 Broad Street, Newark, New Jersey 07102; and Pitney, Hardin & Kipp, 163 Madison Avenue, Morristown, New Jersey 07960. Any member of the Class who does not make his objection in the manner provided above shall be deemed to have waived such objection and shall be forever foreclosed from making any objection to the fairness or adequacy of the proposed settlement or to the request of plaintiff's counsel for fees, allowances and disbursements.

EXAMINATION OF PAPERS AND INQUIRIES

For a more detailed statement of the matters involved in the above-entitled action, reference is made to the pleadings, to the Stipulation and Agreement of Compromise and Settlement, and to the other papers filed in this action, all of which may be inspected at the Office of the Clerk of

SAMPLE COURT ORDERS & NOTICES

the United States District Court for the District of New Jersey, Fourth and Market Streets, Camden, New Jersey 08101, during the hours of each business day.

The Court has appointed a settlement administration committee consisting of Leonard Barrack, Dickinson R. Debevoise and William D. Hardin. Any contact by members of the Class should be with the Committee through the office of Heffler & Company, P.O. Box 30, Philadelphia, Pennsylvania 19105 (Tel. 215-665-8870). No inquiry should be directed to the Clerk of the Court or to Judge Stanley S. Brotman.

PROOF OF CLAIM

1. TO RECEIVE ANY PAYMENTS FROM THIS SETTLEMENT, YOU MUST SIGN AND HAVE NOTARIZED THE ATTACHED PROOF OF CLAIM FORM, AND SUBMIT PROPER DOCUMENTATION SUPPORTING YOUR CLAIM.

2. Distribution of the proceeds of any settlement or of any judgment is subject to Court Approval.

3. You must file your completed and signed Proof of Claim on or before March 15, 1979 addressed as follows:

> Singer Settlement Administration Committee
> c/o Heffler & Company
> P.O. Box 30
> Philadelphia, Pennsylvania 19105
> Tel. 215-665-8870

Your Proof of Claim form shall be deemed to have been filed when posted, if mailed by registered or certified mail, postage prepaid, addressed in accordance with the instructions given therein. A Proof of Claim filed otherwise shall be deemed to be filed at the time it is actually received by the person or office designated to receive it in the Proof of Claim.

4. The claim must be filed in the name, or names, of the actual beneficial owner, or owners, of the securities upon which the claim is based. All joint owners must sign this Proof of Claim. Executors, administrators, guardians, and trustees may complete and sign the form on behalf of persons represented by them, but must identify the beneficial owners. Proof of their authority need not accompany the Proof of Claim but their titles or capacities must be stated.

5. You must list all acquisitions of any Class Securities on or after January 20, 1973 through December 29, 1975 and all dispositions of any Class Securities at any time.

6. If you acquired any Class Securities by gift, inheritance or operation of law, you are to report them as if you acquired them at the actual cost of your transferor.

SAMPLE COURT ORDERS & NOTICES

7. Brokerage commissions, stock transfer taxes or other miscellaneous charges (excepting accrued interest) usually incurred in connection with either a purchase or a sale of the Class Securities shall be included in the cost and the sales price of such Class Securities.

8. Your Proof of Claim must be under oath, and must be accompanied by the documents called for therein.

Dated this _____ day of _____, _____.

_____
JUDGE

THIS ENTIRE FORM (OTHER THAN SIGNATURES)
MUST BE TYPED OR PRINTED

UNITED STATES DISTRICT COURT
FOR THE DISTRICT OF NEW JERSEY

THOMAS BULLOCK, on behalf of himself and all others similarly situated,

Plaintiff,

vs.

DONALD P. KIRCHER, JOSEPH B. FLAVIN, GILBERT W. FITZHUGH, ARTHUR H. FREDSTON, EDWIN J. GRAF, WILLIAM G. HAMILTON, JR., LLOYD L. KELLEY, IAN K. MacGREGOR, JAMES W. McKEE, JR., DONALD E. MEADS, WILLIAM H. MORTON, DONALD G. ROBBINS, JR., ARTHUR J. SANTRY, JR., F. WAYNE VALLEY, THE SINGER COMPANY,

Defendants.

Herein designated as the "Claimant"

The undersigned, being duly sworn, deposes and says that the following is true, correct and complete to the best of his knowledge, information and belief.

I. IDENTITY OF CLAIMANT:
    A. Claimant's name,* mailing address and telephone number are as follows:

---

* If stock or debentures are held jointly, give the names of all persons interested in the stock or debentures.

SAMPLE COURT ORDERS & NOTICES

  B. Claimant is (check one)—
  _____ An Individual
  _____ Two or more persons holding stock or debentures jointly
  _____ Partnership
  _____ Corporation
  _____ Executor or Administrator
  _____ Trustee
  _____ Other (specify)_____

II. STATEMENT OF CLAIM:

  A. Claimant (or person from whom Claimant acquired shares by gifts or inheritance, or deceased person for whom Claimant is acting as executor or administrator) made the following purchases of (i) Common Stock of The Singer Company, par value $10 per share, (ii) $3.50 Cumulative Preferred Stock of The Singer Company, stated value $13 per share and (iii) The Singer Company's 8% Sinking Fund Debentures due January 15, 1999, during the period January 20, 1973 through December 29, 1975. *Claimant has included information as to all such purchases made during such period.*

Number of shares and amount of debentures purchased (list each type of security separately)	Date of purchase (trade date)	Price for the purchases, shares or debentures (including commissions)

	Type of Security		
Name in which shares or debentures registered	Common	Preferred	Debenture

  B. Claimant sold the following (i) Common Stock of The Singer Company, par value $10 per share, (ii) $3.50 Cumulative Preferred Stock of The Singer Company, stated value $13 per share and (iii) The Singer Company's 8% Sinking Fund Debentures due January 15, 1999, referred to Paragraph II A above. *Claimant has included information with respect to all such sales, and such shares and debentures are still held by the Claimant to the extent that their sale is not listed below.*

Number of shares and amount of debentures sold (list each type of security separately)	Date of sale (trade date)	Price for the sold shares or debentures (including commissions and expenses)

	Type of Security		
Name in which shares or debentures registered at time of sale	Common	Preferred	Debenture

SAMPLE COURT ORDERS & NOTICES

III. ADDITIONAL PROOF REQUIRED:

CLAIMANT MUST ANNEX TO THIS PROOF OF CLAIM COPIES OF BROKER'S CONFIRMATION, MONTHLY ACCOUNT STATEMENTS, DELIVERY RECEIPTS, OR OTHER DOCUMENTATION ESTABLISHING EVIDENCE OF ALL PURCHASES AND SALES INCLUDED IN PARAGRAPH II OF THIS PROOF OF CLAIM.

IV. THE FOLLOWING PARAGRAPHS APPLY TO ALL CLAIMANTS:

A. By the filing of this Proof of Claim, Claimant hereby submits to the jurisdiction of the United States District Court for the District of New Jersey.

B. Claimant understands that the information contained in this Proof of Claim is subject to investigation and discovery pursuant to the Federal Rules of Civil Procedure and that Claimant may be required to furnish additional information to support this Proof of Claim.

C. Claimant hereby certifies that neither he (it) nor any purchaser of shares or debentures of The Singer Company which are the subject of this Proof of Claim was (i) an employee of The Singer Company who purchased his shares pursuant to a stock option plan, stock purchase plan or executive incentive plan sponsored or adopted by Singer, or (ii) an individual defendant in this action, or (iii) a spouse, child, parent, brother, sister, officer, director, partner, or controlling person of any named defendant or a subsidiary or affiliate of a named defendant, or (iv) an underwriter, purchasing for its own beneficial account, with respect to any of the securities which are the subject of this Proof of Claim.

D. By the filing of this Proof of Claim, and in consideration of the right to participate in the distribution of the Settlement Fund, Claimant hereby waives and releases all claims and demands which he (it) may have against any defendant in the Action, or against the officers, directors, employees, agents, attorneys and representatives of any of such defendants, or against any other person or business entity, arising from or related to the matters complained of in the above-entitled action or the consummation of the terms of the Stipulation and Agreement of Compromise and Settlement entered into in said action.

Sworn to before me this _____ day of 19__.	Signed _____ (Name(s)—all registered joint owners must sign)
Notary Public	(Address)

THIS PROOF OF CLAIM MUST BE FILED NO LATER THAN MARCH 15, 19__ AND MUST BE MAILED TO:

SAMPLE COURT ORDERS & NOTICES

Singer Settlement Administration Committee
c/o Heffler & Company
P.O. Box 30
Philadelphia, Pennsylvania 19105 **

1.45 Additional Sample Sections That May Be Used in Settlement Notices

In addition to the sections contained in the sample notices of settlement set out above, the Court may desire to use one or more of the following sections:

(a) Section on reasons for settlement [6]

REASONS FOR SETTLEMENT: Defendants disclaim any liability and any wrongdoing of any kind whatsoever and have denied the allegations in both actions and have asserted defenses that they believe are meritorious, but they consider it desirable that this action and the claims alleged therein be settled upon the terms and conditions set forth in the Settlement Agreement, in order to avoid further expenses, and burdensome, protracted litigation, and to put at rest all claims that have been or might be asserted by any member of either class arising from the subject matter of the complaints herein. The proposed settlements and this Notice are not to be construed as admissions of liability of any kind whatsoever by any of the defendants.

Counsel for plaintiffs and the classes represented by them have thoroughly investigated the facts and circumstances underlying the issues raised by the pleadings herein and the law applicable thereto, have conducted extensive discovery, and have concluded that, taking into account the risks involved in establishing, in whole or in part, a right to recovery on behalf of the named plaintiffs and the classes they represent against the defendants and the likelihood that this litigation will be further protracted and expensive, it would be in the best interests of the named plaintiffs and the classes they represent to settle these actions upon the terms and conditions set forth in the Settlement Agreement and that such terms are fair, adequate, and reasonable.

Once again, the Court has not expressed any opinion concerning the merits of the claims or defenses herein.

(b) Section on effect of failure to file proof of claim form [7]

If you do not exclude yourself and also do not file a valid Claim Form, you will be included in the Class, but you will not receive any

---

** A Proof of Claim shall be deemed to have been filed when posted, if mailed by registered or certified mail, postage prepaid. A Proof of Claim filed otherwise shall be deemed to be filed at the time it is actually received by the Singer Settlement Administration Committee at the address set forth above.

[6] From an order used in Weisberg v. APL Corp., Civil Action No. 74-C-1794 (E.D.N.Y.).

[7] From an order used in Friedman v. Zale Corp., Civil Action No. 3-77-0850-C (N.D.Tex.).

SAMPLE COURT ORDERS & NOTICES

portion of the Net Settlement Fund, and you will be bound by the Final Judgment in this Litigation, the Settlement Stipulation, and the releases therein, and you will be barred from any further assertion of released and settled claims. To receive a portion of the Settlement Fund you must file a Claim Form in a proper manner and mail it so that it is received on or before _____ _____, 19__.

(c) Section on effect of failure to file proof of claim form and filing objections to settlement [8]

TO ALL PERSONS WHO PURCHASED COMMON STOCK OF GIANT STORES CORP. DURING THE PERIOD APRIL 16, 1971 THROUGH AND INCLUDING MAY 23, 1973.

PLEASE TAKE NOTICE that a hearing will be held on May 9, 1979 at 9:30 a. m. before the Honorable Charles M. Metzner, Judge of the United States District Court for the Southern District of New York, at the United States Courthouse, Foley Square, New York, New York in Room 519. The purpose of the hearing is to determine whether the two proposed settlements of the above-entitled Consolidated Class Action for sums aggregating $4,750,000, which will constitute the entire recovery to the class members, pursuant to two Stipulations of Settlement, should be approved by the Court as fair, reasonable, and adequate, and to consider the application of plaintiffs for the award of counsel fees and expenses. If you have not excluded yourself from the class, you may be entitled to share in the distribution of the settlement fund. TO SHARE IN THE DISTRIBUTION OF THE SETTLEMENT FUND, YOU MUST FILE A PROOF OF CLAIM ON OR BEFORE JUNE 15, 1979, establishing that you purchased common stock of Giant Stores Corp. during the period April 16, 1971 through and including May 23, 1973.

Objections to the settlement or the award of counsel fees, expenses, and disbursements must be filed no later than April 27, 1979 as provided in the detailed notice referred to below.

A more detailed notice describing the proposed settlements of this consolidated class action, the fees and expenses requested, the hearing thereon, and the requirement that a proof of claim be filed, has been mailed to all persons appearing on the transfer records of Giant Stores Corp. as record purchasers during the period April 16, 1971 through and including May 23, 1973. If you have not received a copy of that notice, *you may obtain one and a Proof of Claim form by making a written request to* Clerk of the Court, P.O. Box 1220, General Post Office, New York, New York 10001.

Re: Giant Stores Corp., *or* Attorneys for Plaintiffs,

One Pennsylvania Plaza, New York, New York 10001

Attention: Jared Specthrie, Esq.

---

[8] From an order used in Goldberg v. Touche Ross & Co., Civil Action No. 74 Civ. 1483 (S.D.N.Y.).

Part VI

Illustrative Litigation Problem *with* Sample Documents

Introduction

The purpose of the illustrative problem is three-fold: to give a general picture of the flow of litigation; to present a series of sample documents in the context of a factual setting; and, finally, to demonstrate how specific procedural matters may arise during the course of an actual case. The problem is broken into four sections: Jurisdiction, Pleadings, Pretrial Discovery and Motions, and Trial, Verdict, and Attacks on Verdict. Each section contains a number of questions to focus attention on the problems raised.

Stage I. Jurisdiction

Plaintiff Thomas A_____, filed an action in a state court. His complaint read as follows:

IN THE SUPERIOR COURT, DELTA COUNTY, STATE OF ARVADA

Thomas A_____,
   Plaintiff
   vs.
Reginald B_____, Daniel C_____, and D_____ Corporation,
   Defendants

Civil P 15163
COMPLAINT

COUNT ONE

I

On or about June 1, 1992, plaintiff Thomas A_____ was involved in a motor vehicle collision with an automobile driven by defendant Reginald B_____ and with a bulldozer operated by defendant Daniel C_____ who was acting within the scope of his employment with defendant D_____ Corporation. The collision occurred on Public Highway 10 in the state of Arvada, approximately twenty miles east of the City of Diego.

ILLUSTRATIVE LITIGATION PROBLEM

II

Defendants and each of them have informed plaintiff that they suffered injuries to persons and property in a total amount of $100,000 and have demanded that plaintiff remit the amount of such damages or face institution of legal action against him for their recovery.

III

Defendants have informed plaintiff that their injuries are proximately due to the plaintiff's negligence in that at the time of the collision, plaintiff was operating his vehicle in excess of the speed limit.

IV

Plaintiff is an agent of the Federal Bureau of Investigation. At the time of the collision he was proceeding at a speed of 80 miles per hour along Public Highway 10 pursuant to orders, duly issued, to assist in the apprehension of escaped federal prisoners. Plaintiff's speed, although in excess of the state speed limit, was necessary in order for him to carry out his assigned duties.

WHEREFORE, Plaintiff prays for a declaration:

(1) That he was not negligent at the time of the collision.

(2) That he is immune from liability because his acts were required within the scope of his federal duties.

(3) Awarding him such other relief to which he is entitled.

James L. W_____
Attorney for Plaintiff

Question:

On the basis of facts stated in the complaint could plaintiff have maintained suit in a federal district court?

Plaintiff A_____ is a citizen of the State of Mindon, defendant B_____ is a citizen of the State of Arvada, defendant C_____ is a citizen of the State of Lamar, and the D_____ Corporation, which does considerable business in all three states is incorporated in Lamar where its equipment is housed and where all of its 2000 workmen reside. Its administrative offices, however, are located in Mindon, which is the residence of its 10 executive officers and 25 office workers.

ILLUSTRATIVE LITIGATION PROBLEM

Questions:

1. How does the information regarding the citizenship and activities of the parties affect the ability of plaintiff to bring his action in a federal court? In the federal court of Arvada?

2. Assuming that Arvada has enacted the broadest possible statutes permitting service of process on out-of-state residents, can the courts of Arvada constitutionally assert personal jurisdiction over all the defendants in this action by personally serving them where they reside? Is the extension of jurisdiction to cover such a case a wise policy?

After filing his action, but prior to attempting service of process, plaintiff's attorney called defendant C_____ at his house, informed him of the pending suit, and requested a meeting in Arvada in order to arrange a settlement. The attorney promised that C_____ would be paid a substantial sum but only if he tacitly agreed to take a job in another part of the country and to resist all efforts by his codefendants to induce him to testify against plaintiff. C_____ agreed to the meeting. Immediately upon his arrival in Arvada, however, he was greeted by a process server who handed him a summons to appear in plaintiff's action. (For a form summons see Federal Rules of Civil Procedure Form 1, in Part I, supra.) When C_____ arrived at the attorney's office, he was told by the secretary there that the scheduled meeting was canceled and would be rescheduled. C_____, justifiably angry, stormed out of the office to return home. Before leaving Arvada, however, he tarried long enough to look at 100 acres of unimproved real estate that was for sale. Several days after returning home, he purchased the property for $5,000 in a transaction handled through the mail.

Questions:

1. Is the service made on C_____ in Arvada sufficient to bring him before the state courts? What arguments might he make if he wishes to avoid being sued in Arvada?

2. May C_____'s purchase of the property in any way assist plaintiff in bringing his action against C_____?

ILLUSTRATIVE LITIGATION PROBLEM

The original complaint was served on all defendants on June 30, 1992. On July 31, 1992, prior to the filing of any response by defendants, and without leave of court, plaintiff filed a "First Amended Complaint" containing all the information in the original complaint and adding the following new counts:

COUNT TWO

I

Plaintiff incorporates herein the allegations contained in paragraphs I and IV of Count One.

II

Defendant C_____ negligently stopped the bulldozer along the side of Public Highway 10. As a direct and proximate result thereof, plaintiff was unable to avoid striking the vehicle driven by defendant B_____ which in turn caused plaintiff to strike the bulldozer.

III

As a direct and proximate result of defendant C_____'s negligence, plaintiff suffered severe physical injuries involving his head and right shoulder. Plaintiff has endured great pain and suffering and will have large hospital and doctor bills in an amount as yet unascertained.

WHEREFORE, Plaintiff prays for damages in the amount of $160,000 against defendant C_____ and such other relief to which plaintiff is entitled.

COUNT THREE

I

On July 15, 1992, plaintiff deposited the sum of $2,500 cash with the Efficiency Bank of Mindon as trustee, to deliver said sum to defendant B_____ upon his execution of a release form provided by plaintiff.

II

On July 17, 1992, the Efficiency Bank paid B_____ $2,500 cash. The Bank did not receive the executed form from defendant B_____ then or at any subsequent time.

WHEREFORE, Plaintiff prays that the court order defendant B_____ to execute such release form or in the alternative to hold the $2,500 as a constructive trustee for plaintiff or for any other relief to which plaintiff is entitled.

Attached to the amended complaint and labeled "Exhibit" was the following document:

ILLUSTRATIVE LITIGATION PROBLEM

RELEASE FORM

Whereas B_____ is alleging a claim for personal injury and property damage against A_____ arising from an automobile collision, and whereas both parties wish to avoid litigation,

B_____ hereby acknowledges receipt of $2,500 from A_____ and in consideration therefor, forever releases A_____ from any and all liability to B_____ arising from any cause whatsoever occurring on or before the date of this instrument.

_____   _____
Date   Signature

Question:

May defendants, or any one of them, when served with the amended complaint have the entire case removed to the federal court in Arvada?

Stage II. Pleadings

Five days after receiving the amended complaint, defendant B_____'s attorney filed the following document and sent a copy to each of the parties through their attorneys:

IN THE SUPERIOR COURT, DELTA COUNTY STATE OF ARVADA

Thomas A_____, Plaintiff	Civil P 15163
vs.	
Reginald B_____, Daniel C_____ and D_____ Corporation, Defendants	NOTICE OF MOTION TO STRIKE

To Thomas A_____, plaintiff, and to his attorneys, W_____ and B_____.

You and each of you will please take notice that on August 10, 1992, at the hour of 9:00 A.M. in the above entitled court, defendant Reginald B_____ will move to strike the First Amended Complaint. The motion is made on the ground that the said Amended Complaint was filed without leave of court as required by Rule 15 of the Arvada Rules of Civil Procedure.

In the alternative, defendant B_____ will move to strike Count Three of the First Amended Complaint on the ground that it is improp-

ILLUSTRATIVE LITIGATION PROBLEM

erly joined with Counts One and Two in violation of section 20 of the Arvada Civil Practice Act.

Louis F_____
Attorney for Defendant B_____

Attached to the motion was the following supporting document which is required of all motions to strike in Arvada courts:

STATEMENT OF POINTS AND AUTHORITIES SUPPORTING MOTION TO STRIKE

I

1. Rule 15(a) of the Arvada Rules of Civil Procedure provides that a complaint cannot be amended without leave of court "after defendant's answer has been filed."

2. This rule should logically be interpreted to prohibit amendment without leave of court if the normal time for answer has elapsed, whether or not such answer is filed.

3. Under Rule 12(a) of the Arvada Rules of Civil Procedure the time for answer is twenty days after service. Plaintiff's First Amended Complaint was filed on July 31, 1992, whereas the original complaint was served on June 30, 1992.

II

1. Section 20 of the Arvada Civil Practice Act permits joinder of causes all of which fall within one of the following classes:

   (1) Contracts, express or implied
   (2) Physical injury to person
   (3) Injury to property
   (4) Injury to character
   (5) Matters arising out of the same transactions or occurrences.

2. Count Three of plaintiff's First Amended Complaint does not appear in any of the statutory categories in which Counts One and Two appear.

Questions:

1. How likely is it that the court will grant the motion to strike the entire complaint? See Federal Rule 15(a) and the comparative state materials, supra.

2. What chance does defendant have on his motion to strike Count Three? See Federal Rule 18(a) and the comparative state materials, supra.

ILLUSTRATIVE LITIGATION PROBLEM

At the same time that he filed his notice of motion, defendant B_____'s attorney filed and served on all parties the following:

IN THE SUPERIOR COURT, DELTA COUNTY, STATE OF ARVADA

Thomas A_____,
              Plaintiff
    vs.
Reginald B_____, Daniel C_____
  and D_____ Corporation,
              Defendants

Civil P 15163

DEMURRER

Defendant B_____ demurs to the First Amended Complaint on file herein as follows:

I

Count One does not state facts sufficient to constitute a cause of action.

II

Count Three does not state facts sufficient to constitute a cause of action.

III

There is a defect of parties in plaintiff's Count Three.

IV

The court has no jurisdiction over the matters in Count Three because an Indispensable Party has not been joined.

                      Louis F_____
                      Attorney for Defendant B_____

Under Arvada rules, defendant need not set the date for the demurrer; instead the clerk of the court must notify all parties as to the time the hearing will be held.

Questions:

1. Assuming that this case, if properly pleaded, would justify declaratory relief under Arvada law, and further assuming that Arvada follows the classic rules of code pleading, what chance does defendant B_____ have on his challenge to the sufficiency of Counts One

ILLUSTRATIVE LITIGATION PROBLEM

and Three? What possible defects may he point to in arguing that the demurrer should be sustained? Would the result be different if the court was operating under the Federal Rules of Civil Procedure?

2. How successful will B_____ be regarding his challenges as to joinder of parties? Does anything turn on whether or not the Efficiency Bank is subject to personal jurisdiction in Arvada? See Federal Rule 19, supra.

After hearing arguments on both the motion to strike and the demurrer, the trial judge issued the following order, which was prepared at his direction by defendant B_____'s attorney:

IN THE SUPERIOR COURT, DELTA COUNTY STATE OF ARVADA

Thomas A_____,
                                Plaintiff
        vs.   Civil P 15163
Reginald B_____, Daniel C_____
  and D_____ Corporation,   ORDER
                                Defendants

The motion of defendant Reginald B_____ to strike the First Amended Complaint or in the alternative to strike parts therefrom and his demurrer to counts One and Three having come on regularly for hearing before the undersigned this 10th day of August, 1992, at the hour of 10 A.M., upon notice duly and regularly served and plaintiff Thomas A_____ appearing by his counsel James. L. W_____ and defendant Reginald B_____, appearing by his counsel, Louis F_____, and no appearance having been made on behalf of the other named defendants and the matter having been argued and submitted and good cause appearing therefore,

IT IS HEREBY ORDERED, AS FOLLOWS:

(1) That defendant's motion to strike be denied in all particulars.

(2) That defendant's demurrer to Count One be denied.

(3) That defendant's demurrer to Count Three be sustained on the ground that it fails to state facts constituting a cause of action.

(4) That the demurrer otherwise be denied in all particulars.

(5) That plaintiff has leave to file an amended complaint in ten days from the date hereof and that defendant is granted twenty days from the date hereof to file his Answer.

ILLUSTRATIVE LITIGATION PROBLEM

Dated: August 10, 1992

                             Learned W_____
                             Judge of the Superior Court

Questions:

1. What choices does plaintiff now have with regard to the Court's ruling on Count Three of his complaint? What will be the consequences of an amendment if he later wishes to claim that the trial court erred? If he fails to amend, will he be prohibited from bringing any new action against B_____ for the same damages?

2. What chance does plaintiff have to appeal immediately the ruling as to Count Three? If it is within the trial or appellate court's discretion to permit an amendment, should it be allowed?

On August 20, 1992, plaintiff filed a Second Amended Complaint changing only the allegations of Count Three as follows:

COUNT THREE

I

On July 15, 1992, plaintiff deposited the sum of $2,500 cash with the Efficiency Bank of Mindon. The money was held in trust to deliver said sum to defendant B_____ upon his execution of a specific release form provided by plaintiff. The release form is attached to this complaint as an "Exhibit" and is made a part hereof as if set forth in full herein.

II

On July 17, 1992, the Efficiency Bank paid the $2,500 held in trust to defendant B_____. The Bank did not receive the executed form from defendant B_____ then or at any subsequent time.

WHEREFORE, Plaintiff prays that the court order defendant B_____ to execute such release form or in the alternative to hold the $2,500 as a constructive trustee for plaintiff or for any other relief to which plaintiff is entitled.

Once again defendant B_____ demurred to the complaint on the ground that Count Three failed to state a cause of action. The demurrer was overruled.

ILLUSTRATIVE LITIGATION PROBLEM

Questions:

1. To what extent does this amendment cure any defects in the prior complaint?

2. What choices does B_____ have with regard to the court's ruling on Count Three? If he answers does he waive the defense that Count Three doesn't state a valid cause of action? What if he fails to answer? See Federal Rule 8(d).

3. What opportunity does B_____ have to appeal immediately the overruling of his demurrer to Count Three? Should a trial or appellate court in its discretion permit the appeal?

On August 22, 1992, defendant C_____ filed and served on all other parties the following Answer and Cross-Claim:

IN THE SUPERIOR COURT, DELTA COUNTY STATE OF ARVADA

Thomas A_____,
Plaintiff
vs.
Reginald B_____, Daniel C_____ and D_____ Corporation,
Defendants

Civil P 15163

ANSWER AND CROSS–CLAIM

Defendant Daniel C_____ Answers and alleges as follows:

I

Admits the allegations of paragraph I of Count One of plaintiff's complaint.

II

Admits the allegations of paragraphs II and III of Count One of plaintiff's complaint and alleges the truth of those facts in paragraph III of Count One of which plaintiff alleges defendant C_____ informed him and further alleges that defendant C_____ was severely injured, endured great pain and suffering and medical expenses, none of which can presently be ascertained with certainty but which will amount at a minimum to $25,000.

III

Admits so much of paragraph IV of Count One of plaintiff's complaint that alleges that plaintiff drove in excess of the state speed limit;

has no information as to plaintiff's employment at the time of the collision and on that ground denies the allegation relating to plaintiff's employment as an FBI agent; and denies that a speed of 80 miles per hour was required by defendant's duties or was in any way reasonable or non-negligent.

IV

Refuses to admit or deny each and every allegation of paragraph II of Count Two of plaintiff's complaint and demands that plaintiff be put to his proof.

V

Has no information or belief as to the allegations of paragraph III of Count Two of plaintiff's complaint, and on that ground denies the allegations of said paragraph III.

CROSS–CLAIM

Defendant C_____ as a Cross-Claim alleges as follows:

I

At the time of the collision which is the subject of plaintiff's action, defendant Daniel C_____ was stopping his bulldozer on the shoulder of Public Highway 10 in the State of Arvada, to assist defendant Reginald B_____ whose vehicle had stalled on the highway.

II

Defendant B_____ was instructing and directing defendant C_____ in parking the bulldozer in order that it would not be a hazard to vehicles approaching along the highway. Defendant C_____ followed such instructions as given by defendant B_____. C_____'s reliance on such instructions was reasonable.

III

Plaintiff in this action seeks damages from defendant C_____ on the grounds that said bulldozer was improperly stopped so as to create an unreasonable risk to passing traffic. The position of the bulldozer when stopped was the direct and proximate result of defendant B_____'s negligence in giving the aforesaid instructions.

WHEREFORE, Defendant C_____ prays as follows:

1. That plaintiff take nothing by his action.

2. That defendant B_____ be held liable to indemnify defendant C_____ for all amounts, if any, which defendant C_____ is ordered to pay plaintiff on the basis of his complaint herein.

3. That defendant C_____ be awarded such damages and other relief to which he is entitled.

Samuel R_____
Attorney for Defendant C_____

ILLUSTRATIVE LITIGATION PROBLEM

Questions:

1. Could plaintiff successfully move for a judgment on the pleadings against defendant C_____? What arguments does plaintiff have that all of the essential elements of his case have been admitted?

2. Suppose the case had been brought in a federal court and that B_____ had not been named as a codefendant by plaintiff. Could the cross-claim still have been maintained by defendant C_____? See Federal Rule 14. How would your answer be affected if the Arvada law, on the basis of the facts alleged, clearly prohibited C_____'s claim against B_____ for indemnity but permitted C_____ to recover damages for his own personal injuries from B_____? Could C_____ sue for such injuries on a cross-complaint? See Federal Rules 13(g) and (h).

Shortly after defendant C_____ filed his Answer and Cross-Claim, defendants B_____ and D_____ Corporation filed separate answers to Counts One and Two of plaintiff's complaint, asserting that the sole cause of the accident was plaintiff's negligence. Both B_____ and D_____ Corporation demanded, by way of counterclaim, payment for the damages they suffered. In addition defendant B_____ generally denied allegations in Count Three of the complaint.

B_____ then filed an answer to defendant C_____'s Cross-Claim as follows:

IN THE SUPERIOR COURT, DELTA COUNTY STATE OF ARVADA

Thomas A_____,	
Plaintiff	Civil P 15163
vs.	
Reginald B_____, Daniel C_____ and D_____ Corporation,	ANSWER TO CROSS-CLAIM
Defendants	

Defendant B_____ for an Answer to the Cross-Claim filed by Defendant C_____:

I

Denies each and every allegation therein stated.

ILLUSTRATIVE LITIGATION PROBLEM

II

Alleges that defendant C_____ was negligent in stopping the bulldozer and that said negligence was a direct and proximate cause of plaintiff's injuries.

WHEREFORE, Defendant B_____ prays that defendant C_____ take nothing from defendant B_____ on his cross-action.

Louis F_____
Attorney for Defendant B_____

Question:

Should any of the parties file further pleadings? To what extent are they permitted to do so? See Federal Rule 7(a) and the accompanying state materials, supra.

Stage III. Pretrial Discovery and Motions

On September 1, 1992, defendant B_____ filed and served on all parties the following document:

IN THE SUPERIOR COURT, DELTA COUNTY STATE OF ARVADA

Thomas A_____, Plaintiff vs. Reginald B_____, Daniel C_____ and D_____ Corporation, Defendants	Civil P 15163 NOTICE OF MOTION

To plaintiff Thomas A_____ and his attorney, James L. W_____:

You are hereby notified that on September 6, 1992, at the hour of 10 A.M. in the courtroom of the above entitled court, defendant Reginald B_____ will move this court for an order directing plaintiff to submit to a physical examination by Dr. William M_____, whose office is at 420 D_____ Avenue, in the City of Diego, State of Arvada. The purpose of the examination is to determine the state of plaintiff's mental health at the time of the collision described in the Complaint herein. The motion is based upon Rule 35 of the Arvada Rules of Civil Procedure. The examination is necessary to determine whether plaintiff was mentally capable of safely operating a motor vehicle at a speed of 80 miles per hour; whether he was aware of his ability or inability to do so; and whether he is capable of truthful testimony. The motion is made upon the affidavit of Louis F_____, Attorney for defendant Reginald

ILLUSTRATIVE LITIGATION PROBLEM

B_____, and upon evidence, oral and documentary, to be presented at the hearing of this motion.

                                        Louis F_____
                                        Attorney for Defendant B_____

AFFIDAVIT

STATE OF ARVADA   ⎫
                        ⎬ ss.   Civil P 15163
COUNTY OF DELTA ⎭

Louis F_____, being first duly sworn, states that he is attorney for defendant Reginald B_____ herein and is familiar with the issues to be tried.

In this action plaintiff seeks a declaration that he was not negligent in operating a vehicle although he was traveling at a high rate of speed in excess of the state speed laws. The ability of an individual to control a motor vehicle at high speeds depends upon his individual psychological make-up which determines his reaction time. Defendant is without expert information as to these matters regarding plaintiff.

Plaintiff further alleges that his speeding was reasonable. This will in part depend on whether plaintiff knew he created an unreasonable risk by driving much faster than was necessary under the circumstances. Defendant B_____ can ascertain such knowledge on the part of plaintiff only through an examination by an expert.

The undersigned is informed and believes that plaintiff will testify during trial on his own behalf. Defendant B_____ is unable without the examination here requested, to obtain evidence as to whether plaintiff is a pathological liar or is otherwise psychologically unable or unlikely to tell the truth.

Dr. M_____ is a practicing clinical psychologist, with a Ph.D. degree from Midwestern University. He is licensed to practice under the laws of the State of Arvada and has been practicing in the State for the past 12 years and enjoys an excellent reputation in his field.

                                                        Louis F_____

Subscribed and sworn to before me this First day of September, 1992

    [*Signed*] Rita N_____   [*Notary Seal*
    Notary Public In and For the   *of the State*
    State of Arvada, Delta County   *of Arvada*]

ILLUSTRATIVE LITIGATION PROBLEM

Questions:

How likely is the court to grant the motion? Assuming that Federal Rule 35 is applicable, what arguments could be made by A_____ to avoid such examination?

Defendant B_____'s attorney subsequently learned that the lawyer for defendant D_____ Corporation has done considerable investigation of every aspect of the case. B_____'s attorney therefore sent the following interrogatories to D_____ Corporation (Assume that Arvada has not as yet adopted amended Federal Rule 26(a) requiring automatic disclosure of potential witnesses.):

IN THE SUPERIOR COURT, DELTA COUNTY STATE OF ARVADA

Thomas A_____,
             Plaintiff
       vs.   Civil P 15163
Reginald B_____, Daniel C_____
  and D_____ Corporation,   INTERROGATORIES
            Defendants

To D_____ Corporation:

Please take notice that the following interrogatories are submitted pursuant to Rule 33 of the Arvada Rules of Civil Procedure; answers are required by said Rule 33 within 30 days of the receipt hereof:

1. What are the names and addresses of persons, if any, other than the named parties to this action, whom you are aware witnessed the activities of plaintiff and defendant C_____ just prior to, at the time of, and immediately subsequent to the collision which is the subject of plaintiff's action?

2. What are the names and addresses of those persons, if any, other than the parties named in this action, whom you are aware witnessed the activities of defendant B_____ just prior to, at the time of, and immediately subsequent to the collision which is the subject of plaintiff's action and defendant C_____'s counterclaim?

3. What information concerning the events in this action has D_____ Corporation or its attorneys voluntarily turned over to defendant C_____ or his attorneys?

4. What is the nature of the conspiracy, if any, between defendant C_____ and defendant D_____ Corporation or their attorneys regarding a concerted effort to avoid liability by placing all blame for the accident on plaintiff and defendant B_____?

ILLUSTRATIVE LITIGATION PROBLEM

5. It is true that two days after the collision defendant C_____ told an investigating attorney for D_____ Corporation that the only instruction given by him by B_____ just prior to the accident was "Get the hell off of the road!"?

6. What is the substance of the reports of any experts hired by defendant D_____ Corporation regarding the speed and exact location of the vehicles involved in the accident just prior to and at the time of the collision?

7. What are the names and addresses of any experts referred to in Interrogatory 6 above?

                                      Louis F_____
                                      Attorney for Defendant B_____

D_____ Corporation responded to these interrogatories as follows:

IN THE SUPERIOR COURT, DELTA COUNTY STATE OF ARVADA

Thomas A_____, Plaintiff vs. Reginald B_____, Daniel C_____ and D_____ Corporation, Defendants	Civil P 15163 OBJECTIONS TO INTERROGATORIES

To defendant Reginald B_____ and Louis F_____, his attorney:

Please take notice that defendant D_____ Corporation, objects to the interrogatories which were served by you on September 1, 1992, and said defendant will on September 6, 1992, at the hour of 10 A.M. in the above entitled Court, move for an order striking said interrogatories for the following reasons:

1. Interrogatories may not be served by one defendant on a codefendant in an action.

2. Interrogatory Number 2 is irrelevant as to matters between D_____ Corporation and B_____.

3. Interrogatories Numbers 3, 4, 5, 6 and 7 request information within the work-product privilege.

                                      Paul Y_____
                                      Attorney for Defendant
                                      D_____ Corporation

Question:

Assume that the Arvada discovery rules are the same as the federal discovery rules. What are defendant

ILLUSTRATIVE LITIGATION PROBLEM

D_____ Corporation's chances on its motion? See Federal Rule 33(a) and the accompanying Notes, supra.

On September 10, 1992, defendant B_____ moved for summary judgment on the cross-claim filed by defendant C_____. The motion was supported by an affidavit of one William G_____, which read as follows:

AFFIDAVIT

STATE OF ARVADA } ss.   Civil P 15163
COUNTY OF DELTA

William G_____, being first duly sworn deposes and says:

That on June 1, 1992, he was a passenger in a vehicle driven by Reginald B_____; that said vehicle was involved in a collision on Public Highway 10, East of the City of Diego; that just prior to the collision, the vehicle driven by B_____ was required to stop on the highway because the pavement was blocked by a bulldozer crossing over the road; that B_____ had shouted a few words to the bulldozer operator; that said operator had shouted back and waved his fist in an angry manner; that B_____ had then said, "I told him to get the hell out of the middle of the road"; that thereupon another vehicle approaching from the opposite direction at a high rate of speed struck the bulldozer and careened into the car driven by B_____.

William G_____

Subscribed and sworn to before me this First day of September, 1992

[Signed] Rita N_____   [Notary Seal
Notary Public In and For the   of the State of
State of Arvada, Delta County   Arvada]

Defendant C_____ filed no answering affidavits; at the hearing his attorney argued that the affidavit was insufficient to justify summary judgment, that the failure of B_____ to file his own affidavit was in itself sufficient reason to deny the motion, and that C_____'s pleadings clearly contradicted the statements in the affidavit. The court took the matter under advisement and one week later signed an order granting the motion in favor of B_____.

ILLUSTRATIVE LITIGATION PROBLEM

Questions:

Was the decision of the trial judge appropriate? Should it be reversed on appeal?

The filing of G_____'s affidavit was the first notice to defendant D_____ Corporation that he had been a witness to the collision. The Corporation's attorney sent copies of the following document to all other parties:

IN THE SUPERIOR COURT, DELTA COUNTY STATE OF ARVADA

Thomas A_____, Plaintiff vs. Reginald B_____, Daniel C_____ and D_____ Corporation, Defendants	Civil P 15163 NOTICE OF TIME AND PLACE OF DEPOSITION

To Thomas A_____, plaintiff, and to James W_____, his Attorney; to Reginald B_____, defendant and Louis F_____, his Attorney; to Daniel C_____, defendant, and Samuel R_____, his Attorney:

YOU AND EACH OF YOU will please take notice that on September 17, 1992, at the hour of 9 a.m., at the office of Irma W_____, Notary Public, whose address is 13 W_____ Drive, City of Diego, State of Arvada, defendant D_____ Corporation will take the deposition of William G_____, whose address is 280 F_____ Street, City of Diego, State of Arvada, upon oral examination before the above named Irma W_____, Notary Public said deposition to continue from day to day until completed.

Paul Y_____
Attorney for Defendant
D_____ Corporation

The following document was prepared by D_____ Corporation's attorney for service on William G_____:

IN THE SUPERIOR COURT, DELTA COUNTY STATE OF ARVADA

Thomas A_____, Plaintiff vs. Reginald B_____, Daniel C_____ and D_____ Corporation, Defendants	Civil P 15163 SUBPOENA

ILLUSTRATIVE LITIGATION PROBLEM

The People of the State of Arvada to

William G_____

280 F_____ Street

Diego, Arvada

GREETING:

You are commanded to appear and attend proceedings of the above entitled Court to be held on September 17, 1992, at the hour of 9 A.M. at the office of Irma W_____, Notary Public, whose address is 13 W_____ Drive, City of Diego, State of Arvada, then and there to give testimony on deposition as a witness produced by defendant D_____ Corporation in said action now pending in said Court.

And you are advised that disobedience of said subpoena may be punished as a contempt by the above entitled Court and for such disobedience you will also forfeit to any party or parties aggrieved thereby the sum of all damages suffered due to your failure so to attend.

September 13, 1992

                                      Angus B_____
                                           (Clerk)

                                    By Solomon D_____
                                          (Deputy Clerk)

Questions:

Is it necessary to subpoena every witness for deposition? Is it wise to do so? See Federal Rule 30(g)(2).

Stage IV. Trial, Verdict, and Attacks on Verdict

After all of the parties engaged in and completed their discovery and defendants B_____ and C_____ submitted voluntarily to physical examinations by plaintiff's doctor, defendant B_____ filed the following document on October 12, 1992:

Thomas A_____,
                                  Plaintiff

vs.

Reginald B_____, Daniel C_____ and D_____ Corporation,
                                  Defendant

Civil P 15163
MEMORANDUM TO SET FOR TRIAL AND DEMAND FOR JURY TRIAL

ILLUSTRATIVE LITIGATION PROBLEM

The Court is requested to set the above entitled case for trial. Jury is hereby demanded on all factual issues.

I hereby represent to the Court that this cause is at issue; that all affirmative pleadings have been answered; that to my knowledge no new parties will be served with summons prior to time of trial, and I know of no further pleading to be filed and know of no reason why the cause should not be tried as soon as the calendar of the Court will permit. I certify that the party filing this memorandum has completed all discovery proceedings.

October 12, 1992

Louis F_____
Attorney for Defendant B_____

Plaintiff then filed a special memorandum taking the position that a jury trial was not appropriate on the issued involved in Count Three of his complaint. The trial court, on October 18, 1992, issued an order setting the case for trial by jury on January 20, 1993. The order specified that jury trial was denied as to the issues contained in Count Three.

Questions:

If the case had been brought in a federal court would the Constitutional right to trial by jury extend to the issues in Count Three? Would the demand for jury trial have been adequate?

At the trial testimony was given by A_____, B_____, C_____ and their medical experts, the highway patrolmen who arrived at the scene shortly after the accident, and G_____. The evidence, in addition to bearing on the question of which of the parties was at fault and the purported settlement agreement between A_____ and B_____, showed that all three participants, A_____, B_____, and C_____ had suffered serious personal injuries and that both the bulldozer and B_____'s car had been badly damaged. In addition, on cross-examination, A_____'s attorney adduced the following testimony from one of the highway patrolmen who had been called as a witness by C_____'s attorney:

Q. Now you say that plaintiff's car struck the bulldozer head-on?

ILLUSTRATIVE LITIGATION PROBLEM

A. Yes.

Q. Are you certain that the car didn't hit the side of the bulldozer which was projecting out toward the roadway?

A. I don't think it did.

Q. How do you know?

A. Well, plaintiff's car appeared to have struck something head-on; the impact was directly in front. I looked at the wreck.

Q. Did you see evidence of a second impact?

A. No.

Q. You mean to say that you disagree with the testimony of every participant in the collision that plaintiff's car hit the bulldozer and bounced into the automobile driven by B_____?

A. I guess so. The car was in awful shape. Really too bad. It was a brand new model. I have one just like it myself. Worth $13,800. Total wreck.

Court: Just answer the questions please.

Q. Then you really couldn't tell where the initial impact was?

A. I guess not.

After all parties had rested and the final arguments were about to begin, defendant B_____ requested that the court reopen the case to take additional testimony from witnesses on a "new" point. On the promise that the new presentation would take no more than one hour, the court granted permission, subject to a motion to strike if the evidence was unfair to any of the other parties. B_____'s attorney first called to the stand the owner of the largest construction company in Arvada who testified that the custom of every local construction company was to plant flares to warn approaching traffic when a piece of heavy equipment was crossing the road. Then three people testified. Each was the driver of a vehicle that had preceded plaintiff's car by a few minutes on Highway 10 on the day of the accident. Each remembered passing the site where the accident subsequently took place. They remembered seeing a huge bulldozer as it was moving along the road. The testimony of witness H_____ is typical.

Q. As you approached the area where the bulldozer was located did you see a warning flare?

A. No. Not that I recall. I don't remember seeing it.

Cross-examination by C_____'s attorney.

Q. How far had you driven?

A. 200 miles.

Q. Had you passed other construction sites?

ILLUSTRATIVE LITIGATION PROBLEM

A. Sure.

Q. Did you see flares there?

A. I may have. I guess I did.

Q. Were you looking to see if flares were or were not present at construction sites?

A. No, of course not. If a flare was present, I'd slow down.

Q. Was there anything unusual about the construction site in question here?

A. No.

Q. How much farther did you drive after you passed the site?

A. About 150 miles.

Q. When did you realize that an accident occurred there shortly after you passed?

A. Not until a few days ago when one of the lawyers here tracked us down. I'll never know how he did it!

After this evidence was presented, defendant C_____'s attorney moved to strike on the ground that it raised a new issue regarding the use of flares, that he was unable, because of such short notice, to "scour the countryside" for other witnesses to rebut the testimony given, and that since none of the parties had mentioned the seeing of or the setting of flares in their testimony, the new evidence was all improper. He rejected the judge's offer to grant a two-day continuance on the ground that it would be "futile."

The trial court denied the motion. Each of the parties then made final arguments, and moved for directed verdicts, which were denied; and the court then gave its instructions. The instructions on negligence, causation, and respondeat superior were general in form but correct, and no specific instructions were requested. After instructing on how to compute damages the court added the following as Instruction 46:

Ladies and gentlemen of the jury. You will be given a number of verdict forms. One asks whether or not plaintiff should collect from defendant C_____, and if so how much. Another does the same regarding defendant D_____ Corporation. Then you have three other forms asking whether any of the three defendants should collect on counterclaims against plaintiff. You must answer each of these. If you find liability, there is a place where you set down the amount of damages. You are required to decide how much is for personal injury and how much for property damage. These forms are to aid you in making a proper verdict; you may write additional information on them as you wish.

ILLUSTRATIVE LITIGATION PROBLEM

Defendant C⎯⎯⎯ objected to the instruction insofar as it permitted plaintiff to collect damages for his vehicle on the ground that such damages had never been pleaded or proved. Plaintiff objected to that part of the instruction permitting defendant C⎯⎯⎯ to collect any damages whatsoever against plaintiff on the ground that defendant C⎯⎯⎯ had failed to file a counterclaim therefor.

Defendant B⎯⎯⎯ objected on the ground that the court should have left to the jury those issues involved in Count Three of plaintiff's complaint.

The Court denied the objections of C⎯⎯⎯ and B⎯⎯⎯, but granted plaintiff's motion and ordered the jury to find that in no event would plaintiff A⎯⎯⎯ be liable to Defendant C⎯⎯⎯.

While the jury was debating the court said: "I find for plaintiff on Count Three of his complaint. However, the equitable relief sought by plaintiff is totally inappropriate. There is clearly an adequate remedy at law. Defendant B⎯⎯⎯ never intended to sign a release of liability. Therefore I find that defendant B⎯⎯⎯ has been unjustly enriched by the amount of $2,500 and I hereby award plaintiff that sum against defendant B⎯⎯⎯."

The jury then returned with its verdict. It found for plaintiff on all points, awarding $150,000 for physical injuries and $13,800 for property damage against C⎯⎯⎯ and D⎯⎯⎯ Corporation. The jury foreman wrote on the verdict sheet, "We find defendant C⎯⎯⎯ negligent because of his failure to set out warning flares. Since defendant C⎯⎯⎯ was operating within the scope of his employment with D⎯⎯⎯ Corporation, we find against D⎯⎯⎯ Corporation too. Everybody else seemed reasonable to us."

Defendant C⎯⎯⎯ then filed the following motion:

IN THE SUPERIOR COURT, DELTA COUNTY STATE OF ARVADA

Thomas A⎯⎯⎯, Plaintiff vs. Reginald B⎯⎯⎯, Daniel C⎯⎯⎯ and D⎯⎯⎯ Corporation, Defendants	}	Civil P 15163 NOTICE OF MOTION FOR JUDGMENT N.O.V. AND FOR NEW TRIAL

To plaintiff A⎯⎯⎯, and his Attorney James W⎯⎯⎯:

YOU AND EACH OF YOU ARE NOTIFIED that on the 30th day of January, 1993, at the hour of 10 A.M. in the above entitled Court, defendant Daniel C⎯⎯⎯ will move for an order for judgment notwith-

ILLUSTRATIVE LITIGATION PROBLEM

standing the verdict on Counts One and Two of the Complaint, and if the same be denied, for a new trial. In addition defendant C_____ will move for a new trial for the purposes of collecting damages for his injuries as alleged in his Answer and Cross-Claim. Said motions are based on the insufficiency of the evidence to sustain or legally justify a ruling that defendant was negligent on the ground specified by the jury in its special verdict, that it was error for the court at the end of trial to admit and not to strike the evidence pertaining to the use of flares, that it was error to instruct the jury that plaintiff could collect damages for his vehicle, and that the Court erred in instructing the jury that defendant C_____ failed to state a valid claim for damages against plaintiff.

> Samuel R._____
> Attorney for Defendant C_____

Defendant B_____ filed his own motion for new trial as to Count Three on the ground that he was denied his constitutional right to a trial by jury.

Defendant D_____ Corporation filed a motion to dismiss the action for failure of the complaint to state a cause of action for collection of damages against the corporation. In the alternative it requested a new trial on the same ground.

All of the motions were consolidated for hearing.

Questions:

1. What argument does defendant C_____ have to support his motion for a judgment N.O.V.? Is he likely to be successful? Has C_____ failed to include any significant error in the trial as a basis for seeking a new trial?

2. What arguments will the various parties make regarding the other motions? In considering defendant B_____'s motion assume that the right to jury trial in Arvada is identical to that in the federal courts.

Shortly after arguments on these motions the court made the following order:

ILLUSTRATIVE LITIGATION PROBLEM

IN THE SUPERIOR COURT, DELTA COUNTY STATE OF ARVADA

Thomas A_____, Plaintiff
vs.
Reginald B_____, Daniel C_____ and D_____ Corporation, Defendants

Civil P 15163
ORDER

The motion of defendant C_____ for a judgment N.O.V. and for a new trial and the motions of defendants B_____ and D_____ Corporation for a new trial and dismissal having come on regularly for hearing before the undersigned on the 30th day of January, 1993, at the hour of 10 A.M., upon notice duly and regularly served and plaintiff A_____ appearing by James L. W_____, his counsel, and defendant C_____ appearing by Samuel R_____, his counsel, and defendant B_____ appearing by Louis F_____, his counsel, and defendant D_____ Corporation appearing by Paul Y_____, its counsel, and the matter having been argued and submitted and good cause appearing therefor,

IT IS HEREBY ORDERED that defendant C_____'s motion for judgment notwithstanding the verdict be denied, and that defendant C_____'s motion and defendant B_____'s motion for new trial be denied.

IT IS FURTHER ORDERED that defendant D_____ Corporation's motion to dismiss plaintiff's complaint for failure of plaintiff to allege a claim for damages against D_____ Corporation is granted without leave to amend.

Dated: January 30, 1993

Learned W_____
Judge of the Superior Court

The Court then rendered the following judgment:

IN THE SUPERIOR COURT, DELTA COUNTY STATE OF ARVADA

Thomas A_____, Plaintiff
vs.
Reginald B_____, Daniel C_____, and D_____ Corporation, Defendants

Civil P 15163
JUDGMENT

ILLUSTRATIVE LITIGATION PROBLEM

The above entitled cause came on regularly for trial before the undersigned sitting with a jury on January 20, 1993. Upon the jury being duly sworn and impaneled, evidence was presented, the matter argued and the jury instructed by the undersigned.

The Court, after deliberation, rendered the following verdict on issues not triable to a jury: that plaintiff recover the sum of $2,500 from defendant B_____.

The jury, after deliberation, rendered the following verdict: We the jury find for the plaintiff and against defendants Reginald B_____, Daniel C_____ and D_____ Corporation, and declare that plaintiff was not negligent. We further find that plaintiff suffered damages against defendants C_____ and D_____ Corporation in the amount of $150,000 for personal injuries and $13,800 for property damage.

The Court then dismissed plaintiff's claim for damages against defendant D_____ Corporation on the ground that the complaint failed to state a claim for such relief.

IT IS HEREBY ORDERED ADJUDGED AND DECREED that plaintiff have judgment as follows:

1. Plaintiff is declared to have been not negligent in his conduct toward defendants B_____, C_____ and D_____ Corporation.

2. Plaintiff is entitled to damages against defendant B_____ in the amount of $2,500, plus interest thereon, from the 28th day of January, 1993, until paid, at the rate of 7% per annum, and for his costs of action.

3. Plaintiff is entitled to damages against defendant C_____ in the amount of $163,800 plus interest thereon from the 28th day of January, 1993, until paid, at the rate of 7% per annum, and for his costs of suit.

Dated: February 10, 1993

Learned W_____
Judge of the Superior Court

Defendants C_____ and D_____ Corporation decided to appeal this decision. Their attorneys filed the following documents which were duly served on plaintiff:

ILLUSTRATIVE LITIGATION PROBLEM

IN THE SUPERIOR COURT, DELTA COUNTY STATE OF ARVADA

Thomas A_____,)
    Plaintiff)
  vs.) Civil P 15163
Reginald B_____, Daniel C_____,) NOTICE OF APPEAL
 D_____ Corporation,)
    Defendants)

To Angus B_____, County Clerk;

Notice is hereby given that defendants Daniel C_____ and D_____ Corporation appeal from that part of the judgment relating to Counts One and Two of plaintiff's Complaint and also to that part of the judgment denying to said defendants Daniel C_____ and D_____ Corporation damages for their injuries to person and property.

Dated: February 25, 1993.

    Samuel R_____
    Attorney for Defendant Daniel C_____
  Paul Y_____
    Attorney for Defendant
    D_____ Corporation

IN THE SUPERIOR COURT, DELTA COUNTY STATE OF ARVADA

Thomas A_____,)
    Plaintiff) Civil P 15163
  vs.)
Reginald B_____, Daniel C_____,) NOTICE TO PRE-
 and D_____ Corporation,) PARE TRANSCRIPT
    Defendants)

To Angus B_____, Clerk of the above entitled Court:

Please take notice that defendants Daniel C_____ and D_____ Corporation have commenced an appeal and in connection therewith require a reporter's transcript of the proceedings and testimony in the above entitled case which transcript shall also include the instructions to the jury which were given and those which were refused, all statements, orders, requests, rulings and remarks of the court, counsel, the parties or any witnesses, and all exhibits introduced into evidence during the course of trial.

ILLUSTRATIVE LITIGATION PROBLEM

                Samuel R_____
                Attorney for Defendant
                Appellant Daniel C_____
Paul Y_____
                Attorney for Defendant
                Appellant D_____
                Corporation

    While the appeal was pending plaintiff brought a new action against D_____ Corporation for damages of $163,800, alleging the negligence of C_____ and the fact that C_____ had been acting within the scope of his employment. The Corporation filed an answer denying both these allegations, alleging that plaintiff had been contributorily negligent, and that the action was barred by res judicata. Both parties then moved for summary judgment in their favor on the entire case or as to those issues which could be so decided. Each party supported its case solely with a certified copy of the entire record in the first suit.

Question:

Should the court grant a full summary judgment to either party? If not, to what extent, if any, is a partial summary judgment appropriate?

    The trial court, after a hearing, rendered a decision granting summary judgment for the plaintiff. Shortly thereafter the appeal in the first action was argued and submitted. Within two weeks the appellate court handed down a decision setting aside the verdict in the first action and ordering a new trial on all issues.

Question:

What steps should D_____ Corporation's lawyer now take with regard to the summary judgment rendered in the second action? See Federal Rule 60(b)(5).

Part VII

Local Rules for the United States District Courts for the Southern and Eastern Districts of New York*

General Rules

Rule		Page
1.	Clerk's Office—Court Sessions	383
2.	Admission to the Bar	384
3.	Attorneys of Record and Parties Appearing	385
4.	Discipline of Attorneys	386
5.	Duty of Attorneys—Default Sanctions—Imposition of Costs on Attorneys	387
6.	Fees of Clerks and Reporters	389
7.	Photographs, Radio, Recordings, Television	389
8.	Procedural Questions	389
9.	Disclosure of Interested Parties	390

Civil Rules

1.	Filing Papers	390
2.	Address of Party or Original Owner of Claim to Be Furnished	390
3.	Motions	391
4.	Class Actions [Revoked]	393
5.	Fees in Stockholder and Class Actions	393
6.	Orders	393
7.	Form of Orders, Judgments and Decrees	394
8.	Submission of Orders, Judgments and Decrees	394
9.	Preparation and Entry of Judgments, Decrees and Final Orders [Revoked]	395
10.	Default Judgment	395
11.	Taxable Costs and Disbursements	395
12.	Stenographic Transcript	398
13.	Entering Satisfaction of Judgments or Decrees	398
14.	Order of Taking Depositions [Revoked]	399
15.	Counsel Fees on Taking Depositions in Certain Cases	399
16.	Deposition for Use Abroad [Revoked]	399
17.	Commission to Take Testimony [Revoked]	399
18.	Filing of Discovery Materials	399

* Many of these rules have been reworded slightly. Only alterations of substance have been included here.

FEDERAL LOCAL COURT RULES

Rule		Page
19.	Masters	400
20.	Oath of Master, Commissioner, etc.	400
21.	Marked Pleadings	401
22.	Six Member Jury Trials; Assessment of Juror Costs	401
22.	Assessment of Jury Costs	401
23.	Proposed Findings of Fact and Conclusions of Law	401
24.	Custody of Exhibits	402
25.	Removal of Cases From State Courts	402
26.	Transfer of Cases to Another District	403
27.	Review of Cases; Dismissal for Want of Prosecution	403
28.	Actions by or on Behalf of Infants or Incompetents	403
29.	Settlements, Apportionments and Allowances in Wrongful Death Actions	404
30.	Proceedings to Enjoin Expulsion in Deportation and Exclusion Cases	404
31.	Service of Writ or Order Enjoining Expulsion of an Alien [Eastern District Only]	405
32.	Habeas Corpus and Motions Pursuant to 28 USC § 2255	405
33.	Notice of Claim of Unconstitutionality	406
34.	Three-Judge Court	406
35.	Publication of Advertisements	407
36.	Notice of Sale	407
37.	Sureties	408
38.	Approval of Bonds of Corporate Sureties	408
39.	Security for Costs	409
40.	Appeals	409
41.	Supersedeas [Revoked]	409
42.	Remand by an Appellate Court	409
43.	Contempt	409
44.	Order of Summation	411
45.	Exemption From Mandatory Scheduling Order [Eastern District Only]	411
46.	Interrogatories [Southern District Only]	411
47.	Uniform Definitions in Discovery Requests	412

Rules for Proceedings Before Magistrate Judges

1.	Jurisdiction—28 USC § 636	414
2–5.	[Omitted. These Rules Relate Primarily to Criminal Matters.]	414
6.	Issuance of Subpoenas	414
7.	Notice of Determination and Objections Thereto [Revoked]	414
8.	Consent Jurisdiction Procedure	414
9–11.	[Omitted. These Rules Relate Primarily to Criminal Matters.]	415
12.	Rotation of Assignments—Southern District Only	415
13.	General Pretrial Supervision	415
14.	Appeals From Cases Heard on Consent	415

GENERAL RULES — Rule 1

Rule		Page
15.	Entry of Mandatory Scheduling Orders [Eastern District Only]	416
16.	Entry of Mandatory Scheduling Orders [Southern District]	417

Rules for the Division of Business Among District Judges
Southern District

1.	Individual Assignment System	417
2.	Assignment Committee	417
3.	Part I	417
4.	Civil Actions or Proceedings (Filing and Assignment)	418
5.	Civil Proceedings in Part I	418
6–8.	[Omitted. These Rules Relate Primarily to Criminal Matters.]	419
9.	Cases Certified for Prompt Trial or Disposition	419
10.	Motions	420
11.	[Omitted. The Rule Relates Primarily to Criminal Matters.]	420
12.	Assignments to New Judges	420
13.	Assignments to Senior Judges	420
14.	Assignments to Visiting Judges	420
15.	Transfer of Related Cases	421
16.	Transfer of Cases by Consent	422
17.	Transfers From Senior Judges	422
18.	Transfer Because of Disqualification, etc.	422
19.	Transfer of Cases Because of Death, Resignation, Prolonged Illness, Disability, Unavoidable Absence, or Excessive Backlog of a Judge	422
20.	Transfer of Cases to the Suspense Docket	422
21–33.	[Omitted. These Rules Relate to Assignment of Cases Among Courthouses Within the Same District]	

Local Rules, Southern and Eastern Districts of New York
Effective October 26, 1983

GENERAL RULES

Rule 1. Clerk's Office—Court Sessions.

(a) The offices of the clerk are open from 8:30 a.m. to 5:00 p.m. Monday through Friday. The offices of the clerk are closed Saturdays, Sundays, and legal holidays. The Clerk of the Court shall maintain an automatic time and date stamp at a night depository * * *. After hours, papers may be submitted for the district court only, in a night depository located in the courthouse lobby. These papers will be considered to have been filed for the district court as of the time and date stamped thereon which shall be deemed presumptively correct.

(b) The court is open for trials and motions at 9:30 a.m. and closes at 5:00 p.m. except as otherwise directed by the sitting judge.

Rule 2. Admission to the Bar.

(a) A member in good standing of the bar of the state of New York, or a member in good standing of the bar of the United States district court in New Jersey, Connecticut or Vermont and of the bar of the State in which such district court is located, provided such district court by its rule extends a corresponding privilege to members of the bar of this court, may be admitted to practice in this court on compliance with the following provisions:

Each applicant for admission shall file with the clerk, at least ten (10) days prior to hearing (unless, for good cause shown, the judge shall shorten the time), a verified written petition for admission stating: (1) applicant's residence and office address; (2) the time when, and court where, admitted; (3) applicant's legal training and experience; (4) whether applicant has ever been held in contempt of court, and if so, the nature of the contempt and the final disposition thereof; (5) whether applicant has ever been censured, suspended or disbarred by any court, and if so, the facts and circumstances connected therewith; and (6) that applicant has read and is familiar with (a) the provisions of the Judicial Code (Title 28, U.S.C.) which pertain to the jurisdiction of, and practice in, the United States district courts; (b) the Federal Rules of Civil Procedure for the district courts; (c) the Federal Rules of Criminal Procedure for the district courts; (d) the Federal Rules of Evidence for the United States Courts and Magistrates; (e) the Rules of the United States District Court for the Southern and Eastern Districts of New York; and (f) that applicant has read the Code of Professional Responsibility of the American Bar Association, and will faithfully adhere thereto.

The petition shall be accompanied by a certificate of the clerk of the court for each of the states in which the applicant is a member of the bar, which has been issued within thirty (30) days and states that the applicant is a member in good standing of the bar of that state court. The petition shall also be accompanied by an affidavit of an attorney of this court who has known the applicant for at least one year, stating when the affiant was admitted to practice in this court, how long and under what circumstances the attorney has known the applicant, and what the attorney knows of the applicant's character and experience at the bar. Such petition shall be placed at the head of the calendar and, on the call thereof, the attorney whose affidavit accompanied the petition shall personally move the admission of the applicant. If the petition is granted, the applicant shall take the oath of office and sign the roll of attorneys. [Amended 1-27-86.]

(b) [Southern District] A member in good standing of the bar of either the Southern or Eastern District of New York may be admitted to the bar of the other district without formal application (1) upon filing in that district a certificate of the clerk of the United States district court for the district in which the applicant is a member of the bar, which has been issued within thirty (30) days, and states that the applicant is a member in good standing of the bar of that court and (2) upon taking the oath of office, signing the roll of attorneys of that district, and paying the fee required in that district.

(b) [Eastern District] A member in good standing of the bar of any district court in the Second Circuit may be admitted to the bar of the Eastern District of New York without formal application: (1) upon filing in the Eastern District a certificate of the Clerk of the United States District Court for the district in which the attorney is a member of the bar, issued within thirty days, that the applicant is a member in good standing of the bar of that court and that the attorney was required to present a certificate of good standing in a state bar within the Second Circuit in order to be admitted to membership in the federal bar in question; and (2) upon taking the oath of office, signing the roll of attorneys of this district, and paying the fee required in this district. [Amended 10-21-86.]

(c) A member in good standing of the bar of any state or of any United States District Court may be permitted to argue or try a particular case in whole or in part as counsel or advocate, upon motion and upon filing with the Clerk of the District Court a certificate of the court for each of the states in which the applicant is a member of the bar, which has been issued within thirty (30) days and states that the applicant is a member in good standing of the bar of that state court. Only an attorney of this court may enter appearances for parties, sign stipulations or receive payments upon judgments, decrees or orders. [Amended 1-27-86.]

(d) If an attorney changes his or her residence or office address, the attorney shall immediately notify the clerk of the district in which the attorney is admitted.

Rule 3. Attorneys of Record and Parties Appearing.

(a) [Southern District only] If a judge of this court so requires, an attorney not having an office within the Southern or Eastern District of New York shall not appear as attorney of record without designating a member of the bar of either district having an office within either district upon whom service of papers may be made. [Amended 7-5-88.]

(b) A party appearing pro se shall file with that party's initial notice of pleading either (1) a designation of an address within the Southern or Eastern District of New York at which service of papers may be made upon that party, in which case service may be made upon that party at that address in like manner as service may be made upon an attorney or, (2) a designation of the clerk of this court as the person upon whom service may be made, and an address to which the clerk may mail any papers so served upon the clerk. The clerk within three (3) days of the receipt of papers so served shall mail them to the party at that address.

Any application for leave to serve any papers in less than five (5) days before the return day, upon a party who has so designated the clerk, shall contain a statement of such designation.

(c) An attorney who has appeared as attorney of record for a party may be relieved or displaced only by order of the court and may not withdraw from a case without leave of the court granted by order. Such an order may be granted only upon a showing by affidavit of satisfactory reasons for withdrawal or displacement and the posture of the case, including its position, if any, on the calendar.

Rule 4. Discipline of Attorneys.

(a) The chief judge shall appoint a committee of the board of judges known as the committee on grievances, which under the direction of the chief judge shall have charge of all matters relating to discipline of attorneys. The committee on grievances may entertain complaints in writing from any source. Complaints, and any files based on them, shall be treated as confidential. The chief judge shall appoint a committee of attorneys who are members of the bar of this court to advise or assist the committee on grievances. Members of this committee will investigate complaints, and will serve as members of hearing panels.

(b) If it appears, after notice and opportunity to be heard, that any member of the bar of this court has been convicted of a felony in any federal court, or in the court of any state, territory, district, commonwealth or possession, the member's name shall be struck from the roll of members of the bar of this court.

(c) If it appears, after notice and opportunity to be heard, that any member of the bar of this court has been convicted of a misdemeanor, in any federal court or in the court of any state, territory, district, commonwealth, or possession, the member may be disciplined by this court, in accordance with the provisions of paragraph (g).

(d) If it appears, after notice and opportunity to be heard, that any member of the bar of this court has been disciplined by any federal court or by the court of any state, territory, district, commonwealth or possession, the member may be disciplined by this court, in accordance with the provisions of paragraph (g).

(e) If it appears, after notice and opportunity to be heard, that any member of the bar of this court has resigned from the bar of any federal court or the court of any state, territory, district, commonwealth or possession while an investigation into allegations of misconduct by the attorney were pending, the member may be disciplined by this court, in accordance with the provisions of paragraph (g).

(f) If, in connection with activities in this court, any attorney is found guilty by clear and convincing evidence, after notice and opportunity to be heard, of conduct violative of the Codes of Professional Responsibility of the American Bar Association or the New York Bar Association from time to time in force, the attorney may be disciplined by this court, in accordance with the provisions of paragraph (g).

(g) Discipline imposed pursuant to paragraphs (c), (d), (e), or (f) may consist of suspension or censure. In the case of an attorney who is a member of the bar of this court, it may also consist of striking the name of the attorney from the roll. In the case of an attorney admitted pro hac vice, it may also consist of precluding the attorney from again appearing at the bar of this court. Upon the entry of an order of preclusion, the clerk shall transmit to the court or courts where the attorney was admitted to practice a certified copy of the order, and of the court's opinion, if any.

Discipline may be imposed by this court with respect to paragraphs (d) and (e) unless the member of the bar concerned establishes by clear and convincing evidence: (1) with respect to paragraph (d) that there was such an infirmity of proof of misconduct by the attorney as to give rise to the clear conviction that this court could not consistently with its duty accept as final the conclusion of the other court; or (2) that the procedure resulting in the investigation or discipline of the attorney by the other court was so lacking in notice or opportunity to be heard as to constitute a deprivation of due process; or (3) that the imposition of discipline of this court would result in grave injustice.

(h) If it appears, after notice and opportunity to be heard, that any lawyer not a member of the bar of this court has appeared at the bar of this court without permission to do so, said lawyer may be precluded from again appearing at the bar of this court. Upon the entry of order of preclusion, the clerk shall transmit to the court or courts where the attorney was admitted to practice a certified copy of the order, and of the court's opinion, if any.

(i) Complaints in writing alleging that any member of the bar of this court is in a category described in paragraphs (b) through (e), or that any attorney practicing in this court has committed the misconduct referred to in paragraph (f), will be directed to the chief judge, who shall refer such complaints to the committee on grievances, which may designate an attorney selected from the panel of attorneys to investigate the allegations if it deems investigation necessary or warranted. If, with or without investigation, the committee on grievances deems that the charges require prosecution, a statement of charges shall be served on the attorney concerned together with an order to show cause why discipline should not be imposed. Upon the respondent attorney's answer to the charges the matter will be scheduled for prompt hearing before a panel of attorneys, which will report findings and recommendations. After such a hearing and report, or if no timely answer is made by the respondent attorney or if the answer raises no issue requiring a hearing, such action shall be taken as justice and this rule may require.

(j) Any attorney who has been suspended or whose name has been struck from the roll of the members of the bar of this court may apply in writing to the chief judge, for good cause shown, for the lifting of suspension or for reinstatement to the rolls. The committee on grievances shall act upon the application, either immediately or after receiving findings and recommendations from a hearing panel of attorneys to which the application has been referred.

(k) Misconduct of any attorney in the presence of this court or in any manner in respect to any matter pending in this court may be dealt with directly by the judge in charge of the matter or at said judge's option referred to the committee on grievances, or both.

(l) Whenever it appears that an attorney admitted to practice in the court of any state, territory, district, commonwealth or possession, or in any other federal court, has in this court been convicted of any crime or disbarred, suspended or censured the clerk shall send to such other court or courts a certified copy of the judgment of conviction or order of disbarment, suspension or censure, and a statement of the attorney's last known office and resident address.

Rule 5. Duty of Attorneys—Default Sanctions—Imposition of Costs on Attorneys.

(a) *Duty of Attorneys in Related Cases.* It shall be the continuing duty of each attorney appearing in any case to bring promptly to the attention of the clerk all facts which said attorney believes are relevant to a determination that said case and one or more pending cases should be heard by the same judge, in order to avoid unnecessary duplication of judicial effort. As soon as the attorney becomes aware of such relationship, said attorney shall notify the clerk in writing, who shall transmit that notification to the judges to whom the cases have been assigned.

(b) *Default Sanctions.* Failure of counsel for any party, or of a party appearing pro se, to appear before the court at a conference, or to complete the necessary preparations, or to be prepared to proceed to trial at the time set, may be considered an abandonment of the case or failure to prosecute or defend diligently, and an appropriate order may be entered against the defaulting party either with respect to a specific issue or on the entire case.

(c) *Imposition of Costs on Attorneys.* If counsel fails to comply with Rule 5(a) or a judge finds that the sanctions in paragraph (b) are either inadequate or unjust to the parties, the court may assess reasonable costs directly against counsel whose action has obstructed the effective administration of the court's business.

Rule 6. Fees of Clerks and Reporters.

(a) The clerk shall not be required to render any service for which a fee is prescribed by statute or by the Judicial Conference of the United States unless the fee for the particular service is paid to the clerk in advance or the court orders otherwise.

(b) Every attorney appearing in any proceeding who orders a transcript of any trial, hearing, or any other proceeding, is obligated to pay the cost thereof to the court reporters of this court upon rendition of the invoice unless at the time of such order, the attorney, in writing, advises the court reporter that only the client is obligated to pay. Any attorney who fails to pay as provided shall be subject to disciplinary action under Rule 4 of the General Rules.

Rule 7. Photographs, Radio, Recordings, Television.

[This rule has been repealed in favor of Rule 7 as set out below.] [Eastern District only] The taking of photographs and the use of recording devices in the courtroom or its environs, except by officials of the court in the conduct of the court's business, or radio or television broadcasting from the courtroom or its environs during the progress of or in connection with judicial proceedings or otherwise, whether or not court is actually in session, is prohibited.

Environs as used in this rule, shall include the entire United States Courthouses at Foley Square and 225 Cadman Plaza East, including all entrances to and exits from the buildings.

Rule 7. Photographs, Radio, Recordings, Television.

No one other than court officials engaged in the conduct of court business shall bring any camera, transmitter, receiver, portable telephone or recording device into any courthouse or its environs without written permission of a judge of that court.

Environs as used in this rule, shall include the entire United States Courthouse property, including all entrances to and exits from the buildings.

[Amended 7–5–88.]

Rule 8. Procedural Questions.

Whenever a procedural question arises which is not covered by the provision of any statute of the United States, or of the Federal Rules of Civil Procedure, or of the Rules of the United States District Courts for the Southern and Eastern Districts of New York, it shall be determined, if possible, by the parallels or analogies furnished by such statutes and rules. If, however, no such parallels or analogies exist, then the procedure prevailing in courts of equity of the United States shall be applied. In default thereof and in the discretion of the court, the procedure which prevails in the Supreme Court or the Surrogates Court of the State of New York may be applied.

Rule 9. Disclosure of Interested Parties.

To enable judges and magistrates of the court to evaluate possible disqualification or recusal, counsel for a private (non-governmental) party shall submit at the time of initial pleading a certificate of identification of any corporate parents, subsidiaries, or affiliates of that party which are publicly held.

[Amended 9–30–91 (SDNY), 10–16–91 (EDNY).]

CIVIL RULES

Rule 1. Filing Papers.

(a) Unless a judge of this court shall otherwise direct, papers submitted for filing must (1) be plainly written, typed, printed, or copied without erasures or inter-lineations which materially deface it, (2) bear the docket number and judge's initials, if any, assigned to the action or proceeding and (3) bear endorsed upon the cover the name, office and post office address and telephone number, the initials of the first and last name, and the last four (4) digits of the social security number of the attorney of record for the filing party.

(b) All pleadings, motions, and other papers that are submitted for filing must be signed by an attorney of record in said attorney's own name and must show the attorney's address and telephone number. Failure to sign any document will result in the clerk refusing to accept the document for filing.

[Amended, effective 6–12–90 (EDNY), 7–1–90 (SDNY).]

Rule 2. Address of Party or Original Owner of Claim to Be Furnished.

A party shall furnish to any other party, within five (5) days after a demand, a verified statement setting forth said party's post office address and residence, and like information as to partners if a partnership is involved and, if a corporation or an unincorporated association, the names, post office addresses, and residences of its principal officers. In case of an assigned claim, the statement shall include the post office address and residence of the original owner of the claim and of any assignee. Upon non-compliance with the demand, the court, on ex parte application, shall order the furnishing of the statement, and in a proper case, on motion, may direct that the proceedings on the part of the non-complying party be stayed, or make such other order as justice requires.

Rule 3. Motions.

(a) [Repealed. The rule had read, "Except as otherwise provided by statute, rule or order of the court, notice of motion in all actions or proceedings shall be in the time and manner provided in the Federal Rules of Civil Procedure."]

(b) Upon any motion the moving party shall serve and file with the motion papers a memorandum setting forth the points and authorities relied upon in support of the motion divided, under appropriate headings, into as many parts as there are points to be determined. The opposing party shall serve and file with the papers in opposition to the motion and an answering memorandum, similarly divided, setting forth the points and authorities relied upon in opposition. Failure to comply may be deemed sufficient cause for the denial of the motion or the granting of the motion by default.

(c) The notice of motion, supporting affidavits and memoranda, with proof of due service, shall be served in accordance with the following:

(1) All motions and exceptions under Rules 26 through 37 inclusive of the Federal Rules of Civil Procedure, and under Rules 27 and 30 (insofar as they apply to interrogatories), 31, 32, 32A, 32B, and 32C of the Federal Rules of Practice in Admiralty and Maritime Cases, shall be served at least five (5) days before the return day unless otherwise provided by statute or directed by the court. Where such service is made, opposing affidavits and answering memoranda of law shall be served no later than noon of the day preceding the return day.

(2) Unless otherwise provided by subparagraph (1), statute, or the Federal Rules of Civil Procedure, and except for petitions for writs of habeas corpus, in all civil motions and exceptions, the notice of motion, supporting affidavits, and accompanying memoranda of law shall be served at least fifteen days before the return day unless otherwise directed by the court. Where such service is made, opposing affidavits and answering memoranda shall be served at least seven days, and reply papers, if any, at least two days before the return day. [Effective 8-1-89].

(3) No papers, either in support of or in opposition to the motion, which have not been served as provided will be accepted for filing or received by the court except upon special permission granted by the court for good cause shown.

(4) No order to show cause to bring on a motion will be granted except upon a clear and specific showing by affidavit of good and sufficient reasons why procedure other than by notice of motion is necessary.

(d) Upon any motion based upon rules or statutes the notice of motion or order to show cause shall specify the rules or statutes upon which the motion is predicated. If such specification has not been made, the motion may be stricken from the calendar.

(e) Upon any motion, objections or exceptions addressed to interrogatories, answers to interrogatories or requests for admissions, under Rule 37(a), Federal Rules of Civil Procedure, the moving party shall specify and quote verbatim in the motion papers each interrogatory, answer or request to which the objection or exception is taken and immediately following each specification shall set forth the basis of the objection or exception.

(f) No motion of the type described in subparagraph (1) of paragraph (c) of this rule shall be heard unless counsel for the moving party files with the court at or prior to the argument an affidavit certifying that said counsel has conferred with counsel for the opposing party in an effort in good faith to resolve by agreement the issues raised by the motion without the intervention of the court and has been unable to reach such an agreement. If part of the issues raised by motion have been resolved by agreement, the affidavit shall specify the issues so resolved and the issues remaining unresolved.

(g) Upon any motion for summary judgment pursuant to Rule 56 of the Federal Rules of Civil Procedure, there shall be annexed to the notice of motion a separate, short and concise statement of the material facts as to which the moving party contends there is no genuine issue to be tried. Failure to submit such a statement constitutes grounds for denial of the motion.

The papers opposing a motion for summary judgment shall include a separate, short and concise statement of the material facts as to which it is contended that there exists a genuine issue to be tried.

All material facts set forth in the statement required to be served by the moving party will be deemed to be admitted unless controverted by the statement required to be served by the opposing party.

(h) Motions marked off the calendar shall not be restored by consent or stipulation.

(i) The judge may direct the parties to submit motions and may determine them without oral hearing.

(j) A notice of motion for reargument shall be served within ten (10) days after the docketing of the court's determination of the original motion and shall be served at least the same number of days before the return day as was required for the original motion. There shall be served with the notice of motion a memorandum setting forth concisely the matters or controlling decisions which counsel believes the court has overlooked. No oral argument shall be heard unless the court grants the motion and specifically directs that the matter shall be reargued orally. No affidavits shall be filed by any party unless directed by the court.

(k) A motion for leave to bring in a third party defendant under Rule 14 of the Federal Rules of Civil Procedure shall be made within six (6) months from the date of service of the moving party's answer to the complaint or reply to the counterclaim, except that motions of this nature may be granted after the expiration of such period in exceptional cases upon showing of special circumstances and of the necessity for such relief in the interest of justice and upon such terms and conditions as the court deems fair and appropriate. [Revoked, effective 1–25–90 (SDNY), 6–12–90 (EDNY).]

(*l*) (Southern District Only). No motion of the type described in subparagraph (1) of paragraph (c) of this rule shall be heard unless counsel for the moving party has first requested an informal conference with the court and such request has either been denied or the discovery dispute has not been resolved as a consequence of such a conference. [Added, effective 2–1–85.]

Rule 4. Class Actions. [Revoked.]

[Revoked, effective 11–27–89 and 1–25–90 (SDNY), 6–12–90 (EDNY).]

Rule 5. Fees in Stockholder and Class Actions.

(a) Fees for attorneys or others shall not be paid upon the recovery or compromise in a derivative or class action on behalf of a corporation or class except as allowed by the court after a hearing upon such notice as the court may direct. The notice shall include a statement of the names and addresses of the applicants for such fees and the amounts requested respectively and shall disclose any fee sharing agreements with anyone. The court, in its discretion, may direct that the notice also be given the New York Regional Office of the Securities and Exchange Commission. Where the court directs notice of a hearing upon a proposed voluntary dismissal or settlement of a derivative or class action, the above information as to the applications shall be included in the notice.

(b) All applications for attorneys' fees and expenses, pursuant to 28 U.S.C. Sec. 2412(d)(1)(B), and all petitions for leave to appeal an agency fee determination, pursuant to 5 U.S.C. Sec. 504(c)(2), must be filed within thirty (30) days after the date of the final judgment of the court or of the agency fee determination. Any response shall be filed within fifteen (15) days after service of such application or petition.

Rule 6. Orders.

(a) A memorandum signed by the judge of the decision on a motion that does not finally determine all claims for relief shall constitute the order unless the memorandum directs the submission or settlement of an order in more extended form.

Rule 6 — FEDERAL LOCAL COURT RULES

The notation in the appropriate docket of such memorandum, or of an oral decision, which does not direct the submission or settlement of an order in more extended form, shall constitute the entry of an order. The notation in the appropriate docket of an order in more extended form, as required to be submitted or settled by such memorandum, shall constitute the entry of the order.

(b) No ex parte order shall be granted, unless based upon an affidavit showing cause therefor, and stating whether a previous application for similar relief has been made.

Rule 7. Form of Orders, Judgments and Decrees.

The form of an order, judgment or decree shall be entitled substantially as follows:

UNITED STATES DISTRICT COURT

_____ DISTRICT OF NEW YORK

CAPTION:	Docket No.

The date shall immediately precede the signature of the judge, magistrate, referee or clerk and shall be substantially as follows:

"Dated: _____, New York, July 1, 1983"

Rule 8. Submission of Orders, Judgments and Decrees.

(a) Proposed orders, judgments and decrees shall be presented to the clerk, and not presented directly to the judge. Unless the form of order, judgment or decree is consented to in writing, or unless the court otherwise directs, two days' notice of settlement is required. One day's notice is required of all counter-proposals. Unless adopted by the court, such proposed orders, judgments or decrees shall not form any part of the record of the action.

(b) The attorneys causing the entry of an order of judgment shall append to or endorse upon it a list of the names of the parties entitled to be notified of the entry thereof and the names and addresses of their respective attorneys.

(c) Order for Deposit—Interest Bearing Account.

(1) Whenever a party seeks a court order for money to be deposited by the Clerk in an interest-bearing account, the party shall personally deliver the order to the Clerk or Financial Deputy who will inspect the proposed order for proper form and content and compliance with this rule prior to signature by the judge for whom the order is prepared.

(2) Proposed orders directing the Clerk to invest such funds in an interest-bearing account or other instrument shall include the following:

(i) the exact United States dollar amount of the principal sum to be invested;

(ii) [Repealed]

(iii) [Repealed]

(iv) wording which directs the Clerk to deduct from the income earned on the investment of a fee, not exceeding that authorized by the Judicial Conference of the United States and set by the Director of the Administrative Office at equal to the first 45 days income earned on the investment, whenever such income becomes available for deduction in the investment so held and without further order of the court.

[Subsec. (c) added, effective 7–31–89 (SDNY), 6–12–90 (EDNY).]

Rule 9. Preparation and Entry of Judgments, Decrees and Final Orders. [Revoked.]

[Revoked, effective 11–27–89 (SDNY), 6–12–90 (EDNY).]

Rule 10. Default Judgment.

(a) *By the Clerk.* When a party is entitled to have the clerk enter a default judgment pursuant to Rule 55(b)(1), Federal Rules of Civil Procedure, said party shall submit with the form of judgment a statement showing the principal amount due which shall not exceed the amount demanded in the complaint, giving credit for any payments and showing the amounts and dates thereof, a computation of the interest to the day of judgment, and the costs and taxable disbursements claimed. An affidavit of the party or said party's attorney shall be appended to the statement showing: (1) that the party against whom judgment is sought is not an infant or an incompetent person; (2) that said party has made default in appearance in the action; (3) that the amount shown by the statement is justly due and owing and that no part has been paid except as therein set forth; and (4) that the disbursements sought to be taxed have been made in the action or will necessarily be made or incurred therein. The clerk shall thereupon enter judgment for principal, interest and costs.

(b) *By the Court.* An application to the court for the entry of a default judgment, pursuant to Rule 55(b)(2), Federal Rules of Civil Procedure, shall be accompanied by a clerk's certificate of the notation of the default, and by a copy of the pleading to which no response has been made.

Rule 11. Taxable Costs and Disbursements.

(a) *Request to Tax Costs.* Within thirty (30) days after final judgment, or in the case of an appeal by either party, within thirty (30) days after the disposition of the appeal, the party recovering costs shall file

Rule 11 FEDERAL LOCAL COURT RULES

with the clerk a request to tax costs indicating the date and time of taxation. Costs will not be taxed during the pendency of any appeal. Any party failing to file a bill of costs within this thirty (30) day period will be deemed to have waived costs. The bill of costs shall include an affidavit of counsel that the costs claimed are allowable by law, are correctly stated and were necessarily incurred. Bills and cancelled checks in payment shall be attached as exhibits. Proof of service upon opposing counsel shall be indicated. Service of the bill of costs by mail is sufficient and constitutes notice as provided in Rule 54(d) of the Federal Rules of Civil Procedure.

(b) *Objections to Bill of Costs.* A party objecting to any cost item may serve objections in writing prior to or at the time for taxation. The clerk will proceed to tax costs at the time noticed and allow such items as are properly taxable. In the absence of objection, any item listed may be taxed within the discretion of the clerk. The taxation of costs by the clerk shall be final unless modified on review by the court on motion filed within five (5) days thereafter pursuant to Rule 54(d) of the Federal Rules of Civil Procedure.

(c) *Items Taxable as Costs.* [EDNY only]*

* [Rule 11(c) was revoked, effective Nov. 27, 1989, as to SDNY only. By a Standing Order (M–10–468) the Board of Judges of the Southern District ordered "that the following items will be taxable as costs by the Clerk as a matter of course in any Civil Case unless otherwise directed by the assigned Judge or Magistrate.

"(1) Transcripts. Fees of the Court Reporter for any part of the original stenographic court transcript of a trial necessarily obtained for use in the case in this Court. The fees for transcripts of court proceedings prior to or subsequent to trial are taxable only when authorized in advance or ordered by the assigned Judge or Magistrate.

"(2) Depositions. Fees of the Court Reporter for the original of a deposition, and one copy, if the deposition was used at the trial or received in evidence, whether or not it was used or read in its entirety, or if used by the Court in ruling on a motion for summary judgment or similar substantive motion. Fees for depositions not so used are not taxable. Counsel's fees and expenses in attending the taking of a deposition are not taxable except as provided by statute, rule or order of the court. Fees, mileage and subsistence for a witness at a deposition are taxed at the same rate as for attendance at trial if the deposition is received in evidence or read from at trial, or used by the Court in ruling on a motion for summary judgment or similar substantive motion.

"(3) Witness Fees, Mileage and Subsistence. Witness fees if the witness testifies. Subsistence, pursuant to 28 U.S.C. § 1821, if it is not practical for the witness to return to his or her residence from day to day during the trial. No party to the action may claim witness fees, mileage or subsistence. Fees for expert witnesses, in excess of those taxable for ordinary witnesses, are taxable only when authorized or ordered in advance by the assigned Judge or Magistrate.

"(4) Interpreting Costs. The reasonable fee of a competent interpreter for a witness if the fee of that witness is taxable. The reasonable fee of a document translator if the document translated is admitted into evidence.

"(5) Exemplification, Certification and Copies of Papers. Fees for exemplification, certification and copies of an exhibit if the original was not available and the copy was admitted into evidence, and fees for a search and certification or proof of the non-existence of a document in a public office are taxable. The cost of copies used for the convenience of counsel is not taxable.

"(6) Maps, Charts, Models, Photographs and Summaries. The cost of photographs, 8″ × 10″ in size or less, if admitted into evidence. Enlargements greater than 8″ ×

396

(1) *Transcripts.* The cost of an original trial transcript or a transcript of matters prior to or subsequent to trial is taxable only when authorized in advance or ordered by the court.

(2) *Depositions.* The original transcript of a deposition, plus one copy is taxable if the deposition was received in evidence whether or not it was read in its entirety. Costs for depositions are also taxable if they were used by the court in ruling on a motion for summary judgment. Costs for depositions taken solely for discovery or used only for impeachment purposes are not taxable. Counsel's fees and expenses in attending the taking of a deposition are not taxable except as provided by statute, rule or order of the court. Fees, mileage, and subsistence for the witness at the deposition are taken at the same rate for attendance at trial if the deposition taken is received in evidence.

(3) *Witness Fees, Mileage and Subsistence.* Witness fees are taxable if the witness takes the stand. Subsistence pursuant to 28 U.S.C. Sec. 1821 is allowable if it is not practical for the witness to return to his or her residence from day to day. No party to the action may receive witness fees or subsistence. Fees for expert witnesses are taxable only to the extent of fees for ordinary witnesses unless prior court approval was obtained.

(4) *Interpreting Costs.* The reasonable fee of a competent interpreter is taxable if the fee of the witness involved is taxable. The reasonable fee of a translator is also taxable if the document translated is admitted into evidence.

(5) *Exemplification and Copies of Papers.* A copy of an exhibit is taxable if the original was not available and the copy was admitted into evidence. The cost of copies used for the convenience of counsel are not taxable. The fee for certification or proof of non-existence of a document is taxable.

10" are not taxable except by order of the assigned Judge or Magistrate. Costs of models are not taxable except by order of the assigned Judge or Magistrate. The costs of compiling summaries, statistical comparisons and reports are not taxable, unless directed by the assigned Judge or Magistrate.

"(7) Docket Fees to Attorneys. Statutory docket fees pursuant to 28 U.S.C. § 1923 are taxable. Other attorney costs, fees and paralegal expenses are not taxable except by order of the assigned Judge or Magistrate.

"(8) Masters, Receivers and Commissioner Fees. Fees to masters, receivers and commissioners are taxable as costs unless otherwise ordered by the assigned Judge or Magistrate.

"(9) Costs for Title Searches. A party to whom costs are awarded in an action to foreclose a mortgage on real property or an action for partition of real property is entitled to tax necessary disbursements for the expenses of searches made by title insurance, abstract or searching companies, or by any public officer authorized to make official searches and certify same, or by the attorney for the party to whom costs are awarded, taxable at rates not exceeding the cost of similar official searches.

"(10) Miscellaneous. Reasonable and actual fees of a Marshal, Sheriff, or Process Servers."]

[Dated April 20, 1990].

(6) *Maps, Charts, Models, Photographs and Summaries.* The cost of photographs, 8" × 10" in size or less, is taxable if admitted into evidence. Enlargements greater than 8" × 10" are not taxable except by order of court. Costs of models are not taxable except by order of court. The cost of compiling summaries, statistical comparison and reports is not taxable.

(7) *Docket Fees to Attorneys.* Statutory docket fees pursuant to 28 U.S.C. Sec. 1923 are taxable. Other attorney costs, fees and paralegal expenses are not taxable except by order of the court.

(8) *Masters, Receivers and Commissioner Fees.* Fees to masters, receivers and commissioners are taxable as costs, unless otherwise ordered by the court.

(9) *Costs for Title Searches.* A party to whom costs are awarded in an action to foreclose a mortgage on real property is entitled to tax necessary disbursements for the expenses of searches made by title insurance, abstract or searching companies, or by any public officer authorized to make official searches and certify to the same, or by the attorney for the party to whom costs are awarded, taxable at rates not exceeding the cost of similar official searches.

Rule 12. Stenographic Transcript.

Subject to the provisions of Rule 54(d), Federal Rules of Civil Procedure, the expense of any party in necessarily obtaining all or any part of a transcript, for purposes of a new trial, or for amended findings or for appeal shall be a taxable cost against the unsuccessful party at the rates prescribed by the Judicial Conference.

Rule 13. Entering Satisfaction of Judgments or Decrees.

Satisfaction of a money judgment recovered or registered in this district shall be entered by the clerk as follows:

(a) Upon the payment into the court of the amount thereof, plus interest, and the payment of the clerk's and marshal's fees, if any.

(b) Upon the filing of a satisfaction executed and acknowledged by (1) the judgment creditor; or (2) said judgment creditor's legal representatives or assigns, with evidence of their authority; or (3) said judgment creditor's attorney if within ten (10) years of the entry of the judgment or decree.

(c) If the judgment creditor is the United States, upon the filing of a satisfaction executed by the United States attorney.

(d) In admiralty, pursuant to an order of satisfaction, but such an order will not be made on the consent of the attorneys only, unless such consent is given within ten (10) years from the entry of the decree to be satisfied.

(e) Upon the registration of a certified copy of a satisfaction entered in another district.

Rule 14. Order of Taking Depositions. [Revoked.]

[Revoked, effective 11–27–89 (SDNY), 6–12–90 (EDNY).]

Rule 15. Counsel Fees on Taking Depositions in Certain Cases.

(a) When a proposed deposition upon oral examination, including a deposition before action or pending appeal, is sought to be taken at a place more than one hundred (100) miles from the courthouse, the court may provide in the order or in any order entered under Rule 30(b), Federal Rules of Civil Procedure, that prior to the examination, the applicant pay the expense of the attendance including a reasonable counsel fee of one attorney for each adversary party at the place where the deposition is to be taken. The amounts so paid, unless otherwise directed by the court, shall be a taxable cost in the event that the applicant recovers costs of the action or proceeding.

(b) An order pursuant to Rule 27(a)(2), Federal Rules of Civil Procedure, appointing an attorney to represent the absent expected adversary party and to cross-examine the proposed witness, shall fix said attorney's compensation and expenses; the compensation so fixed shall be paid by the petitioner prior to the appearance of such attorney upon the examination.

Rule 16. Deposition for Use Abroad. [Revoked.]

[Revoked, effective 11–27–89 (SDNY), 6–12–90 (EDNY).]

Rule 17. Commission to Take Testimony. [Revoked.]

[Revoked, effective 11–27–89 (SDNY), 6–12–90 (EDNY).]

Rule 18. Filing of Discovery Materials.

(a) Pursuant to Rule 5(d) of the Federal Rules of Civil Procedure, depositions, interrogatories, requests for documents, requests for admissions, and answers and responses shall not be filed with the clerk's office except by order of the court.

(b) A party seeking relief under Rule 26(c), or seeking to determine sufficiency under Rule 36, or seeking to compel under Rule 37(a)(2) of the Federal Rules of Civil Procedure shall file only that portion of the deposition, interrogatory, requests for documents, or requests for admissions that are objected to.

(c) When discovery material not on file is needed for an appeal, upon an application and order of the court or by stipulation of counsel, the necessary portion of discovery material shall be filed with the clerk.

Rule 19. Masters.

(a) *Agreement on a master.* The parties to a civil action may stipulate in writing for the appointment of a master to report on particular issues, or upon all the issues. The stipulation may suggest the master, in which case the court may appoint the person named. The procedure covering such a reference shall be the same as that governing any other reference to a master.

(b) *May sit outside district.* A master may sit within or outside the district. Where the master is requested to sit outside the district for the convenience of a party and there is opposition by another party, said master may make an order for the holding of the hearing, or a part thereof, outside the district, upon such terms and conditions as shall be just. Such order may be reviewed by the court upon motion of any party, served within ten (10) days after notice to all parties by the master of the making of the order.

(c) *Report.* [Revoked, effective 11-27-89 (SDNY), 6-12-90 (EDNY).]

(d) *Fees taxable.* After a master's compensation and disbursements have been allowed by the court, the prevailing party may pay such compensation and disbursements, and on payment the amount thereof shall be a taxable cost against the unsuccessful party or parties. Where, however, the court directs by order the party against whom, or the proportion in which such compensation and disbursements shall be charged, or the fund or subject matter out of which they shall be paid, the party making the payment to the master shall be entitled to tax such compensation or disbursements only against such parties and in such proportions as the court has directed, and to payment of such taxable cost only out of such fund or subject matter as the court has directed.

(e) *Order of reference.* Whenever an order of reference to a master is made, the attorney procuring the order shall, at the time of filing, deposit with the clerk a copy to be furnished to the master.

(f) *Filing of report.* Upon the filing of the report the master shall furnish the clerk with sufficient copies of a notice of filing addressed severally to the parties or their attorneys, to enable the clerk to mail copies to them.

(g) *Confirmation or rejection of master's report.* A motion to confirm or to reject, in whole or in part, a report of a master shall be heard by the judge appointing such master.

Rule 20. Oath of Master, Commissioner, etc.

Every person appointed master, special master, commissioner, special commissioner, assessor or appraiser shall before entering upon those duties take and subscribe an oath, which, except as otherwise prescribed by statute or rule, shall be to the effect that those duties will be faithfully and impartially discharged and in conformance with the order of appointment and to the best of the master's ability and understanding. Such an oath may be taken before any federal or state officer authorized by federal law to administer oaths and shall be filed in the office of the clerk.

Rule 21. Marked Pleadings.

Counsel for plaintiff shall at least one day before a case is actually scheduled to go to trial (unless a shorter time is allowed by the judge) supply to the judge designated to preside at the trial a copy of marked pleadings which shall consist of the following:

(a) A copy of the complaint or libel and of any third party complaint or third party libel briefly indicating in the margin at each numbered paragraph or article, the manner in which the defendant or respondent, or any third party defendant or respondent impleaded who has filed an answer, treats the allegations contained in said paragraph of the complaint or libel or third party complaint or third party libel.

(b) A complete and accurate copy of each answer filed by the defendant or respondent or any third party defendant or respondent impleaded in the case, similarly marked in case a reply has been filed.

(c) A complete and accurate copy of each reply has been filed in the case.

Rule 22. Six Member Jury Trials; Assessment of Juror Costs.

[This separate rule, applicable only to the Federal District Court for the Eastern District of New York, has been revoked.]

Rule 22. Assessment of Jury Costs.

All counsel in civil cases must seriously discuss the possibility of settlement a reasonable time prior to trial. The trial judge may, in his discretion, assess the parties or counsel with the cost of one day's attendance of the jurors if a case is settled after the jury has been summoned or during trial, the amount to be paid to the clerk of the court. For the purposes of interpreting this paragraph, a civil jury is considered summoned for a trial as of noon of the business day prior to the designated date of the trial.

Rule 23. Proposed Findings of Fact and Conclusions of Law.

In any civil action, where findings of fact and conclusions of law are required, the court may require from either or both parties, before or after the announcement of its decision, proposed findings of fact and conclusions of law, for the assistance of the court, but, unless adopted by the court, such proposed findings of fact and conclusions of law shall not form any part of the record of the action.

Rule 24. Custody of Exhibits.

(a) Except upon appeal and in proceedings before a master or commissioner, and unless the court orders otherwise, exhibits shall not be filed with the clerk, but shall be retained in the custody of the respective attorneys who produced them in court.

(b) In the case of an appeal or other review by an appellate court, the parties are encouraged to agree with respect to which exhibits are necessary for the determination of the appeal. In the absence of agreement and except as provided in subdivision (c), a party upon written request of any other party, or by order of the court, shall make available at the office of the clerk all the original exhibits in said party's possession, or true copies, in order to enable such other party to prepare the record on appeal, at which time and place such other party shall also make available all the original exhibits in that party's possession. All exhibits made available at the clerk's office which are designated by any party as part of the record on appeal shall be filed with the clerk who shall transmit them together with the record on appeal to the clerk of the Court of Appeals. Exhibits not so designated shall remain in the custody of the respective attorneys who shall have the responsibility of promptly forwarding same to the clerk of the Court of Appeals upon request.

(c) Documents of unusual bulk or weight and physical exhibits, other than documents, shall remain in the custody of the attorney producing them, who shall permit their inspection by any party for the purpose of preparing the record on appeal and who shall be charged with the responsibility for their safekeeping and transportation to the appellate court.

(d) Exhibits which have been filed with the clerk shall be removed by the party responsible for them (1) if no appeal is taken, within ninety (90) days after a final decision is rendered, or (2) if an appeal has been taken, within thirty (30) days after the mandate of the final reviewing court is filed. Parties failing to comply with this rule shall be notified by the clerk to remove their exhibits and upon their failure to do so within thirty (30) days, the clerk may dispose of them as the clerk may see fit.

Rule 25. Removal of Cases From State Courts.

(a) [Revoked, effective 11–27–89 (SDNY), 6–12–90 (EDNY).]

(b) If the court's jurisdiction is based upon diversity of citizenship (28 U.S.C. Sec. 1332) the petition for removal shall set forth the states of citizenship and residence, address of each party named in the caption and, in the case of a corporation, the state of incorporation and of its principal place of business, regardless of whether service of process has been effected on all parties. If such information or a designated part is unknown to defendant, defendant may so state, and in that case plaintiff within twenty (20) days after removal shall file in the office of the clerk a statement of the omitted information.

(c) Within twenty (20) days after filing the petition and bond, the petitioner shall file with the clerk a copy of all records and proceedings in the state court.

(d) Upon the entry of an order, remanding the case to the state court, the plaintiff shall deposit with the clerk a copy to be certified and mailed by the clerk to the clerk of the state court.

Rule 26. Transfer of Cases to Another District.

In a case ordered transferred from this district, the clerk, unless otherwise ordered, shall upon the expiration of five (5) days mail to the court to which the case is transferred (1) certified copies of the court's opinion ordering the transfer, of its order, and of the docket entries in the case, and (2) the originals of all other papers on file in the case.

Rule 27. Review of Cases; Dismissal for Want of Prosecution.

Civil cases which have been pending for more than one year and are not on the trial calendar may be called for review upon not less than fifteen (15) days' notice addressed to the attorneys or proctors of record by mail, by telephone, or in person. Notice of the call of such cases shall be published in the New York Law Journal, or otherwise as the court directs. The court may enter an order dismissing the case for want of prosecution, or continuing it, or may make such other order as justice may require.

Rule 28. Actions by or on Behalf of Infants or Incompetents.

An action by or on behalf of an infant or incompetent shall not be settled or compromised, or voluntarily discontinued, dismissed or terminated, without leave of the court embodied in an order, judgment or decree. The proceeding upon an application to settle or compromise such an action shall conform, as nearly as may be, to the New York State statutes and rules, but the court, for cause shown, may dispense with any New York State requirement.

The court shall authorize payment of a reasonable attorney's fee and proper disbursements from the amount recovered in such an action, whether realized by settlement, execution or otherwise and shall determine the said fee and disbursements, after due inquiry as to all charges against the fund.

The court shall order the balance of the proceeds of the recovery or settlement to be distributed as it deems may best protect the interest of the infant or incompetent.

Rule 29. Settlements, Apportionments and Allowances in Wrongful Death Actions.

In an action for wrongful death:

(a) The court shall apportion the avails of the action only where required by statute.

(b) The court shall approve a settlement only in a case covered by subdivision (a).

(c) The court shall approve an attorney's fee only upon application in accordance with the provisions of the Judiciary Law of the State of New York.

Rule 30. Proceedings to Enjoin Expulsion in Deportation and Exclusion Cases.

(a) *The Petition or Complaint.*

(1) Any application to enjoin an alien's expulsion must be verified and, if made by someone other than the alien, must show either that the applicant has been authorized by the alien to make the application, or that the applicant is the parent, child, spouse, brother, sister, attorney or next friend of the alien.

(2) The application must state in detail why the alien's expulsion is invalid. This shall include a statement describing the irreparable harm the alien will suffer if the application is not granted and setting forth the reasons it is believed the application has a probable chance to succeed on the merits. The application shall also state in what manner the applicable administrative remedies have been exhausted and whether any prior application to the court for the same or similar relief has been made.

(3) The application shall recite the source of the factual allegations it contains. If the Immigration and Naturalization Service has been requested to grant the alien, the alien's attorney or the alien's representative access to the alien's records and access has been refused, the application shall state who made the request to review the records, when and to whom it was made, and by whom access was refused. In the event it is claimed that insufficient time was available to examine the alien's records, the application shall state when the alien was informed of his expulsion and why he has been unable to examine the records since that time.

(4) Every application to enjoin the alien's expulsion shall contain the alien's immigration file number and the decision, if any, the alien seeks the court to review. In the event this decision was oral, the application shall state the nature of the relief requested, who denied the request, the reasons for the denial and the date the request was denied.

(b) *Commencement of the Proceeding.* In any proceeding to enjoin the expulsion of an alien, the original verified petition or complaint shall be filed with the clerk. In addition to service pursuant to Rule 4, Federal Rules of Civil Procedure, a copy of the petition or complaint, and application for a writ of habeas corpus or order to show cause shall be delivered to the United States attorney prior to the issuance of any writ or order enjoining the expulsion; if the United States attorney's office is closed, delivery shall be made before 10:00 A.M. the following business day, unless the court otherwise directs.

(c) *Procedure for Issuance of an Order or Writ.*

(1) In the event the court determines to enjoin temporarily an alien's expulsion, it shall briefly set forth why the order or writ was issued, endorse upon the order or writ the date and time it was issued, and set the matter for prompt hearing on the merits.

(2) All orders or writs temporarily enjoining an alien's expulsion shall expire by their terms within such time after entry, not to exceed ten (10) days, as the court fixes, unless within the time so fixed the order, for good cause shown, is extended for a like period or unless the government consents to an extension for a longer period.

Rule 31. Service of Writ or Order Enjoining Expulsion of an Alien.

[Eastern District Only] [Revoked, effective 11–27–89, as to SDNY only.]

(a) In all cases except those described in Rule 30(b) of the Federal Rules of Civil Procedure, service of the writ or order upon the United States attorney's office within the time specified by the court shall be sufficient service to enjoin an alien's expulsion.

(b) After delivery of an alien for expulsion to the master of a ship or the commanding officer of an airplane, the writ or order enjoining the alien's expulsion shall be addressed to and served upon only such master or commanding officer. Notice to the respondent, or the United States attorney's office, of the allowance of the writ or issuance of the order shall not operate to enjoin an alien's expulsion if the alien is no longer in the Government's custody. Service of the writ or order may not be made upon a master after the ship has cast off her moorings or upon a commanding officer once the airplane has closed its doors and left the terminal.

Rule 32. Habeas Corpus and Motions Pursuant to 28 USC § 2255.

(a) The petition in all habeas corpus proceedings shall set forth whether or not applications previously have been made for writs or for similar relief, stating to what court or judge they were made, the determination in each case, and any new facts upon the present application that were not previously shown.

(b) The original verified petition shall be filed with the clerk. In addition to the service on the respondent of the writ of habeas corpus or order to show cause why such a writ should not issue in all cases where an official or employee of the United States is respondent, a copy of the petition and writ or order to show cause shall be delivered to the United States attorney prior to issuance of the writ or granting of the order; if the office of the United States attorney is closed, these papers shall be delivered there before 10:00 A.M. on the following business day unless otherwise ordered by the court.

(c) All pro se petitions for writ of habeas corpus by state prisoners and by federal prisoners and all pro se motions under 28 USC Sec 2255 by persons in custody shall be deemed to include a petition for leave to appear in forma pauperis and the clerk is directed to file all such petitions without prepayment of fees, unless the appropriate judge otherwise directs.

(d) Applications for a writ of habeas corpus made by persons under the judgment and sentence of a court of the State of New York shall be filed, heard and determined in the district court for the district within which they were convicted and sentenced provided, however, that if the convenience of the parties and witnesses requires a hearing in a different district, such application may be transferred to any district which is found by the assigned judge to be more convenient. The clerks of the Southern and Eastern District Courts are authorized and directed to transfer such applications to the District herein designated for filing, hearing and determination. [Added 12-1-86.]

Rule 33. Notice of Claim of Unconstitutionality.

[Revoked, Southern District only, 1-30-92.]

If, at any time prior to the trial of any action, suit or proceeding, to which neither the United States nor any agency, officer or employee thereof is a party, a party draws in question the constitutionality of an act of Congress affecting the public interest, such party shall notify the chief judge in writing of the existence of such question (to enable the court to comply with 28 U.S.C. Sec. 2403) giving the title of the case, a reference to the questioned statute sufficient for its identification, and the respects in which it is claimed that the statute is unconstitutional.

If, at any time prior to the trial of any action, suit or proceeding, to which neither a state nor any agency, officer or employee thereof is a party, a party draws in question the constitutionality of any statute of that state affecting the public interest, such notice shall also be given.

Rule 34. Three-Judge Court.

Whenever upon an application for injunctive relief counsel is of opinion that the relief is such as may be granted only by a three-judge court, the petition shall so state, and the proposed order to show cause (whether or not continuing a stay), or the notice of motion, shall include a request for a hearing before a three-judge court. Upon the convening of a three-judge court, in addition to the original papers on file, there shall be handed up three copies of the pleadings, three copies of the motion papers and three copies of all briefs.

Rule 35. Publication of Advertisements.

All advertisements except notices of sale of real estate or of any interest in land shall, in civil and admiralty causes, be published in a newspaper published in the City of New York and which has a general circulation or a circulation calculated to give public notice of a legal publication. The court may direct the publication of such additional advertisement as it may deem advisable.

Unless otherwise ordered, notices for the sale of real estate or of any interest in land shall be published in a newspaper of general circulation in the county in which the real estate or the land in question is located.

Rule 36. Notice of Sale.

In any civil action, the notice of any proposed sale of property directed to be made by any order or judgment of the court, unless otherwise ordered by the court, need not set out the terms of sale specified in the order or judgment, and the notice will be sufficient if in substantially the following form:

UNITED STATES DISTRICT COURT

_____ District of New York

NOTICE OF SALE

Pursuant to ....of the United States
             (Order or Judgment)

Court for the ....District of New York, filed in the office

of the clerk on ....
                              (Date)

in the case entitled ....
                      (Name and Docket Number)

....................................the undersigned will sell

at ....
                 (Place of Sale)

on ....
              (Date and Hour of Sale)

the property in said ....
               (Order of Judgment)

described and therein directed to be sold, to which ....
                                     (Order of Judgment)

reference is made for the terms of sale and for a description of the property which may be briefly described as follows:

Dated:

_____

Signature and Official Title

The notice need not describe the property by metes and bounds or otherwise in detail and will be sufficient if in general terms it identifies the property by specifying its nature and location. However, it shall state the approximate acreage of any real estate outside the limits of any town or city, the street, lot and block number of any real estate within any town or city, and a general statement of the character of any improvements upon the property.

Rule 37. Sureties.

(a) Whenever a bond, undertaking or stipulation is required, it shall be sufficient, except in bankruptcy or criminal cases, or as otherwise prescribed by law, if the instrument is executed by the surety or sureties only.

(b) Except as otherwise provided by law, every bond, undertaking or stipulation must be secured by the deposit of cash or government bonds in the amount of the bond, undertaking or stipulation, or the undertaking or guaranty of a corporate surety holding a certificate of authority from the Secretary of the Treasury, or the undertaking or guaranty of two individual residents of the district in which the case is pending, each of whom owns real or personal property within the district worth double the amount of the bond, undertaking or stipulation, over all his or her debts and liabilities, and over all obligations assumed by said surety on other bonds, undertakings, or stipulations, and exclusive of all legal exemptions.

(c) In the case of a bond, or undertaking, or stipulation executed by individual sureties, each surety shall attach the surety's affidavit of justification, giving the surety's full name, occupation, residence and business addresses, and showing that the surety is qualified as an individual surety under paragraph (b) of this rule.

(d) Members of the bar, administrative officers or employees of the court, the marshal, the marshal's deputies or assistants, shall not act as surety in any suit, action or proceeding pending in this court.

Rule 38. Approval of Bonds of Corporate Sureties.

Except as otherwise provided by law, all bonds, undertakings and stipulations of corporate sureties holding certificates of authority from the Secretary of the Treasury, where the amount of such bonds or undertakings has been fixed by a judge or by court rule or statute, may be approved by the clerk.

Rule 39. Security for Costs.

The court, on motion or in its own initiative, may order any party to file an original bond for costs or additional security for costs in such an amount and so conditioned as it may designate. For failure to comply with the order the court may make such orders in regard to non-compliance as are just, and among others the following: an order striking out pleadings or staying further proceedings until the bond is filed or dismissing the action or rendering a judgment by default against the non-complying party.

Rule 40. Appeals.

(a) A notice of appeal shall exhibit the names of the several parties to the judgment, and the names and addresses of their respective attorneys of record. Upon the filing of the notice of appeal the appellant shall furnish the clerk with a sufficient number of copies thereof to enable the clerk to comply with the provisions of Rule 3(a), Federal Rules of Appellate Procedure.

(b) Whenever a notice of motion to enforce the liability of a surety upon an appeal or a supersedeas bond is served upon the clerk pursuant to Rule 8(b), Federal Rules of Appellate Procedure, the party making such motion shall deposit with the clerk one additional copy for each surety to be served.

Rule 41. Supersedeas. [Revoked.]

[Revoked, effective 11–27–89 (SDNY), 6–12–90 (EDNY).]

Rule 42. Remand by an Appellate Court.

Whenever an appellate court has remanded a case or matter to the district court, and further proceedings not requiring the trial of an issue of fact are appropriate, an application, whether made on motion or otherwise, shall be referred for such further proceedings to the judge who heard the case or matter below unless the appellate court otherwise directs. [Southern District only]

Any other order or judgment of an appellate court, when filed in the office of the clerk of the district court, shall automatically become the order or judgment of the district court and be entered as such by the clerk without further order except if such order or judgment of the appellate court requires further proceedings in the district court other than a new trial, an order shall be entered making the order or judgment of the appellate court the order or judgment of the district court.

Rule 43. Contempt.

(a) A proceeding to adjudicate a person in civil contempt of court, including a case provided for in Rules 37(b)(1) and 37(b)(2)(d), Federal

Rules of Civil Procedure, shall be commenced by the service of a notice of motion or order to show cause. The affidavit upon which such notice of motion or order to show cause is based shall set out with particularity the misconduct complained of, the claim, if any, for damages occasioned thereby, and such evidence as to the amount of damages as may be available to the moving party. A reasonable counsel fee, necessitated by the contempt proceedings, may be included as an item of damage. Where the alleged contemnor has appeared in the action by an attorney, the notice of motion or order to show cause and the papers upon which it is based may be served upon said attorney; otherwise service shall be made personally, in the manner provided for by the Federal Rules of Civil Procedure for the service of a summons. If an order to show cause is sought, such order may upon necessity shown, embody a direction to the United States marshal to arrest the alleged contemnor and hold such person in bail in an amount fixed by the order, conditioned on the appearance of such person at the hearing, and further conditioned that the alleged contemnor will hold himself or herself amenable to all orders of the court for surrender.

(b) If the alleged contemnor puts in issue his or her alleged misconduct or the damages thereby occasioned, said person shall upon demand, be entitled to have oral evidence taken, either before the court or before a master appointed by the court. When by law such alleged contemnor is entitled to a trial by jury, said person shall make written demand on or before the return day or adjourned day of the application; otherwise said person will be deemed to have waived a trial by jury.

(c) In the event the alleged contemnor is found to be in contempt of court, an order shall be made and entered (1) reciting or referring to the verdict or findings of fact upon which the adjudication is based; (2) setting forth the amount of damages to which the complainant is entitled; (3) fixing the fine, if any, imposed by the court, which fine shall include the damages found, and naming the person to whom such fine shall be payable; (4) stating any other conditions, the performance whereof will operate to purge the contempt; and (5) directing the arrest of the contemnor by the United States marshal and confinement until the performance of the condition fixed in the order and the payment of the fine, or until the contemnor be otherwise discharged pursuant to law. Unless the order otherwise specifies, the place of confinement shall be the Metropolitan Correction Center. No party shall be required to pay or to advance to the marshal any expenses for the upkeep of the prisoner. Upon such an order, no person shall be detained in prison by reason of the non-payment of the fine for a period exceeding six months. A certified copy of the order committing the contemnor shall be sufficient warrant to the marshal for the arrest and confinement. The aggrieved party shall also have the same remedies against the property of the contemnor as if the order awarding the fine were a final judgment.

(d) In the event the alleged contemnor shall be found not guilty of the charges, said person shall be discharged from the proceeding and, in the discretion of the court, may have judgment against the complainant for costs and disbursements and a reasonable counsel fee.

Rule 44. Order of Summation.

After the close of evidence in civil trials, the order of summation shall be determined in the discretion of the trial judge.

Rule 45. Exemption From Mandatory Scheduling Order [Eastern District Only].

Matters involving habeas corpus petitions, social security disability cases, motions to vacate sentences, forfeitures, and reviews from administrative agencies are exempted from the mandatory scheduling order required by Rule 16(b) of the Federal Rules of Civil Procedure.

Rule 46. Interrogatories [Southern District Only].

(a) At the commencement of discovery, interrogatories will be restricted to those seeking names of witnesses with knowledge or information relevant to the subject matter of the action, the computation of each category of damage alleged, and the existence, custodian, location and general description of relevant documents, including pertinent insurance agreements, and other physical evidence, or information of a similar nature.

(b) During discovery, interrogatories other than those seeking information described in paragraph (a), above may only be served if they are a more practical method of obtaining the information sought than a request for production or a deposition.

(c) At the conclusion of each party's discovery, and prior to the discovery cut-off date, interrogatories seeking the claims and contentions of the opposing party may be served unless the court has ordered otherwise. Questions seeking the names of expert witnesses and the substance of their opinions may also be served, if this information has not been previously obtained.

(d) No part of an interrogatory shall be left unanswered merely because an objection is interposed to another part of the interrogatory.

(e)(1) Where an objection is made to any interrogatory or sub-part thereof or to any document request under Fed.R.Civ.P. 34, the objection shall state with specificity all grounds. Any ground not stated in an objection within the time provided by the Federal Rules of Civil Procedure, or any extensions thereof, shall be waived.

(2) Where a claim of privilege is asserted in objecting to any interrogatory or document demand, or sub-part thereof, and an answer is not provided on the basis of such assertion:

(i) the attorney asserting the privilege shall in the objection to the interrogatory or document demand, or sub-part thereof, identify the nature of the privilege (including work product) which is being claimed and if the privilege is being asserted in connection with a claim or defense governed by state law, indicate the state's privilege rule being invoked; and

(ii) the following information shall be provided in the objection, unless divulgence of such information would cause disclosure of the allegedly privileged information:

(A) for documents: (1) the type of documents; (2) general subject matter of the document; (3) the date of the document; (4) such other information as is sufficient to identify the document for a subpoena duces tecum, including, where appropriate, the author of the document, the addressee of the document, and, where not apparent, the relationship of the author and addressee to each other;

(B) for oral communications: (1) the name of the person making the communication and the names of persons present while the communication was made and, where not apparent, the relationship of the persons present to the person making the communication; (2) the date and place of communication; (3) the general subject matter of the communication.

(f) Whenever a party answers any interrogatory by reference to records from which the answer may be derived or ascertained, as permitted in Fed.R.Civ.P. 33(c):

(1) The specification of documents to be produced shall be in sufficient detail to permit the interrogating party to locate and identify the records and to ascertain the answer as readily as could the party from whom discovery is sought.

(2) The producing party shall make available any computerized information or summaries thereof that it either has, or can adduce by a relatively simple procedure, unless these materials are privileged or otherwise immune from discovery.

(3) The producing party shall provide any relevant compilations, abstracts or summaries in its custody or readily obtainable by it, unless these materials are privileged or otherwise immune from discovery.

(4) The documents shall be made available for inspection and copying within ten days after service of the answers to interrogatories or at a date agreed upon by the parties.

[Added, effective 2-1-85.]

Rule 47. Uniform Definitions in Discovery Requests.

(a) The full text of the definitions and rules of construction set forth in paragraphs (c) and (d) is deemed incorporated by reference into all discovery requests, but shall not preclude (i) the definition of other terms specific to the particular litigation, (ii) the use of abbreviations or (iii) a more narrow definition of a term defined in paragraph (c).

(b) This Rule is not intended to broaden or narrow the scope of discovery permitted by the Federal Rules of Civil Procedure for the United States District Courts.

(c) The following definitions apply to all discovery requests:

(1) *Communication.* The term "communication" means the transmittal of information (in the form of facts, ideas, inquiries or otherwise).

(2) *Document.* The term "document" is defined to be synonymous in meaning and equal in scope to the usage of this term in Federal Rule of Civil Procedure 34(a). A draft or non-identical copy is a separate document within the meaning of this term.

(3) *Identify (With Respect to Persons).* When referring to a person, "to identify" means to give, to the extent known, the person's full name, present or last known address, and when referring to a natural person, additionally, the present or last known place of employment. Once a person has been identified in accordance with this subparagraph, only the name of that person need be listed in response to subsequent discovery requesting the identification of that person.

(4) *Identify (With Respect to Documents).* When referring to documents, "to identify" means to give, to the extent known, the (i) type of document; (ii) general subject matter; (iii) date of the document; and (iv) author(s), addressee(s) and recipient(s).

(5) *Parties.* The terms "plaintiff" and "defendant" as well as a party's full or abbreviated name or a pronoun referring to a party mean the party and, where applicable, its officers, directors, employees, partners, corporate parent, subsidiaries or affiliates. This definition is not intended to impose a discovery obligation on any person who is not a party to the litigation.

(6) *Person.* The term "person" is defined as any natural person or any business, legal or governmental entity or association.

(7) *Concerning.* The term "concerning" means relating to, referring to, describing, evidencing or constituting.

(d) The following rules of construction apply to all discovery requests:

(1) *All/Each.* The terms "all" and "each" shall be construed as all and each.

(2) *And/Or.* The connectives "and" and "or" shall be construed either disjunctively or conjunctively as necessary to bring within the scope of the discovery request all responses that might otherwise be construed to be outside of its scope.

(3) *Number.* The use of the singular form of any word includes the plural and vice versa.

Rule 48. [Omitted—The rule involves discovery in actions brought by prisoners pro se.]

RULES FOR PROCEEDINGS BEFORE MAGISTRATE JUDGES

Rule 1. Jurisdiction—28 USC § 636.

Full-time magistrates shall have jurisdiction to discharge the duties set forth in 28 U.S.C. Sec. 636.

Rules 2–5. [Omitted—These rules relate primarily to criminal matters.]

Rule 6. Issuance of Subpoenas.

Magistrates may issue subpoenas, writs of habeas corpus ad testificandum or ad prosequendum or other orders necessary to obtain the presence of parties or witnesses or evidence needed for court proceedings, either civil or criminal and may sign in forma pauperis orders.

Rule 7. Notice of Determination and Objections Thereto. [Revoked.]

[Revoked, effective 11–27–89 (SDNY), 6–12–90 (EDNY).]

Rule 8. Consent Jurisdiction Procedure.

(a) When a civil action is filed with the clerk, the clerk shall give the filing party notice of the magistrate's consent jurisdiction in a form approved by the court, with sufficient copies to be served with the complaint on adversary parties. A copy of such notice shall be attached to any third-party complaint served by a defendant. [SDNY only.]

(b) [Revoked, effective 11–27–89 (SDNY), 6–12–90 (EDNY).]

(c) When a completed form has been filed, the clerk shall draw by lot the name of a magistrate, unless a magistrate has previously acted in the matter, and forward the consent form with the name of such magistrate for final approval to the judge to whom the case is assigned. When the judge has approved the transfer and returned the consent form to the clerk's office for filing, the clerk shall forward a copy of the consent form to the magistrate to whom the case is assigned. The clerk shall also indicate on the file the name of the magistrate to whom the case has been assigned. [SDNY only.]

(d) The magistrate may hear and determine any and all pretrial and post-trial matters which are filed by the parties, including case-dispositive motions in a case which has been assigned upon consent of the parties. [SDNY only.]

PROC. BEFORE MAGISTRATES   Rule 14

(e) Appeals, if made to the district court from a magistrate's judgment, shall be heard by the judge to whom the case was originally assigned. [SDNY only.]

Rules 9–11. [Omitted—These rules relate primarily to criminal matters.]

Rule 12. Rotation of Assignments—Southern District Only.

See provision of Southern District's Civil Justice Expense and Delay Reduction Plan.

Rule 13. General Pretrial Supervision.

Any case referred to a magistrate by a district judge for general pretrial supervision shall confer on the magistrate the jurisdiction set forth in 28 U.S.C. Sec. 636(b)(1)(A) unless specifically stated otherwise in the order of reference.

Rule 14. Appeals From Cases Heard on Consent. [SDNY.]

(a) *Appeal to the Court of Appeals.* [Revoked 11-27-89.]

(b) *Appeal to a District Judge.*

(1) *Notice of Appeal.* In accordance with 28 U.S.C. Sec. 636(c)(4), the parties may consent to appeal any judgment in a civil case to be disposed of by a magistrate to the district judge to whom the case was initially assigned, rather than directly to the Court of Appeals. In such case the appeal shall be taken by filing a notice of appeal with the clerk of the district court within thirty (30) days after entry of the magistrate's judgment. If the United States or an officer or agency thereof is a party, the notice of appeal may be filed by any party within sixty (60) days of the judgment. A notice of cross appeal shall be filed within fourteen (14) days after the first timely notice of appeal was filed. For good cause shown, the magistrate or the judge may extend the time for filing the notice of appeal or cross appeal for an additional twenty (20) days. Any request for such extension, however, must be made before the original time period for such appeal has expired.

(2) *Record on Appeal.* The record on appeal shall comply with the provisions of Rules 10 and 11 of the Federal Rules of Appellate Procedure.

(3) *Briefs.* The appellant shall within twenty (20) days of the filing of the notice of appeal file a typewritten brief with the clerk of the district court together with two (2) additional copies, stating the specific facts, points of law, and authorities on which the appeal is based. The appellee shall file an answering brief within fifteen (15) days of the filing of the appellant's brief. The appellant may serve and file a reply brief within seven (7) days after service of appellee's brief and at least three

(3) days before any scheduled argument. The court may extend these time limits upon a showing of good cause made by the party requesting the extension. Such good cause may include reasonable delay in the preparation of any necessary transcript. If an appellant fails to file his brief within the time provided by this rule, or any extension thereof, the court may dismiss the appeal.

(4) *Oral Argument.* After the appellee's brief has been filed, the chambers of the district judge will inform the parties of the time and place of any oral argument. By agreement of the parties and the judge, cases may be submitted for decision without oral argument.

(5) *Disposition of the Appeal by a Judge.* The judge shall consider the appeal on the record, in the same manner as if the case had been appealed from a judgment of the district Court of Appeals and in accordance with the provisions of 28 U.S.C. Sec. 636(c)(4).

(6) *Rehearing.* A petition for rehearing must be filed within seven (7) days after judgment is entered on the appeal.

Rule 14. Appeals from Cases Heard on Consent. [EDNY.]

(a) *General.* The practice on an appeal from a judgment in any civil case decided by a magistrate on consent of the parties pursuant to 28 U.S.C. § 636(c), as governed by Fed.R.Civ.P. 74–76, is supplemented by the following local rules of practice.

(b) *Briefs.* The appellant shall within twenty (20) days of the filing of the notice of appeal file a typewritten brief with the clerk of the district court together with two (2) additional copies, stating the specific facts, points of law and authorities on which the appeal is based. The appellee shall file an answering brief within fifteen (15) days of the filing of the appellant's brief. The appellant may serve and file a reply brief within seven (7) days after service of appellee's brief and at least three (3) days before any scheduled argument. The court may extend these time limits upon a showing of good cause made by the party requesting the extension. Such good cause may include reasonable delay in the preparation of any necessary transcript. If an appellant fails to file his brief within the time provided by this rule, or any extension thereof, the court may dismiss the appeal.

(c) *Oral Argument.* After the appellee's brief has been filed the chambers of the district judge will inform the parties of the time and place of any oral argument. By agreement of the parties and the judge, cases may be submitted for decision without oral argument.

[Amended, effective 6–12–90.]

Rule 15. Entry of Mandatory Scheduling Orders [Eastern District Only].

Magistrates are empowered to enter scheduling orders pursuant to Rule 16(b) of the Federal Rules of Civil Procedure.

Rule 16. Entry of Mandatory Scheduling Orders [Southern District].

Magistrates may make and modify for good cause shown, scheduling orders pursuant to Federal Rules of Civil Procedure 16(b) in any case referred to them by a judge.

RULES FOR THE DIVISION OF BUSINESS AMONG DISTRICT JUDGES SOUTHERN DISTRICT

These rules are adopted for the internal management of the case load of the court and shall not be deemed to vest any rights in litigants or their attorneys and shall be subject to such amendments from time to time as shall be approved by the court.

Rule 1. Individual Assignment System.

This court shall operate under an individual assignment system to assure continuous and close judicial supervision of every case. Each civil and criminal action and proceeding, except as otherwise provided, shall be assigned by lot to one judge for all purposes. The system shall be administered by an assignment committee in such a manner that all active judges, except the chief judge, shall be assigned substantially an equal share and kind of the work of the court over a period of time. There shall be assigned or transferred to the chief judge such matters as the chief judge is willing and able to undertake, consistent with the chief judge's administrative duties.

Rule 2. Assignment Committee.

An assignment committee is established for the administration of this assignment system. The committee shall consist of the chief judge and two other active judges selected by the chief judge, each to serve for one year. The chief judge shall also select two other active judges, each to serve for a period of one year, as alternate members of the committee.

The assignment committee shall supervise and rule upon all problems relating to assignments under this system, in accordance with these rules, as amended from time to time by the board of judges.

Rule 3. Part I.

A Part I is established for hearing and determining certain emergency and miscellaneous matters in civil and criminal cases and for processing criminal actions and proceedings through the pleading stage.

Judges shall choose assignment to Part I from an appropriate schedule, in order to (sic) their seniority, for periods not to exceed three weeks in each year. The assignment committee may, on consent of the judges affected, change such assignments, if necessary, to meet the needs of the court.

Part I shall be open from 10:00 A.M. to 5:00 P.M. Monday through Friday except on holidays and a magistrate shall be available at the courthouse on Saturdays up to 12:00 P.M. The judge presiding in Part I shall be available for emergency matters.

The judge presiding in Part I may fix such other times for any proceeding as necessary.

Rule 4. Civil Actions or Proceedings (Filing and Assignment).

(a) *Filing with the Clerk.* All civil actions and proceedings shall be numbered consecutively by year upon the filing of the first document in the case.

When a complaint or the first document is filed in a civil action or proceeding, counsel shall complete and file an information and designation form, in triplicate, indicating: (1) the title of the action; (2) the residence address and county of each plaintiff and defendant; (3) the basis of federal jurisdiction; (4) whether the action is a class action; (5) a brief statement of the nature of the action and amount involved; (6) whether the action is claimed to be a related case within the meaning of Rule 15, infra, and if so, the docket number and name of the judge assigned to the earlier filed related action; (7) the category of the case; (8) the name of the sentencing judge, if brought under 28 U.S.C. Sec. 2255; and (9) the name, address, and telephone number of the attorney of record and of the attorney's firm, if any. Forms for this purpose will be on file in the office of the clerk of the court and shall be furnished to counsel. [Amended 3-30-89.]

(b) *Assignment by the Clerk by Lot.* All civil actions and proceedings, except applications for leave to proceed in forma pauperis, upon being filed and all appeals from the bankruptcy court upon being docketed in this court shall be assigned by lot within each designated category to one judge for all purposes.

An action, case or proceeding may not be dismissed and thereafter refiled for the purpose of obtaining a different judge. If an action, case or proceeding, or one essentially the same, is dismissed and refiled, it shall be assigned to the same judge. It is the duty of every attorney appearing to bring the facts of the refiling to the attention of the clerk.

Rule 5. Civil Proceedings in Part I.

Admissions to the bar and civil matters other than emergencies shall be heard on Tuesdays commencing at 10:00 A.M. Naturalization proceedings shall be conducted on Wednesday, commencing at 10:30 A.M.

(a) *Miscellaneous Civil Matters.* The judge presiding in Part I shall hear and determine all miscellaneous proceedings in civil matters, such as application for naturalization, for admission to the bar, for relief relating to orders and subpoenas of administrative agencies and shall purge jurors in the central jury part as and when required. When a modification or further action on such determination is sought, it shall be referred to the judge who made the original determination even though said judge is no longer sitting in Part I.

(b) *Civil Emergency Matters.* The Part I judge shall hear and determine all emergency matters in civil cases which have been assigned to a judge when the assigned judge is absent or has expressly referred the matter to Part I because said judge is unavailable due to extraordinary circumstances. Depending on which procedures the Part I judge deems the more efficient, the Part I judge may either dispose of an emergency matter only to the extent necessary to meet the emergency, or on consent of the assigned judge and notice to the clerk, transfer the action to himself or herself for all further proceedings.

(c) *Subsequent Emergency Proceedings.* If a civil emergency matter is brought before the Part I judge and the judge concludes that for lack of emergency or otherwise the proceeding should not be determined in Part I the party who brought the proceeding shall not present the same matter again to any other Part I judge unless relevant circumstances have changed in the interim in which case the party shall advise the judge of the prior proceedings and changed circumstances.

Rules 6–8. [Omitted—These rules relate primarily to criminal matters.]

Rule 9. Cases Certified for Prompt Trial or Disposition.

Immediately after assignment to a judge, civil and criminal actions shall be screened by the assignment committee for the purpose of identifying cases which are likely to be subject to delays and which, because of exceptional and special circumstances, demand extraordinary priority, prompt disposition, and immediate judicial supervision in the public interest.

When a case has been so identified by the assignment committee, the committee shall certify that the case requires extraordinary priority and a prompt trial or other disposition within sixty (60) days and shall so advise the judge to whom the case has been assigned. The judge so assigned shall advise the assignment committee whether said judge can accord the case the required priority. In the event the judge so assigned advises the assignment committee that he or she cannot accord the required priority, the case shall immediately be assigned to another judge by lot and the same procedure followed until the case is assigned to a judge able to accord it the required priority. The name of the judge to be so assigned shall be drawn by lot in the same manner as other civil and criminal actions are initially assigned.

[Third paragraph repealed, effective 11–27–89.]

Rule 10. Motions.

(a) *Civil Motions.* Civil motions shall be made within the time required by the Federal Rules of Civil Procedure and the Civil Rules of this court. Motions shall be made returnable before the assigned judge.

(b) *Criminal Motions.* Motions in criminal actions shall be made returnable before the assigned judge at such time as said judge directs. Criminal motions must be made within the time required by the Federal Rules of Criminal Procedure and the Criminal Rules of this court, except that the time for motions otherwise required by such rules to be made before the entry of a plea shall be made within ten (10) days after the entry of a plea, or at such other time as the assigned judge directs.

Rule 11. [Omitted—The rule relates primarily to criminal matters.]

Rule 12. Assignments to New Judges.

When a new judge is inducted, the assignment committee shall transfer to the new judge an equal share of all cases then pending (including cases on the suspense docket). The cases shall be taken equally, by lot, from the dockets of each of the judges' most recent chronological list of cases which have been designated by the transferor as eligible for transfer. No case shall be transferred without the consent of the transferor judge. The assignment committee shall also direct the clerk to add the name of the new judge to the random selection system for assigning new cases to active judges.

Rule 13. Assignments to Senior Judges.

If a senior judge is willing and able to undertake assignment of new cases for all purposes, said judge shall advise the assignment committee of the number and categories of new cases which said judge is willing and able to undertake. New cases in the requested number in each category shall then be assigned to said judge in the same manner as new cases are assigned to active judges.

If a senior judge is willing and able to undertake assignment of pending cases from other judges, said judge may (1) accept assignment of all or any part of any case from any judge on mutual consent, or (2) advise the assignment committee of the number, status, and categories of pending cases which said judge is willing to undertake. Such cases will be drawn by lot from current lists provided to the assignment committee by the judges wishing to transfer cases under this rule. If a senior judge does not terminate any action so transferred, it shall be reassigned to the transferor judge.

Rule 14. Assignments to Visiting Judges.

When a visiting judge is assigned to this district, said judge shall advise the assignment committee of the number and categories of pending cases which said judge is required or willing to accept. The assignment committee shall then transfer to said judge the required number of cases in each category by drawing them equally and by lot from each judge's list of cases ready for trial, but no case shall be so transferred without the consent of the transferor judge. If the visiting judge does not terminate the action, it shall be reassigned to the transferor judge.

Rule 15. Transfer of Related Cases.

(a) Subject to the limitations set forth below, a civil case will be deemed related to one or more other civil cases and will be transferred for consolidation or coordinated pretrial proceedings when the interests of justice and efficiency will be served. In determining relatedness, a judge will consider whether (i) a substantial saving of judicial resources would result; or (ii) the just efficient and economical conduct of the litigations would be advanced; or (iii) the convenience of the parties or witnesses would be served. Without intending to limit the criteria considered by the judges of this Court in determining relatedness, a congruence of parties or witnesses or the likelihood of a consolidated or joint trial or joint pre-trial discovery may be deemed relevant.

(b) Criminal cases are not treated as related to civil cases or vice versa. Criminal cases are not treated as related unless a motion is granted for a joint trial. Bankruptcy appeals are not considered related merely because they arise from the same bankruptcy proceeding.

(c) When a civil case is being filed or removed, the person filing or removing shall disclose on an appropriate form, to be furnished by the Clerk's Office, any contention of relatedness. A copy of such form shall be served with the complaint or notice of removal. A case filed or removed and designated as related shall be forwarded to the judge before whom the earlier filed case is then pending who shall accept or reject the case in his or her sole discretion. Cases rejected by the judge as being not related shall be assigned by random selection. Any party believing its case to be related to another may apply on notice in writing to the judge assigned in its case for transfer to the judge having the related case with the lowest docket number. If the assigned judge believes the case should be transferred, he or she shall refer the question to the judge who would receive the transfer. In event of disagreement among the assigned judges, a judge (but not a party) may refer the question to the Assignment Committee. Litigants will not be heard by the Assignment Committee.

(d) Motions in civil and criminal cases to consolidate, or for a joint trial, are regulated by the Federal Rules. A defendant in a criminal case may move on notice to have all of his or her sentences in this district imposed by a single judge. All such motions shall be noticed for hearing before the judge having the lowest docket number, with courtesy copies to be provided to the judge or judges having the cases with higher docket numbers.

(e) Nothing contained in this rule limits the use of Rule 1, infra, for reassignment of all or part of any case from the docket of one judge to that of another by agreement of the respective judges.

[Amended 3-30-89]

Rule 16. Transfer of Cases by Consent.

Any active or senior judge, upon written advice to the assignment committee, may transfer directly any case or any part of any case on said judge's docket to any consenting active or senior judge except where Rule 18 applies.

Rule 17. Transfers From Senior Judges.

When an active judge becomes a senior judge, or later as the judge chooses, the judge may keep as much of his or her existing docket as said judge desires and furnish the assignment committee with a list of all cases which the judge desires to have transferred. The assignment committee will distribute these cases as equally as is feasible, by lot, to each active judge.

Rule 18. Transfer Because of Disqualification, etc.

In case the assigned judge is disqualified or upon request, if said judge has presided at a mistrial or former trial of the case, upon written notice to it, the assignment committee shall transfer the case by lot.

Rule 19. Transfer of Cases Because of Death, Resignation, Prolonged Illness, Disability, Unavoidable Absence, or Excessive Backlog of a Judge.

The assignment committee shall, in the case of death or resignation, and may, in the event of prolonged illness, disability, unavoidable absence of an assigned judge, or the build-up of an excessive backlog, transfer any case or cases pending on the docket of such judge by distributing them as equally as is feasible by lot, to all remaining active judges and to such senior judges who are willing and able to undertake them.

Rule 20. Transfer of Cases to the Suspense Docket.

A civil case which, for reasons beyond the control of the court, can neither be tried nor otherwise terminated shall be transferred to the suspense docket. In the event the case becomes activated, it shall be restored to the docket of the transferor judge if available, otherwise it shall be reassigned by lot.

Rules 21-33 [Omitted—These rules relate primarily to assignment of cases among various courthouses within a District.]

Part VIII

RECENT COURT DECISION

TABLE OF CONTENTS

Court Opinion

Matter of Rhone–Poulenc Rorer Incorporated
(No. 94–3912, 7th Cir., March 16, 1995)

Certification of Class Actions—Basic Standards
Review by Mandamus of Interlocutory Orders—When Appropriate

IN THE MATTER OF: RHONE–POULENC RORER INCORPORATED, ET AL.*

United States Court of Appeals, Seventh Circuit, 1995.
51 F.3d 1293.

POSNER, CHIEF JUDGE. Drug companies that manufacture blood solids are the defendants in a nationwide class action brought on behalf of hemophiliacs infected by the AIDS virus as a consequence of using the defendants' products. The defendants have filed with us a petition for mandamus, asking us to direct the district judge to rescind his order certifying the case as a class action. We have no *appellate* jurisdiction over that order. An order certifying a class is not a final decision within the meaning of 28 U.S.C. § 1291; it does not wind up the litigation in the district court. And, in part because it is reviewable (at least in principle—the importance of this qualification will appear shortly) on appeal from the final decision in the case, it has been held not to fit any of the exceptions to the rule that confines federal appellate jurisdiction to final decisions. In short, as the Supreme Court made clear in *Coopers & Lybrand v. Livesay,* 437 U.S. 463, 98 S.Ct. 2454, 57 L.Ed.2d 351 (1978), and *Gardner v. Westinghouse Broadcasting Co.,* 437 U.S. 478, 480–82, 98 S.Ct. 2451, 2453–54, 57 L.Ed.2d 364 (1978), it is not an

---

* Note that the printed case was not formally prepared for publication and therefore included a number of typographical errors and incomplete citations. The authors have taken the liberty of correcting errors and completing citations when appropriate.

appealable order. Those decisions involved the denial rather than the grant of motions for class certification, but the grant is no more final than the denial and no more within any of the exceptions to the final-decision rule. *Hoxworth v. Blinder, Robinson & Co.,* 903 F.2d 186, 208 (3d Cir.1990); 7B Charles Alan Wright, Arthur A. Miller & Mary Kay Kane, *Federal Practice and Procedure* § 1802, pp. 484–86 (2d ed. 1986). Still, even nonappealable orders can be challenged by asking the court of appeals to mandamus the district court. Indeed, as a practical matter *only* such orders can be challenged by filing a petition for mandamus; an appealable order can be challenged only by appealing from it; the possibility of appealing would be a compelling reason for denying mandamus. For obvious reasons, however, mandamus is issued only in extraordinary cases. Otherwise, interlocutory orders would be appealable routinely, but with "appeal" renamed "mandamus." *Kerr v. United States District Court,* 426 U.S. 394, 403, 96 S.Ct. 2119, 2124, 48 L.Ed.2d 725 (1976); *Eisenberg v. United States District Court,* 910 F.2d 374, 375 (7th Cir.1990).

How to cabin this too-powerful writ which if uncabined threatens to unravel the final-decision rule? By taking seriously the two conditions for the grant of a writ of mandamus. The first is that the challenged order not be *effectively* reviewable at the end of the case—in other words, that it inflict *irreparable* harm. *Kerr v. United States, supra,* 426 U.S. at 403, 96 S.Ct. at 2124; *In re Sandahl,* 980 F.2d 1118, 1119 (7th Cir. 1992); *Eisenberg v. United States District Court, supra,* 910 F.2d at 375. The petitioner "must ordinarily demonstrate that something about the order, or its circumstances, would make an end-of-case appeal ineffectual or leave legitimate interests unduly at risk." *In re Recticel Foam Corp.,* 859 F.2d 1000, 1005–06 (1st Cir.1988). Second, the order must so far exceed the proper bounds of judicial discretion as to be legitimately considered usurpative in character, or in violation of a clear and indisputable legal right, or, at the very least, patently erroneous. *Gulfstream Aerospace Corp. v. Mayacamas Corp.,* 485 U.S. 271, 289, 108 S.Ct. 1133, 1143–44, 99 L.Ed.2d 296 (1988); *Allied Chemical Corp. v. Daiflon, Inc.,* 449 U.S. 33, 35, 101 S.Ct. 188, 190, 66 L.Ed.2d 193 (1980) (per curiam); *United States v. Spilotro,* 884 F.2d 1003, 1006–07 (7th Cir.1989); *In re Sandahl, supra,* 980 F.2d at 1121; *Maloney v. Plunkett,* 854 F.2d 152 (7th Cir.1988). We shall not have to explore these gradations; it will be enough to consider whether the district judge's order can fairly be characterized as usurpative.

The set of orders in which both conditions are satisfied is small. It certainly is not coterminous with the set of orders certifying suits as class actions. For even though such orders often, perhaps typically, inflict irreparable injury on the defendants (just as orders denying class certification often, perhaps typically, inflict irreparable injury on the members of the class), irreparable injury is not sufficient for mandamus; there must also be an abuse of discretion that can fairly be characterized as gross, very clear, or unusually serious. But it is not an empty set. The point of cases like *Coopers & Lybrand* is that irreparable harm is not enough to make class certification orders *automatically* appealable under 28 U.S.C. § 1291, not that mandamus is *never* appropriate in a class certification setting. There is a big difference between saying that *all* class certification rulings are appealable as of right because they are final within the meaning of section 1291 (the position rejected in *Coopers & Lybrand*) and saying that a handful are—the handful in which the district judge committed a clear abuse of discretion. Mandamus has occasionally been granted to undo class certifications, see, e.g., *In re Fibreboard Corp.*, 893 F.2d 706 (5th Cir.1990), and we are not aware that any case has held that mandamus will *never* be granted in such cases. See *In re Catawba Indian Tribe*, 973 F.2d 1133, 1137 (4th Cir.1992); *DeMasi v. Weiss*, 669 F.2d 114, 117–19 and n. 6 (3d Cir.1982). The present case, as we shall see, is quite extraordinary when all its dimensions are apprehended. We shall also see that when mandamus is sought to protect the Seventh Amendment's right to a jury trial in federal civil cases, as in this case, the requirement of proving irreparable harm is relaxed.

The suit to which the petition for mandamus relates, *Wadleigh v. Rhone–Poulenc Rorer Inc.*, arises out of the infection of a substantial fraction of the hemophiliac population of this country by the AIDS virus because the blood supply was contaminated by the virus before the nature of the disease was well understood or adequate methods of screening the blood supply existed. The AIDS virus (HIV—human immunodeficiency virus) is transmitted by the exchange of bodily fluids, primarily semen and blood. Hemophiliacs depend on blood solids that contain the clotting factors whose absence defines their disease. These blood solids are concentrated from blood obtained from many donors. If just one of the donors is infected by the AIDS virus the probability that the blood solids manufactured in part from his blood will be infected is very high unless the blood is treated with heat to kill the virus. * * *

Some 300 lawsuits, involving some 400 plaintiffs, have been filed, 60 percent of them in state courts, 40 percent in federal district courts under the diversity jurisdiction, seeking to impose tort liability on the defendants for the transmission of HIV to hemophiliacs in blood solids manufactured by the defendants. Obviously these 400 plaintiffs represent only a small fraction of the hemophiliacs (or their next of kin, in cases in which the hemophiliac has died) who are infected by HIV or have died of AIDS. One of the 300 cases is *Wadleigh,* filed in September 1993, the case that the district judge certified as a class action. Thirteen other cases have been tried already in various courts around the country, and the defendants have won twelve of them. All the cases brought in federal court (like *Wadleigh*)—cases brought under the diversity jurisdiction—have been consolidated for pre-trial discovery in the Northern District of Illinois by the panel on multidistrict litigation.

RECENT COURT DECISION

The plaintiffs advance two principal theories of liability. The first is that before anyone had heard of AIDS or HIV, it was known that Hepatitis B, a lethal disease though less so than HIV–AIDS, could be transmitted either through blood transfusions or through injection of blood solids. The plaintiffs argue that due care with respect to the risk of infection with Hepatitis B required the defendants to take measures to purge that virus from their blood solids, whether by treating the blood they bought or by screening the donors—perhaps by refusing to deal with *paid* donors, known to be a class at high risk of being infected with Hepatitis B. The defendants' failure to take effective measures was, the plaintiffs claim, negligent. Had the defendants not been negligent, the plaintiffs further argue, hemophiliacs would have been protected not only against Hepatitis B but also, albeit fortuitously or as the plaintiffs put it "serendipitously," against HIV.

The plaintiffs' second theory of liability is more conventional. It is that the defendants, again negligently, dragged their heels in screening donors and taking other measures to prevent contamination of blood solids by HIV when they learned about the disease in the early 1980s. The plaintiffs have other theories of liability as well, including strict products liability, but it is not necessary for us to get into them.

The district judge did not think it feasible to certify *Wadleigh* as a class action for the adjudication of the entire controversy between the plaintiffs and the defendants. Fed.R.Civ.P. 23(b)(3). The differences in the date of infection alone of the thousands of potential class members would make such a procedure infeasible. Hemophiliacs infected before anyone knew about the contamination of blood solids by HIV could not rely on the second theory of liability, while hemophiliacs infected after the blood supply became safe (not perfectly safe, but nearly so) probably were not infected by any of the defendants' products. Instead the judge certified the suit "as a class action with respect to particular issues" only. Fed.R.Civ.P. 23(c)(4)(A). He explained this decision in an opinion which implied that he did not envisage the entry of a final judgment but rather the rendition by a jury of a special verdict that would answer a number of questions bearing, perhaps decisively, on whether the defendants are negligent under either of the theories sketched above. If the special verdict found no negligence under either theory, that presumably would be the end of all the cases unless other theories of liability proved viable. If the special verdict found negligence, individual members of the class would then file individual tort suits in state and federal district courts around the nation and would use the special verdict, in conjunction with the doctrine of collateral estoppel, to block relitigation of the issue of negligence.

With all due respect for the district judge's commendable desire to experiment with an innovative procedure for streamlining the adjudication of this "mass tort," we believe that his plan so far exceeds the permissible bounds of discretion in the management of federal litigation as to compel us to intervene and order decertification. The plaintiffs' able counsel argues that we need not intervene now, that it will be time enough to intervene if and when a special verdict adverse to the defendants is entered and an appeal taken to us. But of course a verdict as such is not an appealable order. Only when a final judgment is entered, determining liability and assessing damages, will the case, including interim rulings such as the certification of certain issues in the case for determination in a class action, be appealable to us. Since without a final judgment the special verdict would not (with an exception noted later in this opinion) even have collateral estoppel effect, *Amcast Industrial Corp. v. Detrex Corp.*, 45 F.3d 155, 158 (7th Cir.1995), the district judge may have intended that the special verdict would be followed by a trial on any remaining liability issues, and on damages, limited to Wadleigh and the other named plaintiffs in the *Wadleigh* case. The trial would culminate in a final judgment, which would both be appealable to us and impart collateral estoppel effect to the special verdict. The members of the class, other than the named plaintiffs, would take the special verdict back to their home districts and use it to limit the scope of the individual trials that would be necessary—for remember that the district judge has refused to certify the case as a class action for a final adjudication of the controversy between the class and the defendants—to determine each class member's actual entitlement to damages and in what amount.

* * * The reason that an appeal will come too late to provide effective relief for these defendants is the sheer *magnitude* of the risk to which the class action, in contrast to the individual actions pending or likely, exposes them. Consider the situation that would obtain if the class had not been certified. The defendants would be facing 300 suits. More might be filed, but probably only a few more, because the statutes of limitations in the various states are rapidly expiring for potential plaintiffs. The blood supply has been safe since 1985. That is ten years ago. The risk to hemophiliacs of having become infected with HIV has been widely publicized; it is unlikely that many hemophiliacs are unaware of it. Under the usual discovery statute of limitations, they would have to have taken steps years ago to determine their infection status, and having found out file suit within the limitations period running from the date of discovery, in order to preserve their rights.

Three hundred is not a trivial number of lawsuits. The potential damages in each one are great. But the defendants have won twelve of the first thirteen, and, if this is a representative sample, they are likely to win most of the remaining ones as well. Perhaps in the end, if class-action treatment is denied (it has been denied in all the other hemophiliac HIV suits in which class certification has been sought), they will be compelled to pay damages in only 25 cases, involving a potential liability of perhaps no more than $125 million altogether. These are guesses, of course, but they are at once conservative and usable for the limited purpose of comparing the situation that will face the defendants if the class certification stands. All of a sudden they will face thousands of plaintiffs. Many may already be barred by the statute of limitations, as we have suggested, though its further running was tolled by the filing of *Wadleigh* as a class action. *American Pipe & Construction Co. v. Utah*, 414 U.S. 538, 554, 94 S.Ct. 756, 766, 38 L.Ed.2d 713 (1974). (If the class is decertified, the statute of limitations will start running again. *Glidden v. Chromalloy American Corp.*, 808 F.2d 621, 627 (7th Cir.1986); *Barrett v. U.S. Civil Service Comm'n*, 439 F.Supp. 216, 218–19 (D.D.C. 1977); cf. *American Pipe & Construction Co. v. Utah, supra*, 414 U.S. at 552, 561, 94 S.Ct. at 765, 770; *Crown, Cork & Seal Co. v. Parker*, 462 U.S. 345, 354, 103 S.Ct. 2392, 2398, 76 L.Ed.2d 628 (1983).)

Suppose that 5,000 of the potential class members are not yet barred by the statute of limitations. And suppose the named plaintiffs in *Wadleigh* win the class portion of this case to the extent of establishing the defendants' liability under either of the two negligence theories. It is true that this would only be prima facie liability, that the defendants would have various defenses. But they could not be confident that the defenses would prevail. They might, therefore, easily be facing $25 billion in potential liability (conceivably more), and with it bankruptcy. They may not wish to roll these dice. That is putting it mildly. They will be under intense pressure to settle. * * *

We do not want to be misunderstood as saying that class actions are bad because they place pressure on defendants to settle. That pressure is a reality, but it must be balanced against the undoubted benefits of the class action that have made it an authorized procedure for employment by federal courts. We have yet to consider the balance. All that our discussion to this point has shown is that the first condition for the grant of mandamus—that the challenged ruling not be effectively reviewable at the end of the case—is fulfilled. The ruling will inflict irreparable harm; the next question is whether the ruling can fairly be described as usurpative. We have formulated this second condition as narrowly, as stringently, as can be, but even so formulated we think it is fulfilled. We do not mean to suggest that the district judge is engaged in a deliberate power-grab. We have no reason to suppose that he *wants* to preside over an unwieldy class action. We believe that he was responding imaginatively and in the best of faith to the challenge that mass torts, graphically illustrated by the avalanche of asbestos litigation, pose for the federal courts. But the plan that he has devised for the HIV-hemophilia litigation exceeds the bounds of allowable judicial discretion. Three concerns, none of them necessarily sufficient in itself but cumulatively compelling, persuade us to this conclusion.

The first is a concern with forcing these defendants to stake their companies on the outcome of a single jury trial, or be forced by fear of the risk of bankruptcy to settle even if they have no legal liability, when it is entirely feasible to allow a final, authoritative determination of their liability for the colossal misfortune that has befallen the hemophiliac population to emerge from a decentralized process of multiple trials, involving different juries, and different standards of liability, in different jurisdictions, and when, in addition, the preliminary indications are that the defendants are not liable for the grievous harm that has befallen the members of the class. These qualifications are important. In most class actions—and those ones in which the rationale for the procedure is most compelling—individual suits are infeasible because the claim of each class member is tiny relative to the expense of litigation. That plainly is not the situation here. A notable feature of this case, and one that has not been remarked upon or encountered, so far as we are aware, in previous cases, is the demonstrated great likelihood that the plaintiffs' claims, despite their human appeal, lack legal merit. This is the inference from the defendants' having won 92.3 percent ($^{12}/_{13}$) of the cases to have gone to judgment. Granted, thirteen is a small sample and further trials, if they are held, may alter the pattern that the sample reveals. But whether they do or not, the result will be robust if these further trials are permitted to go forward, because the pattern that results will reflect a consensus, or at least a pooling of judgment, of many different tribunals.

For this consensus or maturing of judgment the district judge proposes to substitute a single trial before a single jury instructed in accordance with no actual law of any jurisdiction—a jury that will receive a kind of Esperanto instruction, merging the negligence standards of the 50 states and the District of Columbia. One jury, consisting of six persons (the standard federal civil jury nowadays consists of six regular jurors and two alternates), will hold the fate of an industry in the palm of its hand. This jury, jury number fourteen, may disagree with twelve of the previous thirteen juries—and hurl the industry into bankruptcy. That kind of thing can happen in our system of civil justice (it is not likely to happen, because the industry is likely to settle—whether or not it really is liable) without violating anyone's legal rights. But it need not be tolerated when the alternative exists of submitting an issue to multiple juries constituting in the aggregate a much larger and more diverse sample of decision-makers. That would not be a feasible option if the stakes to each class member were too slight to repay the cost of suit, even though the aggregate stakes are very large and would repay the costs of a consolidated proceeding. But this is not the case with regard to the HIV-hemophilia litigation. Each plaintiff if successful is apt to receive a judgment in the millions. With the aggregate stakes in the tens or hundreds of millions of dollars, or even in the billions, it is not a waste of judicial resources to conduct more than one trial, before more than six jurors, to determine whether a major segment of the international pharmaceutical industry is to follow the asbestos manufacturers into Chapter 11.

We have hinted at the second reason for questioning whether the district judge did not exceed the bounds of permissible judicial discretion. He proposes to have a jury determine the negligence of the defendants under a legal standard that does not actually exist anywhere in the world. * * * If one instruction on negligence will serve to instruct the jury on the legal standard of every state of the United States applicable to a novel claim, implying that the claim despite its controversiality would be decided identically in all 50 states and the District of Columbia, one wonders what the Supreme Court thought it was doing in the *Erie* case when it held that it was *unconstitutional* for federal courts in diversity cases to apply general common law rather than the common law of the state whose law would apply if the case were being tried in state rather than federal court. *Erie R.R. v. Tompkins,* 304 U.S. 64, 78–80, 58 S.Ct. 817, 822, 82 L.Ed. 1188 (1938). The law of negligence, including subsidiary concepts such as duty of care, foreseeability, and proximate cause, may as the plaintiffs have argued forcefully to us differ among the states only in nuance (though we think not, for a reason discussed later). But nuance can be important, and its significance is suggested by a comparison of differing state pattern instructions on negligence and differing judicial formulations of the meaning of negligence and the subordinate concepts. * * *

The "serendipity" theory advanced by the plaintiffs in *Wadleigh* is that if the defendants did not do enough to protect hemophiliacs from the risk of Hepatitis B, they are liable to hemophiliacs for any consequences—including infection by the more dangerous and at the time completely unknown AIDS virus—that proper measures against Hepatitis B would, all unexpectedly, have averted. This theory of liability, which draws support from Judge Friendly's opinion in *Petition of Kinsman Transit Co., supra,* 338 F.2d at 725, dispenses, rightly or wrongly from the standpoint of the Platonic form of negligence, with proof of foreseeability, even though a number of states, in formulating their tests for negligence, incorporate the foreseeability of the risk into the test. See, e.g., *Fawley v. Martin's Supermarkets, Inc.,* 618 N.E.2d 10, 13 (Ind.App.1993); Comment Note, "Foreseeability as an Element of Negligence and Proximate Cause," 100 A.L.R.2d 942 (1994). These states follow Judge Cardozo's famous opinion in *Palsgraf v. Long Island R.R.,* 248 N.Y. 339, 162 N.E. 99 (1928), under which the HIV plaintiffs might (we do not say would—we express no view on the substantive issues in this litigation) be barred from recovery on the ground that they were unforeseeable victims of the alleged failure of the defendants to take adequate precautions against infecting hemophiliacs with Hepatitis B and that therefore the drug companies had not violated any duty of care to them.

The plaintiffs' second theory focuses on the questions when the defendants should have learned about the danger of HIV in the blood supply and when, having learned about it, they should have taken steps to eliminate the danger or at least warn the hemophiliacs or their physicians of it. These questions also may be sensitive to the precise way in which a state formulates its standard of negligence. If not, one begins to wonder why this country bothers with different state legal systems.

Both theories, incidentally, may be affected by differing state views on the role of industry practice or custom in determining the existence of negligence. * * *

The plaintiffs argue that an equally important purpose of the class certification is to overcome the shyness or shame that many people feel at acknowledging that they have AIDS or are HIV-positive even when the source of infection is not a stigmatized act. That, the plaintiffs tell us, is why so few HIV-positive hemophiliacs have sued. We do not see how a class action limited to a handful of supposedly common issues can alleviate *that* problem. Any class member who wants a share in any judgment for damages or in any settlement will have to step forward at some point and identify himself as having AIDS or being HIV-positive. He will have to offer jury findings as collateral estoppel, overcome the defendants' defenses to liability (including possible efforts to show that the class member became infected with HIV through a source other than the defendants' product), and establish his damages. If the privacy of these class members in these follow-on proceedings to the class action is sought to be protected by denominating them "John Does," that is something that can equally well be done in individual lawsuits. The "John Doe" device—and with it the issue of privacy—is independent of class certification.

The third respect in which we believe that the district judge has exceeded his authority concerns the point at which his plan of action proposes to divide the trial of the issues that he has certified for class-action treatment from the other issues involved in the thousands of actual and potential claims of the representatives and members of the class. Bifurcation and even finer divisions of lawsuits into separate trials are authorized in federal district courts. Fed.R.Civ.P. 42(b); *Sellers v. Baisier,* 792 F.2d 690, 694 (7th Cir.1986). And a decision to employ the procedure is reviewed deferentially. * * *

The plan of the district judge in this case is inconsistent with the principle that the findings of one jury are not to be reexamined by a second, or third, or nth jury. The first jury will not determine liability. It will determine merely whether one or more of the defendants was negligent under one of the two theories. The first jury may go on to decide these additional issues with regard to the named plaintiffs. But it will not decide them with regard to the other class members. Unless the defendants settle, a second (and third, and fourth, and hundredth, and conceivably thousandth) jury will have to decide, in individual follow-on litigation by class members not named as plaintiffs in the *Wadleigh* case, such issues as comparative negligence—if any class members knowingly continued to use unsafe blood solids after they learned or should have learned of the risk of contamination with HIV—and proximate causation. Both issues overlap the issue of the defendants' negligence. * * * A second or subsequent jury might find that the defendants' failure to take precautions against infection with Hepatitis B could not be thought the *proximate* cause of the plaintiffs' infection with HIV, a different and unknown bloodborne virus. How the resulting inconsistency between juries could be prevented escapes us.

The protection of the right conferred by the Seventh Amendment to trial by jury in federal civil cases is a traditional office of the writ of mandamus. *Beacon Theatres v. Westover*, 359 U.S. 500, 510–11, 79 S.Ct. 948, 956–57, 3 L.Ed.2d 988 (1959); *Dairy Queen, Inc. v. Wood*, 369 U.S. 469, 472, 82 S.Ct. 894, 897, 8 L.Ed.2d 44 (1962); *Maloney v. Plunkett, supra; First National Bank v. Warren*, 796 F.2d 999 (7th Cir.1986). When the writ is used for that purpose, strict compliance with the stringent conditions on the availability of the writ (including the requirement of proving irreparable harm) is excused. In *Beacon*, for example, if the judge had gone ahead and tried the equitable claims first and made his decision collateral estoppel in the subsequent jury trial, the losing party would have been entitled to a new trial, wiping out the judge's decision. There was no irreparable harm, yet mandamus was granted—which is one reason why in cases like *Maloney* and *Sandahl* we have said that the use of the writ cannot be reduced to formula. But the looming infringement of Seventh Amendment rights is only one of our grounds for believing this to be a case in which the issuance of a writ of mandamus is warranted. The others as we have said are the undue and unnecessary risk of a monumental industry-busting error in entrusting the determination of potential multi-billion dollar liabilities to a single jury when the results of the previous cases indicate that the defendants' liability is doubtful at best and the questionable constitutionality of trying a diversity case under a legal standard in force in no state. We need not consider whether any of these grounds standing by itself would warrant mandamus in this case. Together they make a compelling case. * * *

The defendants have pointed out other serious problems with the district judge's plan, but it is unnecessary to discuss them. The petition for a writ of mandamus is granted, and the district judge is directed to decertify the plaintiff class.

ROVNER, CIRCUIT JUDGE, dissenting. The majority today takes the extraordinary step of granting defendants' petition for a writ of mandamus and directing the district court to rescind its order certifying the plaintiff class. Although certification orders like this one are not immediately appealable (*see Coopers & Lybrand v. Livesay*, 437 U.S. 463, 98 S.Ct. 2454, 57 L.Ed.2d 351 (1978)), the majority seizes upon our mandamus powers to effectively circumvent that rule. Because, in my view,

RECENT COURT DECISION

our consideration of Judge Grady's decision to certify an issue class under Fed.R.Civ.P. 23(c)(4) should await an appeal from the final judgment in *Wadleigh*, I would deny the writ.

The Supreme Court has consistently cautioned that mandamus is a drastic remedy to be employed only in the most extraordinary of cases. *See, e.g., Gulfstream Aerospace Corp. v. Mayacamas Corp.,* 485 U.S. 271, 289, 108 S.Ct. 1133, 1143–44, 99 L.Ed.2d 296 (1988); *Allied Chem. Corp. v. Daiflon, Inc.,* 449 U.S. 33, 34, 101 S.Ct. 188, 189–90, 66 L.Ed.2d 193 (1980) (per curiam); *Kerr v. United States District Court for the Northern District of California,* 426 U.S. 394, 402, 96 S.Ct. 2119, 2123–24, 48 L.Ed.2d 725 (1976). The writ traditionally has been used only "to confine an inferior court to a lawful exercise of its prescribed jurisdiction" and is justified only by "exceptional circumstances amounting to a judicial 'usurpation of power.'" *Will v. United States,* 389 U.S. 90, 95, 88 S.Ct. 269, 273, 19 L.Ed.2d 305 (1967); *see also Gulfstream Aerospace Corp.,* 485 U.S. at 289, 108 S.Ct. at 1143–44; *Allied Chemical,* 449 U.S. at 35, 101 S.Ct. at 190; *Kerr,* 426 U.S. at 402, 96 S.Ct. at 2123–24. "To ensure that mandamus remains an extraordinary remedy," the Supreme Court requires the proponents of a writ to "show that they lack adequate alternative means to obtain the relief they seek," and that their right to relief is "clear and indisputable." *Mallard v. United States District Court for the Southern District of Iowa,* 490 U.S. 296, 309, 109 S.Ct. 1814, 1822, 104 L.Ed.2d 318 (1989) * * *.

Even when a petitioner's right to relief is sufficiently clear, a writ should not issue if an adequate alternative is available. *See Maloney v. Plunkett,* 854 F.2d 152, 154 (7th Cir.1988); *In re American Airlines, Inc.,* 972 F.2d 605, 608 (5th Cir.1992) ("unless [petitioner] demonstrates that it lacks an adequate alternative means to obtain relief, we need not consider whether its right to a writ of mandamus is 'clear and indisputable.'"), *cert. denied,* ___ U.S. ___, 113 S.Ct. 1262, 122 L.Ed.2d 659 (1993). We observed in *Maloney,* for example, that clear error is a necessary but not sufficient condition for the issuance of the writ: "Not only must the error be clear; it must be irremediable by the regular appellate remedies." 854 F.2d at 154; *cf. Will,* 389 U.S. at 104, 88 S.Ct. at 278 ("Mandamus, it must be remembered, does not run the gauntlet of reversible errors." (internal quotation omitted)). And when review of the challenged order is available by direct appeal after entry of a final judgment, "it cannot be said that the litigant 'has no other adequate means to seek the relief he desires.'" *Allied Chemical Corp.,* 449 U.S. at 36, 101 S.Ct. at 191; *see also In re City of Springfield, Illinois,* 818 F.2d 565, 568 (7th Cir.1987); *J.H. Cohn & Co. v. American Appraisal Assoc., Inc.,* 628 F.2d 994, 999 (7th Cir.1980); *Campanioni v. Barr,* 962 F.2d 461, 464 (5th Cir.1992).

The majority concedes that this court would have an opportunity to review the certification order on appeal from a final judgment addressed to the named plaintiffs in *Wadleigh.* * * * Yet the majority finds this avenue inadequate because "it will come too late to provide effective relief to the defendants." * * * This is so because class treatment of plaintiffs' claims will pose a liability risk of such magnitude that defendants "will be under intense pressure to settle." * * * And if that risk produces the predicted settlement, the district court's certification order would evade this court's review. * * * Because of the likelihood of a settlement, then, the majority believes that the first condition for issuance of a writ of mandamus has been satisfied, and it proceeds to consider whether the district court's discretionary decision to certify a class amounts to a "judicial usurpation of power." * * *

I find the majority's reasoning troubling in several respects. First, it means that the preliminary requirement for mandamus—the lack of an alternative means of obtaining relief—will be satisfied by virtually every class certification order, which then authorizes the court to assess the relative merits of the order to determine whether it is "usurpative." The majority's complaint about Judge Grady's order—that it will make a settlement more likely than if defendants' negligence were to be determined by separate juries in individual trials—is true of most every order certifying a large plaintiff class. Certification orders almost always increase the likelihood of settlement by expanding the scope of defendants' exposure. Yet that does not make the order any less reviewable if defendants resist the temptation to settle and litigate to final judgment. *See In re Sugar Antitrust Litigation,* 559 F.2d 481, 483 n. 1 (9th Cir.1977). Indeed, in concluding that certification orders are not immediately appealable under 28 U.S.C. § 1291, the Supreme Court observed that any order certifying a large plaintiff class "may so increase the defendant's potential damages liability and litigation costs that he may find it economically prudent to settle and to abandon a meritorious defense." *Coopers & Lybrand,* 437 U.S. at 476, 98 S.Ct. at 2462. Yet that did not stop the Court from finding that "orders granting class certification are interlocutory" and thus not immediately appealable as of right. *Id.* But the majority here would override *Coopers'* edict, making certification orders reviewable on mandamus simply because the likelihood of a settlement makes the order unreviewable at the end of the case. I cannot reconcile this conclusion with *Coopers & Lybrand* or with the Supreme Court's mandamus cases. * * * I thus cannot agree that the possibility of a settlement satisfies defendants' burden under the first of the two requirements for mandamus.

I am also wary of the majority's application of a "settlement theory" in this case, as defendants did not offer that rationale in support of their petition. * * * The possibility of a settlement was raised for the first time by the court itself at oral argument. Generally, arguments not raised in a party's brief, but only at oral argument, are waived. *See, e.g., United States v. Rodriguez,* 888 F.2d 519, 524 (7th Cir.1989). But even assuming that we may consider the argument (*see ante* at ___-___), I fail to see how counsel's vague statements at oral argument about the possibility of a settlement can be said to satisfy defendants' substantial burden of establishing that they will suffer irreparable harm. The only "evidence" supporting counsel's assertion has been supplied by the majority's own statistical conjecturing, to which plaintiffs have had no opportunity to respond. *Cf. LB Credit Corp. v. Resolution Trust Corp.,* ___ F.3d ___ (7th Cir.1995) (refusing to consider argument raised for the first time in a post-judgment motion because the opposing party had no opportunity to test the assumptions underlying the argument). The burden of proving irreparable harm lies with the party seeking mandamus relief, not with the court, and defendants wholly failed to meet that burden here.

Furthermore, even if the possibility of a settlement were relevant to the first mandamus requirement, and even if it had been asserted by defendants in support of their petition, I still cannot agree with the majority's premise that Judge Grady's order in fact will prompt a settlement. Contrary to the clear implication of the majority's opinion * * * the class portion of the anticipated trial in this case would not go so far as to establish defendants' *liability* to a class of plaintiffs; it would instead resolve *only* the question of whether defendants were negligent in distributing tainted clotting factor at any particular point in time. Even if defendants were faced with an adverse class verdict, then, a plaintiff still would be required to clear a number of hurdles before he would be entitled to a judgment. For example, defendants no doubt would contest at that stage whether a particular plaintiff could establish proximate causation or whether his or her claim is in any event barred by the statute of limitations. Thus, contrary to the majority's implication, a class verdict in favor of plaintiffs would not automatically entitle each member of the class to a seven-figure judgment. * * * The defendants will thus have ample opportunity to settle should they lose the class trial. And that would seem to me an advisable strategy in light of the success they have had in earlier cases. * * *

Finally, although the availability of review on direct appeal after final judgment makes it unnecessary for me to discuss the merits of the certification order, the majority's arguments addressed to the propriety of forcing "defendants to stake their companies on the outcome of a single jury trial" or of allowing a single jury to "hold the fate of an industry in the palm of its hand" seem to me at odds with Fed.R.Civ.P. 23 itself. * * * That rule expressly permits class treatment of such claims when its requirements are met, regardless of the magnitude of potential liability. And I see nothing in Rule 23, or in any of the relevant cases, that would make likelihood of success on the merits a prerequisite for class certification. * * * The majority's preference for avoiding a class trial and for submitting the negligence issue "to multiple juries constituting in the aggregate a much larger and more diverse sample of decision-makers" * * * is a rationale for amending the rule, not for avoiding its application in a specific case. *Cf. Coopers &*

Lybrand, 437 U.S. at 470, 98 S.Ct. 2458–59 (policy arguments addressed to the benefits and burdens of class litigation are matters only for legislative consideration). * * *

In the final analysis, I think it significant that the majority recognizes the need for limits on the mandamus power—"if uncabined," that power has the potential "to unravel the final-decision rule" of 28 U.S.C. § 1291. * * * The way to cabin that power, the majority explains, is "[b]y taking seriously the two conditions for the grant of a writ of mandamus." * * * Yet in holding that the possibility of a settlement satisfies the first condition, the majority, regrettably, has failed to heed its own counsel. I respectfully dissent.

Part IX

UPDATES TO COUND, FRIEDENTHAL, MILLER AND SEXTON, CIVIL PROCEDURE, CASES AND MATERIALS, 6TH EDITION

TO

CONFORM TO THE 1993 AMENDMENTS TO THE FEDERAL RULES

When the 6th Edition of the Cound, Friedenthal, Miller & Sexton *casebook* was published, there had not been final approval of the proposed 1993 rules. Although the proposed rules are discussed at length throughout the *casebook,* a number of changes in the numbering of sections of the amended rules and alterations of wording have taken place. Therefore, in this section, for the sake of accuracy, these very minor changes are reflected.

The affected *casebook* pages are as follows:

190	394	779	812
207	395	780	815
210	403	785	816
211	406	787	819
214	586	788	840
215	761	790	843
218	763	791	844
219	769	795	848
221	770	796	870
222	772	797	
226	773	798	

Page 190. Note 5 should read as follows:

5. In response to the Supreme Court's invitation in *Omni,* new Rule 4(k)(2) was adopted in 1993. How would this provision have affected the outcome in *Omni?* Would it correct the anomalous results discussed in note 4, supra?

Pages 207–208. Note 10 should read as follows:

10. The means of communicating notice differ from the prescribed content of the notice. Is the Due Process Clause also concerned with the content of the notice given? The Restatement (Second), Judgments § 2 (1982) states that notice is adequate only if the notice is "official in tenor."

Rule 4(a) generally prescribes the contents of the summons to be used in federal actions, and the Supreme Court has approved an illustrative form of summons, Official Form 1, which is reproduced in the Supplement. If a party fails to comply with the form of summons prescribed in Rule 4(a), the amendment policy expressed in Rule 4(a) can be used to alleviate errors of a technical nature in the form of the summons that are not misleading or prejudicial to the recipient. See 4A Wright & Miller, *Federal Practice and Procedure: Civil 2d* §§ 1088, 1131 (1987).

Page 210. Add the following new paragraph after the runover paragraph:

Mason never signed and returned the acknowledgment form. At the same time, Genisco sent Mason's counsel a letter enclosing a copy of the summons and complaint and stating that Mason was being served pursuant to Federal Rule 4(e) and Cal.Code Civ.Proc. § 415.40. Mason's counsel sent a letter to Genisco acknowledging receipt of the summons and complaint. In April, 1989, the district court granted the requested declaratory relief in a default judgment.

[Note that subsequent to this decision, Rule 4 was rewritten. In reading this opinion, and the notes that follow, it is important to recognize that Rules 4(c) and 4(e) now cover different matters. Current Rule 4(d) is the successor rule.]

Pages 211-212. Notes 1 and 2 should read as follows:

1. As stated in *Mason,* the general rule is that service by mail under Rule 4(c)(2)(C)(ii) [current Rule 4(d)(2), (4)] is valid only if the defendant returns the acknowledgment form and the plaintiff files it with the court. See, e.g., Audio Enterprises, Inc. v. B & W Loudspeakers, 957 F.2d 406 (7th Cir.1992). Plaintiffs generally are not allowed to establish jurisdiction based on defendant actually having received the summons and complaint, regardless of whether the acknowledgment form is returned. The Second Circuit, however, holds otherwise. In Morse v. Elmira Country Club, 752 F.2d 35, 40 (2d Cir.1984), the court held that "strong factors of justice and equity push toward reading Rule 4(c) as providing for effective mail service where * * * the recipient actually receives the mail service but refuses to acknowledge it properly." In fact, in Lee v. Carlson, 645 F.Supp. 1430, 1432–33 (S.D.N.Y.1986), affirmed 812 F.2d 712 (2d Cir.1987), Judge Weinfeld held that even if plaintiff fails to include an acknowledgment form, the service is still valid so long as the defect can be cured by an admission, or other proof, that in fact the summons and complaint were received. Is this view consistent with the Rule? Consider the role that the acknowledgment form is meant to play. Does it constitute a waiver by the defendant of the requirement of personal service? Or is it evidence of valid service under a distinct mode of service of process—service by mail? Should the Rule be amended to provide that failure to acknowledge the mail service does not affect the validity of the service? See Comment, *Morse v. Elmira Country Club: Dealing With the Uncooperative Recipient of Mailed Service of Process Under the 1983 Amendments to the Federal Rules of Civil Procedure,* 47 Ohio St.L.J. 713 (1986).

2. The *Mason* court also joins the majority of courts in holding that a defective mailing under prior Rule 4(c)(2)(C)(ii) caused by defendant's failure to return the acknowledgment form could not be recharacterized as effective service under state law pursuant to Rule 4(c)(2)(C)(i). As the Fifth Circuit has said: "it is obvious from the wording of the rule itself * * * that in the event the defendant elects not to complete and return the [acknowledgment] form, then an alternative mode of service will be made *subsequently*— not *previously* and not *contemporaneously*." Carimi v. Royal Carribean Cruise Line, Inc., 959 F.2d 1344, 1347 (5th Cir.1992). However, the wording of Rule 4(c)(2)(C)(ii) seems to prohibit the subsequent attempts from being made pursuant to state law. The courts have split on this question. Compare Electrical Specialty Co. v. Road & Ranch Supply, Inc., 967 F.2d 309, 313 (9th Cir.1992) (subsequent service under Rule 4(c)(2)(C)(i) permitted provided new summons is issued), with Combs v. Nick Garin Trucking, 825 F.2d 437, 443–

44 (D.C.Cir.1987) (subsequent service under Rule 4(c)(2)(C)(i) not permitted). In both the context of recharacterization, note 1, supra, and the context of subsequent service, what interest does a federal court have in preventing a plaintiff from benefitting from a less restrictive state rule in instances when the plaintiff easily could have used that rule at the outset?

Pages 214–215. Subsection c. should read as follows:

c. Service on a Person Residing in Defendant's Dwelling House or Usual Place of Abode

As an alternative to personal delivery, Rule 4(e)(2) permits service of process to be made upon an individual by leaving a copy of the summons and complaint at his "dwelling house or usual place of abode with some person of suitable age and discretion then residing therein." Despite the length of time these words have been a part of federal practice, the decisions do not make clear precisely what they mean, and the facts of a particular case often prove to be crucial.

ROVINSKI v. ROWE, 131 F.2d 687, 689 (6th Cir.1942). Rowe brought suit against Rovinski in a Michigan state court, service of process being effected under the state's nonresident motorist statute. Rovinski moved to dismiss on the ground that he was a resident of Michigan, and hence not amenable to service under the statute. After the action was dismissed, Rowe commenced a diversity action against Rovinski in a federal court. Service of process was made under Federal Rule of Civil Procedure 4(d)(1) [now 4(e)(2)] by leaving a copy of the summons and complaint with Rovinski's mother at the address that he had given as his residence in an affidavit supporting his motion to dismiss in the prior state action. Rovinski again challenged the propriety of service, contending that his "dwelling place and usual place of abode" had been in Minnesota for the past two years, and that he had returned to his mother's house only to visit, even though he considered it his legal residence. The District Court held the service of process valid, and the Sixth Circuit affirmed:

> In construing * * * Rule 4(d)(1) [now 4(e)(2)] liberally, the district court effectuated the declared purpose of the Supreme Court Advisory Committee in submitting a service of process rule, which would provide "a good deal of freedom and flexibility in service." * * * That the rule should be liberally construed seems logical, when consideration is given to the fact that uncertainty of its applicability to varying situations would be increased by strict construction. This is apparent from the irreconcilable conflict among state courts upon the meaning and interpretation of the expression "usual place of abode." * * *
>
> The wide diversity of opinion may be illustrated by two examples. On the one hand, delivery of process to defendant's wife at an apartment in Miami Beach, Florida, where his family had been living for about two months and where he had previously visited them, but from which he had departed to his permanent home in

another state, was held *sufficient* under a Florida statute * * *. On the other hand, delivery of service of process to the father of a minor defendant at the family home where the defendant had lived up to the time of his enlistment in the United States Army less than one month previously was held *insufficient* under a New Jersey statute * * *.

The only pertinent reported Federal decision is Skidmore v. Green, D.C.N.Y., 33 F.Supp. 529, 530, wherein service was upheld under Rule 4(d)(1) against a peregrinating policeman, who, after retiring from the New York force, spent most of his time traveling about the country in an automobile and trailer. Process had been delivered at the home of defendant's brother which, in the application for his New York automobile license, defendant had given as his address. In his application for his South Carolina automobile license, he had stated that he was a resident of New York. The district judge commented that "so far as the migratory nature of his life" permitted of any place of abode or dwelling house, that place was his brother's home.

Pages 218-219. The first paragraph of Justice Black's dissent should read as follows:

MR. JUSTICE BLACK, dissenting.

* * * I disagree with * * * [the Court's] holding, believing that (1) whether Mrs. Weinberg was a valid agent upon whom service could validly be effected under Rule 4(d)(1) [now 4(e)(2)] should be determined under New York law and that we should accept the holdings of the federal district judge and the Court of Appeals sitting in New York that under that State's law the purported appointment of Mrs. Weinberg was invalid and ineffective; (2) if however, Rule 4(d)(1) [now 4(e)(2)] is to be read as calling upon us to formulate a new federal definition of agency for purposes of service of process, I think our formulation should exclude Mrs. Weinberg from the category of an "agent authorized by appointment * * * to receive service of process"; and (3) upholding service of process in this case raises serious questions as to whether these Michigan farmers have been denied due process of law in violation of the Fifth and Fourteenth Amendments.

Pages 219-220. Justice Brennan's dissent should read as follows:

MR. JUSTICE BRENNAN, with whom THE CHIEF JUSTICE and MR. JUSTICE GOLDBERG join, dissenting.

I would affirm. In my view, federal standards and not state law must define who is "an agent authorized by appointment" within the meaning of Rule 4(d)(1) [now 4(e)(2)]. * * * In formulating these standards I would, *first,* construe Rule 4(d)(1) [now 4(e)(2)] to deny

UPDATES TO CASEBOOK

validity to the appointment of a purported agent whose interests conflict with those of his supposed principal * * *. *Second,* I would require that the appointment include an explicit condition that the agent after service transmit the process forthwith to the principal. Although our decision in Wuchter v. Pizzutti * * * dealt with the constitutionality of a state statute, the reasoning of that case is persuasive that, in fashioning a federal agency rule, we should engraft the same requirement upon Rule 4(d)(1) [now 4(e)(2)]. *Third,* since the corporate plaintiff prepared the printed form contract, I would not hold the individual purchaser bound by the appointment without proof, in addition to his mere signature on the form, that the individual understandingly consented to be sued in a State not that of his residence. * * * It offends common sense to treat a printed form which closes an installment sale as embodying terms to all of which the individual knowingly assented. The sales pitch aims solely at getting the signature on the form and wastes no time explaining or even mentioning the print. * * *

Page 221. The first paragraph of Subsection e. should read as follows:

e. Service on Artificial Entities: Corporations, Partnerships, and Unincorporated Associations

Rule 4(h) authorizes service upon corporations, partnerships, and unincorporated associations that are subject to suit under a common name. The most frequently invoked portion of the rule is the part permitting service by delivery of process to an officer, a managing agent, or a general agent.

The first quoted paragraph should read as follows:

Rule 4(d)(3) [now Rule 4(h)] has been liberally construed by the courts and, as interpreted, does not require rigid formalism. To be valid, service of process is not limited solely to officially designated officers, managing agents or agents appointed by law for the receipt of process. Rather, "[r]ules governing service of process [are] to be construed in a manner reasonably calculated to effectuate their primary purpose: to give the defendant adequate notice that an action is pending. * * * [T]he rule does not require that service be made solely on a restricted class of formally titled officials, but rather permits it to be made 'upon a representative so integrated with the organization that he will know what to do with the papers. Generally, service is sufficient when made upon an individual who stands in such a position as to render it fair, reasonable and just to imply the authority on his part to receive services.'" * * *

Page 222. Note 1 should read as follows:

1. Is the court's willingness to disregard labels and conclusory terms such as "general" and "managing" agent consistent with the clear requirements of Rule 4(d)(3)

UPDATES TO CASEBOOK

[now Rule 4(h)]? Should the court simply have held that the claims adjuster could be regarded as a "managing" agent of the defendant? See also Direct Mail Specialists, Inc. v. Eclat Computerized Technologies, Inc., 840 F.2d 685, 688 (9th Cir.1988).

Page 226. The first paragraph should read as follows:

As a separate matter, it is noteworthy that new Rule 4(j) [now 4(m)], adopted in 1983, requires a federal court to dismiss without prejudice an action when the defendant has not been served within 120 days of the filing of the complaint, if the plaintiff fails to show "good cause" for not completing service within that time. If the statute of limitations expires during that period, and if the plaintiff's action is dismissed, can the plaintiff refile the complaint and thus still maintain the action? See Burks v. Griffith, 100 F.R.D. 491 (N.D.N.Y.1984) (attempt at refiling civil rights action met with a successful statute of limitations challenge; court observed that the problem could have been avoided had plaintiff utilized Rule 6(b) and requested an extension of time to serve her summons and complaint).

Page 394. The first paragraph of Chief Justice Warren's opinion should read as follows:

Mr. CHIEF JUSTICE WARREN delivered the opinion of the Court.

The question to be decided is whether, in a civil action where the jurisdiction of the United States District Court is based upon diversity of citizenship between the parties, service of process shall be made in the manner prescribed by state law or that set forth in Rule 4(d)(1) [now Rule 4(e)(2)] of the Federal Rules of Civil Procedure.

Page 395. The second full paragraph should read as follows:

We conclude that the adoption of Rule 4(d)(1) [now Rule 4(e)(2)], designed to control service of process in diversity actions, neither exceeded the congressional mandate embodied in the Rules Enabling Act nor transgressed constitutional bounds, and that the Rule is therefore the standard against which the District Court should have measured the adequacy of the service. Accordingly, we reverse the decision of the Court of Appeals.

Pages 395–396. The last paragraph, beginning on page 395, should read as follows:

In Mississippi Pub. Corp. v. Murphree, 326 U.S. 438, 66 S.Ct. 242, 90 L.Ed. 185 (1946), this Court upheld Rule 4(f) [now Rule 4(e)(2)], which permits service of a summons anywhere within the State (and not merely the district) in which a district court sits:

Page 403. Note 6 should read as follows:

6. In MARSHALL v. MULRENIN, 508 F.2d 39 (1st Cir.1974), the First Circuit challenged the Supreme Court's interpretation of the Massachusetts statute applied in *Hanna* and held the Massachusetts rule for amendments changing the party against whom

a claim is asserted to be controlling over Federal Rule 15(c). The decision meant that the plaintiff could maintain the action against the substituted defendants even though these defendants had not received actual notice of the institution of the action within the applicable statute of limitations as required by Rule 15(c)(1) and (2) [as they then read] because the Massachusetts rule allows any amendment "which may enable the plaintiff to sustain the action for the cause for which it was intended to be brought." Given *Hanna*, is the *Marshall* decision correct? Can these two cases be explained by the fact that both permitted an adjudication on the merits? For an analysis of *Marshall* and its relationship to *Hanna*, see Comment, *Federal Rules of Civil Procedure—The Erie Doctrine—State Relation-Back Provision Found Controlling Over Rule 15(c)—Marshall v. Mulrenin*, 50 N.Y.U.L.Rev. 952 (1975). In 1991, Rule 15(c) was amended. See pp. 573–579 *infra*.

Page 406. The fourth paragraph should read as follows:

Ragan was not our last pronouncement in this difficult area, however. In 1965 we decided Hanna v. Plumer * * *, holding that in a civil action where federal jurisdiction was based upon diversity of citizenship, Rule 4(d)(1) [now 4(e)(2)] of the Federal Rules of Civil Procedure, rather than state law, governed the manner in which process was served. * * *

Page 586. The second paragraph should be amended as follows:

Rule 11 (in both its 1983 form and its earlier incarnation [and more recently in still another version adopted in 1993—see the note on page 598]) attempts to curb abuse of the federal pleading rules by imposing affirmative duties on attorneys and by raising the possibility of sanctions for failure to discharge them. As is clear from *Surowitz,* the pre–1983 incarnation of Rule 11 employed a subjective standard to judge attorney conduct—so long as attorneys acted in good faith, they were not subject to sanctions if it later became clear that their legal theory was faulty or that the facts did not support their claims.

Page 761. The first paragraph should read as follows:

Read Federal Rules of Civil Procedure 26(a), 26(b), 26(f), 27(a)(1), 32(a), 37(c)(1), and the accompanying materials in the Supplement.

Page 763. The first full paragraph should read as follows:

In 1993 a series of proposed amendments to the Federal Rules on discovery went into effect. Changes were made in response to comments, and the amendments were sent to the Supreme Court in October 1992. The amendments were approved by the Supreme Court in April 1993 and sent to Congress for final approval. The main focus of the amendments was to revise the rules relating to discovery to make the discovery process more efficient, less costly, and less time-consuming. In the words of the Advisory Committee that drafted the proposals:

The last paragraph should read as follows:

To achieve this goal, the amended rules introduce several innovations in the discovery process. They require that each party make certain disclosures "without awaiting a discovery request." These disclosures include the identity of individuals "likely to have discoverable information," a description of all relevant documents, and the identity of and copies of reports by expert witnesses. The parties also are required to meet "as soon as practicable" to discuss certain matters, including "the nature and basis of their claims and defenses and the possibilities for a prompt settlement or resolution of the case." In addition, the parties must develop "a proposed discovery plan." These and other changes introduced by the proposed amended rules—which we will discuss later in this chapter—are designed to curtail discovery abuses while promoting the important goals that discovery seeks to achieve. Many of these changes—including the requirement of disclosure by parties without awaiting a discovery request—were adopted in 1992 by the State of Arizona. See Ariz.R.Civ.P. 26.1, which is reproduced in the Supplement.

Add after the last paragraph:

THE REVIVED SIGNIFICANCE OF DETAILED PLEADING

Identical clauses in amended Rules 26(a)(1)(A) and (B) require automatic disclosure of certain information "relevant to disputed facts alleged with particularity in the pleadings." How does this mesh with Federal Rule 8(a)(2) and the general adoption of "notice pleading" throughout the federal courts? Recall the discussion of pleading requirements in Chapter 8, Section A, parts 1 and 2. Will the clauses in Rule 26 result in tactical utilization of general or detailed pleadings depending upon a party's desire for automatic disclosure? Will the provisions of Rule 26(f) avoid such problems or will they require parties to return to the days of "fact pleading" before needed information can be obtained?

LOCAL OPTION AND THE LOSS OF UNIFORMITY

The most significant amendments to the discovery provisions adopted in 1993, Rules 26(a), (b)(2), and (f), each contains a clause permitting it to be superseded by local rule. Local rules in many of the 94 federal districts have prescribed details of discovery and other procedures in the past, but there have never before been formal "opt-out" provisions that undercut the fundamental principle of national uniformity that has underlain the Federal Rules since their inception.

The impact of these provisions is particularly significant in light of the 1990 Civil Justice Reform Act, 28 U.S.C. §§ 471–482, by which Congress ordered each of the federal judicial districts to form local advisory committees to study the problems of delay and inefficiency in their courts and to formulate and adopt plans to ensure the speedy and just resolution of civil cases. It is not at all clear that Congress intended that the results of these efforts would result in the substantial elimination of uniformity with regard to the basic rules of discovery, see generally, Robel, *Fractured Procedure: The Civil Justice Reform Act of*

1990, 46 Stanford Law Review 1447 (1994). However, given the opportunity specifically provided throughout Rule 26 itself, it appears that over half of the federal districts have determined not to implement, or to delay implementation of, the 1993 amendments to the federal discovery rules. Is this a sound development? What are the reasons favoring uniformity among all federal courts? Do they outweigh the value of local controls tailored to the specific conditions faced by local federal judges? For additional discussion of the uniformity issue see, Tobias, *Improving the 1968 and 1990 Judicial Improvements Acts,* 46 Stanford Law Review 1589 (1994).

Page 769. Note 1 should read as follows:

1. In what way would the decision in Grant v. Huff have been altered if Georgia had adopted Federal Rule 26(a)(1)(D)? Over the years there has been considerable controversy regarding the discoverability of liability insurance. What are the competing arguments on this question? See the comments of the Advisory Committee on Rule 26(b)(2) [now Rule (a)(1)(D)] set forth in the Supplement [in the note on the 1970 amendments to Rule 26]. See also the discussion in Cook v. Welty, 253 F.Supp. 875, 877 (D.D.C.1966), in which the court said: "It is not to be doubted that information concerning liability insurance coverage and its extent is conducive to fair negotiations and to just settlements." Is this statement accurate in all contexts? When might the reverse be true? For a general review of the authorities, see 8 Wright & Miller, *Federal Practice and Procedure: Civil* § 2010 (1970).

Page 770. Notes 4 and 5 should read as follows:

4. Under the amendments to the discovery rules, Rule 26(b)(2) has been replaced with new Rule 26(a)(1)(D), which provides that, without awaiting a discovery request, the defendant must make its insurance policies available to the plaintiff for inspection and copying pursuant to Rule 34.

5. What reasons justify the decision in Grant v. Huff refusing to permit discovery of the names of witnesses whom defendant intended to call at trial? Compare Federal Rule 26(a)(3)(A). Note the exception in 26(a)(3) for evidence to be used solely for impeachment. What is the reason for the exception? Should evidence for impeachment generally be excluded from discovery? How should "impeachment" be defined?

Page 772. Note 1 should read as follows:

1. The *Zinsky* case was decided prior to the 1970 amendment to Federal Rule 33, which added the second paragraph of Rule 33(b) [now 33(c)]. Read the Advisory Committee's Note on Rule 33(b) [now 33(c)] in the Supplement. Would *Zinsky* have been decided any differently under the amended rule? Compare JOSEPH v. NORMAN'S HEALTH CLUB, INC., 336 F.Supp. 307, 319 (E.D.Mo.1971), in which the court upheld an interrogatory asking whether one defendant had ever assigned any promissory notes to another. In overruling an objection that the interrogatory called for a legal conclusion, the court held:

> The final sentence of Rule 33(b) [now 33(c)] added by amendment in 1970 * * * does not authorize interrogatories calling for legal conclusions as such. * * * [T]he only kind of interrogatory that is objectionable without more as a legal conclusion is one that extends to "legal issues unrelated to the facts of the case."

What is a legal conclusion unrelated to the facts of the case? Does it encompass the cases upon which a party intends to rely? See Fishermen & Merchants Bank v. Burin, 11 F.R.D. 142 (S.D.Cal.1951). Consider ROGERS v. TRI–STATE MATERIALS CORP., 51 F.R.D. 234, 246 (N.D.W.Va.1970), in which defendant sought to discover any "presumption of law or fact" upon which plaintiff intended to rely. The court upheld the interrogatory as follows:

UPDATES TO CASEBOOK

Plaintiff may not be schooled on the meaning of the term "res ipsa loquitur" but counsel, largely responsible for preparation of answers to interrogatories, will be able to explain that a state of facts may speak for itself under certain circumstances.

Compare Estate of May v. Zorman, 5 Wash.App. 368, 487 P.2d 270 (1971) (defendants held not required to answer questions asking whether their conduct was negligent).

Page 773. The first paragraph of Subsection 3 should read as follows:

Read Federal Rules of Civil Procedure 26(b)(2), (c), (d) and the accompanying material in the Supplement.

Page 779. Note 3 should read as follows:

3. Under Rule 26(b)(2)(iii) what weight should a court give to "the parties' resources" in setting limits on discovery? Is a discovery request that otherwise would be barred as disproportionate to the needs of a case permissible simply because the party from which the discovery is sought has a "deep pocket"? On the other hand, should a relatively wealthy litigant be able to buy additional discovery by offering to pay the expenses of a financially weak litigant? Should relatively wealthy antagonists be permitted to stipulate to unlimited discovery?

Page 780. Note 4 should read as follows:

4. The 1993 amendments to the discovery rules for the first time, placed self-executing limits on the extent to which parties can make use of the discovery devices. Thus, amended Rules 30(a)(2)(A) and (B) and 33(a) provide that, unless the parties agree otherwise, leave of court must be obtained if a party wishes to take more than ten depositions, to take the deposition of a witness more than once, or to serve on any other party more than 25 interrogatories, including all discrete subparts. In addition, amended Rule 26(b)(2) provides that, in determining whether to limit discovery, the court must consider "the importance of the proposed discovery in resolving the issues."

Page 785. The first paragraph should read as follows:

Study Federal Rules of Civil Procedure 26(d), 29(1), 30, and 31 and the notes on 1993 amendments to these Rules in the Supplement.

The third paragraph should read as follows:

Under modern discovery rules, an attorney schedules a deposition merely by serving a notice on the opposing attorney. The notice must include the name and address of the deponent, if known, and the date, time and the place of the deposition. If the deponent is a party, the notice is sufficient to require the party's appearance, and a subpoena is unnecessary. The notice may include a demand that the party produce documents and other items of evidence at the deposition, in which case the procedure of Rule 34 applies (although it is not clear whether the 30-day period of Rule 34(b) applies to a response to a demand for production under Rule 30(b)(5)).

Page 787. Note 3 should read as follows:

3. Rule 30(c) states that testimony objected to shall be "taken subject to the objections." Is Rule 30(c) necessary to expedite the process of taking depositions? How strictly should it be enforced? Are there circumstances when it is proper for an attorney to instruct a deposition witness to refuse to answer a question notwithstanding the rule? See

UPDATES TO CASEBOOK

Eggleston v. Chicago Journeymen Plumbers' Local Union No. 130, 657 F.2d 890 (7th Cir.1981); International Union of Electrical, Radio & Machine Workers v. Westinghouse Elec. Corp., 91 F.R.D. 277 (D.D.C.1981). Note that amended Rule 30(d)(1) permits a party to instruct a deponent not to answer a question only in order to preserve a privilege, to enforce a court-ordered limitation on the scope of discovery, or to allow a motion to be made to the court addressing alleged improper conduct of the deposition.

Pages 787–788. Note 5 should read as follows:

5. Ever since modern discovery rules first appeared, courts have been faced with the situation in which the parties are vying to take the first deposition, each attempting to pin down the opponent or the opponent's key witness before submitting himself or his own witnesses to the discovery process. Is there really a substantial advantage to deposing first? Does this advantage exist for an honest party as well as for an unscrupulous party who will deliberately color his testimony? See generally *Developments in the Law— Discovery,* 74 Harv.L.Rev. 940, 954–58 (1961).

Prior to 1970, the federal courts generally had held that the party who first served a notice of a deposition was entitled to priority as to that deposition. This is still the situation in many states. See, e.g., N.Y.C.P.L.R. 3106. The problem is complicated by the fact that in most of these jurisdictions plaintiff is prohibited, without leave of court, from serving a notice of deposition for a specific period of time in order to permit defendant to learn of the suit and employ counsel. That was the situation in the federal courts between 1970 and 1993. Leave of court normally has been permitted only under exceptional circumstances. Since there is no comparable restriction on defendant, he will receive priority merely by serving notice during the period plaintiff must wait. Would elimination of plaintiff's waiting period eliminate the priority problem? If one party normally is to have priority if that party wants it, who should it be, plaintiff or defendant? Is there any satisfactory way to solve the priority question?

For extensive discussions of the priority problem in the past see 8 Wright & Miller, *Federal Practice and Procedure: Civil* §§ 2045–47 (1970); *Developments in the Law— Discovery,* 74 Harv.L.Rev. 940, 954–58 (1961).

The 1993 amendments to the federal discovery rules abolished plaintiff's waiting period. Instead, they provide that, unless the deponent is expected to depart from the country or leave of court is obtained, neither party may commence discovery until all parties have met and conferred to discuss possible resolution of the dispute, to arrange for the disclosures required by the new amendments, and to develop a proposed discovery plan. See Federal Rules 26(d) and 30(a)(2)(C). Do you think that this new approach will eliminate bickering between the parties as to priority of discovery?

Page 788. The last paragraph should read as follows:

Read Federal Rules of Civil Procedure 45(c) and (e) in the Supplement.

Page 790. Note 2 should read as follows:

2. The party who gives notice of the taking of a deposition is not required to subpoena even a nonparty witness whose testimony is sought. If no subpoena is issued, however, and the witness fails to attend, Federal Rule 30(g)(2) permits certain sanctions to be imposed upon the party who failed to use a subpoena. What tactical reasons might motivate a party to refrain from serving a subpoena on a witness? Note that under Rule 45(d)(2) [now 45(a)(2)] if a witness refuses to cooperate, so that she must be subpoenaed, the deposition may have to be held in a district other than the one in which the case has been filed. Suppose the witness disobeys the subpoena. If she appears but refuses to answer questions properly put to her, the parties may seek assistance under Rule 37(a). According to Rule 37(a)(1), application for judicial assistance must be made to the court where the deposition is being held as opposed to the court where the action is filed. What is the purpose of this provision? Note that if the witness is a party, Rule 37(a)(1) specifies the court where the action is pending as the proper court to issue orders relating to the deposition. Is there any reason for distinguishing between party and nonparty witnesses? See 62 Colum.L.Rev. 187 (1962).

UPDATES TO CASEBOOK

Page 791. Note 2 should read as follows:

2. Does the use of tape-recorded depositions raise any special problems? Who should provide and be in charge of the recording equipment? Is there ever a need for more than one recording machine? Reread Federal Rules 30(b)(2), (3). See Colonial Times, Inc. v. Gasch, 509 F.2d 517 (D.C.Cir.1975); Champagne v. Hygrade Food Products, Inc., 79 F.R.D. 671 (E.D.Wash.1978); Barham v. IDM Corp., 78 F.R.D. 340 (N.D.Ohio 1978).

The last paragraph should read as follows:

Read Federal Rule of Civil Procedure 33 and the accompanying materials in the Supplement.

Pages 795–796. Note 2 should read as follows:

2. Federal Rule 33(c) [currently 33(d)] as amended in 1970 addressed the problem of burdensome interrogatories by expressly providing a party the option of producing its business records in lieu of answering. Thus Rule 33(b) was adapted from Cal.Code Civ.Proc. § 2030(f)(2), which appears in the Supplement. The Federal Rule differs in that it adds the requirement that "the burden of deriving or ascertaining the answer" must be "substantially the same for the party serving the interrogatory as for the party served." What is the justification for this additional requirement?

An informative discussion of Rule 33(c) [now 33(d)] is found in IN RE MASTER KEY ANTITRUST LITIGATION, 53 F.R.D. 87 (D.Conn.1971):

> * * * Since a respondent is required to answer proper interrogatories, it is not plausible to assume that a response that an answer may (or may not) be found in its records, accompanied by an offer to permit their inspection is sufficient. This is little more than an offer to play the discredited game of blindman's bluff at the threshold level of discovery. * * *
>
> I conclude that the option afforded by Rule 33(c) is not a procedural device for avoiding the duty to give information. It does not shift to the interrogating party the obligation to find out *whether* sought after information is ascertainable from the files tendered, but only permits a shift of the burden to dig it out once the respondents have specified the records from "where the answer" can be derived or ascertained. If the answers lie in the records of the defendants, they should say so; and if, on the other side, they do not, they should say that. * * *

Id. at 90.

Page 796. Note 4 should read as follows:

4. Interrogatories have been cited as the most abused of the available discovery devices. In response, many federal district courts have adopted local rules providing that, except on leave of court, no party shall serve on any other party more than a fixed number of interrogatories, often 20. See, e.g., Local Rule 9(g), Northern District of Illinois, adopted June 20, 1975. For an interesting opinion explaining and defending one such rule, see Crown Center Redevelopment Corp. v. Westinghouse Elec. Corp., 82 F.R.D. 108 (W.D.Mo. 1979).

The 1993 amendment to Rule 33(a), for the first time, imposed a presumptive limit on the numbers of interrogatories that a party may serve. It provides that, unless the parties stipulate otherwise or leave of court is obtained, a party may serve on any other party no more than 25 interrogatories, "including all discrete subparts." The original draft proposed by the Advisory Committee established a limit of 15 interrogatories; in response to comments by the bench and bar, the number was increased to 25. The Notes of the Advisory Committee indicate that although parties cannot evade the limitation "through the device of joining as 'subparts' questions that seek information about discrete separate subjects," nevertheless "a question asking about communications of a particular type should be treated as a single interrogatory" even though it asks for a number of specific details regarding the particular communication.

UPDATES TO CASEBOOK

Page 797. The first paragraph should read as follows:

Read Federal Rules of Civil Procedure 34 and 45 in the Supplement.

Page 798. Add to the end of the runover paragraph:

Rule 45(c)(2)(A) specifically provides that unless his or her testimony is sought, the individual need not appear in person.

Page 812. The first paragraph of Subsection 5 should read as follows:

Read Federal Rule of Civil Procedure 36 and the accompanying materials in the Supplement.

Pages 815–816. Subsection 6 should read as follows:

Read Federal Rule of Civil Procedure 26(e) and the accompanying materials in the Supplement.

Rule 26(e), first adopted in 1970, was designed to eliminate inconsistent decisions regarding the existence and scope of the duty to update discovery answers. Note that the Rule is not all-encompassing. What information obtained subsequent to the original responses is not covered by it? See 8 Wright & Miller, *Federal Practice and Procedure: Civil* § 2049, at 323 (1970).

Note that amended Rule 26(e) broadens the requirement to supplement discovery responses. It requires that disclosures and responses to interrogatories, requests for production, and requests for admissions be supplemented "if the party learns that in some material respect the information disclosed is incomplete or incorrect" and if the updated information has not otherwise been made known to the other parties.

Why should there be any duty to supplement answers given in the course of discovery? Some states have refused to impose it. See, e.g., Clay v. McCarthy, 73 Ill.App.3d 462, 30 Ill.Dec. 38, 392 N.E.2d 693 (3d Dist.1979). Doesn't this duty constitute an undue burden on a responding party? Why isn't it enough that the discovering party simply can send a later set of interrogatories or engage in discovery immediately before trial if it wants up-to-date replies from another party? Would it be wise to limit the duty to the giving of names of any newly discovered witnesses? See *Developments in the Law—Discovery*, 74 Harv.L.Rev. 940, 961–63 (1961). Should the duty continue until and even during trial? See Everett v. Morrison, 478 S.W.2d 312 (Mo.1972) (party must disclose identity of witness discovered after trial was in progress).

What is the appropriate sanction for a breach of a duty to supplement answers? Most courts merely have prohibited the admission of the undisclosed evidence or prohibited the undisclosed witnesses from giving testimony. The original language of Rule 37 did not seem to permit this sanction, but courts have justified the imposition of this sanction on their inherent powers of control over the discovery process. See 8 Wright & Miller, *Federal Practice and Procedure: Civil* § 2050 (1970). The amended Rule 37(c)(1) specifically provides that a party may not use any witness or any information not disclosed to the other party or not supplemented as required by Rule 26(e)(1).

As an alternative to imposing sanctions upon the offending party, a court usually has the option of postponing the trial of a case, or granting a continuance or recess, so that the other side may complete discovery and prepare to meet any new testimony. See, e.g., Shelak v. White Motor Co., 581 F.2d 1155, 1159 (5th Cir.1978) (defendant permitted additional time to prepare for trial when interrogatory answers were supplemented three days before trial); Washington Hospital Center v. Cheeks, 129 U.S.App.D.C. 339, 394 F.2d 964 (D.C.Cir.1968) (trial recessed to permit the taking of the deposition of expert witness whose name had not been previously given). Is this procedure ordinarily better than sanctions?

Page 816. The first paragraph of Subsection 7 should read as follows:

Read Federal Rules of Civil Procedure 32, 36(b), and 30(e) in the Supplement.

Page 819. Note 5 should read as follows:

5. Florida Rule of Civil Procedure 1.330(a) follows Federal Rule 32(a) with one exception, which is spelled out in Rule 1.390(b) as follows:

> The testimony of an expert or skilled witness may be taken at any time before the trial in accordance with the rules for taking depositions and may be used at trial, regardless of the place of residence of the witness or whether he is within the distance prescribed by Rule 1.330(a)(3). No special form of notice need be given that the deposition will be used for trial.

What is the purpose of this rule? In the August 1991 draft of the proposed amendments to the Federal Rules, the Advisory Committee proposed to amend Rule 32(a)(3) to provide that the deposition of an expert may be used at trial even if the expert could be made available to testify in person. 137 F.R.D. at 119–21. However, this provision encountered "substantial opposition," and in May 1992 the Advisory Committee decided to eliminate this proposed change.

Page 840. The first paragraph of Subsection 3 should read as follows:

Read Federal Rule of Civil Procedure 26(b)(4) and the Advisory Committee's Notes on it, which appear in the Supplement.

Page 843. Note 4 should read as follows:

4. Prior to the 1993 amendments Federal Rule 26(b)(4)(A)(i) provided for limited discovery regarding information of experts who will be called to testify. Discovery limited to interrogatories has been found to be inadequate and unsatisfactory:

The results of the survey indicate that the actual practice of discovery of expert witnesses expected to be called at trial varies widely from the two-step procedure of Rule 26(b)(4)(A). The interrogatory overwhelmingly is recognized as a totally unsatisfactory method of providing adequate preparation for cross-examination and rebuttal. In practice, full discovery is the rule, and practitioners use all available means of disclosure including both the discovery of expert's reports and depositions.

Graham, *Discovery of Experts Under Rule 26(b)(4) of the Federal Rules of Civil Procedure: Part Two, An Empirical Study and a Proposal,* 1977 U.Ill.L.F. 169, 172. See also McLaughlin, *Discovery and Admissibility of Expert Testimony,* 63 Notre Dame L.Rev. 760 (1988). The amended Rule 26(a)(2)(B) requires disclosure of written reports of any "witness who is retained or specially employed to provide expert testimony." The report would have to include "a complete statement of all opinions to be expressed and reasons therefor." In addition, the proposed amended Rule 26(b)(4)(A) provides that "[a] party may depose any person who has been identified as an expert whose opinions may be presented at trial." What are the arguments for and against this expanded discovery of the opinions of expert witnesses?

Page 844. The first paragraph of Section D should read as follows:

Read Federal Rules of Civil Procedure 26(g) and 37 in the Supplement.

Pages 848–849. Note 2 should read as follows:

2. Many local court rules require attorneys to attempt to resolve discovery disputes informally before the counsel seeking discovery can file a motion to compel discovery. See, e.g., Rule 230-4 of the United States District Court for the Northern District of California, and Rule 12(k) of the General Rules of the United States District Court for the Northern District of Illinois, reproduced in the Supplement. Such a requirement is now imposed by amended Rule 37(a)(2), which provides that any motion to compel disclosure or discovery "must include a certification that the movant has in good faith conferred or attempted to confer" with the party against whom relief is sought in an effort to obtain the requested matter without court action.

Page 870. The paragraph following the Notes and Questions should read as follows:

Read the excerpts from the Civil Justice Reform Act of 1990, 28 U.S.C. §§ 471–479 in the Supplement.

Part X
PROPOSED RULE AMENDMENTS

FEDERAL RULES OF CIVIL PROCEDURE *

AMENDMENTS TO FEDERAL RULES OF CIVIL PROCEDURE

EFFECTIVE DECEMBER 1, 1995

SUPREME COURT OF THE UNITED STATES

Thursday, April 27, 1995

ORDERED:

1. That the Federal Rules of Civil Procedure for the United States District Courts be, and they hereby are, amended by including therein amendments to Civil Rules 50, 52, 59, and 83.

2. That the foregoing amendments to the Federal Rules of Civil Procedure shall take effect on December 1, 1995, and shall govern all proceedings in civil cases thereafter commenced and, insofar as just and practicable, all proceedings in civil cases then pending.

3. That THE CHIEF JUSTICE be, and hereby is, authorized to transmit to the Congress the foregoing amendments to the Federal Rules of Civil Procedure in accordance with the provisions of Section 2072 of Title 28, United States Code.

PROPOSED AMENDMENTS TO RULES OF CIVIL PROCEDURE

Rule 50. Judgment as a Matter of Law in Jury Trials; Alternative Motion for New Trial; Conditional Rulings

* * *

---

* Editor's Note: Observing the method of rule prescription outlined in 28 U.S.C.A. §§ 2072–2074, the Supreme Court adopted and on April 27, 1995, submitted to the Congress Amendments to the Federal Rules of Civil Procedure. Be alert to the fact that Congress may postpone, decline to approve, or change these amendments, otherwise effective December 1, 1995.

PROPOSED RULE AMENDMENTS

(b) Renewing Motion for Judgment After Trial; Alternative Motion for New Trial. If, for any reason, the court does not grant a motion for judgment as a matter of law made at the close of all the evidence, the court is considered to have submitted the action to the jury subject to the court's later deciding the legal questions raised by the motion. The movant may renew its request for judgment as a matter of law by filing a motion no later than 10 days after entry of judgment—and may alternatively request a new trial or join a motion for a new trial under Rule 59. In ruling on a renewed motion, the court may:

   (1) if a verdict was returned:

   (A) allow the judgment to stand,

   (B) order a new trial, or

   (C) direct entry of judgment as a matter of law; or

   (2) if no verdict was returned:

   (A) order a new trial, or

   (B) direct entry of judgment as a matter of law.

(c) Granting Renewed Motion for Judgment as a Matter of Law; Conditional Rulings; New Trial Motion.

* * *

(2) Any motion for a new trial under Rule 59 by a party against whom judgment as a matter of law is rendered shall be filed no later than 10 days after entry of the judgment.

* * *

Rule 52. Findings by the Court; Judgment on Partial Findings

* * *

(b) Amendment. On a party's motion filed no later than 10 days after entry of judgment, the court may amend its findings—or make additional findings—and may amend the judgment accordingly. The motion may accompany a motion for a new trial under Rule 59. When findings of fact are made in actions tried without a jury, the sufficiency of the evidence supporting the findings may be later questioned whether or not in the district court the party raising the question objected to the findings, moved to amend them, or moved for partial findings.

* * *

Rule 59. New Trials; Amendment of Judgments

* * *

(b) Time for Motion. Any motion for a new trial shall be filed no later than 10 days after entry of the judgment.

(c) Time for Serving Affidavits. When a motion for new trial is based on affidavits, they shall be filed with the motion. The opposing party has 10 days after service to file opposing affidavits, but that period may be extended for up to 20 days, either by the court for good cause or by the parties' written stipulation. The court may permit reply affidavits.

(d) On Court's Initiative; Notice; Specifying Grounds. No later than 10 days after entry of judgment the court, on its own, may order a new trial for any reason that would justify granting one on a party's motion. After giving the parties notice and an opportunity to be heard, the court may grant a timely motion for a new trial for a reason not stated in the motion. When granting a new trial on its own initiative or for a reason not stated in a motion, the court shall specify the grounds in its order.

(e) Motion to Alter or Amend Judgment. Any motion to alter or amend a judgment shall be filed no later than 10 days after entry of the judgment.

Rule 83. Rules by District Courts; Judge's Directives

(a) Local Rules.

(1) Each district court, acting by a majority of its district judges, may, after giving appropriate public notice and an opportunity for comment, make and amend rules governing its practice. A local rule shall be consistent with—but not duplicative of—Acts of Congress and rules adopted under 28 U.S.C. §§ 2072 and 2075, and shall conform to any uniform numbering system prescribed by the Judicial Conference of the United States. A local rule takes effect on the date specified by the district court and remains in effect unless amended by the court or abrogated by the judicial council of the circuit. Copies of rules and amendments shall, upon their promulgation, be furnished to the judicial council and the Administrative Office of the United States Courts and be made available to the public.

(2) A local rule imposing a requirement of form shall not be enforced in a manner that causes a party to lose rights because of a nonwillful failure to comply with the requirement.

(b) Procedures When There Is No Controlling Law. A judge may regulate practice in any manner consistent with federal law, rules adopted under 28 U.S.C. §§ 2072 and 2075, and local rules of the district. No sanction or other disadvantage may be imposed for noncompliance with any requirement not in federal law, federal rules, or the local district rules unless the alleged violator has been furnished in the particular case with actual notice of the requirement.

PROPOSED RULE AMENDMENTS

FEDERAL RULES OF APPELLATE PROCEDURE *

AMENDMENTS TO THE FEDERAL RULES OF APPELLATE PROCEDURE

EFFECTIVE DECEMBER 1, 1995

SUPREME COURT OF THE UNITED STATES

Thursday, April 27, 1995

ORDERED:

1. That the Federal Rules of Appellate Procedure be, and they hereby are, amended by including therein amendments to Appellate Rules 4, 8, 10, and 47.

2. That the foregoing amendments to the Federal Rules of Appellate Procedure shall take effect on December 1, 1995, and shall govern all proceedings in appellate cases thereafter commenced and, insofar as just and practicable, all proceedings in appellate cases then pending.

3. That THE CHIEF JUSTICE be, and hereby is, authorized to transmit to the Congress the foregoing amendments to the Federal Rules of Appellate Procedure in accordance with the provisions of Section 2072 of Title 28, United States Code.

PROPOSED AMENDMENTS TO THE FEDERAL RULES OF APPELLATE PROCEDURE

Rule 4. Appeal as of Right—When Taken

(a) *Appeal in a Civil Case.*

* * *

(4) If any party files a timely motion of a type specified immediately below, the time for appeal for all parties runs from the entry of the order disposing of the last such motion outstanding. This provision applies to a timely motion under the Federal Rules of Civil Procedure:

(A) for judgment under Rule 50(b);

---

* Editor's Note: Observing the method of rule prescription outlined in 28 U.S.C.A. §§ 2072–2074, the Supreme Court adopted and on April 27, 1995, submitted to the Congress Amendments to the Federal Rules of Appellate Procedure. Be alert to the fact Congress may postpone, decline to approve, or change these amendments, otherwise effective December 1, 1995.

PROPOSED RULE AMENDMENTS

(B) to amend or make additional findings of fact under Rule 52(b), whether or not granting the motion would alter the judgment;

(C) to alter or amend the judgment under Rule 59;

(D) for attorney's fees under Rule 54 if a district court under Rule 58 extends the time for appeal;

(E) for a new trial under Rule 59; or

(F) for relief under Rule 60 if the motion is filed no later than 10 days after the entry of judgment.

A notice of appeal filed after announcement or entry of the judgment but before disposition of any of the above motions is ineffective to appeal from the judgment or order, or part thereof, specified in the notice of appeal, until the entry of the order disposing of the last such motion outstanding. Appellate review of an order disposing of any of the above motions requires the party, in compliance with Appellate Rule 3(c), to amend a previously filed notice of appeal. A party intending to challenge an alteration or amendment of the judgment shall file a notice, or amended notice, of appeal within the time prescribed by this Rule 4 measured from the entry of the order disposing of the last such motion outstanding. No additional fees will be required for filing an amended notice.

* * *

Rule 8. Stay or Injunction Pending Appeal

* * *

(c) *Stay in a Criminal Case.*—A stay in a criminal case shall be had in accordance with the provisions of Rule 38 of the Federal Rules of Criminal Procedure.

Rule 10. The Record on Appeal

(a) *Composition of the Record on Appeal.*—The record on appeal consists of the original papers and exhibits filed in the district court, the transcript of proceedings, if any, and a certified copy of the docket entries prepared by the clerk of the district court.

(b) *The Transcript of Proceedings; Duty of Appellant to Order; Notice to Appellee if Partial Transcript is Ordered.*

(1) Within 10 days after filing the notice of appeal or entry of an order disposing of the last timely motion outstanding of a type specified in Rule 4(a)(4), whichever is later, the appellant shall order from the reporter a transcript of such parts of the proceedings not already on file as the appellant deems necessary, subject to local rules of the courts of appeals. The order shall be in writing and within the same period a copy shall be filed with the clerk of the

district court. If funding is to come from the United States under the Criminal Justice Act, the order shall so state. If no such parts of the proceedings are to be ordered, within the same period the appellant shall file a certificate to that effect.

* * *

Rule 47. Rules of a Court of Appeals

(a) *Local Rules.*

(1) Each court of appeals acting by a majority of its judges in regular active service may, after giving appropriate public notice and opportunity for comment, make and amend rules governing its practice. A generally applicable direction to a party or a lawyer regarding practice before a court shall be in a local rule rather than an internal operating procedure or standing order. A local rule shall be consistent with—but not duplicative of—Acts of Congress and rules adopted under 28 U.S.C. § 2072 and shall conform to any uniform numbering system prescribed by the Judicial Conference of the United States. The clerk of each court of appeals shall send the Administrative Office of the United States Courts a copy of each local rule and internal operating procedure when it is promulgated or amended.

(2) A local rule imposing a requirement of form shall not be enforced in a manner that causes a party to lose rights because of a nonwillful failure to comply with the requirement.

(b) *Procedure When There Is No Controlling Law.*—A court of appeals may regulate practice in a particular case in any manner consistent with federal law, these rules, and local rules of the circuit. No sanction or other disadvantage may be imposed for noncompliance with any requirement not in federal law, federal rules, or the local circuit rules unless the alleged violator has been furnished in the particular case with actual notice of the requirement.

Part XI

Index to Comparative Provisions

Federal Provisions

	Page
United States Constitution 7th Amendment	123
United States Code	
Tit. 15, § 15(a)	251
United States Supreme Court Rule 10.1	243
United States District Court, Eastern District, California, Local Civil Rule 271	126
United States District Court, Northern District, California, Local Civil Rule 230–4	120
United States District Court, Northern District, Illinois, Local	
General Rule 9(g)	109
General Rule 12k	121
United States District Court, Eastern District, Michigan, Former Local Rule 5(b)	126
Proposed Consumer Class Action Act	252

State Provisions

Alabama Code	
§ 12–2–13	291
Arizona Rules of Civil Procedure (26.1)	91
California Constitution	
Art. 6, § 11	241
Art. 6, § 12	241
California Civil Procedure Code	
§ 382	74
§ 386	66
§ 396	43
§ 415.30	22
§ 425.10(b)	28
§ 430.10	46
§ 431.30(d)	31
§ 436	154
§ 437c	152
§ 446	31
§ 469	52
§ 470	52
§ 471	52
§ 583.210	127
§ 583.310	127
§ 583.320	127
§ 583.330	127
§ 583.360	127
§ 583.410(a)	127
§ 583.420	127
§ 597	45
§ 597.5	45

COMPARATIVE PROVISIONS

Page

California Civil Procedure Code—Continued
- § 909 291
- § 2023 121
- § 2030(f)(2) 109

California Rules of Court
- 28 241
- 29 243
- 228 136

Colorado Rules of Civil Procedure
- 8(e)(1) 31

Connecticut Rules for the Superior Court
- § 390 282

Delaware Superior Court Rules (Civil)
- 9(b) 34

Florida Rules of Civil Procedure
- 1.500 150

Georgia Constitution
- Art. VI, § 1, ¶ 8 243
- Art. VI, § 5, ¶ 5 243
- Art. VI, § 6, ¶ 2 244
- Art. VI, § 6, ¶ 3 244
- Art. VI, § 6, ¶ 5 244

Georgia Code Annotated
- § 5-5-24 141
- § 9-10-111 39
- § 9-11-8(a)(2) 28
- § 9-11-8(e)(2) 32
- § 9-11-11(b) 38
- § 9-11-54(c)(1) 149
- § 9-11-60 159
- § 19-5-5(a) 39

Illinois Compiled Statutes 5/2
- 104(a) 259
- 104(b) 44, 259
- 201(a) 18
- 202 18
- 203(a) 19
- 204 19
- c. 110, ¶ 2-205 19
- 205.1 19
- 206 20
- 207 21
- 208 20
- 211 19
- 212 20
- 301 44
- 603(b) 36
- 604 29
- 610 30
- 613(a) 35
- 616(d) 54
- 1009(a) 125

Illinois Compiled Statutes 5/4
- 101 21
- 126 21

459

INDEX

	Page
Illinois Supreme Court Rules	
Rule 20	265
Rule 239	141
Indiana Rules of Trial Procedure	
Trial Rule 8(E)(3)	43
Trial Rule 41(E)	128
Trial Rule 50	139
Kansas Statutes Annotated	
§ 60–203(a)	12
Maryland Rules	
2–321	42
Massachusetts General Laws Annotated	
c. 233, § 45	268
Michigan Court Rules	
2.113(F)	36
2.113(G)	36
2.203	60
2.203(B)	49
2.206(A)	65
2.302(B)(4)(d)	106
2.308(A)	107
Minnesota Constitution	
Art. 1, § 4	136
Minnesota Rules of Civil Appellate Procedure	
103.03	247
Minnesota Rules of Civil Procedure	
4.04(b)(2)	45
26.02(c)	92
33.01(a)	110
35.01	113
51	141
59.01	158
59.03	158
Mississippi Code Annotated	
§ 11–7–155	141
Missouri Statutes Annotated	
§ 510.330	158
Missouri Rules of Civil Procedure	
55.25(a)	42
78.01	160
Nebraska Revised Statutes	
§ 25–701	61
§ 25–702	61
§ 25–803	27
§ 25–804	29
§ 25–806	42
§ 25–807	43
§ 25–808	43
§ 25–810	43
§ 25–811	49
§ 25–820	27
§ 25–833	46
§ 25–842	31

COMPARATIVE PROVISIONS

	Page
Nebraska Revised Statutes—Continued	
§ 25–1223	135
§ 25–1224	135
§ 25–1227(1)	135
§ 25–1228(1)	135
New Jersey Civil Practice Rules	
4:5–8(b)	34
4:9–3	52
4:17–7	93
4:25–1	57
4:41–5(b) & (c)	146
New York Civil Practice Law and Rules	
216	67
302(a)	285
320(c)	44
602	128
1002(a) & (b)	65
1002(c)	129
3013	29
3015	33
3016	33
3017(c)	29
3018(a)	31
3018(b)	31
3019(b)	49
3024(b)	46
3025(a) & (b)	52
3041	30
3043	30
3101	92
3102(c)	95
3106	93
3120	112
3121(b)	114
3130	109
3211	46
3219	168
3220	168
3221	168
4103	123
4317	146
4404(a)	139
5205	169
5206	171
5601	244
5602	242
5701	248
6201	163
6301	166
6401	166
North Carolina General Statutes	
§ 1–75.2	286
§ 1–75.4	286
§ 1–75.7	289
§ 1–75.8	289

INDEX

	Page
North Carolina Rules of Civil Procedure	
Form (3) Complaint for Negligence	195
Ohio Revised Code Annotated	
§ 2307.27	78
Oklahoma Statutes Annotated	
Tit. 12, § 611	143
Pennsylvania Constitution	
Art. 1, § 6	123
Pennsylvania Rules of Civil Procedure	
1024	39
Rhode Island General Laws Annotated	
§ 9–5–33(a)	289
South Carolina Code	
§ 14–7–1020	136
Texas Rules of Civil Procedure	
301	149
Virginia Code	
§ 8.01–359	136
Virginia Constitution	
Art. 1, § 11	123
Wisconsin Statutes Annotated	
§ 801.63	258
§ 805.12(1)	137
§ 805.12(2)	138

Uniform Acts

Uniform Declaratory Judgments Act	
§ 6	283
Uniform Enforcement of Foreign Judgments Act (1964 Revision)	
§ 2	281
§ 6	281
Uniform Interstate and International Procedure Act	
§ 1.02	290
§ 1.03	290
§ 1.05	290
Uniform Parentage Act	
§ 8(b)	290

†